BIG BOOK OF
QUILTING

kp
krause

Iola, Wisconsin

Table of *Contents*

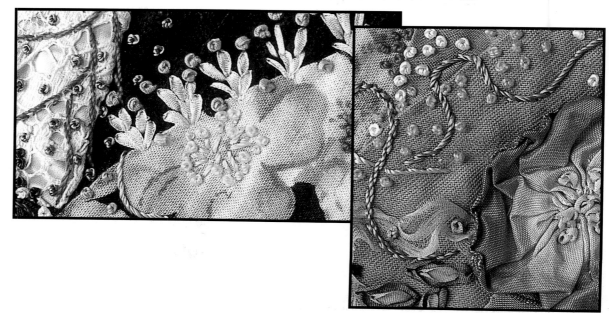

Kaye Wood's
Strip-Cut Quilts *296*

Fast-Folded

389

Flowers

Introduction

Whether you're a beginner or a long-time quilter, you appreciate the time, creativity, and know-how it takes to create a one-of-a-kind quilt. We've made it easy by bringing you the most complete collection of quilting tips, tricks, and techniques. From fabric selection to sewing the last stitch, the *Big Book of Quilting* will guide you step-by-step through patterns and construction to help you create an inspired work of art that reflects your personality.

Inside this book you'll find inspiration and explanation of the skills necessary to make a quilt. Step-by-step instruction and clear illustrations combined with innovative ideas and techniques will help you complete the quilt of your dreams. The *Big Book of Quilting* is packed with a wealth of information, specific patterns, tips, and projects. Be sure to check out the table of contents at the beginning of each section so you don't miss an opportunity! No matter your level of experience, the 500+ pages will guide you in creating a variety of quilts from simple to lavish. Learn, experiment, enjoy!

The Essential
Guide to
Practically Perfect
Patchwork

Everything You Need to Know to Make Your First Quilt

Michele Morrow Harer

FOREWORD

I feel I've always known and loved quilting, although I was around thirty, married, and had three children when I discovered quilt making in the revival of the '70s. My love of quilting is more than just an enjoyment of the fabrics, colors, or the process. I love everything quilting stands for. I love the history—of being connected to our foremothers through over two centuries of quilting. I love that quilting is a symbol of recycling, of conservation, of making do. I love that quilting is taking common scraps of fabrics and turning them into beautiful works of art. I love the traditions of fellowship that quilting encompasses.

Quilting, to me, is an expression of love, because when you've made a quilt, you realize no one would make one just to pass the time. The work is too compelling, time-consuming, and all involving. A quilt is a warm covering of love for someone you care about. A quilt is an expression of emotions that cannot be put into words. A quilt is a legacy. Besides turning out three wonderful young adults to help make this a better world, my quilts are also one small part of me I can leave behind in memoriam. And at times during my life, quilting was the only thing I did that stayed done!

I have found that quilters are a group of the best people in the world. They are helpful and generous. They share ideas, techniques, their time, their work and (best of all), their fabrics. And that is why I came to write this book. I wish to share with you my love of quilting and the practical methods I have learned that help to ensure the successful completion of a quilt. It is my wish that you, too, will come to love quilting and all it stands for. I hope to infect you with "quilt pox" so that you will enjoy the creativity and personal satisfaction I have found in my beloved hobby. I hope these lessons will be an enjoyable, no-pressure experience for you. I know you will have fun while you learn to make the quilts of a lifetime.

I'd like to share a quote from Texas quilter, Mary White, from a book entitled, *The Quilters—Women and Domestic Art* by Patricia J. Cooper and Norma Bradley Allen. For me, it embodies the truth of quilting, and has brought me comfort through good times and not-so-good times.

"You can't always change things. Sometimes you don't have no control over the way things go. Hail ruins the crops or fire burns you out. And then you're just given so much to work with in a life and you have to do the best you can with what you got. That's what piecing is. The materials is passed on to you or is all you can afford to buy … that's just what's given to you. Your fate. But the way you put them together is your business."**1**

Blessings to you as you embark on this wonderful journey.

Michele

TABLE OF CONTENTS

INTRODUCTION

The Essential Guide to Practically Perfect Patchwork will give you quilt making power. This book is intended to be an introduction into quilting for beginning quilters, and those who have been quilting but want to know how to stitch patchwork blocks with more ease and accuracy. The lessons offer a basic understanding of what constitutes "practically perfect" block construction and includes tips and techniques developed to help you succeed.

Many times my students have told me they were afraid to take a quilt class for fear they would encounter too many rules and face an overly critical examination of their work. Well, there are no quilt police here. If you follow the assembly instructions and use the "tricks" developed to outwit fabric's perversities, your quilt will be as accurate and beautiful as you make it.

There are no bad quilts. There are quilts for different purposes. If you are making a quilt to enter into competition, naturally you will try for excellence. But if you're making a quilt to be loved and used, doing the best you can is enough. If anyone should be so rude as to point out a flaw in your quilt, you can just tell them (as the Amish do) that you left the error in on purpose so that your work wouldn't approach perfection and thus be an affront to God.

In a simple, straightforward way, the patterns included in each lesson will teach all the basic types of seams you will ever need to successfully sew any patchwork block. The blocks are grouped according to the technique or skill to be learned.

Each lesson builds upon the lesson before it, and the whole book is intended to give support at each advancing stage of quilt making. The last four lessons demystify finishing steps and set forth some easy-to-understand tips and techniques that are thoroughly explained and diagrammed so you can use the power of "practically perfect patchwork" to *finish* your quilt. So, if you begin with Lesson 1 and continue through Lesson 10, your quilt will be done!

Whether you choose to make a whole quilt using one block pattern from this workbook or a sampler quilt using many of the patterns, you can finish your quilt using *The Essential Guide to Practically Perfect Patchwork* as your manual through a step-by-step process to success.

The Practically Perfect Bunny

My underlying philosophy as a quilting teacher is to make everything as simple as possible. Over the years, I have accumulated many valuable short cuts and timesaving techniques that make sewing patchwork less difficult, and I want to share them with you.

These helpful hints have multiplied like rabbits, so watch for my bunny helper within each lesson. She will remind you of skills already learned. She will teach you some new tricks. She will even tell you of past mistakes, from which we get our best and longest-lasting instruction.

While our bunny friend will help you hop over the hurdles of patchwork construction, she won't do anything about the dust bunnies that may accumulate in your house while you are sewing. But then, dust bunnies are some of her best friends.

Supply List For Lessons 1 – 6: Making the Blocks

- Template patterns from this book
- X-Acto or red-handled craft knife with size 24 or equally substantial blade
- Paper scissors
- 2-ply, medium weight illustration board or dense cardboard, 1/8" thick
- 5 sheets medium or fine grade sandpaper
- Rubber cement with brush in the cap
- Emery board
- Hard, textured surface cutting board (not a rotary mat)
- .5 mm mechanical pencil with H or HB lead
- 12" or 18" metal ruler with cork backing
- Colored pencils, markers or crayons to color in quilt block diagrams
- Pad of small self-stick notes, 1-1/2" x 2"
- Sewing machine in good working order
- 12/80 machine sewing needles
- Iron and ironing board
- Fabrics for quilt top
- Good fabric scissors
- Long, thin straight pins

- 28 mm rotary cutter
- Rotary cutting mat
- 2 rotary grid rulers: 3" x 18" rectangle, 15" square (You won't need the square until Lesson 7, so watch for sales or ask for it as a special gift. Note: if you buy different sizes of rulers, always choose the same brand to keep your measurements consistent.)
- Temporary fabric marking pens and pencils
- Seam ripper
- Neutral color threads
- Freezer paper
- 120" tape measure

Optional items you may want to add to the list:
- A second smaller mat (less than 12" x 12")
- Rotary point cutter
- Rubber cement "pick-up"
- Thread snips

"Gold and Black Sampler"
57-1/2" X 72-1/2"
made by author

How Patchwork Quilts Came to Be

The quilting tradition in the United States began in the early 1700s as pioneer women searched for ways to keep their families warm in a new land where fiber resources for clothing and blankets were scarce. It was this scarcity of materials that created the serendipitous invention of patchwork quilts as a unique and practical art form. Early quiltmakers, who presumably were untrained in sophisticated design, sewed scraps of fabric together to make bed covers producing many beautiful works of practical art and displaying an inborn talent for pattern, color, harmony, and geometric form.

Quilts were made mostly by women who took pleasure and comfort in quiltmaking as one of the few creative outlets that were allowed to them. Many of the early patchwork patterns reflected the political and moral beliefs their makers cherished but were not allowed to express. I can remember reading about an early 1800s colonial woman, who was the wife of a devout Democrat in favor of an overly strong presidency. She made a beautiful "Whig Rose" quilt for her husband to sleep under. (The Whigs, precursors to the Republican Party, were in favor of strong states rights.) Every night she exerted her silent choice, while her husband slept peacefully under her quilt.

But What Exactly is a Quilt?

A quilt is made of two layers of fabric arranged in sandwich fashion with batting in between. It is held together by thread stitches or ties. Two factors work together to create the beauty of a quilt: 1) the quilt top, the part that is pieced together in interesting combinations of design, color and pattern, and 2) the actual stitching of the three layers together, called quilting, which adds texture and an additional design element to the surface. Piecing and quilting complement each other.

A quilt can be any size, but it must be made of three layers stitched together. Therefore, you can make a quilt for a pillow top, a wall hanging, or your bed. Size is not a restriction.

One-Patch, Two-Patch, Four, Five, Seven, Nine ...

You will discover in your exploration of quilting that block patterns are categorized by the arrangement of the patches. As a teacher, I have found this confusing for the beginner, so don't feel you have to understand and know how to classify blocks. In the future, you can investigate the many fine books written to help you design and draft your own quilts. Two excellent resource books are Dolores Hinson's *A Quilter's Companion*, and Jinny Beyer's *Patchwork Patterns*. Nevertheless, I have categorized many of the blocks in this workbook as an introduction to block classification.

The Sampler

A sampler quilt, also known as an album quilt, is one in which no two blocks are the same. So, how did the "sampler" quilt originate? One common belief is that when a quilter wanted to remember a block she had seen, she made a copy of it out of fabric rather than draw it on paper, another scarce early American commodity. These blocks were her "reference library" from which she could recall patterns for future quilts, although she may not have recorded the block's original name. So, while a block may have started out with the name "Bear's Paw," it may have acquired various other names along the way—"Duck's Foot in the Mud" or "Hand of Friendship"—like stories changing as they pass from person to person. You can see how many traditional patterns came to be known by more than one name. When the quilter who had made a copy of "Bear's Paw" referred back to *her* pattern—blame it on poor memory or that she wanted to put her own spin on the design by naming it differently, somehow the various patterns got renamed and renamed. Later, in pioneer tradition of "waste not, want not," these orphan quilt blocks were sewn together into a bed covering creating the sampler-type quilt we will be making during this series of lessons.

For our purposes, the "Practically Perfect Patchwork" sampler we'll be creating will become your beginning library of patterns to use, and will provide many happy hours of creating beautiful quilts for yourself and loved ones. This book contains all the templates you will need to make over 45 different blocks, so you have the choice of which ones you want to include in your sampler quilt. Later, you may want to use just one block and make a complete quilt with it.

Size Counts

When I made my first sampler quilt, I decided it had to be big enough to cover my queen-sized bed … and, embarrassingly, I am still hand-quilting it. Originally, I embraced the whole hand-quilting tradition and was determined to make my quilt the "old-fashioned way." Well, I do not live an old-fashioned life. My life—and no doubt, yours too—speeds by faster and faster the older I get. When I do get a chance to sit down, I just may fall asleep. That's how I came to develop my theory of "machine quilt where it doesn't show, and hand quilt where it does."

I recommend that you restrict your quilt size to no larger than 60" by 70". You only need to make twelve blocks; with borders, the quilt would be suitable as a topper for a queen-size mattress, or quilt for a smaller bed. Still, it won't be so prohibitively large that you'll lose interest. You will be encouraged as you see your work transformed into a completed quilt. Plus, this smaller size will make it easier to machine quilt your sampler, if you choose.

Planning Ahead

It's very helpful to begin with a definite diagram or scale drawing of the layout and size of the quilt you want to make. Look ahead to Lesson 7, "Make a Blueprint of Your Quilt," for how to draw it. Of course, you are not committed to any layout you might choose now, but it is a good idea to have some sort of target. You may end up making more blocks than required, and want to include them in your quilt, or you may make fewer and finish them into a wall hanging. I've included a few examples of possibilities for you to consider.

Quilt Layout Possibilities and Size Guidelines

THROW: ± 40"x ± 75"
CRIB OR   36" x 44"
WALL-   40" x 54"
HANGING   45" X 60"

Mattress sizes:
CRIB: 27" x 52"
TWIN: 39" x 75"
DOUBLE: 54" x 75"
QUEEN: 60" x 80"
KING: 76" x 80"

QUILT = size of mattress PLUS number of inches you want the quilt to drop on both sides and bottom.

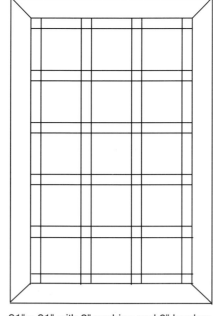

91" x 91" with 3" sashing and 6" borders

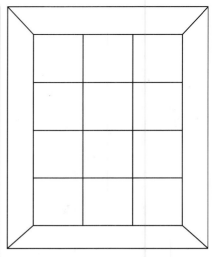

60" x 48" with 6" borders and no sashing

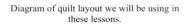

Diagram of quilt layout we will be using in these lessons.

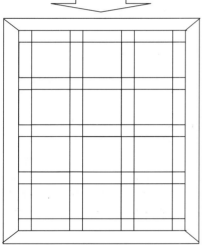

71" x 56" with 3" sashing and 4" borders

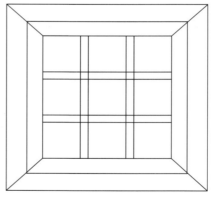

60" x 60" with 2" sashing and 4" plus 6" double border

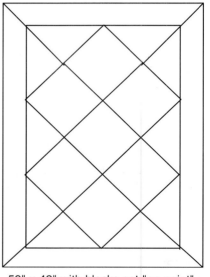

59" x 42" with blocks set "on point", 4" borders, corner triangles made with 12RT

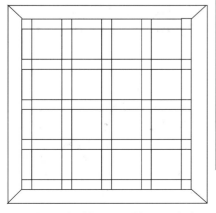

65" x 65" with 3" sashing and 4" borders

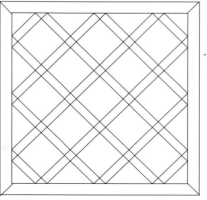

Approx. 71½" X 71½" on point with 2" sashing and 4" borders, 12RT on sides and MOM#1 at corners

By using wider sashings, wider borders, and/or multiple borders, you can increase the size of your quilt without making more blocks.

Choosing Fabrics

One of my favorite sayings (and a truth I have learned the hard way) is, "Your work is only as good as your tools." I am especially referring to fabric. Some fabric manufacturers produce three grades of fabric. The fabric that is first run through the printing process is a loose-woven cotton or blend. This run-through is for adjusting the registration of the colors. You'll find the resulting fabrics are not wrapped on bolts but sold as flat-folds in discount department stores, etc. In the second run-through, the mill uses better quality cotton, but it is still fairly loose-woven, also. This production refines the printing process, and the resulting fabric is sold on bolts at chain fabric stores and discount stores. The last-run printing process uses the best, highest denier (more threads-per-inch) fabric. All the errors in printing have been corrected by this time. This bolt fabric goes to independent fabric shops and costs more, but you definitely get a higher-quality material.

I'm not recommending that you purchase your fabrics only from quilt shops. That wouldn't be reasonable. You should purchase the type of fabric appropriate to the quilt you will be making. When you give a quilt as a gift, you want the recipient to use your beautiful quilt, but you lose control of the care it will receive. Making a quilt requires an investment of many hours of work, and if you intend for it to be an heirloom that will be passed down in your family, I encourage you to purchase the best fabrics you can afford—and your first quilt may just become an heirloom.

When choosing your fabrics, always check the label on the end of the bolts to see where it is manufactured. If you see that the fabric is imported, assess how well it is made. Does the fabric have a nice feel *because it is closely woven, or because it is treated with sizing* (a finish that is applied to the surface of fabric to make it look and feel "crisp," but which will wash out)? Scrunch up a corner in the palm of your hand. If the wrinkles remain, it probably contains a lot of sizing. Be aware that fabric of lesser quality is more difficult to work with.

Fabric Colors and Patterns

Fabric manufacturers are closely tied to the fashion industry, and you'll find that colors and patterns go in and out of vogue frequently. That beautiful, vivid spring-green fabric that you just love may not be available next year when you really need it for a future quilt. If you see a fabric you love, buy it (at least 1/2 yard), because it may not be seen again for years. And after all, there *are* worse bad habits you can acquire besides fabric addiction!

Today, we are fortunate that there are so many beautiful, one hundred percent cotton fabrics from which to choose. They come in a myriad of color and design. Some patterned fabrics are made in more that one color combination—called a "colorway." Also, fabric manufacturers produce groupings of fabrics with colors and patterns made to go together. This helps us in coordinating our quilt fabrics.

When I work with beginning quilters, I find many are intimidated by the two most creative and effective components of a quilt: fabric designs and color choices. They feel unsure when they begin selecting specific fabrics for their quilts. Choosing the colors and patterns of fabrics can be the most enjoyable and exciting part of making your quilt. Actually, we all live with color, texture and pattern every day, and I can assure you that you know more than you think you do about them. You can successfully combine almost all fabrics as long as you understand and employ the principles of color value and pattern value as they relate to fabric choices.

Keep in mind that you will be spending many exacting hours sewing small patches of fabrics together to make an overall design. To make that design or block well defined and pleasing to look at, you will want to choose fabrics in colors that contrast. Select light-, medium-, and dark-colored fabrics—this is color value. If you used fabrics that were all one value (for example, all medium hues), from any distance you would not be able to distinguish one shape from another. Imagine that a block has a medium background. In order to make the patchwork design within the block visible, you would want to use light and/or dark fabrics to contrast against the medium background. This same principal holds true for light as well as dark backgrounds. **Contrast** is the key to making your patchwork designs distinct and recognizable.

Choose fabrics for pattern value by including **larger**, **medium**, and **smaller** prints. Many of the patches we will be cutting are small, so it is unwise to choose fabric that is patterned in a very large-scale print with spread-out colors. The smaller patches you cut will not contain all the colors you chose the fabric for and might not blend well within a block.

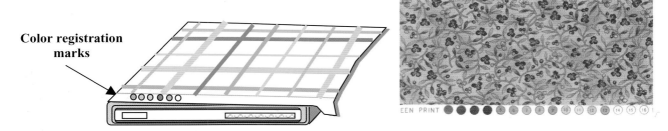

Color registration marks

The easiest way I know to choose fabrics for your quilt is to walk through the fabric shop and select your inspiration fabric first. This fabric will be one that you just "fall in love with" and will become the touchstone for colors in your quilt. Choose colors for the other fabrics that will coordinate with that inspiration piece. You can use the color registration marks on the margin or selvage edge of the fabric you have chosen to help you select complementary fabrics for your quilt. What are color registration marks? They are the little circles of colors in the selvage margin of fabric yardage. The little circles show all the colors contained in that fabric. When the fabric is printed, the dots of colors must fall within the circle outline to ensure the printing will be aligned.

Try to choose fabrics that enhance each other. They don't necessarily have to exactly match the colors in your inspiration fabric; you already have those shades. Choose fabrics that are darker and lighter in color value, and contain a variety of print patterns.

Gather your fabrics together so you can see the development of your fabric palette. Stack and "fan" them exposing a proportionate amount of each that you expect to use in your blocks. If you are undecided about a fabric choice, place it with your other fabrics, and then take it away. Ask yourself, "do I miss it?" If your answer is "yes," put it back. If you don't miss it, you probably like it for reasons other than how well it goes with your developing palette.

Over the next few lessons, you can continue to add fabrics to your collection, but by the time you have made the first third of your quilt blocks, you should have introduced all the fabrics you will use. This doesn't mean that you can't substitute one very similar fabric for another. In fact, done carefully, this adds interest to your blocks, but these "like-substitute" fabrics must have scale and coloration that is interchangeable.

The following is a list of fabric identifiers that will help you in adding variety to your fabric palettes:

Inspiration or theme fabrics—choose a fabric that beckons you to own it.

Stripes, geometric, graphic—these provide motion and carry direction, bringing the eye in or out.

Lights, mediums, darks—use your inspiration fabric to pick complementary fabrics; watch the scale of prints you choose, and include some (not too) large, medium and small prints.

Solids—use with care they can say a lot and weigh heavily in a quilt. Their uncluttered surface demands attention and cries for quilting and that's why I like to use solid substitutes.

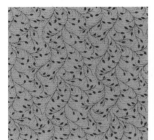

Solid substitutes or tone-on-tone—are printed fabrics with designs that are subtle and give the impression they are a solid color, but require much less quilting and lend support to a block.

"Zinger"—usually a bright, attention-grabbing fabric (use sparingly).

Whimsical and pictorials—these give interest, pull the eye in.

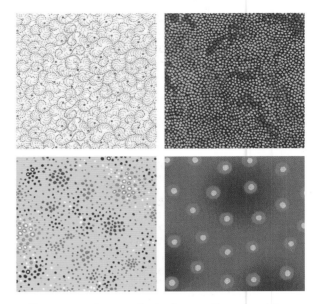

Dots, spots, and circles —these add fun, whimsy, interest; try to use one in every quilt.

Light givers—light, medium, and dark colors all in one fabric (plaids can be light givers).

Some quilters are comfortable with more, but you need at least eight fabrics for variety and contrast. I'm from the "more is better" school, and have used over 30 in one sampler quilt. Seek *your* comfort zone.

MATERIALS

 ✳ Two yards of your inspiration fabric or 2-1/2 to 3 yards if it will also be your border fabric, (which will help keep expenses in line). See the border and sashing cutting diagram.

 ✳ At least 1/2 to 1 yard of each of the fabrics you have chosen (1/2 yard of each if you purchase more than eight fabrics; one yard if you have chosen fewer).

 ✳ Only 1/4 yard of a "zinger" fabric.

 ✳ If you prefer, you can choose border and backing fabric later after your top is assembled and you know how big your quilt will be.

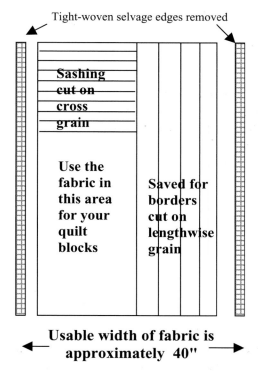

Tight-woven selvage edges removed

Sashing cut on cross grain

Use the fabric in this area for your quilt blocks

Saved for borders cut on lengthwise grain

Usable width of fabric is approximately 40"

Again, the more fabrics you purchase, the less you need of each, but 1/4 yard is the least amount you should buy, and this should be a "zinger" fabric, which every quilt needs—but not much of it!

Many years ago I made a Baltimore Album quilt. The colors I used were vibrant jewel tones. I did not pre-wash the fabrics. After the quilt top was completed, I sprayed it with water to remove the wash out marker I had used. Some of the fabrics bled onto the white background and it was impossible to remove all the stains.

Getting the Fabric Ready

I always rinse my fabrics after I bring them home from the store. Don't run them through a wash cycle, you'll loose a lot of fabric at the cut edges and it's not necessary. No matter how careful the mill is, some intensely colored fabrics will bleed. I wet my fabric down one piece at a time in an old, large, white porcelain dishpan where I can see if the colors run. If a fabric doesn't bleed, it gets wrung out and goes in the dryer with the other fabrics. If it does run, I rinse it over again once or twice until the rinse water is clear. If it still runs, I soak it in 1/4 cup white vinegar to a gallon of water then rinse again. If it still runs after that, I don't use it.

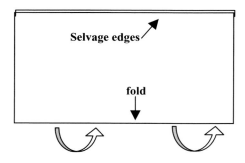

Selvage edges

fold

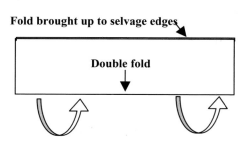

Fold brought up to selvage edges

Double fold

After the fabric is dry, square up the yardage and fold the piece in half meeting selvage edge to selvage edge so that the folded cloth hangs or lays wrinkle-free and straight. You may have to stretch the fabric on the bias to help it regain its "square." Spray with fabric sizing, and press it with an iron from selvage edge to the fold. Match the folded edge up to the two selvage edges, press again, and your fabric is ironed and folded in fourths ready to use. If you consistently do this, you can attack your stash and start working on a quilt in a moment's inspiration, confident that your fabric is pre-shrunk and ready to use.

Threads

You are not going to want to keep changing thread colors in your sewing machine to match fabrics as you piece your blocks, so I recommend that you purchase a neutral color thread that will blend with your fabrics. If your quilt will have mostly warm colors in it, try a taupe or beige. If the colors will be cool, try a gray. If you are using intense or very dark colors, you might want to use darker browns or grays. Of course, if your quilt fabrics are light in color, you can use white or off-white. See what looks the best. You don't want the thread to contrast with the fabrics you are using; you want it to blend in and disappear.

Needles

What size sewing machine needle? The most versatile size machine needle to use is 12/80. A 10/70 needle is also a good choice, but if you should accidentally hit a straight pin as you are sewing a seam, it will break more easily.

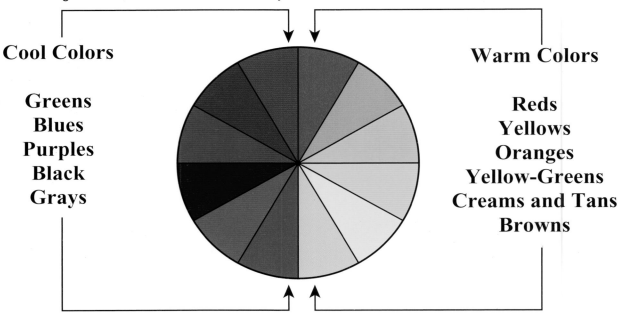

Cool Colors

Greens
Blues
Purples
Black
Grays

Warm Colors

Reds
Yellows
Oranges
Yellow-Greens
Creams and Tans
Browns

Remember to fill a couple of bobbins before you begin sewing. It seems you always run out of thread at the most inconvenient time.

Templates
LESSON 2

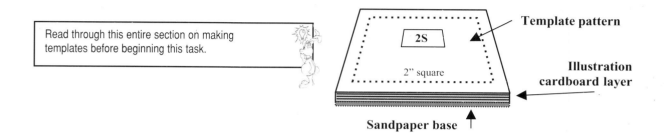

Read through this entire section on making templates before beginning this task.

Template pattern

2S

2" square

Illustration cardboard layer

Sandpaper base

Practically Perfect Templates

In **The Essential Guide to Practically Perfect Patchwork**, templates are the patterns we use to cut most fabric patches. They consist of three layers: the paper pattern, illustration or cardboard in the middle, and a sandpaper base. Manufactured Plexiglas, plastic and metal templates are available for purchase; you are limited, however, to the specific blocks for which they were made. You can make your own templates, and you can make them to last your quilting lifetime. You only need to take your time and make them with care. When you have completed your templates, you will have durable tools that you can easily identify and use over and over again.

When cutting many identical patches, I have found it is easier to make a template for each shape and assembly-line cut from layers of folded fabric. This is not only easier, it is more accurate and less wasteful. Some quilters prefer to cut patches using only a rotary cutter and grid ruler, and we will employ this technique when making blocks such as the **Log Cabin**. But, we'll use a little trick to help line up the grid ruler to cut the correct size shapes every time.

You may wonder about the "different" identifiers used to label most of the templates. I don't know how many times I've looked through my personal collection for a group of templates I made from another source only to find most of them labeled "A", "B", "C", etc., and couldn't figure out which ones went together. Practically Perfect templates are labeled to reflect their type and **finished** measurements. Therefore, a square is identified as "S." A three-inch square is 3S. A two-inch by four-inch rectangle is labeled as 2X4R, and a two-inch by four-inch right triangle is labeled 2X4RT. Please remember that the **actual** measurements of all templates are 1/2" larger to reflect the addition of 1/4" seam allowances.

Be Accurate!

Your work will only be as good as your tools. Templates are tools. Patchwork is all about accuracy. All through these lessons you will be checking measurements, so start with accurate templates.

At the end of Lessons 3 through 6, you will find paper template patterns to make into durable templates. They begin with the easiest shapes, squares, and advance to more complicated ones. To make your templates you will need:

MATERIALS
for making templates

* ✶ X-Acto or red-handled craft knife with a 24 blade or equivalent (a snap-off-type tool used for wallpaper allows the blade to wiggle and is not suitable for exact cutting)
* ✶ Paper scissors
* ✶ Medium weight cardboard or illustration board approximately 1/8" thick
* ✶ 5 sheets of medium or fine grade sandpaper
* ✶ Rubber cement with brush in the cap

* ✶ Rubber cement "Pick-Up" (optional) to clean up excess rubber cement
* ✶ Emery board
* ✶ Hard, textured surface like a cutting board or piece of Masonite at least 8" x 11" (Use the textured side of the Masonite)
* ✶ 12" or 18" metal ruler with cork backing
* ✶ .5 mm mechanical pencil with H or HB lead
* ✶ Template patterns from this book

Step 1: Separating the Paper Templates

As you begin Lessons 3 - 6, preserve each set of templates by making xerographic copies of them. **Be sure that the copies are exactly the same size as the originals.** Consistently use first copies, not a copy of a copy. With each lesson, cut the paper template copies apart from each other. **Do not cut on the bold lines; just separate the shapes from each other.** There are two 2S template patterns included so that you have one extra for practice. Making templates is just another skill you will acquire as you continue through these lessons.

Step 2: Rubber Cementing

Rubber cement is tricky stuff, but it is the only glue that won't wrinkle your paper template. (We're after accuracy here.) Additionally, if used as instructed, it will hold forever.

To create your first templates, lay your cut-out paper templates right side up on the illustration or cardboard. With a pencil, lightly draw around each piece. Leave about 1/4" between each template. You are designating a space on the cardboard where you will adhere the paper template. Remove your templates and flip them upside down onto scrap paper, getting them ready for cementing.

Brush rubber cement evenly and thinly on the backs of the template pieces. Then, brush rubber cement evenly and thinly onto the receiving areas you drew around them on the illustration board. Let both surfaces dry thoroughly. It will take a few minutes, depending upon how thickly you applied the rubber cement and how much humidity is in the air. Recap that rubber cement; it outgases and is flammable.

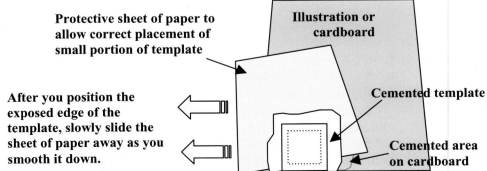

Protective sheet of paper to allow correct placement of small portion of template

After you position the exposed edge of the template, slowly slide the sheet of paper away as you smooth it down.

Illustration or cardboard

Cemented template

Cemented area on cardboard

Once two dried rubber-cemented surfaces touch each other, they will never come apart. To ensure proper placement of the paper template, place a clean sheet of any lightweight paper (typing/copy) over its cemented receiving spot on the cardboard. Expose a small area where you will adhere the first side of the template. Carefully align the template to the cemented receiving area you drew on the cardboard, and press to adhere. Slowly slide the clean sheet of paper away as you carefully smooth the rest of the template onto the cardboard. The back of the template and the cemented cardboard will adhere as soon as they touch each other. This sounds more complicated than it actually is, but it's the only safe way to avoid misplaced paper templates.

Continue to adhere all the pattern pieces to the illustration or cardboard in the same manner.

Take advantage of the straight edges of both the template and the cardboard. With scissors, cut the paper template on one straight line then adhere that edge to a straight cardboard edge. You can also use this trick for corners by cutting two 90 degree sides of the template and aligning them to a cardboard corner. Saves cutting with the craft knife!

Step 3: Cutting Out the Templates

Now, we have to cut the patterns apart so we can use them. For this we will need the red-handled craft knife and the metal ruler with the cork backing. (The cork backing prevents slipping.) Use a hard surface such as a cutting board or the wrong side of a piece of Masonite with its irregular non-slip surface. **Do not use a rotary cutting mat.**

Remember, a sharp blade is an accurate blade. A dull blade is a boo-boo waiting to happen.

NOTE: Only use a metal ruler with a cork backing when cutting out templates!

Be very careful how you place your fingers. Keep them well away from the action edge of the ruler.

Always place the ruler on top of the paper template. This keeps the knife blade at the outside edge of the bold cutting line and **protects the integrity of its shape.** Position the ruler **exactly on each line** you will cut. **Cut on the outside edge of the line.** Hold the craft knife securely, pressing the side of the blade against the ruler as a guide. Draw the **tip** of the blade down the ruler, slightly cutting into the cardboard. You don't have to use extreme pressure, and you don't have to cut all the way through with the first pass. Without moving the ruler, repeat the same cut, going deeper each time until you have cut through all layers of the cardboard. **Each pass will automatically cut deeper.** As you do cut deeper, the groove formed by the cut will help hold your blade in line. **Do not remove the ruler until you've made each cut all the way through the cardboard.** Repeat this process on all sides of the pattern piece until it is liberated from the rest of the cardboard. Follow this procedure for all pattern pieces. **When you are cutting narrowly-pointed pattern pieces, always cut toward the point.**

Step 4: Improved Non-skid Templates

You're almost done! We could use the templates you have made as they are now, but we can improve them so that they won't slide when we cut around them with our rotary cutters.

Take all your newly made templates and lay them right side up on the smooth side of a sheet of sandpaper. The sandpaper is going to become the bottom layer of our templates. Again, draw around each template onto the sandpaper. Repeat the cementing process. Lightly brush cement on the areas you just drew and on the bottoms of your template pieces. When both are dry, again use the clean paper sheet to carefully place the templates onto the receiving areas you drew for them on the sandpaper. This won't be as touchy as it was when you adhered the pattern pieces to the cardboard.

Carefully cut, freehanded (no ruler), around each template with the craft knife. Since you have been so careful in preparing the templates, you do not want the non-skid sandpaper base to be larger than your template. Therefore, **slant** the tip of the blade at an angle toward the template and **cut only the sandpaper.** This actually makes the sandpaper layer a little smaller than the template itself. Now you have a non-skid template!

Step 5: Finishing Touches

You can use an emery board to carefully smooth any rough edges. Also, there is a product called rubber cement "Pick-Up" found in art supply stores that will remove any excess rubber cement; simply rubbing off the excess with your fingers will accomplish the same task. Keep in mind, though, that dried rubber cement erases just like an eraser.

Homework

Make templates for Lesson 3—Squares, Rectangles, and Half-Square Triangles—which begins on the next page. You don't have to make a template for the 6" square if you don't want to. (I don't always make a cardboard template for minimum-use, larger patches. We will cut that patch with our rotary ruler and cutter.) Also have your fabric pre-shrunk, pressed, folded, and ready for the next lesson. We will be constructing:

•**Log Cabin** or **Courthouse Steps** block to identify accurate seam allowances.
•**Four-Patch** block to learn perfect intersections.
•A block containing half-square triangles to learn how to eliminate bias.
•Challenge: one other block of your choice just for fun.

> Our lessons build on all the templates in this workbook. We will be using some of them in more than one lesson. By choosing which blocks you want to construct, you can limit how many templates you will have to make for each lesson. Instructions for each block show which templates are needed. Just make sure that you choose to make a block from each construction technique category.

Squares, Rectangles, and Half-Square Triangles
LESSON 3

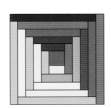

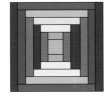

Find and Use Accurate Seam Allowances

Log Cabin Traditional Set
"Logs" are sewn in a clockwise fashion around the center square.

Courthouse Steps Set
"Logs" are attached to the center square: top, bottom, left, right.

Make Perfect Intersections

Four-Patch
This humble little block is the foundation of many patchwork quilt block patterns.

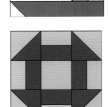

Half-Square Triangles – NO BIAS!
Bluebell
Another log cabin assembly similar to Thistle.

Thistle
This block is similar to a log cabin with larger "logs." It is assembled off-center.

Hole in the Barn Door
You'll build confidence making this block – no diagonal intersections to match.

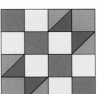

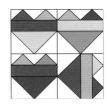

CHALLENGES

Snowball & Nine-Patch
Here you can practice joining diagonal seams to perpendicular seams.

Road to Oklahoma
A complete quilt top of this block makes an over-all directional pattern.

Loop the Loop
Assembled edge-to-edge Loop the Loop makes a wonderful "fool the eye" quilt.

Four Hearts
This block requires careful piecing. Be sure you use a *scant* 1/4" seam allowance!

A completed block will measure 12-1/2" X 12-1/2"; when it is sewn into the quilt top, its finished measurements will be 12" X 12".

In this lesson, we begin to cut the patches we'll sew into blocks that will be assembled into our quilt top. We'll start with squares, rectangles, and half-square triangles because they are the easiest shapes to work with. We will use the rotary cutter, mat, ruler, and templates instead of scissors because we can more quickly and accurately cut out many identical patches at the same time from pressed and folded fabric as shown in the first lesson.

Occasionally straighten and trim off the crosswise edge of your prepared fabrics perpendicular to the selvage and folded edges to ensure patches will be cut on grain.

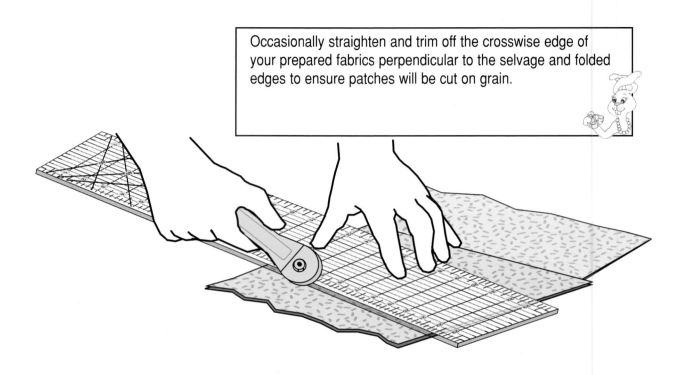

Rotary Cutter Safety

A dull rotary cutter is like a dull knife; both do the best job if they are sharp and can be the cause of damage if they are not. Unfortunately, as expensive as they are, rotary blades become dull with use fairly quickly, so watch for sales and have a supply on hand when you begin a project. Actually, you can purchase rotary blade sharpeners, but blades can be sharpened only a limited number of times.

When you were using the craft knife to cut your templates, you positioned bent fingers on top of the ruler well away from the ruler edge. This is the same position you must use when cutting with the rotary cutter. Expose the blade facing the ruler for cutting. Always cut away from yourself, and always retract the blade after each cut. Anchor your "ruler" hand by placing your ring and little fingers off the ruler on the fabric. When making a long cut, "crawl" your fingers up the ruler parallel to the rotary cutter; in other words, cut as far as across from your fingertips, crawl your "ruler" hand up the ruler (retaining pressure on the ruler and being careful not to move it) as many times as necessary to complete the cut.

Having an additional small cutting mat is so helpful for the detail work of rotary cutting patches. You can place your partially-cut fabric patch on the smaller mat and turn the mat instead of the fabric. The little mats are inexpensive, and having the flexibility to turn your work to a more accessible angle without disturbing the fabric ensures you won't cheat and cut across or toward yourself.

All fabrics are made with tightly-woven selvage edges on both long (lengthwise) sides; therefore, the lengthwise grain of fabric runs parallel to the selvage edges. The lengthwise grain does not stretch. The crosswise grain runs perpendicular to the selvage edges of fabric and "gives" a little. True bias is 45 degrees from either lengthwise or crosswise grain and stretches a great deal. By being aware of these fabric characteristics, we can use them to our advantage and limit the amount of difficulty their improper use can cause.

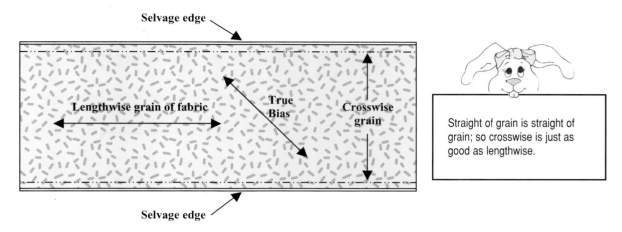

Straight of grain is straight of grain; so crosswise is just as good as lengthwise.

You will notice that each template pattern included in this book has an arrow on it that indicates straight of grain (crosswise or lengthwise). When placing and cutting your patches, pay attention to the grainline arrows marked on each template. Orient each template squarely on the straight of either grain. Although you might be tempted to use the selvage edge of your fabric because you can be certain your patches will be cut on the straight of grain, you will regret using it because its extra-tight weave will act differently from the rest of the material in the patch and cause problems. Use the selvage edge only as a ***reference*** of grainline.

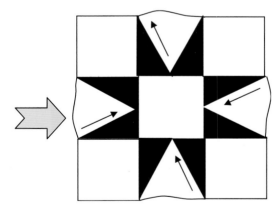

Also, be mindful to control where the bias sides of patches will appear. This means that as we construct our patchwork blocks, the lengthwise or crosswise grain should be at the outside edges of the assembled units as well as the completed block; ***no*** bias on any outside edges, unless you want ruffles.

A Little Patchwork Terminology

In this instruction, **patches** are the individually shaped pieces we will cut and assemble into **sub-units**. Sub-units will be assembled into larger groupings called **units**. Units will be assembled into **blocks**.

How to Cut Patches

Begin with a straight new cut **on the crosswise grain** (perpendicular to the folded and selvage edges) of your prepared fabric pieces.

Be careful when cutting patches; you don't want to cut into your cardboard templates. Take your time. Don't "attack" the fabric. Use the template edges as barriers to guide the rotary cutter as you cut. Treat your templates as tools that you must use carefully so they will retain their accuracy.

• Using the **Four-Patch** block as an example, you can see from the color diagram on the first page of this lesson that it is made of 16 squares using only four colors of fabric. You'll need four squares of two colors; six squares of one color; and two squares of a fourth color.

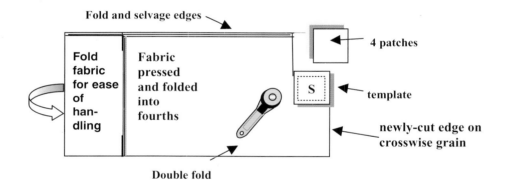

• After you have cut one set of patches, you can use the remaining cut edge as the first cut line for another set of patches.

• Open your folded fabrics if you need less than four patches. You can layer your fabrics and cut two or more different colors at the same time.

• When cutting, hold the template firmly, keeping your fingers away from the edges. Cut away from yourself. **Gently pull excess fabric away from that which is under the template.** You can see if your cut is complete without disturbing the patch. If the fabric is not cut all the way through, you can re-cut. Use more downward pressure with the next cut.

• After making a cut, **always** close the blade.

- You don't have to use templates if you're only going to cut one or two patches like the 6" square for **Snowball and Nine-Patch**, or if the block you will be making consists of strips easily measured and cut using the rotary ruler, as in the **Log Cabin** and **Courthouse Steps** blocks. See the individual instructions for these blocks.

Patchwork's Golden Measure

We will use a straight machine stitch to sew our patches together, but before you begin to sew, it is important to understand the necessity for accuracy in seam allowances. **The patterns in this book use a scant 1/4" seam allowance. The completed blocks measure 12-1/2" by 12-1/2" before assembly into the quilt.** You can imagine if you make only 1/16th of an inch error on each seam multiplied by eight seams, for example, your completed block will be 1/2" off in size. (Don't fear, though, if your blocks are slightly off, there is a fix-up remedy that will be presented in Lesson 7.) Do try your best to sew consistent, scant 1/4" seam allowances.

Where is the Scant Quarter-Inch Mark on the Machine?

There isn't one! But, we can find it. You can buy a special foot for most machines whose left edge is a scant 1/4" from the needle. You would use that left edge as a guide to make a scant 1/4" seam. If you don't have a special foot, you can find the scant quarter-inch mark on your sewing machine by using your rotary ruler. Since you will be using your rotary ruler during the quilt-making process, always use it as your uniform measuring tool. If you purchase other rulers later because you need a different shape or size, buy the same brand to avoid discrepancies from one manufacturer to another.

Place the ruler under the presser foot and drop the foot down to hold the ruler, positioning

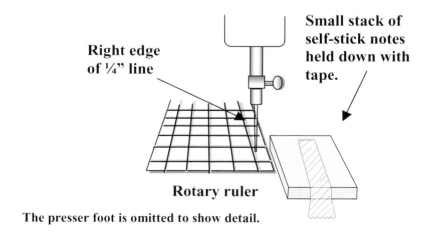

Right edge of ¼" line

Small stack of self-stick notes held down with tape.

Rotary ruler

The presser foot is omitted to show detail.

the needle hole under the 1/4" line at the right edge. Slowly rotate the flywheel to move the needle down to touch the right side of the 1/4" line. A small stack (four to six) of little self-stick notes taped alongside the edge of the ruler and in front of the foot helps you line up your patches, and guides them straight toward the needle. You can also purchase self-stick guides or use a strip of moleskin. Observe where the scant 1/4" mark is in relation to the edge of your machine's foot or feed dogs, and make a mental note.

Stitch a sample 1/4" seam joining two 2" square scraps of fabric. Press the patches open. Check the measurement across the middle of the patches. It should be 4-1/2". If it isn't, make adjustments using the same procedure.

Next Step — Pinning

Select the first two pieces that will be sewn to each other, overlay them right sides together matching raw edges on the side to be sewn, and pin them together with the pin slightly away from the outer edge. Don't take too big a "bite" as it distorts the edges when sewing. Don't sew over pins. You will break your needles and bend your pins. Sewing over pins also distorts the seam line.

OK, I confess. I do sew over pins occasionally. I'm very careful to do it slowly. Sometimes a point just needs to be held while you sew over it. Also, I don't keep my straight pins corralled on a magnet anymore. My friend, Debbie, told me it magnetizes the pins, and when you sew over them, they're sure to attract the needle and break it! She's right!

Correct pin placement

Take Me to Your Leader

What's a scrap leader? It's a piece of scrap fabric you use when beginning to sew your fabric patches together. Start sewing with a doubled-over scrap of fabric, and then feed your layered patches into the needle. The scrap at the beginning prevents the needle from punching the leading edge of the upcoming fabric patches into the needle hole. Plus it gives you something to hold on to when keeping the threads taut as you begin a line of stitching.

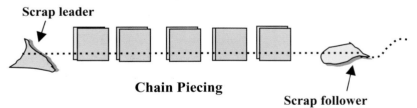

Scrap leader

Chain Piecing

Scrap follower

Chain Piecing

Chain piecing is a streamlined technique that enables you to sew many two-patch sub-units together very quickly. Simply pin a number of two patches together, then sew assembly line fashion almost butting each successive sub-unit one after another. Leave a few stitches of thread between each sub-unit and sew a "scrap follower" at the end of your chain. Clip off the patches leaving the "scrap follower" to become the next "leader."

Pressing Your Patchwork: Seam Allowances — Step to One Side!

I know you think you're learning how to sew patches, but in truth, you'll be using your iron almost as much as you use your sewing machine in patchwork construction. Did you know there's a difference between ironing and pressing? Ironing is what you do to clothing. Pressing is how you "iron" patchwork.

After sewing two patches together, press the seam line as sewn to "set in" the stitches and make it easier to press the patches apart. **In almost all applications, seam allowances will be pressed to one side with the right side of the fabric facing up as you press. This strengthens seams.** Seam allowances are not pressed "open." If seam allowances would be pressed open, the only thing that would hold patches together would be the thread that joined them. By pressing seams to one side, other seams that cross the seam allowances will strengthen the join.

Do not slide the iron back and forth over your assembled seams. This will stretch and distort your work. Press your patchwork with a kind of up-and-down motion. Use **no steam** as it also stretches fabric and burns fingers. When you complete each block, you can spray it with

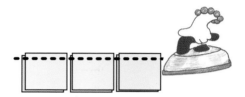

Pressing and "setting in" a line of stitching

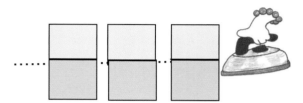

Pressing sub-units open with seam allowance to darker fabric, if possible

fabric sizing, square it up, and give it a good overall press.

Floating Seam Allowance

If you have a choice, you will want to position the joined patches so that the seam allowances will be pressed to the darker fabric to keep them from shadowing through the lighter patches on the quilt top. Sometimes you will need to press one seam allowance in two different directions to press to the dark fabric. This is called a floating seam allowance.

Although pressing to the darker fabric is the ideal, my practical advice is to press seam allowances for ease of construction. If a sliver of darker fabric shadows through to the top under a lighter fabric, trim away the offending darker fabric.

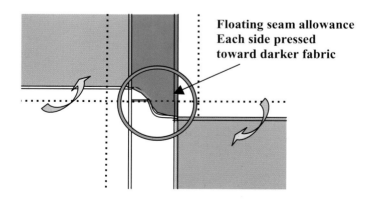

**Floating seam allowance
Each side pressed
toward darker fabric**

The key to making intersections meet perfectly is opposing seam allowances. To accomplish this, use the press to nest principal. This one technique and its applications will give you the power to control how easy it is to construct your patchwork blocks.

You will be sewing many pieced units together with other like units; when joined, you will want the resulting points at seam intersections to meet perfectly, not overlap or not quite touch each other. To accomplish this "miraculous feat," simply place two pieced units that are to be joined, right sides together. Since you have already pressed the seam allowances to one side, just make sure the sides will end up in opposition; in other words, both units will have their seam allowances pressed to the right, but when you stack them right sides together, the seam allowances will be facing in opposite directions. This is called nesting. Feel for a tight nesting fit at the seam, and place pins into the seam allowances on both sides of the seams through all layers as shown. Sew the joining seam, removing each pin after the sewing machine needle is **within each seam allowance**, but just before the needle reaches the pin. Removing the pin after the machine needle is within the seam allowance will prevent any shifting.

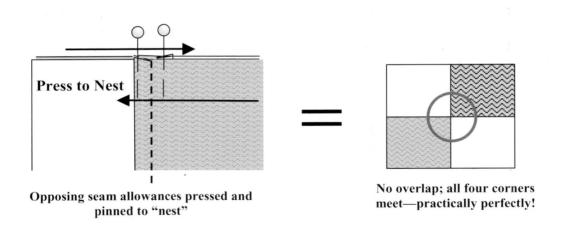

Press to Nest

Opposing seam allowances pressed and
pinned to "nest"

No overlap; all four corners
meet—practically perfectly!

Creative Pressing

When you press your seams to one side, it may make a difference how "perfect" they look depending upon which direction the seam allowance is pressed. After sewing, you can press those seam allowances to make YOU look good! Don't forget to trim any allowance that shadows through to the front.

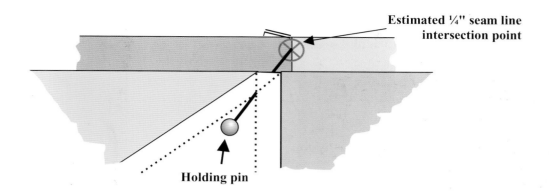

Estimated ¼" seam line
intersection point

Holding pin

The Holding Pin

Matching other configurations such as diagonal and/or straight seams at intersections presents a real challenge. Let's use the example of joining a unit consisting of two squares to another sub-unit of one square and half-square triangles.

In the illustration, two joined squares are face-up behind the square/half-square triangle unit. First, anticipate in which direction you will need the "square/half-square triangle unit" seam allowance pressed so that you can see the triangle intersection you will be matching. Then press the seam allowances of the "squares" sub-unit in opposition. With right sides together, insert a holding pin in the apex of the angle of the top sub-unit. Estimate where the 1/4" seam line will fall on the "squares" sub-unit. Continue to insert that same pin in the anticipated 1/4" seam line on the second sub-unit. Nest seam allowances in the same way we did for squares and rectangles, and pin. Sew 1/4" seam **one thread** above apex (closer to the cut edge) to provide "turning space."

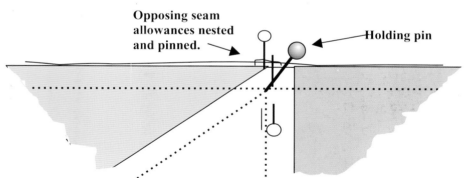

Opposing seam
allowances nested
and pinned.

Holding pin

Holding pin shown in correct position. Note seam line is sewn one thread above intersecting seams. Remove holding pin after machine needle is into seam allowance just before needle would hit it.

Always sew units together with the points you are trying to match visible on top of the layered patches.

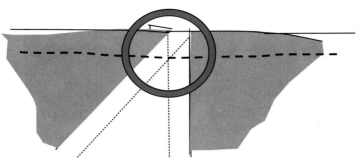

**More than ¼" to raw edge at apex of join—seam
allowance gets gradually wider to cross one thread
above target point, then returns to ¼".**

If you encounter a sub-unit with a target intersection point that is slightly more or less than 1/4" from the raw edge, gauge your distance and ***gradually*** decrease or increase the seam allowance to within one thread of the apex, then ***gradually*** return to 1/4" as you finish the seam. Stop and remove holding pin after your needle is **into** the seam allowance and just before you will cross at apex.

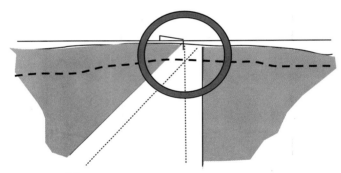

**Not quite ¼" to raw edge at apex of join—seam
allowance gets gradually narrower and crosses one
thread above target point, then returns to ¼".**

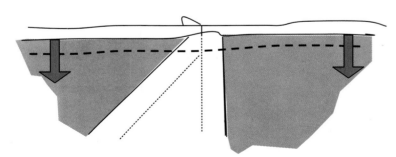

Drop smaller unit down and sew standard ¼" seam

If both units are just slightly smaller than needed, you can adjust the seam allowance where necessary by sewing a seam narrower than 1/4". If only one unit is small, just drop that unit down slightly and pretend it's the right size, then sew your 1/4" seam. Check to ensure there is enough fabric in the seam allowance (at least 1/8") to keep the units from pulling apart. Fear not if you can't make any correction at this time. As long as your blocks are sewn securely together, there are a few tricks we will learn later to alter the size of the finished blocks.

Making Half-Square Triangles

In Lesson 4, you will learn how to deal with triangle patches and their natural inclination to stretch out of shape. For this lesson, though, we will use the "half-square triangle" method to make triangle patches. I always use this technique whenever I need to make small triangles. It is a little wasteful, but very accurate, and you can use your leftovers for "scrap leaders."

Light square on top

Dark square on bottom

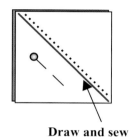

Draw and sew

To make half-square triangles, start with two square patches of the same size. Layer the squares with right sides together. Using your ruler and a .5mm mechanical pencil, draw a diagonal line through the center of the top square. Even though you draw the line diagonally from corner to corner, usually one triangle side of the line will be a little larger than the other (possibly caused by the distortion created by drawing on fabric instead of paper). The larger side is the side you will keep. To help you remember, pin the patches together in the larger side.

Sew the two patches together on the right edge of the drawn line, **favoring the side you will be using.** This gives the seam "turning space." Cut off the excess triangle shape, leaving 1/4" seam allowance.

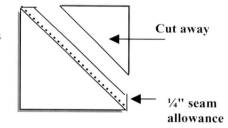

Cut away

¼" seam allowance

Wrong Side

Right side

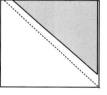

Press seam allowance to dark patch

This is how the half square triangle sub-unit should look.

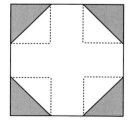

Smaller squares placed over corners of larger square and sewn on diagonal.

Square placed over rectangle, sewn together on diagonal of square.

The half-square triangle technique can be used with a square + rectangle, and a small square + large square. The most important thing to remember in using this technique is to look at the block pattern and determine which way the diagonal line should go when drawn on the wrong side of one square, so that it will be oriented correctly on the right side of the sub-unit. Just like carpenters do, check it twice, cut it once.

When sewing patches together, it is not desirable to backstitch at the beginning and end of each seam, as you would do in garment construction. The "backward" stitches hardly ever go into the same line of stitching, so the width of the seam allowance could be affected. Instead, choose a shorter stitch length that is about 12 stitches to an inch. Because patches are so small, I hardly ever take out stitches. Most of the time I'll just re-cut the patches and start over. As you are assembling your blocks, you will eventually come to a point where you'll have to take out stitches or cut and sew more units and sub-units, and 12 per inch isn't too difficult to remove.

In Lesson 5 we will backstitch at the beginning and ending of seams that undergo stress as they are sewn. But, as my Mom used to say, we don't have to buy that ticket until we board the train.

The Patterns and Instructions

All of the block patterns presented in this workbook appear twice, once grouped in color at the beginning of each lesson so you can see how the patches that make them up are used, and once as a line drawing next to the specific directions for making the blocks. It will be very helpful to you if you color in the line drawings with crayons, colored pencils or markers approximating your fabric colors to aid you in assembling your patches. Keep your diagram in front of you as you stitch your blocks together.

Each pattern gives a little information about the block, indicates which templates to use and some list how many patches you will need to cut. Additional assembly instructions, tips, and techniques are shown as you will need them.

Homework

The patterns and templates for Lesson 3, Squares, Rectangles and Half-Square Triangles, follow. Now, for your assignment, should you choose to accept it:

• Make either the **Log Cabin** traditional set or **Courthouse Steps** blocks. Remember the importance of accurate scant 1/4" seam allowances ... any discrepancy will show here. Read the instructions beside the black and white line drawing. Watch for the "magic trick" you can perform as you attach the last two logs.

• Make the **Four-Patch** block. It will give you the practice you need to make "perfect" intersecting seams.

• Choose and make a half-square triangle block. Here is where you'll master the diagonal/straight seam intersection. Use the "holding pin" technique for combination seam intersection construction.

• Optional: Choose and make any other block from the Challenges.

• Make templates for Lesson 4, Triangles.

If one of your fabrics tends to stretch, sew with the "difficult" fabric placed against the feed dogs. Pin the beginning and ending edges squarely and let the feed dogs do the work of easing in excess fullness. You will be surprised how this little trick will automatically take care of any unruly fabric patches. This method also works when sewing two units together if one is slightly larger than the other.

You'll soon be wondering why I had you go to all the trouble of making durable templates when you see the first two patterns. Both **Log Cabin** and **Courthouse Steps** could be made using templates, but why bother making them when it's so much easier to cut strips with your rotary cutter? Don't worry! There are plenty of opportunities coming up to use templates. I just wanted to make you aware of other options. As mentioned, plastic templates are commercially available for some of the shapes I've given you in this book. But, you're limited to specific sizes, and it becomes quite expensive to purchase all the template shapes you can make from this book, if you can find them.

Just as the pioneers first cut down many trees for logs to build their cabins, we're going to pre-cut an assortment of fabric "logs" with our rotary tools before we construct our blocks. Having our fabrics pressed and folded in fourths is going to make this preparation work easy.

When using the grid rotary ruler to cut patches, it's helpful to place a few small self-stick notes on the under side of the ruler along the grid line you will be referencing. Position the sticky edge right on the line, having the rest of the note extend away from that line. Then, when you align your ruler against the raw edge of a fabric to cut each "log," the note will act as a flag so you won't line up to the wrong measurement. It will also act as a "stop" so that the ruler won't slide.

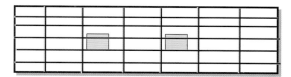

You may want to remember and use this technique whenever you need a number of shapes easily cut with rotary tools, including squares, rectangles, and triangles of various sizes that are quite large; i.e., the 12-1/2" square or triangle you will need in upcoming lessons.

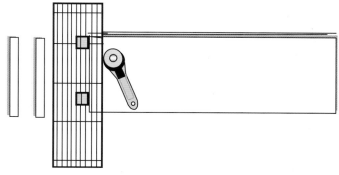

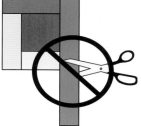

Strip width for the Log Cabin-type blocks finishes 1", which means we have to cut them 1-1/2" to include two 1/4" seam allowances. Strip lengths are given in the pattern and include seam allowances. Don't be tempted to sew a strip onto the growing center square and then cut it off using the already-sewn patches as a gauge. That's not an accurate way to measure length because there's the possibility that the narrow strips will stretch.

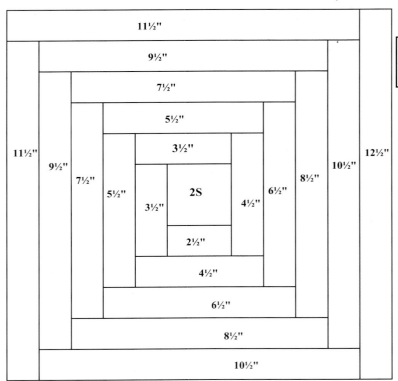

Templates: 2S
There are no other templates.

About this block: Log Cabin is a basic block that will teach the importance of accurate seam allowances. The contrast of light and dark plays an important role when it is made into a whole quilt. Depending upon how you arrange them, numerous secondary designs, known by such names as **Barn Raising**, **Straight Furrows**, etc., can be created. Here, the dark fabrics are on the top and right side, and the light fabrics are on the bottom and left side. In traditional blocks, the center square (2S) was either red to denote "fire in the hearth" or yellow to denote "light in the window" of the log cabin. Color this line drawing to approximate your fabrics repeating colors (fabrics) as needed.

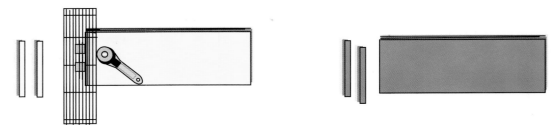

Step 1: Using the grid ruler, cut strips that are 1-1/2" wide from the folded and pressed fabrics you prepared. The number of strips you cut will be determined by how many fabrics you will use. Fabric "logs" can be repeated. Just keep darks with darks and lights with lights. Start with one long strip of each light and dark fabric. Unfolded, those strips will be 1-1/2" by approximately 40". Remember, you don't want to use the selvage edge in a patch.

Step 2: Cut one **each** light and dark "logs" that are **1-1/2" wide** by **3-1/2", 4-1/2", 5-1/2", 6-1/2", 7-1/2", 8-1/2" 9-1/2", and 10-1/2"**. Cut one light log that is **2-1/2"** long and another that is **11-1/2"** long. Don't cut the last **11-1/2"** and **12-1/2"** dark logs until you have assembled the rest of the block. All these measurements include the 1/4" seam allowance.

Step 3: With a scant 1/4" seam allowance, begin sewing the center 2S patch to the 2-1/2" light log. Continue to attach logs as shown in the diagram alternating light, dark, dark, light, etc., around the center square in clockwise fashion. Make previously attached logs fit the new ones by placing the larger log against the feed dogs and easing in fullness. As you add each log, press seam allowances away from the center.

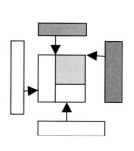 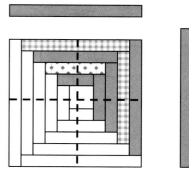

Step 4: Before you attach the last two "logs," press your block well and measure across the **middle** of your almost-completed block from:

side to the side = _____ inches **and top to the bottom** = _____ inches

Your almost-finished **Log Cabin** block should measure 11-1/2" X 11-1/2". If it doesn't, the last two logs may need to be cut **wider** than 1-1/2". (Don't worry, when assembled into your quilt top, no one will be able to tell they are wider.) With this adjustment, you can be certain your finished block will be 12-1/2" X 12-1/2".

Subtract your **side-to-side** measurement from the goal of 12-1/2". Do the same for the **top to bottom** measurement. Add 1/2" for seam allowances to each remainder, and you will get the exact width you will need to cut each of the last two logs.

Insert your measurements:

	12-1/2"ideal side		12-1/2" ideal top to bottom
	-_____" Actual		-_____" actual
	difference		difference
	+ 1/2"seam allowance		+ 1/2"seam allowance
New width of	_____" last side log		_____" last top log

Step 5: If necessary, cut and attach the last two dark logs using your calculated new width measurement. The lengths of the logs should still be 11-1/2" and 12-1/2". **OR....**

If your almost-finished block is larger than 11-1/2" X 11-1/2", go ahead and cut the last two logs 1-1/2" by 11-1/2" and 12-1/2", respectively, then attach as before. Your block will be larger than 12-1/2" square and will be trimmed to size later when we assemble the top. Since your block is larger, go back and correct the seam allowance reference line you marked on your machine.

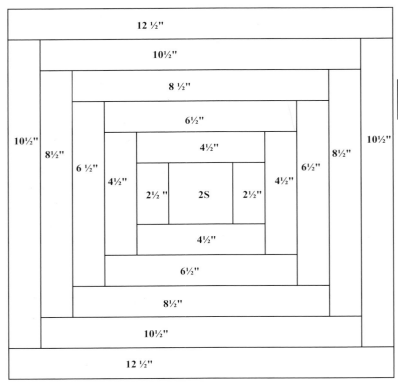

Templates: 2S
There are no other templates.

About this block: As you can see from the color illustration of blocks at the beginning of this lesson, **Courthouse Steps** has coloration that is also light versus dark, but here the lights and darks are opposite each other with light on top and bottom and dark on the sides. This creates the optical illusion of depth. Because this block, too, has so many seams, you probably guessed that making it will impress you with the importance of accurate seam allowances.

Step 1: Prepare and cut 1-1/2" fabric strips as for traditional **Log Cabin**.

Step 2: Cut two **each** light and dark logs that are **1-1/2" wide** by **4-1/2"**, **6-1/2"**, **8-1/2"**. Cut one dark log **1-1/2" wide** by **10-1/2"** long. Cut two dark logs that are **1-1/2" wide** by **2-1/2"** long. Cut one light log **1-1/2" wide** by **12-1/2"** long and two that are **10-1/2"** long.

Step 3: Instead of attaching logs clockwise to the center 2S patch, these logs are sewn first side-to-side then top and bottom, repeating until after you attach the third 10-1/2" log.

Step 4: Follow the instructions detailed in the **Log Cabin Traditional Set** directions for measuring and cutting the width of the last 10-1/2" log and the last 12-1/2" log. Unfortunately, you will have to make your calculations twice: Once when you measure to add the last 10-1/2" log, then again when you add the last 12-1/2" log.

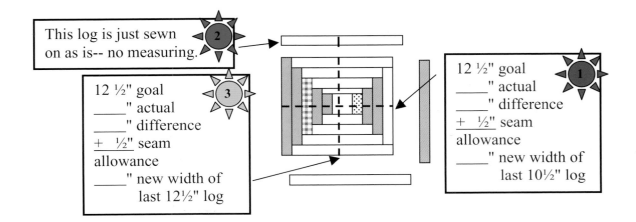

1	2		
3	4		

Simple Four-Patch Block

> **Templates: 3S = Cut 16 patches**

About this block: The **Four-Patch** is one of the most basic traditional blocks. It is believed to be the first block taught to a young girl just learning to piece patchwork. The form of this block is used as a foundation for much more intricate block combinations, which you will see as you progress through this book. Color in this diagram to help you decide fabric placement. By sewing this block, you will learn how to make perfect intersections.

Step 1: Join eight sets of two squares together **according to your colored diagram** to get eight rectangle units. Assembling this block presents an excellent opportunity to practice chain piecing as shown in this lesson.

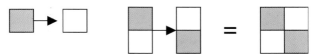

Step 2: Following your color guide, sew two rectangle sub-units together to get a four-patch square. Press to nest to create perfect intersections. Create floating seam allowances or press for ease of construction. If necessary, use "imaginative seam allowances." Repeat this process three more times to make (four) four-patch units. You've almost completed this block!

Step 3: In the same way you joined the rectangle sub-units into a square, nest and pin, then sew two sets of four squares together. You now have two halves of the block that measure approximately 12-1/2" X 6-1/2".

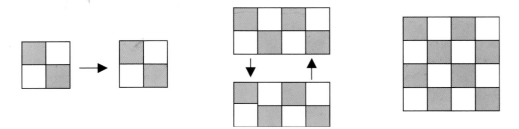

Step 4: Join the two halves together pressing to nest, and you are finished. Congratulations!

It is more accurate to assemble patchwork (or even whole quilts) in block segments as we did units 1, 2, 3, and 4. If assembled in rows, the seams will take on a wavy look.

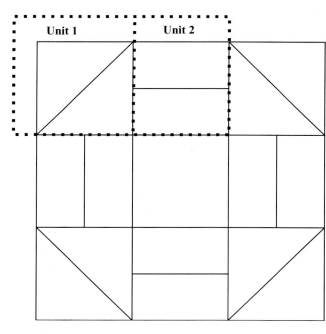

Unit 1   Unit 2

Templates: 4S =
Cut 4 of one color
Cut 5 of second color
  2X4R =
Cut four of each color

About this block: Hole in the Barn Door is also known as Churn Dash. It is a nine-patch, which is another basic, traditional block. Choose two colors that contrast well for your patches. By stitching this block, you will be practicing the half-square triangle technique.

Step 1: Refer to half-square triangle instructions and make four half-square triangles. Press seam allowances to darker fabric. This is Unit 1.

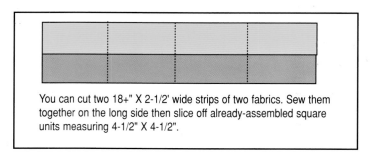

You can cut two 18+" X 2-1/2' wide strips of two fabrics. Sew them together on the long side then slice off already-assembled square units measuring 4-1/2" X 4-1/2".

Step 2: To make Unit 2 you can cut and join two different color rectangles on the long sides, or you can follow the short cut above. Make four like units. Press seam allowances to darker fabric.

Step 3: Assemble the first and third rows of this block by joining two of Unit 1 to opposite sides of Unit 2. Press seam allowances to the darker fabric.

Step 4: Assemble the middle row by rotating the remaining Units 2 and attaching to opposite sides of 4S. Put your press to nest method to work here. If you have pressed the seam allowances in rows 1 and 3 **away from** the center unit, press the seam allowances in row 2 **towards** the center square, or vice versa.

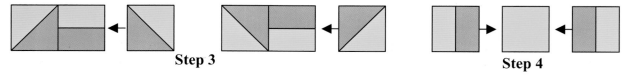

Step 3   Step 4

Step 5: Join rows 1and 3 to row 2, nesting seams. "Creative Press" the long seam allowances to whichever sides give the face of the block the most accurate look.

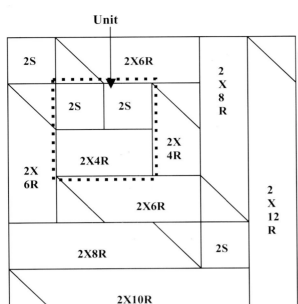

Unit

2S	2X6R		2 X 8 R
2S	2S		
	2X4R	2X 4R	
2X 6R	2X6R		2 X 12 R
2X8R		2S	
2X10R			

Templates:
2S   =Cut 12
2X4R =Cut 2
2X6R =Cut 2
2X8R =Cut 2
2X10R= Cut 1
2X12R=Cut 1

Or you can cut strips as in Log Cabin.

About This Block: Using the color picture of Thistle at the beginning of this lesson, color the diagram to resemble your fabrics. This will help you correctly orient squares on the rectangles to use the half-square triangle technique. **Thistle** is assembled like an off-center **Log Cabin** block.

There is one whole 2X4R patch and four whole 2S patches in this block. There are eight 2S patches that are used to make half-square triangles at the ends of the rectangles. Do you see why it is so helpful to be able to refer to a color diagram as you cut out the patches to make **Thistle**? It's a challenge, but I know you can do it. As you cut your patches, arrange them into the **Thistle** block laying the 2S patches on top of the rectangles you will be joining to them.

Step 1: Join two of the **2S** patches that make part of the **Thistle** flower and add 2X4R to make Unit 1.

As you make Thistle, press the seam allowances to expose diagonal intersecting points. You may have to change the direction you pressed some prior seam allowances as you continue assembly.

Step 1

Step 2

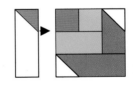

Step 3

Step 2: To make the rest of the flower, pin 2S patches right sides together at the correct ends of 2X4R and 2X6R, referring to your color diagram. **Be sure to draw the diagonal line in the proper direction.** Pin, sew, trim, and press. Then attach the 2X4R sub-unit to the right side of Unit 1. Press seam allowance toward Unit 1. Make and sew 2X6R sub-unit to the bottom of Unit 1 in the same way. Press the seam allowance also toward Unit 1.

Step 3: Make and add the 2X6R sub-unit that is part of the left edge of the block. When you are sewing this unit to Unit 1, you won't be able to see both diagonal and straight intersections. Use the hold pin technique. The hold pin insertion point denotes where the seam should be sewn.

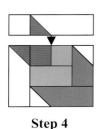

Step 4

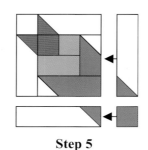

Step 5

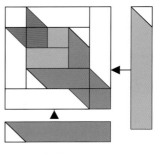

Step 6

Step 4: Make another 2X6R sub-unit, attach a 2S background patch and sew to the top edge of the block using the hold pin technique. You again have a square.

Step 5: Continue by making two 2X8R sub-units with 2S in the leaf color attached to the correct end of each rectangle. Attach 2S in the leaf color to the bottom sub-unit and sew to the block.

Step 6: Make the leaf sub-units which complete the block using 2X10R + 2S and 2X12R + 2S and attach.

Would you like to try another similar block all by yourself?

Unit 1

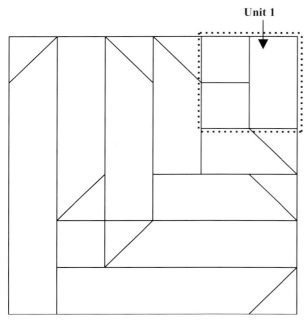

Bluebell — Another Modern Log Cabin Block

> **Templates:**
> 2S   =Cut 11
> 2X4R=Cut 2
> 2X6R=Cut 2
> 2X8R=Cut 3
> 2X10R= Cut 1
> 2X12R=Cut 1
> **Alternatively, you can cut strips as in Log Cabin.**

See if you can tell what size rectangles are used to make up this block. Hint: the left side sub-unit is 2X12R + 2S. Label this diagram before you color it in.

Use the same methods to make **Bluebell** as described for **Thistle**.

The "center" (Unit 1) for **Bluebell** is the three-patch unit in the upper right hand corner and consists of two 2S patches and one 2X4R rectangle. You use the half-square triangle technique to make each rectangle that you add alternately to the left and bottom sides of the block.

You're really making progress!

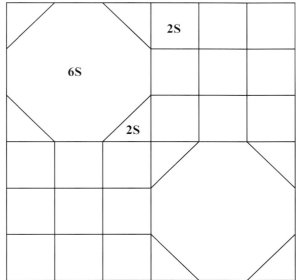

Snowball and Nine-Patch — 4-Patch

Templates:
2S = Cut ____ of one color
       Cut ____ of second color
6S = Cut 2 OR...
It's easier to cut the 6" squares with your rotary cutter and ruler than it is to make the template. Just remember, 6" is the finished measurement. The squares you cut should be ____" X ____".

About this block: The **Snowball and Nine-Patch** block is composed of two individual blocks. Can you tell which is which? Although both are nine-patch blocks, put together in this configuration the completed block becomes a four-patch. I told you it was confusing!

You already know the importance of coloring and referring to the diagram. You also have learned enough about what patches make up a block to be able to tell how many of each kind are in this block, including the extra eight 2S patches you will need to make the Snowballs.

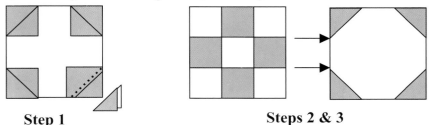

Step 1   **Steps 2 & 3**

Step 1: Let's make the Snowball Block first. You can see the corners of 6S are cut off diagonally in another application of the half-square triangle technique. Right sides together, squarely position a 2S patch at each corner of 6S. Make sure their two common edges are even. Pin within the half-square triangle you want to save. Draw the diagonal sewing line, sew, cut, and press. **Voila** – a snowball! Make two.

Step 2: The nine-patch is assembled in the same way as the **Four-Patch** block.

Step 3: Now for the difficult part. Using the holding pin technique, you have to match up diagonal seams with perpendicular seams as you join one nine-patch to a Snowball unit. Not only that, you have to join the resulting half blocks to each other and match even more diagonal to perpendicular seams. Using the holding pin technique should take most of the pain away ... and there's always the seam ripper to make corrections. Do the best you can, and don't forget "Creative Pressing."

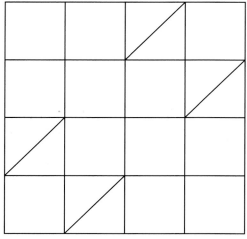

Road to Oklahoma

Template: 3S = Cut 20

All totaled, you will need twenty 3" squares.

Begin by making four half-square triangles.

Assemble the four, four-patch units. Two will be just like the **Four-Patch** block and two will contain half-square triangles. Always press for ease of construction, so you can see points and intersections when you are joining units.

Don't forget all the helpful techniques you've learned: pressing to nest, holding pin, creative pressing, imaginative seam allowances, etc.

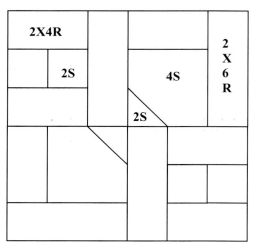

Loop the Loop

Templates:
2S = Cut 6
4S = Cut 2
2X4R = Cut 6
2X6R = Cut 4

This block is a four-patch made up of two different units, as you can see in the line drawing. Magic happens when you make a whole quilt of this block, rotating one to another 1/4 turn as you sew the blocks together.

Assemble both like units then join together nesting seams and matching intersections.

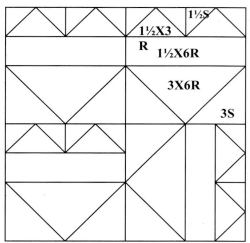

Four Hearts

Templates:
1-1/2S = Cut 16
1-1/2X3R = Cut 8
1-1/2X6R = Cut 4
3X6R = Cut 4
3S = Cut 8

This is not an easy block —a cute block, yes, but not an easy one. You have the skills and the knowledge to make it. By the time you finish the fourth heart, you'll be an expert. Good luck!

1½ S

1 ½" square

2S

2" square

2S

2" square

3S

3" square

4S

4" square

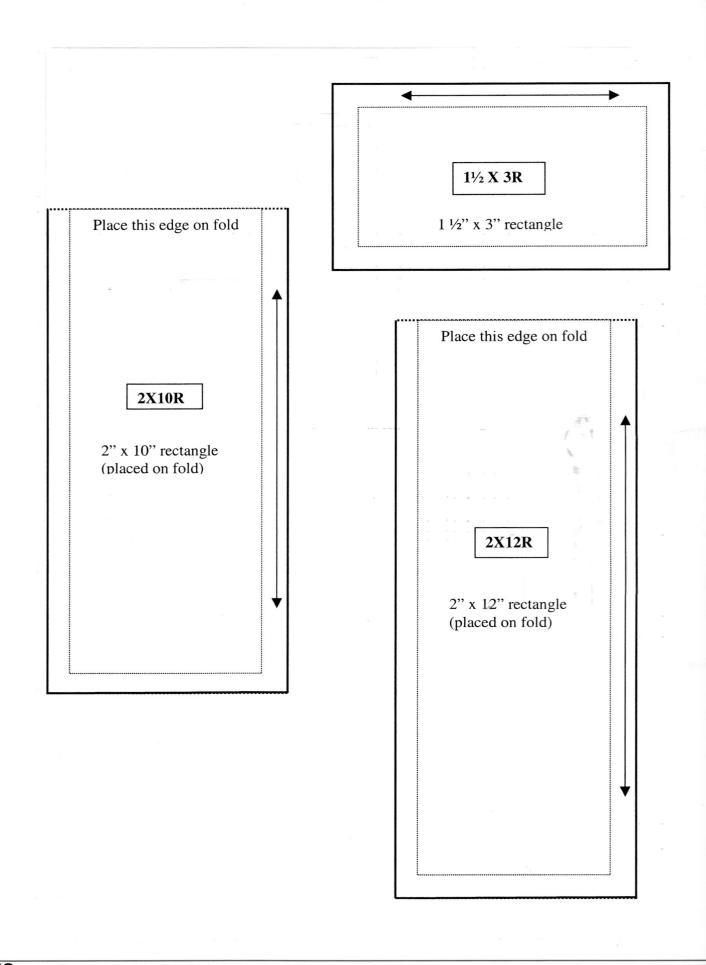

1½ X 3R

1 ½" x 3" rectangle

Place this edge on fold

2X10R

2" x 10" rectangle
(placed on fold)

Place this edge on fold

2X12R

2" x 12" rectangle
(placed on fold)

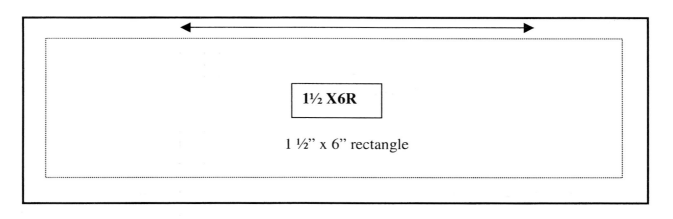

1½ X6R

1 ½" x 6" rectangle

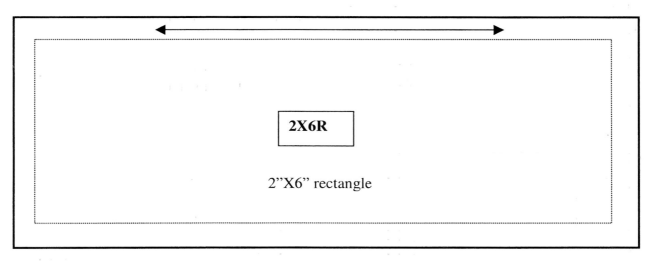

2X6R

2"X6" rectangle

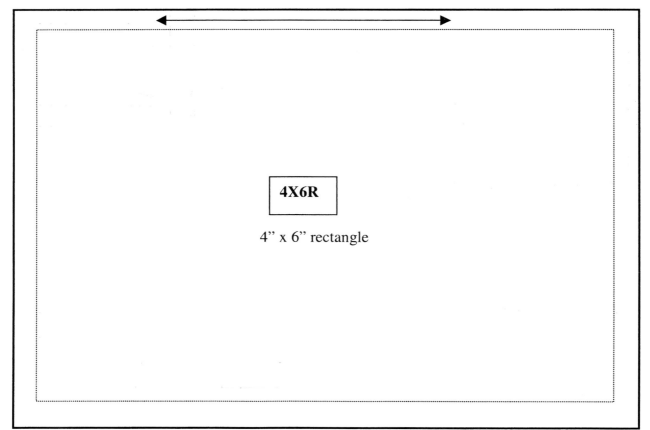

4X6R

4" x 6" rectangle

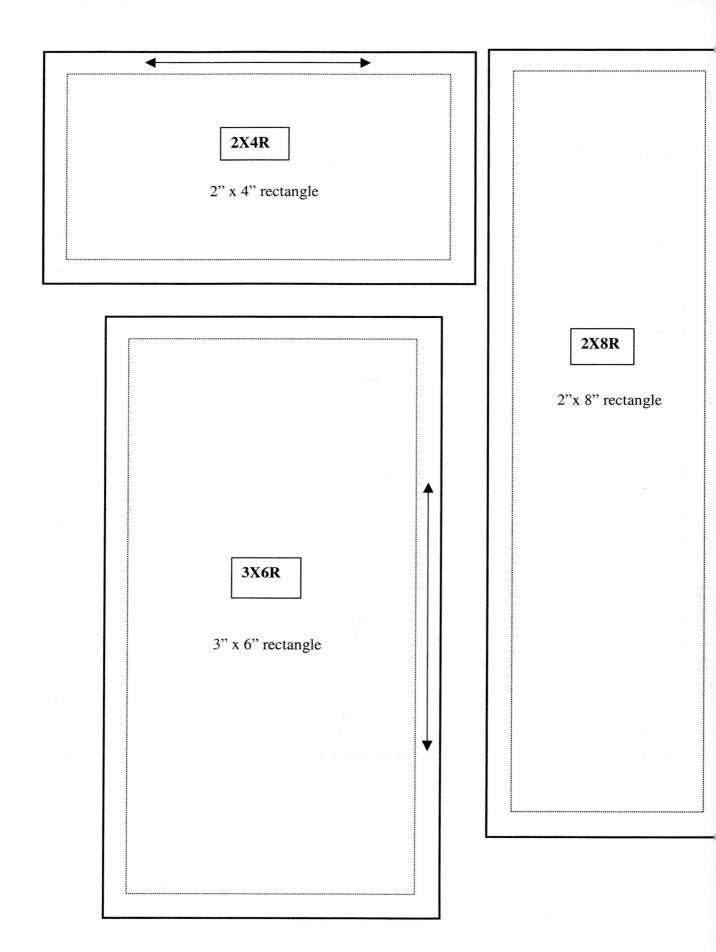

2X4R

2" x 4" rectangle

3X6R

3" x 6" rectangle

2X8R

2"x 8" rectangle

Remember, you don't have to make this large template if you don't want to.

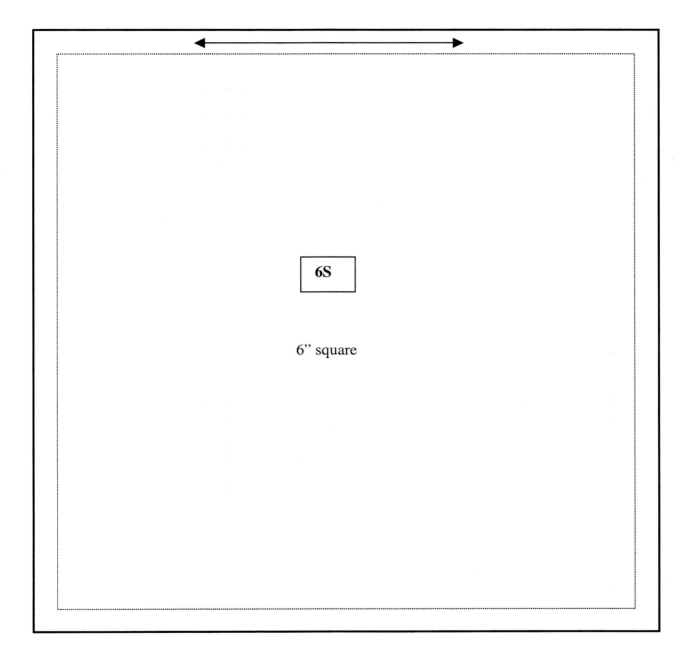

6S

6" square

Working with Triangles:
Try one of the blocks in this column first to practice working with bias.

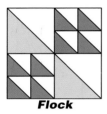

Flock

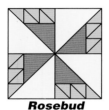

Rosebud

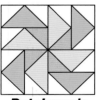

Dutchman's Puzzle

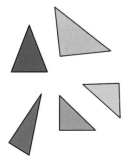

These are all different arrangements of a basic block known as Variable Star.

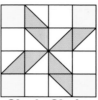

Clay's Choice

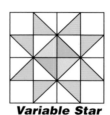

Variable Star

Broken Dishes

Pinwheel

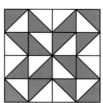

Barbara Fritchie Star

Can you see that these three nine-patch blocks are very similar?

Ohio Star

Sweet Gun Leaf

Card Trick

Here are the Challenge Triangle blocks:

54-40 or Fight

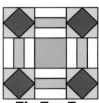

Tic-Tac-Toe

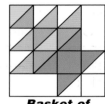

Basket of Triangles

The stem in Sweet Gum Leaf is made using freezer paper appliqué. You can learn how in this lesson.

Triangle shapes used in patchwork are versatile. Blocks containing triangles can be used to show direction. They can be used together to create the illusion of curves. They come in so many happy three-sided shapes. They can be sturdy and solid, or they can be slender and graceful. You can see by the number of triangle blocks included in this lesson how much I enjoy working with them.

Sewing patchwork triangles can be a real challenge. In Lesson 3, you learned how to create triangle units using the half-square triangle method that eliminated the complications of working with patches that have side(s) cut on fabric bias. In this lesson you will learn how to deal with the idiosyncrasies of bias fabric. Don't be tempted to use the half-square triangle technique when constructing the blocks. It's important that you learn how to work with triangles' bias sides that, guaranteed, will easily stretch out of shape.

Do you remember where bias is in fabric? If not, go back to Lesson 3 to review. Although true bias runs at a 45 degree angle, any cut of fabric that is not on the lengthwise or crosswise grain should also be treated as bias because it, too, will stretch. I can't stress strongly enough that an understanding of the inherent characteristics of fabrics will help you use their idiosyncrasies to your advantage.

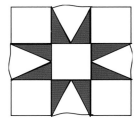

As mentioned before, whenever we cut fabric patches that will have bias side(s), we must think ahead to where the patch will appear in a sub-unit, unit, or even in a block. We do not want any bias on the outside edges of our blocks.

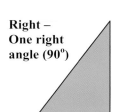

Our templates have arrows showing grainline to help you in orienting them on your fabric before cutting. By placing the templates on your fabric and aligning the arrows to either the crosswise or lengthwise grain, your patches will be cut correctly.

A Triangle is a Polygon with the Least Number of Sides

There are specific names for triangles of different shapes. They are classified by the angles they contain (see illustrations below).

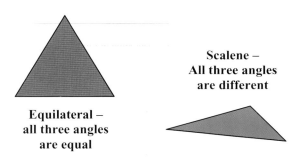

Equilateral –
all three angles
are equal

Scalene –
All three angles
are different

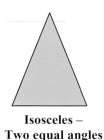

Isosceles –
Two equal angles

Right –
One right
angle (90°)

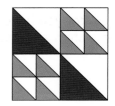

We will use the **Flock Block** as an example to demonstrate how to work with triangles. Three-inch and six-inch right triangles make up the block. Cut eight 3" triangles (3RT) from two fabrics. Cut four 6" triangles (6RT) from two fabrics.

Okay, let's go for those little 3" triangles. Overlay, right sides together, eight 2-color sets of 3RT. When joining these triangles, it is a simple matter to match all the angles. Pin your triangle patches together at the beginning and end of the seam line as shown. The pins act as "handles" for you to hold to keep the seam straight. This is especially important at the end of the seam where the patch will tend to move sideways as it exits the presser foot. Hold onto those handles removing them just before the needle reaches them.

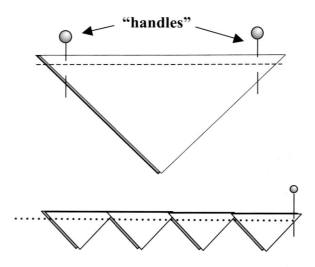

Now is a good time to use the chain piecing technique. As you guide the patches one after another between the presser foot and the feed dogs, slightly overlap the triangles (as shown). A continuous feed of fabric helps keep the patches from skewing sideways by giving the feed dogs something to "bite" onto. Enough thread is stitched between patches to make a secure seam. Don't forget to use your scrap "leaders" and "followers."

Use a stiletto, seam ripper, or sharpened wooden chopstick to help you hold those little patches as you sew.

After you have sewn all 3RT together, press seam allowances of six sub-units in one direction and the seam allowance of the other two sub-units in the other direction. This will allow you to see intersections when you join them together later.

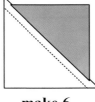
make 6

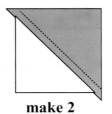
make 2

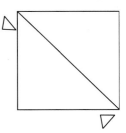

After pressing, you will see that you have little triangles overhanging at the seam. I call these "bunny ears" (what else?). Trim off the overhanging "ears" to make a square. (Some quilters prefer to cut off the bunny ears prior to assembly. I don't; I use those little triangular tips to help me correctly align patches.)

Next, sew the 3RT sub-units together as you did when you made the **Four-Patch** block. Be sure to employ the "hold" pin technique you learned in the last lesson. You'll notice this unit is quite similar to one in **Road to Oklahoma**, but you have twice the number of diagonal-to-straight seam intersections to match. Make two four-patch units.

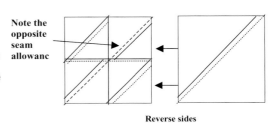
Note the opposite seam allowanc

Reverse sides

Make two 6RT triangle squares. Press the diagonal seams opposite each other and attach to the correct side of each four-patch unit.

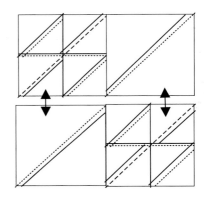

Sew the two block halves together, nesting and matching seams. Use your "imaginative seam allowance" trick, if necessary. "Creative press" the final seam join to get the best look on the right side. You're done!

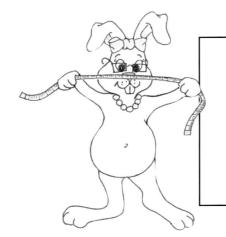

As you continue piecing each block, always check the dimensions of your assembled units to see if they "measure up" to the pattern.

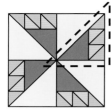

When joining triangles to assembled units that take on a new shape, as in the **Rosebud Block,** you will have to *offset* your patches by the 1/4" seam allowance. This exemplifies why I don't like to trim the bunny ears off my triangles before sewing; those little corners help you judge where to set your patches and place your seam.

Rosebud is made from 2", 4", and 6" right triangles. To begin, sew two sets of 2RT together on the long side as shown for **Flock** making two squares. Orient the colors correctly, and join the two squares to make a rectangle. Don't forget to use your "handles."

As you look at your rectangle sub-unit, check your colored-in pattern to determine which side to attach 4RT. Overlay the 4RT patch matching right angles and offsetting the overhanging corner by *approximately* 1/4". Pin, and sew beginning at the offset. Trim the bunny ear as shown, and press the seam allowance to the darker color (or the direction that makes your piecing look the best).

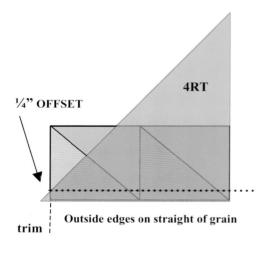

¼" OFFSET

4RT

Outside edges on straight of grain

trim

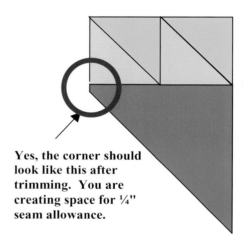

Yes, the corner should look like this after trimming. You are creating space for ¼" seam allowance.

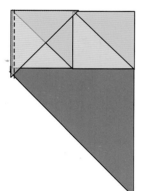

In the same way you attached 4RT, attach another 2RT to the left edge of the rectangle sub-unit matching right angles and offsetting the overhanging corner by approximately 1/4". You can trim the offset angle, but it's not necessary if you press the seam allowance toward the pieced rectangle. It should fall in line with the long side of 4RT.

This is how your pieced triangle should look when completed. Notice there appears to be an extension on the long side of the assembled unit that allows for the ¼" seam.

Making one-fourth of the **Rosebud** block is a simple matter of sewing two 6RT together, one pieced by **you**. Make three more and sew them together matching and nesting seams as shown for **Flock**, and your block will be done. You'll be getting lots of experience using imaginative seam allowances and creative pressing for practically perfect patchwork.

There are two more types of seams encountered when piecing triangle blocks in this lesson.

The diagram below shows bias sides of two differently shaped triangles being sewn together. You will encounter this configuration in **Dutchman's Puzzle**, and **54-40 or Fight**. When sewing

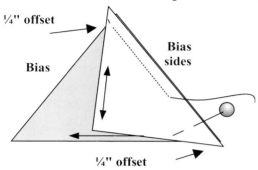

¼" offset

Bias

Bias sides

¼" offset

these types of patches together, offset and pin the two end points, then stitch while holding the seam taut. (I won't use the word "pulling." What you want to do is keep the raw edges even and patches aligned as you sew.) This type of unit is an example of the "no outside bias edges" rule. Remember, if one of the patches is extra stretchy; sew with it on the bottom against the feed dogs. Let the feed dogs do the easing in.

Tic-Tac-Toe brings you another type of triangle seam to conquer. Compared to sewing two bias triangle sides together, this seam is a cinch! For clarity, the diagram shows the triangle being sewn on top, but give the feed dogs on your machine something to do by placing the triangle under the square for stitching.

Again, at times you might have to alter the direction you pressed a seam when you sew your completed units into blocks. You'll be creating "floating" seam allowances within some of the blocks in this lesson.

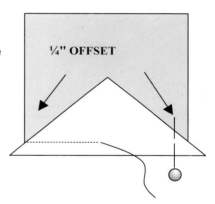

¼" OFFSET

Homework

The patterns and instructions for Lesson 4 – Triangles, follow. Your assignment in developing triangle block-making skills is:

* Complete your choice of **Flock**, **Rosebud**, or **Dutchman's Puzzle**.
* Choose and make a variable star block from those shown on page 50. All the variable star adaptations are more intricate versions of the **Four-Patch** block we learned in Lesson 3.
* Make one of the Nine-patch blocks: **Ohio Star**, **Card Trick**, or **Sweet Gum Leaf**.
* *Optional*: Choose, and make, one of the Challenge Blocks: **Tic-Tac-Toe** (not such a challenge), **54-40 or Fight,** or **Basket of Triangles**.
* Make templates for Lesson 5, Polygons.

Refer back to your chosen quilt diagram to see if you're on track in the number of quilt blocks you will need to finish your quilt. I've found that you will want to make more blocks than required because some just won't look that good with the rest. You can make pillows out of the orphans.

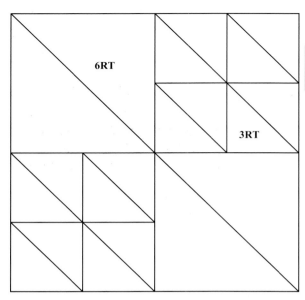

Flock

Templates: 3RT = Cut 8 of two colors
6RT = Cut 2 of two colors

About this block: The quilter who made up this four-patch block must have loved watching the birds flock up to fly South for the winter. She reduced her piecing work by substituting one large 6" triangle for four smaller 3" triangles. (There were many chores early quiltmakers had to do besides making all their family bedcovers.)

Using the color example, choose your fabrics to contrast well so you can see the "flying birds" design.

Arrange and assemble as you learned in this lesson.

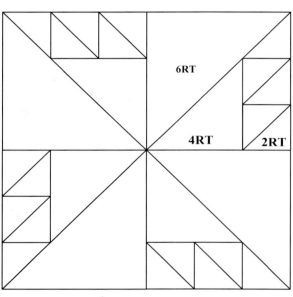

Rosebud

Templates: 2RT = Cut 20 of two colors
4RT = Cut 4
6RT = Cut 4
Okay, you can use 2S for the half-square triangles, I'll never know. But don't cheat yourself in learning how to piece the smaller triangles.

About this block: This large pinwheel-type block is another four-patch variation.

Using the instructions in this lesson, assemble the four units positioning each unit a quarter turn from the one next to it.

POWER CHECKLIST

√ *Chain piecing*
√ *Press to nest*
√ *Match points with imaginative seam allowances*
√ *Creative press for the best look*

√ *Measure completed units for accuracy*
√ *Use "hold" pin*
√ *Trim bunny ears*

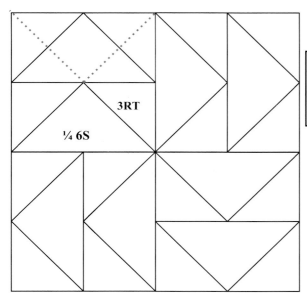

Dutchman's Puzzle

> **Templates: 1/4 6S = Cut 8**
> **3RT = Cut 16**
> **Experiment with your color choices to create a secondary pinwheel pattern.**

About this block: Even though template 1/4 6S is a right triangle, what it is **not,** as you can see, is half a square as used in this block. 1/4 6S is a triangle you get when you divide a square diagonally with an "X". It's **a fourth** of a square. 1/4 6S is smaller than 6RT. The patches aren't interchangeable. This example shows the importance of knowing whether a triangle is used as half of a square or a quarter of a square.

Step 1: Cut eight 1/4 6S with the longest side on the straight of grain. Cut 16 of 3RT with right angle sides on straight of grain.

Step 2: To make the rectangular sub-unit, stitch 3RT to both short sides of 1/4 6S using the handle and offset techniques shown in the lesson. This is another good time to do your chain piecing. Make eight pieced rectangles. Press seams to 3RT.

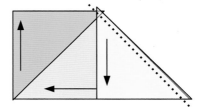

Step 3: Stitch two rectangle sub-units together using the imaginative seam technique, if necessary. As you join the sub-units, you want to have your seam line cross just above the apex of 1/4 6S (see circle in diagram below) to make a perfect intersection. Use creative pressing to get the best look. You can readjust the seam allowance to expose the outside angle when sewing the units together. Remember, always sew with the points you are trying to match visible on top. In this way, make four units.

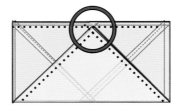
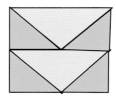

You won't see this target point

But you will see these two

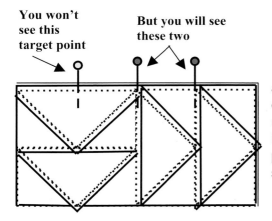

Step 4: Adjust and create floating seam allowances as you pin and get ready to sew the two halves. You will only be able to see two target intersections on the top unit. Nest and use a hold pin for the exact middle intersection and the visible target point. Place another pin to indicate the hidden target point and stitch the seam.

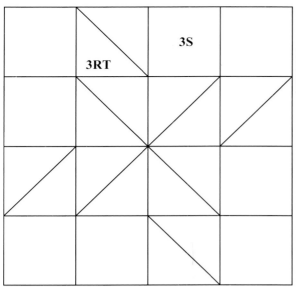

Clay's Choice

Templates: 3RT = Cut 16
3S = Cut 8

About these blocks: The five four-patch blocks on this page and the next are classified as variations of the **Variable Star** block. **Clay's Choice** and **Variable Star** have triangle shapes replaced by squares, thus reducing the number of patches. **Barbara Fritchie Star, Pinwheel,** and **Broken Dishes** are only three examples of the many patterns you can make by altering the arrangement and coloration of the triangle patches.

You have the skills to make any of these five blocks. They are shown in order of difficulty. Just remember your helpers: chain piecing, trimming bunny ears, "hold pin," matching points with imaginative seam allowances, floating seams, pressing to nest, and creative pressing for the best look.

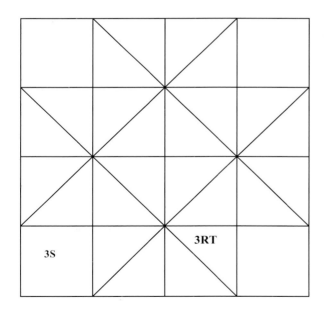

Variable Star

Templates: 3S = Cut 4
3RT = Cut 24

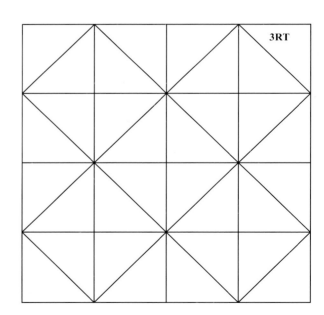

Broken Dishes

Template: 3RT = Cut 32

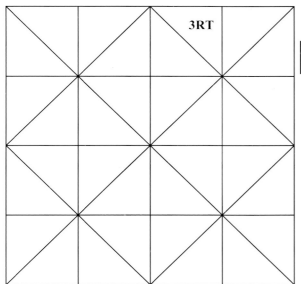

Pinwheel

Template: 3RT = Cut 32

Aren't you glad we have rotary cutters?

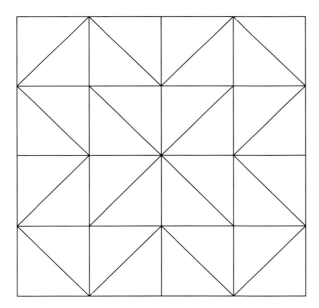

Barbara Fritchie Star

Templates: 3RT = Cut 32

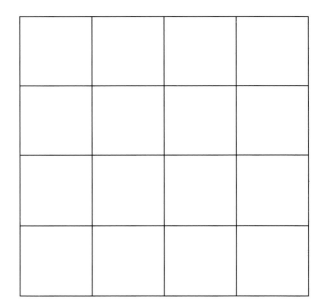

You're a Star!

Templates: Make up your own block.

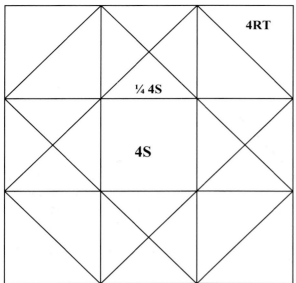

Ohio Star

Templates:
1/4 4S = Cut 16
4RT = Cut 4
4S = Cut 1

About this block: Although similar, this star differs from the **Variable Star** in that it's a nine-patch instead of a four-patch block. After piecing 16 sub-units, you'll appreciate making only nine for this block – and the center square is **not** pieced!

Remember correct cutting placement of the long side of 1/4 4S to keep outside edges on the straight of grain.

Card Trick

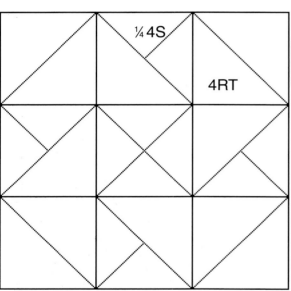

Templates:
4RT = Cut 12
1/4 4S = Cut 12

About this block: Yet another block that uses 1/4 square triangles. Note the placement of the long side of 1/4 4S. It always appears as the outside edge of the unit/block, so you know you'll have to cut those triangles with the long side on the straight of grain. **Card Trick** is a variation of **Ohio Star**. Broken down into its component parts, you can see how easy it is to construct. Use of color here is very important to achieve the illusion of interlocking "cards."

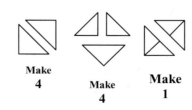

Make 4   Make 4   Make 1

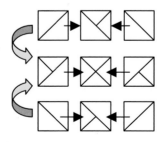

Refer to diagrams as you assemble sub-units.

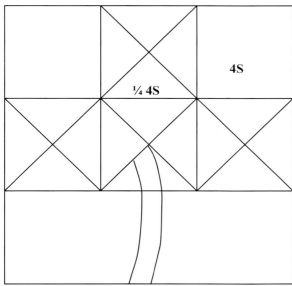

Sweet Gum Leaf

Templates:
1/4 4S = Cut 16
4S = Cut 2
Stem Pattern
4X6R = Cut one on fold
(less 1 seam allowance*)
Or cut: 4-1/2" X 12-1/2" rectangle

About this block: The quarter square sub-units of this block are pieced the same as the center block in **Card Trick**. To make the 4-1/2" X 12-1/2" rectangle at the bottom, use the 4X6R template and cut on the fold. The fold eliminates the need for a center seam. Cut as shown:

Stem for Sweet Gum Leaf

Trim where needed

Into Seam

Step 1: To make the stem, get a piece of freezer paper from your kitchen drawer and place it over this stem pattern with the shiny side down. Trace the stem onto the paper side of the freezer paper and cut on the outside lines. This is a freezer paper template. Pin the paper side of the stem template against the wrong side of the fabric you chose for the stem. Cut out your fabric stem, adding 1/4" seam allowances to the two long sides.

Step 2: With your iron on the "dry" setting, press the fabric seam allowances over onto the shiny side of the freezer paper. It will stick, yet won't leave any residue on the patch: you have just made freezer paper applique.

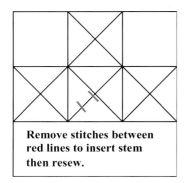

Remove stitches between red lines to insert stem then resew.

Step 3: To sew the stem in place, remove stitching between the red lines shown in the diagram. Insert the raw edge of one stem end, position it, and pin the stem in place.

Step 4: Replace the top thread in your machine with a color that matches the stem. Sew the stem to the block on both long sides as close as you can to the outside edges. Pull out the freezer paper template.

Step 5: Sew the insertion point closed through the stem end; how about that?

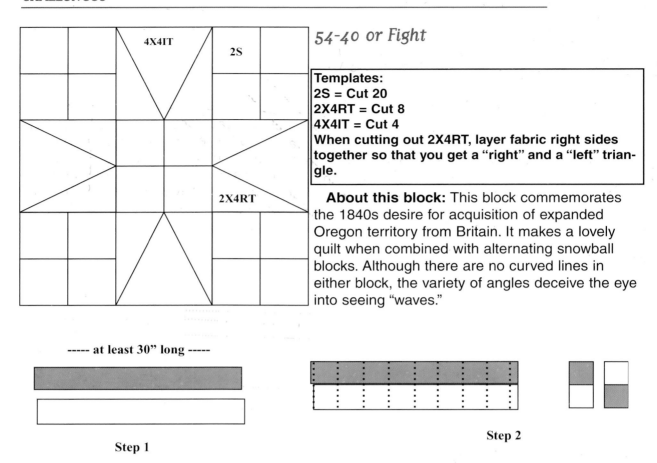

54-40 or Fight

Templates:
2S = Cut 20
2X4RT = Cut 8
4X4IT = Cut 4
When cutting out 2X4RT, layer fabric right sides together so that you get a "right" and a "left" triangle.

About this block: This block commemorates the 1840s desire for acquisition of expanded Oregon territory from Britain. It makes a lovely quilt when combined with alternating snowball blocks. Although there are no curved lines in either block, the variety of angles deceive the eye into seeing "waves."

Step 1: For an easy way to get the four-patch blocks, use the strip piecing technique. This time you will cut two strips about 30" long by 2-1/2" wide.

Step 2: After you've sewn two strips together on the long side, slice off already-assembled rectangle units that measure 2-1/2" X 4-1/2". Reverse one, and place two pieced rectangles right sides together, nest seams, and sew to make the four-patch sub-unit.

Step 3: To make the triangle subunits, offset the small angle on 2X4RT by 1/4" (approximately – it's bias; it stretches). The angle of 2X4RT will match the angle of 4X4IT at the apex for 1/4".

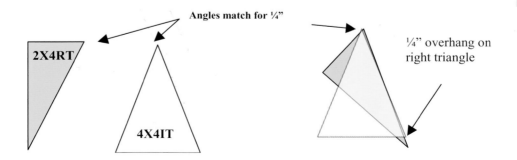

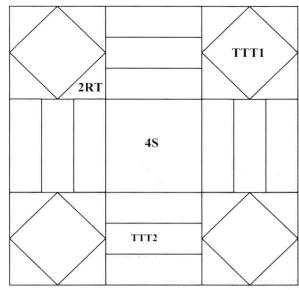

Tic-Tac-Toe

Templates:
4S = Cut 1
2RT = Cut 16
Tic-Tac-Toe1 = Cut 4
Tic-Tac-Toe 2 = Cut 12
Or: make strips, sew, and cut

About this block: Tic-Tac-Toe is a fun block to make and is graphically interesting. It reminds me of a game board. You can use the same shortcut to make the "bar" units as you did for **Hole in the Barn Door**. Cut the unfinished strips 1-7/8" wide by approximately 20" long.

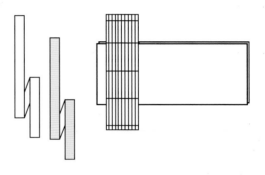

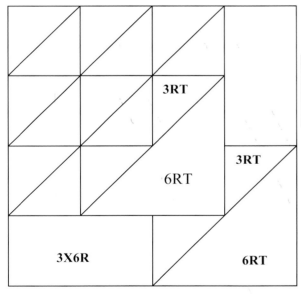

Basket of Triangles

Templates:
3RT = Cut 16
6RT = Cut 2
3X6R = Cut 2

About this block: The challenge of **Basket of Triangles** is in matching seam intersections. Join the basket to the triangle "flowers" to make a square. Then attach the background with basket base ends. Finally, add the 6RT corner background.

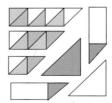

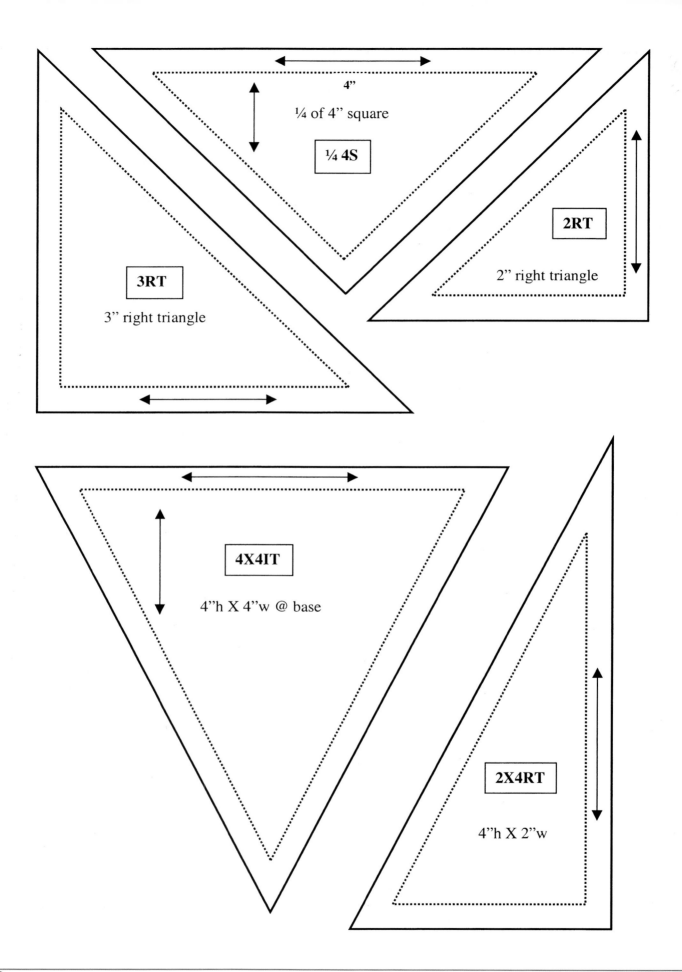

4"

¼ of 4" square

¼ 4S

2RT

2" right triangle

3RT

3" right triangle

4X4IT

4"h X 4"w @ base

2X4RT

4"h X 2"w

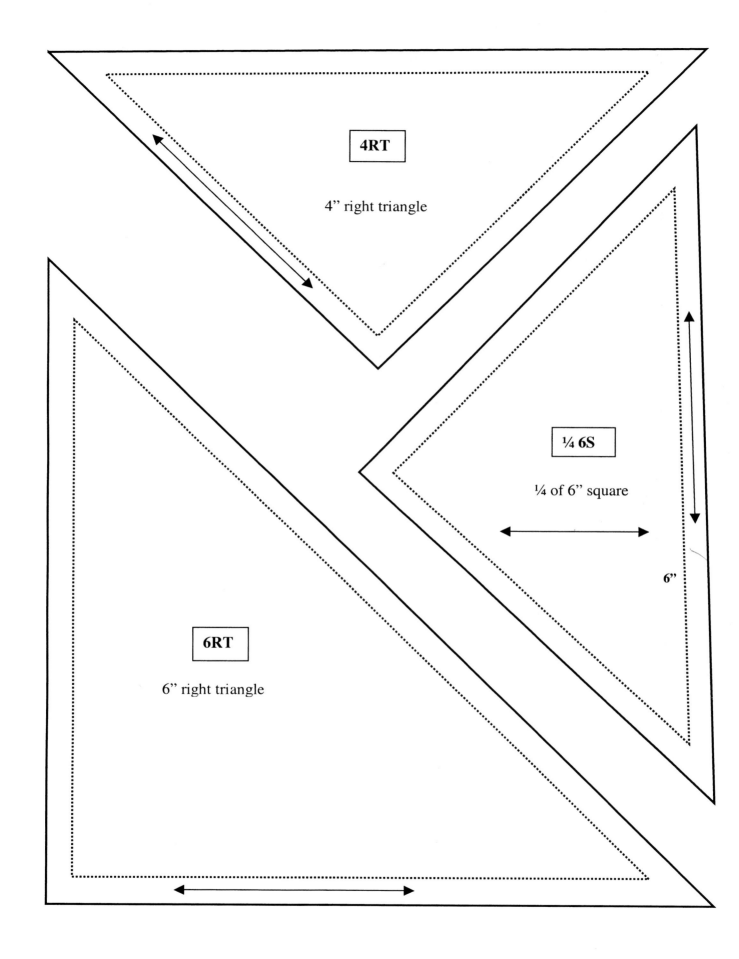

4RT

4" right triangle

¼ 6S

¼ of 6" square

6"

6RT

6" right triangle

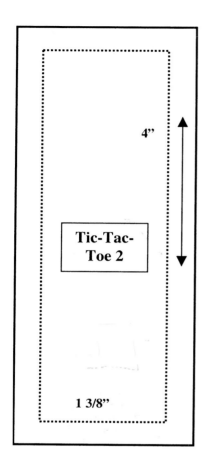

4"

Tic-Tac-
Toe 2

1 3/8"

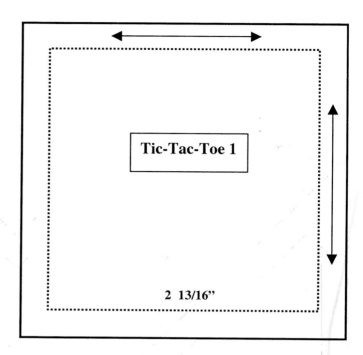

Tic-Tac-Toe 1

2 13/16"

POWER CHECKLIST

√ *Chain piecing*
√ *Press to nest*
√ *Match points with imaginative seam allowances*
√ *Creative press for the best look*

√ *Measure completed units for accuracy*
√ *Use "hold" pin*
√ *Trim bunny ears*

LESSON 5

Parallelograms resemble two joined right triangles. They reduce the number of patches and seams. But *watch out*: there are left ones and right ones!

Trapezoids join squares or rectangles with triangles and also can be directional

Challenges

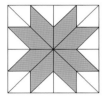

Joined Variable Star

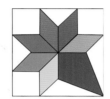

Bouquet of Flowers

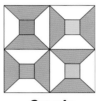

Spools

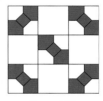

Bow Tie

Windblown Square

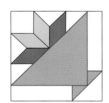

Flower Pot

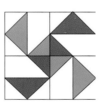

Next-Door Neighbor

House on the Hill

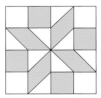

Shooting Star

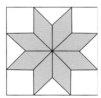

8-Pointed Star

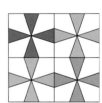

Light and Shadow

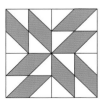

Alsace Lorraine

Diamonds are like two joined isosceles triangles If you can successfully sew blocks containing diamonds, there isn't any patchwork block you won't be able to conquer!

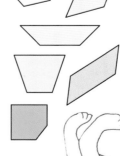

Webster's definition of a polygon is "a closed plane figure bound by straight lines." We have specific names for the most common polygons.

Many of these shapes appear as templates in this guide. You have already conquered squares and triangles, so let's move on to the specific polygon shapes of diamond, parallelogram, trapezoid, and pentagon introduced in this lesson.

I view all polygons as timesavers in cutting and sewing patchwork by reducing the number of patches needed to construct a block. They are combinations of the simpler shapes we have already mastered. Their larger area allows for more opportunities to create design interest. You can use larger prints for these patches, and they can provide a canvas for your quilting motifs. In this lesson you will even learn how to manipulate a diamond template to create a type of kaleidoscope block.

As you grow in your understanding of patchwork design, you'll want to create your own blocks. Being able to break shapes down into easy-to-draw figures will help you transfer your ideas into patterns. All you'll need is graph paper, a pencil, and a ruler.

Generally, the more complicated the shape, the more skill required to assemble it into blocks. We'll discover new techniques and tricks as we build upon construction methods you have already learned. *You can do it!*

Parallelograms

Looking at the blocks for this lesson on page 69, you can see they are grouped in rows according to the skill to be learned, with three additional blocks offered as challenges. The blocks in the first row contain parallelograms, which are the easiest of these new shapes to sew. Be careful, though: Parallelograms are devious. There are right- and left-facing varieties.

Look at the four parallelograms in **Windblown Square**. They are all the same shape facing in the same direction. That means you have to cut your patches with the right side of your fabric facing up.

The parallelogram patches on **Shooting Star** likewise are the same shape facing in the same direction, but not the same direction as Windblown Square. These patches are "reverse," and must be cut with the right side of your fabric facing down.

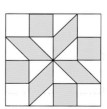

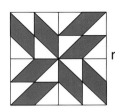

How would you cut the eight parallelograms for **Alsace Lorraine?** That's right; they would all be cut on the right side of the fabric.

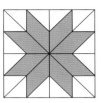

How would you cut the parallelograms for **Joined Variable Star**? Here you're safe, because there are an equal number of right and left parallelograms, so you cut these patches as you normally would, with wrong sides of your fabric facing each other.

> You probably noticed as you made the templates for Lesson 5 that some were labeled "# & #R." Adding an "R" designation to a template means it is also used in "reverse" for left- and right-facing patches. When cutting, you reverse the fabric not the template.

Making Parallelogram Units

Joined Variable Star is a good block to begin working with parallelograms because you can cut eight PAL1 & 1R from your fabric in the usual way (with wrong sides together). Remember, this gives you right and left facing patches. You will also cut sixteen 3RT patches.

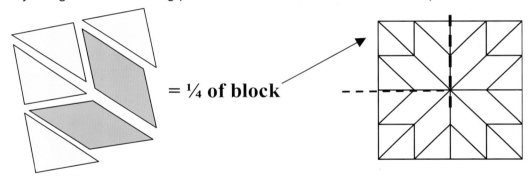

= ¼ of block

To this day, I find working with right/left parallelograms to be confusing, so I always lay out my patches as they should be assembled, using the line drawing in the pattern section as a guide.

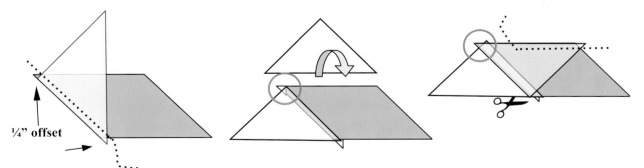

¼" offset

We will apply the offset technique we learned in Lesson 4, and treat the diagonally-cut ends of parallelograms as triangles to be offset when attached to another patch. Join 3RT to PAL 1&1R, right sides together, offsetting the two angles as shown. Press the seam allowances away from PAL 1 to expose point intersections for later matching. *Don't* clip bunny ears yet.

Use the offset bunny ear shown in the red circle to help you place the next 3RT onto the sub-unit. Just match the angles with right sides together, offset the opposite angle, and sew the seam. If easing is necessary, sew with the difficult patch against the feed dogs. Again you can see why I don't like templates that already have their bunny ears cropped. Now you can trim bunny ears and press the seam allowance toward the triangle.

Are we having fun yet? We've learned to make a larger pieced triangle out of two smaller triangles and a parallelogram. Sew one more as a mirror image of the unit you just made.

By pressing seam allowances away from the parallelogram, the seam crossing point at the edge of the block is exposed and the block will lie flat when finished—but we have created a problem for ourselves: how are we going to join these two units since there are no cross seams to reference or opposing seam allowances to nest? You could readjust your seam allowances into floating seams so they do nest (and risk the block not lying flat), or we can use our helpful holding pin technique.

Invisible Matching Points

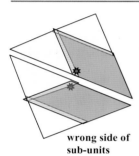

wrong side of
sub-units

I'll bet you didn't know you had the skill to sew a perfect intersection without nesting seam allowances. The trick is in finding where the stitching *should* cross a seam. On the wrong side of both patches, use your rotary ruler (it's nice to have a small 6" one by the same manufacturer for things like this) to measure 1/4" in from the outside edge. Mark those points on the **seam** with a pencil or disappearing fabric marker.

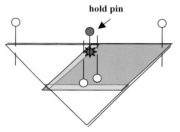

hold pin

Next, line up your patches, right sides together. Take a pin and insert it through the first mark then through to the mark on the second patch. Keep this hold pin perpendicular, and pin on either side, as usual.

Attach your handles to the ends of the triangle and sew the seam crossing over the invisible matching point. Don't remove the hold pin until your machine needle is almost on top of it. Press this seam to the left. You've successfully made one quarter of the **Joined Variable Star** block! Repeat these steps three more times to get four units.

To join two of the four units together, again find the invisible matching points, mark, pin, and stitch the perpendicular seam. Press this seam to one side. Sew the other two blocks together, but press the perpendicular seam in the opposite direction for nesting.

Because you pressed the diagonal seams all in one direction and made opposing perpendicular seams, the two block halves will nest.

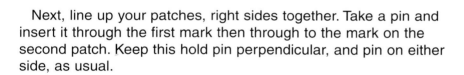

Use the hold pin technique at all matching points, including the center, to finish your block.

Since you can make the **Joined Variable Star** block, you'll also be able to make **Windblown Square, Shooting Star,** and **Alsace Lorraine.** The patterns for these, and all the other polygon blocks begin on page 78.

Diamonds are a Quilter's Best Friend

Diamonds are especially *my* best friend. When our youngest child was about 12, I went back to work (like taking care of a family and a home isn't work!). While this job was an opportunity to help my kids through college, it represented a loss of quilting time. I did get to make a few quick projects, most of which were baby quilts that were given away. Fifteen years later, my husband and I were involved in a car accident that aggravated an old neck injury I'd nursed for 20 years, and I eventually had to quit working.

Coincidentally, the same year I "retired," Viking Sewing Machines and JoAnn Fabric Stores co-sponsored a quilt contest entitled, "Diamonds are Forever." Entries had to relate to diamonds, and I entered the contest as a personal challenge to see if I could even complete a quilt that would qualify for the first prize—a Lily Viking sewing machine, which I certainly needed because my old machine was wearing out.

With my family's encouragement I persevered, making my entry for the contest. It was the first time in my life I gave myself permission to try to achieve a goal of my own. Well, long story short, my "Quilt Queen of Diamonds" won the grand prize … the beautiful Lily sewing machine. My family and I were thrilled.

While I waited for delivery from the manufacturer, one day I decided to visit my local sewing shop to see what the Lily looked like. The store had been notified that someone in its sales area had won the contest. When I went in, of course they first tried to sell me a new machine, but I told them I had won one. They asked if I was the winner of the "Diamonds are Forever" contest, then they asked me if I'd ever thought about teaching quilting. They offered me an opportunity to teach classes in their shop!

And that's how this book was born—because I wanted to teach quilting the way I wish I had learned. I sent my students home with handouts to help refresh their memories of class content; at the end of the 8-week session, I had a lot of handouts! One of my students said, "You ought to write a book." So I did. And that was the beginning of my wonderful new life.

Here is "Quilt Queen" to which I owe so much.

Okay, enough sidebar … let's get back to work!

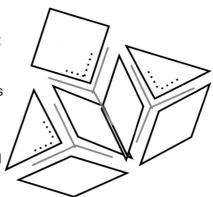

Blocks containing diamonds are among the more difficult to sew. Stitching diamond shapes to each other is tricky, and attaching the background patches presents an entirely different challenge. Each background square and triangle must be "set in." What is set in? If you sew clothing, you know that sleeves can be set in. Gussets can be set in. So can bound buttonholes and pockets. In patchwork, setting in means that two patches are sewn together, leaving space (seam allowance partly sewn) for insertion of a third patch so that no seams cross. All patches fit together and the block lies flat. This is accomplished by what is known as a "Y" seam.

Looking at the "Y" diagram here, wouldn't it be easier to assemble these patches by using right triangles? Then you'd just sew triangles to the sides of the diamonds and assemble the block like **Joined Variable Star.** You can do that, but if you follow a few simple rules, "Y" seams aren't that difficult, and having this skill in your repertoire will open a world of design possibilities. Besides, fewer seams make for better-looking blocks and save piecing, and that's what we're learning in this lesson of combined shapes.

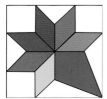

Let's use **Bouquet of Flowers** to illustrate the construction of a diamond block with "Y" seams. Bouquet is a variation of the traditional **Eight-Pointed Star** block. It combines two of the diamonds into a polygon handle, and it offers the opportunity to work with three different set-in shapes.

As always, it is a good plan to color the line drawing on the pattern on page 79 with your fabric colors. This helps you organize the block patches. Begin by cutting six 12D diamonds from different fabrics. You can stack pieces of your fabrics and cut once. Also cut three 3-1/2 S, two 1/4 5S and two BF2 from the chosen background fabric. Cut one BF1 for the handle.

There is a trick to be learned about sewing diamond patches together. You just can't sew a 1/4" seam when joining two diamonds. I think it has something to do with all that bias. If you make perfect 1/4" seams, when you sew the last diamond to the first, you'll get a bump in the middle. So you have to "adjust" the seam allowance, *and* you also have to prepare those diamonds to set in the background patches.

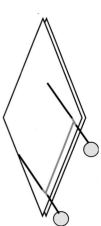

Here we go! On the wrong side of three diamond patches, use your grid ruler and pencil or fabric marker to draw the seam allowance line (shown in red on the diagram). Draw only the seam line and indicate where it should start and stop 1/4" in from the outside edges. Since two patches are layered and sewn together, you only need to mark half the diamonds. Employ the "handle" trick by pinning patches together at the ends of the drawn seam line to help you see where these points are when you sew.

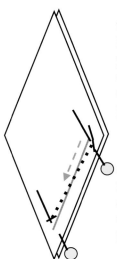

Starting at the widest part of the diamond, sew three sets of diamonds together, backstitching at the beginning and end of each drawn seam line. Begin with the machine needle touching the right side of the drawn line. As you sew, guide the patches so that the machine needle crosses over the drawn line halfway point and finishes touching the **left** side of the line. **The dotted line in the diagram is an exaggeration to show you seam placement.**

The object is to make a slightly wider seam at the block center where the diamond points join. This minor manipulation will ensure no bump in the middle of your joined diamonds. After you've made three of these two-diamond sets, press the seams open. **This is one of the few instances in which you will press the seams open to reduce bulk at the center of the block.**

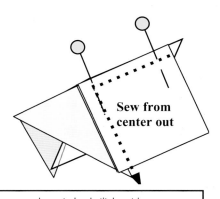

Now for the "Y" seam. In the same way you drew the seam line on the diamonds, draw the **corner** seam lines on the wrong sides of the squares and triangles. You don't need to draw the whole line because here you can stitch to the outside edge.

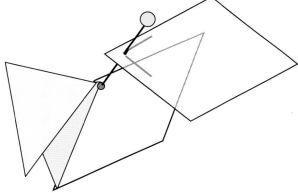

Last stitch hole is represented by red dot.

To set in the corner squares, adjust the left diamond out of the way, and overlay the square on the right diamond with right sides together as shown. Insert a pin where the drawn seam lines meet in the corner of the square. Since the diamonds are free from each other for 1/4", you will be able to continue inserting that pin into the first stitch hole you made on the right diamond. Offset the narrow end point of the diamond with the square and pin.

Starting at the center of the "Y", drop the machine needle into the last stitch hole as you pull out the pin, make a few forward stitches, backstitch, and sew the square to the right diamond, sewing off the raw edge.

Flip the square around and match raw edges to the second diamond. Adjust the first diamond patch out of the way and insert the pin into the first stitch hole in the corner of the square then into the stitch hole on the second diamond. You will sew this seam with the wrong side of the diamond facing up. Again, drop the machine needle into the first stitch hole, stitch, backstitch, and sew from the center out. Press seams toward the square so that you can see the point intersections when you assemble the block into your quilt.

Sew from center out

The reason we have to backstitch set-in seams is that they really get a workout during assembly. If we don't secure the beginning and ending stitching, the little patches would pull apart and our blocks could be ruined.

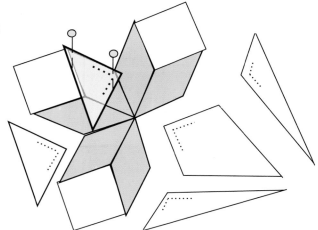

After you have inset all the squares, sew the three diamond units together as before—only on the seam lines, backstitch at the beginning and ending of the seam. Press the seam allowances open.

The triangle background patches and the handle are set in exactly as you did the squares. After you've set them in, attach the long background triangles to finish the block also using the set-in method.

Press all set-in seam allowances away from the diamonds. The diamond points on the wrong side of the very center of the block will open and twirl in a kind of pinwheel shape. Just touch the center with the tip of your iron to flatten.

Trapezoids

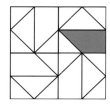

There are two types of trapezoids to learn in this lesson. One looks like a parallelogram missing one triangle end, and appears in **Next-Door Neighbor** where it is joined to a triangle. You don't know it, but you're already the expert here. All you have to do is match the long triangle side to the trapezoid angle. Do you recognize the combination? Yes, it is exactly the same way the triangle and parallelogram are sewn together in **Joined Variable Star**. The resulting sub-unit can then be treated as what it has become—a rectangle.

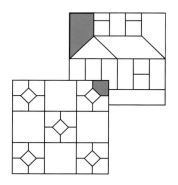

The trapezoids appearing in **House on the Hill** are also shaped like parallelograms missing one triangle end, but are set in as you have learned working with diamonds. See the specific pattern instructions at the end of this lesson to make both of these blocks.

The trapezoids in **Spools** and the pentagon "bow" in **Bow tie** are not the same shape, yet the same setting-in technique is used to make their blocks. Because the patches are larger, we will use **Spools** to learn how to set in trapezoids.

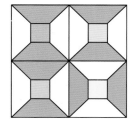

For this block you will need to cut four 2S and sixteen TRAP2. Color in the pattern at the back of this lesson with your fabric colors and keep it in front of you to help with patch placement.

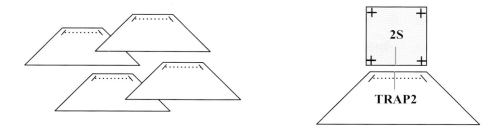

In the same way you marked the beginning, end, and the stitching lines in **Bouquet of Flowers,** mark the stitching lines on wrong side of the shorter parallel edge of TRAP2.

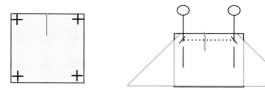

Fold one TRAP2 in half and pinch the center of the short side as shown by the red line. Also fold and pinch the middle of 2S. Instead of drawing them this time, let's try to "eyeball" the corner intersecting points on 2S.

Layer TRAP2 over 2S right sides together matching centers and raw edges. With the wrong side of TRAP2 facing you, insert pins at the ends of the drawn seam line. Continue to insert those same pins into the "eyeballed" 1/4" seam intersections. You'll know you did it right if two tiny bunny ears appear evenly on both sides of the top edge. Sew the seam only on the drawn line. Backstitch at the beginning and end of the seam. These two edges are cut on the straight of grain and should not stretch out of shape. Rotate the sub-unit one half turn and attach another TRAP2 to the opposite side of 2S.

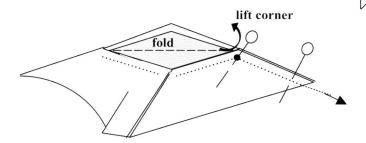

Without catching adjoining TRAP2 patches, attach the last two trapezoids to 2S. You'll get a comical unit that looks like it should be able to fly. All that's left to do is sew those floppy diagonal sides to each other.

Begin by folding 2S diagonally in half—this helps keep flying trapezoid ends away from each other so you don't catch them as you sew. Lift the corner edge of 2S up out of the way, too. Pin and stitch from the inner last needle **holes** to the outside edges. (Yes, holes. As you added each TRAP2 to the square, you ended each line of stitching where the adjoining TRAP2 was attached—same hole—or close.) Don't forget to backstitch as you start sewing this diagonal seam. Rotate the unit a quarter turn, refold 2S, and then sew until all four sides are completed.

Make three more spools. Depending upon your choice of block arrangement, press (or repress) your seams to nest and complete this amusing little block using the hold pin technique to match points.

Homework

Using the patterns and instructions that follow, practice working with polygons by:

- Making one block from the parallelogram grouping.
- Choose and make one diamond block.
- Make one of the trapezoid blocks, or make one of the Challenge blocks.
- Optional: make another Challenge block.
- Make templates for Lesson 6: Circles, Curves, and Arcs.

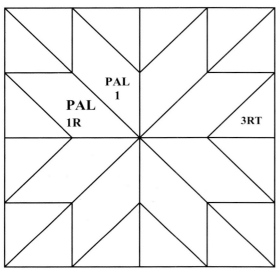

Joined Variable Star

> **Templates:**
> **3RT = Cut 16**
> **PAL 1&1R = Cut 4 each**

About these four blocks: You could make these four-patch blocks using only triangles, as we learned in Lesson 4. Combining shapes into one template eliminates some cutting and sewing. It also creates an opportunity to learn new, sophisticated piecing techniques.

As you cut out the patches for all the variable star derivatives, pay close attention to the grain lines shown on the templates.

Follow the instructions in this lesson to complete the block.

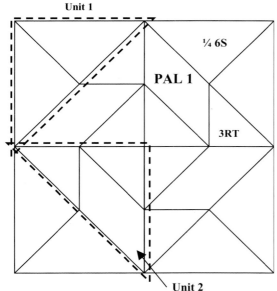

Windblown Square

> **Templates:**
> **3RT = Cut 8**
> **1/4 6S = Cut 8**
> **PAL 1 = Cut 4**

About this block: Before cutting PAL 1, be sure your fabric is right side up. The parallelograms in this block face the same direction.

Make Unit 1 by joining two 1/4 6S. To make Unit 2, stitch one 3RT to PAL 1 to make a trapezoid, then attach another 3RT to the shorter parallel side.

If you use solid color fabrics for the parallelograms, you won't need to worry about right and left-facing templates!

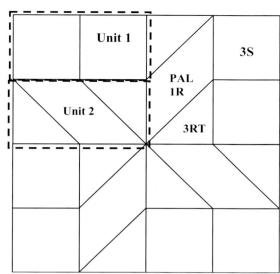

Shooting Star

Templates:
3RT = Cut 8
3S = Cut 8
PAL 1R = Cut 4

   About this block: Before cutting, be sure your fabric is wrong side up. These parallelograms are one-way patches.

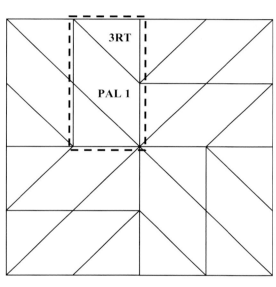

Alsace Lorraine

Templates:
3RT = Cut 16
PAL 1 = Cut 8

   About this block: Remember the rule about template orientation on grain line for PAL 1. What side of the fabric should face up for cutting?

   There is only one unit in this block. Use floating seams to create opposing seam allowances and press to nest.

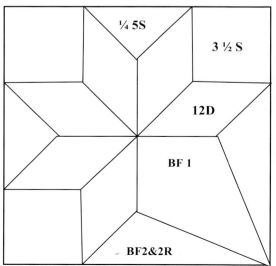

Bouquet of Flowers

Templates:
12D = Cut 6
3-1/2 S = Cut 3
1/4 5S = Cut 2
BF 1 = Cut 1
BF 2&2R = Cut 2

   About this block: Instructions for completing this block begin on page 74.

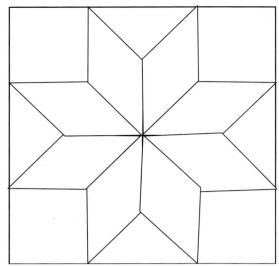

Eight-Pointed Star

Templates:
12D = Cut 8
3-1/2 S = Cut 4
1/4 5S = Cut 4

About this block: You can do something very exciting and different with this block. You can make it a kaleidoscope, and here's how.

Purchase a sheet of semi-transparent template plastic. Trace 12D onto the plastic with a template marking pencil or indelible pen. Transfer all markings **especially the seam allowance line** and cut it out with paper scissors.

Let's **fussy-cut**! Use one of your fabrics that contains larger design elements such as flowers, paisley, etc. Find an area of the fabric you like that would fit nicely within the 12" diamond. Place your plastic template over that area and trace enough of the design elements so that you can find the same repeat over the surface of your fabric. Now, match up the traced design over the fabric. DRAW the cutting lines, then cut each diamond with scissors, or place your rotary ruler on the lines you drew and use your rotary cutter. I know you have to cut out that diamond eight times, but you'll see it's worth it. Your fabric will look like Swiss cheese, too, but it's still worth it! Sew the diamonds together as instructed for **Bouquet of Flowers** and you'll be amazed at your beautiful kaleidoscope star.

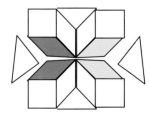

Another instruction about assembling this block: Join two sets of four diamonds only on the seam lines and press seams open. Inset the two squares and one triangle on each half block. You must join the half-blocks together as you did each diamond set – **only on the seam line of the diamonds, not across seam allowances.** You'll actually have a tiny pinhole in the very center because seams did not cross. After the half-blocks are joined, press seams open and inset the side triangles.

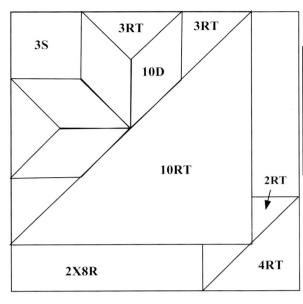

Flower Pot

Templates:
3S = Cut 1
2RT = Cut 2
3RT = Cut 4
4RT = Cut 1
10RT = Cut 1
2X8R = Cut 2
10D = Cut 4

About this block: Flower Pot is complex. Its assembly should remind you of **Thistle** or **Bluebell** from Lesson 3. The diamond "flowers" unit 1 and 10RT triangle make a 10" block. By adding background patches 2X8R and 4RT, and 2RT triangles for a base, the 10" flower and pot becomes a 12" block.

Step 1: Make Unit 1 as instructed for **Bouquet of Flowers**. You will only have to set in two triangles and a square. The 3RT triangles on either side of the flower are offset, as you learned with parallelograms.

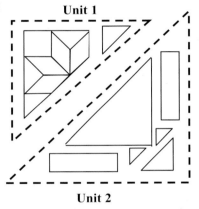

Step 2: Unit 2 patches are assembled like a log cabin. Attach 2RT to the 2X8R in the proper orientation, then attach each to 10RT. Match centers and sew 4RT to complete the triangle unit.

Step 3: Find the Center of 10RT's long side and pin to the exact center of the diamond points. Match corner angles and place a few pins along that outside edge to help control the bias. Join the two units with Unit 1 on top so you can see seam intersections. This time you can sew right across seam allowances being careful to cross one thread above the sewn points.

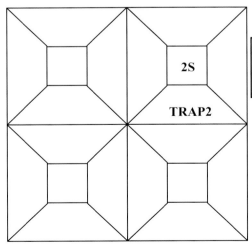

Spools

Templates:
2S = Cut 4
TRAP2 = Cut 16

About this block: The directions for making **Spools** appear in this lesson. As you can see from the tiny illustration above, this block creates the optical illusion of depth. It might be fun to use your fabric colors to make a block of four "tunnels." Just make the top trapezoid dark, the bottom light, the side trapezoids medium, and the center square very light or very dark.

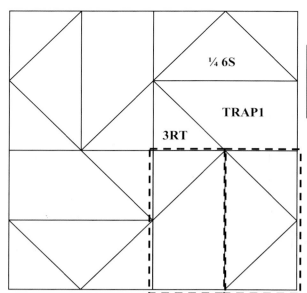

Next-Door Neighbor

Templates:
TRAP 1 = Cut 4
3RT = Cut 12
1/4 6S = Cut 4

About this block: You'll find this block easy to do as long as you press seam allowances toward 3RT to expose matching points.

I suppose you've noticed by now that most four-patch blocks are made up of four identical units that are placed a quarter of a turn from the one next to it.

CHALLENGES

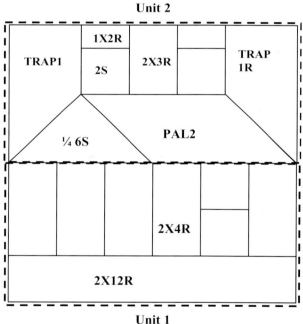

Unit 2

Unit 1

House on the Hill

Templates:
PAL 2 = Cut 1
2S = Cut 4
1X2R = Cut 2
TRAP 1&1R = Cut 2
2X3R = Cut 1
2X4R = Cut 5
2X12R = Cut 1
1/4 6S = Cut 1

About this block: Sometimes when I build this house, I cut appropriate fabric strips for the squares and rectangles with my rotary cutter and ruler, then slice off patches of the length needed. This is one of the reasons I label templates with measurements.

It's fun to choose fabrics that mimic sky, bricks, wood, shingles, and grass. You might even want to add embellishments to this block such as little snips of lace for curtains at the window. You could add a button doorknob and put an embroidered bird in the sky.

Step 1: There's nothing difficult in making Unit 1. You can do it with one hand tied behind your back. If you will be adding fabric embellishments, baste them to the patches before you assemble. Pin anything out of the way that might be caught when sewing seams.

Unit 2 is another matter.

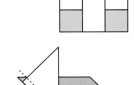

Step 2: You know how to make the chimneys with the "sky" patch in between.

Step 3: You also know how to sew a triangle onto the PAL2 roof.

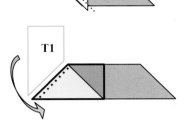

Step 4: Now it gets confusing. In fact, the first time I taught this block, I showed everyone how to put the TRAP1 sky on *backwards*. If you lay out your patches just like the drawing, it's a simple matter of flipping TRAP1 over right sides together with 1/4 6S. TRAP 1's lines and angles match up with the gable and the roof. Pin and sew the seam from the points to within 1/4" of the roof ridge, and **backstitch 1/4".**

Step 5: This is your lucky opportunity to set in a pieced rectangle! Not only that, you get to set in TRAP1R. Draw your seam lines on the left chimney as shown then set in the pieced rectangle. When you sew the seam joining the "roof ridge" to the pieced rectangle, stop and backstitch 1/4" from the edge. Set in TRAP1R.

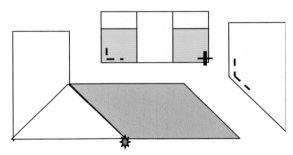

Step 6: Complete **House on the Hill** by sewing Unit 1 to Unit 2. You only have one point to match.

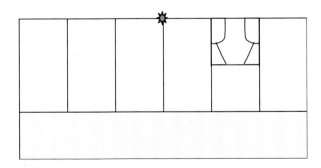

That was hard work, and you did a great job! Bet you didn't know you were a carpenter as well as a quilter!

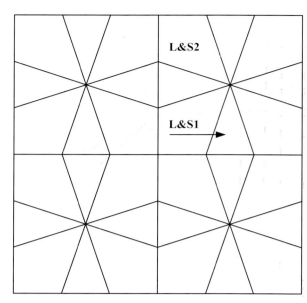

Light and Shadow

Templates:
Light & Shadow 1
Light & Shadow 2

About this block: **Light & Shadow** is a favorite of Amish quiltmakers. It is made in a very different way. You might think of it as an irregular eight-point diamond block with background squares and triangles already attached.

Experiment with different ways of coloring the patches. When blocks are placed edge to edge, the straight lines of the isosceles triangles almost appear curved.

   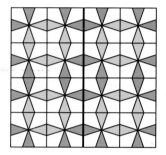

Step 1: Arrange the patches to make one fourth of the block wrong side up. Draw the seam line from the outside edge to within 1/4" of the inside point on the right edge of all patches.

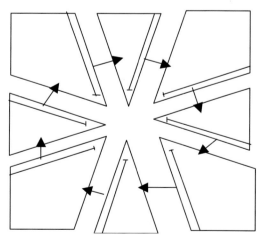

Step 2: Refer to the instructions for sewing a diamond star seam by slightly increasing the seam width at the center. For strength, begin stitching and backstitch 1/4" from the narrow point, then sew to the raw edge.

The unit is put together by sewing one patch to the next, to the next, etc., until you have all eight attached in a series. As you attach each successive piece, place a pin in the seam starting point of the to-be added patch and through the hole that was made by the first stitch in the one you're sewing it to. Stitch the last patch to the first to complete the block. Press the seams open.

Step 3: Make four of these units. To make it easier when you sew them together to finish the block, change some of the open seams to floating seams to allow for nesting.

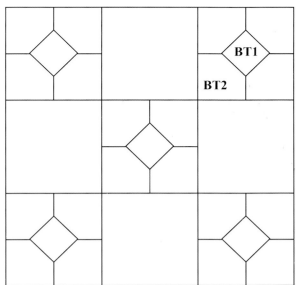

Bow Tie

Templates:
Bow Tie 1 = Cut 4
Bow Tie 2 = Cut 20
4S = Cut 4

About this block: The "bows" of the bow tie are pentagons that are sewn to the center square in exactly the same way as trapezoids are attached in **Spools.**

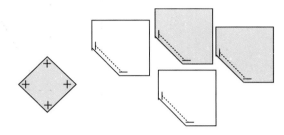

Step 1: Draw seam lines on the diagonal side of "bow." Indicate 1/4" start-and-stop points.

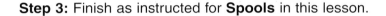

Step 2: With the **Bow Tie 2** on top, sew two identical BT2 to opposite sides of BT1 backstitching at the beginning and ending of the drawn seam line for reinforcement.

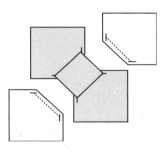

Step 3: Finish as instructed for **Spools** in this lesson.

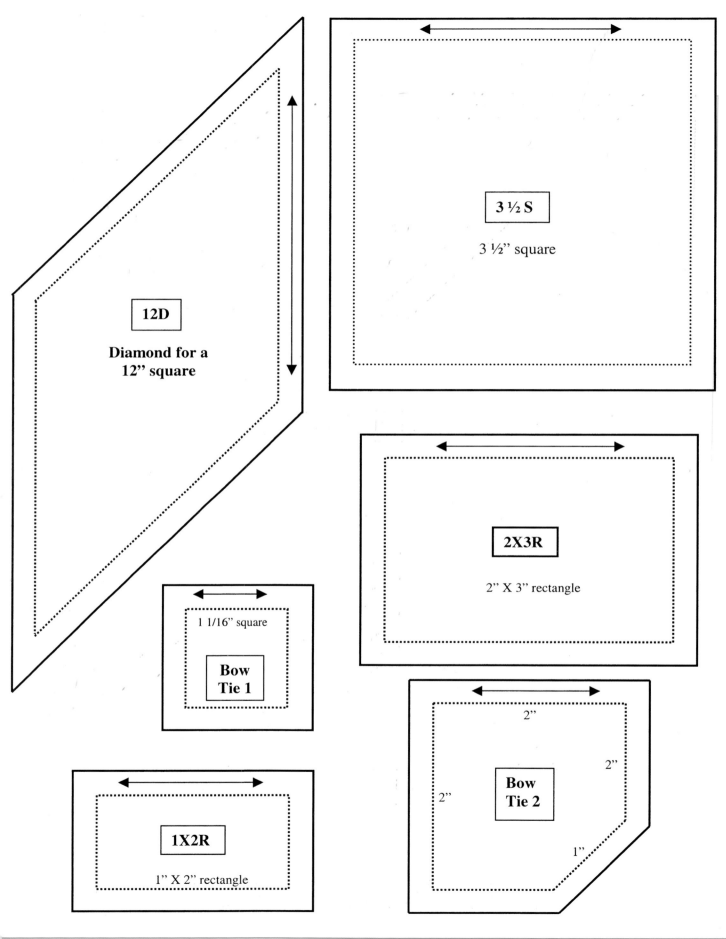

12D

Diamond for a 12" square

3 ½ S

3 ½" square

2X3R

2" X 3" rectangle

1 1/16" square

Bow Tie 1

2"

2"

2"

Bow Tie 2

1"

1X2R

1" X 2" rectangle

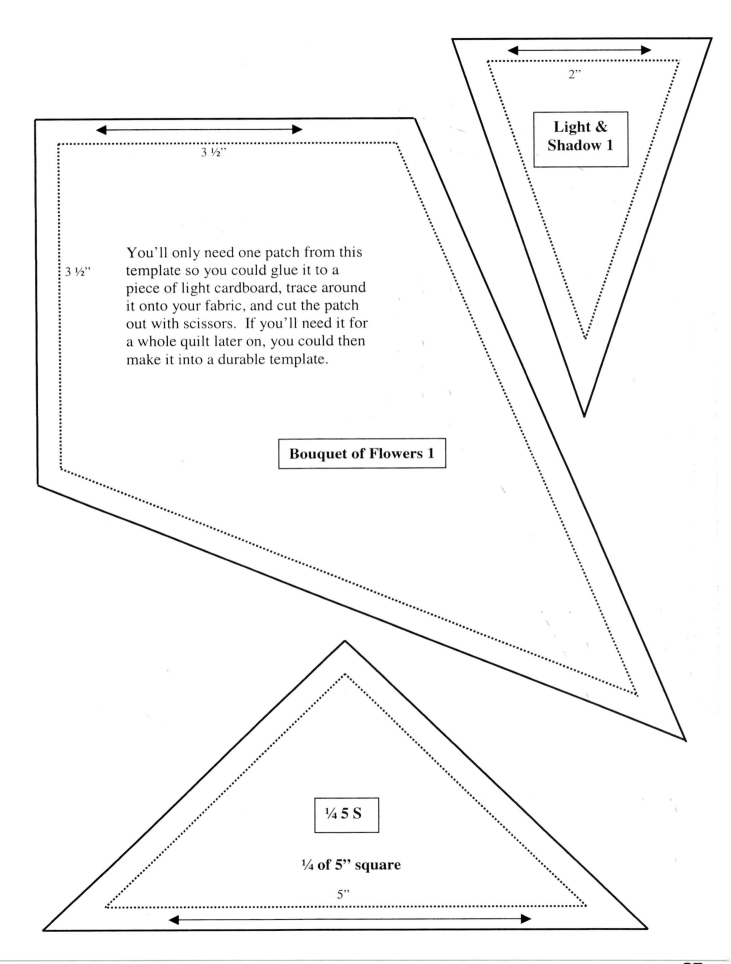

2"

Light & Shadow 1

You'll only need one patch from this template so you could glue it to a piece of light cardboard, trace around it onto your fabric, and cut the patch out with scissors. If you'll need it for a whole quilt later on, you could then make it into a durable template.

3 ½"

3 ½"

Bouquet of Flowers 1

¼ 5 S

¼ of 5" square

5"

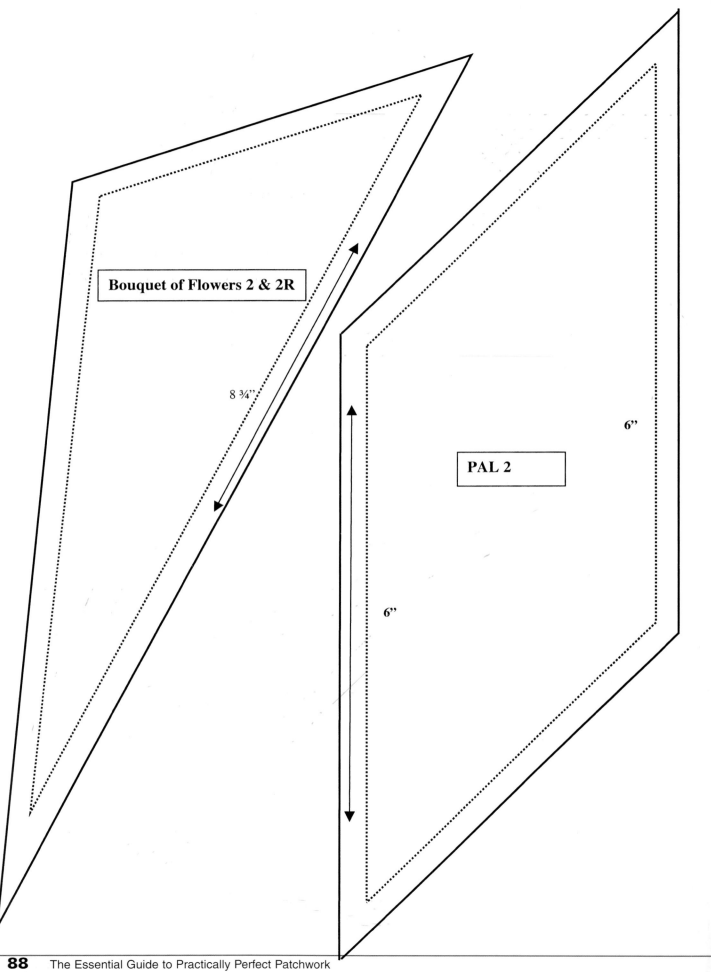

Bouquet of Flowers 2 & 2R

8 ¾"

PAL 2

6"

6"

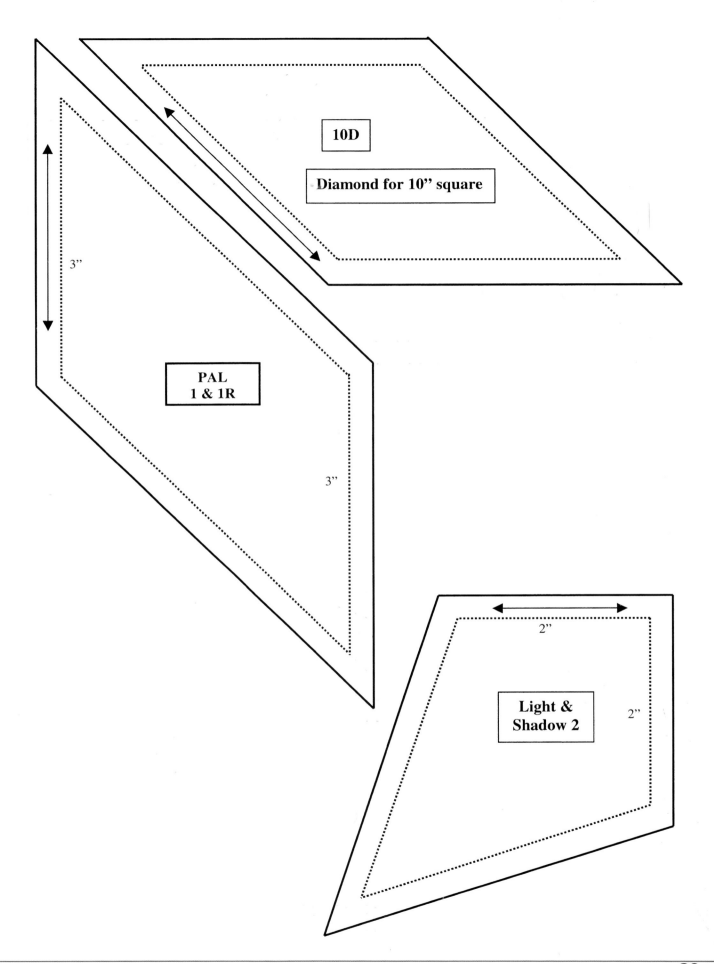

10D

Diamond for 10" square

3"

PAL
1 & 1R

3"

2"

Light &
Shadow 2

2"

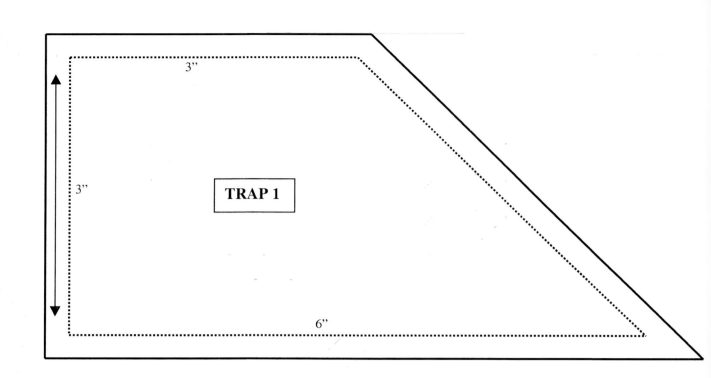

TRAP 1

3"

3"

6"

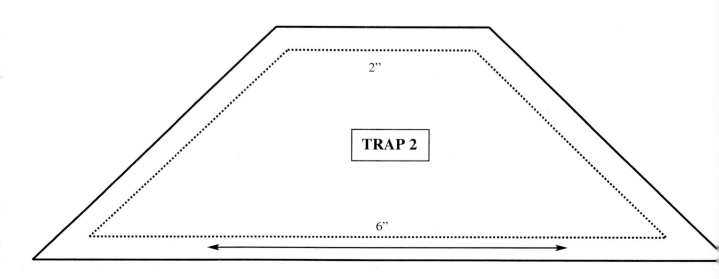

TRAP 2

2"

6"

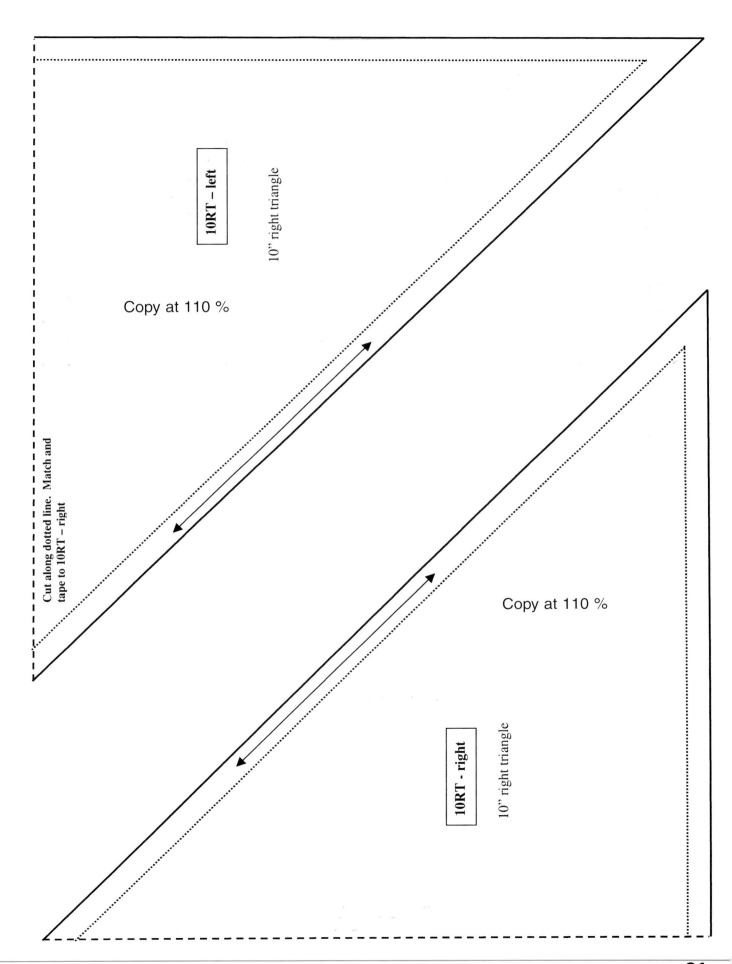

10RT – left

10" right triangle

Copy at 110 %

Cut along dotted line. Match and
tape to 10RT – right

Copy at 110 %

10RT - right

10" right triangle

Circles, Curves, and Arcs

LESSON 6

These larger quarter-circles are easy to sew if you remember that concave goes over convex.

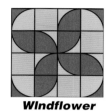
Windflower

Baby Buds contains both gradual and tightly-curved patches.

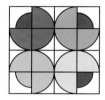
Baby Buds

Moon Over the Mountain

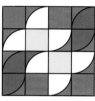
Trillium

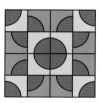
Around the World

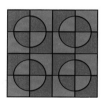
Snowball

Pictures in the Stairwell

Spinning Pinwheel

CHALLENGES
There are so many traditional two-patch curve-in-a- square block designs. Here are four – try making up a few of your own.

Grandmother's Fan

These blocks contain patches with gradual curves and are very stitch-friendly.

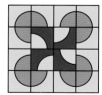
Wonder of the World

Drunkard's Path

Circles, Curves, and Arcs

To be truthful, this will be your most difficult sewing lesson. Fabric is woven in straight lines. Machines are manufactured to sew in straight lines. Cutting implements for the most part cut in straight lines. When you go about making straight things into curves, it seems contrary to nature, but it's not impossible. You need to know how to create curved seams if you want to have complete command of all the patchwork skills. There are time-proven methods and techniques to help us sew circles, curves, and arcs, and you will understand how and be able to do it well after you complete your blocks from this lesson.

Concave Versus Convex

What's concave? What's convex? These terms are used to describe the two types of curved patches you will learn to sew together.

This curved patch contains a concave arc. It looks like a "bite" has been taken out of it. An easy way to remember concave is that a cave is an indentation in a rock.

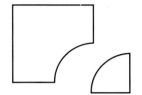

This patch contains a convex curve. It looks like a piece of pie and fills the "bite" taken out of the concave patch.

Negative Templates and "The Bite"

A new cutting method for making two of the concave patches is introduced in this lesson. We've certainly been using our rotary cutters to cut clean, straight lines. Rotary cutters will also make convex cuts. They will even make **easy** concave cuts. They will not make **tight** concave cuts.

For years I made patches containing tight concave curves by cutting straight and convex template lines with a rotary cutter, then drawing the concave curve with a pencil, removing the template, pinning the patches together, and cutting on the drawn curve line with scissors.

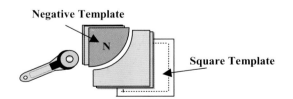

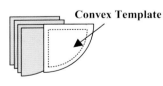
Convex Template

Negative Template

Square Template

Then I thought of using a negative template. I reasoned that every concave cut is really the other side of a convex cut, if only you had the right size template to take the "bite" out of the square.

The convex template that fills the "bite" couldn't be used because it includes seam allowances. You can't cut those off. Negative templates do not include any seam allowances, so they are smaller than the template used to cut the convex patches and take just the right amount of "bite" out of the square.

Negative templates are identified with an "N" preceding the template name/measurements, and tell you what other template to use for whole patches before you take out the "bite." N4X4QC (QC = quarter circle) takes the "bite" out of 6S (from Lesson 3) to cut the large concave patches for **Pictures in the Stairwell.** Negative template N2X2QC takes the bite out of 3S to make the concave patch for **Around the World, Snowball, Wonder of the World,** and **Drunkard's Path.** Both of these negative templates are used for **Baby Buds.**

All you have to do is cut the square as usual. Position the special negative template at one corner of the stack of squares and carefully cut only the curve. *Voila* – there are the concave patches! A paper template is provided with the patterns to compare with your cut patches for accuracy.

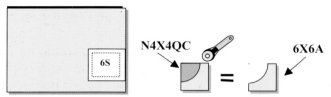

If you're wondering why a negative "bite" template isn't needed to cut the sky background in **Moon Over the Mountain,** it's because the patch is cut on the fold and has a concave curve easily cut with a rotary cutter. **Windflower, Trillium,** and **Pinwheel** also have the same type of gentle arc that can be cut with a rotary cutter.

Cutting Concave Fabric Patches

Just as you had to take special care in cutting those curved template lines, you have to take that same extra care in cutting the curved fabric patches. Only the smaller 28mm rotary cutter is able to perform this task. You could also try the rotary point cutter, a new instrument on the market, which seems to have been made for the job of accurately cutting gently arched concave curves. There are a few guidelines to follow for the use of each tool. With both instruments, always make the concave cut first. Just in case you might have cut the curve too deeply, check to see if you need to reposition the template on the curved cut edge before you make the straight cuts.

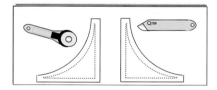

If you are using the rotary cutter, hold it at a comfortable angle and slowly, almost haltingly, cut the fabric, being careful not to cut into the template. If you do nick the template, stop—don't cut a chunk out. Back the cutter out of the slit, and set it back on track. After you have completed cutting the whole patch, you can repair the slit by filling it with white glue. When the glue has dried, you can add a bit of transparent tape to the paper side. You may need to file the edge smooth again.

The new rotary point cutter almost eliminates the chance of accidentally cutting into your cardboard template. A new blade will cut four layers of fabric cleanly, and does do a fine job of cutting those concave curves. Use the tip of the pie-shaped blade and follow the curved edge of the template as you cut. Continue to cut the straight edges of the template with your rotary cutter.

If this is just way too much fooling around for you, do as I used to do: Cut the concave template straight sides with the rotary cutter, draw the concave cut line, remove the template and pin the layers of fabric together, then cut the curve with your scissors.

Basic Curve-in-a-Square Instructions

Even though there are four different configurations of curves, all use the same basic Curve-in-a-Square Principle for assembly, so there's only one new set of sewing instructions to follow to help you make curved seams. (Hooray!)

To stitch a curved seam, remember one basic principal: **Always sew the two patches together with the concave patch on top.** The convex curve does not change its shape when sewn to the concave patch, so it can be placed on the bottom against the feed dogs. You don't have to worry about adjusting it. The concave patch, on the other hand, changes its shape considerably as it is sewn to the convex patch, and you will have to watch for puckering and catching tucks in the seam line. This is contrary to placing the "fussy" fabric against the feed dogs for easing, but placed on top, you can easily see what is happening as you sew the seam.

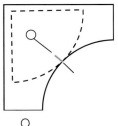

Step 1: Mark the centers of the arcs on both patches by folding each one in half and pinching. Pin the two arcs right sides together at the centers. Make sure the convex patch is on the bottom and right sides are facing each other.

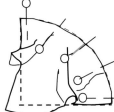

Step 2: Adjust and pin the arc of the concave patch so that raw edges are even and the end corners of the curves are "squared" up to each other. The sides adjacent to the arcs of both patches are straight, so align them and pin. Even though you aligned the beginning and ending of the arc, you may see a slight offset of the patches as your needle enters and exits. This is correct.

Step 3: As you start sewing the 1/4" seam, you will be **clearing the pathway for the needle**. Begin and end the seam with a few backstitches. **Take your time.** Using a stiletto or sharpened chopstick like an extra-long finger helps hold the fabric edges.

Step 4: Leaving the machine needle "down" in the fabric, stop sewing as necessary to see if you have caught any tucks in the concave patch. Make any readjustments and complete the seam. This is kind of a stitch/adjust/stitch effort. Use the last pin as a handle to keep the subunit from skewing sideways as it exits the needle. You'll soon get so good at sewing these curved seams, you'll be able to do them in one fell swoop using only three pins!

Step 5: According to the placement diagram for the block you are making, press all seam allowances to nest for ease of assembly.

This lesson is short and sweet. As I said before, the basic curve-in-a-square instructions hold true for sewing all curved patches together. Larger curved patches, and patches that are gently curved are easier to sew than tighter, smaller curved patches. The easy arc of the patches in **Windflower, Trillium,** and **Spinning Pinwheel** are easier to sew than the tighter curves of **Around the World, Snowball, Wonder of the World,** and **Drunkard's Path,** although the curves in **Around the World** and **Drunkard's Path** don't touch, so you won't have to match many intersections. **Pinwheel** has no seams to match, and a small, appliquéd circle covers the center! What more could you ask? Have fun making these blocks.

Homework

Follow the individual instructions for each block and learn how to sew curved patches.
- Make one block containing a large quarter circle.
- Make one of the "easy" curve blocks in the second column of the color page.
- Make one of the traditional two-patch curve-in-a-square blocks. Each of these five blocks contains 16 subunits. You can see that **Baby Buds** is easiest.
- NO MORE TEMPLATES TO MAKE!

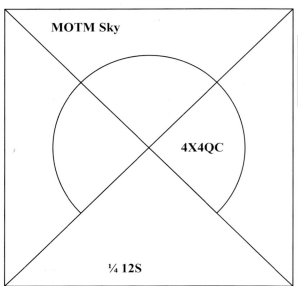

Moon Over the Mountain

Templates:
4X4QC = Cut 3
1/4 12S = Cut 1
MOTM Sky = Cut 3 on fold

About this block: Moon Over the Mountain is such a fun block to make. You can choose fabrics that mimic sky, moon, and grassy mountain.

See basic instructions for joining curved patches.

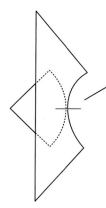

Step 1: Fold and pinch the centers of the arcs on 4X4QC and MOTM Sky. Match centers right sides together placing the concave "sky" over the convex "moon." Pin. Adjust the arc of the sky patch to fit the curve of the moon, square up ends and pin as instructed in this lesson. Carefully stitch seam easing in fullness. Make three. Press the curved seam of two patches to the sky and one to the moon. The sub-unit with the curved seam pressed to the moon will be at the top of the block.

Step 2: Pin the top sky subunit to the right sky subunit right sides together. Because you pressed the one curved seam allowance in opposition to the other two, the curved seams will nest just like straight seams. Sew from the moon patch to the outside edge using the last pin as a handle. Press the seam in whichever direction makes your unit look the best.

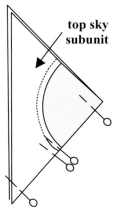

top sky subunit

Step 3: Right sides together, join the third sky unit to the left side of the mountain patch. Press the resulting seam in opposition to the two-piece sky unit you just made. You've got two pieced half-square triangles!

Step 4: Pin and stitch your two pieced 12" right triangles together to complete the block. Trim all bunny ears and press the seam towards the darker fabric or whichever way looks best.

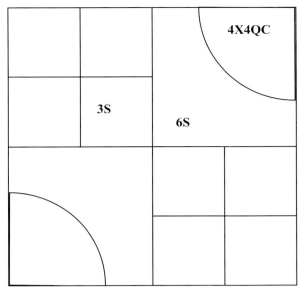

Pictures in the Stairwell

Templates:
3S = Cut 8
4X4QC = Cut 2
6S = Cut 2
N4X4QC for the "bite"

About this block: Pictures in the Stairwell should be quite easy for you to stitch. Two little four-patch units make up half the block. You only have to set in two curved patches to complete the rest. This is a four-patch block made of two four-patch units and two two-patch units.

I know you can make this block by following the instructions you learned in this lesson. Just compare your concave patches with 6X6A. You're already an experienced in making four-patch units, pressing seams to nest and making perfect intersections. You don't need me for this one!

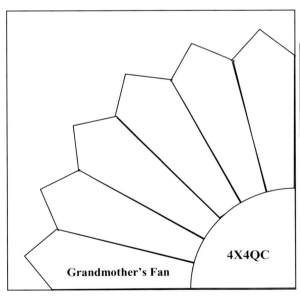

Grandmother's Fan

Templates:
4X4QC = Cut 1
Grandmother's Fan = Cut 6
12-1/2" X 12 -1/2" Background
Square = Cut 1

About this block: This quaint little block makes a beautiful quilt all by itself and is great for hand quilting and embellishments. The fan blades are sewn together to make a **pieced** concave patch. I think you'll be proud of yourself for making **Grandmother's Fan.**

Take notice of the grainline arrow on the fan blade template. *One* long side of each blade should be on the straight of grain. When you sew the blades to each other, stitch a straight-of-grain edge of one blade to an off-grain edge of the second. This will help keep the fan from stretching out of shape. You will need to plan ahead for color placement before you cut your patches.

Step 1: If you like, cut each fan blade from a different fabric. I know you're wondering how we're going to get that point on the blade. We could just fold and press it under, but chances are the six points would not be uniform. Let's try this little trick:

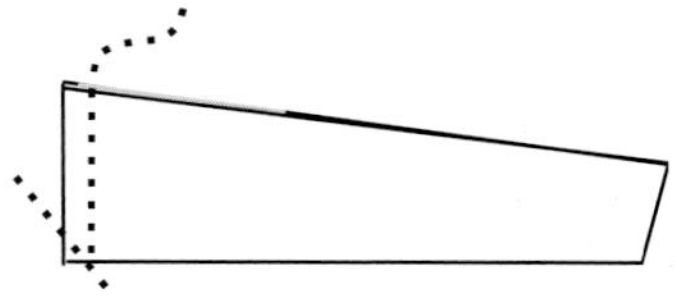

Fold and lightly press each fan blade in half lengthwise right sides together. Pin, backstitch and sew a 1/4" seam across the wide end from the fold to the raw edge. **Trim** the angle at the fold being careful not to cut into stitching.

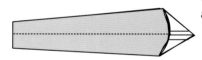

Press the seam allowance open.

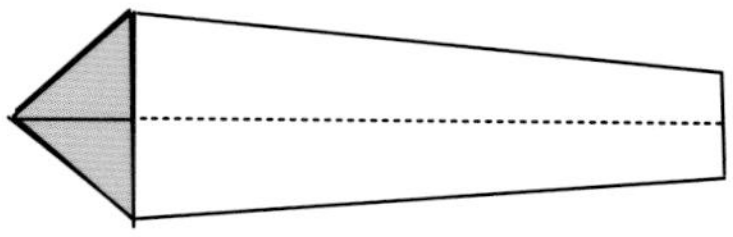

Turn the point right side out. On the wrong side, match the seam line to the center fold of the blade and press the point while pressing away the fold line.

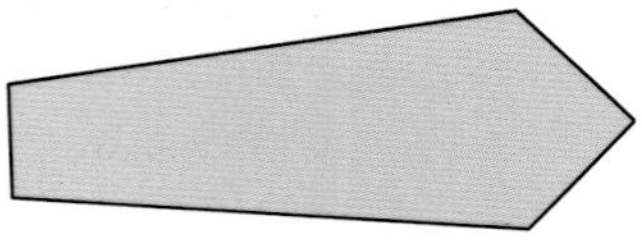

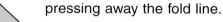

Look at the right side. You have a perfectly shaped fan blade. Make five more.

Step 2: Match two fan blades right sides together and pin. Beginning at the folds of the points, backstitch and join the two patches together on one long side. You don't need to backstitch at the end of the seam line. In this way, join all six fan blades together pressing seam allowances to the darker patch.

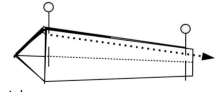

Because you planned ahead and sewed a bias side to a straight of grain side, there shouldn't be very much stretching. If there is a little discrepancy at the small ends of the blades, you can trim after all six have been connected, but it won't show because the fan unit will be joined to the quarter circle. You **do** want the "V" where the seam joins the blades to meet perfectly.

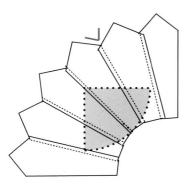

Step 3: Even though the fan unit is pieced, it is now treated as one concave patch. Use the basic curve-in-a square instructions to attach the 4X4QC fan base.

Press the curved seam toward 4X4QC.

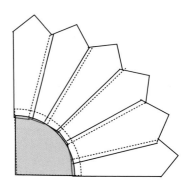

Step 4: We've got the fan but we need to attach it to a background. Cut your background square 12-1/2" X 12-1/2" on the straight of grain using your rotary ruler and cutter. (You might find it easier to cut the square on a fold, in which case you would cut a rectangle that is 6-1/4" X 12-1/2".) Fold the square in half diagonally and lightly press the fold line.

Step 5: Pin the completed fan unit onto the background square aligning the fan center with the diagonal fold and right and bottom edges. Baste the two outside edges together.

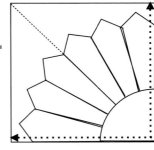

Right side of block

Step 6: We need to attach the fan unit to the background square. This attachment is called "applique." For practical quilts, I like to machine applique. The process is speedy and holds patches very securely. Since it's a real bother to keep changing thread colors to topstitch applique, I recommend you use nylon thread. Some nylon threads are difficult to work with and have a mind of their own. I prefer Wonder Invisible® monofilament thread by YLI brand for its strength and compliant characteristics. Choose clear for light colors and smoke for intense or dark colors. You will sew with this thread on the top through the needle. The bobbin thread is the same dressmaker type you have been using for piecing. Later, we'll use this nylon thread when we machine quilt our sampler.

Machine applique is very simple and straight forward. Pin the fan blades flatly and securely to the background fabric. On the right side using the monofilament thread, topstitch each blade point as **close to the edge as possible**. If you see your needle drop off the edge of the fold, **stop** sewing, lift your needle, place it back on track and continue. You'll see that the stitching line is hardly noticeable. Remove the basting stitches at the right and bottom edge of the block.

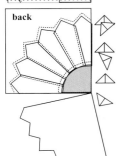

Step 7: Most of my students are afraid to do this next step. Have courage. There is an extra thickness of fabric in your block that you don't need. If you intend to hand quilt your finished sampler, you're not going to appreciate stitching through an extra layer of fabric. The background color you have chosen also may shadow through the fan applique so that the seam allowances will show. We need to cut out the background fabric that is under the applique. We also need to cut off the back folds of the fan blade tips. But we need to cut away these pieces of fabric **leaving a 1/4" seam allowance.**

You do have to be very careful not to cut any part of the fan while leaving 1/4" seam allowances, as shown. You can do it. If not now, maybe just before you assemble your quilt top. A duck-billed applique scissors is perfect for this job, but not absolutely necessary – careful cutting is your best tool.

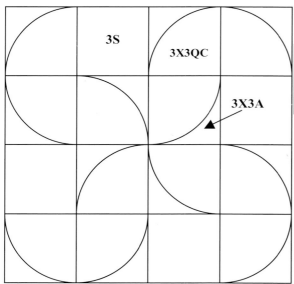

Windflower

Templates:
3S = Cut 4
3X3QC = Cut 12
3X3 Easy Arc = Cut 12

About this block: The graceful arcs of these curved patches make such beautiful patchwork blocks and afford limitless design possibilities when creating your own.

See basic instructions for joining curved patches.

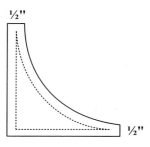

Step 1: Cut the 3X3 Easy Arc patches as described in the lesson for cutting concave curves. There's not much to these patches. The ends of the curve side are quite narrow, and that's good *and* bad. The good part is the patch is very compliant and will stretch easily to conform to 3X3QC. The bad part is they're delicate and could fray, so treat them tenderly. As you can see, the curve ends are only 1/2" wide. That means each end is really two seam allowances. Putting in backstitching at the beginning and ending of the seam line will keep the ends from disintegrating. Make 12 two-patch curve sub-units.

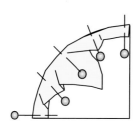

Before assembly, the sub-unit will look something like this. Why, you may ask, is the left pin shown placed in the opposite direction from the others? When I pin the two patches together, I hold them with my left hand, and spread the fullness evenly along the convex curve pinning as I go. First, I pin the centers, then start pinning at the right side of the curve. Because my left thumb is holding the last corner areas of the two patches on the left, I can't let go to put the pin in from right to left. So I put the pin in from left to right. It's a simple matter to remove that pin first after I start the seam.

Step 2: Finish the block as learned in this lesson.

When you match 3S with the pieced two-patch subunit in preparation for joining, you'll automatically be checking the two-patch for correct size.	

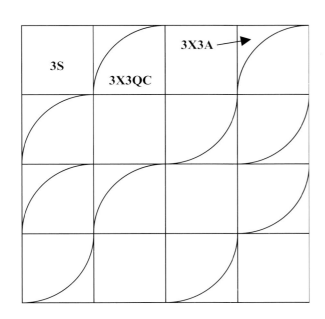

3S

3X3QC

3X3A

Trillium

Templates:
3S = Cut 6
3X3QC = Cut 10
3X3 Easy Arc = Cut 10

About this block: Spring is so welcome after the long winters of upstate New York where I live. I know the "back of winter is broken" when I see the wild Trillium beginning to bloom. I designed this block to remind me of the promise of spring.

POWER CHECKLIST

√ *Chain piecing*
√ *Use "hold" pin*
√ *Press to nest*
√ *Trim bunny ears*

√ *Match points with imaginative seam allowances*
√ *Creative press for the best look*
√ *Measure completed units for accuracy*

Your Block

Templates:
3S = Cut _____
3X3QC = Cut _____
3X3 Easy Arc = Cut _____

About this block: Try your hand at designing a two-patch curve block. You could cut out 16 paper squares with this easy curve drawn on some or all of them and create a new block by just rearranging them like a puzzle.

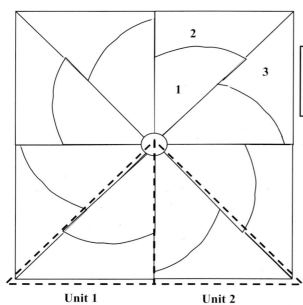

Unit 1   Unit 2

Spinning Pinwheel

Templates:
Spinning Pinwheel 1 = Cut 8
Spinning Pinwheel 2 = Cut 4
Spinning Pinwheel 3 = Cut 4

About this block: I find this old block from the '30s very interesting because the same curved wedge is attached to two differently-shaped background patches. **Spinning Pinwheel** makes a lively scrap quilt with a white background. Follow the basic curve-in-a-square assembly instructions. **Cut all patches with the fabric right side up.** If you use a solid color fabric for the background, be careful not to flip Spinning Pinwheel 2 and 3 over and try to use the wrong side.

Step 1: This is the way the units should look as you match centers and begin to pin them together. The curve corners will show a slight offset. When you complete the seams, press the seam allowance toward Pinwheel 1 to make the pinwheels puff forward from the background. Make four of each unit.

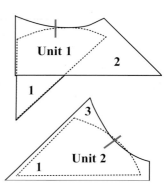

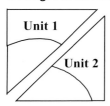

Step 2: Sew Unit 1 to Unit 2 right sides together in a diagonal seam. Press diagonal seam allowances in the same direction so they will nest. Make the four quarters of the block.

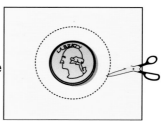

Step 3: Finish the block as you would a four-patch.

Step 4: To make the center circle, place a quarter on the wrong side of a scrap of fabric you've chosen for the **Spinning Pinwheel** center. Draw a larger circle around it, as shown. Cut out the fabric circle. With a threaded and knotted needle, sew a running stitch around the outside edge of the fabric circle. Stitch past your starting point. Pull the thread to gather the fabric tight around the quarter. Turn the fabric-covered quarter over, spray starch and press the smooth side with an iron. Loosen the gathers to remove the quarter, draw them up again, knot the thread, and clip. Topstitch the center circle gathered side down onto the block.

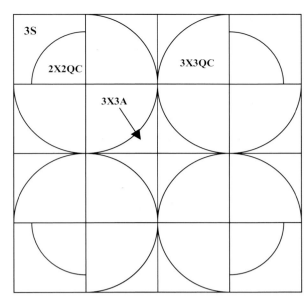

Baby Buds

Templates:
3S = Cut 4
2X2QC = Cut 12
3X3A Easy Arc= Cut 12
N2X2QC for the "bite"

About this block: **Baby Buds** combines both the gentle curved patches found in **Windflower** and **Trillium** with the traditional tight curve-in-a-square patch. Make this block and ease into those challenging little tight curves. You'll get to use the negative template technique to cut four background patches.

Follow the basic curve-in-a-square instructions. Assemble the block in quarters, then join the quarters to complete the block. You might have difficulty meeting the bud outside curves when sewing the quarter blocks together. Just press your seam allowances to nest and use your imaginative seam technique. (See red circle.)

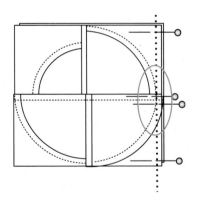

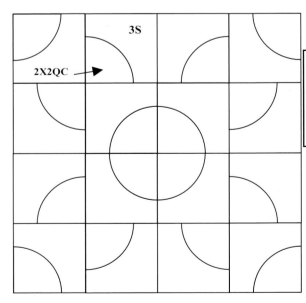

Around the World

Templates:
3S = Cut 16
2X2QC = Cut 16
N2X2QC for the "bite"

About this block: Besides the four presented in this lesson, there must over 30 variations of this 16-unit block. They have names such as **Love Ring**, **Vine of Friendship**, **Nonesuch** and **Fool's Puzzle**. Their only differences are coloration and arrangement of the two-patch sub-units.

Compare your concave patches with 3X3A for accuracy. **Follow the basic curve-in-a-square instructions.** Always refer to your colored diagram while assembling. Press seam allowances for nesting, especially joining the center circle seams. Don't forget to make the block in quarters, then join the quarters to complete the block.

Snowball

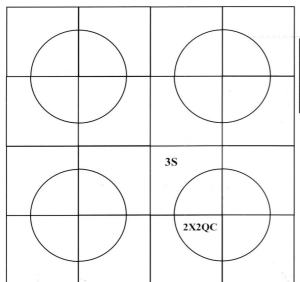

Templates:
3S = Cut 16
2X2QC = Cut 16
N2X2QC for the "bite"

About this block: Every seam in **Snowball** makes an intersection!

All four two-patch curve-in-a-square blocks use the same construction techniques.

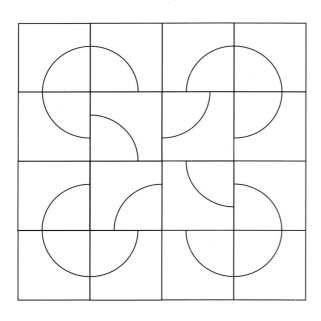

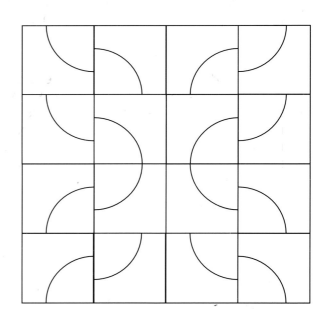

Wonder of the World

Templates:
3S = Cut 16
2X2QC = Cut 16
N2X2QC for the "bite"

Drunkard's Path

Templates:
3S = Cut 16
2X2QC = Cut 16
N2X2QC for the "bite"

It's a little more difficult to make curve and arc templates. They don't have to look beautiful, they just have to be accurate. As you follow Super Bunny's directions, do the best you can. You'll have these templates for a long time. Hopefully, you'll only have to make them once, so be gentle while using them. Remember how precious they were to come by.

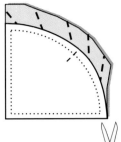

For Quarter-Circle Templates

First, see how well your paper scissors can cut a small piece of scrap cardboard. If it will cut cleanly for about 1/2", you can cut your quarter-circle templates as follows:

After the pattern has been cemented to the cardboard, cut the outside curve of QC and "N" templates with scissors. The scissors won't make that left curve to cut the entire line, so cut as far as you can then shoot off straight, as indicated by the dashed lines in the drawing. Repeat until the curve is cut. Finish the straight lines with the metal ruler and craft knife. Apply the sandpaper layer as usual and trim. Clean up the edges with an emery board.

If your scissors won't cut the cardboard you'll have to cut the convex curves in the same way you will cut the easy concave curves.

For Easy Arc Concave Curves

Hold the red-handled craft knife perpendicular to the cemented cardboard and template. With the very tip of the blade, slowly make the first cut in the concave line of the template. Repeat, increasing pressure with each pass. It becomes easier as the deepening groove you are cutting stabilizes the blade. Take your time. It's the repeats that cut cleanly, more than the pressure. Cut the straight sides with the knife and metal ruler. Attach sandpaper when finished and trim. Clean up edges with emery board.

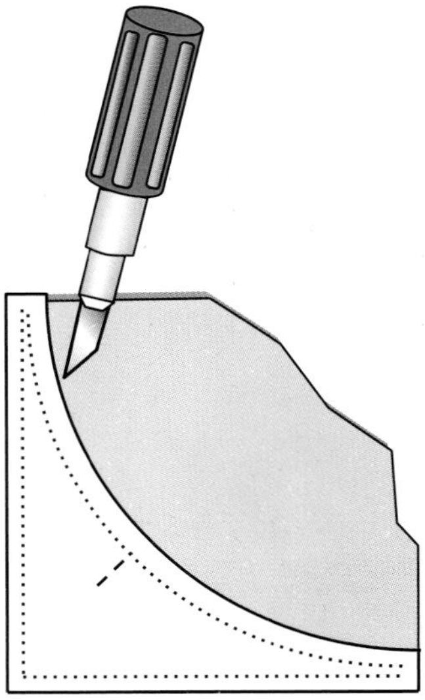

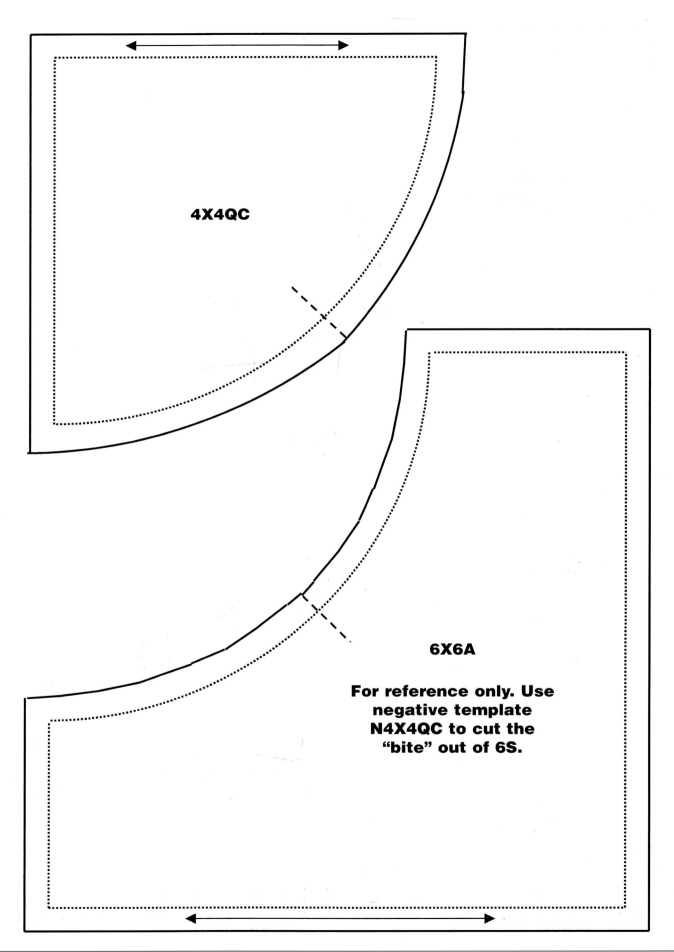

4X4QC

6X6A

For reference only. Use negative template N4X4QC to cut the "bite" out of 6S.

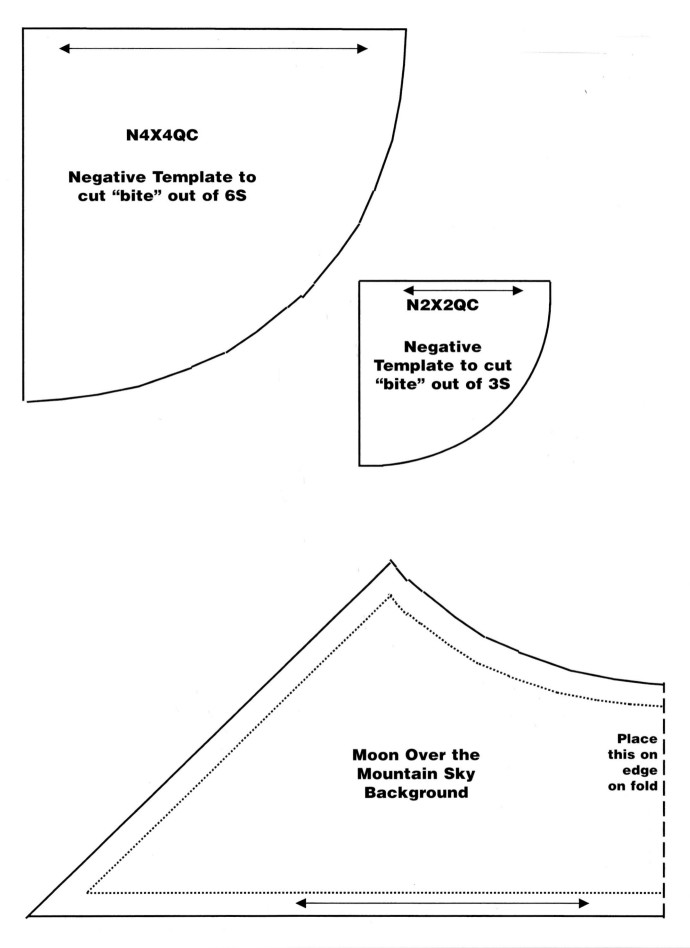

N4X4QC

Negative Template to cut "bite" out of 6S

N2X2QC

Negative Template to cut "bite" out of 3S

Moon Over the Mountain Sky Background

Place this on edge on fold

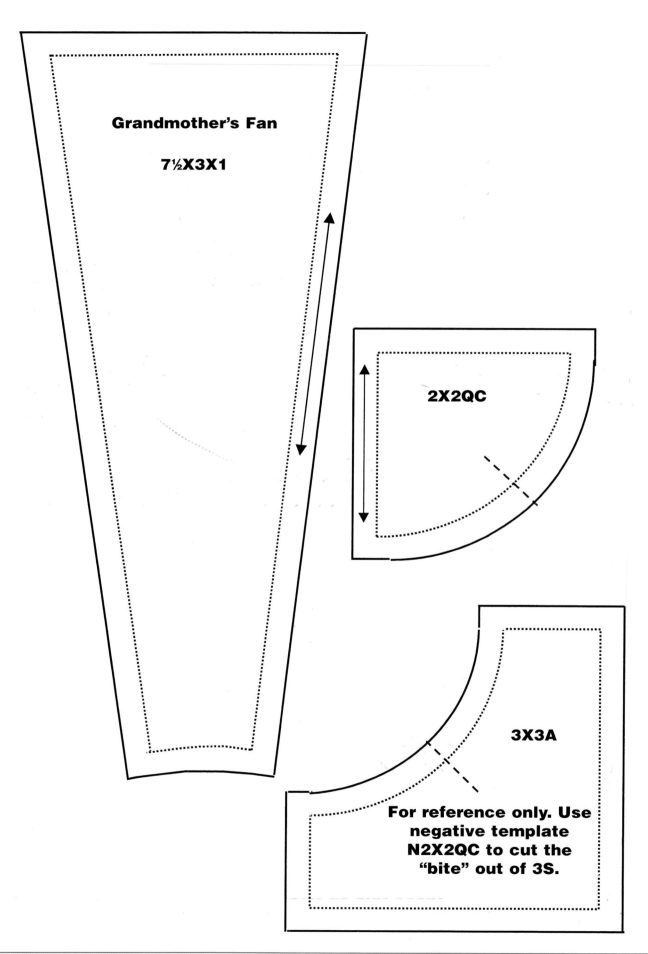

Grandmother's Fan

7½X3X1

2X2QC

3X3A

For reference only. Use negative template N2X2QC to cut the "bite" out of 3S.

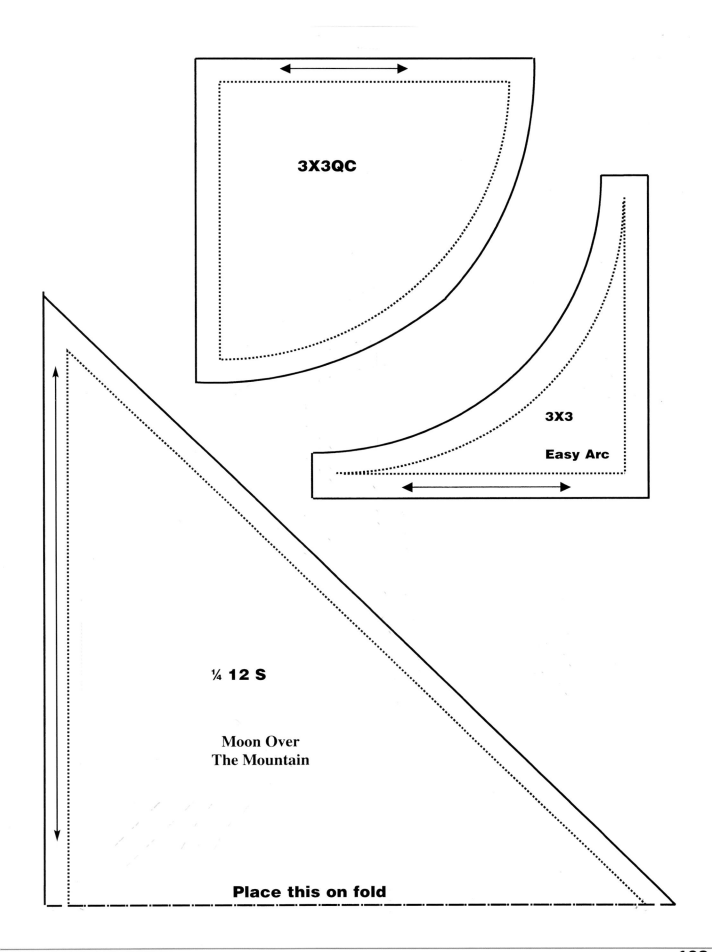

3X3QC

3X3

Easy Arc

¼ **12 S**

**Moon Over
The Mountain**

Place this on fold

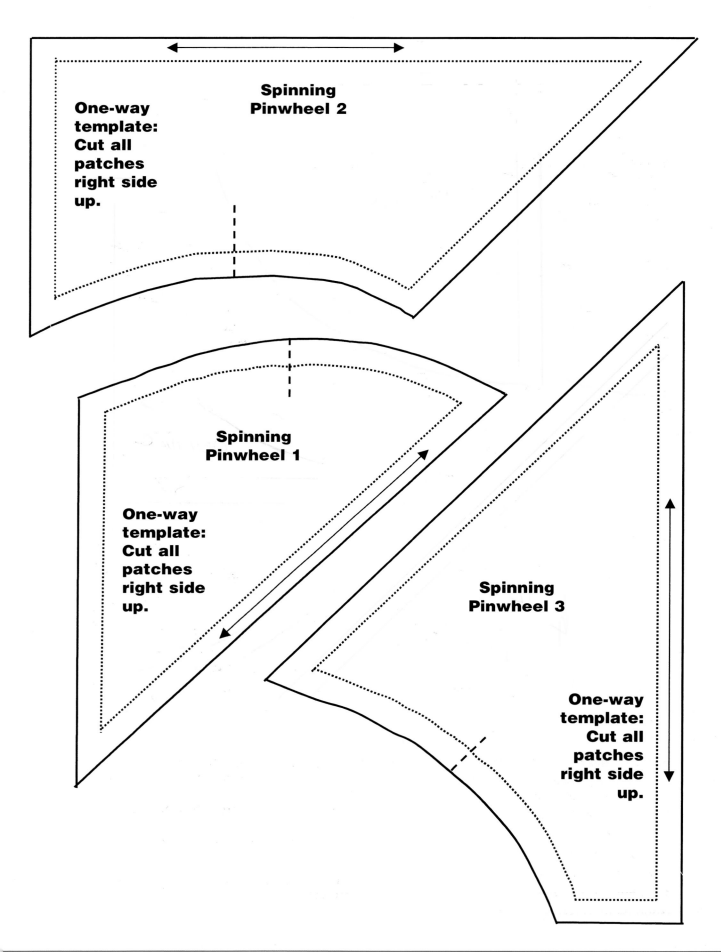

Spinning Pinwheel 2

One-way template: Cut all patches right side up.

Spinning Pinwheel 1

One-way template: Cut all patches right side up.

Spinning Pinwheel 3

One-way template: Cut all patches right side up.

LESSON 7
Finishing the Quilt Top

MATERIALS
Lessons 7 & 8

* Fabric for sashing and borders

* Fabric to make backing that is 6" larger than finished quilt top

* .5 mm mechanical pencil

* Quadrille ruled graph paper

* Rotary grid ruler

* Rotary Cutter and mat

* 15" square rotary grid ruler

* Good fabric scissors

* YLI Wonder Invisible Thread: clear if quilt colors are light; smoke if the colors are bright or dark

* Batting that is 6" larger than finished quilt top

* Size #1 nickel-plated safety pins

* Masking tape

* Large Binder clips (found in office supply stores)

Finishing the Quilt Block

You have reached an exciting moment in the birth of your quilt. The time has arrived to sew all your blocks together and transform them into a quilt top. Quilt blocks sewn together, with or without sashings and/or borders, are referred to as a quilt top. Only after the top is layered over batting and backing, and either stitched or tied together, does it become a quilt. For our example quilt, sashings will be used to join blocks together.

Let's Play "Block Doctor"

No matter how careful you are in constructing your blocks, fabric patches sometimes have a mind of their own and, when assembled, might not "measure up." Often, the sides of our blocks have uneven edges. There are a variety of causes for this, including varying seam allowances, looseness of fabric weave, and patches cut too large or too small. These minor discrepancies can be easily corrected. So, let's "operate" and shape them to the correct size. The goal is to adjust the blocks so that they are within 1/4" of each other, more or less, with sides as straight as possible. Don't get crazy about it. The later addition of sashing will also help adjust size.

Measure each of your finished blocks **across the centers:** top to bottom and side to side. Write down these measurements on a piece of paper. Look at the written dimensions of your blocks. What size are the majority of them? These are **your goal measurements.** While you are measuring, sort your blocks into three piles: too large, too small, and "practically perfect."

If your blocks are approximately 1/8" larger or smaller than your goal measurements, I consider that a home run, and you will not need to fix them.

Here are the measurements for the blocks in the Gold and Black Sampler quilt I made for this book:

Fan =	12-1/2"	x	12-1/2"
Flower =	12-1/2"	x	12-1/2"
Road to Oklahoma =	12-1/2"	x	12-1/2"
Around the World =	12-1/2"	x	12-1/2"
Bouquet =	12-1/4"	x	12-3/8"
Snowball & 9-Patch =	12-1/2"	x	12-1/2"
Pinwheel =	12-3/4"	x	12-5/8"
Windblown Square =	12-3/8"	x	12-1/2"
Basket =	12-1/2"	x	12-1/2"
Joined Variable Star =	12-1/2"	x	12-5/8"
Spools =	12-1/2"	x	12-1/2"
Spinning Pinwheel =	12-5/8"	x	12-1/2"

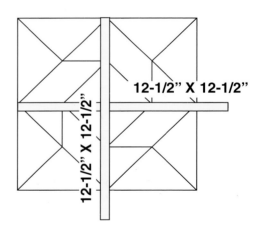

12-1/2" X 12-1/2"

12-1/2" X 12-1/2"

Even though I've been sewing patchwork for 30 years, you can see my blocks still don't come out perfectly. You may have a larger difference because, after all, this is one of your first attempts at sewing patchwork. It's reassuring to know that there's something you can do to make your blocks approximately all the same size.

Blocks too Small? This is an easy fix. All you need to do is add a narrow border around all four sides of an undersized block. For example, this **Road to Oklahoma** block is 12-1/8" square and we want to bring it up to our goal size of 12-1/2" x 12-1/2". The block is 3/8" too small on both the width and the length. You can't just add two 3/8" strips to only two sides because it wouldn't look balanced.

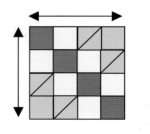

We could make a lot of mathematical calculations here, but basically what we're after is a larger block. We know we'll need to add **half of 3/8" to each side**, include the seam allowances we'll take away from the existing block (1/4" x 2) **plus** add the seam allowances for the fill strips (another 1/4" x 2). I know from experience that narrow strips are hard to apply, so **cut 2" strips** and sew them to all sides just as we learned to add "logs" to the log cabin-type blocks. Then trim the block to the correct size.

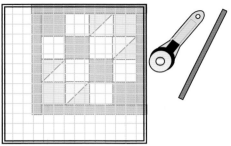

Think about how this "special" block will look in the quilt because the added border will draw attention to it. If you want it to go with the rest of the blocks, make the border out of the least noticeable color that will blend with the block itself.

This square rotary ruler is almost indispensable when "operating" on your blocks. It makes it so easy to "square-up" and trim off the excess. The 15" size is perfect. I know they're expensive, but you'll be grateful for it now and later when we use it to make your quilt "square" while pin-basting the layers

Creative press the border seam allowances after you add each to the block. What does the newly-enlarged block measure across the centers? Correct the top/bottom, then the side/side by subtracting your block size goal number (12-1/2") from the new block measurements, and divide the remainder by 2 (sides). Use your grid ruler and rotary cutter to trim off excess, i.e., **1-5/16"** from each side. Remember, measure twice, and cut once.

Top/Bottom:	Example	Yours
New Measurement =	15 1/8"	
Goal Measurement =	12-1/2"	
Difference =	2 5/8"	
Divided by 2 sides =	1 5/16"	
Cut off top/bottom:	1 5/16"	

Side/Side:	Example	Yours
New Measurement =	15 1/8"	
Goal Measurement =	12-1/2"	
Difference =	2 5/8"	
Divided by 2 sides =	1 5/16"	

Blocks too large? This presents a different problem. If you just cut off the excess, you might cut off the points of patches in the block that you want to touch the sashing strips. Examine each block that is too large. Can you re-sew joining units with a slightly wider seam to bring its' measurements into line? Remember, the amount you stitch into the increased seam allowance will be doubled because you are affecting two layers (patches).

If you can manipulate your too-large blocks to within approximately 1/4" over your target measurements, you will be able to "quilt out" any fullness. That means the fluff of the batting will take up the excess fullness as you quilt.

Blocks have uneven outside edges? When you sew your blocks to the sashing strips, you will pretend that the outside edges are straight. In order to make your points touch, you may have to anticipate where you will be sewing seam intersections, and maneuver the block as you did when assembling patch units using the imaginative seam allowance and holding pin techniques. As long as there is at least 1/8" of block seam allowance beyond the seam line, the seam won't separate. Use a shorter stitch length with these narrow seams. Even though the block seam allowance may be only 1/8", the seam allowance on the sashing strip should remain 1/4".

If you haven't done so already, you will need to draw a sketch or blueprint of the quilt you want to make. This will be your guide. It doesn't have to be fancy. I like to use 4:1 (4 squares equal 1") graph or quadrille paper to make my quilt diagram. It helps me see the exact proportions of the parts of my quilt top. Assign a value to each square on the grid. One square could equal three inches, which fits these blocks well. Therefore, a 12" block would be represented by 16 little grid squares—four across and four down.

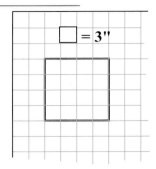

= 3"

There are few rules for creating your own top layout, and you have many options. Balance is probably the most important factor. Do you want sashing in between the blocks or no sashing? Sashing separates the blocks so the viewer can appreciate each individual design. Do you want a wide border, a narrow border, or no border? If you choose to add sashing, a width that can be evenly divided into the finished block size looks the best. Usually, if you have sashing, the border should be wider. But I've seen beautiful quilts that break all the rules, and this is your quilt, so follow your instincts.

If you want a large quilt, consider placing your blocks "on-point" and/or adding wider borders or a series of borders. Placed on-point, your quilt's measurements will be based upon the diagonal measurement of your blocks (approximately 17" instead of 12"), and that will make your quilt much larger. Be aware that if you choose the on-point layout, you'll have fill-in triangles that beg for a quilting motif. Look at the examples in Lesson 1 again to help you decide.

A larger quilt means more fabric will be needed for the borders. To cut the borders on the lengthwise grain, which you must do to keep your quilt square, you'll have to buy yardage equivalent to the measurement of your longest border plus at least an additional 1/2 yard.

One of the quilt diagrams shown in Lesson 1 was this on-point setting. Only seven blocks are needed for this wall-hanging size quilt. Ten half-square triangles are used to complete the rectangle. Use the 12RT template for the fill-in triangles included with the stencil patterns at the back of this book

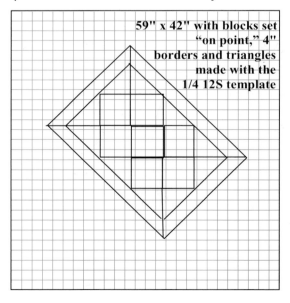

59" x 42" with blocks set "on point," 4" borders and triangles made with the 1/4 12S template

A challenge for the very brave: You can expand on this arrangement and make a bed-size quilt set on-point. A scale drawing is your first step to success. It took me quite some time to realize I had to use the grid lines to draw my blocks, then tilt the paper to draw the outside lines indicating the borders and edges diagonally on the grid.

My choice for the Gold and Black quilt was 3" sashing (which divides evenly into the 12" block size), with a 4" border width (wider than the sashing). I also decided to make little nine-patch blocks at the sashing intersections, expanding on the shortcut method shown in **54-40 or Fight**.

The Gold and Black Sampler will be used as the teaching example for finishing your quilt.

Reserving Border Fabric

I'll bet when you first saw this illustration in Lesson 1, you didn't have a clue what it meant other than you couldn't use most of the fabric you chose for sashing and borders in your quilt blocks. Here comes the best example of using the inherent qualities of fabric to your advantage.

There are good reasons why we use the lengthwise grain for our borders and the crosswise grain for the sashing. Remember that the lengthwise grain does not stretch. The borders will be corralling your quilt top, and no matter what's stretching there, the borders will contain it and make your quilt top square.

Sashing cut on the crosswise grain, on the other hand, will stretch a little, and that's exactly what we need to accommodate the differently sized blocks sewn to the same sashing strip. Isn't that great!

Before we make either the borders or the sashing strips, we have to get rid of the tightly woven selvage edges. It's difficult to cut them off evenly with scissors or a rotary cutter, but it's a breeze to tear them off "on grain." So make a little snip just past where you can see that the fabric threads are woven closer to each other and rip away! Save those strips and cut them into short lengths. They're great for tying up your tomato plants and long-stemmed flowers. Another thing I like to do in the spring is hang the little strips on tree and bush branches. The birds love to weave them into their nests, and you'll soon see colorful strips of your fabrics in the trees.

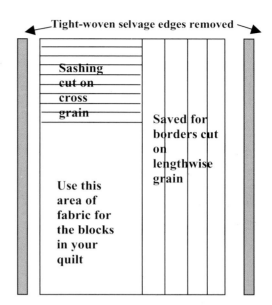

Usable width of fabric is approximately 40"

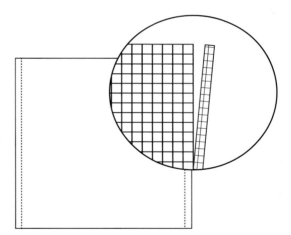

Since we're on a "tear," let's tear off and reserve the border fabric. To make the example quilt, we'll need to save about 20" of lengthwise grain fabric for the borders. Add 2" to make allowance for any mistakes and tear off 22" on the lengthwise grain. (Insert your measurements if your quilt has different dimensions.)

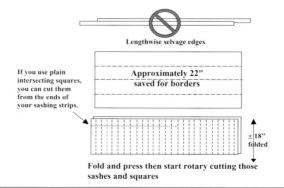

Fold and press then start rotary cutting those sashes and squares

I prefer using short individual sashing strips for each block rather than long strips that run either from the top to the bottom or side-to-side. The reason is that it's very difficult to attach two blocks exactly across from each other on one long sashing strip, especially blocks that may not be the same exact size. Improper alignment can make you disappointed in that quilt you worked so hard on.

Use your hand-drawn diagram as a guide to determine how many sashing strips you will need. The width of those strips is your choice, but the length of the strips will be determined by your length/width block goal measurement; for example, if your "doctored" blocks share common measurements of approximately 12-1/2" x 12-1/2", then your sashing strips will be 12-1/2" long.

If you choose plain sashing strips and intersection squares, you may want to omit the perimeter sashes and squares, and attach the borders directly to your blocks—especially if they will be made from the same fabric. You won't notice those other seams, so why make them? Save work wherever you can.

This particular quilt diagram contains sashing strips that are 3" wide. You have reserved 22" on the lengthwise grain for 4" **borders** and have at least another 18" to use for sashing strips. You can get one sashing strip and one corner square out of each length. Use your rotary cutter and mat to cut the number of sashing strips (17) and intersecting squares (6) you will need from the crosswise grain of your folded fabric.

Do You Want to Make Pieced Sashing and Intersection Squares?

Don't let this step intimidate you. To make the Gold and Black quilt layout, you will have to make 31 pieced strips and 20 nine-patch intersection squares. You can use the quick assembly tricks you learned in **54-40 or Fight** to make two different sets, and then cut strips from those sets for squares and sashes.

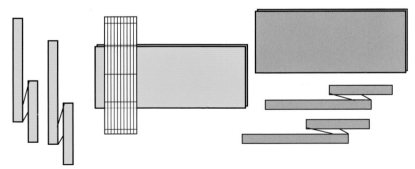

To begin, cut 1-1/2" strips from two fabrics and prepare Sets 1 and 2, from which you will cut the sashing and the nine-patch intersections, also known as "cornerstones."

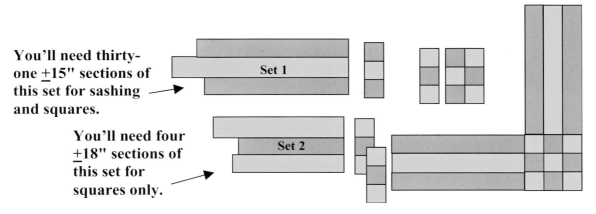

You'll need thirty-one ±15" sections of this set for sashing and squares.

You'll need four ±18" sections of this set for squares only.

Sashing strips and setting squares have to nest too, so press seam allowances to the darker color, and nesting will be automatic. Don't attach the squares to the strips yet.

How Does Your Quilt Top Look So Far?

Once all the sashing strips are cut and pieced (if necessary), **sew one strip to the bottom of each of your quilt blocks.** You'll get a better idea of how the blocks will look in final form attached to their sashes. Stitch with the wrong side of the blocks on top. Use the same tricks and techniques to meet points and match seam intersections as you did when constructing the blocks. Make the blocks fit the strips.

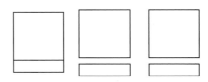

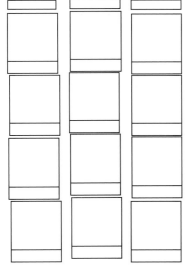

This next step is kind of fun. Lay your blocks out on a large surface and rearrange them to achieve a pleasing combination. Try to balance color and block busy-ness. Some of your blocks might not look that great with all the others. That's why I recommended you make a few extra ones. Turn the orphans into pillows and gifts.

When you find the arrangement you like, sew a sash to the top of each block in the first row. Assemble your quilt top in uneven quarter sections as shown. Don't assemble it in strips. That could lead to "wavy" seams.

Your quilt top is almost finished. Sit back and admire it!

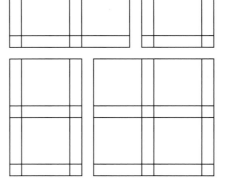

Borders: Does Your Quilt Really Need Them?

A border is to a quilt what a frame is to a painting. Some paintings are so full of color and design that an overly ornate frame would detract from its beauty. Some paintings are too small for the wall, so the addition of a wide frame would nicely fill the space. Some paintings need no frame at all. And some frames are of such beautiful design that they meld with a painting and both complement each other.

Borders can help you achieve these same effects. If your quilt is bright, colorful, and busy, all you would need for a border would be a simple frame of fabric that controls the interior action within a boundary. (What a surprise if a bit of that interior action might escape and fall into the border with the interjection of a small, matching pieced block!) Perhaps you have a quilt top that makes such a strong statement, a border would be superfluous. All that would be necessary to finish this quilt would be a narrow binding. If your quilt top is too small to cover a bed, the addition of a border or number of borders will bring it up to the correct size. Borders are limited only by your imagination—and how much fabric you have left!

> Speaking of leftovers, save pieces of your quilt fabrics.
> You never know when you'll need a repair patch.

Measuring for Borders with Mitered Corners

Well-executed, mitered borders amaze quilt admirers and judges alike, and it isn't that difficult to accomplish. This treatment really does give your quilt a frame. Beauty aside, we must never forget that borders fulfill many practical requirements, not the least of which is to keep our quilt square.

To construct our border, we need to know the top's correct measurements. How do you measure your quilt top? Remember when we measured our individual blocks—we didn't hold the tape along one side, we measured across the centers. Spooky things can happen at the outside edges of our quilt, but its true dimensions are always found right across the middles.

Your quilt measures
_____ **inches top to bottom**
_____ **inches side to side**

Find the correct size to cut your border strips for mitering by using this formula:

How wide will your border be?   _____ inches.

For length of top and bottom border strips:

Side to Side measurement =   _____ inches
    Plus border width x 2 =   + _____ inches
    Add 3" (seam allowances and safety margin)   + 3 inches
    Length of top and bottom border strips   _____ inches

For length of side border strips:

Top/bottom measurement =   _____ inches
    Plus border width x 2 =   + _____ inches
    Add 3" (seam allowances and safety margin)   + 3 inches
    Length of side border strips   _____ inches

To see how this formula works, let's insert the measurements from the example quilt.

Gold and Black top measures   ____64____ " top to bottom
                                              ____49____ " side to side

To find the correct length to cut border strips for mitering, use this formula:
How wide will your border be?   ____4____ "

For top and bottom border strips:
Side measurement = ___49___ " plus width of 2 borders = ___8___ " plus 3" extra = _60___ "

For side border strips:
Top/bottom measure = ___64___ " plus width of 2 borders = ___8___ " plus 3" extra = _75__ "

Don't forget to add 1/2" for seam allowances to your border width when cutting. These borders should be cut 4-1/2" wide.

Using your calculated measurements, cut or tear border strips for your quilt top from the lengthwise grain. Tearing will ensure on-grain strips. The torn edges will be a little raggedy and the fabric print could be slightly distorted, but true straight of grain borders are what we're after.

NOTE: If you are planning to add a series of borders around your quilt, tear the strips from the fabrics you will be using. Sew them together then treat each pieced border as one complete unit.

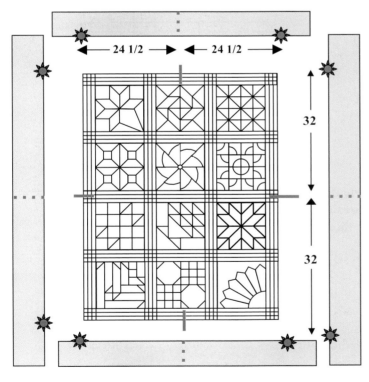

24 1/2   24 1/2

32

32

Attaching the Borders

Find the centers of each side of your quilt and mark with a pin. Fold each border strip in half and mark the centers.

We always use the across-center measurements for the size of our quilt. The side-to-side measurement is 49". To attach the top and bottom border strips, calculate half the side-to-side measurement, 24-1/2", then measure 24-1/2" from the center of the top border to each end and mark. Repeat for the bottom strip.

Half the top-to-bottom measurement of 64" is 32". Measure from the center of the side strips and place a mark at the 32" point at each end. Repeat for the other side.

If you are sewing the border right to the blocks with no perimeter sashing strips, use the point matching and creative seam allowance techniques you have learned.

With the wrong side of the quilt facing up, match one side center mark to the center of its border and pin. Align the outside corners of that side of the quilt top to the 32" mark on the border and pin. Ease in fullness and pin the side as necessary. Sew the seam **starting and stopping 1/4" in from the outside edge of the quilt top and backstitch at both seam ends**. Repeat on all four sides. Press the seam allowances toward the borders. Doesn't the quilt with its detached border corners now resemble a large version of a **Spools** unit?

You have just corralled your quilt and it will be square because you used the across-the-middle measurements. Congratulations!

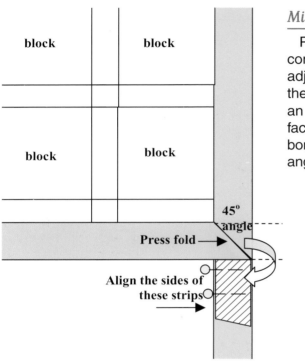

Mitering the Corners

Position your quilt right side up. We'll miter one corner at a time. Lay one border strip across the adjoining one. Flip the top strip down and away from the quilt, aligning it with the second strip to create an automatic 45° miter. The right sides of the strips face each other. Press the resulting fold and pin the border extensions to secure positioning. Check the angle of the fold with your rotary ruler.

To sew the miter, lift and diagonally fold that corner of the **quilt** right sides together matching the outer long border edges. Secure with additional pins. When you sewed the border onto the quilt, you stopped stitching 1/4" from the top's outer corners. Begin stitching the border miter seam in the last stitch holes, backstitch, then follow the pressed fold line, and finish the seam at the raw edge.

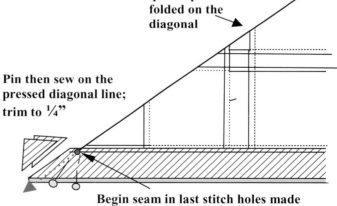

Pin then sew on the pressed diagonal line; trim to ¼"

Begin seam in last stitch holes made when borders were sewn to quilt top.

Open the quilt and look at the right side of the miter you just made. Again, use the 45-degree line on your rotary ruler to check for accuracy and a square border corner. If it needs no correction, return the quilt to the wrong side and trim excess seam allowance to 1/4". Press the seam open.

Don't Want Mitered Corners?

You can make borders with square corners by cutting squares the width of your border plus 1/2" for seam allowances. (If your borders are 4" wide, the square would be 4-1/2" x 4-1/2".) The top and bottom border strips must be cut to your exact crosswise quilt measurements plus 1/2" for seam allowances. The side borders must be cut your exact lengthwise quilt measurement. Add the squares to the top and bottom borders first. Sew the side borders to the quilt then add the joined top and bottom borders nesting seam intersections.

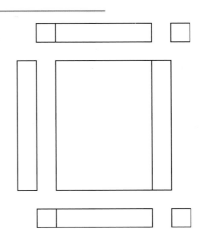

Always make the outer edge of the quilt fit the borders to make your quilt square.

You can also make plain borders. To do this, begin with one across-the-center measurement. (You save fabric if you add the long sides first.) Cut the side borders and add them to the quilt. Measure your quilt again from side-to-side including the new side borders. Cut your top and bottom borders using that measurement, and add them to your quilt so as to make the quilt fit the borders.

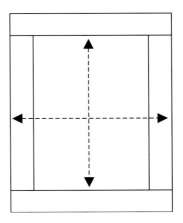

Your Quilt Top is Done!

Give your beautiful **completed** quilt top a good steam pressing. You can use starch or sizing, too. Take final center measurements in preparation for the next lesson, The Three B's—Backing, Batting, and Basting.

Your finished quilt top is _____" long and _____" wide.

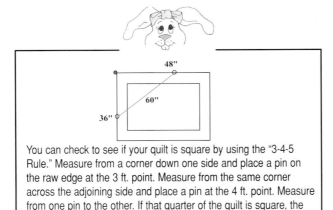

You can check to see if your quilt is square by using the "3-4-5 Rule." Measure from a corner down one side and place a pin on the raw edge at the 3 ft. point. Measure from the same corner across the adjoining side and place a pin at the 4 ft. point. Measure from one pin to the other. If that quarter of the quilt is square, the cross measurement will be 5 ft. Check all four corners. If there is a discrepancy, determine the cause. Now is the time to fix it.

Backing, Batting, and Basting

This lesson will teach you how to make your quilt into a "sandwich" in preparation to be quilted. Because a quilt is made up of three layers—the top, the batting in the middle, and the backing—we need to make choices on the best types of batting and backing material to purchase for the kind of finish we want to give our quilts.

Choosing a Fabric for the Backing

The fabric you choose for your quilt's backing should be of the same fiber content and quality as the fabrics you used in your quilt top, and that would preferably be a good 100 percent cotton. Don't be tempted to use a cotton sheet just because it's large enough to make a backing with no seams. Some sheets can be very tightly woven and impossible to quilt through. Many contain a mix of cotton and polyester that, with wear, will form little "pills" of fiber on its surface. Some 100 percent cotton sheets are too soft and stretchy for use as a backing.

You can find a few 90"-wide fabrics available, although color and pattern choices are limited. Most quilters choose a 45" cotton fabric that goes well with their top, and piece it to accommodate the quilt's measurements. Janet Yantch, one of my students, took all the larger leftover fabric scraps from her quilt top, pieced them together, and made a backing of simple patchwork squares and rectangles. It was quite wonderful, and her skill in keeping all the backing seam lines straight and perpendicular with the edges of the quilt top was very evident.

What color fabric should you pick for your quilt back? If you want to hand quilt your entire quilt, you should use a light, solid color. Only a plain cotton fabric will reveal the stitching and shadows created by your hand quilting. If you're going to go to all the trouble of hand quilting, you want your hard work to show on the back as well as the front.

Our beginner quilt will contain some hand quilting. It will also be machine quilted in keeping with my philosophy of **"machine quilt where it doesn't show and hand quilt where it does."** In this way, people who look at your quilt will think it is completely hand quilted. But simple machine quilting in the ditch will hurry the chore along so that you will be able to finish your quilt in a relatively short time. Finishing a quilt encourages all of us, especially beginners, to continue making more quilts instead of being hung up on hand quilting for months at a time.

Although the next lesson will concentrate on the actual quilting processes, we have to keep in mind what specific techniques we plan to use in order to purchase the correct backing fabric and quilt batting.

Since this could be your first experience with any type of quilting at all, I suspect your stitch might not be perfection. Mine certainly wasn't when I began quilting—far from it! So let's buy backing fabric that disguises our learning experience. A non-directional, busy print fabric is great for this. Choose a color that blends well with the fabrics you used in your top. It's really great if you can find one that has its design printed in the color of the hand quilting thread you plan to use. This combination is the best camouflage.

Examples of backing fabric

How Much Backing Fabric To Buy

The backing for a quilt should be at least 6" larger (after pre-shrinking) than your quilt top. Why? When you quilt, the top and backing will get smaller as its surfaces are taken up slightly by the stitching and batting. If we made the backing the same size as the top, at the end of the quilting process, the backing could be smaller than the top. We don't want to have to cut the top down to fit the backing. It's better to cut the backing down to fit the top.

In Lesson 7, you measured your completed quilt top after adding the borders. What were your measurements? The finished Gold and Black Sampler top measured 57-1/2" wide by 72-1/2" long. The cotton fabric I wanted to use was 45" wide. (Me, thinking: "So, the quilt is 72-1/2" long— that's a smidge over 2 yards. Twice 2 yards is 4 yards plus the additional 6" [3" x 2 edges] **for each length of fabric**, 12"—that's 1/3 yard more.") I needed 4-1/3 yards, so I bought 4-1/2 yards. It's better to have more than you need than not enough.

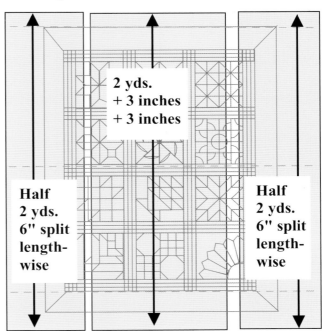

2 yds.
+ 3 inches
+ 3 inches

**Half
2 yds.
6" split
length-
wise**

**Half
2 yds.
6" split
length-
wise**

You might wonder why you wouldn't just sew two lengths of fabric with one seam down the middle. You could do that, but a middle seam will carry the weight of the entire quilt as it would lie on a bed. Even though there's batting between the back and top, after time, a wear line tracing the center backing seam could appear on the top. By supporting the weight of the quilt between two backing seams, a wear line is less likely.

Choosing the Batting — Match Fiber Content to Quilting Method

The most readily available quilt batts contain fibers that are all cotton, all polyester, or a combination of polyester and cotton. For practical purposes, I'll omit silk, wool, and down as choices because of expense, accessibility, and/or potential allergy problems. Let's take a moment to discuss the attributes of cotton versus polyester.

Batting made of cotton, a natural fiber, captures less air and is generally less voluminous than polyester. It will not separate if you follow the manufacturer's instructions for quilting distances. Its' fibers will not migrate through the top or backing fabric. Cotton batting gives your quilt a flatter, more traditional look. **The thicker and more dense the cotton batting, the more difficult it is to hand quilt.** Machine quilting through this type of batt looks beautiful, provides the feed dogs with something sturdy to grip onto as it sews, and gives the quilt a substantial and warm look. You will get a good "relief" of shadow and stitch with a dense, cotton batting, but the quilt will be heavier. If I am going to completely machine quilt, I prefer this type of batting for even-stitch results.

Cotton battings come in white or natural (cream) colors. Thick or thin, many are chemically glazed, heat treated, or manufactured so that you can space your quilting up to 8"-10" apart with no danger of bunching or separation. Some brands contain broken seed particles, and the manufacturer recommends that you wash it before use to eliminate the possibility of released oils staining your quilt top. Other brands of cotton batting have been manufactured with the same non-bunching features and do not contain seed particles.

Read the manufacturers' package directions before use. Be especially mindful of how much the cotton quilt batting is expected to shrink. If you want a traditional look for your quilt, a minor amount of shrinkage is desirable and will contribute to the shadowing and "relief" texturing effect.

Polyester Quilt Batting

Polyester, a synthetic fiber, has its attributes, too. It dries faster, retains its volume after washings, does not mildew, won't shrink, and helps keep your quilt from looking wrinkled. Polyester traps more air, thus making your quilt warmer with less weight. You don't have to pre-wash polyester, although you might want to toss the batt into the dryer on low for a few minutes just before you baste it into your quilt to remove the wrinkles caused by packaging.

If you plan to hand quilt, it is much easier to stitch through a 100 percent polyester batt. This characteristic is referred to as "needling quality." Leave the "high," "ultra," and "extra" loft batts for tied quilts. These thicker polyester batts puff up and hide hand quilting. If it's not going to be seen, why do it? Tying a puffy quilt with embroidery floss, heavy cotton thread, yarn or narrow (1/8") ribbon is a perfectly acceptable form of attaching the three layers of a quilt together, and its effective use can become part of the total design of your quilt top.

Polyester battings are also manufactured with surfaces that are heat bonded or treated with a finish that holds their fibers in place. This treatment, too, is intended to prevent bunching, and inhibit the migration of fibers through your quilt fabric and cause what is referred to as "bearding." Inexpensive polyester batting with no surface treatment can ruin a quilt. Minute fibers will continually work their way through the fabric weave and give an unsatisfactory "fuzzy" look. You'll never be able to get those fibers off because brushing, using a "de-fuzzer," or one of those tape garment rolls will just pull more fibers to the surface.

The bearding won't be as noticeable if you use a white batting on a mostly white or light quilt, but will be quite noticeable when used under darker or more intense colors. There are charcoal-colored polyester batts available which make it more difficult to see the "bearding" on these darker quilts, and I highly recommend their use if you want to entirely hand quilt one. Be aware, though, that the dark batting will shadow through and affect the color of any light patches in your quilt.

Glazed or bonded, whatever stabilizing treatment is given to the surface, if you're going to use a polyester batt, the small additional expense is worth paying when you consider how much time and work you will put into making your beautiful quilt.

Cotton-Polyester Blend

Almost all major batting manufacturers have produced a hybrid batt that contains both cotton and polyester fibers. The ratio is cotton in the 80 percent range with around 20 percent polyester and will give your quilt the characteristics of a traditional low-loft look. This type of batting produces good results and is a realistic compromise between cotton and polyester battings offering the advantages of both fibers.

Your choice of batting depends upon the finished look you want to give to your quilt. For a successful outcome, it is essential to always **read and follow the manufacturer's instructions** before you choose and use a quilt batting.

No matter what the fiber content, be aware that some people can be allergic to the chemicals used in surface treatment methods. If this is a concern, you can try one of the new batts with heat-treated surfaces.

What Size Batt Should You Purchase?

Purchase a batt that is at least 6" larger than your quilt—the same size you made your backing. The manufacturer prints the size of the batting on its packaging. Larger is better than smaller. You can always use leftover scraps in other small projects. Don't trim down your batting until after it's placed onto the backing during basting.

If you can't find a big enough batt or you have leftovers of the same fiber content you'd like to join and use, follow these simple instructions to make one large batt from smaller pieces.

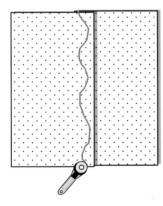
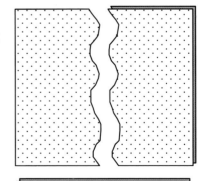

Step 1: Overlap batting pieces at least 2". Using your rotary cutter, cut a curvy line through BOTH batting pieces at the same time. Save scraps for stuffing pillows, etc.

Step 2: Butt the two curved edges together. They will match exactly because you cut them at the same time.

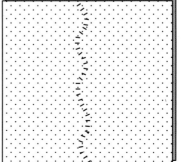

Step 3: With needle and matching thread, hand sew pieces together with large crisscross stitches (herringbone stitch). Don't pull the thread so tightly that it puckers the batting.

Okay, you're home with your 4-1/2 yards of backing material and quilt batt. You pre-shrank your quilt top fabrics; so don't forget to pre-shrink your backing fabric. A simple wet-down with warm water is sufficient. Be sure to check for color-fastness as you did before. If the fabric doesn't transfer color into the rinse water, wring it out and toss it in the dryer. If it does, rinse it until the water runs clear—or don't use it!

Now we're ready to transform the 4-1/2 yards of fabric into a backing. The first thing you will do is t**ear it**! The tightly woven selvage edges need to be removed before we can sew the backing together. So, as we removed them in Lesson 7, tear off the selvage edges. Here we don't have to be concerned with distortion of the fabric pattern caused by tearing because all these torn edges will either be hidden by a 1/2" **seam** or trimmed off after the quilting process. Iron the yardage with no folds or creases.

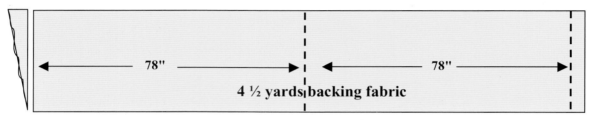

Square up one end of the backing fabric by tearing or cutting a straight edge across the width. Measure the **length** of your quilt plus 6" from the straightened end. For the example quilt, that measurement would be 78". Cut off 78". Measure and cut off a second length of 78". You now have two pieces of fabric that are each 6" longer than your quilt.

Add 6" to the **width** measurement of your quilt for shrinkage. The width of the example quilt is 57-1/2" plus 6" shrinkage allowance requires a backing width of 63-1/2". Each of the fabric pieces after removal of the selvage edges has about 43 useable inches, so we need to add at least 30" from the second piece to reach that goal. We mustn't forget to include seam allowances, and **these seams will be 1/2" wide**. Two seams will join four seam edges using 1/2", that's two more inches. We need to add 32" to the center fabric strip. Half of 32" is 16"—we will cut off two 16" lengths from the second piece of backing fabric. Keep the 11" strip of fabric in case you want to add a hanging sleeve to the back of your quilt later. (See Lesson 10, page 152)

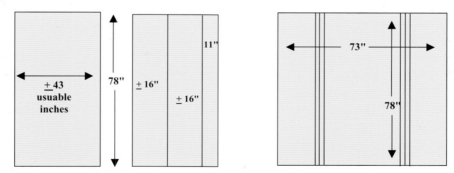

Using a 1/2" seam allowance, sew a 16" strip to each side of the 43" panel. Press the seams open. Those seams add extra bulk, and you don't want to quilt through five layers if pressed to one side.

We have our three layers—the top, the batting and the backing. We're ready for the next stop on the road to a completed quilt.

If you want to completely hand quilt your top, you will want to hand baste the layers together. Thread basting will not interfere with later securing the sandwich into a hoop or frame, a necessity for hand quilting. You will need guidance and help, so I encourage you to join a quilt club where you can find wonderful support and inspiration. Most quilt shops have a listing of clubs with contact names and telephone numbers within their sales areas.

Before machine quilting became a common way to attach a quilt top, batting, and backing, quilts were either tied or hand quilted using a basting frame and many quilting friends. These basting bees were a fun gathering for women, and one of the few social outlets available to them in the 1700s and 1800s. The old-fashioned basting frame consisted of four lengths of dimensional lumber, usually 2" x 2". These boards were covered with a sturdy, closely woven material such as canvas or denim, which stopped approximately 4" from each end and extended evenly along the length like a little "flap." Traditionally, two boards would be 8 ft. and the other two would be 10 ft. By sliding these boards back and forth perpendicular to each other, the frame could be adjusted to fit any size quilt. Four "C" clamps were used to hold these boards together at the corners, where great care was taken to ensure they were perfectly square.

After the frame was assembled, made square, and adjusted to fit the size quilt that was to be basted, it would be placed on the high backs of four chairs (seats facing toward the center of the frame) or attached to upright stanchions made for the purpose of supporting the frame.

Centers of each side of the frame were marked on the fabric coverings. Then centers were marked on each four sides of the quilt top and the backing fabric. Matching center points, the backing was stretched wrong side up and firmly pinned to the fabric flaps of the frame. Again, care was taken to ensure square corners.

Then the batting was unrolled and centered onto the backing fabric. Any necessary trimming of the batting was done at this time to make it the same size as the backing. With the quilt top facing right side up, its centers were aligned to those of the backing, and the top was carefully centered, smoothed, stretched over the batting, and pinned through to the backing. The whole stretched unit was tight enough to bounce a quarter tossed onto its surface.

Now the quilt could be basted! Many hands made light work, and a number of "needle basters" would take their positions at all four sides of the frame with their double-threaded long needles. They would take long, running stitches across the width and down the length of the quilt sandwich. These rows of stitches would be placed about a hand's-width apart. When the basters could no longer reach toward the center of the quilt, each short side, one at a time, would be released from the "C" clamps, and the basted part of the quilt would be carefully rolled onto the 8 ft. boards (one rolled over, one rolled under). Before re-attaching the "C" clamps, the accuracy of new "square" corners would again be checked. In this fashion, the quilt top would be completely basted with thread in a checkerboard pattern ready for hand quilting.

If the quilt were to be tied instead of basted, the volunteers would fill large-eyed needles with perle cotton, embroidery floss, or yarn, and the quilt would be "tied" to completion. The addition of a binding edge finish by its maker was all that remained to be done.

Today with so many women working, it is difficult to find the time to get together with fellow quilters to baste a quilt let alone to hand quilt it. That is why so many quilters have turned to pin basting and machine quilting.

One person can do pin basting, although the company of two or more helpers is definitely more enjoyable and easier on one's back and neck. Essentially, the same procedure as thread basting is followed with safety pins replacing needle and thread, and one or two long tables substituting for the basting frame.

You can use your dining room table fully extended with all its leaves. You'll have to cover your tabletop with a pad or cardboard to protect it from scratches. Many quilt shops have long tables and space available to quilters who want to pin baste their quilts. Also, churches and community centers that have long tables and recreation rooms are willing to let you use their facilities. Call for information. I find these organizations are very welcoming and accommodating.

I use the tables at my town's recreation center for basting. It's great fun, and passersby always stop to admire the quilts and learn about quiltmaking. I've even gotten interested visitors to become students, who are also now using the tables for their quilts.

We can't pin the backing edges to the table, so we use large binder clips for fastening the layers. These binder clips can be found at stationery and office supply stores and are inexpensive. They'll be stiff to open at first, but they will loosen up with use—for the **next** quilt. You'll need at least 12 clips.

Use #1 nickel-plated safety pins for the actual basting. The pin size is very important. It should be thin and very sharp so that no tiny broken thread holes will be made in your quilt top or backing. There are special basting pins available that have a bend in the closure part. The students in one of my classes did a comparison when pin-basting their quilts. We found that, with or without the bend, it made no difference on how difficult it was to close the pins. So if the specialty pins cost more, it's probably not worth the expense. I've found some very nice pins at the dollar-type store. Just make sure they're nickel-plated. You'll be using about 400 pins placed **3 to 4 inches apart** for the standard 60" x 75" quilt diagrammed in this book.

If you encounter a blunt safety pin while you're basting, throw it away. Also, as you remove a pin while machine quilting, don't close it again. Put the open pins in a secure container and store it away from children and pets. You'll find it an unnecessary bother to have to open pins as you are basting, and another bother to close them again after you remove them from your quilt only to open them again for the next basting. In fact, you can purchase "open" pins through catalogs, but they cost twice as much as "closed" ones!

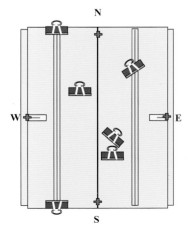

Setting Up for Pin Basting

First, find the centers on all four sides of your quilt backing and mark with a safety pin. Place a short strip of masking tape at the outside center edge of each side of the table(s). If you're using two tables, of course, the top and bottom centers will be where they meet. If the quilt is too small for two tables, center your backing onto one table with even amounts of overhang on opposite sides. I'll describe the basting procedure assuming the use of two long (6 ft.) tables pushed together.

Find the centers of the "west" and "east" table sides again. There should be a piece of masking tape there. Make a mark onto the masking tape at the exact center.

With the backing wrong side up, match backing center pins and table center marks. The E and W sides will probably hang over the table edges; so reset the backing center pins toward the middle until they meet the table markings. Make sure those adjusted backing side center points are accurate.

Using the binder clips, clamp the backing to the tables. If you have a helper, work in tandem across from each other. This will keep even tension on the backing as you secure it to the tables. If the binder clips can't catch the top and bottom edges of the quilt, secure them to the table with short strips of masking tape.

After securing all sides of the backing to the table, lay your prepared batting evenly on top of the backing, removing then reattaching each clamp to include the two layers. Be careful to keep the backing fabric smooth and undisturbed. If you know the batting is too large, arrange it so you'll only have to cut off excess from two sides. Doing this will result in larger scrap pieces that may be used later.

Finally, mark the edge centers of your **quilt top** with safety pins. Fold the top in half and carefully lay it over the batting. Open the top matching its centers to the centers of the backing. Smooth the top to remove wrinkles and square it up. Where you can, remove and reattach binder clips over the three layers without disturbing them. Clamp the quilt sandwich taut, but do not stretch it. If the top isn't as long as the tables and you can't secure its "north" and "south" edges, leave the backing and batting clipped or taped and secure only the "east" and "west" sides. We'll attach the top and bottom with pins.

You'll be bumping into the binder clip handles, so flip them over onto the quilt to get them out of the way.

Last Chance to Make Your Blocks Square

With your quilt sandwich clamped to the tables, this is the last chance you will have to affect how straight your blocks and sashing strips will look. We know that we made the quilt square with our careful measuring and attachment of lengthwise grain borders. Still, you might see less than straight lines either within or at the sashing edges of the blocks. We can fix this using our 15" square grid ruler.

To keep from having bloody fingers, insert the pin with your right hand, pushing toward your tummy, and close it with that thumb nail. If you insert the pin away from yourself, you'll have to close it with the forefinger and thumb of your other hand, which will get sore and bleed before all 400 pins are in position. If you're really having trouble with sore fingers, use the bowl of a spoon to help you close pins.

Use the 15" grid square ruler to test the **top center** of the quilt. Align the unclamped quilt top border edge and its seam to the table and secure though to the backing with pins. Adjust any sashing seams above the center block in the first row so they are parallel with the table edge and lines on the ruler and pin. Avoid pinning on top of seams, as you will be machine quilting them "in the ditch." If a seam is wavy, straighten it with your fingers and place a pin on **the side you moved the seam to**. If it's extra wavy, you may have to place many pins on both sides of a seam to keep it straight. Later, when you're quilting, the number of pins in an area will be a sign to you that a problem exists there, and you can hold the seam straight as you quilt.

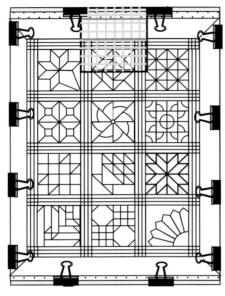

Align border edge and seam to table edge.

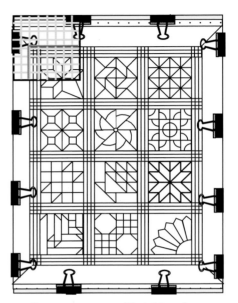

Square seams with table edges

Continue this same procedure as you move to adjust the left then right corners testing and squaring up the quilt edge and border seams with the table edges. Then invite your quilting buddy to work with you pinning the rest of the quilt. Sharing the grid ruler, work opposite each other here, too, in an organized fashion. **Always reference your grid ruler to seam lines you know are straight and square.**

The binder clips are not sacred, they can be moved. Occasionally, you may have to release and reclamp. The quilt may flatten as you're pinning causing the quilt/border seams to move towards the long sides of the table. That's okay; just keep seam lines straight and parallel with the sides of the table.

Basting within Blocks

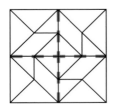

Move down to address the first row of blocks. Use the grid square to check the center block in that row, **Windblown Square**. At the same time, you'll be looking at the adjoining sashing to make sure it is also straight. The major axis lines within the block should be parallel to the sides. Make corrections, straighten seams, and pin baste the interior of the block. Also square up, check, and adjust the sashing strips, if necessary. Remember, pins are placed 3" to 4" apart and should be **filled** with quilt sandwich (take a good-sized bite) to keep the layers from shifting. If some patches within a block are a little too big after you adjust and pin its sides straight, gently pat down the puff of excess fabric and pin. Don't worry, it will quilt out.

The pin basting process continues by first pinning the center block of each successive row. Square its perimeter by referencing seams you know are accurate. Address patches within the block and make their seam lines **appear** straight. Move to the adjoining sashings to check for and adjust straight lines. Go to the blocks on each side; make any adjustments, then progress to its adjoining sashings. Finally, align the side border seam to the table edge.

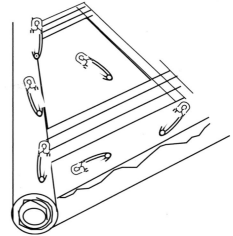

When you come to the bottom border, repeat the same procedure you used to square, straighten, and pin the top border. Make sure, also, that the pinned-side border seams are still parallel to the table edges.

Finally, stand at each side of your basted quilt and look down the rows of sashing strips for a final "straight" check. It doesn't have to be perfect; it just has to give the impression of being straight.

Remove the binder clips. I hope you have a few pins left because it's a good idea to roll and pin the extra backing over the batting and quilt edges. This protects them from fraying and catching on your sewing machine foot while quilting.

Next stop…Quilt Central!

You know, there are very nice people who will take your quilt top and pieced backing, supply the batting and machine quilt it for you. The cost depends upon the size and quilting design you choose. If you have this done with an overall quilting pattern that doesn't trace each blocks' design, pick a motif and thread color that doesn't detract from your piecing. Ask at your local quilt shop for a reference.

ℒESSON 9

Quilting

We have a little work ahead of us as we learn how to both hand and machine quilt. Treat this stage in completing your quilt as a job that will be both creatively and physically challenging.

You will need the following supplies to begin machine and hand quilting. Most of the items you have been using all along or have around your home. A few will be new to you. We'll begin with machine quilting.

• **Sewing machine** in good working order. Although a smaller featherweight-size sewing machine is wonderful for piecing, it is not heavy enough for machine quilting.

• **Walking or even-feed foot** for straight line, in-the-ditch machine quilting. This foot is indispensable; you cannot do a good job of machine quilting without it. Some brands are quite expensive. Mine was, and I had to view its purchase as a long-term investment in quality workmanship. Quilt shops and sewing catalogs carry generic models that may fit your machine. Follow the manufacturer's guidelines and instructions for attaching it.

• A good **14 (90) machine quilting needle**. These needles are especially made for quilting. If you cannot find the specific machine quilting needle, you can substitute a regular 14 (90) needle.

• Threads: **YLI Wonder Invisible Thread for top; dressmaker thread to match the backing in the bobbin.** Choose YLI "clear" if your fabrics are light; "smoke" if they are dark or intense. You may have to use both and change colors at times, depending upon the fabric colors in the areas you will be quilting. A **thread stocking** (small plastic net sleeve) will help control the YLI monofilament thread from unwinding.

• **Thread snips.** They're nice to have handy to snip the thread tails as you quilt.

• An old pair of **tweezers** will help you get out of tight situations with closed basting pins showing up in awkward positions.

• As you have been working with your fabrics, you may have noticed that your hands lose natural oils, become dry, and have less "traction." Also, "older" fingertips evidence the decline of pronounced fingerprint indentations caused by years of hard work and thinning skin. These factors make it more difficult to grip onto and guide your quilt's flat surfaces during machine quilting. That's why you need to use either **rubber fingers, latex gloves, cotton gloves with gripper dots made for machine quilting,** or **two 6" squares of mesh rubber shelf liner.**

The purpose of these little helpers is to aid you in holding the top surface of the quilt so you can slightly spread the seams apart as you stitch in-the-ditch. Each notion has its advantages and disadvantages. The gloves cover all your fingers. The latex gloves make your hands perspire; the cotton gloves don't. Mesh rubber shelf liner squares are helpful, but take some getting used to and can hide the target seams. I prefer the rubber fingers sold as quilting notions. You get eight progressive sizes in a package, and I use seven—none on the index finger of my right hand—so I can thread needles and feel for high or low sides of the seams. None are needed on either of your little fingers.

> Keep a tiny "sample" container of talcum powder with your rubber gloves or fingers. When you finish a machine quilting session, dust the inside and outside with a little bit of the powder. This will absorb any moisture and keep the rubber surfaces from sticking together and ready for the next use.

• **Large rubber bands**, the kind the mail carrier bundles your mail with. Now you have a recycling use for them!

• Optional: **Bicycle clips** to hold the rolled-up edges of your quilt while you're quilting. You don't have to go to a bicycle shop; you can find these at quilt shops and fabric store notion displays. The metal clips won't work very well until they're wrapped with strips of leftover cotton fabric or muslin. All types lose their usefulness as the thickness of the rolled quilt edge they're holding diminishes.

• Place **a table or ironing board** alongside your sewing machine to help support the quilt as you work on it. You want to keep the weight of the quilt off the floor so it isn't pulling against the needle, making it difficult for you to sew.

• Optional: A **Quilter's table** is a clear, Plexiglass surface on short, adjustable legs that surrounds the bed of your sewing machine and expands the work area while supporting your quilt as you sew. It's another expensive quilting aid. You can machine quilt without it, but it's very helpful, especially if you later want to try free-motion machine quilting of decorative motifs in open areas. A quilter's table would be a very nice gift—hint to someone who might buy you one! Of course, if your sewing machine drops into a cabinet, you already have a larger area to work on.

Now is the time to begin planning for hand quilting designs; i.e., stencils. Initially, I have no idea what hand quilting motifs I'll put in the open areas of my quilts, but during the machine quilting process, the blocks begin to "tell" me what they need. At the end of this book you will find my offering of a few quilting designs for some of the blocks in this book.

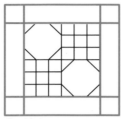 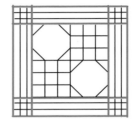

"In-the Ditch" Machine Quilting

We will machine quilt the sashing seam lines that join to the blocks, indicated by the red lines in the illustrations. This will create a secure framework that will hold our three layers together as we add more machine or hand quilting within each block. (If your sashing is pieced, you need only quilt the seams that join the sashings to the blocks.) After the framework quilting is done, we will stitch along some of the seam lines within each block. All of this quilting will be done "in-the-ditch."

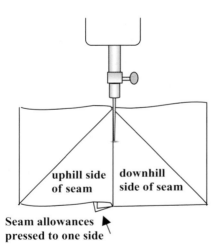

uphill side of seam | downhill side of seam

Seam allowances pressed to one side

The term "in-the-ditch" refers to quilting stitched almost right on top of the seam line. This type of quilting does not show and makes both the design and the background appear puffy. It can also be done by hand, but lends itself extremely well to machine quilting—especially by a beginner.

Because we pressed the seam allowances in our blocks in one direction, each seam line or "ditch" will have a high and low side. Your needle will automatically favor the downhill side of the ditch and, try as you may, you won't be able to make it sew a straight, invisible line on the uphill side. So don't fight it; go with the flow. **Always stitch in the downhill ditch.** That's one of the reasons I don't cover my right index finger; I want to be able to feel for the downhill side of seams. Sometimes those downhill sides aren't where you would expect them to be.

Physical Comfort and Well-Being

It won't take you long to understand the physical challenges of machine quilting, so let's start off with a few ergonomically correct rules. Dr. Susan Delaney Mech, author, quilter, and physician, recommends in her book, *Rx for Quilters: Stitcher Friendly Advice for Every Body*, that good posture is by far the most important factor in alleviating fatigue and muscle strain while you are quilting. Your chair should be adjusted so that your knees bend at a 90-degree angle and your feet rest flatly on the floor. You should provide lumbar support for the small of your back by either adjusting your chair or securing a small pillow to the back of your chair so that you can move your hips to the rear of the seat.

Your work surface should be about 4" below your bent elbow, which also should be at a 90-degree angle. Set your machine on a lower desk or table where your shoulders can be relaxed and your fingers rest lightly on the throat plate as your arms and hands guide the fabric. I have an armless secretary's chair, which I love. I can adjust the height up or down and move the back in close enough to force me to sit up straight. My husband bought me the chair at a used office furniture sale where he works. It's of higher quality than I would have bought for myself in a brand new chair.

Okay, we're sitting with feet flat on the floor and backs straight. Our shoulders and neck are relaxed. Well, don't sit there for too long! Dr. Mech also advises that we should stand up, walk around, drink a glass of water and perform a few stretching exercises once every hour for about 10 minutes. By doing this, she says you can expect to accomplish 25% more. I have to second that statement. With my neck injury, if I don't give myself regular breaks, I really suffer for it later, especially in loss of quilting time waiting for neck spasms to go away.

Another helpful hint from Dr. Mech before we begin: you may need more light to be able to see as you quilt either by hand or machine. Direct an extra lamp or task light over your work area to reduce eyestrain. Don't forget to wear your eyeglasses, too.

One last suggestion is that you should machine quilt early in the day when you're not tired. It's difficult to "drive" straight down those ditches—and more difficult when you're a little weary; don't forget those hourly breaks!

Quilters, Adjust Your Engines!

Let's adjust our sewing machine settings before we prepare our quilt sandwich. If you haven't already done so, attach the walking foot according to manufacturer's instructions. If your machine has a setting which allows you to choose whether it stops with the needle down or up, choose "down." Reduce the presser foot pressure slightly. Make adjustments to the stitch length, setting for approximately 8 to 10 stitches to an inch. Too long a stitch can be caught and broken; too short a stitch can cause tearing.

Check your settings to see what kind of stitches you'll get. Mimic your quilt sandwich by pinning together scraps of backing, batting, and a patch fabric of a size sufficient to practice on. Try quilting the practice piece with the walking foot to get a feel for the process. If necessary, make any further adjustments to the stitch length and presser foot so that the layers move securely and smoothly, and stitches are spaced approximately eight to an inch. Then write all your setting numbers on the sample with an indelible pen. Keep this record of your machine quilting settings as a reference for the next time. Don't forget to change the numbers if you later change adjustments.

If applicable, lower your ironing board and put it behind your sewing machine. If you have a low table, you can use that. You want to keep the weight of the rolled quilt up off the floor as it feeds out from under the needle so it won't engage you in a tug of war as you're trying to sew. If needed, use whatever additional support you can devise to carry the weight of the quilt.

> Whenever you are machine quilting, always begin and end a line of stitching for 1/4" with the stitch length setting at almost "0" then return the length back to 8 stitches per inch. This will secure your thread ends so they cannot be pulled out.

Preparing the Sandwich for Quilting

First we will stitch the sashing seams in the ditch to isolate our quilt into four sections, just as if we had drawn imaginary lines from the center to the top, from the center to the bottom, and from the center to each side. Depending upon the layout of your quilt, you may or may not have seams exactly in the centers; therefore, treat the closest sashing seams that run from the exact middle to the borders as the center lines of your quilt.

To reduce the bulk to a manageable size and control overhang, we must "package" our quilt. We will use large rubber bands at the ends of each roll and bicycle clips wrapped with strips of cotton fabric to hold the middles. Wrapping keeps the clips from sliding and loosening their grip on the rolled quilt. Rubber banding the ends won't hurt the quilt.

Diagram of quilt divided into quarter sections.

Evenly roll the right and left sides of your quilt and secure with rubber bands and bicycle clips leaving an area right down the middle exposed and flat as shown in the illustration below. The center to top and center to bottom quilting lines will be stitched first.

The First Line of Machine Quilting

To quilt the center-to-bottom seam, carefully slide the top flat area of your packaged quilt under the even feed foot and move to where the off-center starting point is under the needle. Support the top end on the ironing board, and hold the rest of the packaged quilt either in your lap or draped over your shoulder. Don't let the weight of the quilt drag.

Keep the exposed part of the quilt flat and don't let it shift. Drop the presser foot lever. Take one stitch to pull the bobbin thread through to the top and initially hold onto both the bobbin and top threads. Reduce the stitch length to almost "0" and stitch for 1/4" to secure the threads. If your machine has a "fix" feature, use that instead.

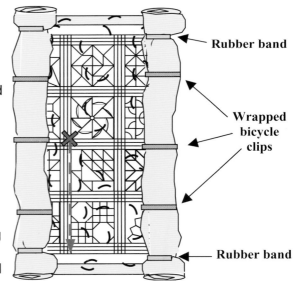

Rubber band

Wrapped bicycle clips

Rubber band

After you have completed the 1/4" locking stitches, place your hands on the quilt in front of and to the sides of the foot slightly fanning out your fingers (using rubber fingers/gloves/pads). Spread the uphill from the downhill sides exposing the seam line and helping the fabric remain pucker free as it is fed under the needle. Don't pull or push the fabric, let the walking foot and feed dogs do their job, just open a path on the seam line and guide the fabric as it moves along. Sew slowly; take your time. The needle has to go in and out of a thick layer of fabrics, and you want every stitch to be complete. You'll ultimately sew faster with more practice, and you'll definitely be getting more experience before you're finished!

Stitch close to the seam on the "downhill" side of the ditch from the center towards the bottom edge of your quilt. Again, your needle will automatically favor the "downhill" side of a seam. After quilting when the two sides of the seam come back together, your stitching will be hidden. If you have borders, stop just before them and lockstitch at almost "0" for 1/4", or use the fix feature. If you have no borders, you can stitch off the quilt edge with a backstitch.

When you anticipate stitching quite near a basting pin, remove it just in advance of getting too close. Don't think you'll be able to avoid it. Pins can get caught on the wider walking foot, when you won't be able to take them out easily and could chance tearing your quilt. Encountering trouble like this can affect the straightness of a seam, and one thing you don't want to do is start and stop a line of stitching if you don't have to. If this does happen, keep an old pair of tweezers nearby to help you open and remove the basting pin.

A concentration of basting pins in one area will be a sign that a major correction was made to a pin-basted seam. How will you make the correction? Hold the seam straight from behind as well as in front of the needle. Don't pull it, just hold it taut. If you really can't remove an upcoming pin because its positioning is crucial to keeping the seam straight, at least open it for removal at the last minute. You may have to sew this seam haltingly, starting and stopping to remove pins and make adjustments.

What If Your Stitching Goes Off-Track?

Depending upon which way seam allowances are pressed, you will have to "switch

> Snip the top threads at the beginning and ending of a seam as you quilt. They're difficult to find later, and you don't want to stitch those tails down when you're quilting in a different direction. Be very careful not to cut the quilt top.

lanes" as you sew alongside patches and come to intersections. So go "jogging."
When you come to an intersection where seam allowances change direction, simply slow down or stop, and move the quilt sandwich slightly to the left or right as you sew. The resulting "jog" will not be noticeable on the front, and barely noticeable, if at all, on the back.

If you see that your stitching is beginning to go where no other has gone before, STOP. Lift the foot and reposition the needle. You'll be surprised how unnoticeable the correcting point will be. If you're having a hard time "steering," you might be tired, or the seam allowance unexpectedly flipped and you're trying to stitch on the uphill side of the ditch. Don't fret over a few misplaced stitches. You may know where they are, but no one else will even see them.

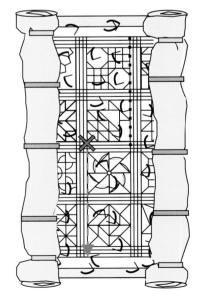

After this first seam is completed, remove your quilt and rotate it, being careful not to create wrinkles in the backing. Machine quilt the center to top seam.

Now you can unroll the left and right sides of your quilt, and roll and secure the top and bottom sides toward the center, leaving a flat area sideways across the middle in which to quilt the crosswise center lines.

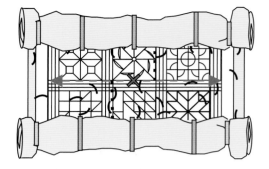

Quilt the crosswise centers from the middle out to each side.

You have now isolated your quilt into four sections. Open it up and check the back for any glaring errors and sewn-in wrinkles. If you see a wrinkle, evaluate how noticeable it is against the busy print of the backing. If it's minor, ignore it. If you see a large tuck of backing fabric, remove only as much of the stitching as you need to release it. Smooth out the fabric and iron out the wrinkle. This is important because the wrinkled fabric has a memory, and you could get another tuck on that seam when you re-quilt it.

Pin-baste the affected area on the **backing**. You know where you'll have to quilt the replacement seam, so don't place pins in the path of the bottom feed dogs. Turn the quilt right side up and, using the beginning and ending lockstitch over the thread that remained, re-quilt the removed seam. Clip thread tails and remove back pins.

Using the same techniques you have just learned, you can now prepare to machine quilt each "quarter" of your quilt. Always start at the original middle crosswise or lengthwise quilted lines of the entire quilt, not in the middle of one of the quarters.

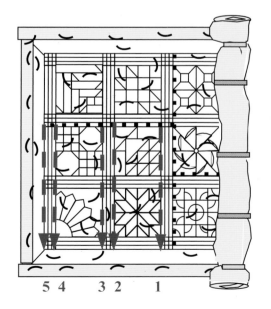

5 4   3 2   1

To machine quilt sashing seams in each quarter, roll and band one side of your quilt. You can loosely roll any other sides if that will help you, or you can leave them free.

Let's use the quilt's lower right quadrant as an example.

With the quilt packaged in the configuration shown on the previous page, machine quilt lines **1, 2, 3, 4, and 5**, **in that order.** The rolled edge will be hard to maneuver because it will rest under the machine arm, so wrap it tightly.

You will have to repackage to sew lines **6, 7, 8, and 9**, **in that order too**, but with no bulky quilt roll under the machine arm.

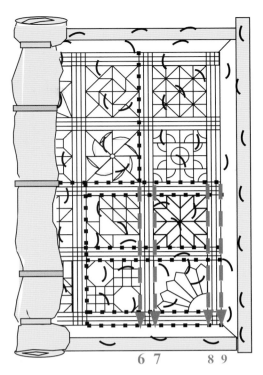

6 7   8 9

You can see that to keep the quilt square and eliminate bunching and catching puckers in the backing, all quilting lines must be sewn away from the lengthwise and crosswise center lines of the quilt. Sometimes you will have a large, bulky roll of quilt under your machine's arm; other times you won't. Do the best you can. Once you have all the sashing/block seams quilted, you will be able to machine quilt within the blocks in relative freedom from rolling. So finish quilting the sashing seams in the other three sections, then we'll move on to quilting the blocks.

Machine Quilting in the Blocks

The blocks also will be machine quilted in the ditch following some of its design elements. You don't have to machine quilt all the seam lines. The only restriction you really have is the one spelled out by the quilting distance requirements of the batting. Since we will be machine and hand quilting, we'll let both methods satisfy the restriction.

The in-the-ditch sash quilting has provided a framework to keep the quilt layers from shifting, but puckers can still occur when sewing within the blocks. I usually begin by stitching within a middle block of my quilt, progressively working out to adjoining blocks. Quilting blocks from the middle out limits shifting and stitched-in wrinkles.

When you are quilting the middle block(s), you'll have to roll and secure the side that will lie under the machine arm. Nothing formal, just keep the bulk confined. Give yourself an unencumbered flat plane to work on by arranging, smoothing, and flattening the block you will be stitching. Feel for any wrinkles or puckers on the backing before sewing.

Quilt the major intersecting lines of each block first. This is just another orderly step to prevent shifting and wrinkles. You do not have to sew these lines from the center out as you did when quilting the sashing seams; edge-to-edge is fine. Remove basting pins as usual.

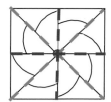

Spinning Pinwheel is one of the center blocks in the example quilt. It has two sets of intersecting seams. I would quilt both the diagonals and the N-S, E-W seams, but I would leave the curves and the rest of the block available for the addition of a little hand quilting. There, one block is done!

Sometimes a block's major intersecting lines are difficult to determine or there really aren't any at all. In **Grandmother's Fan**, for example, I would make sure the block was pinned securely because it contains a large, flexible open space that I'd want to hand quilt later. Well-placed basting pins will have to hold it for machine quilting. Stitch all the seams in-the-ditch: the zigzag line of the fan tips, the curve of the fan base and the seams joining each fan blade.

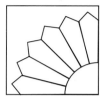

You're finally able to pivot the quilt while stitching to reduce the number of starts and stops. Keep the needle in the "down" stopping position, or turn the flywheel to insert the needle into the layers before you release the presser foot to turn your work. It's fun to figure out how far you can go with one beginning and one ending lockstitch.

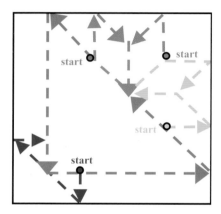

You don't have to cut the invisible thread after you lockstitch each continuous quilting line. Just move to the next starting point, 1/4" lockstitch, and sew on to the next ending lockstitch. You'll want to cut the thread tails occasionally while you are quilting so the even feed foot doesn't get caught up on them. While checking for puckers, cut all the tails, back and front, after you complete machine quilting each block.

> If the nylon top thread breaks at an inopportune time and you have difficulty re-threading, hold a small piece of white paper behind the needle to make it easier to see the needle's eye.

Why Stop Now When We're Having So Much Fun?

You could call an end to your quilting at this point as long as your quilt's open, and unquilted areas are within the parameters recommended by the manufacturer of the batting you used. But by adding hand quilting after the machine work is done, your quilt will give the impression of being completely hand quilted.

Hand Quilting Supplies

The tools used for hand quilting haven't changed in over three centuries. There have been a few innovative aids developed to make hand quilting a little easier, but the basic thread, needle, thimble, and hoop are all you really need. See the photograph at the beginning of this lesson for a display of these supplies:

• **Hoops:** There are many types, sizes, and shapes of quilting hoops. Every quilter has a favorite. There are round, oval, and rounded square hoops made of wood or plastic, large and small. There are "fanny" hoops that are supported by a short pedestal that lifts the weight of your quilt up off your lap. There is even a special border hoop. (When you are ready to quilt your border, don't deny yourself this special tool.) Additionally, you can purchase wooden floor stands to which you can attach your quilting hoops for "lap-free" quilting.

I have found that too large a hand-held hoop is difficult to balance and reach across. My favorite hand-quilting hoop is oval and about 20" at its longest dimension and 13" at its shortest. This size and shape is excellent especially if you have some physical limitations that might prevent you from extending your head over a floor frame. Sitting in a comfortable position, you can place your feet on a footstool, balance the hoop on your knees, lean your head back and still quilt.

Before you choose the hoop that's right for you, test out different sizes and types. Ask your quilting friends if you could use one of theirs to see how it fits your style. Your hoop will become one of your favorite tools—a personal and comfortable "friend."

No matter what hoop you use, you must always remember to remove your quilt from it at the end of each quilting session. If you leave your quilt stretched in a hoop for any length of time, portions of it can become distorted and stretched out of shape.

You don't have to use a hoop to quilt, although it certainly makes the task easier once you've learned how to use it. The "no hoop" method of hand quilting, sometimes referred to as lap quilting, may feel more comfortable when you are first learning to quilt because you can also use your non-dominant hand to manipulate the quilt "sandwich" onto the needle with each stitch.

In 1988, during the Reagan administration, President and Mrs. Reagan chose a quilt made by Julia H. Spidell of Sparta, NC, as a gift from the United States to Soviet Premier Mikhail Gorbachev and his wife Raisa. Julia's 90" x 90" gorgeous "Piece Baskets" quilt was entirely lap quilted with no hoop! Julia came to quilting with a background in art education. To find a way to make additional income while caring for her handicapped husband at home, she began quilting. Little did she know just how good a quilter she was! Julia is one of my personal heroes and an example of what quilting is all about: creating a quilt or a life out of the "materials" given to you. 2

•   **Thimbles:** There is an ever-growing selection of thimbles. The benchmark thimble for hand quilting is made of metal with an indented top encircled by a raised ridge. This "lip" catches the quilting needle and helps you reinsert it back into the quilt. Usually, a thimble is worn on the middle finger of your dominant hand. The direction of quilting is across your body from either right to left (if you're a "righty"), left to right (if you're a "lefty") and towards yourself. Some very experienced quilters can quilt away from themselves using only a thimble on their dominant thumb. (I can't even do this, but I sure wish I could. More practice called for here.)

You will use the fingers of your "underhand" to feel for the needle tip as you stitch to be sure the needle has penetrated all three quilt layers. These repetitive little needle sticks can eventually sting, but you'll soon develop calluses on your fingertips—a recognition and badge of honor among quilters. To protect your "underhand" fingers, you can use wraps, oval self-stick protective plastic shields, or leather, metal and small plastic thimbles to deflect the needle back up through your quilt as you are quilting. Additionally, the use of a rubber fingertip on your index finger helps you grab and pull a stubborn quilting needle through your quilt.

My favorite is an inexpensive flesh-colored plastic thimble made especially for those quilters who have longer fingernails. This thimble can also be warmed and stretched to fit over arthritic knuckles. It has an open, adjustable side that allows for circulation of air.

I mentioned in the machine quilting section how constantly handling fabrics removes natural oils from your fingers and hands. For dry sore hands, two wonderful products to include in your sewing basket are Bag Balm® or Udder Cream®. Yes, these are repackaged bovine products, but they're great for us quilters. Bag balm is a salve that contains antiseptic and is so healing for sore fingers. Udder cream is also soothing for dry hands and is not greasy or sticky.

An occupational hazard of hand quilting is pricked fingers. It's a trade secret, but if you get a drop of blood on your quilt, your own saliva is the best solvent. Just dab a little cold water on the spot after removal to avoid later discoloration.

• **Needles and Threads** : Historically, the quilt stitch is executed with a single strand of thread and a sharp, thin, very short needle called a "between." The shorter the needle, the smaller and closer together you can work the stitches. It's always a balancing act between hand quilting skill and how small a needle eye we can thread when choosing the size of quilting needle to use. Betweens come in sizes from #3 through #12—the largest number is the smallest needle. Most experienced quilters use betweens in the #8 to #12 range.

Quilting needles are made of tempered steel, gold, or platinum. Choose good quality, realistically priced needles because they all break. As you quilt, you will notice that your needle may develop a "bend," which I like because it bends to fit my fingers. Of course, with use that "bend" eventually breaks, and you start over again with a new needle. Needles, too, become dull. If stitching becomes more difficult, it's probably time to replace the needle.

Quilting thread is made from strong, long cotton fibers that have been treated to make its surface glide through the layers of your quilt. It is the thread of choice. But you are not restricted to using *only* quilting thread. You can use embroidery and decorative threads as additional design elements to accent different areas of your quilt. Care should be taken when using these specialty threads because they are more fragile than quilting thread. You may not be able to load your needle with a very long strand because of breaking and fraying.

For the quilt we will be making in these lessons, I would like you to use single strands of **size #8 Perle Cotton,** an unorthodox thread for quilting. The look that thicker perle cotton gives longer beginner stitches is very pleasing, decorative, and more substantial than quilting thread. You will find the perle cotton in needlework and yarn shops. Also, some fabric and quilt shops might carry it in limited colors. It is inexpensive, and one ball is more than enough for a whole quilt—the way we do it.

Because of the thickness of perle cotton, you'll have to use a needle with a large eye, so try betweens in sizes #5, #6, or maybe #7. It's difficult to find the larger betweens in packets of all the same size, but packages of mixed sizes will contain the larger ones.

I find that beginners have a hard time executing the 10—12 stitches per inch of traditional hand quilting. They worry about evenness and how close the stitches are to each other. You cannot get close stitches using a #5 or #6 between and size #8 perle cotton thread! Experience with students, and my own work, has led me to encourage the revival of the old-fashioned "Depression" stitch in favor of getting hand quilting done more quickly. From its' name, you probably realized that the Depression stitch was born in that period of our country's history. This simple, larger quilting stitch made it possible then, and now, to finish quilts in less time.

• Don't forget **needle threaders**. There's a reason why four needle threaders come in some packages. They are going to break because we will put them through the difficult task of squeezing a fat thread through the needle's eye. (Hold onto the wire part as you pull the thread through the eye.) Buy a few packages of needle threaders. Don't buy the fancy ones for this project. Save the "fancies" for use later with regulation quilting and sewing threads.

- **Thread Heaven® or beeswax** add additional conditioning to the perle cotton or any quilting threads. Stroking your thread over either one lubricates it and allows it to glide more easily through the fabric, reducing tangling, fraying, and breaking.

- **Fabric marking implements:** Water or air-erasable pens, chalk, or white charcoal art pencils, wash-out pencils of appropriate colors, **pencil sharpener** (sharp points are very important for accuracy), soap sliver, .5 mm mechanical lead pencil, etc. As usual, test your marking instrument on a fabric sample to make sure it will wash out.

- **File folders and freezer paper** to help you transfer designs to the quilt top.

- **Stencils and quilting designs**: Choose quilting designs that compliment each patchwork block and the borders. There is a large sheet of stencils in the back of this book designed specifically for the blocks we have created. There are innumerable resources available to you for stencil patterns in stores, books, and magazines, even on the Internet at some quilt-related Web sites. You can also use some of your templates for quilting designs. You can buy plastic quilting stencils, or you can make your own. (More about that later.) Helen Squire, a well-known quilter and author, has written a series of large, inexpensive, very user-friendly stencil pattern books containing beautiful and easy-to-execute designs. I highly recommend her patterns and instructions to new quilters.

How Much Quilting? Fill the Spaces ....

As we've noted, the manufacturer of your batting has determined how close you need to place your lines of quilting. Since you have already machine stitched most of the seams in your top, you really won't have too many open spaces in which to hand quilt. Looking at the example Gold and Black Sampler, you can see that some blocks have more open areas than others. **Pinwheel** has no large open areas that require hand quilting. **Grandmother's Fan**, on the other hand, has a large area that would be enhanced with a quilting motif.

There are a few fundamental and practical rules for hand quilting:

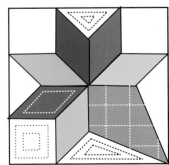

1. If it won't show, don't put much time and effort into hand quilting an area. A large, darkly colored or highly patterned patch like the handle in **Bouquet of Flowers,** needs some quilting to meet the batting requirements, but that quilting just won't show very much unless its done with contrasting thread. A basic one or two-inch grid will hold the layers together, and add texture without consuming too much quilting effort.

The colorful diamond "flowers" will also hide any decorative quilting designs, but their area is still too large to leave unquilted. Simple outline stitching placed a little more than 1/4" away from the seam line will do the job here. Why +1/4"? Because you won't want to quilt through seam allowances where you don't have to. The background patches are also quilted with an outline that follows the seams. Their areas needed more quilting for balance, so a double outline was used.

2. If you want your quilting to show, use a contrasting color thread. Conversely, if you don't want your quilting to appear pronounced until you get better at it, use a color thread that will blend in with the background fabric.

3. A quilting design that fills open areas looks better than one that is too small, *and*, more importantly, larger designs are easier to quilt.

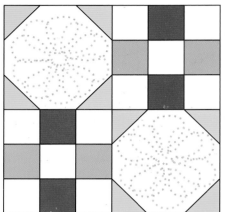

The two open hexagons in **Snowball and Nine-Patch** begged for a decorative quilting motif. I designed the flower for this block and quilted it in white perle cotton just as a first quilter with not too much confidence in her ability might do. I didn't want the quilting to stand out, but I also didn't want the area to look empty! Well, it looked empty and out of balance with the other elements of the block. Far be it from me to take out perfectly good quilting stitches! I just rotated the stencil and traced another flower on top of the first, then quilted it using tan perle cotton. The resulting double flower was even better than the single one. A happy accident!

Blocks have to be quilted enough to hold the batting and also contain an equivalent *sum* of machine and hand quilting to look balanced with other blocks and itself.

Marking the Blocks for Quilting

There are many marking tools to transfer quilting patterns to your quilt. If the fabric you are working on is dark, I recommend a white charcoal or white chalk pencil that can be sharpened to a fine point. For lighter fabrics, you may choose to use a wash-out marker, an air-erasable pen, or one of the many other marking instruments available today. You could even try a "pouncer" (a cloth bag filled with powdered chalk) when using a quilter's stencil. No matter which way you mark your top, no one method is perfect for every application. Chalk shows very well on darker patches but has a very short marking "life," and will brush off easily as you work. Lines made by water- or air-erasable pens will become permanent if exposed to heat or reappear after time if not completely washed out.

I prefer to use my old faithful .5mm mechanical lead pencil with HB or H lead for a marking tool. The lines created with a light touch of this pencil hardly show after quilting, and can be easily washed out. In any event, try your marking instruments on a sample of your fabrics to ensure they can be removed.

You can mark your basted quilt as you go along (that's what I usually do), or you can completely mark your quilt top before basting. Hold the stencil tight against the quilt top to reduce distortion as you trace. A few pieces of masking tape will help hold it in place. Use a delicate touch when marking.

Stencils

You can purchase plastic stencils or you can make your own. A grid stencil is a lot of trouble to make with all it's "bridges" to hold its cutouts together, so it's a good idea to purchase one. Stencils of other shapes are easy to make or trace from many sources. I transfer my designs onto manila file folders and outline them with indelible black pen. Instead of cutting slots, sometimes I cut the designs out individually.

The illustration at the right represents the stencil for the open area in **Grandmother's Fan**. I drew it onto the paper side of a piece of freezer paper. I cut out the freezer paper pattern then ironed it, shiny side down, onto the block. I outlined the design with my .5mm pencil, then removed the stencil to use again. The freezer paper will not leave any residue.

Hooping it Up

As we did with machine quilting, we will begin hand quilting in the center of our quilt. Loosen the screw that holds the ends of the outer hoop together and separate the two pieces. With the right side of your quilt facing up, place the inner hoop under the exact center. Overlay the outer hoop with the screw clamp away from your body (so thread won't get tangled in it as you quilt) and press it down around the inside hoop. Pull at the edges of the quilt extending past the outer hoop to square up the block, and tighten the quilt over the inner hoop. When the center area is straight, smooth, and taut, tighten the hoop screw. You want the area of the quilt contained in the hoop to be under tension but still have a little "give." If you're going to mark your blocks as you quilt, it's easier to do so with the quilt in the hoop.

Itching to Stitch

Insert the end of a strand of perle cotton 6" beyond the needle's eye with the help of the needle threader. Unspool a length of thread that reaches from your fingers to your elbow and cut off. You'll be able to work this length (approximately 18") of thread into your quilt before it begins to fray and break. Not only does repeatedly being sewn through the quilt sandwich wear on the thread, so does traveling through the needle's eye. It's a good idea to occasionally slide the needle to different positions along the thread to reduce wear and tear. Your thread will twist after you've quilted for a while, so stop, invert the hoop, let the thread and needle dangle to unwind.

> Always use thread as it unwinds, tying a knot in the end that came off the spool last. Thread is wound onto the spool with a warp. If you were to sew against that warp, your thread would continually tangle, twist and knot.

With your thimble on and your needle threaded you are now ready to quilt! I hope you are sitting in a comfortable chair that gives good back support. A small footstool that raises your knees helps to reduce fatigue and improve your posture. Good light is a must. Remember what Dr. Mech says, only quilt for an hour, then get up and walk around to give yourself a break. You'll be much more productive when you return.

Don't expect to become an instant expert quilter. Quilt stitching skill comes only with time and practice. Require no more from yourself than to just relax and enjoy the rhythm of placing running stitches in and out of your quilt top. Don't try to make your stitches too close together, but do try to make them evenly spaced. Four or five to an inch is perfect. And don't think the stitches on the back have to be the same size as those on the front.

For all the rules and techniques you have been learning in quiltmaking, there are very few for actual hand quilting. The needle goes in; the needle touches your "underhand" finger; the needle comes out; the needle goes in again. Hand quilting is a skill you basically teach yourself, and learning to quilt is like learning to roller skate: your progress is slow in the beginning, but soon you'll be zipping along with speed and rhythm. You'll find hand quilting is very relaxing—and portable!

Eventually, you will switch to a smaller needle and regular quilting thread to achieve tinier, more uniform stitches. To get to that point faster, purchase a magnifying lamp and look through the lens as you quilt. You'll be surprised how quickly your stitches improve because it's much easier to see.

Knots!

Continuous lines of hand quilting are secured at the beginning and end by imbedding just the right size knot in the batting layer of the quilt. Let's learn how to make this quilter's knot.

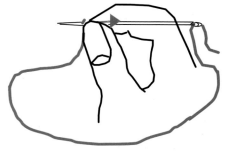

Hold your threaded needle between your forefinger and thumb. Take the "tail" end of the thread with your left hand and make it into a circle, laying the tail on top of the needle and pointing toward the eye. Pinch the thread end against the needle with the right fingers. With your left hand, wrap the thread around the needle tip four or five times for regular quilting thread, two times for perle cotton. Move your right hand fingers up to pinch the coil of thread that is wrapped around the needle. Now, take your left hand, and pull the needle through the pinched coil, and slide the coil down the thread length to the end. A nice, tight "quilter's knot" will be formed. If the leftover tail is too long past the knot, snip it off.

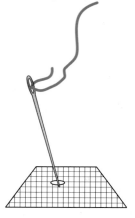

Because the perle cotton thread is thicker than normal quilting thread, it presents a problem when it comes to hiding knots. There are two ways to resolve this problem, and you'll use both during the course of your hand quilting. The knotted ends are going to need a little assistance going though the top of your quilt, so help it by enlarging the weave with the tip of your needle—just stick the needle in between threads and wiggle it. This insertion point should be about 3/4" away from where you want to start stitching to give the knot a little distance in which to catch and entwine itself within the batting. Slide the needle tip to where you want to begin quilting and bring it out. "Scratch" the tiny opening closed.

With a rocking motion, take even running stitches, gathering about four onto your needle before you pull the thread through. With each stitch, the needle should go through the backing where it will touch one of your fingers. Your "underhand" finger will feel that the needle has gone completely through the layers to make a good stitch. In one with this motion, help the needle back through the quilt layers to the top with an "underhand" finger (or thumbnail).

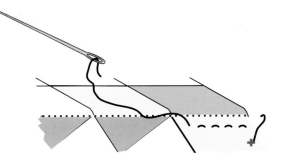

Ending a Line of Stitching with a Knot

When you see you are running out of thread, make that same quilter's knot close to the last "out" stitch. Wiggle an opening in the weave at the correct distance to finish the stitch. Insert the needle into the batting and bring the needle back out about 3/4" away. Tug the knot below the first layer. You might hear a little "pop" as the knot is pulled into the batting. Pull gently on the threaded needle, and hold your snips or scissors slightly open right on the thread but don't cut it by moving the snips or scissors; cut the thread by moving it into the blades. When your scissors are so close to the surface, it's too easy to accidentally cut the top. The tension of the taut thread end on the blade of your snips or scissors will cut the thread, and the thread will relax and slip under the surface of your quilt. Scratch the entry hole closed.

No Knots!

You can quilt with "no knots" by beginning and ending a line of stitching with a series of minute backstitches hidden in a seam line. Insert your needle into the top layer of your quilt an inch or so away from where you wish to start stitching. Bring the needle out right in the middle of a nearby seam line and pull the thread only until the tail end disappears under the quilt surface. Take a very small backstitch again in the seam line hiding the stitch as you tighten it. Don't pull too hard; this stitch doesn't have to be too tight, it's just the

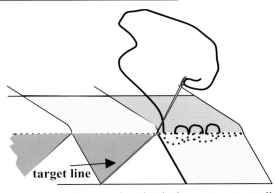

target line

anchor. Repeat this procedure two more times. As you place each new backstitch, you can pull a little harder and see that the stitches won't pull out. When you exit your final backstitch you should be at the point where you wanted to begin your line of quilting.

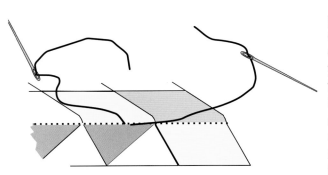

Expanding on the no-knot method, cut a piece of thread twice as long as the finger-to-elbow length, and load two needles on it. Take one stitch in the middle of the line of stitching you want to do, and pull the thread halfway through so that you have half the thread length and one needle on each side of the entry point. Then you can stitch with both ends. (I know I said you should thread your needle from the spool as it was wound, but this is one trick that breaks the rule. I'd rather deal with a few tangles to reduce the number of knots. Use the thread conditioner to limit twisting.)

Ending a No-Knot Line of Quilting

My preferred ending of a line of stitching is using the same backstitch method. You have to anticipate when you're going to run out of thread, and allow yourself enough length to secure the last inch or so within a nearby seam. Take a backstitch as your last running stitch, then slide your needle through the batting between the top and backing to a nearby seam. Take a series of three invisible in-the-ditch backstitches in the same manner as you began your quilting line. Tug on the threaded needle and snip the thread so the clipped end will slide below the quilt surface.

Traveling

If you have quite a bit of thread on your needle at the end of a line of quilting, traveling is how to get your thread from where it is to where you want to be. All you have to do after you secure the last quilting stitch with a backstitch is slide the needle between the layers to its destination. If the distance is further than the needle is long, slide the needle as far as you can in the right direction. Do the weave-opening trick to bring the needle up through the top, then return the needle back in the same hole and close it with your fingernail until you get to the next starting point. If the distance is ridiculously long, it's better to end the stitching and start over. I always check the quilt back after a traveling stitch to be sure it didn't come through to the backing.

Stabbing

Quilting though layered seam allowances is unavoidable, and you'll have to use a different quilting stitch called "stabbing." This entails making single stitches when crossing seams by perpendicularly inserting the needle all the way through to the back and returning it to the top of the quilt with your underhand. You may want to switch hands and use your "smart" hand underneath. This is where using the rubber finger really comes in handy. Pulling the needle and perle cotton thread through all those layers will take determination. Some quilters use this stitch exclusively. Ouch!

A Few More Random Thoughts

• You can end lines of quilting on the back as well as the front using either the knot or no-knot methods. For the no-knot method, just hide the tiny backstitches on a part of the backing fabric design that matches your thread.
• Don't worry about not getting one little stitch all the way through to the back—it's just one little stitch, and the front of the quilt is what you're interested in.
• Use a number of needles going in different directions within one hooped area as you quilt. This reduces starts and stops, and you can continue those same loaded needles into the next hooped area.
• As you hand quilt, you'll find and can cut off the machine quilting thread ends you missed.
• Always rotate the hoop to a comfortable quilting angle.
• If you quilt one block a night or one border in two nights, you should be able to finish a 12-block quilt in approximately two weeks of evenings. Think about your next quilt project while you're finishing this one.
• Finally, you don't want hand quilting to be perfect, you want it to look hand done.

Quilting the Border

When you've finished hand quilting the blocks that need it, you'll want to quilt the border. This quilting in particular convinces others that your quilt has been completely hand quilted. Prior planning is required to mark borders with a quilting design. Choose a simple, widely spaced motif that is at least 3/4" smaller than the border width so you won't have to quilt through seam allowances. I've included two easy ones in the back of the book. To use one, trace it onto an open manila file folder and cut out on the dashed lines. If the design crosses over the fold, tape it on both sides for reinforcement.

The quilting motif must be centered on each side. All ends must match to be worked into a corner design. I like to use freezer paper to plan and draw my border layout because I can get 72 and more uninterrupted inches to draw on. (That's not the only reason I use freezer paper. More on that coming up.)

To make your border layout, cut off a length of freezer paper that measures the length of your top before the borders were added and cut it down to a strip that is 2" wider than the border width. Draw a line 2" away from one long side. Fold the paper strip in half across the width. Open it and center your border stencil on the fold line. Place pencil marks on the paper at the ends of the design, then "space out" the stencil aligning end marks along the full length of the strip. Does the design or any of its repetitive parts fit evenly on the border layout? If it does, great! If not, you'll have to make adjustments to the design, which probably will be nothing more than adding or subtracting space between design element repeats, not whole stencil repeats.

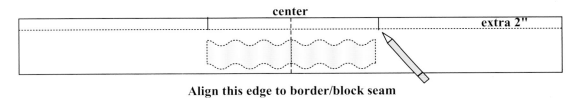

Align this edge to border/block seam

As you trace your layout plan, use the extra 2" we added to make notations on how you adjusted the stencil. Remember, your quilt should look hand made, not manufactured.

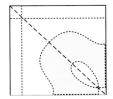

You'll need to plan on how you will turn the corner with your quilting design. Cut a square of freezer paper the measurement of your border width plus 2". (A 4" border will need a 6" square.) Transfer your corner design onto the freezer paper square, aligning diagonal centers. The outside edges that will join to the border must align.

Match your border layout to your corner and make any adjustments you feel are necessary. That's it! You've made your plan. By folding, you can adapt this layout plan to fit the shorter border and won't have to make two. Just use the 2" area to write instructions to yourself for changes. Using the file folder stencil, trace your design with an appropriate removable marking instrument onto the border fabric following your adjustment instructions.

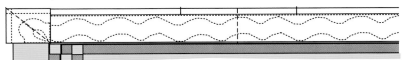

Do you recall that I showed you how to cut a small quilting motif out of freezer paper so you could iron it onto **Grandmother's Fan** and trace around it? Well, you can use this same idea and machine quilt your borders. You'll have to make four correctly sized border and corner patterns, because you will iron them in place and machine quilt right through them! Do one border and corner at a time. I like to use double decorative threads, like Sulky Ultra Twist® through the needle. It makes a better-looking stitch. Carefully tear the paper away after you finish each side.

For the Free Spirit

Here's an old, tried-and-true pattern to use called "teacups" that requires no planning ahead, but you have to like the random look. The stencil is made by drawing around a teacup onto a piece of lightweight cardboard. Cut out and fold the circle into quarters, notching the outside ends of each fold line. Now you can use this stencil to experiment and create an easy design for your border. Line the circles and notches up to each other in any way. Doing so will create rhythm to your design. You can draw and quilt one circle at a time.

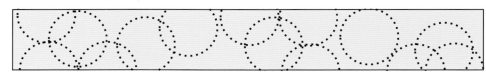

You don't have to do anything to the borders if the space between the blocks and the outside edge is less than the quilting distance required by the batting, but quilting looks so lovely.

Hand Quilting the Border

The quilt hoop to the right is especially made for quilting borders. It's a perfect example of the right tool for the right job. The raw edge of the border is safety pinned to the strip of heavy white fabric that is stapled to the wooden frame.

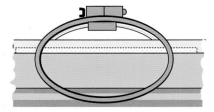

You can see that our favorite oval frame falls short in its ability to keep the border taut for hand quilting. But we can fix that.

Pin a rectangle of tightly woven, doubled-over fabric to the border edge you will be quilting. Then place that area in your hoop. The added fabric strip has to be about as thick as the quilt layers for the hoop to hold it tightly.

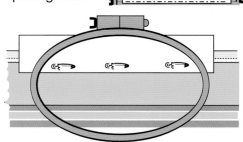

Hand quilt the border design. You'll find it's enjoyably easy to do because you only have to cross seams at the corners. Also, start and end each line of stitching at the raw edge so you don't have to deal with hiding knots … we'll let the binding do that!

Can you believe it? After you complete quilting your borders, all there is left to do is add a hanging strip (if you would like), bind the edges, and add a label … the next lesson.

Chong Blind has been my friend for over 30 years A career
woman, she always wondered why I would cut up fabric into
little pieces, then sew them back together to make a blanket.
She finally took my class and made this striking sampler,
which she completely finished the day after her last class!

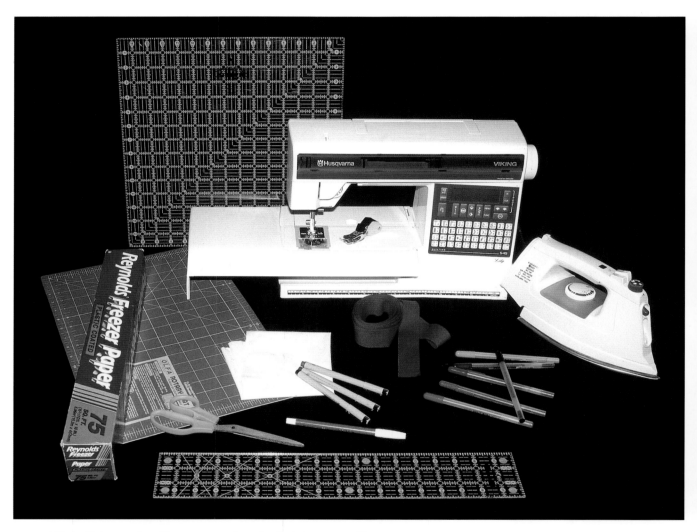

We will be using these supplies to finish our quilt:

- Sewing machine
- Binding fabric
- Rotary rulers and cutter
- Fabric and paper scissors
- Pins
- Removable marking instruments

- Freezer paper
- Scrap of tightly woven cotton for label
- Fabric markers or gel pens
- OPTIONAL: Backing fabric for sleeve

Cutting Off the Excess Batting and Backing

Let's take a look at our almost completed quilt. Are the **quilt top** corners still square? Do the sides wiggle? Use your large grid rulers to check.

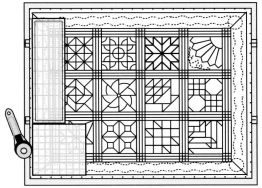

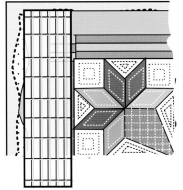

You may have to make a few corrections that could include "borrowing" batting and backing to make the sides straight. The binding we will apply to finish the quilt edges should be filled with batting and fabric, otherwise it will wear too easily. Don't be concerned if you have to cut away a little of the border fabric to straighten the sides and make the corners "square." The quilting process caused these changes.

You can use your rotary cutter, ruler and mat or good old-fashioned scissors for trimming. If you use the rotary cutter, place the rulers on top of the quilt to protect it as you cut away the backing and batting. If you want to be extra cautious, draw the cutting lines and use scissors. *Optional*: you can machine baste a scant 1/4" line of stitching all around the outside edges after trimming.

Do You Want a Hanging Sleeve?

If you would like to hang your quilt on the wall, or if you might want to enter it into a show, you'll need to add a hanging sleeve to the back. Use the 11" strip you had leftover from making the backing. Most quilt shows require a minimum 3" wide hanging sleeve, so the leftover strip will be more than wide enough. Cut a rectangle 7" inches wide and as long as the width measurement of your quilt. Fold in 1" on both short outside edges, then fold it in half lengthwise. Match the raw edges to the top edge and baste it to the back. Later, you can carefully hand baste the folded edge to the backing layer.

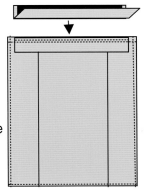

For a professional way to display your quilt, attach a flat sash curtain rod to the wall. The hanging rod can be slipped in between the layers of the sleeve so it will not wear against the quilt backing. The rod ends won't show because the sleeve doesn't extend to the edges of the quilt.

Making the Binding

Binding is the finishing strip of fabric that folds over the outside raw edges of your quilt. Double-fold binding is more durable than single-fold. Binding can be cut on straight or bias grain lines. If your quilt has straight sides and square corners, use binding cut on the straight of grain. Bias cut binding should be used on quilt edges that are curved. For your first quilt, you don't need to deal with the stretchy attributes of bias binding applied to a straight-sided quilt. Later, as you explore more options for finishing your quilts, I'd like to suggest that you read Mimi Dietrich's book, *Happy Endings*, for well-illustrated and comprehensive instructions on a variety of finishing techniques.

Double-fold binding is usually cut 2-1/2" wide. To determine how much fabric you will need, add up the measurements of all four sides of your quilt. Include at least 2" more for turning each corner. The example quilt measures 72-1/2" by 57-1/2", or 260". Add at least 8" for the corners and another 8" to compensate for seam allowances used when joining the strips to make the binding. This brings the total up to 276". Also, include extra binding for the invisible seam finish and the inches lost by cutting the strip ends at a 45-degree angle. I'd be comfortable with at least 290".

Cutting binding on the crosswise fabric grain is more economical than from the lengthwise grain. Since we know that there are approximately 40 usable fabric inches on the crosswise grain, we'll need to divide the anticipated perimeter binding total of 290 by 40 to get 7.25 strips. It's always better to have too much than not enough, so cut eight strips. Since the strips will be 2-1/2" wide, eight strips x 2-1/2" = 20" – you will need to purchase a minimum of 2/3 yard of binding fabric, but it's always reassuring to have a little extra, especially if the fabric isn't cut straight from the bolt, so get a yard.

Prepare the binding fabric as usual: preshrinking (check for color-fastness), drying, ironing, and folding. Remove the selvage edges. With the rotary cutter and ruler, cut eight 2-1/2" strips. Unfold and, using the 45-degree angle line on the ruler, cut off the ends of each strip as shown. All the cuts are slanted in the same direction.

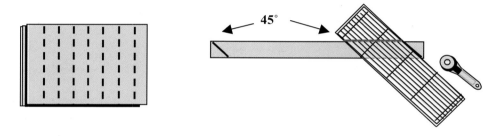

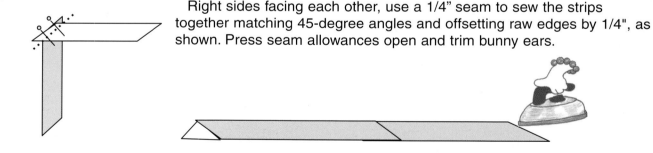

Right sides facing each other, use a 1/4" seam to sew the strips together matching 45-degree angles and offsetting raw edges by 1/4", as shown. Press seam allowances open and trim bunny ears.

After you make the binding, fold it in half and press, being careful not to let one side drift away from being square to the other. Roll up the binding to make it easier to handle.

Applying the Binding to the Quilt

The width of the seam allowance you use to sew the binding onto your quilt depends on how thick the combined quilt and binding layers are. Let's figure out how wide the seam allowance should be by doing a little test with one end of the prepared binding.

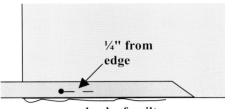

¼" from edge

back of quilt

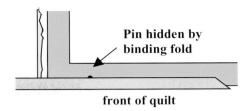

Pin hidden by binding fold

front of quilt

On the back of the quilt, match binding raw edges to quilt raw edges. Measure 1/4" up from the outer edges and place a parallel pin, which represents the future seam. Fold the binding over the raw edges to the front of the quilt making it "full of quilt sandwich." We want the binding fold edge to slightly surpass the line of stitching that will attach the binding to the quilt in order to hide it. If you can't see the shaft of the pin, a 1/4" seam allowance is correct for your application. If you can see the shaft, adjust the seam depth and repin until you find the correct width of your binding seam.

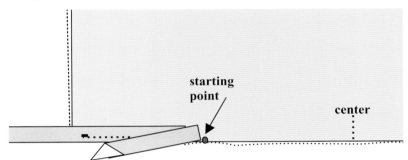

starting point

center

Use your walking foot and thread that matches the binding. Always backstitch at the beginning and ending of seams when applying binding.

Choose a point at the bottom of the quilt back that is halfway between the center and left corner; that will be your starting point for stitching. Leave about 8" of binding unattached, and begin sewing to the quilt using your pre-determined seam allowance. Stop and backstitch at your seam allowance measurement from the left edge. Translation: if your seam allowance is 3/8", stop 3/8" from the left edge of the quilt. Remove the quilt from under the needle.

Turning the Corner: An Automatic Miter

Mitering the binding corners is a cinch. It happens automatically if you follow these instructions:

Fold the binding out and away from the quilt so that its raw edge continues in a straight line with the quilt's raw edge. Place a pin through all layers at the bottom of the quilt. Refold the binding up so that all raw edges are aligned again. Pin this new arrangement in place.

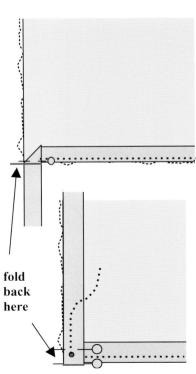

fold back here

Return the quilt back under the needle and begin stitching at **your** seam allowance measurement from both corner edges; i.e., if your seam allowance is 3/8", then you will begin stitching 3/8" from the bottom and 3/8" in from the left side. Don't forget to backstitch. When we flip the seam allowance to the right side of the quilt, we'll have to tug on it a little, and you don't want the stitching to come out.

Sew all four corners in the same way. When you have turned the last corner and are back to the bottom of your quilt, stop and backstitch about 6" from the right quilt edge.

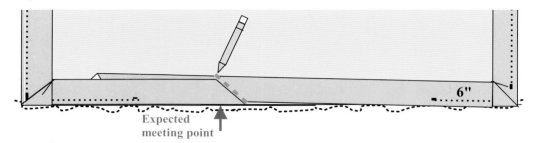

If you have too much binding remaining on the right side so that it extends past your original starting point, cut some off. Don't cut it too short; you want to allow the right-hand binding to lie smooth and flat under the left-hand binding. Trace the overlap line of the left-hand binding onto the right-hand binding.

Open the folds of both binding ends. Extend the 45-degree line you drew up onto the other side of the right-hand binding. Using your grid ruler, align and draw a second 45-degree line 1/2" away from the first, making the right binding longer. With the addition of this 1/2", you have compensated for two 1/4" seam allowances needed to join these two ends together.

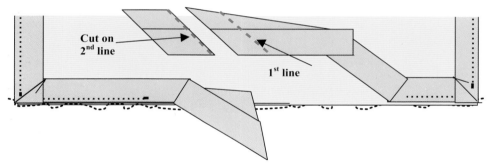

Check first to see if your measurements are correct by re-folding the right binding and overlapping the ends again. If the second drawn line is 1/2" past the cut edge of the left binding, go ahead open and cut the right binding on that <u>second</u> line.

Unfold the left binding end. Place both ends right sides together to sew the "invisible" seam. These two pieces will be offset just as they were when you joined the strips to make the binding. After the seam is completed, press it open, trim bunny ears, and return the binding to its original folded formation. Stitch down the remainder of the binding to the quilt. This angled seam will be practically imperceptible unlike overlapped or square-sewn seams. With a steam iron, press the binding away from the quilt on all sides.

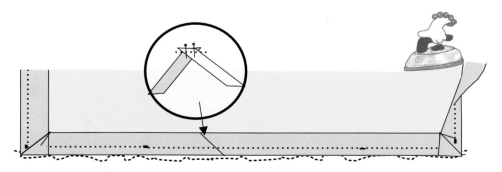

Topstitching the Binding in Place

The binding is sewn to the back of the quilt, so we need to flip it to the front and topstitch it down to finish the edge. We also want to slightly overlap the stitching we just made to hide it. This topstitching should be placed quite close to the fold.

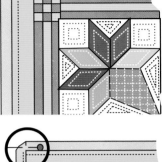

You will see that your binding is curving over the corners of the quilt. This is correct because we put a mitering tuck in each corner. If you feel a bound corner on the back, you'll notice that the little fold created by the miter is turned toward one side. When you hand miter the binding on the front, be sure you tuck that little flap to the opposite side distributing the bulk.

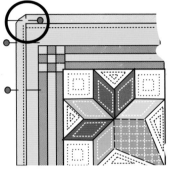

Working on one side and corner at a time, turn the quilt right side up and begin wrapping and pinning the binding over the raw edge hiding the stitching line that sewed it on. About 10" away from the corner, begin to topstitch the binding down with a continuous seam. You will probably need to readjust the wrapped binding as you sew. Backstitch when you reach the quilt edge and remove it from the machine.

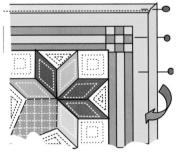

To hand miter the first front corner, fold the binding on the upcoming side over the quilt and the binding you just topstitched. Adjust the back tuck in the opposite direction of the one on the front. Press and pin. You may have to encourage the fold into a 45-degree angle. Continue to topstitch the binding to the second side just as you did the first. Stop with a backstitch at the next edge of the quilt. Repeat this procedure until the binding on all four sides is topstitched down.

To make the corner miters more secure, you can hand stitch them closed, if you like.

Some people prefer to machine sew the binding to the front of the quilt and flip it to the back. Instead of topstitching, they hand stitch the entire binding fold edge in place at the seam line with a blind stitch. I do like this method, but prefer finishing the binding by machine for quilts that will receive a lot of use. The directions given here work for front or back application.

Labels

Quilts are a symbol of someone who cared. People put so much work, time, talent, and love—so much of themselves—into a quilt. Because a quilt is treasured and preserved, it could lovingly be handed down to descendants who may not remember or even know the story of its maker. I hope you will put a label on this and all your quilts to say who you are, where you lived when you made it, the date you made it (or finished it), for whom it was made and why.

Labels are messages written on cloth that are traditionally sewn on the backs of quilts, but you don't have to relegate your information to the back of your quilt. A quilt block that contains writing concerning the quilt of which it is part is called a dedication block and performs the same function as a label. Besides quilting, this is another way to fill up a larger open block patch. If you would like to put a dedication block into your quilt, write the words on it before you sew it in…just in case.

You can find books filled with inspirations for quilt labels and make your own. You can purchase pre-printed labels in packages on the notions wall of your fabric store or quilt shop. There is yardage available printed with a number of labels for you to cut out, fill in, and sew on.

If you have a computer and a printer, making a label is magically easy. You can purchase fabric sheets made to feed through your printer just like paper. You could design a label using all of the different choices your word processing, photo, and graphic programs have to offer. Follow the manufacturer's instructions to print your label. Use the freezer paper technique shown here to sew it to the back of your quilt.

A friend of mine made just such a label. She scanned a photograph of herself holding her grandchild and the lovely pinwheel quilt she made for the little girl. She then printed it onto a special fabric sheet. She cut out the picture, adding an area in which to write information about the quilt and a special message for her granddaughter. What a lovely memento this will be for her little one to treasure for a lifetime.

High-quality, closely woven 100 percent cotton fabric is the best choice for labels. There's just one little trick to remember that will make writing on fabric seem like writing on paper. It involves our versatile friend, freezer paper. On the paper side, draw then cut a square or whatever shape you choose for your label. If you want an irregular shape, draw a mirror image because the shiny side is the right side. Iron the shiny side onto the wrong side of your label fabric, then cut out the fabric adding 1/4" all around.

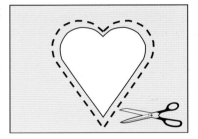

At this point, I use my computer in a different way to make labels. I choose a font I like, then type the sentiment within the size limitations of my label and print it out on paper. I tape the printed sheet onto my light table, center it, and tape the paper-backed fabric over that, fabric side up. Then I trace the letters onto the fabric. The result looks like hand-done calligraphy, not computer generated print.

You'll need special writing instruments to mark on fabric, which you can find at fabric stores, quilt shops, craft stores and discount stores. They contain permanent pigment color and do not run or wash out. My favorite is archival gel pens. They come in a myriad of shades, so you could add colorful drawings to your labels, if you'd like. Test them on a fabric scrap first.

After your information and any drawings have been placed on your label, peel off the freezer paper. If the paper shape is reversible, like this heart or a square, rectangle, etc., flip it around shiny side up, center it onto the back of your label patch, and pin it in place. Turn the outside fabric edges onto the shiny surface of the freezer paper and iron them to create turned-under seam allowances. You will have to clip curved edges and inverted points. If the shape you chose is not reversible, make a second pattern by flipping the first over and tracing a mirror image onto the paper side of another piece of freezer paper so you can use this technique.

All that is left to do is blind stitch the label to the back of your quilt. Leave the freezer paper attached to your label while you hand sew it on. It will force your needle to the very edge of the patch, helping you make tiny, invisible stitches. When you've only got a few inches to sew before the label is completely stitched on, use a tweezers to pull out the freezer paper template. Tuck the unsewn raw edges back under and stitch the opening closed.

The Blind Stitch

The blind stitch is the most commonly used hand appliqué technique. It is worked from the right to the left, and is fast and easy.

Use a single strand of thread that matches the label patch. Thread and knot your needle and take a stitch under where you want to position the label to secure. Bring the needle up and catch a few threads on the very edge of the label patch. Then take a small stitch through only the backing fabric and up again just under the fold of the patch. Take another small stitch on the patch edge, then another small stitch through the backing, etc. You don't have to pull the full length of the thread through the fabric with every stitch—try after every 3 or 4 stitches. When you have attached the entire patch, make a tiny knot just under the edge of the label and clip the thread.

'Bye for Now ...

I hope you have enjoyed these lessons as much as I have. You have come such a long way in a relatively short period of time, and you have your beautiful quilt to show for it. Let this learning experience be a continuation of the legacy of quilting threaded through time connecting us with our foremothers who made their beautiful quilts mostly for practical reasons, but always with love.

BIBLIOGRAPHY

Beyer, Jinny. Patchwork Patterns. McLean VA: EPM Publications, 1983

Brackman, Barbara. Encyclopedia of Pieced Quilt Patterns. Paducah, KY: American Quilters Society, 1993.

Chalfant-Payne, Suzzy and Susan Aylsworth Murwin. Quick and Easy Patchwork on the Sewing Machine. New York, NY: Dover Publications, Inc., 1979

Cooper, Patricia J. and Norma Bradley Allen. The Quilters – Women and Domestic Art, An Oral History. Lubbock, TX: Texas Tech University Press, 1999

Dietrich, Mimi. Happy Endings. Bothel, WA: That Patchwork Place, 1997

Field, Carol, ed. Better Homes & Gardens 101 Full-Size Quilt Blocks & Borders, Des Moines, IA: Meredith Publishing, 1998

Frager, Dorothy. The Book of Sampler Quilts. Radnor, PA: Chilton Books, 1983

Hassel, Carla, You Can Be a Super Quilter. Radnor, PA: Wallace-Homestead Book Col., 1980

Hinson, Dolores. A Quilter's Companion. New York, NY: Arco Publishing Co., 1978

Leone, Diana and Cindy Walter. Fine Hand Quilting. Iola, WI: Krause Publications, 2000

Malone, Maggie. 120 Patterns for Traditional Patchwork Quilts. New York, NY: Sterling Publishing Co., Inc., 1983

McKim, Ruby. 101 Patchwork Patterns. New York, NY: Dover Publications, Inc., 1962

Mech, Dr. Susan Delaney. Rx for Quilters: Stitcher-Friendly Advice for Every Body. Lafayette, CA: C&T Publications, 2000

Mills, Susan Winter. Illustrated Index to Traditional American Quilt Patterns. New York, NY: Arco Publishing Co., 1980

Poe, Ann. Quilting School. Singapore: Readers Digest Association, Inc., 1994

Quick Method Quilts. Little Rock, AK: Leisure Arts, unknown date.

Reader's Digest Complete Guide to Needlework, Reader's Digest Association, Inc., USA, 1979.

Squire, Helen. Helen's Guide to Quilting in the 21st Century: Hand and Machine Quilting Designs (Dear Helen Series). Paducah, KY: American Quilters Society, 1997.

The Meetin' Place, Quilters Newsletter Magazine, January 1989, Primedia, Inc., Golden, CO.

Verna, Lois, Lofty Decisions, Quilters Newsletter Magazine, November 1999 – December 1999, Primedia, Inc., Golden, CO.

RESOURCES

C&T Publications, Inc.
POB 1456
Lafayette, CA 94549
www.ctpub.com

For rotary cutters and mats:
Olfa Products Group
Division of World Kitchens
1536 Beech St.
Terre Haute, IN 47804
www.olfa.com
1.800.962.OLFA

For Omnigrid Rulers:
PRYM-Dritz USA
Makers of Omnigrid Rulers and Mats
http://1st-sewingsuppliesandnotions.com/index.htm

For X-ACTO Knives and Blades
Bob Corey Associates
Division of BCA Marketing, Inc.
POB 73
Merrick, NY 11566
www.x-actoblades.com
1.516.485.5544

For Wonder Invisible Thread:
YLI Corporation
161 W. Main St.
Rock Hill, SC 29730
www.ylicorp.com
1.800.296.8139
1.803.985.3100
customerservice@ylicorp.com

For cork-backed metal rulers:
Acme United Corp.
1931 Black Rock Turnpike
Fairfield, CT 06432
203.332.7330

The information in this book is meant to be shared. I've organized the content exactly the same way my classes are organized. Almost all of the students who have taken my courses finished their quilts, which filled my heart with great pride and respect. Not only did they learn the quiltmakers' skills, they developed confidence in their sewing and artistic abilities. They also gained a new understanding and appreciation of their patience and perseverance.

Permission to make a copy of the templates included in these lessons is granted to the purchaser of each book and extends only to the owner for her personal use. Therefore, when using **The Essential Guide to Practically Perfect Patchwork** as a teaching aid, each member of your class will need to purchase her own copy. Just as you place value on your knowledge and time as a teacher, I place that same value on my knowledge and time that this book represents. We both want to share our love of quilting and encourage others to join us in our treasured hobby in an ethical way reflecting the honorable traditions of our quilting foremothers.

A practical suggestion to you for the timing of each lesson would be a lesson a week for the first six weeks. Take a break of a few weeks before continuing with lessons 7, 8, and 9 giving everyone a chance to catch up and fine-tune. Another break between the 9th and 10th lessons is a good idea to allow the new quiltmakers to finish quilting their quilts. I called the 10th lesson "A Binding Reunion" where we covered applying the binding as well as adding a label to the back of the quilt. This play on words was a light-hearted invitation to all, as during this last lesson we shared treats and compliments on each other's handiwork. We even proudly shared "war stories" about the troubles we had making our quilts.

As a quilting teacher, you know the feeling of sisterhood that sharing your knowledge and skills with your students fosters. It was a surprise to me to learn what an impact teaching quiltmaking had on my students—and on my own life, as a matter of fact.

Happy journeys to all.

1 *The Quilters – Women and Domestic Art, An Oral History*, Texas Tech University Press, 1999, p. 20
2 "Quilter's Newsletter Magazine," January 1989, pp. 14, 54

The Magic of

Crazy Quilting

A Complete Resource For Embellished Quilting

J. Marsha Michler

Acknowledgments

My most heartfelt thanks to all of those who contributed in so many ways to this book. Thanks to all the wonderful people at Krause including my editors, Gabrielle Wyant-Perillo and Kris Manty, and book designer Jan Wojtech; my agent, Sandy Taylor for believing in me; Joe Hudgins, who generously shared his knowledge of cigarette silks; Diana Vandervoort for her gracious encouragement; Cindy Smith, **Limerick Public Library**, for her research assistance; Paula Robert of **Copy-It**, Biddeford, Maine; Jeannette Brewster, President of **Valley Needlers Quilt Guild**.

Many thanks to those who generously contributed supplies, photographs and other materials: Kim Kovaly, **The Willow Shop**; Maggie Backman, **Things Japanese**; Anna Baird, **Green Mountain Hand Dyed Linens**; Nancy Kirk, **The Kirk Collection**; Dena Lenham, Design Coordinator of **Kreinik Mfg. Co., Inc.**; Elda O'Connell, Catherine Carpenter; Mary Weinberg.

My deepest thanks to the following businesses, institutions, and people for kindly and generously allowing access to crazy quilts for study and photography:

Betsey Telford, owner of **Rocky Mountain Quilts**
130 York St.
York Village, ME 03909

Richard T. Eisenhour, Curator of Collections
Marcene J. Modeland, Director
Pamela S. Eagleson, Acting Director
The Brick Store Museum
117 Main St.
Kennebunk, ME 04043

Joan Sylvester, owner of **Shiretown Antique Center**
Rt. 202
Alfred, ME 04002

Bonnie Hayward, owner of **Avalon Antiques**
on display at Arundel Antiques
1713 Portland Rd.
Arundel, ME 04046

The Gold Bug Antiques
U.S. Rt. 1
Cape Neddick, ME
http://www.antiques4you.com/~victique/

The Barn at Cape Neddick
U.S. Rt. 1
Cape Neddick, ME 03902

Tina Toomey, **Curator of York Institute Museum**
371 Main St.
Saco, ME 04072

Maine Historical Society
485 Congress St.
Portland, ME 04101

Thanks to **Dover Publications, Inc.** for permission to use Victorian clip art from its "Pictorial Archives.":
Victorian Frames, Borders and Cuts, from the **1882 Type Catalog of George Bruce's Son and Co.,** 1976,
Grafton, Carol Belanger, ed., **Victorian Pictorial Borders**, 1984,
Derriey, Charles, **Borders, Frames and Decorative Motifs from the 1862 Derriey Typographic Catalog**, 1987,
Grafton, Carol Belanger, ed., **Treasury of Victorian Printers' Frames, Ornaments and Initials**, 1984,
Grafton, Carol Belanger, **Victorian Spot Illustrations, Alphabets and Ornaments, from Porret's Type Catalog**, 1982.

Also, my thanks, deepest appreciation and admiration to Limerick's very special "quilters," who are: Kim and Lauren Kovaly, Marian Budzyna, Jane Bryant, Kathy Melzer, Adele and Ruth Floyd, Paul Baresel and Peg Gomane.

Contents

Introduction

The years marked by Queen Victoria's reign, 1838-1901, were characterized by massive and significant social changes. The romance in this age is in the phenomenal opening of trade, the boom in technology and the creation of entrepreneurialism. The "Iron Horse" began to course its way across entire continents. Toilets became flushable, silks became available and affordable and telegraph cables literally connected continents. Electricity created easy lighting of a home and medical discoveries found new ways to save lives. The color mauve was discovered, the sewing machine was invented and the search was on for a synthetic silk.

With industry, art was undergoing major changes. Painters studied the science of light and color. They began juxtaposing colors in ways that the eye would mix them. Artists such as Monet sought to capture the effects of light, while Seurat created paintings entirely of dots. These and other artists were the vanguardists of the modern art movement. They were very different from the prior academic style, of realistically rendering subjects, with layer upon layer of well-oiled paint.

Victorian-age needlework was rich and varied. It is fitting that women in their quilting, reacting to the changes around them, attempted unconventional forms. The play of colors and textures placed on a quilt top, and united with embroidery stitches, are every bit as artistic as the works of the painters. Some crazy quilts of late Victorian times display a range of highly developed needlework skills, combined with a refined sense of color and composition. These quilts often feature ribbonwork, ribbon embroidery, monogramming, embroidery stitches of all types and other forms of needlework. At times, they included paintings on fabric; a complex mix of ingredients.

There is no identifiable "inventor" of the crazy quilt. It seems to have been congruous with the era in which it was born. Similar to the fads that occur today, crazy quilting took off of its own volition. It appears to have originated in America and gained steam from about 1860. The phase culminated around the 1880s and fizzled out in the early 1900s. The appeal of crazy quilting to Victorian ladies must have subsequently inspired the rage. These ladies would have adored the same we do today–that of seeking out a wonderful collection of "finds," fancy fabrics and luxurious threads. These valuables are then assembled into a showpiece quilt.

About Crazy Quilting

Crazy quilting is the placing together of irregular-shaped patches, usually onto a foundation, after which they are usually secured with embroidery stitches. Often used are fancy fabrics from dressmaking, draperies, bridal apparel and other sources. A wide variety of embellishments and embroidery stitches, added to the patches, dramatically bring the patched surface to life.

The true magic of crazy quilting is in the melding of its ingredients and the individuality of each hand's work. There is a magical transformation that takes place with the laying of patches and the addition of embroidery stitches and embellishments. You never truly know what it is going to look like until the final stitches are placed.

The word "crazy" beautifully sums up what is unique about this type of quilt. It is perfect if you feel a little bit crazy while working on one! This form of quilting utilizes your most pure imaginativeness from beginning to end. For those who make these quilts, the joy of creativity will truly blossom.

How to Use This Book

Read this book from front to back or use it as a reference volume. I recommend that beginners read it through to become familiar with the basic procedures and the many options. More experienced workers may prefer to reference individual topics.

I present **The Magic of Crazy Quilting** with the crazy quilt in mind. However, the techniques on the pages apply to a variety of quilt types and many needlework projects.

A showpiece antique crazy quilt. Collection of, and photographed at Rocky Mountain Quilts, York Village,

The Basics of Crazy Quilting

A treadle and an early Singer are still dependable workhorses today. A basket of silks awaits a new project.

Simple Requirements

There are a few essential tools for crazy quilting. If you have done sewing or traditional quilting, there is a good chance they are already part of your repertoire. Essential tools include shears, pins, iron and ironing board, tape measure, cutting mat, and a basic sewing machine. For embroidery, you will need embroidery scissors, needles, pincushion and a hoop. Additional requirements for different types of embroidery and embellishments are covered in Artful Embellishments.

Purchase quality tools and you will find that, with proper care, they will last a lifetime. Quality tools are an excellent investment and make a difference in your level of sewing enjoyment.

Shears and Scissors

The shears I use for patch cutting are 7 inches long, slightly shorter than the standard 8-inch shears. A good shears is very sharp and cuts fabric so easily that cutting is effortless. Mine is all metal, and the blades can be honed to keep them sharp.

There are many different styles and sizes of embroidery scissors. My favorite is a multi-functional 5-inch metal knife-edge scissors with both a narrow and a wide blade. The narrow blade is needle-sharp for picking out unwanted stitches. When trimming thread ends and fabrics on a patched quilt top, place the wide blade next to the fabric. For safety and to protect the

blades when not in use, store the scissors in a sheath or other holder. Purchase a ceramic hone to retain the cutting edges of knife-edge scissors. Be sure to follow the manufacturer instructions.

Add a paper-cutting scissors to your tool collection. Use this to cut out paper patterns and tissue paper. Do not use a fabric shears or embroidery scissors to cut paper, as this horrendously dulls the blades.

A good scissors to treasure,
Is both delight and pleasure.
But in public is not to share -
Too likely to dis-a-pair!

Only a few tools are required for crazy quilting. Some antique tools are still viable today, such as the pincushion/thread stand here.

When traveling with a project, take along an inexpensive thread clippers instead of your good embroidery scissors. Like pens, scissors are often borrowed or they can unknowingly fall out of your bag. Also, a sharp-pointed scissors presents safety concerns.

Needles and Pins

Three types of hand-sewing needles will accommodate almost any technique in crazy quilting: embroidery/crewel, chenille and applique/size12 sharps.

For use with a variety of threads and ribbons, purchase assortments of the embroidery and chenille needles. Needles vary in quality. My favorites, manufactured by Piecemakers®, slide effortlessly through fabric and have smooth eyes.

The purpose of the needle is to make a hole in the fabric that is large enough to easily allow a thread or embroidery ribbon to pass. At the same time, it should hold the thread snug enough to prevent slipping out of the eye.

Although they slip through and stick fingers, evade grasp and often become stuck in the carpet, pins are among the most useful of tools. Having discovered silk pins, I now use them for almost everything. They create little bulge in the fabric and pressing is easier because the heads are smaller. If using pins with beaded heads, choose those with glass beads to prevent melting under the iron.

Embroidery Hoops

An embroidery hoop is essential for handstitching on projects patched onto such lightweight foundations as silk organza and batiste. This also applies to embellishments such as beading and punchneedle. A 3-inch or 4-inch hoop is an excellent size for small, silk ribbon embroideries. Hoops 6 inches or larger are useful for embroidering along patch seams.

I use hoops imported from Germany. These are a smooth wood hoop with a brass screw.

To protect delicate fabrics and prevent hoop marks, wrap the hoop with a strip of clean batiste or another soft fabric. When you set a project aside, always remove the hoop.

Projects worked on a muslin foundation, and patched with firm fabrics, such as satins, velveteen and cottons, do not always require a hoop for embroidery. Try embroidering without a hoop to determine if the piece will stay smooth. Use a hoop if it tends to bunch.

One of my favorite tools is the supported lap hoop. This is a quilting hoop, raised above a base, on supports of wood or metal. Both hands remain free for stitching and doing embellishment work because the hoop rests on your lap or a table. I use a 14-inch round lap hoop, particularly for punchneedle, beading and embroidering silk quilts.

A lap hoop is easily portable. The only drawback is in fastening the ends of embroidery and beading threads. It is a bit clumsy to fasten the ends on the back of the work. Instead of turning the hoop over, secure and conceal ends on the front by making several tiny stitches beneath the edge of a patch or an embellishment.

Laying Tool

Use a laying tool, for embroideries such as Oriental, satin stitch, monogramming, silk ribbon and needlepoint. When pulling the thread or ribbon through the fabric to the back, run it over the laying tool to remove any excess twist. This specialty tool also allows the thread to lie smoothly on the surface of the fabric. In silk work, this is important for the maximum sheen of the fiber to show. The project must be in a supported hoop, since one hand holds the laying tool and the other hand works the stitches.

Iron and Ironing Board

Essential to all patching methods, careful pressing helps ensure a smooth quilt surface. Press all patched quilt tops and embroideries face down on a padded surface. Use a padded ironing board cover or a terry cloth towel placed over the ironing board.

When patching, use a dry iron to avoid scorching your fingers. When steam is required, use a spray bottle and spray the surface of the ironing board. To prevent water-spotting, do not spray the patch.

Use a press cloth on delicate fabrics and on those that pressing may cause a shiny surface.

A laying tool is held in the left hand, while the needle is used in the right. (Reverse for left-handedness). This tool is used to assist thread or embroidery ribbon to lie smoothly on the surface of the fabric. The quilt top is in a lap, or supported hoop.

TIP: "Pressing" is not the same as "ironing." To press, place the iron on the fabric and lightly press for a few seconds. Be careful not to scorch. I do not recommend sliding the iron around on embroidery, embellishments or patches, as this can move materials out of place.

Sewing Machine

Unless you are going to machine embroider around the crazy-quilt patches, a sewing machine with only a simple, straight stitch setting is necessary. The older, smaller machines called "featherweights" are more than ideal. Even a treadle is acceptable!

The machine manual specifies maintenance, necessary operation information and special purpose instructions.

NOTE: Throughout this book, the words "fabric" or "fabrics" describe cloth.
The word "materials" often denotes fabric yardage. However, in this book materials may also include laces, ribbons, threads and miscellaneous items used in a quilt or a project.

A Workspace

Set up a workspace in an area large enough to place an ironing board next to a table or desk. It is far easier to have a permanent space to work than it is to repeatedly set up and take down. An entire room is, of course, the most ideal situation. If this is not possible, a corner or nook is next best. Space in an attic or a basement can be converted, although if you have a basement studio, be sure to monitor the humidity. Too much moisture can cause your tools to become rusty and fibers to become musty.

Lighting is very important. Achieve proper lighting with good fixtures or a combination of windows and fixtures. In the necessary position, place or position a clamp-on light with an adjustable arm. Fit these, or other types, with ener-gy-saving fluorescent bulbs. Choose fluorescent or incandescent lighting according to personal preference. For accuracy, I make my color choices in natural daylight. This allows me to work on the project under any type of lighting.

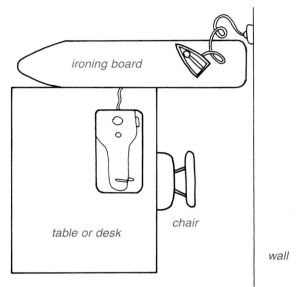

The machine-sewn methods of crazy quilting are easiest with an ironing board placed next to the sewing machine.

For large projects, a table is helpful for hand-patching methods. With an ironing board placed alongside, use a kitchen, dining or fold-up table. Place a large cutting mat on the table to protect it from being scratched by pins and needles.

If you are using a machine method of patching, place the ironing board within reach of the sewing machine. For safety, always set an ironing board and iron against a wall and near an outlet.

A bookcase, or space on a bookshelf, will keep your needlework references handy. Put your magazines or magazine clippings in binders. These materials will inspire project ideas, provide answers, give examples and offer suggestions. In one volume, a good how-to book is equivalent to an entire class or seminar.

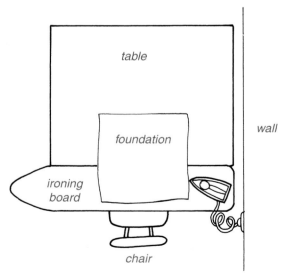

A table placed next to an ironing board is a convenient arrangement for patching a crazy quilt by hand.

Natural Elegance

Crazy quilting is an opportunity par excellence to explore fabrics and colors. Fabric types from Victorian times include silks, cottons, linen and wool. These fabrics were available in a wide variety of textures, weaves and surface finishes. In the late 1800s, in an attempt to imitate silk, it was discovered that rayons and acetate synthetics could be derived of natural materials. Improved in the early 1900s they are invaluable for their beautiful finishes.

The 1800s represented a burgeoning of new fabric weaves, finishes, types and colors. The invention of the jacquard loom came about for making fabrics with woven-in patterning. Experimentation to create a synthetic silk was underway and methods of both printing and photography improved. As William Henry Perkin was trying to make synthetic quinine, he accidentally discovered the color mauve, which in turn caused the invention of Aniline dyes. As they sought scraps for their crazy quilts, Victorian ladies likely drooled over some of these new-fangled fabrics and colors! They began to eschew cotton calicos thinking them "drab." They instead made scrap quilts and crazy quilts out of silks and other fine fabrics.

Involved in the assemblage of a crazy quilt is a combination of textures, finishes and colors. Of these, choosing colors presents a great challenge for many of us. Later in this chapter is some information that may be helpful in selecting fabric colors. Also try the dye experiments in part two of Artful Embellishments. Dyeing is an excellent way to learn about colors.

The "White Rose" quilt, 1862, with its many black and white patches displays a strongly contrasting color scheme softened by touches of color. Photographed at Shiretown Antique Center, Alfred, Maine.

An Overview of Fiber Types

Silk

Amazing, exceptional and unique are a few words with which to describe this fiber. Silk has extremely fine fibers with amazing strength. It is exceptional in its translucency and possesses a uniquely dry, crushy texture. This is a "protein" fiber, made of silkworm cocoons. These cocoons are unraveled into a fine strand many yards long. This strand, called "filament silk," is then plied into threads. In comparison, "spun silks" are carded and spun. The filament silks are capable of the highest sheen, while spun silks tend to be matte or nearly matte in finish.

Habotai, taffeta, jacquard, charmeuse, satin, dupion, noil and velvet are some of the weaves and fabric types in which silk is available. Silk fabrics can be crisp as taffeta, or soft and nearly weightless as lightweight Habotai. Finishes vary from matte to shiny and smooth to coarse, depending on the silk and the weave of the fabric.

Silk in its natural state is highly washable. When washed for the first time, shrinkage can occur and some dyes, especially darker colors, may run. Silk garments and yardage, labeled "dry clean only," may not be colorfast and could shrink. Some surface finishes can change with washing. As with other fabric types, test-wash a small piece before immersing the whole piece. Wash silk in lukewarm water with mild soap.

Iron silks on low heat to prevent scorching. If the fabric is crumpled up and wrinkles have set in, apply steam or mist while ironing. Should static occur, try misting the air with water or set the piece aside until the electricity ceases.

Cotton

Cotton is a seed head that forms on the plant after the flower blooms. I tried growing it in my Maine garden, but cotton requires a longer growing season. The plants flowered, but did not go to seed. The result was no cotton to harvest. If you live in the North and wish to try growing cotton, start the seeds early, indoors. Transplant outdoors after the final frost.

Mercerization, cotton treated with caustic soda, was invented in the mid-1800s. This treatment produces high luster, greater strength and more efficient dye absorption.

Some of the finishes and weaves associated with this fiber include broadcloth, twill, velveteen, gauze and corduroy. Cotton is spun from very fine to heavy and coarse fibers. Fabric types vary from lightweight to heavy and from sheer to opaque. Since the fiber itself is opaque, sheerness is obtained by using extremely fine threads or open weaves.

Cotton fabrics can be washed with agitation in hot or cold water. Some shrinkage in the first washing is normal, as is the loss of some excess dye.

Cotton moiré and chintz have glossy surface finishes which tend to wash-out. These polished surfaces are produced by running the fabric through rollers. Although labeled "dry clean only," I prefer to wash them. Washing produces a natural way to "antique" the finish!

Iron cottons on high heat, but take care to avoid scorching. I find for most crazy quilting purposes, a "wool" setting works well.

TIP: Sateen of 100 percent cotton is a beautiful fabric with a soft sheen and elegant drape. Sateen is often used as borders and backings in antique crazy quilts. Its satin weave creates floats of threads that reflect the light. It is occasionally found, from heirloom sewing sources, in white (consider dyeing it) to dressmaking fabric selections. It heartens me to see it used by known designers in luxury sheets and bedding. I hope this beautiful fabric continues to become more widely available. A high-quality sateen has a luxurious-looking finish and both sides of the fabric are free of pilling or fuzzing.

Linen

Linen fabric comes from the flax plant. A laborious process involves rotting away the non-fibrous parts of the plant, then spinning and weaving the resulting fibers. It is woven into fine handkerchief linens or coarser fabrics and canvas.

Linens often have a distinctive luster, especially when starched and pressed. Because the fiber is firm, bordering on stiffness, it makes an ideal even-weave fabric for cross stitch embroidery. Linen easily accepts dye. Use natural dyes to create a wide range of beautiful, luxurious colors.

Linens, more than other fibers, have survived through time. A long-lasting fiber (Egyptian mummies are wrapped in it), it tends to have a feel of age-old elegance. Linen is highly washable and irons on high heat.

Rayon

First appearing in the late 1800s, rayon is the result of a search for synthetic silk. This early rayon was highly flammable. In 1924, another method of making it was discovered. Rayon consists of cellulose fibers derived from wood or cottonseed.

Rayon fabrics range from the drapey challis types to twills, velvets and other finishes. Rayon is used in combination with silk to create velvet. The drapery fabric bengaline, consists of rayon woven over a cotton core.

Rayon presses easily and holds a crease even with finger-pressing. For this reason, the closely woven types are excellent for appliqué. Although weak when wet, it firms up again when dry. Iron rayon on low heat and use cool temperatures for washing.

Acetate

Acetate, also synthesized of cellulose, is an offshoot of the rayon discovery. Acetate, not used commercially until 1924, is often woven into satin or taffeta. Taffeta is sometimes "calendered," or run through rollers to give it a moiré finish. Acetate satin has high luster and firm drape. The taffeta is crisp and, when rubbed against itself, is noisy.

Although sold as "dry clean only," these fabrics are washable by hand. Moiré and some glossy finishes may partly or completely wash out. I often do this intentionally to cut down on shine or to create an "aged" effect. Because the sheen is created by the weave, satins retain their luster.

Like rayon, press these fabrics on low heat. Acetates retain creases well. Wash in a large basin of cool or cold water. DO NOT WRING or creases may remain, even after pressing.

Wool

Here in Maine, where the weather gets chilly, wool is a favorite fiber. A century ago, there may have been many crazy quilts made of wool. Those I found are mostly bed-size and well worn.

Wool fabrics vary from finely woven challis to heavy types that are used for coats and blankets. Suit-weights and challis make excellent crazy patches. Use the blanket stitch appliqué on blanketing and felted wools to eliminate having to hem their edges. Most patterned wool fabrics are woven in plaids, herringbones and pinstripes. Natural sheep-color browns, grays, tans and off-whites are lovely and useful neutral shades.

Wool holds a crease when steamed and allows sculptural forming by steaming (hats are an example). It has a tendency to felt when it is both wet and subjected to agitation. Shocking with temperature changes when it is wet will surely shrink wool.

Fabrics for Crazy Quilting

Luxury and plain fabrics in a mix of textures and surface finishes. From left are wool, velveteen, bengaline, taffeta, moiré taffeta, rayon/cotton, rayon challis, damask, satin, brocade, velveteen. The folded pieces are Green Mountain Hand natural-dyed linens.

Characteristics of fabrics make some easier to work with than others. These include fabrics that are:
   a) woven,
   b) firm or "crisp" in texture, and
   c) hold a crease when pressed.

Napped fabrics, such as velvets, make beautiful crazy patches. However, while working with them, velvets have a tendency to slip and slide. To keep them in place, carefully pin and baste.

The most useful fabrics are solid colors. Beautifully textured, unprinted fabrics add a great deal to a crazy quilt. Solid fabrics nicely flaunt embroidery and other details.

The following is a list of some of the fabric types that are suitable for crazy patches:

Plush: Velvet
         Cotton Velveteen
         No-wale or fine-wale corduroy

Smooth: Satin
         Taffeta
         Chintz
         Cotton Sateen
         Linen
         Cotton Sheeting
         Quilting cottons

Ribbed: Bengaline
         Corduroy
         Some velvets and
            velveteens

Textured: Jacquard
          Damask
          Moiré
          Silks noil, dupion,
             crepe.
          Brocade
          Twill
          Challis
          All-over laces

Washing Instructions for Washable Fabrics

If you are not sure about the washability of a fabric, first test-wash a small piece. Washing by hand allows you observe if the fabric dulls, bleeds dye or excessively shrinks. I like to prewash fabrics soon after purchase. By doing so, I avoid the question: "Was this prewashed or not?"

When you cut up a piece of clothing to use for crazy patch fabrics, and the label says "dry clean only," this could mean that the *fabric* is washable but

the *garment* is not washable. For example, interior paddings and interfacings in tailored suits can shift about or lose their shape.

Test-iron any unfamiliar fabrics. I've had upholstery fabrics shrink to half their size when slightly touched by a warm iron.

I use the following method for all of my crazy quilting fabrics:

1 Use a large basin for acetates to avoid crinkling. Wash other types in a size in which the fabric fits. Use cool to lukewarm water and mild soap. For all fabrics, especially silks and wools, I suggest using unscented natural shampoo that is found at a natural-food store.

2 Wash silks, rayons, wools and acetates by soaking. Gently move the fabric in the water to work the soap through the fibers. Do not soak dark and light colors together. Cottons and linens can be vigorously washed.

3 Rinse by repeatedly changing the water until it is clear. Always use the same temperature to rinse and wash. Rinse cottons and linens under running water. If dyes run, keep rinsing until the water is clear. If the dye continues to run after you re-soap the fabric, it is not colorfast and should instead be dry cleaned.

4 Do not wring acetate, silk or wool fabrics. Wrap the wet fabric in a towel, roll and gently squeeze. Immediately remove the fabric and hang it over a line to dry. Dry all fabrics out of direct sunlight and away from heat sources.

5 When the fabric is dry, iron at an appropriate temperature. If necessary, use steam.

Mary's Velvet Dilemma

This tale of woe was sent out to nearly 700 members of *Quiltropolis'* crazy quilt email list. The following is an edited version and is used by permission of the author. Mary wrote this spontaneously, the reason for some of the spellings!

"... I was rummaging around today at a yard sale and got a WONDERFUL beautiful deep blue velvet ... coat with a 'furry' white lining and ivory satin sleeves. WHAT A FIND!!!

"Ran home jumped on the bed with a cup of coffee, the tv clicky dude, and SISSORS! Took me the better part of two hours but FINALLY I had everything whacked up.

"Of course at THIS point I have MY TISSUES because there's little tiny tiny NANNO tiny white 'hairs' EVERY-WHRERE ... I'm sneezing ... the Pupper is sneezing .... I run down stairs throw the blue velvet in the washer.

"Took out a HUGH ... KNOT of string and velvet. GRRRRRRRR stand there and untangle.

"Throw in (the dryer) to soften and unwrinkle. Pupper now wants out and the phone rings ... GRAB TISSUES ... *finally* make it back to the dryer open the door and FLUFFFF out FLYS bitty blue fluffles EVERYWHERE .... The inside of the door is solid with blue ... I'm sneezing, the Pupper is sneezing....

"...I've sworn the Pupper to silence or no doggie treats!

"Lesson learned: DON'T cut up velvet ... BEFORE washing!"

-reprinted by permission of Mary Weinberg.

TIP: The nap of velvet and velveteen consists of many short fibers. These fibers are held in place by a woven backing. With cut pieces of these fabrics, use a gentle hand-wash or first machine stitch the edges with a zigzag stitch. A serger will nicely overcast raw edges.

Shopping for Fabrics

The right piece of fabric often inspires an entire project. Buy crazy quilting fabric because you love it. Remember, you don't have to wear it or swath a room. Purchase, and actually use, the most outrageous colors and textures.

Shopping and collecting is as inspiring as diving into a new project. Fabrics are gleaned from a number of sources. Search fabric stores for clothing types, quilt shops for cotton solids, upholstery and drapery fabrics stores and bridal shops. Also seek out factory outlets.

January white sales are good for finding high quality, all-cotton sheets. Sheets are excellent fabrics for borders and backings.

Check out linen departments for damask, allover lace tablecloths and other interesting weaves.

Browse second-hand shops and yard sales for hardly-worn evening and tailored wear, especially those made of natural fibers. Take them apart by ripping out the seams or simply cutting along the seam edges. Search for men's ties, especially silk ones, and carefully rip out the stitching.

Although solids are most useful in crazy quilting, collect some prints. The prints used in the Victorian crazies were usually simple foulards, stripes and somewhat plain-looking florals.

Shopping is greatly simplified if you are willing to dye white or natural-color goods. One yard of white fabric easily becomes two to three dozen different colors. Silks in particular are very easy to dye. When selecting dyes, remember to purchase the correct type for the specific fiber being dyed.

Tips for collecting:

- Buy what you like when you see it. If you go back for it later, it may not be there.
- Save scraps down to the smallest possible

Inspiration for a quilt with an Oriental theme, these fabrics are pieces of worn kimonos, from Katie's Vintage Kimono (see Sources). The designs on the dishes and pottery can be adapted for embroidery designs.

patch-size pieces, especially luxury fabrics such as silks. Use these in miniature quilts, for covering buttons and folded flowers.

- Buy new to have the old: buy the man in your life a new tie, then talk him out of an old one.
- Recycle out-of-style but still good clothing into patch fabric.
- To solicit contributions, announce to friends and neighbors that you are collecting.

Using bias fabrics

When patches are laid onto a foundation, the grainline of the fabric becomes irrelevant. Because of this, bias fabrics, including men's ties, are easily used.

Also, when applied to a foundation, lightweight fabrics are much more stable.

Note: The "straight of grain" is the lengthwise grainline. It is necessary to use the "straight of grain" when cutting garment fabrics and patches for traditional quilting. The "cross grain" is the grainline from selvedge to selvedge.

Choosing Colors

At times, selecting a combination of coordinating colors is the most baffling aspect of crazy quilting. A basic understanding of color theory can be helpful.

Basic guidelines for using colors are taught to students of art and mastered by artists. First, let's study the visual appeal of some antique crazy quilts.

The Colors in Antique Crazy Quilts

The contrast is typically the most immediate recognizable characteristic of attractive antique quilts. The colors range from very light to very dark.

Characteristically, darks, lights and neutral shades are used nearly equally. This creates an overall balance. The appearance is easy to look at even though the maker used many colors. Also, there is usually a balance between warm and cool shades.

Bright golden yellow is used in some Victorian crazy quilts in occasional patches. It is also found in embroidery along the edges of a patch and was sometimes used as the sole color of embroidery thread. Bright golden yellow, used with other jewel-like and deep tones such as burgundy, dark green, violet, red and blue, adds a wonderful touch of contrast and brightness.

A lap quilt in roses, browns, cream, and antique gold will fit almost any home decor.

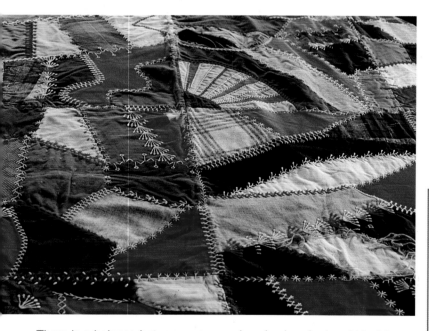

There is a balance between warm and cool colors (red and blue) in this antique wool quilt in which red predominates. Detail. The Brick Store Museum, Kennebunk, Maine.

As follows are the color schemes of two antique crazy quilts. The colors are separated into columns for easy comparison.

Quilt 1

Darks	Lights	Neutrals
red/orange (rust)	antique gold	medium brown
black	gold	beige
orange	white	
blue	pink	
yellow-gold	pale blue	

Quilt 2

Darks	Lights	Neutrals
black	soft yellow	medium brown
blue	yellow	light brown
purple	lt. orange	
red	pale blue	
olive		

Color pointers taken from antique quilts:

- Use vivid colors sparingly (magenta, royal blue, yellow, etc.). Separate with plenty of neutrals or with darker or lighter colors.
- To avoid a monotonous and dull appearance, separate similar shades (i.e. dusty rose and dusty blue) with lights or darks.
- Use a black patch to highlight nearby colors. Black patches in antique quilts were often embroidered with florals, scenes or even painted. The black background seems to highlight the incorporated colors.
- Shades of brown are useful in harmonizing surrounding colors. Browns tend to assume the depth of warm colors and the coolness of cool colors. This assumption thereby "extends" or "improves" a color scheme.

HERE IT IS IN A NUTSHELL

Dark and light,
Warm and cool,
Yellow's bright,
Brown's a tool.
Black is right,
Vivids duel!

This unusual circa mid-19th century quilt is made of many mauve, magenta, and purple fabrics. Some of the patches are set into a "sidewalk" pattern! Detail. The Brick Store Museum, Kennebunk, Maine.

Color Theory

Primary and Secondary Colors

The primary colors are red, blue and yellow, which are the basis for all other colors.

The secondary colors are obtained by mixing two primary colors, as shown in the diagram.

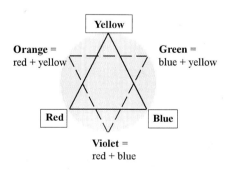

Tertiary Colors

As is evident in their names, the tertiary colors are obtained by mixing a secondary color with a primary: yellow/green, for instance, is made of yellow and green.

There are variations on each. For example, a yellow/green that tends toward yellow more than green is yellow/yellow/green.

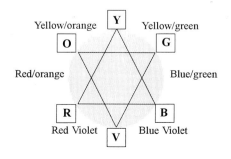

Neutrals

Browns are created by various mixtures to result in yellow/brown, red/brown, taupe, violet/brown and others. These, in addition to gray, black and white, are called "neutral" colors.

Light and Dark Colors

Adding white (water if using dye) or black to a color stretches the range of possible colors. The color choices are nearly infinite.

Add white to create a lighter shade of any color. If dyes are used water creates a lighter shade of any color. The more white or water added to a color, the lighter the color.

Adding black to a color creates a darker color. The tiniest amount of black merely grays the color, while greater amounts deepen it more intensely.

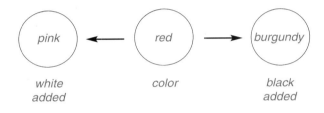

Color Relationships

For the purpose of combining fabrics in a quilt, study the relationships between colors and their successful use.

Analogous colors share characteristics. Red, red-orange and orange are united by the varying degrees of red constituted by each color. Blue-green (peacock), green-blue (teal) and green are united by the common element of green. The analogous colors naturally blend. They easily complete a color scheme by the addition of lighter shades, darker shades and neutrals.

Complimentary colors have no shared characteristics. Red and green are commonly used complimentary colors. The color green is obtained by mixing yellow and blue, neither of which appears in red—a primary or pure hue. Purple and yellow are complimentary (purple consists of red and blue and yellow is a pure hue), as are blue and orange (orange is yellow plus red and blue is a pure hue).

Complimentaries are easily found on a color wheel as direct opposites. There are also in-between complimentary hues, such as blue-violet and yellow-orange.

When placed near each other, complimentary colors tend to "clash" or reverberate. Use a complimentary to create vibrant areas in a quilt. In one antique crazy quilt I saw a fan pieced of royal blue and orange. Royal blue and orange is a striking combination! Tone down the colors to calm the vibrancy. For example, a soft combination is dusty rose used beside celery-green.

Cool colors include blues, purples and blue-greens. Cool colors tend to portray restful, calm, peaceful and relaxed feelings. Warm colors, indicative of action and passion, include reds, yellows, oranges and yellow-greens.

Neutral colors include shades of brown, gray, gray-browns (taupes), black and white. The browns are various mixtures of the pure hues mentioned above. Grays are mixtures of white and black.

When used between other colors in a quilt, browns and grays tend to create restful areas. Both prevent strong colors from overpowering. When placed between bright colors they create smooth transitions.

A balanced color scheme is the hallmark of this elegant mid- to late-19th century crazy quilt. Bright colors are softened by many neutrals. Detail. The Brick Store Museum, Kennebunk, Maine.

Observing Colors in Nature

We live in a colorful world! We are accustomed to an array of colors. How much do we actually think about them?

Many of us learned color "prejudices" at an early age. For instance, while in Kindergarten we were taught that tree trunks are brown. In reality, tree trunks are shades of gray, taupe and olive. Most unlike the blue crayon so diligently used, the colors of lake, ocean and sky are ever-changing.

Notice how nature interposes vast areas in shades such as green and blue. How much sky is there in comparison to everything else? How do these panoramas function as backdrops for the colorful accents of flowers and birds?

Looking into the distance, what happens to the colors of objects? Do they fade, pale or take on grayed shades?

Compare the effects on a particular scene on a gray day and a sunny day. Perhaps a scene through a window. What colors are shadows? Is there inspiration here to translate to a quilt, an embroidery for a patch or a color scheme?

My favorite place to observe colors is the flower garden. Each day there is something new to behold. From vivid spring crocus to heady panicled lilacs, followed by soft sprays of Baby's Breath blooming one day and fading the next, the garden is a summer-long orchestra of colors. When roses bloom, each petal is a wonder to observe. Late in summer, what a surprise when the yellow and black spider has spun its fabulous web overnight. And how a

Garden spiders appear in late summer to spin their elegant webs.

drop of dew glitters on the web. A sight to see! ... and to embroider, perhaps?

Compare the effect of a glossy-leafed plant to one with a soft, fuzzy leaf. Bring these textures to a quilt you are working on! How can you replicate them with fabric choices? Observe also the wildlife attracted to the garden. Birds and insects, butterflies, toads, each of these a study in colors and textures.

Interior decorating and clothing fads and fashions over the years have combined colors in different ways. These are also opportunities to observe and study colors. Everywhere you go, try to see how colors were used in the exteriors and interiors of buildings. Go to museums and look for how colors were once used in clothing and upholstery. Studying colors and textures will heighten your awareness and appreciation of them.

Exercise: Have you ever said "I hate that color!" ? Or is there a color that is not "your" color and you won't use it - for anything? What color is it—chartreuse, fuschia, an off-shade of green, perhaps? Find a piece of fabric in that color. Choose surrounding patch colors that look pretty to you, using neutrals if none others will do. Add a bit of lace to soften, do a little embroidery on it—a small butterfly, perhaps, or some silk ribbon roses.

Do you find yourself beginning to like a color you once thought you didn't like or couldn't use? Continue this exercise with any other disliked colors. Believe it or not, your color horizons will expand. You will start to look at colors with an eye to "where and how can I use that shade?" instead of having a "yuck" reaction.

Foundation Piecing

One theory of crazy quilting is that these quilts are a result of other quilts being patched as they wore out. Another is that the scraps left over from sewing were used as they were, simply assembled into a quilt top. Both of these ideas have been disproved through studying the quilts and the advertising of suppliers of the time. I haven't come across any "over-patching" except that done in recent times as an attempt to preserve quilts. A set of partly finished blocks that were never assembled in my collection clearly shows that crazy patching was intentional. And, both patterns for patching blocks along with the embroidery stitches to put on them, and scrap bag packages of fabrics were sold specifically for crazy quilting.

It is likely that many influences inspired crazy quilting. In the Victorian times, people were exposed to ideas and inventions and new products on almost a daily basis. In England, the great Exhibition of 1851, housed in the temporary structure, The Crystal Palace, brought together examples of the arts and industries of many nations. This was

The Whole-Quilt Style was used for this fancy Victorian crazy quilt, patched with many small patches. It measures 54 inches x 56-1/2 inches. Owned by Avalon Antiques; photographed at Arundel Antiques, Arundel, Maine. Photo by Paul Baresel.

Prince Albert's idea, a monumental event that drew phenomenal crowds, introducing people to many sights they had never seen before. Queen Victoria herself took a personal interest in things India, while trade with the Orient flourished and influenced western art and decorating trends.

Some believe that crazy patching may have been inspired by the crackled, aged glazes on antique pottery, cracked glass or

ice. Whether it is related or not, the Japanese used a method of printing textiles using finely cut paper stencils held together by fine strands of silk which the printing ink ignored. The threads formed a grid of what could be seen as oddly-shaped patches, upon which is the design. There are many other possibilities that may have inspired the "crazed" look including paving stones, stone walls, and patterns in nature.

The Foundation

Except for the Confetti method, crazy quilting consists of applying patches of varying sizes and shapes onto a foundation, a piece of fabric the size of the quilt top or block. The type of foundation to use depends on the quilt or project being made. A foundation fabric should be chosen for the drape, warmth, weight, and firmness it will add to the finished quilt or project.

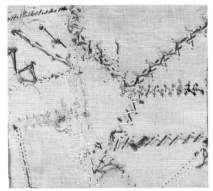

TOP PHOTO: The reverse side of a block from a crazy quilt that was never assembled clearly shows that foundation patching was intentional. The backs of the embroidery stitches, and some basting stitches indicate the Antique method of patching a crazy quilt; 9 inches square. Collection of the author.

BOTTOM PHOTO: The right side of the block.

Foundation Fabrics

Muslin

An excellent choice for beginners, 100-percent cotton muslin provides a firm base, and can be used for any type of crazy quilt, and any patching method. Keep in mind that it provides little drape if you are making a garment. Look for a quality muslin with an even grain. Cheaper muslins can come out unevenly in the wash (assuming the quilt will be washed) if the grain shifts or the fabric continually shrinks.

Batiste

A soft, finely woven, lightweight fabric, 100-percent cotton batiste is perfect for shawls, drapey quilts and clothing. To retain the drape, use soft and lightweight silks and cottons, and challis-type fabrics. Because of its softness, it is liable to bunching. This can be prevented by careful patching and pressing. The Antique or Landscape methods of patching are preferable for projects patched on batiste. Use an embroidery hoop for embroidery and embellishment.

Silk Organza

Crisp, loosely woven, and nearly weightless, silk organza is an ideal foundation for all-silk quilts. A substance from the silk worms creates a crispness that disappears when wet, and reappears as the fabric dries and is pressed. The fabric shrinks significantly in prewashing, so be sure to buy extra yardage. Lightweight silk patches placed onto it will retain their drape, making this an excellent base for silk crazy quilted clothing.

Since organza is loosely woven, use the Antique or Landscape method, squaring it up against a table edge or on a cutting mat to keep the grain even while patching. If you are making clothing, lay the pattern onto the piece periodically to check that it has not shifted out of place. After patching and basting, organza will hold its shape. Use an embroidery hoop for embroidery and sewn embellishments.

Flannel

Cotton flannel doubles as both a lightweight batting and foundation. A wool quilt pieced on flannel will be luxuriously warm, with a double-faced flannel adding slightly more loft than single-face. As with batiste, check often for bunching, because this fabric is soft, not crisp. Flannel is also an excellent choice for a jacket since it provides both drape and warmth. Any patching method can be used, taking care that the foundation stays smooth.

Fusible Interfacings

Fusing the patches to a 100-percent cotton fusible interfacing eliminates the need for basting. It is excellent for small projects such as handbags, book covers, and ornaments. I don't use it for quilts since the fusing unnaturally constricts fabrics, especially in a silk quilt since much of the beauty of silk is in its freedom of movement.

Preparing the Foundation

Prewash cottons in hot, soapy water. Wash silk organza by hand in warm water with mild soap. Rinse well, then line dry, and press. Trim off selvedges that bulge or prevent the foundation from lying flat. Cut the fabric to the size of the quilt top or block including a seam allowance of at least half an inch or more on each side. If the foundation must be pieced, instead of sewing a seam, overlap the raw edges and hand-stitch along the center of the overlap.

Quilt Sizes

Coverlets, throws, and lap robes are practical sizes for a crazy quilt. A coverlet can be the size of the top of the bed, or it can hang over the sides of the bed. Bed-size crazy quilts are easiest to make if the top is divided into blocks that are a convenient size to work on. Decide on the dimensions of the quilt, then choose a border width, and divide the remainder into blocks.

A throw can be about 50-60 inches square, and lap robes the size desired.

Any of these sizes can be used for wall hangings.

A foundation can be of any shape. This "butterfly" is thought to be an unassembled purse. Photographed at The Barn at Cape Neddick, Maine.

RIGHT: Detail of the cotton crazy quilt. Courtesy of The Kirk Collection, Omaha, NE. Photo by Nancy T. Kirk.

LEFT: This aged cotton crazy quilt consists of blocks separated by sashings. Note the border preceding the quilt's binding is not divided into blocks. Courtesy of The Kirk Collection, Omaha, NE. Photo by Nancy T. Kirk.

Quilt Styles

Antique crazy quilts were pieced as entire quilt tops, or were assembled of blocks. There was no standard size for blocks; they vary from one quilt to another from about 12 inches square to about 18 inches on average. To form the quilt top, the blocks were sewn together by machine or by hand. These seams were often finished with a simple row of Feather or Herringbone stitches on the face of the quilt.

Whole-Quilt Crazy Quilts

The Whole-quilt Method is useful for smaller quilts such as crib, lap robes, throws, and wall quilts. I like to use a square based on the width of the foundation fabric. In other words, a 44-inch wide fabric can be used to make a 44-inch square quilt.

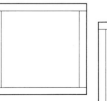

This is about the largest size I like to work on. The Piano Shawl, Victorian, Ladies and Fans, and Butterstamp quilts are made this way (see Gallery).

Laying patches onto a foundation larger than this can get a little cumbersome, but working embroidery and embellishment on them can really prove daunting. Large quilts are much easier to work on if they are first divided into blocks.

The Block Style of Crazy Quilting

For making large quilts, and for the Sew n' Flip method of patching, dividing the quilt top into blocks creates manageable portions. A large quilt can easily be made of blocks of any size. A 13-inch square of foundation will make a 12-inch block (1/2-inch seam allowances), a size that, for beginners, is easy to work on. I prefer blocks that are about 18-22 inches square.

The blocks do not have to be square, or all the same size, as long as they fit together in the end. A large central block can be surrounded by smaller ones. You can also make them as hexagons or diamonds if you like.

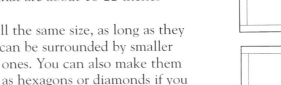

In this 1928 block-style wool quilt, the blocks are staggered. Collection of Rocky Mountain Quilts, York Village, Maine.

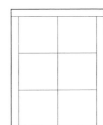

If you want the effect of a whole quilt, allow some patches to hang over the edges, then appliqué them later onto the adjoining blocks.

After the blocks are patched and embroidered, machine sew them with right sides together, then press the seams open. These seams can be embroidered with Feather or other stitching, taking care to keep the seam allowances open and flat.

Blocks can also be assembled with sashing between them, as in the Cousins Quilt.

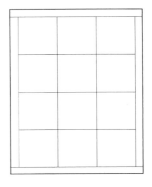

Crazy patches were machine stitched onto diamond-shaped blocks in this vintage crazy quilt. Collection of Rocky Mountain Quilts, York Village, Maine.

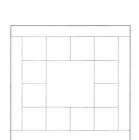

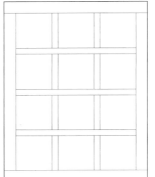

Patching the Crazy Quilt

Most antique crazy quilts were patched by hand, with the patches quilted to the foundation with embroidery stitches. This is the "Antique" Method given below. Patches can be arranged and rearranged, and an entire quilt top can be laid out before anything is fas-

This antique crazy quilt was made in long, narrow strips with velvet sashing between them. The sole embroidery is metallic chenille couched along patch edges. Note the softly rounded shapes of patches. Photographed at Gold Bug Antiques, Cape Neddick, Maine.

tened down. This method finishes to a softer appearance than machined seams, and also allows laces and trims to be added at any time before embroidering. Even though a seam may be already basted, it is easy to take out the basting, insert a trim, and then re-baste.

The "Sew n' Flip" machine method below is a common, modern method. However, embroidery has been 100 years in proving its proficiency in securing seams. In fact, on many deteriorated crazy quilts where some patches have long since disappeared, the embroidery stitches remain. There is no compelling reason to sew patches by machine unless you are making clothing that will be subjected to lots of wear and tear.

Each method has its own particular advantages. The Confetti Method can often be done the quickest, mostly because embroidery is not always needed. Choose a method that fits both the look you want to achieve and the purpose of the quilt.

Cutting Patches

Patches are not cut ahead of time. Cut each as it is needed according to the instructions for the method you are using.

What sizes to make the patches depends on personal preference, the project, and available fabric. My patch sizes are "quilt dependent," in other words larger for one quilt design, smaller for another, and mixed in yet others. If embroidery or embellishment will be added to the centers of the patches, be sure they are large enough for this. If you are a beginner, larger patches will be easier and reduce patching time. Mixing small and large patches creates variety.

Adding Laces and other Trimmings

Sew-on trims including laces, braids, ribbons, rick rack, cording, and so on should be added as the quilt is patched. Some of these must be inserted lengthwise into a seam, while others have cut ends that must be concealed. Both types should be basted or sewn into patch seams.

Battenberg and crocheted motifs are excellent additions, and can be found in craft and sewing shops often in 4" to 12" rounds and heart shapes. The larger ones can be cut in half or in sections, and placed so that cut edges are secured in the patch seams.

Beautiful, heirloom-quality trims will add a touch of elegance to a crazy quilt! Cotton net lace, cotton and rayon Venice laces, cotton eyelet, and several narrow trims are shown here.

Bunching

Bunching is my term for patches and foundation that do not lie smoothly. Either the patch was not laid evenly, or the foundation shifted, causing fabrics to ripple, bulge, or pucker. Velvets, velveteens, and other napped fabrics are sometimes the culprits. It is also common when using a sewing machine where the feed dogs move the fabric along, but the presser foot does not, resulting in a slight unevenness between top and bottom fabrics. Allowing this to happen will tend to "shrink" the finished size of the piece being worked on, making it uneven, and causing a poor fit when blocks are assembled.

To prevent bunching, be sure the foundation remains absolutely smooth (lift your work and check it), pin carefully, hand baste (see "Basting," below), and press often. When using a sewing machine, hold the fabric firmly both in front of and behind the needle while sewing.

If bunching occurs regardless of your best efforts, then make your foundation an inch or so larger than needed. If it finishes too large, then trim it to size.

Pressing

Pressing is important for each of the methods below. It assists in getting patches to lie smoothly, eliminating puckering and bulging that could otherwise occur. Use a padded surface, or lay a terry cloth towel on the ironing board to prevent seam allowances making ridges on the surfaces of the patches. Press, do not iron. Pushing the iron about can dislodge patches, and get your iron full of pin scratches. If a fabric gets a shine from pressing, then use a press cloth.

Patching Methods

Each of the following four methods comes out a little differently. A Potholder pattern follows, a small project with which you can try each of the methods.

Method 1. The Antique Method

This is the method that was most often used in antique crazy quilts. It allows for the greatest versatility in sizes and shapes of the patches. Curved shapes are easy to do, and make a softer looking quilt top than one with all angular pieces. It is sometimes easiest to begin at a corner, and work outwards from there. Patching can also be started in several different areas on the quilt, which come together as more patches are added. And, the entire quilt top can be patched before any stitching. This means you can work with the colors, re-arranging until the entire composition comes together.

The Antique Method of patching.

❶ Begin by cutting and laying a patch wherever on the foundation you'd like to begin - at a corner, an edge, or in the center.

❷ Lay a second patch underlapping or overlapping it with the first by a 1/2 inch or a little more. Repeat with the third and fourth patches. After patching a section, continue with 3, or lay the patches on the entire quilt top or block, and then proceed with 3.

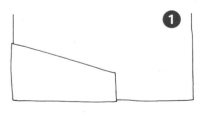

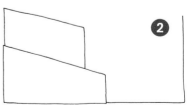

3 Go back to the first patch, and press under the overlapped edges about 1/4 inch, and pin. Continue for each patch, pressing and pinning. If there are any gaps, fit in another patch, replace a patch with a larger one, or add a piece of wide ribbon.

4 Pin on any trimmings desired, baste and embroider.

TIP: If patching becomes puzzling and you get confused over what to do next, here are some suggestions that may help.

• Take a break and come back later with a fresh mind.

• If you were painstakingly trying to fit small pieces together, set them aside and use one larger piece instead, or sew or baste several small ones together and then add them.

• Begin anew on a different area of the foundation, and work towards the original area.

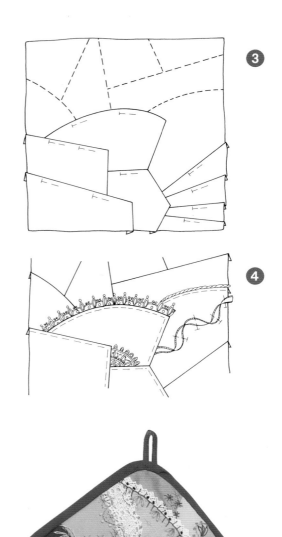

Method 2. Landscape Patching

This is a methodical method that is a little easier than the "Antique" method, because there is no figuring out which edges will be turned under. Each patch is "finished" as it is added. All raw edges are either turned under or inserted under a previous patch. Patches having 90-degree or greater angles are preferred because their corners will finish more easily. Shapes with a rounded edge are also easy to use.

Patches may tend to "landscape," creating the effect of rolling hills or mountain ranges. Varying the sizes of patches, and making some long and narrow, and some more square-shaped can downplay this, or the effect can be used for a pictorial, scenic quilt.

The Landscape Method of patching.

Lay patches as if you were painting with fabric instead of paint. Arrange and re-arrange until the composition looks "right," then pin the fabrics in place. Trims are being added to this landscape piece.

This diagram shows a landscape patched block designed to achieve the effect of rolling hills. The dashed lines indicate patches that were pieced before being added to the block. Turn the page sideways, and then upside down to see the different effects that can be achieved by the orientation of the block.

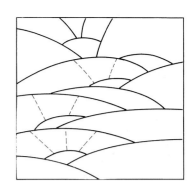

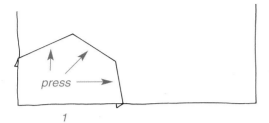

1 Beginning at one corner, cut a patch with a rounded edge, or a square with a corner removed. Press under its edges, except those that become the sides of the block.

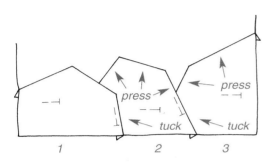

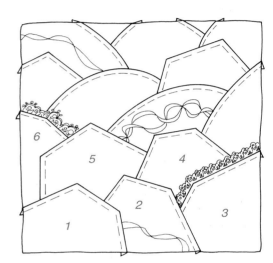

2 Cut the next patch so that one edge can be tucked and the others pressed. Insert this patch under the pressed edge of the first patch, having the remaining raw edges pressed under. Pin. Continue in this manner, trimming any excess seam allowances to about 1/4 inch.

3 Pin on any trimmings desired, baste and embroider.

Hand patching onto fusible interfacing

This is a difference in materials rather than method in which the step of basting is eliminated. Either patching method above can be used. Fusing the fabrics to interfacing creates a firm base for projects such as handbags and ornaments, in which small patches are used.

1 Substituting woven cotton fusible interfacing for the foundation fabric, have the fusible face upwards on your ironing board. Doing a small area at a time, fit a patch, then remove it from the foundation to press its edges under. Place it onto the fusible and pin. Repeat until the foundation is covered.

2 After all of the pieces are in place, fuse them, removing the pins as you press. Follow the directions with your fusible interfacing. The turned-under seam allowances that overlap onto adjoining patches will not be fused, but the patch itself will be held in place, and no further pinning or basting should be needed.

3 After fusing, trims can be inserted under the overlapped edges and basted. Finish with embroidery along patch edges.

TIP: Fusing can be used to create dimensional patches. Lay a patch-size piece of fusible face up on the ironing board. With a piece of lightweight fabric (such as silk), that is larger than the foundation, scrunch, fold, and tuck while pinning it onto the fusible. When finished, press to fasten it all down.

Basting

Basting can "make or break" a project. Done carefully, your quilt top or block will finish smoothly.

The patched block or quilt top should now be completely pinned, with trims added. Lightly press the pinned patches, making sure that everything lies smoothly. Double check that overlapping is sufficient, and no foundation shows through any gaps. Lift the entire piece to check that the foundation is smooth.

Basting is quickest and easiest if it is done on a smooth surface. To protect a table top, use a large rotary cutting mat. Do not use an unprotected dining table, it will get scratched! Lay the block or quilt top right side up on your working surface. Start in one area and work outwards.

Finger-pressing and removing pins, baste each turned-under edge. Stitches can be started and ended on the right side either with knots or one or two small stitches. Use extra pins and stitches to secure velveteen and any other napped patches.

Basting stitches can be of any size that results in a smoothly secured patch. Mine are about 1/2 inch in length.

If your block or quilt top tends to slide about on your working surface, weight it with books or other weights that won't harm the fabrics.

Patches and fans are basted and ready for embroidery in the Ladies and Fans quilt.

Techniques for Basting

① Use a Sharp size 12, or other small-eyed needle.
② Thread the needle with cotton sewing thread that is not doubled. Knot the end.
③ Take several stitches, then pull the thread through. Before each stitch, smooth the patch with your fingers, then hold fabrics down while pulling the thread through.

In stitching, the needle slides along the working surface.

Following these instructions, your basting should result in smooth, unpuckered patches and foundation, with no "shrinkage" of the piece. If a patch becomes distorted while basting, remove the stitches, press, pin, and baste again.

Method 3. Sew N' Flip

Machine Patching

Have your ironing board placed next to your sewing machine. You will want to work with blocks that are not too large or the work will quickly become difficult to handle. About a 10- to 12-inch square is a good size to begin with. Use a firm foundation such as muslin.

The Sew n' Flip Method.

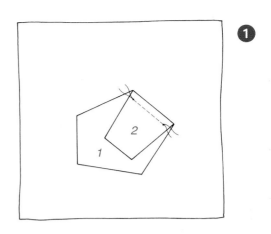

1 Begin with a 5-sided patch at the center of the block. Pin. Lay a second patch onto the first with right sides together, and sew the seam leaving 1/4 inch unsewn at each end. Do not backstitch, since occasionally part of a seam may need to be opened up later on.

2 Add each patch in this manner, trimming out any excess from previous patches. Where edges cannot be sewn by machine, turn them under and press. These edges can later be slipstitched, or held in place with embroidery. Remember to add any trimmings that will be sewn into seam allowances.

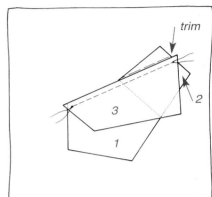

3 It is easiest to have all patches straight-sided (no curved or shaped pieces), and cut into triangular or long, sloping rectangular shapes. As patches are added they often have a tendency to become larger or longer. Two or more patches can be pieced together before they are added.

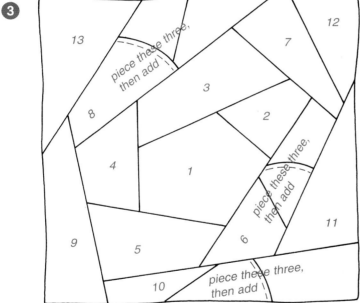

Method 4. "Confetti" Piecing

I enjoy this much more than the Sew n' Flip method. It is quicker, easy, and less puzzling. If you need to make something in a hurry, this is the method to use. It is done completely by machine, without a foundation, and results in all straight seams. Laces and trimmings are not sewn into the seams since they will create too much bulk. A great method for a kid's quilt, it makes a sturdy fabric that will hold up to washing and wear. Cotton fabrics are recommended. In order to understand how the method works, do a "test run" with scrap fabrics.

Use 1/4-inch seam allowances, pressing to one side.

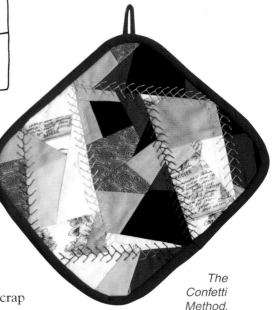

The Confetti Method.

1 Sew together two large patches that are about 9 by 11 inches or so. Press. Add a patch to each end as shown in the following diagram, sew, and press.

2 Cut the piece in half along a straight line. To obtain a straight line, fold the piece and press a crease, or use a pencil and a ruler.

3 Turn the two pieces, and rejoin by sewing, having right sides together. Press.

4 Cut again, and rejoin. When rejoining pieces, it is not necessary to rejoin at an edge. With right sides together, add anywhere onto the piece, then trim off the excess. Rejoin the trimmed-off piece to another area.

To have more than four colors, make two pieces as in 1, using different colors for each. Sew them together, then cut and rejoin. Do this several more times to scramble the two parts.

Finish to have as near a square as possible.

To form a square block, cut a piece of foundation or paper the size of the block, including seam allowances. Align the foundation or paper on top of the sewn piece so it most nearly covers it. Trim off any edges that protrude. Sew the trimmed pieces back on, and continue until the sewn piece is the same size as the block.

Make the required number of blocks for your quilt.

Embroidery along patch seams is optional especially if the patches are very small. A few plain feather stitches can be worked along some of the major seams if desired, although if printed fabrics were used, the quilt may be fancy enough. If the piece will be embroidered by hand or by machine, first baste a piece of foundation to the back of it to cover the seams.

Making a Pattern

For all patching methods except Confetti, a pattern can easily be made for the patches on a block. You can use one pattern for all of the blocks in a quilt, making each look different with embroidery and embellishment, and turning them to face in different directions when assembling the quilt top. Otherwise, a pattern can be drawn for each block, each with its own patch arrangement.

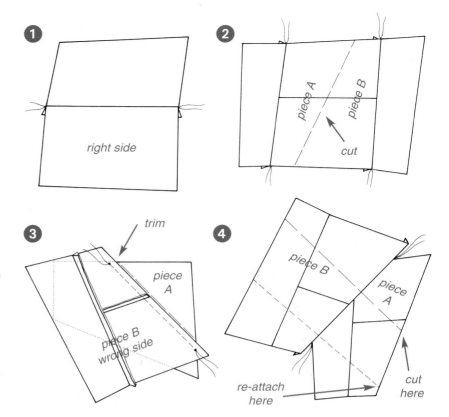

Patterns can be made, or blocks can be patched simply as in this antique wool quilt. These blocks are about 11-1/2 inches square. Detail. Owned by Avalon Antiques, photographed at Arundel Antiques, Arundel, Maine. Photo by Paul Baresel.

To make a pattern:

1 You will need a piece of paper the size of the finished block (without seam allowances). You may need to tape sheets of paper together first.

2 Using the Victorian Stitches plates in the following chapter for block ideas, sketch patch outlines onto the paper. Use a ruler for the straight lines, and freehand the curves. Erase and re-work lines until you have a balanced arrangement.

3 Number each patch. On a separate sheet of paper, sketch a small diagram showing the approximate shapes of the patches, and enter the numbers given each. Set aside the diagram.

4 Cut out the paper patches. Place them onto the patch fabrics with right sides up. Adding a seam allowance of at least 1/4 inch around each, cut out the patches.

5 Cut out the foundation fabric adding a seam allowance of 1/2 inch all around. Following the diagram, place each patch in its numbered place on the foundation. Continue according to the patching method of your choice.

Patched and ready for embroidery and embellishment, the Ladies and Fans quilt-in-progress is clothes-pinned to hangers for viewing.

Viewing Your Work

After the patches are basted onto the foundation of a quilt top or block, I like to hang up the piece, to be able to view it from a distance. An easy way to do that is to clip it to coat hangers using smooth spring-type clothespins. Use as many hangers as needed, and bend the tops so they fit over a door or curtain rod. This is also a good way to store the piece when you are not working on it. Be sure to keep your work out of direct sunlight and away from heat sources.

Potholders Pattern

This pattern is for making four potholders, a small format for trying each of the above patching methods. After making one block of each, it will be easier to decide which to use for quilts and other projects.

Finished size of each: 8-1/2-inches square

Materials:

four 9-inch squares of muslin for foundation
eight or more cotton patch fabrics
cotton laces as desired for methods 1, 2, and 3
four 9-inch squares of 100-percent cotton batting
four 9-inch squares of cotton or linen backing fabric
size 8 pearl cotton, 8 or more colors
five yards of 1/2-inch wide double fold bias tape, matching
  thread

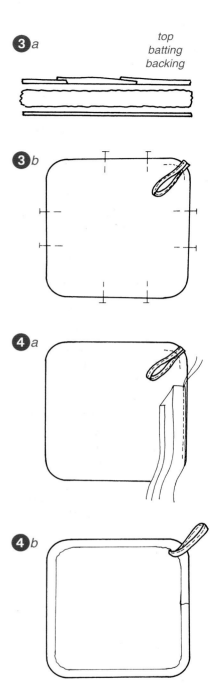

Use a 1/4-inch seam allowance throughout.
Instructions:

1 If desired, round the corners of each muslin, and also those of the batting and backing pieces. Apply patches to each using the Antique method for one, Landscape for another, and Sew n' Flip for the third. Add cotton laces as desired. Construct a fourth using the Confetti method, basting the foundation on afterwards.

2 Embroider, following instructions for Victorian Stitches following. The Confetti potholder may be left plain, or several rows of feather-stitching can be worked along major seams.

3 Assemble the layers with wrong sides together; quilted top, then batting, followed by backing, and pin. Sew a loop for each potholder made of the bias tape, and baste to one corner of each, or add a bone ring afterwards.

4 Open out the bias tape and sew it with right sides together about 1/4 inch from the edge of the potholder. Ease the bias at the corners so it will turn smoothly. Overlap and fold the raw end under. Fold the bias to the back, press, and slipstitch.

Victorian Stitches

Both practical and aesthetic, the rows of embroidery stitches along the patch seams of antique crazy quilts fasten the patches to each other, and at the same time quilt them to the foundation fabric. Although many Victorian crazy quilts featured a single row of feather or herringbone stitches along each seam, the more beautiful ones have a wide variety of stitches, and sometimes multiple rows along each seam. The jewel-like patterning of some of these fancier quilts makes them almost seem to sparkle.

According to Betsey Telford of Rocky Mountain Quilts in York, Maine, the mark of excellence in Victorian crazy quilting was for the needleworker to make at least one hundred different embroidery stitches on a quilt. I think where they ran out of stitches, they made them up!

Threads for Crazy Quilting

When I first began crazy quilting more than 12 years ago, there were only a few variety threads available, and they were hard to find. Now, there are so many it can be difficult to choose, a clear indication of the unrivaled growth of interest and creativity in the needlearts!

Collect a variety of the wonderful thread types available, and try them. You're sure to find some that will become your favorites.

Threads follow the same fiber descriptions as those given for fabric types in chapter two. As with fabrics, the natural

This detail of a circa 1880's crazy quilt shows a range of embroidery stitches. The Brick Store Museum, Kennebunk, Maine.

fibers silk, cotton, wool, and the earliest synthetic, rayon, can be found in various types and finishes. Synthetic and variety threads are also available including those with metallic shine, and some that are "borrowed" from the knitting department such as chenille and kid mohair.

Silk, rayon, and metallic threads are spun of many shorter fibers, or made of long, singular filaments. Cotton and wool threads are always spun, since their fibers by nature are short. Spun fibers are usually more matte in finish, while filaments display more sheen.

TIP: A Ply is a ply, and a strand is a strand. These two terms are often confused with each other. A ply is a single fiber or thread made of a filament such as silk or rayon, or spun of shorter fibers such as cotton or wool. As an example, sewing thread is one strand, however, when you untwist the end, you can see

that the thread divides into separate plies. Plies are not normally meant to be separated.

A strand is one thread of several that are placed together to form a multi-strand skein such as six-strand embroidery floss. Each strand may consist of several plies.

Both twist and number of plies give a thread its strength.

Working with Silk Threads

Twisted types such as Soie Perlee can snag, pulling one ply loose, and causing the thread to appear to disintegrate right before your eyes. If this should happen, hold the thread vertically and drop the needle to the base, where it comes through the fabric. Run your fingers upwards along the thread several times, smoothing it until the plies become even. Bring the needle back up and continue stitching.

Stripping is a way of preparing silk floss for embroidery when more than one strand is used in the needle. Cut a working length of the floss, and individually pull out as many strands as will be used, then lay them smoothly back together again. This allows the full sheen of the thread to show, and helps embroidery stitches such as Satin Stitch lie smoothly. Cotton and rayon flosses also benefit from stripping.

Working with Rayon Threads

Twisted rayon threads such as Pearl Crown benefit from giving the thread a quick snap. First, cut a working length of thread, then hold both ends of it and give a sharp tug, just enough to relax the thread. This helps prevent tangling.

Rayon flosses should be stripped the same as silks as explained above. Some rayon threads, especially skeined flosses appear "kinky" as they are removed from a skein. To remove the kinks, run the thread over a damp paper towel and allow it to dry before using.

Tangling

Tangling can occur with any threads used in hand stitching. Hold up your work and allow the thread to dangle and untwist occasionally. Also, as you embroider, place your left thumb (if you are right-handed) on the thread about 1 inch from where it comes through the fabric. Then, as the stitch is made, release the thread at the last instant.

The "Stab" Method

If threads tend to wear quickly as they are pulled through fabrics, do not "sew" them. Make the stitch in parts, first bringing the needle down through the fabric and pulling the thread through. Then bring the needle up and pull through.

Preparation of Hands

Anyone who enjoys both gardening and embroidery knows that you can't just pick up your embroidery upon coming in from the garden. Threads, especially silks and rayons will snag on rough fingers and fingernails.

Thickly apply a non-greasy hand lotion, rub it in thoroughly, then buff your hands on a clean towel until they feel smooth and dry. Keep an emery board with your sewing things to smooth rough spots on your fingers and nails that appear while stitching.

Thread types

Twisted Threads for Patch Seam Embroidery.

There are three thread types I use almost exclusively for patch seam embroidery. These are Size 8 Pearl Cotton, Soie Perlee, and Pearl Crown Rayon. These can be mixed and matched on one quilt, or used cotton on cotton, silk on silk, and rayon thread on rayon patch fabrics.

Pearl cotton is an all-cotton thread available in a wide color range in skeins or larger spools. Size 8 is ideal for crazy patch embroidery. Pearl cottons are available in other weights including the finer Size 12, and the heavier Size 5. There are several different manufacturers of this thread.

My favorite silk thread for crazy patch embroidery is Soie Perlee, ideal for embroidery on fancy or silk crazy quilts. Slightly finer than the Size 8 Pearl Cotton, it comes on 11-yard spools. It is a modern-day counterpart to the silk buttonhole twist once available from Belding Corticelli. The buttonhole twist seems to have gone out of style, with buttonholes seldom made by hand anymore. Twisted silks are also available

Twisted threads impart an unrivaled texture and definition to stitches worked along patch seams. Included here are Kreinik Soie Perlee and Silk Serica®, DMC® size 8 pearl cotton, Pearl Crown Rayon, Needle Necessities' Pearl 8 Overdyed.

in other weights, such as the finer Soie Gobelin, ideal for miniature work and fine outline embroidery, and the heavier Silk Serica®, similar to Size 5 Pearl Cotton.

Pearl Crown Rayon is a twisted 100-percent rayon thread available on 100-yard spools, and similar in thickness to the Size 8 Pearl Cotton. I like this thread for its high sheen, and find it excellent for most quilts. Fewer colors are available, but it can be used in combination with other thread types. It has a high sheen and shows up brilliantly.

Threads for Other Uses

Flower thread is a matte-finish twisted cotton similar in weight to Size 12 Pearl Cotton. Use it for fine outline embroidery, miniature crazy quilts, monograms, cross stitch embroidery, and sampler work. Flower thread and Size 12 Pearl Cotton were used to embroider the Kate Greenaway figures on the Cousins quilt.

Flosses are multi-stranded skeined threads that can be separated for use, and are available in cotton, silk, rayon, wool, or metallic fibers. In crazy quilting, flosses are excellent for Satin Stitch embroideries on patch centers, and useful as the filler thread for couching. Flosses are not the best threads for patch edge embroidery, since the stitches will not be well defined, lacking the texture of twisted threads.

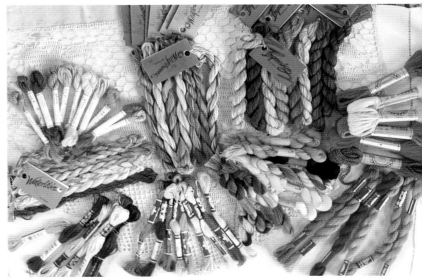

A collection of threads for hand embroidery including flosses: Kreinik's Soie D'Alger, The Caron Collection Waterlilies®, DMC® Rayon Floss.
Flower threads: The Caron Collection's Wildflowers®, DMC® Flower Thread , Wool threads: Impressions®(wool/silk), Needle Necessities' Overdyed French Wool; DMC® Medici wool, Paternayan® Persian wool.

Wool threads can be used for wool embroidery, punchneedle, needlepoint, and embroidery along patch seams in wool crazy quilts. Paternayan® Persian wool, spun for crewel embroidery and needlepoint, is an excellent thread for these purposes. DMC® Broder Medici, and Needle Necessities' Overdyed French Wool are finer threads in multi-stranded skeins ideal for outline, satin stitch, or single-strand fine embroidery.

Some knitting wools can be used for embroidery. Test them by working some embroidery stitches to be sure they are strong enough. Those that are loosely spun, although fine for knitting, will pull apart if used for embroidery. Any knitting wool can be couched.

Metallic threads often consist of a tinsel-like strand that is spun, plied, or wound around a core of nylon or other fiber. There are many different makes and types, from one-ply filaments to twisted threads and flosses, cordings, and ribbons in different weights and thicknesses. "Blending filaments"

are extremely fine and are meant to be knotted into the needle alongside a second thread of another type.

Rarely do metallics embroider easily. Use short lengths for those that can be pulled through fabric. Metallic threads can be couched to make wonderful spiderwebs!

Linen threads with their unique luster used mainly for hardanger and lacemaking, can also be used creatively in embroidery. Green Mountain Hand-dyed Linens offers linen threads that are

Some variety threads can be sewn through fabric, others can be couched. From left to right: Needle Necessities' Charleston, Kreinik metallic ribbons and Japan Gold, Green Mountain's hand-dyed linen thread and Kid Mohair, and DMC® metallic flosses.

hand dyed in natural dyes in a range of exquisite colors.

Yarns made of exotic fibers from angora (bunny), alpaca, mohair (goat), and other animals can often be found in knitting shops. Use them in creative embroideries, for portraying animals, and for couching along patch seams. As with any knitting yarns, be sure they are strong enough for embroidery.

Chenille is a yarn with a pile spun into its core threads. Very popular Victorian embroidery materials, chenilles were couched as filler in embroideries, and along seams of crazy patches. Victorian instructions say to test them for strength before using. Now, as then, run them through your fingers to be sure they hold together well.

Learning the stitches

Most embroidery stitches are easy to learn, although some may appear more complicated than they actually are. Beginners can learn the stitches in the following order from simple to more complicated: Running and Straight, Blanket, Fly, Chain, Lazy Daisy, Outline, Feather, Herringbone, Fishbone, French Knot, Bullion.

On scrap fabric, try making each stitch in very small to very large sizes, then it will be easier to settle on an appropriate size for your own preference. Practice each stitch many times until you feel comfortable and at ease with it.

Scatter your stitching over a quilt top or block, rather than beginning in one area and moving on from there. That way, one area will not stand out if your stitching changes. The same technique can be used to evenly distribute a thread color over a quilt top.

Beginners often find it difficult to make stitches evenly in rows. This is easier if you establish a rhythm as you work. It is often, however, the unevenly-

RIGHT: This Oriental silk embroidery is a gorgeous example of satin stitch embroidery. Collection of Paul Baresel.

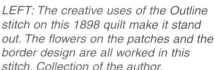

LEFT: If you learn only one stitch, such as the plain Feather Stitch, that is all you really need to complete a quilt top. After achieving proficiency with one stitch, try learning another. Antique block, 9 inches square; collection of the author.

LEFT: The creative uses of the Outline stitch on this 1898 quilt make it stand out. The flowers on the patches and the border design are all worked in this stitch. Collection of the author.

RIGHT: One way to learn the stitches is to work them on an even-weave fabric, using the weave to help make even stitches. This sampler of crazy-quilting stitches was done in size 8 pearl cotton, with the monogram worked in size 12, and embellished with Whimsey seed beads and glass heart beads from Wichelt Imports, Inc. The background fabric is the color, "Spun Silver," a 28-count 100-percent linen also from Wichelt Imports, Inc.

made stitches that are most interesting to look at. Unevenness also becomes less visible as more stitching is added to the quilt.

Thread lengths to use depends on how well a thread holds up to being pulled through the fabric. Use short lengths of about 18 inches for most metallics, silks, and some rayons. Most cottons can be used in one-yard lengths.

If a thread frays at the eye of the needle, pull it a little through the needle and trim off the frayed end. Be sure the needle's eye is smooth. If not, discard the needle.

Ripping out is an essential part of doing needlework of almost any type. If you don't like the stitches you've made, it's better to re-do them or start over with a different stitch or thread. If you leave them in, they will be the focal point of the quilt every time you look at it, although others will be less likely to notice.

About Machine Embroidery

Although antique crazy quilts were embroidered by hand, machine embroidery can be done on modern crazy quilts. Almost any type of sewing machine can be used. The many different techniques include using a heavier thread or silk ribbon in the bobbin (sewn with the piece upside down), free-form darning with the feed dogs lowered, appliqué, couching, cording, built-in embroidery stitch cams, computerized and programmable embroidery stitches, and so on. If you'd like

to try this, your machine's manual will specify what your machine can do.

Machine stitching has a much different character to that of handwork. Try working small samples of each to compare the difference. The machine pulls the layers of fabric tightly together, and places a great many stitches where hand embroidery uses many fewer. Closely placed zig zagging, a common form of machine embroidery, results in a hard, flat surface, compared to the soft and flexible dimensionality of hand stitches. You can choose a method based on either your preference or the use of the finished project.

Catherine Carpenter of Massachusetts designed and stitched a true labor of love in a needlework created for her grand-daughter, Leah C. Carpenter. This waterfall detail demonstrates proficient use of basic embroidery stitches. Photo by Richard Carpenter.

The benefits of hand embroidery.

Some years ago, I spent hours running the sewing machine at high speed to quilt a kimono jacket by zig zagging narrow rayon ribbons onto it. Since then, I've put the machine aside and have embroidered over a dozen quilts, a jacket, and many small projects by hand. And I'm fully convinced that hand embroidery has advantages that machine work cannot touch. These include the pleasures and comforts of stitching away while sitting in the sun in a backyard Adirondack chair, a Victorian rocker on the front porch, in front of the TV in the parlor, my studio on a Sunday morning listening to jazz, and even on camping trips seated on the ground. This is embroidery as it was many years ago, in the company of family and friends.

Note the unusual stitches on this antique crazy quilt block! Collection of Rocky Mountain Quilts, York Village, Maine.

Embroidery Stitch Instructions

BLANKET STITCH—Come up through the fabric at A, and stitch from B to C. The thread is kept under the needle. Working towards the right, stitch from D to E for the following stitch. Repeat. End a row with a short tacking stitch.

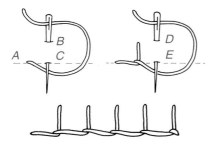

BUTTONHOLE STITCH—Work the same as for the Blanket Stitch, making the stitches very close together.

BLANKET FAN—This is easiest to work upside-down. Use the same hole in the fabric for the top of each stitch, making as many stitches as desired. Finish the fan with a Straight stitch.

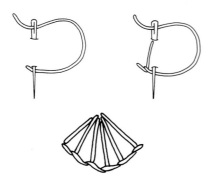

Blanket stitching was used to secure heart-shaped appliqués, in addition to patch-seam embroidery.

CLOSED OR CROSSED BUTTONHOLE —Slant the upper parts of the stitches together in pairs, meeting at the top for the Closed, and overlapping for the Crossed Buttonhole.

DETACHED BUTTONHOLE—Make a Straight Stitch, then work Buttonhole Stitch onto it without piercing the fabric. The Buttonhole Stitch can be worked onto any existing stitch, such as Straight stitch with one making a delicate leaf, and several worked in a circular fashion making a rose.

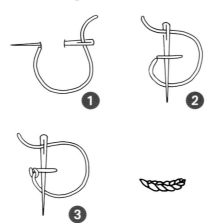

EYELET—Draw a small circle inside a larger one on the fabric. Work the Buttonhole stitch around.

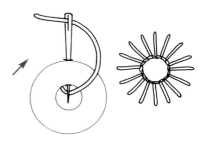

KNOTTED BUTTONHOLE—Wrap the thread once around the needle in the opposite direction of a French Knot, pull snug, and finish the stitch.

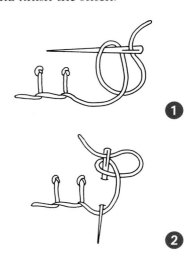

BULLION KNOT—It may take a few tries to learn these, but once you do, they are both fun and easy to make. Come through the fabric at A. Insert the needle from B to A, do not pull through. Wrap the end of the needle evenly enough times to cover the distance between A and B. Hold onto the wraps while pulling the needle through, and continue to hold them until the thread is completely pulled through. Bring the needle down at B. The wraps may be adjusted by tugging on the thread slightly, or by stroking the stitch with the needle.

The Bullion stitch lends itself well to wool embroidery, as here on the Horses and Roses quilt.

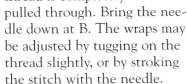

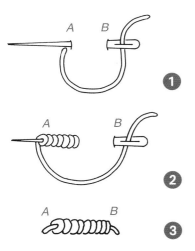

BULLION ROSE—Begin with three short Bullions placed in a triangle. Surround them with longer Bullions in a circular fashion.

LOOPED BULLION—Make the wrapped part of the stitch at least twice as long as the distance between A and B.

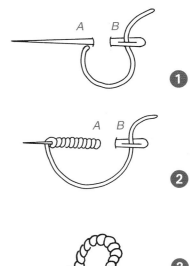

CHAIN STITCH—Come through the fabric at A, and stitch from B to C. Repeat as shown, working towards the left. End with a short tacking stitch.

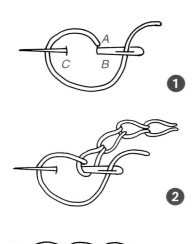

The Chain Stitch and variations of it form an excellent base for additional stitches.

MAGIC CHAIN—Thread the needle with two different types or colors of thread. Working the Chain Stitch, separate the two threads and use one of them to make the first stitch, then the other for the following stitch. Repeat.

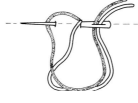

CHAIN STITCH ROSE—Beginning at the center, work the Chain Stitch in a circular fashion until the rose is the size desired.

CABLE CHAIN—Make one Chain Stitch, wrap the thread once around the needle, pull snug, and make the following Chain Stitch not into the first stitch, but just past it. If you are accustomed to making the French Knot, wrap this stitch in the opposite direction.

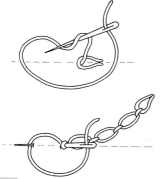

OPEN CHAIN—Come up at A, then stitch from B to C. To begin the following stitch, insert the needle at D, and repeat. End with two tacking stitches to hold the loop open.

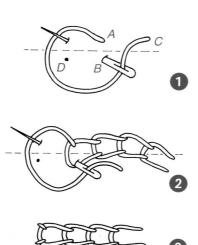

TWISTED CHAIN STITCH—Come up on the line at A. Stitch from B to C having the thread go over, then under the needle. Repeat.

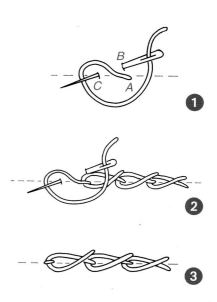

CORAL STITCH–Make a short slanting stitch, having the thread go over, then under the needle. Keep the thread snug while pulling through. Repeat, working towards the left.

CORAL KNOT–Make a short, vertical stitch, wrap the thread over, then under the needle. Pull snug, and pull through. Finish with a short tacking stitch. These can be made in a row, or scattered.

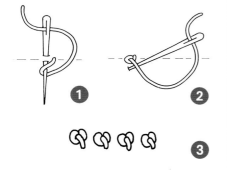

CORAL KNOTTED HERRINGBONE–First make a row of Herringbone Stitch. Fasten on a second thread and work Coral Stitch over the crossed parts of the Herringbone without piercing the fabric.

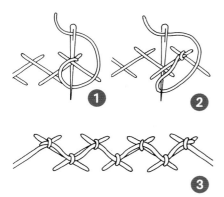

The Zigzag Coral stitch in the Ladies and Fans quilt.

KNOTTED CABLE CHAIN STITCH–this is a combination of Coral, lacing, and Chain stitch. 1. Come up at A, and stitch from B to C to make a Coral Knot. 2. Slide the needle under the thread between A and B without piercing the fabric, and pull through. 3. Insert the needle at D, come up at E having the thread go under the needle. Repeat from 1.

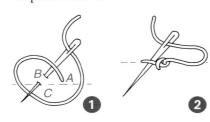

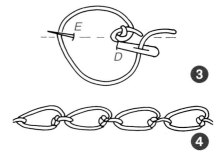

LONG-ARMED SINGLE CORAL STITCH–Make these in rows, clusters, or individually. 1. Come up on the line at A. Insert the needle from B to C, do not pull through. Wrap the thread over, then under the needle as shown. Pull snug, then bring the needle through. 2. Go down at D, just beneath the stitch.

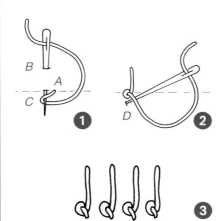

ZIG ZAG CORAL STITCH–1. Make a Coral Stitch at the top of the row. 2. Wrap the thread over the needle, then make a second Coral Stitch wrapping the thread in the opposite direction as shown. Repeat from 1.

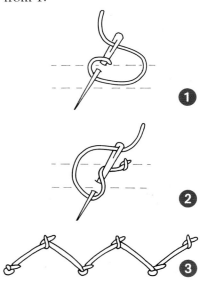

COUCHING. Fasten on the thread to be couched, or secure its ends under patch seams. With a second thread, stitch over the couched thread and through the fabric. Use short Straight stitches, or any embroidery stitch that will secure the couched fibers.

FILLER COUCHING—Long stitches used to fill in an area can be couched at intersections or at intervals to hold them in place.

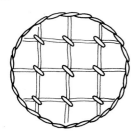

Couching with French Knots and buttons holds ribbons in place on the Victorian quilt.

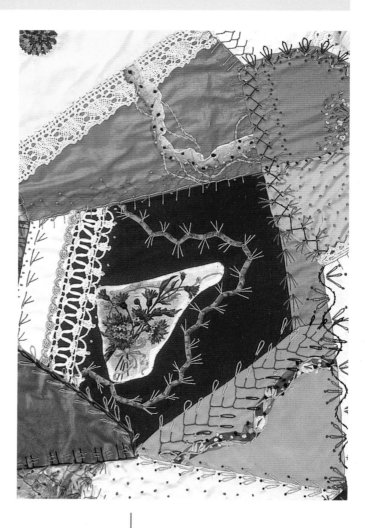

SHEAF STITCH—Make three vertical Straight Stitches, then make a short tacking stitch in the middle.

THORN STITCH—1. Make a long stitch of a heavy thread, shaping it into a curve. 2. With a lighter thread, come up at A, and stitch from B to C, then go down at D. Repeat, spacing the stitches as evenly as possible.

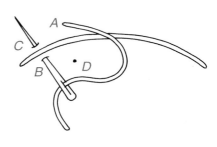

CRETAN STITCH. Working vertically, come up at A. 1. Stitch from B to C with the thread under the needle. 2. Stitch from D to E. Repeat 1 and 2, working first to one side, then the other of an imaginary line, always having the needle pointed towards the center of the stitching. This stitch can be worked closely or spread apart.

The Cretan stitch is one of several that make an ideal base row along patch and border seams.

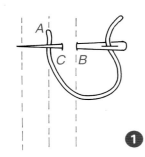

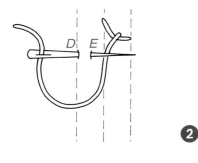

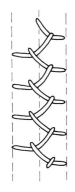

CLOSED CRETAN—Begin by drawing a leaf shape onto the fabric, then follow instructions for the Cretan Stitch, beginning narrow and widening at the center.

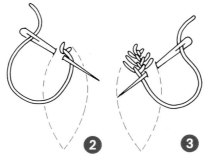

RAISED CRETAN—work two rows of backstitch evenly. Without piecing the fabric work the Cretan Stitch between them. The backstitches can be arranged to form leaf shapes.

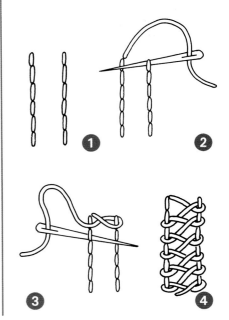

CROSS STITCH. Come up at A, then down at B. Then come up at C and go down at D to make a Single Cross Stitch. To form a row of Cross Stitch, work the A to B part of the stitch across the row, turn, and work back along the row with the C to D part of the stitch.

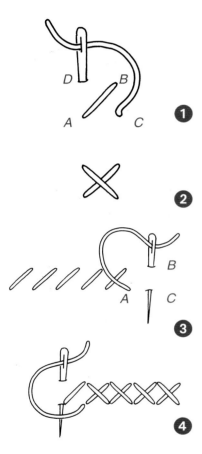

MOSS STITCH—This stitch was invented by Marion Nichols, the author of *Encyclopedia of Embroidery Stitches* (see Bibliography). 1. Make one Cross Stitch as above, bringing the needle up at A, above the stitch. 2. Form a loop, then place the needle over the loop and under the cross stitch without piercing the fabric. Pull

through and go down at B below the stitch.

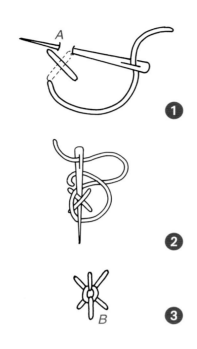

VICTORIAN FRINGE STITCH—Double the thread in the needle. Fasten on to the back of the fabric and bring the needle up between A and B. 1. Hold the thread with your thumb as shown, and stitch from A to B. 2. Then stitch from C to D, and bring the needle down at A. Begin the following stitch between B and E, and use the same holes as B and D. Keep the stitches consistent in size. The loops can be left as they are, or trimmed.

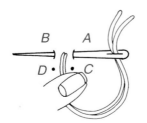

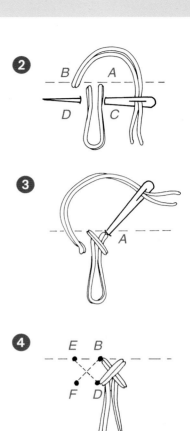

STAR STITCH—Make one Cross Stitch on top of another as shown. A small tacking stitch can be added at the center. Make the "arms" of equal or unequal length.

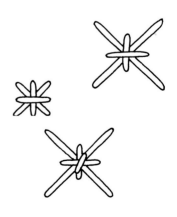

FEATHER STITCH. Working vertically along an imaginary line, come up at A. 1. Make a short, slanting stitch from B to C having the thread under the needle. 2. Make the following stitch from D to E, and repeat 1 and 2. End with a short tacking stitch.

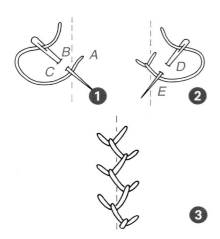

Feather Stitch is an excellent stitch for patch and border seams.

CHAINED FEATHER STITCH—This stitch consists of Long-stemmed Lazy Daisy Stitches in a Feather Stitch formation. Make a Lazy Daisy Stitch, then bring the needle down at the end of the stem, and up at the top of the next Lazy Daisy. Repeat.

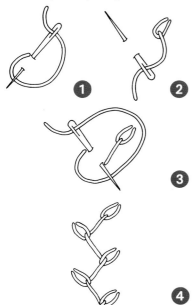

DOUBLE FEATHER STITCH—Begin the same as for the Feather Stitch, then make an extra "arm" on each side of the stitch. A triple feather can be made by adding yet another "arm" to each side. The arms are worked the same as Blanket Stitch.

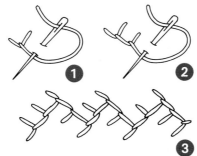

STACKED FEATHER STITCH—Make the Feather Stitch in a leaf-shape, making the stitches close together. A quick way to make leaves! You can begin by drawing a leaf shape onto the fabric, or make them freehand.

STRAIGHT-SIDED FEATHER STITCH—Make this stitch the same as the Feather Stitch, but with vertical "arms."

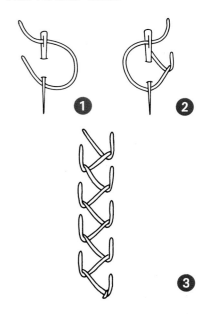

FERN STITCH. There are two ways to make this stitch. It is more quickly formed by beginning with a vertical Straight Stitch followed by a series of Fly stitches.

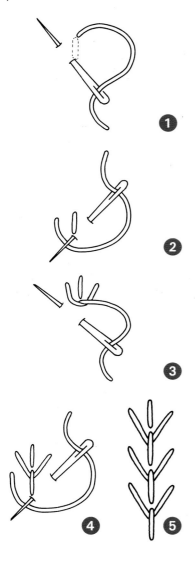

The Fern Stitch is used around an appliqué on the Butterstamp Quilt.

STRAIGHT STITCH FERN—Arrange triads of Straight Stitches one above another.

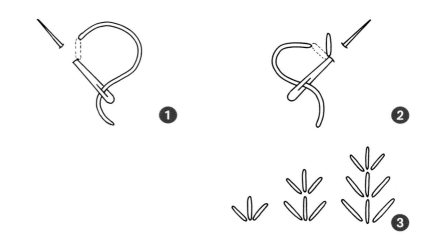

FISHBONE STITCH. First, make a vertical Straight Stitch. Then come up at A, and stitch from B to C. The following stitch is made in the same way in the opposite direction. The stitches will overlap slightly along an imaginary center line.

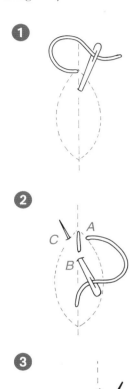

The Closed Fishbone Stitch is used for placing leaf shapes along patch seams, and with roses.

OPEN FISHBONE—This is easiest done by following a drawn line on the fabric. Bring the needle up at A, just to the left of the line. 1. Stitch from B to C. 2. Stitch from D to E having the thread over the needle. 3. Repeat from 1, working downwards.

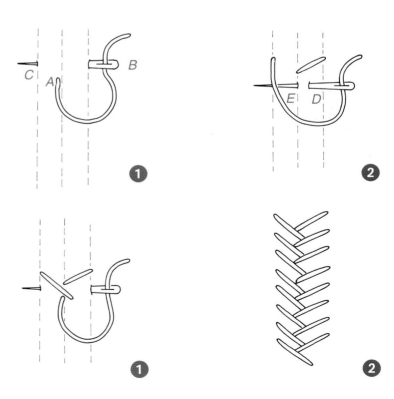

FLY STITCH. Come up at A, and stitch from B to C. Finish with a short tacking stitch. The Fly Stitch can be varied by making the tacking stitch differently–use a French Knot, a small Lazy Daisy, or continue the tacking stitch into Outline stitch.

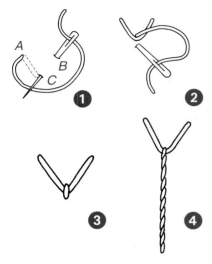

Fly Stitch is one of few stitch types used on this 1898 crazy quilt. These are scattered on a patch. Detail. Collection of the author.

LONG-STEMMED FLY–Make a longer tacking stitch.

CROWN STITCH–Make a wide and shallow Long-stemmed Fly, then add two Straight Stitches.

TÊTE DE BOEUF–This is actually Fly Stitch that is tacked with a Lazy Daisy stitch. The name means "head of the bull." It is sometimes called "Wheat-ear" Stitch.

STACKED FLY STITCH–Make a series of Fly stitches vertically.

FRENCH KNOT. 1. Come up at A. Wrap the thread around the needle once, pull snug. 2. Bring the needle through the fabric at B. Follow the direction of the thread as shown. If wrapped in the wrong direction, the stitch can slip through and disappear. Wrapping the thread two, three or more times around the needle will make a larger stitch.

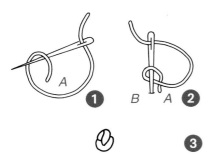

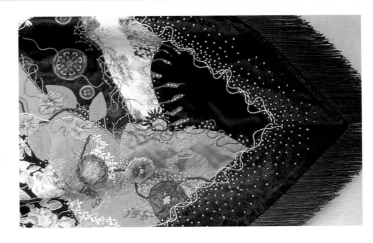

A favorite stitch, the French Knot adds much character to the Piano Shawl.

CONTINUOUS FRENCH KNOT—Form the stitch the same as the French Knot, except finish by making a short stitch, and repeat. Work towards the left. Place the stitches farther apart to make Continuous Pistil Stitch.

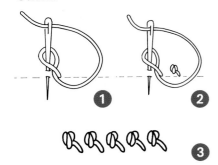

FOUR-LEGGED KNOT STITCH—This is a combination of Cross Stitch and French Knot. Come up at A. 1. Stitch from B to C. 2. Slide the needle under the stitch without piercing the fabric, and loop the thread around the needle. Pull snug, and pull the needle through. 3. Bring the needle down at D.

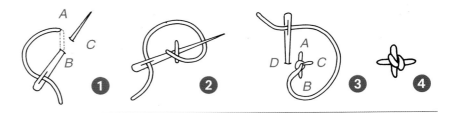

ITALIAN KNOTTED BORDER STITCH—This stitch is actually an elongated Fly Stitch tacked with a French Knot. Come up at A. 1. Stitch from B to C. 2. Form a French Knot. Make the following stitch to the right of the first.

PISTIL STITCH—Form this stitch the same as the French Knot, but sink the thread further away.

HERRINGBONE STITCH. Working towards the right, hold the needle horizontal to the row of stitching, having it pointed towards the previous stitch. 1. Come up at A. At the top of the row, stitch from B to C. 2. At the bottom of the row, stitch from D to E. Repeat 1 and 2.

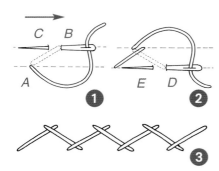

The Herringbone, along with the Feather Stitch, are two of the most common stitches found on antique crazy quilts, such as on this block. They were treated as utilitarian stitches, most often used to hold patches in place. Collection of the author.

CLOSED HERRINGBONE—Make the same as the Herringbone Stitch, but have the stitches meet at the top and bottom of the row. Another way to form this stitch is to work a row of regular Herringbone, then another over it, staggering the stitches to have the second row worked into the spaces left by the first.

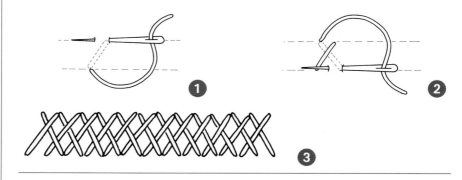

BRETON STITCH—Come up at A, at the bottom of the row. 1. Stitch from B to C. 2. Slide the needle behind the stitch just made without piercing the fabric, and pull through. 3. Stitch from E to D. "E" is at the center line of the following stitch. Repeat steps 1 through 3.

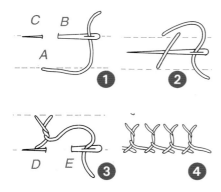

CHEVRON STITCH—Come up at A. 1. With the thread above the needle, stitch from B to C at the top of the row. 2. Stitch from D to E at the bottom of the row keeping the thread above the needle. 3. With the thread below the needle, stitch from F to D. Repeat steps 1 through 3.

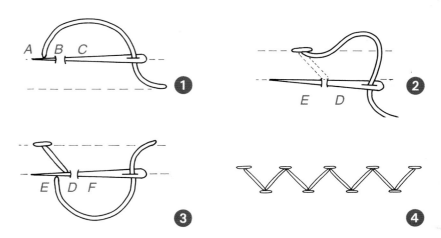

LAZY DAISY STITCH. Come up at A. Stitch from B to C. Finish with a short tacking stitch. This stitch can be varied by using a French Knot, or smaller Lazy Daisy for the tacking stitch, or by making a smaller Lazy Daisy inside a larger one. A Bullion stitch can also be used for the tacking stitch.

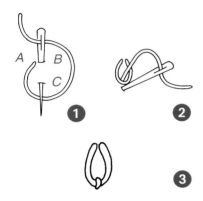

DETACHED TWISTED CHAIN–Follow instructions for the Twisted Chain Stitch, but instead of repeating the stitch, finish with two small tacking stitches.

LONG-STEMMED LAZY DAISY STITCH–Make the tacking stitch longer.

Lazy Daisies almost always seem to have "flower appeal" including here on the Butterstamp Quilt.

BASQUE STITCH–This stitch is worked towards the right. 1. Come up at A, and insert the needle from B to C, do not pull through. 2. Wrap the thread around both ends of the needle as shown, pull snug, and pull through. 3. Insert the needle just beneath the stitch just made, and come up at B. Repeat, forming the following stitch between D and E.

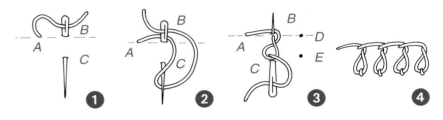

Double Lazy Daisy–Make a short Lazy Daisy, then a larger one outside it. Or, make the smaller stitch inside a larger one.

Kate Greenaway, a turn-of-the-century (1900) artist, drew children in many poses, and these drawings appeared in many crazy quilts worked in Outline Stitch. The embroideries on this quilt are from iron-on transfers published by Dover Publications, Inc. (See Sources).

OUTLINE STITCH. Come up at A, and stitch from B to C. Work towards the right, keeping the thread to one side of the needle, and having the needle pointed towards the previous stitch. The stitches form the Backstitch on the reverse of the work. Stitches can also be overlapped slightly to make a wider stitch, or made further apart for a narrower stitch.

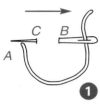

BACKSTITCH—Come up at A, and stitch from B to C. Make the following stitch from C to A, and repeat.

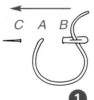

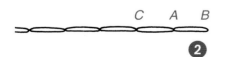

OVERCAST OUTLINE—Work the Outline Stitch and fasten off. Fasten on a second thread. Overcast by sliding the needle under it without piercing the fabric.

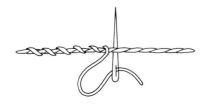

Innovative use of the Outline Stitch, as used on this 1898 crazy quilt. Detail. Collection of the author.

OUTLINE STITCH ROSE—Begin at the center of the rose. Make small Outline Stitches, turning the work for each stitch. Make the stitches longer as the work progresses, making the rose the size desired. You can begin with one color, and change to another to finish. Work the stitches closely so the fabric does not show through the rose.

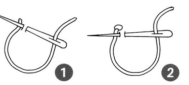

SPLIT STITCH—Work the same as for the Outline Stitch, but run the needle through both fabric and thread for each stitch. This makes a finer outline. The Split Stitch can also be worked as a Backstitch, from right to left, with each stitch piercing the one before it.

TURKEY WORK—Do not fasten the thread to the back of the fabric. 1. Make a short stitch from A to B, pull through, and hold the end with your thumb. Sink the needle at C and come up at A having the thread go under the needle. Make the following stitch to the right of the first. The resulting loops can be trimmed evenly when the stitching is completed.

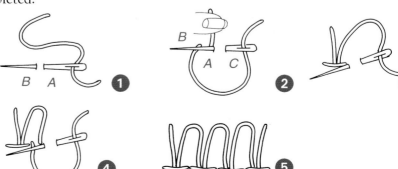

Useful in landscape quilting, the Running Stitch can be like painting with thread.

RUNNING STITCH. Stitch evenly along a line. Make one stitch at a time, or have several on the needle before pulling through.

HOLBEIN STITCH—Make a line of Running Stitch, having the stitches and the spaces between them of equal size. At the end of the row, fasten on a second thread, and make a return row of Running Stitch filling in the spaces left previously.

SATIN STITCH. Bring the needle up at one side of an area to be covered, and down at the other. Repeat, placing each stitch exactly next to the previous one. This stitch also covers the back of the fabric. To conserve thread, the stitches can be made going down, and then up at one side, and repeating at the other side of the design area. To ensure a neat edge, the design can first be outlined in Backstitch or Outline Stitch, working Satin stitch over this.

BASKET SATIN—This consists of groups of Satin Stitches placed perpendicular to each other.

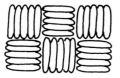

BEETLE STITCH—This is simply the Satin Stitch worked between the same two holes in the fabric. Work enough stitches so they mound up. French knot eyes, straight stitch legs and pistil stitch antennae can be added to form a bug.

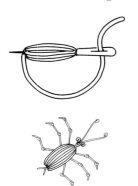

Satin Stitch embroideries make excellent patch decorations. This embroidery is worked from a design in Dover Publications' Traditional Chinese Designs, by Barbara Christopher. The design was transferred using the tissue paper transfer technique.

LACED SATIN STITCH—Work a row of small Satin Stitches spaced evenly. Then, without piercing the fabric, lace a second thread through them.

LONG AND SHORT STITCH—Work the Satin Stitch alternating longer and shorter stitches, to fill in large areas and shade designs.

PADDED SATIN STITCH—Begin by filling the design area with one or more layers of Straight or other stitches. These can also be worked over a small piece of batting for extra loft. Finish with neat, even Satin Stitches to completely cover the padding.

SQUARE STITCH, AND "V" STITCH. These are not stitches as such. They are formed of other stitches such as Straight, Fly, and sometimes Blanket Stitch. Generally, they are made larger and more emphatically than regular stitches, and parts of them are sometimes "tied" with tacking stitches. Found on antique crazy quilts, they may have been an attempt to invent stitches.

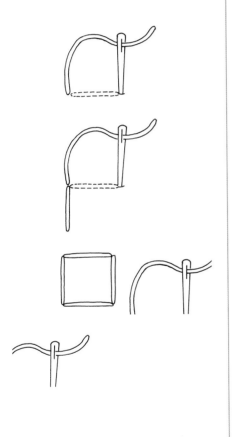

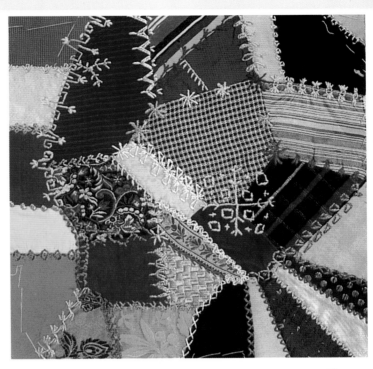

Square and "V" stitches are created using Straight and other stitches. There are many variations of these on antique crazy quilts.

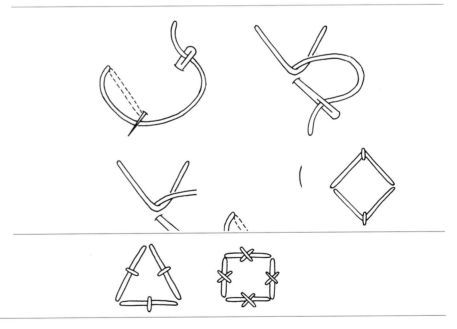

Four-sided Stitch—This stitch consists of Straight or Backstitches to make squares, rectangles, and other geometric shapes. It is easy to work on evenweave fabric.

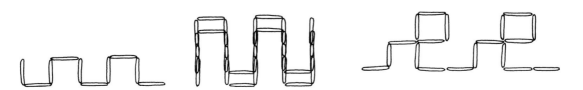

Straight Stitch. Bring the needle up, then down through the fabric. Make stitches in any size desired, placed evenly or randomly.

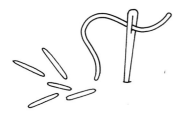

The simplest of stitches, the Straight Stitch has many variations. Antique crazy quilt block is the collection of the author.

ALGERIAN EYE STITCH—Having all stitches converge at the center, make four stitches vertically and horizontally, followed by four diagonal ones. Add shorter stitches in between the longer ones.

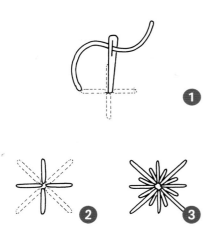

SEED STITCH—this is made by placing two small Straight stitches side by side, and repeating.

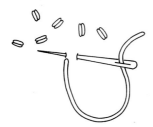

ERMINE FILLING STITCH—Make a vertical Straight Stitch followed by two overlapping diagonal ones. Make them in rows to follow a seam, or scatter them randomly.

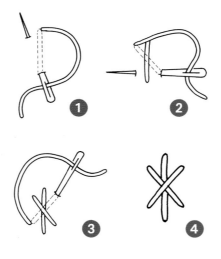

WRAPPED STRAIGHT STITCH—Come up at A, and stitch from B to A. Then pass the needle under the stitch just made without piercing the fabric, and go down at B.

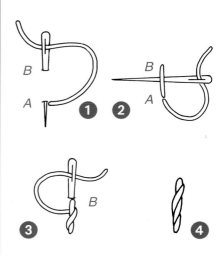

Straight Stitch Fan—All stitches begin at the top of the fan and converge at the base. Fans can be made rounded, tapered, or widened. The number of stitches used can vary from a few to as many as can be fitted.

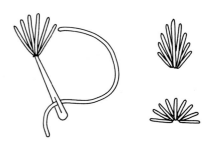

WOVEN AND LACED STITCHES. Begin by making the base stitches. Fasten on a second thread and lace or weave through them. This thread does not pierce the fabric except to begin and end.

DOUBLE-LACED BACKSTITCH—Begin with a row of Backstitching. Fasten on a second thread and pass the needle under each consecutive stitch. Turn, and lace in the reverse direction.

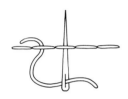

WOVEN SATIN STITCH—Begin by filling an area with Satin Stitch. Fasten on a second thread and weave back and forth until filled in.

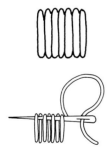

LACED BLANKET STITCHES—Begin with two rows of evenly spaced Blanket stitches. Fasten on a second thread and lace between them as shown.

Woven roses and fans worked in wool threads on the Horses and Roses Wool Quilt.

WOVEN ROSE OR SPIDERWEB STITCH—Begin with an odd number of spokes using Fly Stitches and a Straight Stitch, or all Straight Stitches meeting at the center. Fasten on a second thread at the center; weave over and under spokes until filled in.

PEKINESE STITCH—Begin with a row of Backstitch. Fasten on a second thread, come up at A, pass needle under first Backstitch. Skip one Backstitch; bring needle up under the following stitch, then down under the skipped stitch having the thread over the needle. Repeat.

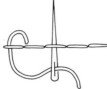 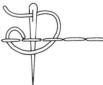 

RAISED SPIDERWEB STITCH—Make any number of spokes of Straight Stitches, overlapping at the center. Fasten on a second thread, come up at the center and work a backstitch over one spoke and under the previous two. Repeat, working clockwise.

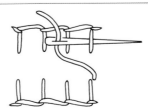  

The Stitch Plates

OTHER NEEDLEWORK: Blanket stitch is used to edge wool blankets and clothing, and to apply appliqués. The Buttonhole stitch is used for buttonholes, appliqué, monogramming and other fine embroidery.

OTHER NEEDLEWORK: Bullion knots are used in dimensional embroidery, especially Wool, and Brazilian embroidery which is worked in rayon threads. Try them in silk ribbon!

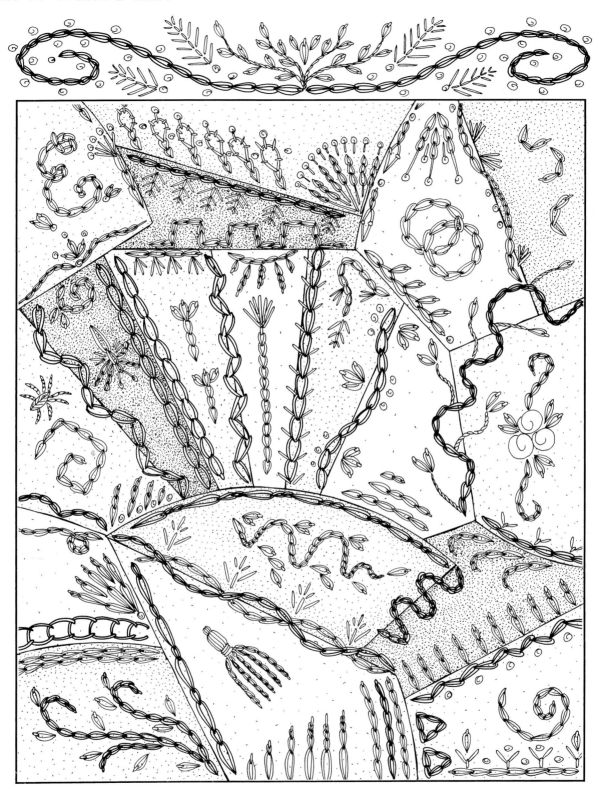

OTHER NEEDLEWORK: Very fine chain stitch worked evenly to form various designs is called "Tambour Work" and was often done using a hook. This was once worked on net or sheer fabric for a lacey effect. Some very beautiful tambour work was done in the late 1700s and early 1800s in the U.S. and Europe to make baby's caps, shawls, collars, and bridal veils.

Chain Stitch is also used for outlining and filler in crewel and other types of embroidery.

OTHER NEEDLEWORK: Excellent in landscape embroideries, the main feature of this stitch is its textural quality. Try it in different thread types and in silk ribbon. This stitch can also be used to couch other threads. Coral Stitch can be worked from left to right by wrapping the thread in the opposite direction.

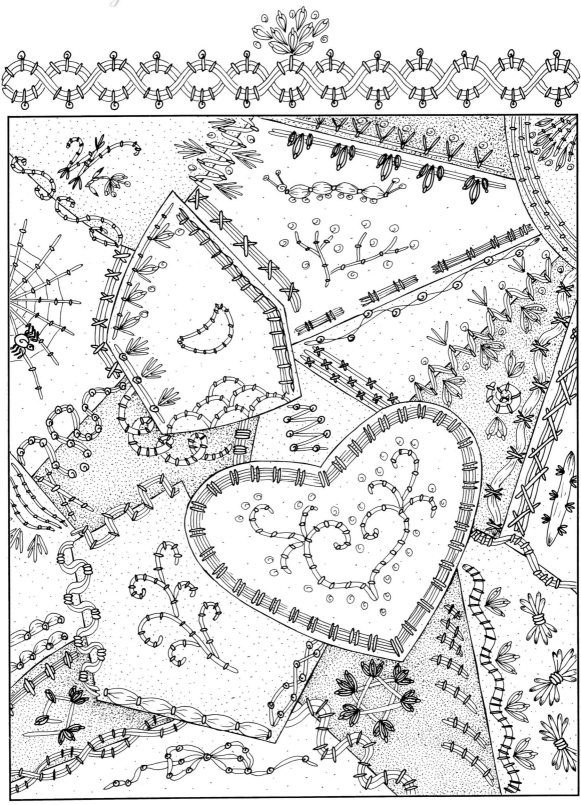

OTHER NEEDLEWORK: Couching was often used in Victorian crazy quilts to fasten on chenille or stranded threads. It is also used in Brazilian embroidery to form fine leaves and branches. In silk and metal embroideries couching is used to secure metal threads that cannot be sewn through fabric. It is also used in silk ribbon embroidery to fasten laid ribbons.

OTHER NEEDLEWORK: The Cretan Stitch is used to make leaves in crewel and other forms of embroidery. The Open Cretan is an extremely versatile crazy quilting stitch, quick to make, and can be "embellished" with additional stitches.

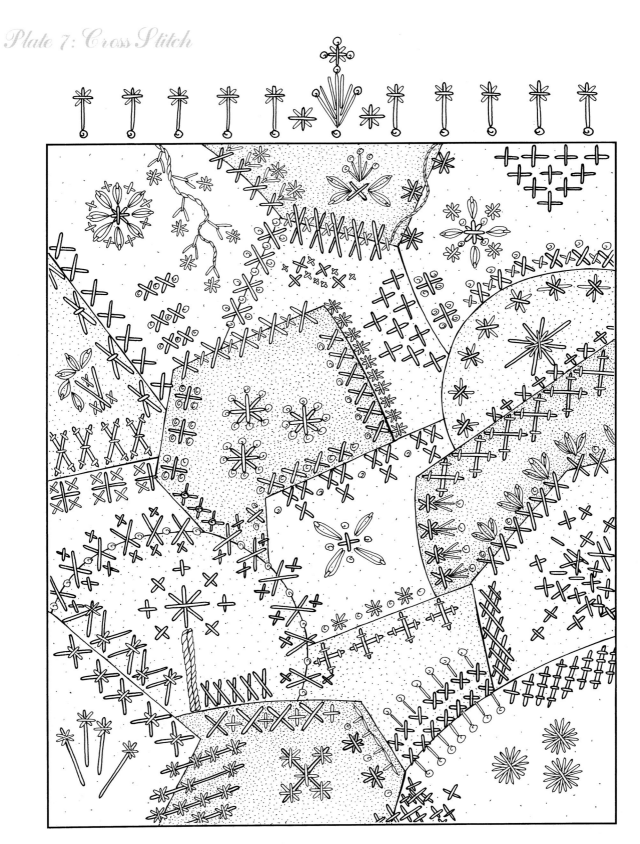

OTHER NEEDLEWORK: Cross stitch is a common form of embroidery worked on Aida cloth or evenweave linen to make pictures, samplers, and many other projects. It can also be worked on plain fabrics using "waste canvas," a lightweight canvas that is basted onto any fabric, embroidered over in cross stitch, then removed by pulling out its individual threads. Double cross stitches made very small appear as dots and are used as filler stitches in crewel embroidery. The 1/2 cross stitch is useful for sewing on beads.

OTHER NEEDLEWORK: A beautiful stitch, and used in many antique crazy quilts, sometimes as the only decorative stitch. This stitch was known as "Coral Stitch" in Victorian times. The Victorian "Feather Stitch" consisted of a straight central line with angled "arms" on one or both sides of the line, identical to a slanted Blanket Stitch.

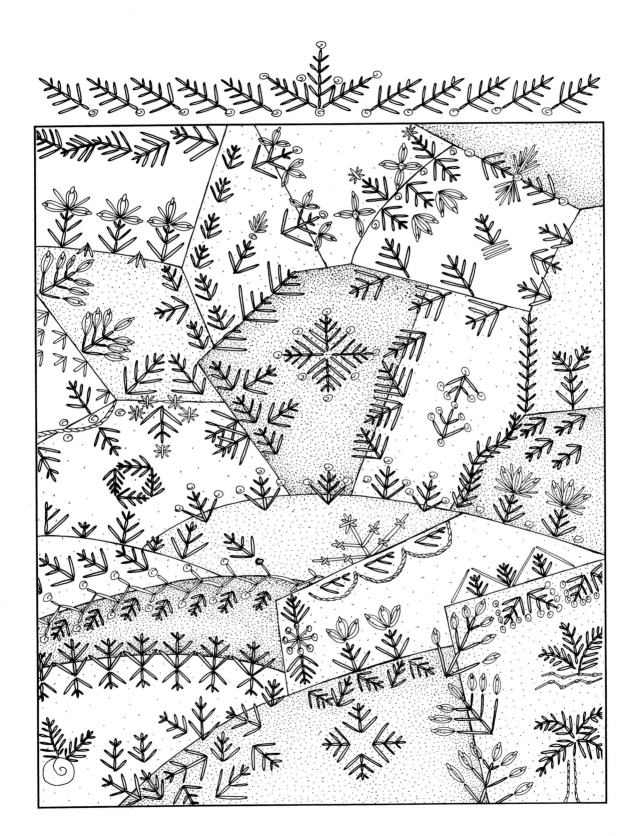

OTHER NEEDLEWORK: This stitch can easily be worked to fit the "grid" of evenweave fabric in cross stitch or needlepoint designs. In silk ribbon embroidery, twist the ribbon to make ferns.

OTHER NEEDLEWORK: The Fishbone stitch defies exact definition. There are several different ways to make the stitch. It can be used to make beautiful leaves in wool, crewel, and other types of embroidery.

OTHER NEEDLEWORK: Among the uses for Fly stitch include its versatility in building up stitch combinations, and its use as a base for a flower or bud. Scatter them for filler stitches.

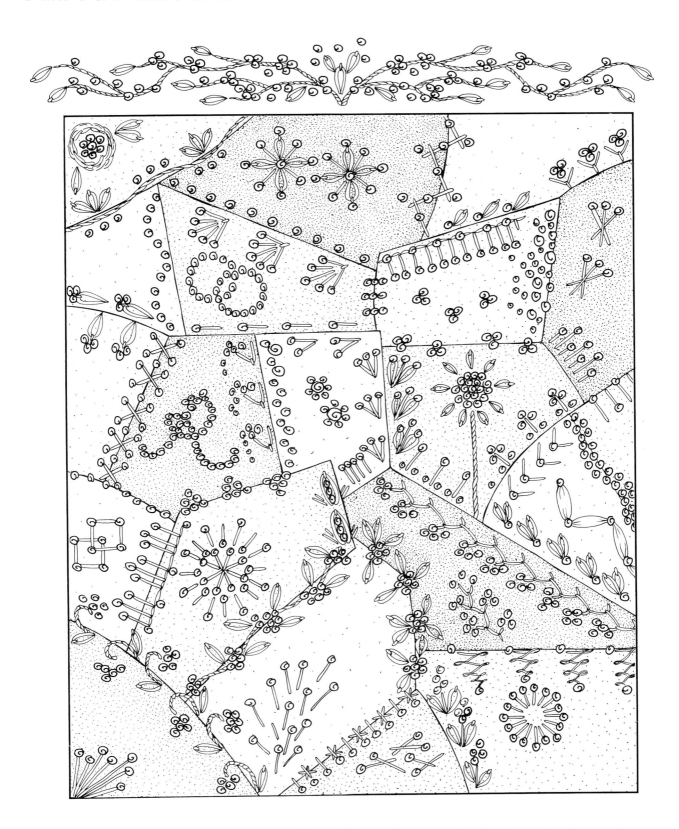

OTHER NEEDLEWORK: The French Knot is used as a filler stitch in crewel and other embroidery, and sometimes in place of Colonial Knot for candlewicking. It can be added to needlepoint and cross stitch. The Pistil Stitch is useful in embroidering flowers.

OTHER NEEDLEWORK: The Herringbone and related stitches are excellent for a base row along crazy quilt patch seams. The Chevron stitch is commonly used in smocking.

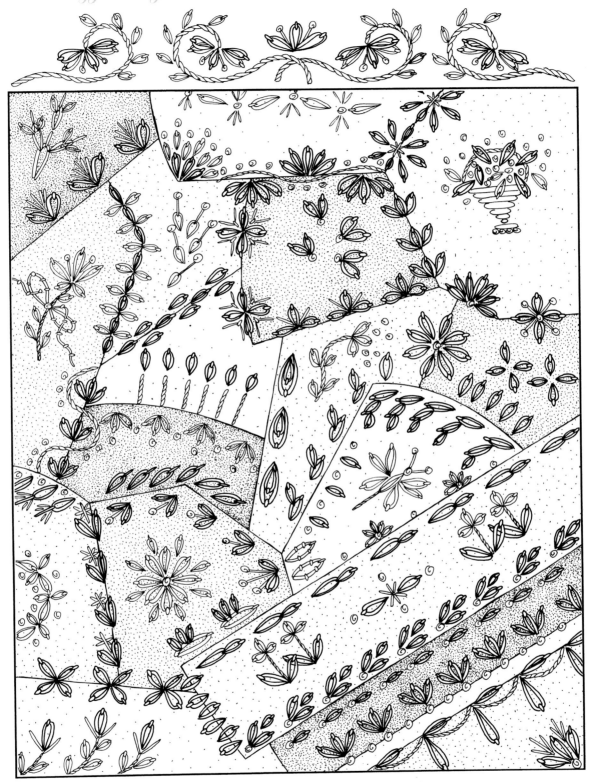

OTHER NEEDLEWORK: This stitch is a single version of the Chain stitch, and is sometimes called "Single Chain," or "Detached Chain." The Victorians termed it the "Picot Stitch." This stitch has many uses, from delineating flower petals, to filler stitches in crewel and other embroideries. It can be worked on top of needlepoint for added dimension, and in cross stitch. Very useful in silk ribbon embroidery to form flowers of many types.

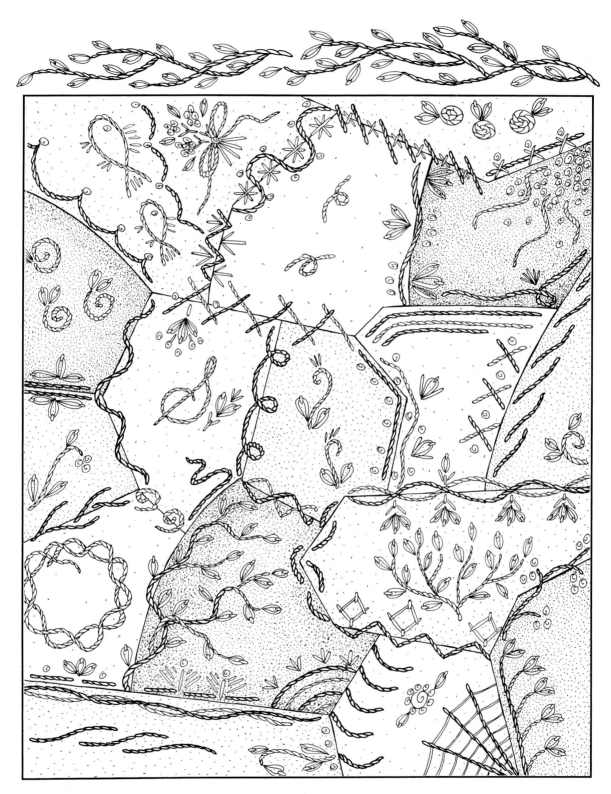

OTHER NEEDLEWORK: Also called "Stem Stitch," the Outline is a much-used embroidery stitch. Kate Greenaway's child-characters were outline stitched onto many Victorian crazy quilts. Turkey work is used in dimensional embroidery. Outline Stitch Roses are often used in Wool or Silk Ribbon Embroidery.

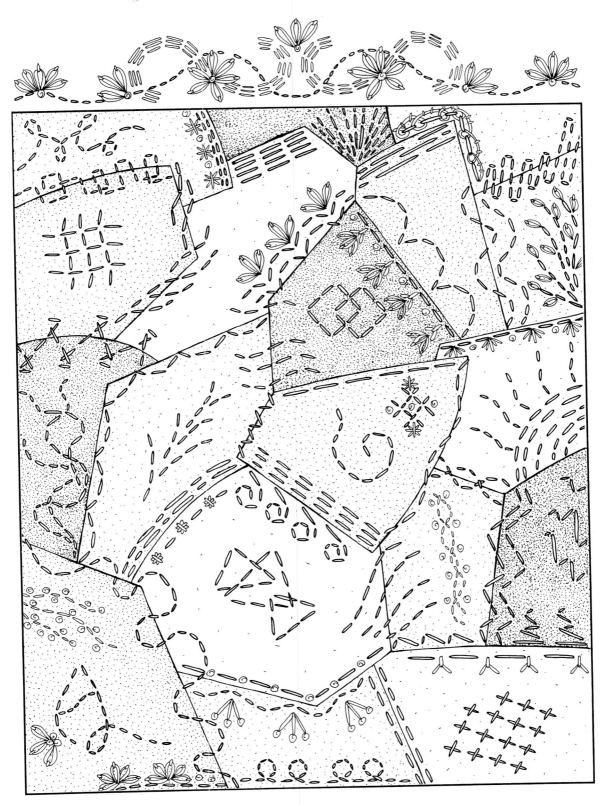

OTHER NEEDLEWORK: Made tiny, and very evenly, this is also the quilting stitch. The same stitch is used for Sashiko, Oriental quilting that is worked in white thread such as a size 8 pearl cotton usually on one layer of indigo-blue fabric. Sashiko is intended to reinforce the fabric rather than quilt layers together. The Holbein Stitch is used in Blackwork.

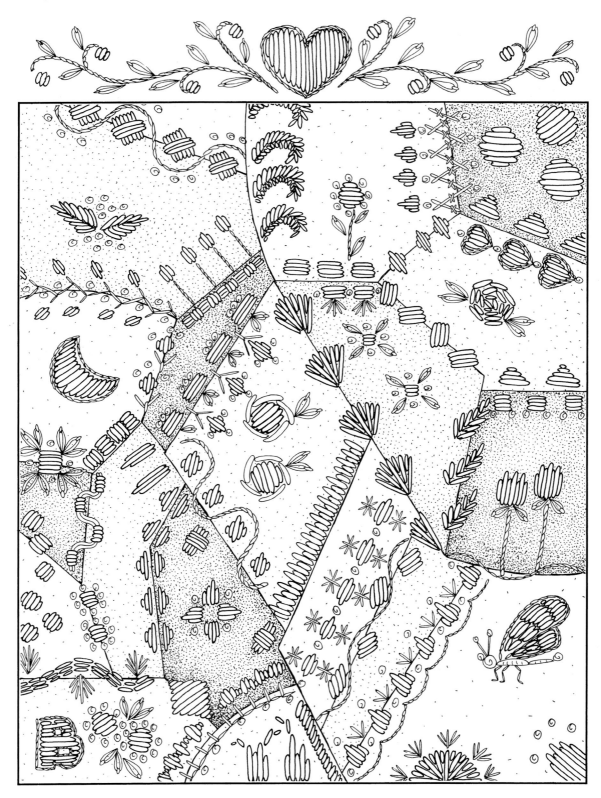

OTHER NEEDLEWORK: Coming from many different embroidery traditions, from most parts of the world, Satin Stitch embroidery is perhaps best known by beautiful and colorful Oriental embroideries worked in lustrous silk threads. Monograms stitched in cotton floss is a western tradition, with many elaborate ones done by the Victorians.

OTHER NEEDLEWORK: These are not stitches as such. They are formed of other stitches such as Straight, Fly, and sometimes Blanket Stitch. Generally, they are made larger and more emphatically than regular stitches, and parts of them are sometimes "tied" with tacking stitches. Found on antique crazy quilts, they may have been an attempt to invent stitches.

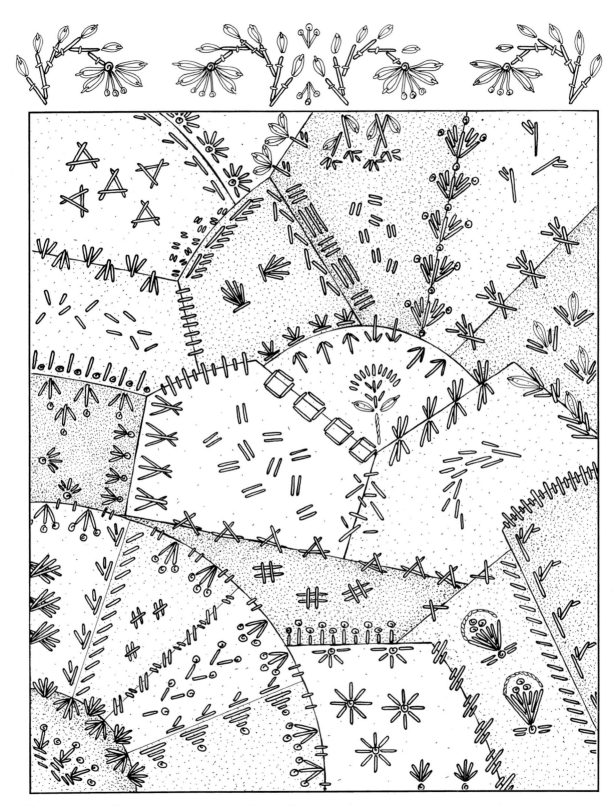

OTHER NEEDLEWORK: One of the most versatile of all stitches, the Straight Stitch can be used to form the Fern Stitch, Box and "V," and Fan stitches. Putting a French Knot at the end of one substitutes for the Pistil Stitch. All of these configurations are found in Victorian crazy quilts, and also as filler stitches in crewel and other embroideries. The Algerian Eye Stitch is traditionally found in needlepoint and cross stitch designs.

OTHER NEEDLEWORK: Woven roses are common to wool and silk ribbon embroidery.

I thought I had invented this method, but then found it in Erica Wilson's books on embroidery! In any case, it has been a foolproof way to get designs onto crazy patches without leaving permanent marks on the fabric. It is ideal for almost any small embroidery design. For larger designs, the paper can sometimes disintegrate too quickly, but can still be done if the design is divided into smaller parts.

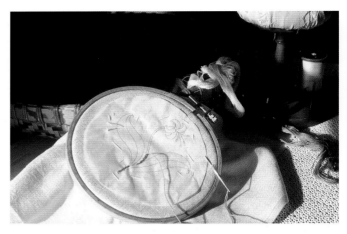

The tissue paper transfer method is easy, effective, and leaves no marks on the fabric.

Trace the design onto tissue paper. I use a hard-lead pencil, making a fine line. If you are doing white on white embroidery, the pencil may come off onto the thread. Do a small sample, then wash it to see whether any pencil remains. If so, experiment with a permanent marker. Do not use a water soluble marker. You can also iron an iron-on transfer design onto the tissue.

Cut around the drawn design leaving about 1/2-1 inch of excess. Place the fabric in an embroidery hoop, and baste the tissue paper onto the fabric.

Embroider the outlines of the design, then tear away the paper. Continue by filling in the design with embroidery if desired.

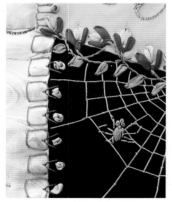

Spiders and spiderwebs are favorite subjects for embroidery on crazy quilts, as here on the Ladies and Fans quilt.

Spiders and Webs

Spiders and webs are not the most-used symbol appearing on Victorian crazy quilts as is sometimes thought. Embroidered fans and rings take precedence by far over spiders and webs on the quilts I've seen.

There are many theories regarding the use of spiders and webs in quilting and the needlearts. I prefer the practical reality–the webs catch nasty bugs. They are symbolic of the ecology of summer, a part of nature's balancing act. Nature weaves an intricate web, and we are part of that intricacy, just a patch in the web of life!

It only stands to reason that spiders can be portrayed in as many ways as there are types of them, and there are many. For starters, spiders are shiny or dull, short- or long-legged, small or large, colorful or gray, patterned or plain, luminescent or hairy. Some have eight eyes, others have none. They all have eight legs!

The same goes for webs. Not all are as perfectly shaped as those of the garden spider. To embroider a web, couch metallic, rayon, or silk threads making the long strands, then the shorter ones.

A spider can be made of embroidery stitches as shown here, or by combining several sizes of beads.

Make two or more French Knots for the head.
Double cross stitch (Star stitch), or a Double Lazy Daisy for the middle.
Padded Satin (Beetle stitch), or Double Lazy Daisy for the end.
Make legs of Coral or Straight Stitches.

Artful Embellishments

I t is artful embellishment that distinguishes the most fanciful of both antique and modern crazy quilts. Satin-stitched monograms interlaced with embroidered flowers, charming Kate Greenaway outlined figures, ribbons fashioned into flowers, and sewn-on beads, buttons, and tassels are some sewn methods. Others include painting, stenciling, and transferring photos onto fabric. In addition to the fancy stitches worked along patch edges, embellishments add dimension, color, texture, and variety to the "crazed china" surface of crazy patching. All of these additions can enliven a quilt by taking its surface beyond the ordinary, explaining why crazy quilts are sometimes referred to as "art quilts".

Like works of art, from simple to complex, a crazy quilt is the unique expression of its maker. Sometimes it doesn't take much. Simple techniques can be extraordinary in their effect, from fastening on a piece of old lace with a particular embroidery stitch, to discovering a fabulous new way to sew a scrap of fabric into the shape of a flower. The individual touches that each pair of hands, like handwriting, bring to a quilt-in-progress are often enough to put a stamp of personality on it.

Sometimes a unique choice of technique can make a difference. Pieces of needlepoint and cross stitch are not the norm for crazy quilt decor, and yet the Wool Quilt demonstrates the efficacy of these as decorative patches. Do you have pieces of unfinished needlework hidden away in a closet or the attic that could be made into crazy patches? Consider making a quilt displaying your favorite of the arts or needlearts, or one that uses up unfinished projects.

We may think of stenciling and other types of printing as being for paper and walls, but they can also be done on fabric, as shown by the Butterstamp quilt.

Try the techniques in both parts of this chapter, experimenting on scraps of fabric and saving them to use later as patches. Is it backwards to embellish the patches before patching the quilt? Not at all! The Victorian

A highly embellished crazy quilt features a central panel with ribbon roses. Other embellishment on this quilt includes painting on silk, cotton and silk floss and chenille embroideries. Courtesy of The Kirk Collection, Omaha, NE. Photo by Nancy T. Kirk.

A needlepoint design by Anne Orr, from Full-Color Charted Designs, published by Dover Publications, Inc., 1984. Anne Orr was a designer of needlework during the early 1900s. This is stitched of silk ribbons, wool, silk, and rayon threads, then used as a patch on the Horses and Roses Wool Quilt.

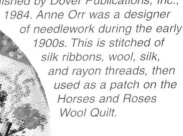

memories quilt was made exactly this way. Far less than perfect, the trial pieces could easily have been thrown out. Instead, they were tossed into a basket, out of which the quilt was patched. This quilt went together quickly with most of its embellishment already finished.

The two parts to this chapter include the applied techniques of ribbonwork, appliqué, dimensional and other embroidery, fabric manipulation, and using beads and buttons in the first. The second features methods that become intrinsic to the fabric, such as dyeing, painting, rubbings, stenciling, and photo transfer.

Learning New Techniques

If you haven't done them before, most of these techniques can be learned easily. But with some, like punchneedle embroidery, you will be lucky to make perfect stitches on the first try. Try, then try again, perhaps with different fabric or thread.

It is very true that challenging things become easy once learned (do you recall learning how to drive!?), and that success happens more easily with an "I can do it" attitude. Indeed, Queen Victoria in this instance may have been likely to recommend that you have the courage of your convictions!

Part 1 : Embroidered and Sewn Techniques

Silk Ribbon Embroidery

NEEDED:

chenille needle size 18, scissors, 4" embroidery hoop, silk ribbons.

One of the many needle arts practiced by Victorian ladies, silk ribbon embroidery is romantic in its appeal, easy to do, and a "must try" if you haven't already! The basic embroidery stitches are used, with silk ribbons in place of threads or floss. The commonest subjects are flowers, with the stitches dimensionally portraying flower parts. A ribbon stitch becomes a leaf or petal, a French knot makes a flower center, or a lazy daisy

Working silk ribbon embroidery using 4mm silk ribbon. In the basket are 4mm and 7mm ribbons, the most common widths used.

stitch a bud, and so on.

Combining these floral stitches into bouquets and other florals, and cottage garden scenes is easy to do and makes beautiful focal points on a crazy quilt. Just as effective is peppering a quilt top with individual silk flowers randomly placed.

Silk has a weightless, airy quality, imparting a painterly characteristic to this needle art, a trait enhanced by using hand-dyed or dye-painted ribbons. Variegated silk ribbons can be purchased, or you can easily dye them yourself. Infinite shade progressions, multi-colorations, and other effects are easy to achieve, and can make your floral embroideries appear almost real. Some of these dye techniques appear in part 2 of this chapter.

Silk embroidery ribbons from Japan, sold under several different brand names, are firmly woven of filament silk for embroidery use. They come in widths of 2mm, 4mm, 7mm, and wider. The 4mm width is available in the widest color range, and is the most common width for embroidery.

Another excellent embroidery ribbon from Japan, a 4mm silk-like synthetic, is available in about 100 colors. Made of a milk-protein based fiber sometimes called "azlon," it is sold under different brand names. This ribbon is lighter in weight than either polyester or rayon, and is washable and colorfast.

There are many other types of ribbons available, of fibers including rayon, nylon, polyester, metallics, and others that are either woven, braided, or knitted. You may want to experiment with some of them for the special effects that can be added to silk ribbon work.

How to Thread the Needle

This technique will keep the silk ribbon secure in the needle while allowing most of its length to be used. Place one end of the ribbon through the eye of the needle, then run the needle through the ribbon, about 1/4 inch from the same end. Pull on the long end of the ribbon to settle the "knot" into place.

To begin, make a tiny stitch on the back of the fabric, then run the needle through the tail of the stitch. OR, leave a tail on the back and work the first stitch through it to secure. Knotting the ribbon should not be done. The needle can hang up on the knots if you happen to stitch into them.

Tips for Silk Ribbon Embroidery

❶ Use short lengths of ribbon, about 12-14 inches. Longer ribbons may begin to wear and fray at the edges.

❷ Use a size 18 Chenille needle when stitching with 4mm and 7mm ribbons. This size needle makes a hole in the fabric that is large enough for the ribbon to slide through easily, reducing wear on the ribbon.

❸ A small, 3-inch or 4-inch embroidery hoop is recommended in order to keep the fabric from being buckled, and is small enough that your fingers can reach the stitches.

❹ Choose embroidery ribbons that are high quality. Those from Japan tend to be smooth and tightly woven, holding up well to embroidery.

❺ Make the stitches loosely, observing each as it forms, and stopping before the ribbon is pulled too tightly.

❻ Allow the ribbon to untwist between stitches. When making Ribbon and Straight stitches, lay the ribbon onto the surface of the fabric, and hold it with your thumb while pulling the needle through.

❼ Ironing the ribbons before embroidering can give a little extra body to them.

❽ To press the finished embroidery, place it face down on a towel-covered ironing board, and press lightly with a dry iron. Take care not to squash the embroidery, and do not use steam.

Silk ribbon was used in combination with Size 12 Pearl Cotton to embroider these moss roses on the Victorian quilt.

Ways to Vary Silk Ribbon Stitches

Stack one stitch directly on top of a previous one. Leaves of Ribbon stitch can be enhanced with a second shade of green in a slightly smaller stitch made on top of the first.

Combine one type of stitch with another, such as French Knots in the centers of Lazy Daisy Stitch.

Twist the ribbon before making a stitch. Straight, Ribbon, and Outline stitches can be twisted once or many times for different effects.

Stitches for Silk Ribbon Embroidery

STRAIGHT STITCH

This corner block detail shows silk ribbon embroidered daisy petals. Collection of Rocky Mountain Quilts, York Village, Maine.

Come up through the fabric at A, then down at B to make one stitch.

This is a simple, but very useful stitch. Group them for flowers, or use them for leaves.

TWISTED STRAIGHT STITCH

Same as the Straight Stitch, but twist the ribbon before going down at B. The ribbon can be loosely or tightly twisted.

Use these for narrow flower petals, leaves, grass, and ferns.

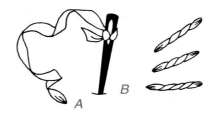

JAPANESE RIBBON STITCH

Smooth the ribbon onto the surface of the fabric, then pierce the end of the stitch and pull through. A variation is to allow the ribbon between A and B to "pouf," making a slightly rounded stitch.

Excellent for leaves and flower petals. Make clusters of them for tree tops.

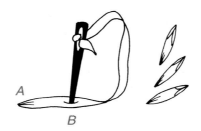

OUTLINE STITCH
TWISTED OUTLINE STITCH

Keep the ribbon to one side of the needle while stitching. Make the stitches shorter to negotiate curves.

Use plain or twisted in straight or curved lines for flower stems, tree trunks, and outlining. Use thread instead of ribbon for very fine stems.

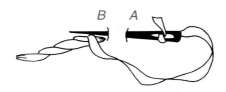

OUTLINE STITCH ROSE

Work the Outline Stitch in a circular fashion, beginning from the center and working outwards. This Rose can also be started around a cluster of French Knots.

LAZY DAISY STITCH
LONG-STEM LAZY DAISY STITCH

The needle passes over the ribbon for the first part of the stitch. A short tacking stitch secures it. A lengthened tacking stitch creates a long-stem stitch.

Use one stitch for a rosebud or a leaf, or group them for flowers.

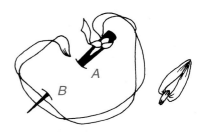

CHAIN STITCH ROSE

Beginning at the center, work Chain Stitch in a circular fashion. This Rose can be started with a French Knot center.

PIERCED LOOP STITCH

Keeping ribbon smooth, pierce ribbon near to A, then pull through, stopping when the loop is the size desired. In a motif, work these last so other stitches won't pull them out.

Make Loop Stitch flowers, and use as filler stitches in florals. French Knots can be used to secure them.

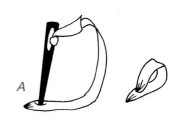

FLY STITCH
LONG-STEM FLY STITCH

Stitch from B to C, with the needle passing over the ribbon. A short tacking stitch secures the stitch. A longer tacking stitch creates a long-stem Fly Stitch.

Use for flower calyxes, or turn upside-down and stack them for Foxglove. Continue the tacking stitch into Twisted Outline Stitch for a stem.

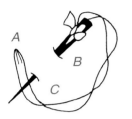

FEATHER STITCH
DOUBLE FEATHER STITCH

Take a stitch first from one side, then the other of an imaginary line. To work the Double Feather Stitch, take two stitches on each side of the line.

Very useful for foliage, shrubbery, and filler in florals.

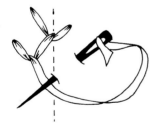

FERN STITCH

Make these as groupings of three Straight Stitches, or one Straight followed by Fly Stitches. Twist the ribbon for a finer stitch.

Add ferns to cottage garden and other florals.

FRENCH KNOT
PISTIL STITCH

Wrap the ribbon one or more times around the needle, pull snug, then bring the needle through. Wrap very loosely once, or several times for a larger, rose-like knot.

Use for Queen Anne's Lace, Lilacs, and filler stitches.

The Pistil Stitch is a variation of the French Knot. Wrap around the needle, then sink the needle farther from the beginning of the stitch.

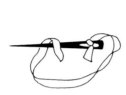

Weaving

Keeping the ribbon smooth, make long Straight Stitches horizontally. Then make vertical stitches while weaving through the horizontal ones.

Use weaving for baskets and to fill in hearts and other objects.

WOVEN ROSE

Make 5 spokes using ribbon or thread. Starting from the center, weave around until the spokes are filled.

COUCHING

Thread two needles with matching or contrasting ribbons. Fasten on the first ribbon and bring the needle through to the front of the fabric. Fasten on the second ribbon, and make French Knots or small Straight Stitches to hold the first ribbon in place. Fasten off both when finished.

Couched streamers and bows are elegant additions to floral embroideries.

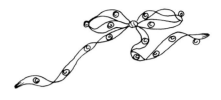

Creating a Rose Motif

Although roses are used here, many other flowers may be represented instead.

❶ Begin with several Outline, Woven, or Chain Stitch roses to establish the placement of the design. Motifs can be made to fit into spaces such as corners and borders by placing these elements appropriately. Add leaves of Lazy Daisy or Ribbon stitches.

❷ Work Feather or Fern Stitches to begin the background. Add several Rosebuds, each consisting of a Lazy Daisy with a Fly Stitch.

❸ Add Twisted Straight Stitch flowers, and finish by scattering French Knots throughout.

Designs for Silk Ribbon Embroidery

These designs can be worked freehand. If you prefer to follow markings, place dots on the fabric using a tailor's chalk pencil, and place the stitches according to the markings.

Detail of a cottage garden scene worked in soft shades of hand-dyed ribbons on a dark green background fabric from Green Mountain Hand-dyed Linens.

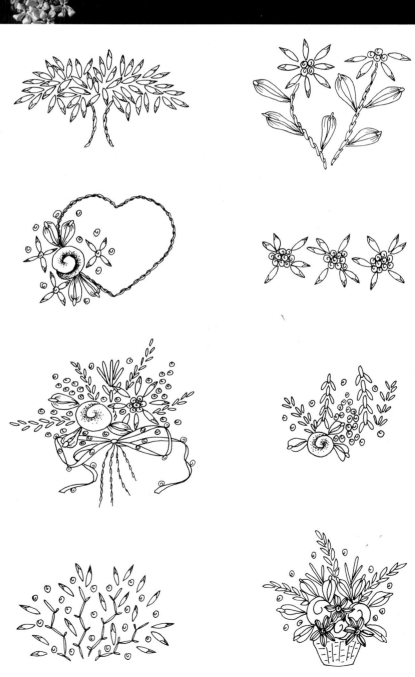

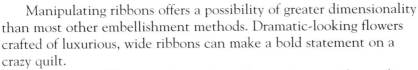

Ribbonwork

NEEDED:

scissors, pins, sewing thread
and needles, ribbons.

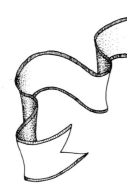

Manipulating ribbons offers a possibility of greater dimensionality than most other embellishment methods. Dramatic-looking flowers crafted of luxurious, wide ribbons can make a bold statement on a crazy quilt.

How to use ribbonwork depends on the result you wish to achieve. One flower with a leaf creates an attractive singular detail, while floral bouquets, sprays, and other arrangements can spread out over a patch or more, even becoming the focus of the quilt. Lengths of ribbon embroidered or couched along patch seams can take the place of embroidery. Used in combination, bolder ribbonwork flowers are soft-ened by the more delicate touches of silk ribbon and other types of embroidery.

Wired, soft rayon, and other ribbons for ribbonwork.

Ribbons for Ribbonwork

Woven ribbons of many fibers and widths are found in sewing, craft, and bridal shops. Be sure to select fabric ribbons for sewing and needlearts, rather than "craft" ribbons. They should be made of fabric that is wash- or dry-cleanable.

Most ribbons can be gathered, folded, scrunched, couched, and some of the narrow ones can be sewn through fabric. Most ribbon types are available in several widths.

Nylon Organdy Ribbons are sheer, appearing soft and shadowy on a quilt's surface. The narrow ones can be sewn through fabric. Form them into accordion roses and gathered flowers, and couch them across patches.

Satin Ribbons are either single or double face. Double-face ribbons have the satin finish on both sides, with single face one side only. Satin is a weave, not a fiber, so these ribbons can be found made of acetate, polyester, silk, or other fibers.

Many satin ribbons are firmly woven, making them suitable for flowers and trims that resist flattening. Some of the imported ones are wide, soft, and have wired edges for making shaped flowers.

Silk embroidery ribbons wider than 7mm make lovely soft flowers. Plain weave silk ribbons are available with finished, or unfinished edges.

Bias-cut, raw edged silk ribbons in attractive variegated shades are ideal for many creative uses, such as embellishment of wall quilts. To use them in functional quilts, their raw edges should be concealed or finished in some way.

Rayon or acetate ribbons from France with wired edges, available in several widths make beautiful flowers. Some of these have ombre shading. The wire can be used to gather the ribbon. For a tighter gather, remove the wire and run a gathering thread instead.

Another type of rayon ribbon, from Japan, is soft and loosely woven. About 1/2-inch wide, it can be sewn through fabric, or used to make soft folded or gathered flowers.

Novelty ribbons made of metallics, velvets, printed fabrics, and ribbons with various edge treatments can also be found. As with other ribbons and trims, be sure they are suitable for the project.

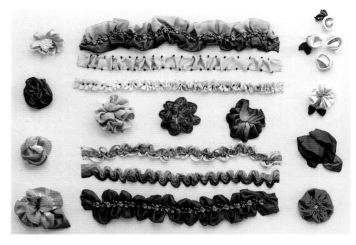

A display of ribbonwork flowers and trims.

Ribbon Trims and Flowers

Experiment with a variety of ribbon types and widths in making the trims and flowers on these pages. Although some are better suited to wide or narrow ribbons, most can be made of many widths.

The length of ribbon to use in making flowers depends on the type of flower and how full you want to make it. For instance, a 2-inch wide ribbon will require a greater length than one that is 1/2 inch in width, to make a gathered flower of equal fullness.

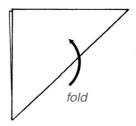

Sew leaves on along with, or before the flowers. French Knots can be added to the centers of flowers, and some flowers can be turned on their sides for side- and three- quarter views.

Cutting bias ribbons.

You can make your own bias ribbons by cutting silk or other lightweight fabrics into strips.

❶ Begin with a square of fabric.

❷ Fold the fabric diagonally as shown.

fold

❸ Press a crease along the fold, then cut along it. Measure, and cut strips as needed.

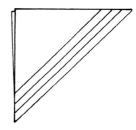

Fold the bias strips lengthwise, and use them to make gathered flowers. Or, sew the strips into tubes, turn the tubes right side out, and press them flat. Ruche or fold these into flowers the same as for ribbons.

Couched Ribbon Trim

Make this trim directly on a crazy patch. Use it in place of the embroidery along patch edges, or lay it across patches, either straight or meandering.

Secure both ends of the ribbon under patch seams, then work embroidery stitches along the ribbon.

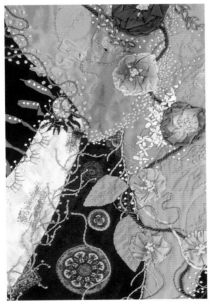

Organdy ribbons wind their way across patches, some couched with French Knots of silk ribbon. Gathered ribbon flowers with appliquéd leaves spill diagonally across the Piano Shawl, interspersed with delicate silk ribbon florals.

Scrunched and Couched Ribbon

Begin by securing one end under a seam, then couch the ribbon while scrunching it. This is easy to do. Make a stitch, such as a French Knot, push the ribbon towards the stitch, and place the following stitch to hold the "scrunch" in place. You can also pin the scrunches, then couch.

Gathered Trims

Velvet ribbons can be shaped and stuffed as demonstrated by this antique velvet pillow. Collection of Rocky Mountain Quilts, York Village, Maine.

Begin with a length of ribbon about twice as long as the finished trim will be.

With matching thread, baste along one or both edges, or along the center of the ribbon. To ruche a ribbon, work basting along it in a zig zag fashion. Pull up the stitches to gather the trim.

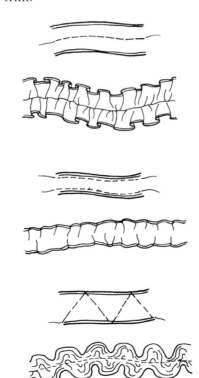

Arrange a gathered trim straight or meandering across a patch. Tuck the ends under patch

edges. Hand-sew or embroider along the trim to secure it into place.

Gathered ribbon trims can also be couched with beads, buttons, and silk ribbon embroidery.

Gathered Flowers

The length of ribbon to use for gathered flowers depends on how full you want the flower to be. A lightly gathered flower will look differently than a very full one made with a longer piece of ribbon. Experiment with various lengths.

❶ Circle Flower. Sew the long ends of a length of ribbon together, then run a gathering thread along one edge. Pull up tightly, and fasten off. Shape the flower while tacking it down.

For a variation of this, use two ribbons of different widths and/or colors held together as one.

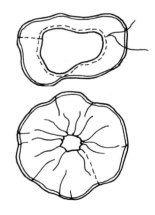

❷ Winding Flower. Edge-gather or ruche a length of ribbon. Sew one end of the ribbon to a crazy quilt patch, then wind the remainder of it around while stitching it down.

3 Double Flower. Following instructions for the Circle or Winding Flower, gather the ribbon along its center. Stitch the gathered line to a crazy quilt patch, folding the two edges upwards to form a double row of petals.

4 Berries and Buds. Sew a short length of ribbon into a circle, then gather both long edges. Sew one or both of the gathered edges to the background fabric. These can be used for buds, berries, and some flower types. A pinch of stuffing can be added inside the berry or flower.

Folded Flowers and Leaf

Accordion Rose.

1 Thread a needle with matching thread and set it aside. Begin at the center of a length of ribbon, using about 9 inches of 3/8-inch ribbon, or 12 inches of 3/4-inch ribbon. Fold the left end of the ribbon down.

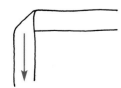

2 Fold the same end upwards and to the back.

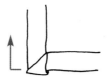

3 Fold the right end backwards. Continue to fold, alternating ends and always folding backwards.

To end, hold the final fold firmly, let go of the previous folds and slowly pull one end downwards. Stop pulling as soon as the rose forms.

Secure by stitching through the base, then the center of the flower. Trim the ends of the ribbon off, and stitch the rose to a crazy patch.

Prairie Point Leaf.

The finished size of the leaf depends on the ribbon's width. Fold, and run a gathering thread as shown. Pull up to gather, fasten off, and trim the ends. Stitch the leaf to a crazy patch, placing a flower over the gathered end.

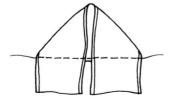

Tea Rose or Rosebud.

A large rosebud can be made of a 14-inch length of 1 1/2-inch-wide ribbon.

Thread a needle with matching thread and set it aside. Remove the wire from the lower edge of the ribbon if it is a wired

ribbon.

1 Fold one end downwards, then wrap the long end of the ribbon loosely around the fold, finishing by folding the end downwards.

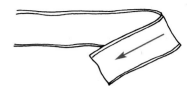

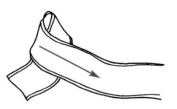

2 Sew through the base several times, then wrap the thread around it several times and fasten off. Trim the ribbon ends close to the stitching.

Fold the lowest petal downwards to conceal the stitching, and sew the rosebud to a patch. Arrange the petals and tack them in place with a few stitches.

Using Crinoline in Ribbonwork

Ribbon flowers can be tacked onto crinoline, a stiffened fabric, as they are made.

Although the crazy patch with its underlying foundation is often a sufficient base, crinoline can be used to provide extra stability to a grouping of flowers. The crinoline is trimmed close to the stitching before it is tacked onto a project.

If crinoline is placed in contact with silks and other fine fabrics, it could saw into the fibers of these fabrics. To prevent this, stitch a piece of fabric over the crinoline before it is tacked on.

Ribbon Flowers and Yo-Yos

Winding Rose.

This is made directly on the crazy quilt patch. Secure one end of the ribbon by putting a needle through it. Make sure the needle is of sufficient length to accommodate the windings. Wind the ribbon around the needle until the flower is as full as you want it. Tuck in the end of the ribbon, thread a second needle, and stitch the "petals" in place.

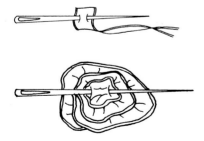

Looped Ribbon Flowers.

Use 1/4-inch satin, or 4mm or 7mm silk ribbon for these. They can be made in hand, or directly on a patch. Holding the center of the flower, fold the ribbon into loops, one loop at a time. Securely sew the loops at the center to keep all of the petals in place. A small gathered flower added to the center will conceal the stitching.

Yo-Yos.

Yo-yos make lovely flowers, as shown on this detail of the Ladies and Fans quilt.

These are made of fabric, not ribbon, but are included here because they make wonderful flowers. Cut a 4-inch circle of fabric—silk jacquards are an excellent choice! Fold the outer edge under about 1/4 inch, and baste close to this edge. Pull up to gather, and fasten off. Slipstitch the yo-yo to a patch with the opening facing upwards.

Yo-yos can be arranged in side and three-quarter views as well as full-face. French Knots can be added inside the opening. Cut smaller, or larger circles to make flowers of other sizes.

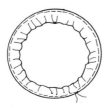

Bias Ribbon Flowers

Ribbon Flower Petals.

Make 4 to 12 petals, depending on the desired fullness of the finished flower. Using wide ribbon or bias scraps of fabric, cut two 2-inch x 3-inch pieces.

❶ Place the two pieces right sides together, and sew as shown. Trim the seam, turn and press the petal. Repeat for the remaining petals.

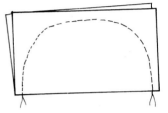

❷ One at a time, baste along the base and pull the thread to gather, then fasten off.

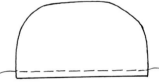

❸ Sew the petals to each other, adding one at a time. Sew the flower onto a crazy patch along with a leaf or two. Take several stitches down through the center of the flower to secure it in place.

Bias Ribbon Rolled Rose.

Thread a needle with matching thread and set it aside. Using about a 6" length of wide ribbon, fold it in two along the center. Roll the folded ribbon 2 or 3 times around the tip of your index finger, having both ends folded downwards so raw edges will be concealed.

fold

Slide the rose off your finger, holding it firmly. Stitch through the base, then wrap the thread around several times and fasten off. Trim close to the thread.

Open out the rose and slipstitch the outer petals to a patch. Then make several stitches down through the center of the rose.

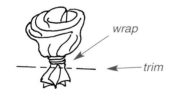

wrap

trim

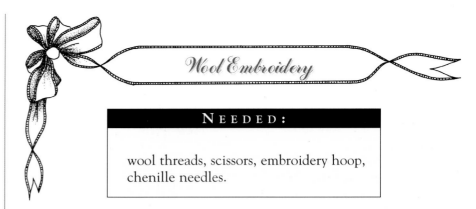

Wool Embroidery

NEEDED:

wool threads, scissors, embroidery hoop, chenille needles.

Recently popularized by needleworkers from Australia and other parts of the world who have done some beautiful designs with it, wool embroidery is now working its way into the U.S. It is not the crewel embroidery we once associated with wool work. Easy to learn, adaptable to many uses, quick to do, and dimensional, it shares many of the characteristics of silk ribbon embroidery. And, like silk ribbon, it is most often used to depict florals, with stitches forming flower parts and leaves.

Wool embroidery is wonderful for embellishing wool and other crazy quilts, worked along seams or on the centers of patches. As a free form technique, flowers and leaves are easily combined into bouquets, sprays, and other configurations.

Wool embroidery is worked on patches and along seams of this wool quilt.

Threads for Wool Embroidery

Use tapestry, persian, and other wool threads made for embroidery. One strand of DMC® Broder Medici produces a very fine stitch. The heavier Paternayan® Persian was used for most of the fancy stitching in the Wool Quilt. Impressions®, from The Caron Collection, is a 50/50 percent wool/silk thread that embroiders like a dream.

Many other types of threads such as silks, cottons, and rayons can also be used for the wool embroidery stitches and motifs.

Tips and Techniques for Wool Embroidery

1 Use a chenille needle that is large enough to make a hole in the fabric for the wool to pass through easily.

2 When working through two layers of fabric, pull the thread all the way through to form each part of a stitch. This reduces wear on the thread.

3 Begin and end by making 2 or 3 tiny stitches on the back of the piece. No knots, please!

4 If you plan to work florals on the centers of patches, it is often easier to do them before the quilt is patched.

5 Learn the Bullion Stitch if you haven't already. It is a common stitch in wool embroidery, and invaluable for its dimensionality and versatility.

Floral Stitches for Wool Embroidery

The sizes of stitches will vary according to the thickness of the thread used, and, for some, the number of times the thread is wrapped around the needle, such as the French Knot and Bullion Stitch.

Many other stitches can also be used. See the preceding chapter, Victorian Stitches, for more stitches, and stitch instructions.

Real flowers, garden and seed catalogs, and gardening magazines are sources of ideas for additional flowers and motifs. I look forward to January when the gardening catalogs arrive, some of their beautiful illustrations invariably inspiring many ideas for flowers and motifs to adapt for embroidery.

Bullion Stitch Roses and Flowers.

Work overlapping Bullion Stitches around a center of two shorter Bullion stitches, French Knots, or padded Satin Stitch. Add various embroidery stitches to the Bullion stitch to make other types of flowers.

Blanket Stitch Flowers.

Make large, rounded flowers by working Blanket Stitch in a circular fashion. This is easiest to do by first drawing the outer circle of the flower onto the fabric with tailor's chalk. French Knots or Pistil Stitches are used for flower centers.

Straight Stitch Flowers.

Groupings of Straight Stitches make different flower forms. Additional embroidery stitches are added to some.

Lazy Daisy Flowers.

Lazy Daisy Stitches make pretty flowers and petals. Add additional embroidery stitches for flower centers and calyxes.

French Knot Flowers.

Lilacs, Wisteria, Queen Anne's Lace, Lupine, and other flowers can be represented by

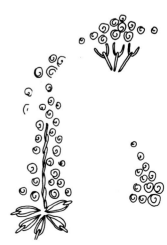

groupings of French Knots. For more natural-looking flowers, vary the sizes of stitches by the number of times the thread is wound around the needle, and by winding the thread loosely for some and tightly for others.

Star Stitch Flowers.

Star Stitch flowers, made very small will appear as dots, and are useful for centers or small flowers.

Stitches for Leaves.

Some stitches that can be used for leaves include: 1. The Fishbone Stitch—these are beautiful in a variegated thread, 2. Feather Stitch, 3. Straight Stitches, 4. Fern Stitch, and 5. stacked Lazy Daisy Stitches.

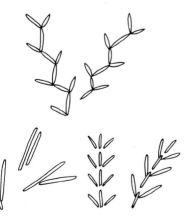

Stems and Branches.

Use Backstitch, Couching, or Outline Stitch for stems and branches.

Weaving.

Weave baskets, vases, and flower centers.

Designs for Wool Embroidery

Wool stitches can be combined into corner motifs, garlands, sprays, baskets, and other shapes. Here are some examples of motifs.

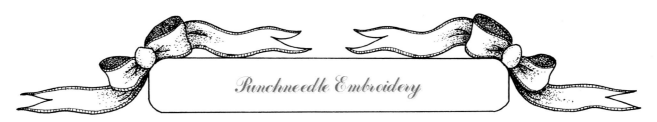

Punchneedle Embroidery

NEEDED:

punch needles, scissors, embroidery hoop, threads, transferred design.

Punchneedle embroidery creates a rug-like pile on the surface of the fabric. It can be worked on any type of crazy quilt, whether wool, silk, or cotton, and in as many types of thread. It can be used to form a solid mat of sheared or looped pile, or to add random looping to other types of embroidery.

Punchneedle is worked on the wrong side of the fabric using a special hollow needle. As the needle is punched through fabric and withdrawn, a loop is formed on the right side.

Punch needles are available in several sizes for different fibers to be used, from crewel yarn to a single strand of embroidery floss. The term, "Russian punch-needle" refers to the finest needle which is used with one strand of silk or cotton floss. Some needles allow the length of the loop to be adjusted.

Threads and Fabrics for Punch Embroidery

Most wool, cotton pearls and flosses, and silk threads work well. Some rayons may be too slippery to hold in the fabric, and metallics can be too coarse to slide through the needle. Following the instructions that came with your needles, experiment with a variety of fibers, using the correct needle size for each. The thread must slide through the eye of the needle easily, but yet not be too loose.

The weave of the background fabric holds the loops in place. Firmly woven linen, cotton, and wool fabrics, and cotton velveteen are excellent choices. Other fabrics such as lightweight silks may be used if they are backed with foundation fabric.

Above: A fruit tree in full bloom is worked in outline stitch and punchneedle embroidery.

Left: Soft and fuzzy creatures are likely subjects for punchneedle embroidery. Here, a chick is worked on the Horses and Roses quilt.

The best designs consist of shapes to be filled in. To fill in large areas, use shading to prevent a "paint by number" look. Also avoid outlining a design in one color and filling in with another, the "coloring book" effect.

Variegated threads are wonderful for punchneedle designs, eliminating the need to change colors for shading. These can be used to achieve natural-looking flowers and trees.

Instructions for Punchneedle Embroidery

1 Draw or transfer a design onto the wrong side of the fabric. Use chalk pencil, an iron-on transfer, or a marking pen intended for needlework.

2 Wrong side up, snugly fit the fabric into an embroidery hoop. Some instructions call for having the fabric "drum-tight." However, I've worked punchneedle with no hoop at all if it is worked into a firm fabric base. To do this, the fabric must be held firmly while punching.

3 To thread the punchneedle, bring the thread down through the shaft, then thread the eye. Hold the needle with the opening facing upwards, or away from yourself. The needle can be held vertically, or at a bit of a slant to prevent working into previously made loops.

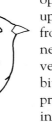

4 Keep the tip of the needle in contact with the fabric between punches, sliding it along the surface of the fabric instead of lifting it. Get into a punch-slide rhythm as you work. Trim thread ends close to the surface of the piece.

Tips for Punch Embroidery

Watch that the thread is not hindered, so it can move freely through the needle.

When filling in solid areas, work from side to side: left to right, then right to left, moving away from yourself.

One way to ensure a neat edge is to work Outline Stitch around a design before punching. Outine Stitch worked on the back will appear as back-stitch on the front of the fabric.

Areas can be punched a second time to fill them in more completely, or to add a second shade or fiber.

If possible, wash the piece afterwards This helps to secure the loops into the weave of the fabric.

Appliqué

Appliqué is the application of one fabric onto another. In crazy quilting, it is most effective used as part of a design with embroidered details added. For instance, a bowl or basket shape is first appliquéd, then filled with embroidered flowers.

The best fabrics are light to medium-weight types that hold a crease easily, and fray minimally. Tightly woven cottons, silks, rayon or wool challis, and taffeta are some examples.

Bold, squared, or rounded shapes are easiest to appliqué. To make narrow strips, use bias cut strips of fabric, pressing the raw edges under.

NEEDED:

scissors, size 12 "Sharp" needle, silk pins, beeswax, cotton or silk sewing thread, tightly woven fabric scraps, dry iron and spray bottle. Optional: freezer paper.

How to Appliqué

1 Cut out the shape, adding a 1/8 to 1/4-inch seam allowance. Clip inside curves almost to the seam allowance. With a dry iron, press the seam allowance under. If steam is needed to hold a crease, lightly spritz the ironing board with water, then press. Pin or baste the appliqué to the ground fabric.

2 Slipstitch, using matching thread. I rarely find an exact match in my thread collection, so use a "blending match" more often than not. Use 100 percent cotton, or a size 50 silk sewing thread. Wax the thread with beeswax to deter tangles.

3 Embroider any details.

How to Slipstitch

Attach the thread to the back of the piece with several tiny stitches, then bring the needle through to the front, coming up at the edge of the appliqué.

To slipstitch, run the needle through the fold of the pressed edge of the appliqué, then pick up a thread or two of the background fabric. The stitches should be very short and nearly invisible.

Some appliqués can be sewn without pressing first. Pin or baste the appliqué to the ground fabric. Begin as above, using the tip of the needle to push the seam allowance under before making each stitch.

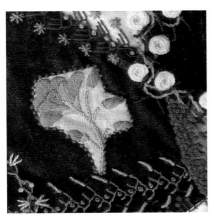

An example of broderie perse, a piece of an unfinished crewel embroidery is appliquéd onto a patch on the Horses and Roses quilt.

Other Techniques for Appliqué

❶ Wool or velveteen appliqués can be finished by edging them with Buttonhole Stitch instead of turning the edges under. Do not add a seam allowance when cutting out the pieces.

❷ To pad an appliqué, add a tiny pinch of stuffing when the slipstitching is nearly finished.

❸ Broderie Perse is cutting out a design from a printed fabric and appliquéing it onto a different background. Use Buttonhole stitches, or turn the edges under and slipstitch around.

❹ Use interesting materials for different effects. Lightweight leather, and lame fabrics are two examples. To appliqué lame, first iron a lightweight cotton fusible interfacing to the back of it.

❺ To use freezer paper, cut out the appliqué design without adding seam allowances. Iron it onto the wrong side of the appliqué fabric. Cut out the fabric adding 1/8" to 1/4" seam allowance all around. Press the seam allowance to the back, over the freezer paper. Pin the appliqué to the background fabric and slipstitch around. Pull out the paper just before the stitching is finished, or cut a slit in the background fabric to remove the paper (without cutting into the appliqué), then stitch the opening closed.

❻ Bias strips can be formed into elaborate Celtic knot designs, basket shapes, or used as stems or trimmings across patches. Use a bias tape maker if you need a large quantity. Pin the bias to the patch, pinning curves. Slipstitch along the edges.

A Victorian Embroidery Design

This design is an adaptation of Victorian embroidery designs with their curving stems, twining vines, and naturalistically posed flowers. Four flowers are appliquéd onto patch fabric, then embroidered details are added.

A Victorian Floral to appliqué and embroider.

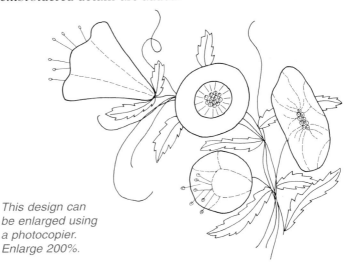

This design can be enlarged using a photocopier. Enlarge 200%.

NEEDED:

embroidery floss and needle, hoop, scissors.

Used to decorate household linens, Monogramming is one of the many needlearts practiced by Victorian stitchers. A finely made monogram can be an attractive enhancement on a crazy patch.

A variety of stitches can be used to embroider a monogram, the most common of them Satin, Backstitch, and Outline stitch. They are sometimes entwined with florals in Outline, Straight, Lazy Daisy, French Knot, and other stitches. Please refer to the chapter, Victorian Stitches for instructions for the individual stitches.

Use cotton, rayon, or silk floss. Very fine stitching can be done using one strand. For greater coverage, use two or three strands. Traditionally a white-on-white technique, monograms can be worked in any color or color scheme.

How to Monogram:

1 Choose an alphabet style that is appropriate for embroidery. Two are given here, and you can also use your own handwriting.

2 If two or more letters will be overlapped onto each other, consider making them two different sizes. Redraw the letter in the size desired. Trace each letter to be used onto tracing paper and cut them out. Taping them onto a sheet of plain paper, arrange the letters so they over-

A monogram and tea rose were combined in this shadowbox detail.

lap onto each other. Be sure the slant and spacing between them is the same, and place a ruler under them to be sure they line up. Make a final tracing.

3 Transfer the letters to the fabric using any transfer method that will be completely concealed by embroidery stitches. The Tissue Paper Transfer Method is recommended since it will leave no marks on the fabric.

4 Choose an embroidery option from the list below.

Techniques for Monogramming:

1 Outline the letter in Outline stitch, and fill in solid areas with Satin or Padded Satin stitch. Victorian instructions call for making Padded Satin stitches thicker at the center of the area, and thinner at the outer edges. This is done by making more of the filler stitches towards the center, and fewer at the edges.

2 Outline a solid letter in Backstitch and work Satin Stitch to fill in the letter, having it cover the backstitching.

3 Outline the letter in Outline stitch and fill in solid areas with French Knots.

4 Outline the letter with Backstitch or Outline Stitch, then work Detached Buttonhole over them. Solid areas can be filled in with French Knots or Satin Stitch.

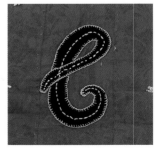
The letter "C" was appliquéd, then embroidered in this Canadian crazy quilt detail. Collection of Rocky Mountain Quilts, York Village, Maine.

A B C D E

F G H I J K

L M N O P

Q R S T U

V W X Y Z

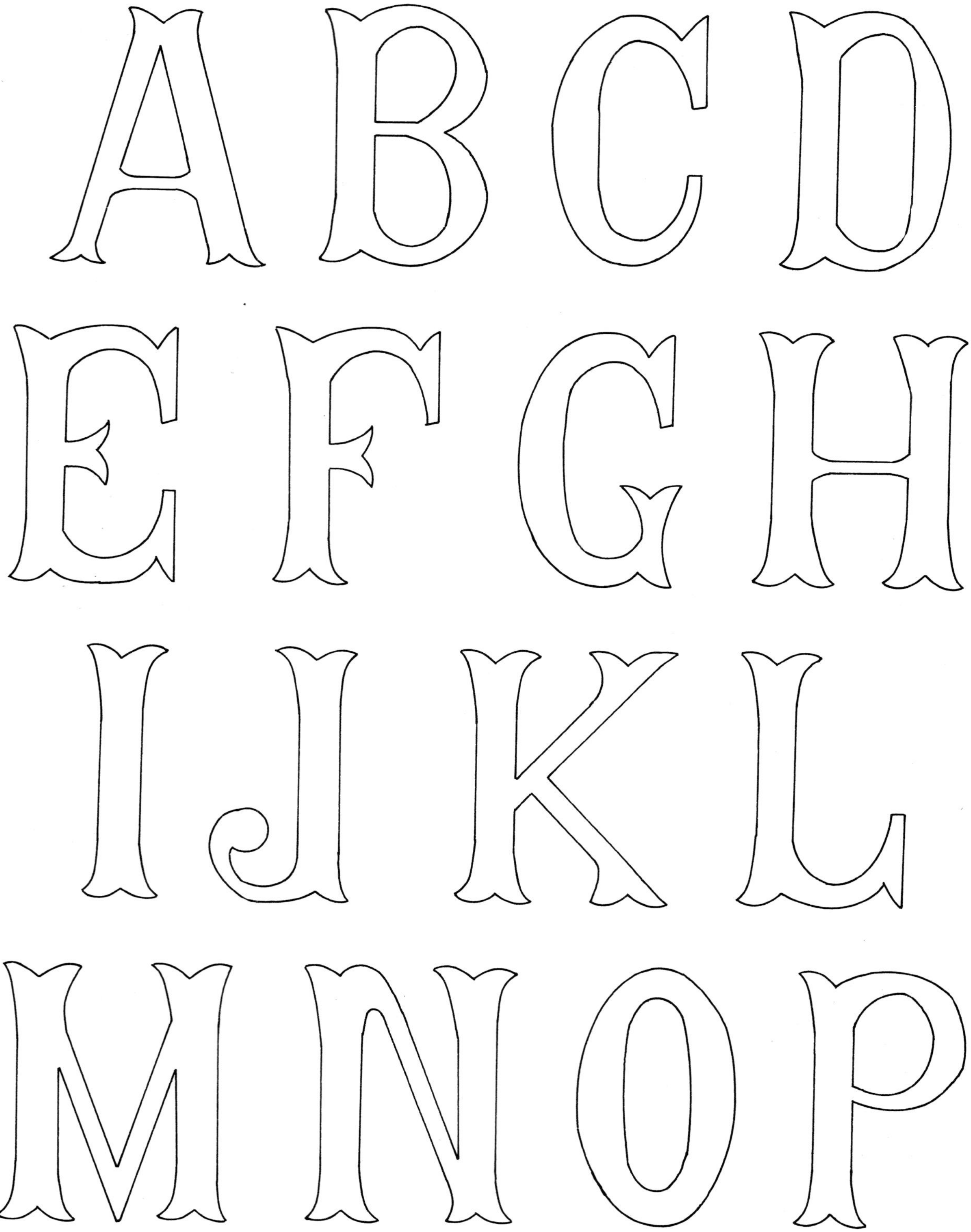

A B C D
E F G H
I J K L
M N O P

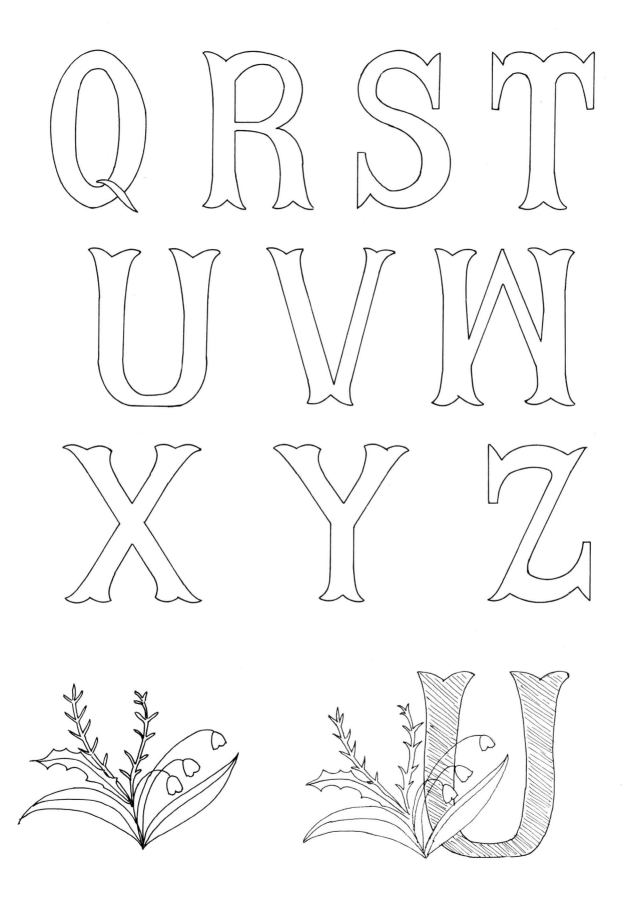

Fabrications

Texturing Fabrics

A fun and easy way to add dimensionality to a quilt top is to add folds, gathers, and scrunches to a patch as it is laid onto the foundation. I prefer to use silk fabrics for these effects. Begin with a piece of patch fabric that is too large for the space. Pin the edges of it on all but one side, leaving the fabric to bulge in the center. Choose a method below:

1 Scrunch and tack the excess fabric, creating "puffs" between tacks. To tack, use French Knots, beads, buttons, or short lines of Feather stitching.

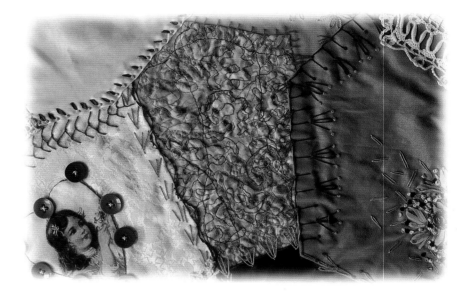

A fabricated patch was made of silk trimmings and organza fabric.

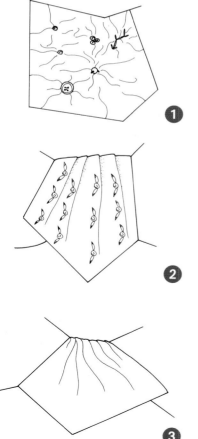

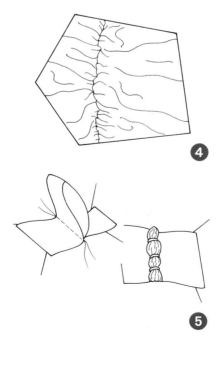

2 Arrange the free end into folds or pleats, pin and baste them in place. Later, as you embroider the quilt, silk ribbon or other embroidery can be worked on the folds to tack them in place.

3 Run a gathering thread along the free end, pull up until the end fits the space, and end off.

4 Run a gathering thread across the patch, pull up to gather, and fasten off.

5 Leaving two opposite sides of the patch free, run a basting thread as shown. Couch the excess fabric with embroidery ribbon or thread.

Finish the patch by hemming the free end, or place the adjoining patch over it. Pin, then baste.

Fabric Overlays

A sheer fabric or all-over lace can be laid onto an opaque fabric and the two used as one crazy patch. Use netting, tulle, gauzes, organza, and other sheer fabrics and laces. These are useful in landscape pieces to create the effects of fog, water, and mist. Wide laces can also be used to partly cover a patch.

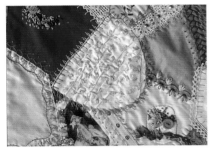

A scrunched patch is held in place by embroidery.

Covering Buttons

NEEDED:
plain plastic 2 or 4 hole buttons, small pieces of fabric and cotton batting, sewing thread.

Cut the organza into two patch-size pieces, each the same. Place the silk trimmings between them (like a sandwich), and work stitching over the entire piece. Have the stitching close enough together so it adequately holds the trimmings in place.

Use the patch as you would any crazy patch, concealing its outer edges under adjoining patches.

These are not the same as the covered buttons used for clothing! These are a great way to use small leftover pieces of your hand-dyed silks. Covered buttons are attractive placed at the corners of patches, on fans, and as flower centers.

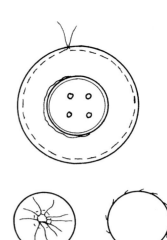

Creating Fabric with Silk Trimmings

The patch shown on the previous page was embroidered on a sewing machine set up for darning, but hand-quilting could also be used. I save all trimmings from silks, considering this material too precious to throw away! Trimmings can also be saved to stuff cloth dolls.

Covered buttons and silk tassels await placement on the Ladies and Fans quilt.

1 Cut a piece of fabric twice as large as the button. (If the button is 1 inch in diameter, cut the fabric into a 2-inch round). Cut a piece of batting the same size as the button. Run a basting thread around the outer edge of the fabric.

2 Place the batting inside the fabric and the button on top of it, and pull up the gathers. Fasten with a few small stitches, then slipstitch the button to a patch.

You can also sew on beads, or work a small motif in silk ribbon embroidery onto the fabric before it is sewn over the button.

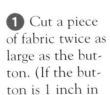

Beads and Baubles

Beads and other "hard" trims were not typically added to Victorian crazy quilts. The majority of the antique quilts feature embroidery as the sole embellishment. Beads and other trinkets are added to many modern crazy quilts and wall hangings as embellishment and to represent themes and other ideas.

NEEDED:

fine needle or beading needle, beading thread, scissors, embroidery hoop, beads.

Beading

Glass beads were used in great quantity by Victorian needleworkers. They used them in needlepoint, crochet, knitting, and sewed them to cross stitch pieces and into elaborate patterns on velveteen.

Wonderful highlights on crazy quilts, beads can be sewn into patterns, used as flower centers, or just scattered about. They can be added to embroidery along patch edges in place of French Knots. Use them to highlight silk ribbon and wool embroideries, and to tack ribbons and lace motifs

The layers of the silk jacket were quilted by sewing beads to the patch seam embroidery.

onto patches. The silk cocoon jacket was beaded to quilt the jacket layers together, a functional use for them.

Czechoslovakian glass seed beads are the most common of the many bead types available. They can be found in transparent, opaque, and silver-lined types in a range of sizes. I prefer size 11 seed beads, which almost perfectly fit a 16-count canvas for beaded needlepoint, and seem about the right size for other applications.

Add beads after embroidery is finished, otherwise threads can catch on them. Also, remember that adding quantities of glass beads to a project will add weight to it.

How to Sew on Beads

Beads added to Outline stitch highlight a feather motif on the Victorian quilt.

Beads can be sewn on one at a time, or several at once. You can also string a length of them and couch them down. Use a fine needle for tiny seed beads, and twisted nylon thread made especially for beadwork.

A supported embroidery hoop can speed the process by allowing the free use of both hands. Place the project into the hoop, and spill out a few beads onto it. To use the beads, pick them up with the needle taking care not to snag the fabrics.

Beaded Needlepoint

Beaded needlepoint takes the form of pansies, nestled into leaves of silk ribbon embroidery on the Victorian quilt.

Beaded needlepoint was a popular Victorian needleart. Worked in glass seed beads in small designs, this technique can make charming, small patch embellishments. Larger pieces can add too much weight to a quilt.

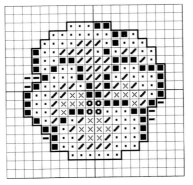

·	lt. amethyst or blue
■	dark amethyst
╱	pink
─	green
✕	dark red
◘	gold

Work beaded pieces on a "soft" canvas such as cotton interlock. There are three ways that beads can be used in a counted design; working the entire design in beads, using beads for all except the background, and using them only for some highlights in a design.

Graphed patterns for cross stitch and needlepoint can be used.

Match the size of the bead to the canvas. For instance, size 11 seed beads fit a 16 count canvas. Using nylon beading thread, sew on the beads using a 1/2 cross stitch to have all the beads slant in the same direction.

A chart for the pansy is included here.

Charms

Charms can be added to silk ribbon and other embroideries on crazy quilts. Although they make attractive accents on wall quilts and projects such as Christmas stockings it is not advisable to use them on bedding quilts and clothing, where they are apt to catch on threads.

Buttons

Buttons of all types and sizes can be sewn onto crazy quilts, especially wall quilts and other projects.

Sew them on in clusters, overlapping them slightly. Use doll-sized mother of pearl buttons for small,

delicate touches, using them for flower and bow centers, and to tack down lace motifs and other trims.

In addition to the common plastic ones found in most sewing departments, buttons are also made of wood, bone, leather, shells, glass, metal, porcelain, and other materials. Some companies make replicas of antique buttons by using the old molds.

In the Cousins quilt, buttons are used in fastening together the layers of the quilt.

Shisha Mirrors

Shisha mirrors are sewn on by making a series of straight stitches overlapping the edges of the mirror. These are then covered with Detached Buttonhole, and additional, decorative stitches may be added around the mirrors.

Like charms, the mirrors are best placed on wall hangings and smaller projects. Handle them carefully, they are made of glass and the edges are not ground smooth.

Tassels

Tassels are fun to add to crazy quilts to decorate patches, fans, or the outer edges or corners of a quilt. They are easy to make and a great way to use up extra threads from earlier projects. A variety of threads and thread types can be combined. Try mixing shiny rayons, metallics, and matte cottons in one tassel. Or use bunka, a knitted rayon cord for tassel-making.

NEEDED:
threads, cardboard, scissors, needle.

How to Make a Tassel

Cut a piece of cardboard to the length of tassel you are making. Wrap the cardboard with thread until it is as thick as you want it to be.

Thread a needle with about one yard of the same or matching thread. Slide the needle under the wrappings, and tie a knot about 6 inches from the end of the thread at the top of the tassel.

Cut across the bottom to remove it from the cardboard.

Holding the tassel together, wrap the long end of the thread near the top. Run the needle through the tassel several times to secure, then under the wrappings through to the top. Tie the ends at the top, and make a loop for hanging.

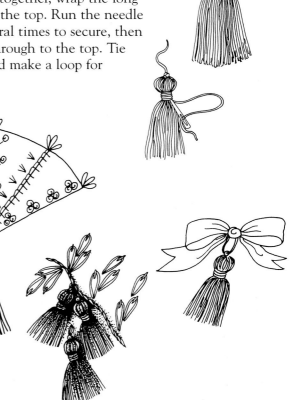

Adding Antiques

Poking around in antiques shops can turn up some interesting trinkets to add to crazy quilt projects. Clothing and other textiles in worn condition can sometimes be salvaged for their still-good parts. (Pieces that are still good and whole should not be cut up) Some dealers sell laces and trims that have been removed from clothing and linens. Hats, belts, and gloves and fabric purses may also have parts worth using, and many types of doilies are commonly found.

Cigarette Silks

Cigarette silks were used as premiums in cigarette packages. In the early 1900s, cigarette advertising became highly competitive, and although it was not quite acceptable for women to smoke they played a large role in sales of cigarettes. You can probably imagine a woman fond of needlework egging her husband to buy a pack of ciggies so she could have the silk! The manufacturers of cigarettes went so far as to print suggestions for needlework projects including table covers, doilies, portiers, and clothing accessories.

There were several types of "silks" made. The smaller ones

Antiques awaiting a crazy quilt project: buttons, cigarette silks and felts, hankie, doily, crocheted laces.

shown here were referred to by one manufacturer as "satin wonders." Close examination of these reveals a heavy base thread that is probably cotton beneath a silk satin surface. In other words, cotton-backed silk satin. The satin surface was printed by a process called chromolithography, capable of hairline details in depicting women, flags, birds, butterflies, flowers, and other subjects.

Another premium is the "felt," actually a piece of cotton

flannel fabric printed with an image. Many of these were flags, but butterflies can occasionally be found. These larger pieces were not in the packages. They had to be sent for.

Although the cigarette silks and felts are part of crazy quilting jargon these days, they weren't made until the early 1900's, as the fad for crazy quilting was ending. They appear in some post-Victorian crazy quilts, and in modern ones.

The silks and felts are now quite delicate and should be handled carefully. Do not turn their edges under. To fasten them onto quilts, lay ribbons over their edges and lightly embroider along them, or tack the ribbons on with sewing thread. Fasten them on in the final stages of making the quilt, and do not sew them onto quilts that will receive active use.

Laces

Laces of many types can be found in many antiques shops, with some shops specializing in them. If you are going to cut them up, find pieces that are beyond repair, in which sections are still useable.

Also consider making your

own motifs of crochet, knitting or tatting, or bobbin or tape lace. Patterns and instructions can be found for all of these.

Hankies

Silk hankies were carried by Victorian ladies. A pretty, whole one in good condition can be tacked onto a central patch on a crazy quilt. Pieces of salvaged ones can be tucked under patches. A shadowbox is an excellent way to display antiques without having to cut and sew them.

Buttons

Antique buttons can sometimes be found in jarfuls, reasonably priced, and this is the way to buy them. You will doubtless find a place for each one on your projects! They may need washing before using. Some may be covered in tiny bits of antique fabrics—these make nice flower centers. Sew on a large one, and attach a tassel.

Needlework

Old needlework in good condition, such as crewel, needlepoint, and other types, can often be used as patches. Full-size pieces can often be used as quilt centers. Unfinished pieces that are not likely to ever be finished, can be cut up and appliquéd or used as patches. If the design seems hopelessly outdated, try adding ribbonwork, or silk ribbon embroidery to them.

A mix of textures and materials are shown in this detail of the Landscape hanging.

Creating Moments

Bringing out the fullest potential of an area of a crazy quilt - staying within that area until it is complete in itself, is what I call "creating a moment."

Small areas of intricate detail draw the eye of the viewer. Detail of the Ladies and Fans quilt.

Much of the beauty of a fancy crazy quilt is in its details, those places on the quilt that attract the eye of the viewer.

One way to begin one of these is to place an embroidery hoop onto a selected area of the quilt. Appliqué on a photo on fabric, a cluster of ribbonwork flowers, or lace motif. Add to it using couched ribbons, silk ribbon or other embroidery, then adding some beads or buttons. Continue to add until the area seems complete, a mini work of art.

These "moments" can be very entrancing to do!

Remember to be kind to yourself.

When doing needlework, I often find myself getting so involved that I forget to notice aching bones. We're now finding that aches can turn into permanent injuries. It is important to change position often; stand up and stretch as much as necessary. Have some lively music playing, and even sit on the floor occasionally. If your neck or wrists are getting strained, find a position that causes no strain. Use adequate lighting to avoid eyestrain. Stitch in natural daylight if possible, either outdoors or by a window.

Oops, an ouch can be too late!
Bigger damage spells the fate.
Joints and bones and sight are dear.
Be kind in work to save a tear!

Part 2:
Paint, Dye, & Transfer Methods

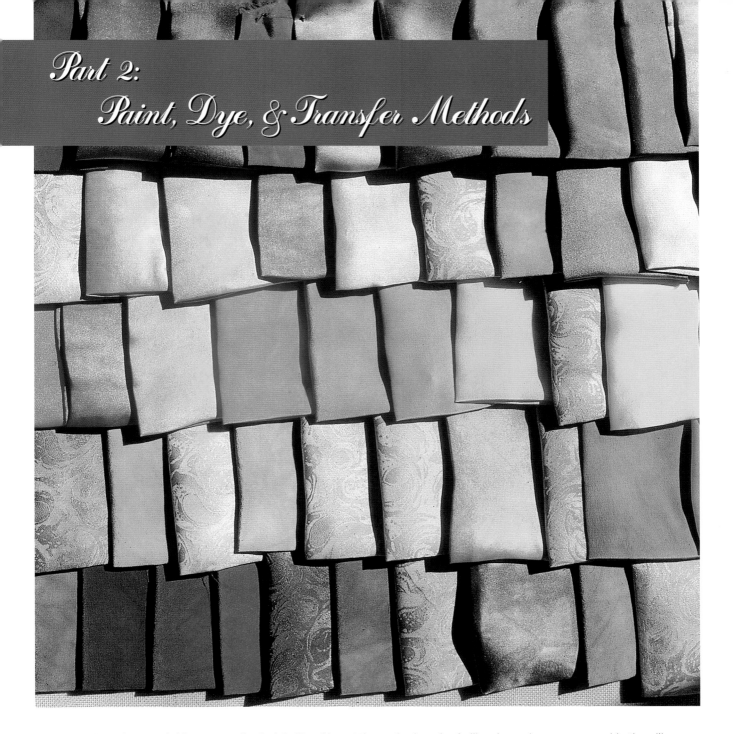

The Dye Experiments yield a range of colorful silks. Almost the entire bunch of silks shown here were used in the silk Ladies and Fans Quilt.

This chapter includes techniques that are the basis of textile design. Becoming a part of the fabric itself, they can be used to transform an ordinary or plain fabric into something extraordinary.

Dyeing and painting fabrics is truly an experience, and small amounts of fabric, ribbons, and trims can be done at a time. This is sometimes the only way to get the color effects you'd like to have, and achieving almost infinite ranges and shades is

easy to do. An hour or two of experimentation can yield sufficient patches, ribbons, threads, and trims to make a small quilt. And do not throw away pieces that might be considered imperfect. Some of my silk dye "mistakes" became surprisingly attractive gathered flowers and yo-yos!

Following are some basic techniques that can be done with minimal tool and materials requirements.

Dyeing

Dyeing Silk Patches, Trims, and Ribbons

If you are looking around for some interesting and even unusual colors for patches, trims, and threads, and feeling limited by those commercially available, then definitely you must try dyeing your own silks. By doing the dye experiments that follow, you can generate shades and mixes of colors that are compatible with each other because they will share characteristics.

There are different types of dyes. One is an instant setting dye that "strikes" almost immediately. Another requires a dye-setting additive after allowing the fabrics to set for 24 hours. Both of these are easy to use, and can be done in small amounts for patch-size pieces of fabric. The instructions given below are for the instant-setting dyes. You can also use any other type of silk dye following any additional instructions that came with them.

Do each of the four dye experiments, and you will end up with 40 or more differently colored patches, enough to make a small wall quilt, several miniatures, or to add to other fabrics for a larger piece.

MATERIALS

Instant-setting silk dyes, 1/2-oz. bottle each of red, yellow, blue, and black.
4 quarter-yard pieces of white or natural silk fabrics such as habotai, satin, jac quard, crepe.
Any desired silk ribbons, trims, threads.
1/2 cup measure.

4 small containers per experiment, jars or plastic, do not re-use in the kitchen.
Distilled water.
8 or more eye droppers.
Rubber gloves or tongs.
Large piece of plastic or plastic tablecloth to protect your work surface.

Procedure:

❶ Cover your work area with plastic. Cut each fat quarter into 12 pieces. Because they will be crazy patches they can be cut into unequal sizes. Prewash silk fabrics, threads, ribbons and trims that will be dyed, and keep them wet or damp.

❷ Follow instructions for each dye experiment following. Each experiment should yield 10 dyed silk patches. Use one eye dropper for each dye bottle, and one for each container of dye. The eye droppers are also used to stir the silks while dyeing.

❸ To dye evenly, stir the silks continuously while in the dye bath. For a mottled effect, crumple the silks into the dye, and

leave them for a couple of minutes. Then, turn them over, and leave them for a few minutes again. With either method, leave the pieces in the dye for several minutes.

❹ Remove silks from the dye with tongs, or just pick them up if you are wearing rubber gloves. Allow them to drip for a minute, then set them aside.

When finished, wash the silks with mild soap and rinse under running water. Roll them in a clean towel to remove excess moisture. Hang over a towel bar and allow to dry, then press. If you are using other than instant-setting dyes, follow instructions that came with the dyes for finishing.

❺ Clean containers, gloves, tongs, and eye droppers with soapy water, and rinse well.

Dye Experiments

With these experiments you will learn how to achieve any color or range of colors that you wish. To replicate a color, keep notes on the quantities of dye and water that were used. The second column in each experiment will result in a pastel shade of the color in the first column, and the browns in the third column will also be pastel. To create deeper browns, repeat the experiments, skipping the second column.

	Column 1	Column 2	Column 3
	To create mixed colors, add several drops of the following, and dye a piece of silk in each:	Then add the following to obtain a lighter shade of the color in column 1, and dye another piece of silk in each:	Then add a drop or two of the following to obtain browned shades, and dye another piece of silk in each:

Dye Experiment: YELLOW

Measure 1/2 cup of distilled water into a container, and add drops of yellow dye. Add and stir until the mixture is a medium yellow. Dye one piece of silk to check that this is a medium shade.

Divide the mixture into each of three containers.

	Column 1	Column 2	Column 3
Container 1	Red (= orange)	water	Blue
Container 2	Blue (= green)	water	Black & Red
Container 3	Black (= chartreuse)	water	Black

Dye Experiment: BLUE

Measure 1/2 cup of distilled water into a container, and add drops of blue dye. Add and stir until the mixture is a medium blue. Dye one piece of silk to check that this is a medium shade.

Divide the mixture into each of three containers.

	Column 1	Column 2	Column 3
Container 1	Red (= royal purple)	water	Black & Yellow
Container 2	Yellow (= green)	water	Red (= lt. moss green)
Container 3	Black (= deep blue)	water	Black

Dye Experiment: RED

Measure 1/2 cup of distilled water into a container, and add drops of red dye. Add and stir until the mixture is a medium red. Dye one piece of silk to check that this is a medium shade.

Divide the mixture into each of three containers.

	Column 1	Column 2	Column 3
Container 1	Yellow (= orange)	water	Blue
Container 2	Blue (= purple)	water	Black
Container 3	Black	water	Black

Dye Experiment: BLACK

Measure 1/2 cup of distilled water into a container, and add drops of black dye. Add and stir until the mixture is a medium gray. Dye one piece of silk to check that this is a medium shade.

Divide the mixture into each of three containers.

	Column 1	Column 2	Column 3
Container 1	Red	water	Blue
Container 2	Blue, Yellow and 1 or 2 drops of Red	water	Black
Container 3	Yellow and 1 drop of Red	water	Red

Tips and Ideas for Dyeing

1 Spread out some silk ribbons and trims on your plastic-covered work surface. Have a spray bottle handy to keep them dampened. As you do the dye experiments, place drops of dye randomly and spaced apart on the ribbons and trims. Select colors to obtain multi-hued ribbons and trims.

2 Some of the Dye Experiment colors will overlap, for instance, green will be derived from both the yellow and the blue experiments, but you can make them different shades each time by adjusting amounts.

3 You may find that the black experiments yield the most interesting shades including teal, mauve, dusty green and purple. You may want to experiment further to find other shades.

4 Working inside a cardboard box, draw a popsicle stick across a dye-loaded toothbrush, splattering dye on a piece of silk.

5 Tie strings or fasten pieces of silk with paper clips before placing them into the dye to achieve tie-dye effects.

6 Lay a large, wet piece of fabric on your plastic-covered work surface. Drip onto it dye mixtures or dye straight from the bottle, allowing the colors to

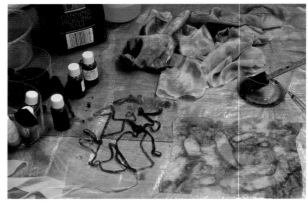

Using dye to create unusual patch fabrics and ribbons.

run into each other. Leave the fabric in place until the dyes set.

7 Add water to a dye bath, adding several times and dyeing with each addition in order to get lighter shades of that color. Especially do this if you've found a color you really like.

8 Overdye already colored silks–either pieces you've done, or commercially dyed silks.

9 Lay a patch-size piece of dampened fabric onto your work surface. Sprinkle salt on the fabric, then, using an eye dropper, place drops of a dye mixture onto it. Allow the dye to set for several minutes, then rinse thoroughly.

Painting

Painting was a skill cultivated by Victorian ladies who did some of their paintings on silk or velvet fabric, and included them in crazy quilts. Sometimes the border of a crazy quilt was beautifully painted.

The Victorians used oil paints. The acrylic paints we have now are more practical, easier and less messy to use. Acrylics are water-based, meaning they can be thinned and cleaned up with water. However, unlike other water based paints such as watercolors and tempera, after

Applying paint to fabric can yield some interesting results.

acrylics dry on the fabric they are not likely to wash out, especially if they are heat-set.

Purchase acrylic paints in artist's tubes, or in small containers that are sold for stenciling. Red, yellow, blue, black, and white make a complete set from which any color can be mixed. See the section on color theory in the chapter, Natural Elegance for how to achieve different colors by mixing the primary and secondary colors.

It isn't necessary to be able to paint scenes,

On a mid-1800's crazy quilt, a rose was painted on black velvet. Detail. The Brick Store Museum, Kennebunk, Maine.

Two miniature paintings by Kim Kovaly of The Willow shop, Limerick, Maine, are beautiful additions to a crazy quilt, but require skill with paints and brushes. The Willow Shop.

A painting on velvet makes an elaborate sashing in this mid-1800's crazy quilt. Detail. The Brick Store Museum, Kennebunk, Maine.

flowers, and other objects. Painting can be used to enhance patch fabrics and create backgrounds for embroidery and other embellishment. You can paint lines and brush strokes that swoop, curve, overlap, fade in and out, and many other fantastical effects that are easy to do. These can make excellent backgrounds for embroidery of all types, landscape quilts, and just interesting patches.

Paints can be used on many fabric types such as cotton, rayon, silk, wool, and others. Begin with scrap fabrics to try some of the following techniques. Remember that embroidery and other embellishments can be added later to enhance your efforts. You can also cut up the pieces and use them in sections.

Heat-setting acrylic paint

Acrylic paints must be heat-set to make them permanent. Before heat-setting, allow the paint to air dry at least 24 hours. Place a press cloth over the painted area. Heat the iron to the correct temperature setting for the fabric, and hold the iron on for 30 seconds. Repeat to cover all of the painted area. The fabric should be left again for 24 hours before it is washed.

Follow the instructions that are on the paint container for clean up. Acrylic paints are water soluble, but are permanent after they dry. For this reason, brushes and work surfaces should be cleaned with soap and water before the paint dries.

MATERIALS

Acrylic paints in tubes or jars in red, blue, yellow, black and white.
Artist's brushes in a variety of sizes.

Bowls or small pots for mixing.
Water.
Pallette or plate for blending colors.

Prewash the fabric, allow it to dry, and press.

There are two basic techniques for painting: wet brush, and dry brush. For dry brush painting, slightly dampen the brush, then dip it into the paint and brush the paint onto the fabric. Depending on how much paint is on the brush, this will leave broad or wispy brush strokes on the fabric. This technique can be used on dry or dampened fabric. If you brush the paint onto very wet fabric, it will act like a wash, and spread.

For the wet brush technique, dip the brush into water and leave it very wet. Use paint that is thinned with water. As the paint is brushed onto the fabric, it will spread out as the fabric absorbs the moisture and the paint runs. This is called a "wash," and achieves a similar effect to dyeing the fabric. Different effects can be obtained by having the fabric either damp, or very wet.

Try the following wet and dry brush experiments using the colors of your choice:

1 Using the dry brush technique, randomly brush paint onto fabric that is dry or slightly damp. Allow it to dry completely. Now, go back over it with a wash.

2 The reverse of 1, paint a wash onto wet fabric, and allow it to dry thoroughly. Then, dry brush in any pattern over the wash.

3 In separate areas of the pallette, mix two different wash colors. Dampen the fabric, or have it wet. Brush on the washes side by side and allow them to run into each other.

4 While the paint is still wet, lift the fabric to allow the paint to run. This can be done with any wash. The wetter the fabric, the more the paint will run. Leave the fabric to dry.

Painting techniques:

1 Stroking with the brush, or dabbing with it will achieve different results, especially using the dry brush technique.

2 Placing two or more colors on the same brush without mixing them together can be used for rainbow-like effects.

3 Instead of brushes, use your fingers, foam brushes, or other implements to apply the paint.

4 Use sponges, crumpled paper, or other materials to dab the paint onto the fabric.

5 Drip paint onto the fabric.

Stencilling

Applying paint to velveteen fabric using stencils produces a clean-edge design with an almost luminescent effect from the paint. I like this effect, but you can also simply paint on the velveteen without using stencils. The stencil designs here are finished with embroidery.

I use freezer paper to make stencils. It is inexpensive, readily available, easy to cut, and the plastic side of the paper prevents the paint from wearing through. Although it will not hold up to heavy use, it is fine for one or two uses. If you are going to use a stencil for more than this, cut it from a sturdier material. To reuse a stencil, first allow it to dry completely.

The type of velveteen I prefer to use is a low-napped all-cotton type, rather than the high plush types.

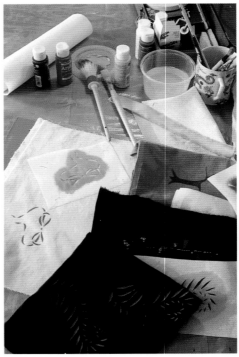

Tools and materials for stenciling on fabrics. A piece of velvet ribbon was painted along its edges.

MATERIALS

Velveteen fabric, prewashed.
Freezer paper, pencil.
Smooth corrugated cardboard larger than the design.
Stencil brush about 3/4" to 1" in diameter.
Acrylic paints in red, blue, yellow, black and white.
Pallette or substitute.
Sewing pins.
Craft knife and smooth cardboard.
Water.

Instructions:

1 Lay a piece of freezer paper over the design to be used, and draw the outlines that will be cut out. Place this on the smooth cardboard or other cutting surface, and cut along the lines using the craft knife. (The freezer paper can be ironed onto smooth fabrics. Do not iron it onto velveteen or other napped fabrics, it will pull out the pile when the paper is removed).

2 Place the velveteen onto the corrugated cardboard, then the stencil on top with the plastic side down. Pin into the cardboard to hold everything in place.

3 Mix the color to be used. For leaves, mix yellow and blue to get green. The green can be shaded with a drop of black, or tinted with white. A drop of red can be added to get a warm, mossy green. Add extra blue if you prefer a teal, or blue-green.

It is advisable to add plenty of white to colors that will be stenciled onto dark velveteens so they show up well. Mixed colors can be left partly unmixed, to give a varied effect to the painting. Do not add much water to the paint. If it is too wet, the color will bleed under the stencil.

4 Dab the brush in the paint, and again alongside the paint on the pallette to remove excess. The brush should be dry, and there should not be a lot of paint on it. Holding the brush vertically, stencil the design by tapping the brush repeatedly until sufficient color is transferred. Remove the stencil and allow the paint to dry.

To do the Hollyhock design, first place pinholes through both patterns at the dots. Place pins through these dots into the cardboard for the leaves stencil. Keep the pins in place when the stencil is removed. Allow the leaves to dry. Place the flower stencil over the leaves, placing the stencil onto the pins at the dots. Mix a rosy or peachy color and stencil the flowers.

Allow the stenciled design to dry, heat-set, and embroider the details.

Work stem in outline stitch

Transfer dots and use to align flowers with leaves

Rubbings

This technique was used for the Butterstamp quilt. I got the idea at The Butterstamp Shop in Wiscasset, Maine where I found plaques, curtain tie-backs, and other objects made from butterstamp impressions. At the same shop were supplies for gravestone rubbings. And I thought, what a great way to transfer the beautifully carved butterstamp designs onto fabric!

A butterstamp wrapped in plastic for doing rubbings on silk fabrics. Dye pastels are from Pentel. Butterstamps collection of Paul Baresel.

Instructions:

Do not use plain crayons or pastels for this. The crayons or pastels must have dye in them to be permanent on fabric.

Follow any instructions with the crayons or pastels.

If you are using wooden butterprints, first cover them with a thin plastic to avoid dyeing the wood. To do a rubbing, hold a piece of silk fabric over the print. Hold tightly, and if necessary, secure the fabric with a rubber band to prevent shifting. Lightly rub the crayon or pastel over the fabric until the design shows up.

Remove the fabric from the print, and iron it between two sheets of clean, white paper on an ironing board that is adequately protected. (Protect your ironing board with extra paper or fabric). This sets the dye and removes the grease from the crayon. Repeat, using clean paper to be sure the grease is removed.

Wash the pieces separately, dry and press.

Patches on the Butterstamp quilt are rubbings taken from antique butterstamps.

Photographic images on fabric is not a new idea. Crazy quilts of the late 1800's often include an image or two that is a photo on silk.

Now, a similar effect can be had by using a special transfer paper. An image is photocopied onto it, then ironed onto fabric. Silk ribbon and other embroidery can be worked around the image on fabric. Add trims, charms, beads, and buttons to embellish.

MATERIALS

Photo transfer paper.
Color photocopier.
Image: color photo or antique postcard.
Iron.

Instructions:

Follow the instructions with the transfer paper. Basically, you will take the paper and your images to a business that does color photocopying, and have them copied onto the transfer paper. You then take this home, and iron the image onto fabric. Each image is good only once, so position carefully, making sure the fabric is not out of kilter.

If you are placing the image onto silk fabric, try a piece of scrap fabric with the iron setting for the time indicated. If the silk scorches, place a sheet of plain paper between fabric and iron. If your test comes out OK, do the transfer.

You may find that some color photos transferred to a quilt appear very bright, and sometimes even garish. To tone down a "loud" photo, trim away some background, border it with embroidery, or paint around with a soft wash to blend it in. If the photos are transferred onto pastel-color fabric, the color of the fabric will show through the light areas of the photo.

Photos of roses from my garden, and antique postcards are waiting to be photocopied onto transfer paper. A rose photo transferred onto the Ladies and Fans quilt has silk ribbon embroidered leaves added to it.

Text and Crazy Quilts

Giving people something to read on a crazy quilt seems to draw them to it. They simply have to read the words! Text can be applied in a number of ways including pens and crayons containing dye, and with outline and other embroidery stitches. If you are using pens, some fabrics are easier to write on than others. For the best results, a smooth cotton should be used. Always heat-set any paint or dye materials that are added to fabric, including fabric pens. To embroider the letters, write the words to be used on a sheet of plain paper, then use the tissue paper transfer method to place them onto the fabric.

You can use:

names of people and pets
poetry
quotes
place names such as states, cities, countries
words relevant to the theme of a quilt

Documenting a quilt.

Documentation is important if a quilt survives through many years. Many antique quilts that have been abandoned, donated, or sold out of the original family are not signed or dated. It is impossible to document where and how they originated, and because of this it is a difficult task for historians to study the place of quilts and quiltmaking in our history.

Your initials, the year the quilt is finished, and the city or state the quilt is made in are important bits of information that can be embroidered or painted on the patches of the quilt. Additional documentation can be written on a piece of fabric such as muslin, using fabric pens. Neatly hem the fabric and slipstitch it to the quilt's backing.

A method that was used for documenting fundraiser quilts was to sew a small pocket to the backing of the quilt for inserting notes written on paper.

Wording placed on a quilt can indicate names, places, and objects.

Finishing Touches

The variety of ways antique crazy quilts are assembled is yet another demonstration that this type of quilt was a creative phenomenon. Made with or without battings, the Victorian crazy quilted tops were finished with borders, bindings, laces, ruffles, or other edgings. They were tied with embroidery or sewn stitches, pearl threads, ribbons, and sometimes were not tied at all. There was no preconceived manner of finishing a crazy quilt.

Because several methods for each step of the finishing are given, please read through the chapter before beginning so you can choose an appropriate procedure for your quilt.

Adding a Border

Borders on some of the antique crazy quilts were extravagantly done, with corner fans, paintings on velvet, embroidery, ribbonwork, patchwork, appliqué, and other techniques. Even plain velvet borders have much to offer these quilts, the plush of the velvet adding a softening touch. Borders act as a frame, provide additional

The 1898 quilt shown here is one of many crazy quilts bordered and backed with cotton sateen fabric. This quilt has a batting. Collection of the author.

area to embellish, expand the size of the quilt, and in some cases, support its theme.

Themes portrayed on a quilt can be reflected by a border design. Early America is the theme suggested by the border of the Butterstamp quilt, with its folk-style patchwork. A trailing vine of roses surrounds the Horses and Roses quilt, and a feminine ruffle decks out the Ladies and Fans quilt.

Borders are sewn onto the quilt after patch embellishment and embroidery are finished.

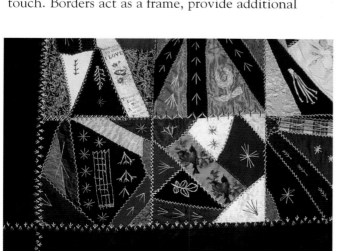

Straight stitch fans decorate the velvet border of the 1862 "White Rose" crazy quilt. Detail. Photographed at Shiretown Antique Center, Alfred, Maine.

Planning the Border

Most of my borders are planned while the quilt is in progress. Beginning with a rough idea of the finished size of the quilt, I try to visualize how different types of borders will look, sketching out some of these ideas. Eventually a particular idea strikes me as something I'd really like to try. Working up a small section as a sample is usually enough to indicate whether the idea will work or not.

If the quilt is for a bed, the dimensions of the border may already have been decided. For other types of quilts, this decision can be reserved for last, when the top is nearing completion. At this point, border colors and widths can be "tried on" the quilt, to determine what will look best.

"Trying on" Borders

To choose a border fabric, take your completed or nearly completed quilt top to a fabric store. Using a cutting table, unroll about a yard or so off a bolt, fold the cut edge under, and lay the quilt top over this leaving a border's width of the fabric protruding. Try several different fabrics and compare how they look with the quilt. Look for both a color and a width that will best enhance your quilt. Be sure to check your color choice in natural lighting before buying.

The principles of color theory given in the chapter, Natural Elegance, also apply to the border. Use black or dark colors for a border that will tend to recede, causing the quilt top to come forward visually, highlighting it. A neutral color will enlarge the quilt without significantly affect-

ing its color scheme. If the border consists of similar colors to those in the quilt top, as in the Butterstamp quilt, a narrow contrasting sashing can be added to differentiate the two.

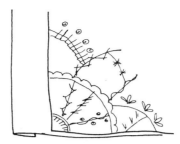

Fabrics for Borders

Cotton sateen must have been considered a "utilitarian" fabric in the late 1800s. It was used for backings and borders on many crazy quilts, and also for vest linings. Now, this gorgeous fabric seems all too rare, unfortunately hard to find. Its weight, satin surface, and elegant drape make it a perfect choice for a finishing a quilt.

Many other fabric types also make excellent borders including velvet, velveteen, satin, silks noil or dupion, linens and wools. Some drapery and decorating fabrics, including bengaline, moiré, and damask with their attractively textured and patterned surfaces are additional possibilities. Take into consideration a fabric's weight, drape, fiber content, and care features, and be sure it will be suitable for any embellishment method that will be used.

Figuring Yardage for Borders

Determine the width of the yardage you will be purchasing. Cottons and acetates are often available as 44-inch widths, but are sometimes up to 60 inches wide.

If you are making a small quilt, and the longest border piece fits across the yardage, up to 9-inch wide borders (including seam allowances) can be cut out of 1 yard of fabric.

For larger quilts, cut the border from the length of the fabric. Purchase the length of fabric required for the longest border piece.

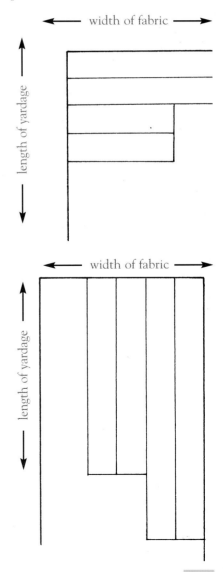

Piecing Fabric for Borders

Whenever possible, I prefer to have my borders of continuous lengths of fabric. This is may require purchasing more fabric, but I think it gives a smoother result. Any left over fabric is saved for future quilts and projects.

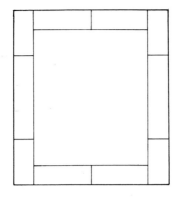

If you are going to piece the border, make the pieces match on both sides of the quilt. Divide the border length in half or in thirds being sure to add seam allowances to the ends of each section. Sew the sections together, then sew the borders to the quilt.

Backing Fabrics, Dimensions and Yardage

Many of the quilts I've made are backed with calico fabrics purchased for traditional quilting.

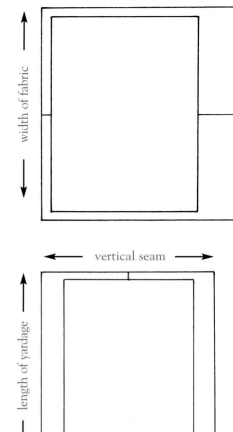

This quilting experience begins and ends with an Amish wall hanging that is tucked away in a closet patched and mostly unquilted. Having discovered that "quilting" has creative counterparts that I enjoy much more, chances are it will stay there unless I choose to work it into a crazy quilt.

Unless you want the back of your quilt to serve a purpose, a quilt's backing can be almost any good fabric. Choose a suitable fabric if you will have signatures, documentation, a pocket, ribbon bows or other embellishment on the back of the quilt.

If you are making a knife-edge quilt, use the same fabric as the border to have it blend in, or as in the Butterstamp quilt, use a contrasting color so a sliver of it shows on the front. This hairline, if it is a dark color, will keep a light-colored wall quilt from blending into the wall.

Cotton sateen was often used in the antique crazy quilts, and is an excellent choice of backing fabric. For a quilt that will be warm and cozy, try a velveteen or corduroy backing. A wool quilt can have either a wool or cotton backing. Silk quilts that have silk batting should also have a silk backing fabric in order to help hold the batting in place.

To calculate the amount of yardage to purchase for backing, first measure the quilt. If the quilt width is the same or less than the width of the fabric, simply purchase the amount required for the length of the quilt.

If the backing must be pieced, purchase fabric that is twice the width of the quilt to have a horizontal seam or, purchase twice the length of the quilt to have a vertical seam.

Always buy a little extra in case of shrinkage.

Interfacing the Border

In order for a border to hang properly, it should be adjusted to approximate the thickness of the quilt top with its multiple layers. If the border is too floppy for a firmly made top, or too firm for a drapey one, it won't look right.

To make this adjustment, interface the border using the same type of foundation fabric that was used in the quilt. Cut the foundation the dimensions of each border piece, place them wrong sides together and proceed as if they were one fabric.

Pressing the Seams

If embroidery will be worked along seams, press them open. If embroidery will not be used, the seams that join the border to the quilt top can be pressed towards the border.

A Plain Border

This border is simple to make. Determine the width of the border including seam allowances. To purchase yardage, two borders will equal the length of the quilt top, and two will be the width of the quilt plus two border widths.

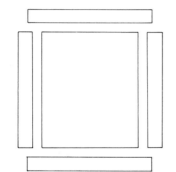
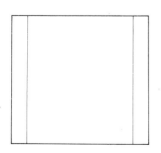
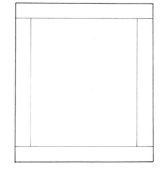

❶ Measure the length of the quilt, including seam allowances. Cut two pieces of border fabric this length. Cut two of foundation fabric and place one of these on the back of each border piece, and handle them as if they were one. Sew each side border to the quilt top. Press the seams.

❷ Measure the width of the quilt including the side borders. Cut two pieces of border

fabric this length. Cut two of foundation fabric, place one on the back of each border piece and handle as one. Sew each to top and bottom of quilt. Press the seams.

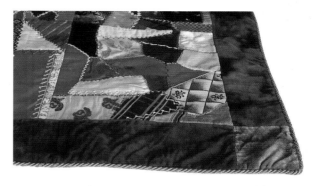

A border made with corner blocks is one of many ways that crazy quilts were finished. This one is attractively edged in gold cording. Detail of an 1885 crazy quilt. The Brick Store Museum, Kennebunk, Maine.

Feather and Herringbone stitches were used along block seams after they were sewn together in this antique wool crazy quilt. This quilt was finished without adding a border. Owned by Avalon Antiques, photographed at Arundel Antiques, Arundel, Maine. Photo by Paul Baresel.

A Border with Corner Blocks

Make this the same as the above method except make two borders the same length, and two the same as the width of the quilt. Sew on the side borders. Make 4 corner blocks, lining them as above with foundation fabric. Sew one corner to each end of the top and bottom pieces, then sew to the quilt top.

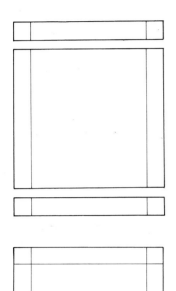

A Border with Mitered Corners

Determine the width of the border. To purchase yardage, two borders will equal the length of the quilt top and two border widths, and the other two will equal the width of the quilt plus two border widths.

❶ Cut two pieces of border fabric the length of the quilt plus two border widths and seam allowances. Cut two of foundation fabric and place one of these on the back of each border piece.

❷ Sew each side border to the

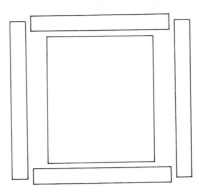

quilt top leaving the quilt's seam allowance at each end unsewn. Press the seams.

Cut two pieces of border fabric the width of the quilt plus two border widths and seam allowances and repeat instruction 1 to add the top and bottom borders.

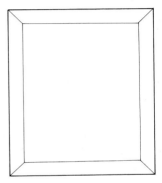

right side of quilt

❸ Place one corner of the quilt on the ironing board. Fold back the two adjoining borders, and make a crease exactly where the seam will be. Repeat for the remaining three corners.

❹ Sew each corner as follows:

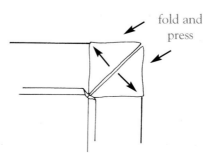

fold and press

with right sides together, line up the crease of each border section and pin. Sew from the outer edge to the inner edge. Trim away excess fabric, and press the seam open.

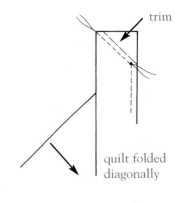

trim

quilt folded diagonally

Embroidered or Appliquéd Border

Before adding batting and backing, work any embroidery or appliqué design.

Scalloped Patchwork Border and Backing

Finish embroidery and embellishment on the quilt top, then add a narrow sashing if desired. Set the piece aside.

Choose the fabrics to be used for the patchwork border.

The pattern for the scalloped patches is 2 inches wide to fit a quilt top that is an even number of inches in width and length. Divide the length of the quilt top (minus the seam allowances) by 2 to get the number of blocks required. If the sewn row of patches doesn't exactly fit the quilt top, the first and last patches can be made either wider or narrower. Or, adjust the width of the pattern by finding a width that is evenly divisible by the quilt top dimensions.

The Butterstamp quilt is a theme quilt displaying folk art images; 1994. Collection of Paul Baresel.

Assemble the border as follows:

1 Copy or trace the pattern onto plain paper and cut it out. Cut out the required number of patches for each border length, and cut an equal number out of foundation fabric. Place one foundation piece on the back of each patch. Sew patches together to make each border. Press seams open.

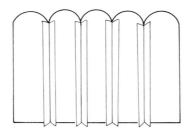

2 Sew the side borders to the quilt top. Sew the corner blocks to the ends of the top and bottom borders, and sew to the quilt top. Press the seams. Work embroidery along the patch seams.

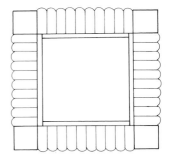

3 The easiest way to install a backing is to make it in two pieces, as in the diagram. Be sure to allow for seam allowances to join the sections. Cut the backing slightly larger than the quilt top.

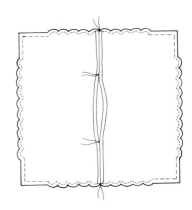

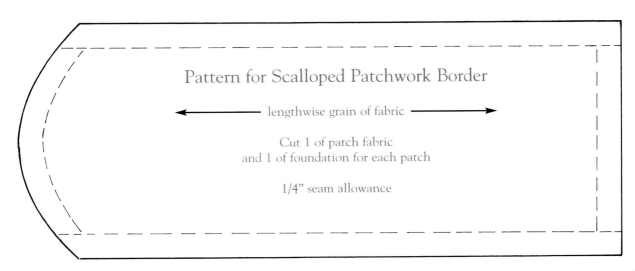

Pattern for Scalloped Patchwork Border

← lengthwise grain of fabric →

Cut 1 of patch fabric
and 1 of foundation for each patch

1/4" seam allowance

With right sides together, sew the seam of the backing leaving the center 24 inches or so open. Press the seam open. Place the backing right sides together with the quilt top, having the quilt on top. Pin carefully all around.

4 Taking your time, sew around the entire outer edge. For the best results, end stitching at each patch seam, and begin stitching on the following patch without leaving a gap.

backing fabric

quilt top

5 Trim excess backing fabric, and trim seams. Turn the quilt right side out, and carefully press the scalloped edges. Slipstitch the center of the backing closed.

6 Finish the quilt by tying the quilt top, having the ties on the back. Embroidery stitches can be worked along the sashings. Here, Straight stitch fans were used.

Types of Batting

A batting can be added along with the backing after the quilt top is finished. Battings are entirely optional; most Victorian crazies did not have them.

There are many types of batting available. My preferences are always with the natural fiber types, such as silk, wool, and cotton.

Silk battings come and go. Years ago I purchased "silk caps" that had to be carefully tugged open. As they were pulled, the fibers gradually released, creating a batting that seemed skimpy but proved to be of sufficient loft for a silk quilt. Then, there were silk battings that could be used straight out of the package. Battings are the same as carded fiber ready for spinning, called rovings. These can be pulled apart to be used as batting. Look for battings and rovings that are made of long fibers if they are to be tugged apart.

Silk crazy quilts require only a thin layer of batting that should be placed between two layers of silk fabrics. Silk batting clings to silk fabrics, helping to hold the layers in place. If, in tying the quilt, the batting comes through the fabric along with the thread, do not keep pulling or the entire batting could come out (how's that for magic!?). Instead, with a sharp embroidery scissors, trim it very closely to the quilt top, then pull up on the fabric to work the batting to the inside of the quilt.

Wool battings have more loft than cotton, and are excellent for bed coverings used in cool climates. Store these quilts in a cedar trunk if they are not in use during the summer.

Cotton battings are excellent for wall hangings, or any size quilt. They are easy to handle because they are not lofty. Some cotton battings must be prewashed to shrink them and to remove the oil from the cotton seeds.

Use only battings that allow plenty of space between ties or quilting stitches. Those that must be closely quilted are not suitable for crazy quilts.

Cotton flannel fabric may be used to add a little extra loft or warmth in place of a batting. Velveteen or corduroy can also be used for the backing fabric for extra warmth and weight.

Joining sections of batting to create a larger piece is done the same for all types. Edges are butted together, sometimes by fluffing each to blend them into each other. Never overlap two pieces of batting, as this can make a long bump in the quilt. Loosely stitching the join with long stitches - about two or more inches in length - will help to keep the pieces joined. Otherwise, be sure to use sufficient ties when tying the quilt.

To Add Lace or Ruffled Edgings

Some antique crazies are made all the more attractive by their lace and ruffled edgings. To add this type of edging to a quilt, choose a cotton or rayon venice lace, or an heirloom cotton lace. Or, better yet, crochet, Battenberg, bobbin, tat, or knit a lace edging if you have any of these skills. Choose a pattern in a width that is suitable for the quilt. Some laces such as the cotton net lace used in the Doll's Quilt are often sold flat, and must be gathered, then sewn into a seam. Start with a length of lace that is 1 1/2 times the finished length, and gather it by running a basting thread along the long raw edge. While pinning the lace to the quilt top, draw up the basting thread, gathering the lace to fit.

Use a knife-edge quilt finish to sew lace into a seam. To add an edging with a finished edge such as crochet, simply stitch it by hand to the finished edge of the quilt.

Pleat, or add extra gathers to the lace or ruffle at each corner of the quilt to have sufficient fullness to turn the corner.

Knife-edge Quilt Finish.

This method creates an edge into which laces and trims may be inserted. It can be used on a quilt top with or without borders.

1 To the finished quilt top, with right sides together, pin any lace or trim that will be sewn into the seam. Sew together the short ends, or overlap and curve the ends outward so the raw ends will be sewn into the seam allowance.

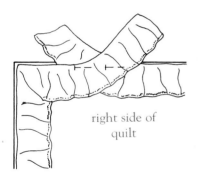

right side of quilt

2 With right sides together, place the backing fabric on the quilt top. If a batting is added, place it on top of the backing. Pin.

3 Sew around, leaving an opening large enough to turn the quilt. Trim corners, and trim the seam allowance if necessary. Turn right sides out, press. Sew the opening closed.

Stack and Bind

Binding is a traditional method of finishing a quilt that was sometimes used to finish Victorian crazy quilts. A binding can be used in place of, or in addition to a border.

Assemble the quilt layers with wrong sides together; quilt top, (batting if used), and backing. Pin, then baste around the outer edges. Measure around the quilt to determine the required yardage.

This 1890's quilt was edged with a simple binding. Courtesy of The Kirk Collection, Omaha, NE. Photo by Nancy T. Kirk.

Detail of the 1890's quilt. Courtesy of The Kirk Collection, Omaha, NE. Photo by Nancy T. Kirk.

1 Make or purchase sufficient 1/2-inch wide bias binding.
2 Open out the binding and sew it with right sides together to the sides of the quilt top, then cut it even with the top and bottom edges of the quilt. Press, folding the bias to the back of the quilt. Pin, and slipstitch invisibly.
3 Sew the bias to the top and bottom of the quilt, leaving about 1/2 inch extra at each end. Fold in the ends and slipstitch for a neat finish. Press and slipstitch as before.

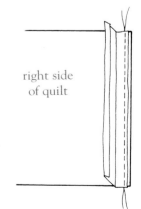

right side of quilt

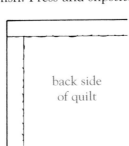

back side of quilt

How to make Bias Binding

Making a bias tape for binding is easy to do, and many different types of fabrics can be used for this including silks, cottons, rayons, and lightweight wool.

1 Begin with a square of fabric. A 36-inch square will yield 24 lengths from 12 inches to 1-1/3 yards long that are 1-1/2 inches wide, sufficient bias for most quilts.

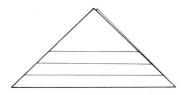

2 Fold the fabric diagonally as shown.

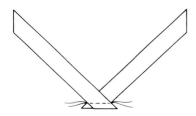

3 Press a crease along the fold, then cut along it. Measure, and cut strips as needed. A 1/2-inch wide binding is made of 1-1/2-inch strips to have 1/4-inch seam allowances. Cut the strip slightly wider if more allowance is needed.

4 Place the strips right sides together and sew 1/4-inch seams as shown. Press the seams open or to one side.

5 To press, first fold the strip in half lengthwise and press the fold. Then, turn in each long raw edge 1/4 inch and press.

Self-binding

Here, the backing fabric is folded to the front of the quilt, forming a self-binding that is slipstitched.

1 Cut the backing 1-1/2 inches larger on each side than the quilt top including borders if it has them. This will add 3 inches to the length and width dimensions of the quilt top. Place the backing and quilt with wrong sides together. If a batting is used, have that in place also. Pin.

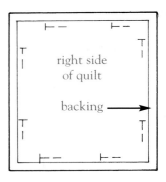

right side of quilt

backing ⟶

2 Fold the backing in 1/2 an inch, and fold again onto the quilt top and pin. Fold corners neatly. Slipstitch invisibly all around.

Tying the Quilt

After assembly, the layers of the crazy quilt must be fastened together. The following methods are the same as those used on the Victorian quilts. You can choose one method or combine several.

First, lay the quilt out flat on a clean floor or other surface that supports the entire quilt. Press it lightly if necessary, and check that both sides lie absolutely smooth. If the quilt is large, safety-pin baste in a few places.

1 With sewing thread and needle, and the quilt right side up, make small tacking stitches here and there over the entire top, having them about 4 inches or so apart. Make the stitches so they are

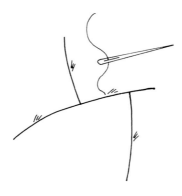

Ways to tie a crazy quilt, including adding stitches, thread and ribbon ties. Vertical strips of cotton fabric help to support a hanging quilt.

An unusual application of crazy quilting: the backing of this antique wool quilt was crazy quilted of black fabrics and embroidered in bright threads. The red stitches are quilting stitches used to join the layers. Detail. Courtesy of The Kirk collection, Omaha, NE. Photo by Nancy T. Kirk.

concealed along the edges of the patches, or under embroidery.

2 Many of the antique quilts have ties that are knotted on the back of the quilt. With the quilt wrong side up, thread a needle with a length of thread, pearl cotton, yarn, or ribbon, and make small stitches about 5-6 inches apart. Cut the thread in the middle between the stitches, and tie the ends. Use square, not granny knots so they won't come loose.

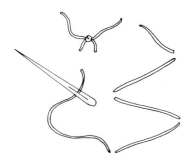

In case you don't want the threads of the ties showing on the surface of the quilt, make the ties "in the ditch," or in the seams between patches. Have the quilt right side up, bring the threaded needle up from the back to the front, and take a stitch to the back.

3 Add embroidery stitches to the face of the quilt, working them through all layers. Thread ends should be finished with a few tiny stitches (no knots) on the back.

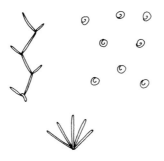

4 If the quilt has a batting, the batting can be quilted to the backing fabric with quilting stitches (short running stitch). After quilting, place the quilt top on it with wrong sides together and sew a binding around the quilt. A few ties can then be added.

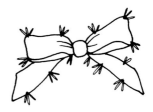

Ties, small stitches, and the ends of embroidery threads can be concealed under small bows tied of 1/4-inch to 1/2-inch wide ribbon, sewn or tacked to the quilt backing.

ABOVE: A pillow made of soft rose, peach, and blue shades will fit into almost any decorating scheme.

Pillow

BELOW: This antique block was formed into a pincushion in the shape of a pillow. Note the unusual stitches. Photographed at The Barn at Cape Neddick, Maine.

MATERIALS

Pillow form the desired size.
Muslin foundation the size of the pillow form plus seam allowances.
Backing fabric the size of the foundation plus about 6 extra inches in one direction.
Optional - edging (fringe or lace), sufficient yardage to go around the pillow.
Patch fabrics in 8 or more colors.
Size 8 pearl cotton in 8 or more colors.
Trims, laces as desired.
Velcro or snap closures.
Sewing thread.

Pillows are easy to make and are a marvelous way of displaying a singular block of crazy quilting. The following pattern can be made the size of your choice. Before beginning the pillow top, purchase a pillow form and make the pillow the same size. If you are a beginner, a small pillow of about 12 inches square is a good size to start with. The one shown here is 18 inches square. It is backed with rose-colored cotton velveteen, and a heavy cotton fringe was sewn into the seams.

Choose fabrics that are washable, and trims that will not catch on anything.
Use 1/2-inch seam allowances for assembly.
Instructions:

1 Patch the foundation according to the method of your choice. Embellish and embroider the patched pillow top.

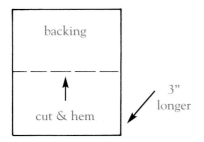

2 Have the backing fabric the same width as the patched pillow top, but 6 inches longer. See the diagram. Cut the backing in half. To hem each, fold under 1/4 inches of each cut edge twice, then sew along the folds.

3 With right sides together, pin lace or fringe around the pillow top, finishing the raw ends.

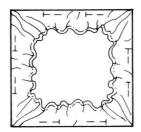

4 With right sides together, pin the backing pieces onto the pillow top matching side, top and bottom edges. The backing will overlap in the middle of the pillow. Sew around. Turn the piece right side out, and insert the pillow form. Sew on Velcro or snap closures to the overlapped edge of the backing.

How to Hang a Wall Quilt

Smaller quilts need only a rod pocket placed along the upper edge of the back of the quilt, and a dowel placed through it. To make a rod pocket, cut a strip of muslin or other fabric the width of the quilt by about 6 inches wide. Fold under the short ends once or twice, and sew. Now, the strip will be narrower than the quilt. Press under the long edges about 1/4 inch, and handstitch to the upper edge of the back of the quilt, centering it.

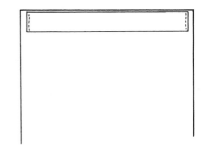

Place two large cup hooks into the wall to support the ends of the dowel. Wooden beads or curtain finials may be glued onto the ends of the dowel to prevent it from slipping off the hooks.

Large quilts hung with a rod pocket should be additionally supported with vertical strips of fabric lightly handstitched to the back of the quilt, running from top to bottom. Have these strips about 2-4 inches wide, and placed about 10 inches apart. Be sure the stitches do not come through to the front of the quilt, but run them through the foundation if possible.

This should be done with any quilt that is weighted with beads and other embellishments, or made of heavy fabrics.

PART TWO
Gallery
of Crazy Quilts

From plain to fancy, useful to decorative, Victorian crazy quilts is a term that covers much territory. Most were made smaller than bed-size and used as decorative throws. These fancy quilts are now sometimes called exhibition, art, or show quilts. Those made of wool, on the other hand, tend to be more plainly embroidered, and were likely to have been used on beds.

I've taken the liberty of some modern interpretations, adapting the crazy quilt to fit many purposes. Refer to previous chapters for construction methods, and embroidery and embellishment details. Any of the quilts can be made the size, colors, embroidery stitches and embellishments of your choice.

Fund-raiser and Commemorative Crazy Quilts

Fund-raiser and commemorative quilts are types that are made by groups rather than individuals. Commemorative quilts can be made to celebrate anniversaries of local importance, such as the founding of a town or city, and raffled off to raise funds. These can be theme quilts, with appliqués and embroideries showing buildings and landmarks that are important to the area's history. Fund-raisers need no theme, although they can be given one.

Fund-raiser quilt made by The Valley Needlers, South Hiram, Maine. 1997.

The Valley Needlers Quilt Guild, members of the Maine State Pine Tree Quilter's Guild, Inc., made a crazy quilt for their annual raffle in 1997. Each block of the quilt was completed by a member of the group. This is a classic crazy quilt in design. Colors, threads and fabrics were chosen by several of the members, and the materials divided sixteen ways for that number of blocks. It took a little over four months with members working on their own and in groups to finish the quilt which was then displayed at the Maine State Quilt Show, and at several fairs and local events. The proceeds from the raffle were used to benefit a local high school.

Theme Crazy Quilts

The antique quilt shown here has a subtly stated theme. "White Rose" is embroidered on one patch, and there is a small embroidered white rose on another. White roses were also important to the previous occupants of the house we live in. There is a rose garden now rescued from thick undergrowth, with all white roses in it, including a once-blooming Alba. All year I await its spectacular blooms and exquisite scent. When it blooms it seems to light up the entire yard, and in moonlight is unforgettable. Something such as this can be both incentive and inspiration for a quilt design.

The "White Rose" quilt is an example of an antique crazy quilt that has a theme. Detail. Photographed at Shiretown Antiques, Alfred, Maine.

A theme can be represented by a central motif, as the Victorian Horse quilt, or by adding appropriate embellishments. The two quilts featured in this Gallery were inspired by antique objects. Here are additional ideas for subjects for theme quilts:

> a favorite vacation spot
> cats, dogs, other animals
> sailing ships and nautical
> flowers, trees, herbs
> sports
> royalty, Egyptian pharaohs, other
> dignitaries
> fairy tales, mythology, angels

Choose a theme, then find ways to represent it. Appliqué, photo transfer, outline embroidery, words and quotes, painted details, are some ways to get your theme onto a quilt.

The Butterstamp Quilt

Butterstamps and buttermolds feature beautifully carved designs including florals, geometrics, cows, swans, initials, and many others. The hand-carved "folk art" designs were once used to imprint a farm family's homemade butter.

As a theme quilt, this piece displays rubbings of the stamps and molds. The rubbings were done with special crayons designed for fabrics, containing dyes.

The Butterstamp quilt is a theme quilt displaying folk art images; 1994. Collection of Paul Baresel.

A few words were also embroidered onto the quilt patches, including "butter prints," "antiques," "folk art," "Americana," and "Limerick," and the quilt is signed and dated.
Quilt size: 56-1/2 inches wide x 58-3/4 inches long, finished size.

Victorian Horse Quilt

An old fashioned horse toy theme makes this quilt suitable for a collector, a child's room, or decoration in almost any room. A pictorial center such as this one displays a theme grandly, making it the central focus of the quilt. In this type of quilt, the crazy quilting forms a border around the center. An additional, outer border, can also be added. The quilt center can also be used as a central patch on a much larger quilt.

The Victorian Horse quilt was photographed after the ice storm of January 1998, with an icy garden horse; 1996.

Crazy Quilts for Children

Until recent history, children were expected to learn adult skills including needlework. The small block shown here is a child's piece, on which she learned how to patch, baste and embroider. Even a small fan is included in the center. What better way to learn a variety of stitches, than by crazy quilting!

As an aside, and since we are on the subject of children, it is interesting to note that Queen Victoria did not enjoy her babies. She was always appalled by what she calls in her writings, "that terrible frog-like action" of her nine children when they were infants! However, she did insist that her daughters learn basic needlework skills.

The Cousins Quilt is a family heirloom; 1997.

The "Cousins" Quilt

The Outline stitched children on this quilt are Kate Greenaway's turn-of-the-century drawings of children. The Kate Greenaway drawings are available as iron-on transfers published by Dover Publications, Inc. See Sources.

The names and dates on this quilt are my son's cousins on the maternal side of the family, courtesy of my Aunt Elda who is researching the family tree. Elda's research has resulted in family reunions (she also publishes a family newsletter!), the only way we get to see each other nowadays. The family is spread out all the way from Oregon to Maine, and some of the names are cousins my son has never met. This was a major impetus to do this quilt, as a reminder that family does indeed exist–somewhere!

Make this quilt the size of your choice. The one shown here is a coverlet for a twin bed. All cotton, it is hand washable. The buttons are optional, ties can be used instead.
Quilt size: 62-1/4 inches wide x 80 inches long, finished size.

This antique block is likely the work of a child learning to crazy patch and work embroidery stitches. In the center, a fan was attempted. Collection of Rocky Mountain Quilts, York Village, Maine.

Confetti Crib Quilt

A "quickie" project, this crib-size child's quilt was completely finished in less than a day. The top was made in one piece using the Confetti method. Fabrics used include printed calicos, plain broadcloths in pink and white, and turquoise cotton flannel. It was not embroidered, since the printed fabrics provide sufficient decoration by themselves.

This is a small quilt, intended for crib, stroller, car, and around-the-house use. Baby may choose to adopt it as a carry around blanket! It could also be used as a wall hanging.

To make a similar quilt choose a batting that does not require close quilting. The cotton batting in this quilt allows quilt ties to be about 10 inches apart.

To make a larger size of this type of quilt, the top can be divided into blocks for easier handling.
Quilt size: 26 inches wide x 38 inches long, finished size.

A confetti crib quilt, 1997, is displayed on a rocking horse made by the author's father, Ray Michler (deceased), and a cotton rag rug woven by the author's mother, Doris Michler of Waupaca, Wisconsin.

Miniature Crazy Quilts

Miniatures can be displayed by hanging them the same as larger quilts, or they can be matted and framed. The miniatures here are true minis, not just smaller quilts. They can be very elegant if stitches are finely made, and fabrics and trims carefully chosen.

Miniatures can also be used as "tools." Working in so small a size is an efficient way to try color schemes, embroidery stitches, patch arrangements, and so on

The pieces shown here are color-scheme experiments, of silk fabrics and embroidered with Soie Gobelin, a twisted silk thread that is finer than Soie Perlee. The only embellishments are several tiny embroidered insects on each picture.

These small pieces can be made close to a 1:1 (1 inch = 1 foot) dollhouse scale, although the patches and embroidery will be slightly larger.

Quilt size: 8-1/2 inches square, finished size.

Miniature quilt 1, 1997.

Miniature quilt 2, 1997.

Miniature quilt 3, 1997.

Embroidering insects:

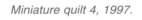

Miniature quilt 4, 1997.

These are tiny! Using Soie Gobelin, make them as follows. Two Bullion stitches about 1/2-3/4 inches long, exactly side by side. Padded satin stitches all worked into the same two holes, about 3/8 inch long. Two or three French knots wrapped about 5 times. Two pistil stitches with two wraps each. Two straight or pistil stitches may be added to the back end of the insect's body. Make wings of a second color of thread, each is a Lazy Daisy stitch, make 4 to 6 wings per bug. Legs can be added using the body color, and making two straight stitches for each.

Shape each insect differently by placing the individual parts of the body and the wings at different angles.

Doll's Quilt

Lightweight silk fabrics adapt well to miniature work, because the smallest patches are relatively easy to handle. This 1:1 miniature doll's quilt is mainly a silk quilt, worked on a silk organza foundation, and including a very thin layer of silk batting.

Quilt size: 9 inches wide x 10 inches long, not including a 2 1/4-inch ruffle on three sides.

Patching a miniature quilt: tiny silk patches are laid onto a silk organza foundation.

All-silk Crazy Quilts

Silk quilts can be very elegant, lightweight and warm. The Victorians had sufficient quantities of this fabric, and began to make their scrap quilts out of it instead of cottons. Silks are a common fabric in most of the fancy antique crazy quilts.

All-silk implies the use of all or mostly silk patch fabrics, foundation, trims, and threads. The silk jacket pictured here is 100 percent silk except for the glass seed beads.

Silk cocoon jacket has silk batting and lining, and is beaded to join the layers; 1995.

Silk Jacket

This cocoon-style jacket was made in one piece. Made of all lightweight silks and a thin silk batting, a jacket can retain much of the exceptional drape that silk is known for. Choose a garment style that relies on draping to achieve a fit, and that can be patched all in one piece. Cocoon and short kimono styles are two that will work well.

Detail of a sleeve.

Ladies and Fans Silk Quilt

Pieced fans found on many antique crazy quilts vary in size and shape, from short and wide to long and narrow. They were pieced of fabrics or ribbons. Many needleworkers also added small embroidered, rounded fans with handles, usually indicated simply in Outline stitch. Fans, and double, triple and quadruple rings seem to have been the most common motifs placed on the quilts, even more so than spiderwebs.

This quilt/wall hanging is finished in the style of a bed quilt with the ruffle placed on three sides only.

Size of quilt: 41-1/2 inches wide x 42-1/2 inches long, not including a 3-inch ruffle on three sides.

The Ladies and Fans quilt displays a feminine side of crazy quilting, with cigarette silks of ladies, pieced fans, silk ribbon florals and baskets, ribbonwork, buttons, tassels, and a silk ruffle finish; 1997. The beautiful marbled silk fabrics in this quilt are the work of Ann Shurtleff of Pagosa Springs, Colorado.

There may have been many crazy quilts made of wool as a practical alternative to the fancy ones. Many were made with very little fancy embroidery stitching, usually only a single row along patch edges. Embellishment, if any, most often consisted of simple outline stitched shapes.

To press under the seam allowances of patches, use a water-filled spray bottle and a dry iron. Place a press cloth over the wool, then spray lightly, and press. The steam will set the crease. The fabric should be allowed to dry before it is moved.

See the section on wool embroidery in Part 1 of Artful Embellishments. This type of embroidery may be worked on some patch seams, with Victorian stitches on others. Wool embroidery is a very attractive addition to a wool quilt. You can also incorporate pieces of unfinished crewel work, needlepoint, and cross stitch as patches or patch appliqués if there are any lurking in your closets. Ask around for donations if you haven't them. Some folks would rather give them up to a purpose such as this in order to free up closet space (and conscience!).

If you haven't quilted with wool, try a small sample, including embroidery before committing to a large project. The wool fiber behaves differently than other fabrics, and is a material of choice for many who like its pliability, warmth, and texture.

Horses and Roses Wool Quilt

I'm pleased to say that this quilt is unfinished! Refusing to buy into a modern notion that everything need be done quickly, I find it very de-stressing to pick up something that is "in progress" and just stitch away.

The idea of things being done quickly I think is ironic. We have available so many appliances, from the kitchen to the sewing room, that speedily do what once took lots of time and human energy. I think this paraphernalia gives the impression that all things in life should also be so quick and easy. The irony is that they were originally intended to free up our time, allowing more time for crazy quilting and other fun things!

This quilt is half finished. It is to be a coverlet for a queen size bed, and there will be 6 additional blocks. The wool embroidery is a winter thing to do, leaving the cross stitch and needlepoint pieces to be done in summer when wool is too heavy to work on.

Quilt size: 73 inches wide x 93 inches long, finished size not including the lace edging.

Horses and Roses. Unfinished. The cross stitch horses are the original works of the author.

The Horses and Roses quilt draped, with the Folk Hearts hanging. Both are at home in a country-style setting.

Art Crazy Quilts

The quilting movement of recent years has given rise to quiltmaking at all levels, some of it better classified as textile arts. This is both exciting and encouraging to those who enjoy the creativity. These quilts are characterized by original patching or piecing that follows no previous conventions, some of them embellished and/or embroidered. Art quilts are a "follow your heart or artistic conscience" type of quilting, a description that easily includes most crazy quilts. Pushing the boundaries of crazy quilting can elevate the artistry involved.

To challenge yourself, try the suggestion given in the chapter on using colors. Choose some colors that make you say "yuck." This is what I did in the Piano Shawl quilt, the light mossy greens and lime greens are colors I did not gravitate to. In addition, greens as a focal color are fairly new to my color agenda which previously included many reds and purples. After making this quilt, I find it easier and more natural to include greens of many shades in my projects.

The Piano Shawl shown "framed" demonstrates the draping potential of crazy quilts if they are made with materials that allow them to do so.

The Piano Shawl

Silks can be substituted for the rayon fabrics. There are many French Knots in this quilt, my favorite stitch. Drape this quilt over a grand piano, or wear it to a party!
This quilt is made of rayon challis and other fabrics, on a foundation of cotton batiste. Quilt size: 42 inches square, finished size, not including a 4-inch fringe.

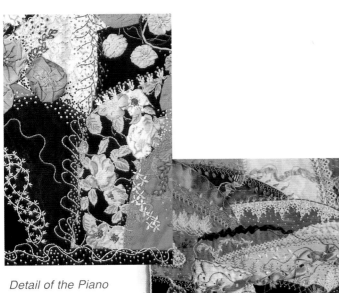

Detail of the Piano Shawl.

The Piano Shawl; 1996.

Landscape hanging; 1998.

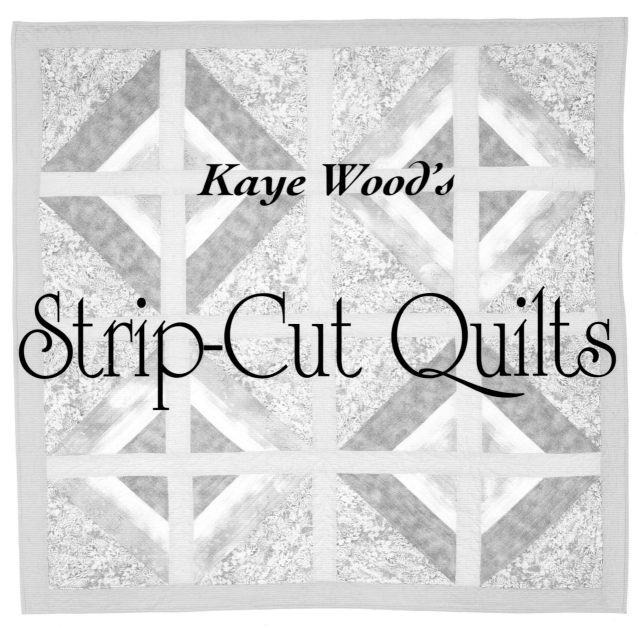

Kaye Wood's

Strip-Cut Quilts

using the 4-angle of the Starmaker 8 Master Template

another book in the *Strip Like A Pro* program,
made up of all of the Strip Quilting books, videos,
Starmaker Master Templates, and quilting tools

by

Kaye Wood

Kaye Wood

You can learn to Strip Like A Pro!

Just follow along with Kaye as she shows you how to simplify both the cutting and the piecing of quilts so your quiltmaking can be more fun, easier, and more accurate. Forget all those sizes of templates; you only need the Starmaker 8 Master Template for all the quilts in this book.

A lot of the quilting techniques that Kaye teaches are easy enough for beginners, but they don't look like beginner projects. That's the fun part for her. The best quilts for a beginner to start with are the "pointless designs." Kaye started to develop and include these designs when she realized that not everyone wants to match points. It is much more important to enjoy the creative process, so some of you have to accept the fact that you are one of the "pointless people" and leave the pointed designs for the "pointed people."

Spools of Lace, made by Kaye Wood. Directions on page 526.

Kaye's *Strip Like A Pro* program is made up of her strip quilting books, videos, three Starmaker Master Templates, and several quilting tools—View-A-Strip, the View-A-Square and the View & Do Shapes (circles, squares, Hexa-Cut, and Octa-Cut) for fussy-cutting.

Starmaker Master Templates

Kaye is especially well-known for her three Starmaker Master Templates, which revolutionized the way lots of quilts are made. The Starmaker Master Template concept has enabled even beginners to make quilts that traditionally took much more skill than Kaye's techniques. The Master Templates are used to strip cut more than 150 different quilt patterns; in fact, most geometric quilt patterns can be strip-pieced using one of the angles or half-angles on the Master Templates.

Since 1978, Kaye has taught her strip quilting techniques internationally. In 1988, a friend asked her when she was going to teach her ideas through television. She thought, "Why not?" and now has the longest running quilting shows on TV—*Strip Quilting, Quilting for the '90s* and *Kaye's Quilting Friends*. In 2000, Kaye completed her 28th season and 364th program for public television. She has also appeared as a guest on several national sewing/quilting/craft TV shows.

Before quilting, Kaye taught clothing construction, pattern drafting and machine embroidery. One day, one of her machine embroidery students asked if she would teach them to make a quilt. Kaye said, "Why not? Next week, bring three half-yard pieces of fabric." And that was the beginning of the first quilting class she taught. The rest is history.

Table of Contents

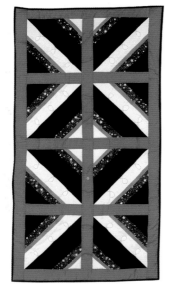

Tablerunner Trio;
see page 311.

Scrap Happy; see page 317.

Glacier Ice; see page 328.

Christmas Tablerunner/Wallhanging; see page 312.

Introduction

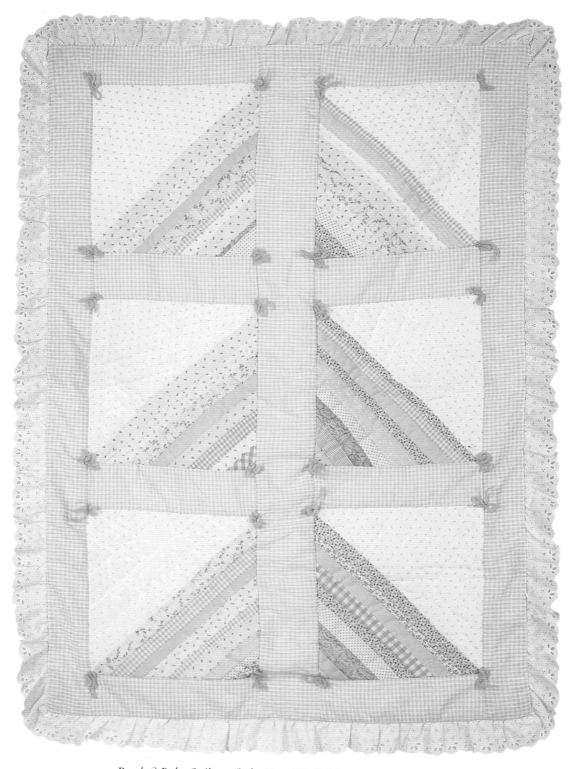

Rosebud Baby Quilt, made by Kaye Wood. Directions on page 319.

Fabric Preparation

Fabric should be washed and dried before using. Just before washing, I cut the four corners off my fabric; this reduces raveling, but most of all, it tells me my fabric has been washed and dried when I later go to use it. Washing and drying fabric removes the sizing, and it reduces the possibility of shrinkage and color bleeding.

Measuring Accurately

Always use the same ruler to cut the width of your strips within any one project. Rulers are not always the same; changing from one ruler to another can result in strips that are not cut the same width. By using the same ruler, your measurements will be more accurate.

Most of the strips used in the designs in this book are cut across the width of the fabric (40 to 44 inches) from selvedge to selvedge. Fabrics with an interesting lengthwise design, such as a stripe, can be cut with the design or across the width.

The View-A-Strip tool can help you decide which way will be more effective.

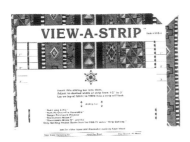

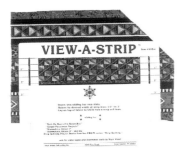

The View-A-Strip tool helps you view strips of varying widths accurately. Here, the tool views a 2 1/4-inch strip on material laid horizontally, and a 2-inch strip on a vertical design.

Cutting Accurately

When rotary cutting, always cut away from you and move the cutter in only one direction. Do not cut back and forth.

To cut strips with the rotary cutter: fold the fabric in half with selvedges together. Lay the folded fabric on the rotary cutting mat. Smooth the fabric out so it lays flat, even if the selvedges don't line up exactly.

Cut the fabric perpendicular (at right angles) to the fold to straighten one edge, using the rotary cutter and a heavy ruler.
Fold the fabric once more by bringing the

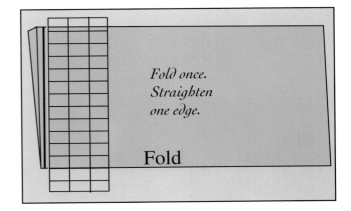

*Fold once.
Straighten
one edge.*

Fold

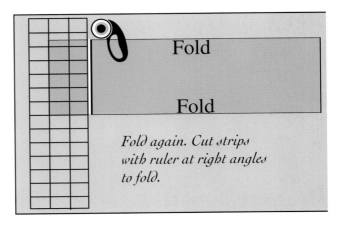

Fold

Fold

Fold again. Cut strips with ruler at right angles to fold.

folded edge to the selvedge. The fabric will now be in four layers and the shorter length will be easier to cut. Every third or fourth cut, unfold the fabric to check to see that your strips are straight.
Cut the strips needed, using the lines on a ruler to cut accurate strips. For example, to

cut 1 1/2-inch wide strips, place the 1 1/2-inch line on the ruler at the cut edge of the fabric. Cut along the edge of the ruler with the rotary cutter.

Make sure the blades are sharp. Dull blades are harder to use and they force the fabric down into the mat causing it to look fuzzy.

Sewing Accurately

Sewing accurately is very important. All your seam allowances should be the same width, preferably a scant 1/4 inch. The size given for each project listed in this book assumes that you will be using a scant (or quilters) 1/4-inch seam allowance. If your seam allowances are wider, that's okay, but your designs will be slightly smaller than the given measurements. For best results, use a 1/4-inch foot or some type of seam guide on your sewing machine. For strip piecing, it is always a good idea to shorten the stitch length to about 2 centimeters, or 10 stitches per inch.

Pressing Accurately

Pressing correctly is important in all kinds of patchwork, and it becomes even more important when you work with angles in your designs.

Seam allowances are usually pressed to one side in patchwork, but before pressing the seam allowances toward one side, press—up and down without sliding the iron—the seamline in the position it was sewn. This will help to keep the stitches locked in the center of the fabric. In some cases, especially when several seam allowances come together, it may be best to press the seams open.

Accurate pressing is ensured by:
1. Pressing with the grain.
Whenever possible, move the iron with the grain of the fabric. Ironing can stretch fabric if it goes along the crosswise grain of the fabric. For instance, moving the iron along the length of the strip will stretch it.

2. Pressing from the right side of the fabric.
Pressing from the wrong side can result in pleats forming at the seamline. Instead set the iron on the right side of the first strip, hold the rest of the strips up in the air. As you slide the iron from the first strip to the next, the seam allowances will be pressed in the right direction.

3. No steam.
Pressing with steam will stretch the fabric.

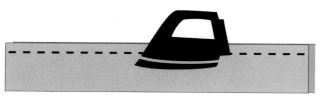

1. Press the seamline as it was sewn

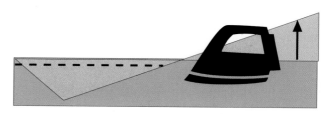

2. Press from the right side of the fabric. Move the iron across the width of the strips (in the direction of the arrow).

All designs in this book are strip cut with the 4-angle and the points or lines of the Starmaker 8 Master Template.

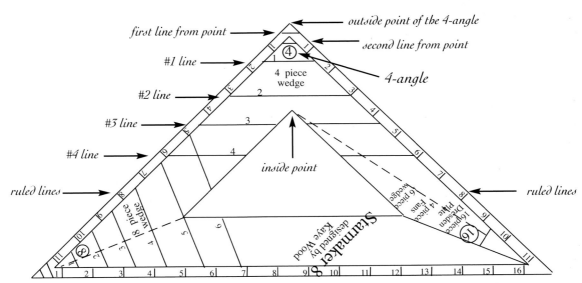

first line from point →
← *outside point of the 4-angle*

#1 line →
second line from point

④
4 piece wedge
4-angle

#2 line →

#3 line →

#4 line →

inside point

ruled lines →
← *ruled lines*

8 piece wedge

16 piece Fans
14 piece Dresden Plate
16 piece

Starmaker 8
designed by Kaye Wood

⑧
⑯

These points and lines on the Starmaker 8 Master Template ensure accurate angles.

Strip cutting shapes with the 4-angle of the Starmaker 8
Look at all the possible shapes.

You may have already used several of these shapes in quilts, but now they are easier to cut.
The strips can be any width or can even be several strips sewn together into a combination strip.

The height of the shape is determined by the width of the strip or combination strip.

To cut these shapes:
1. Place the 4-angle of the Starmaker 8 with the point, or one of the lines, at the top of a strip of fabric.
2. Cut the shape shown.

1. Place the Starmaker 8   **2. Cut the shape**

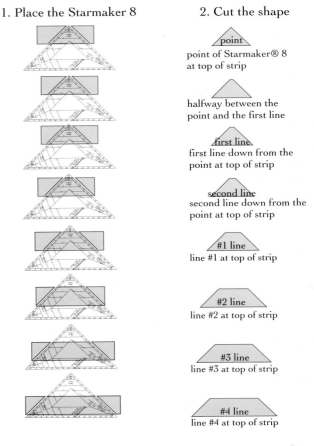

point
point of Starmaker® 8 at top of strip

halfway between the point and the first line

first line
first line down from the point at top of strip

second line
second line down from the point at top of strip

#1 line
line #1 at top of strip

#2 line
line #2 at top of strip

#3 line
line #3 at top of strip

#4 line
line #4 at top of strip

Chapter 1

Horizontal Triangles

Celebration Banner, made by Kaye Wood. Directions on page 314.

Two different triangles are cut from each strip or combination strip. The size of the triangle is determined by the width (height) of the combination strip.

Triangle A
Cut with the point of the 4-angle of the Starmaker 8 at the top of the strip.

Triangle B
Cut with the point of the 4-angle of the Starmaker 8 at the bottom of the strip.

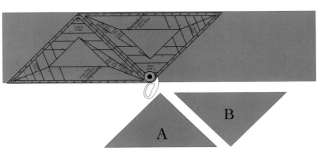

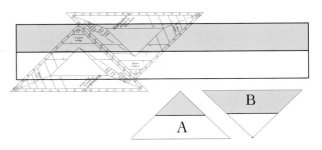

Strips can be one solid fabric, a stripe, or several strips sewn into a combination strip.

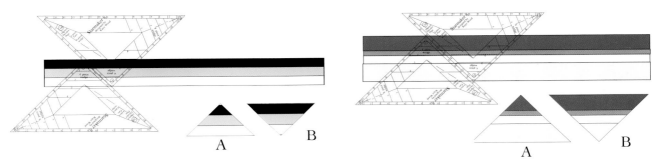

Strips can be all the same width, as shown above, or the combination strip can be made up of several different width strips.

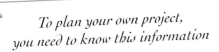

To plan your own project, you need to know this information

How much fabric do I need?

Number of triangles in my quilt?_____
Select the width of strip (height of triangle)
The chart will give you number of triangles per strip.
For example, for 30 triangles with a strip width of 6 inches, you will need five strips.

five strips x 6 inches per strip =
30 inches of fabric

Strip-Cut Triangles

Combination strip width	Number of triangles per 44-inch strip
3 inches	13*
4 inches	9*
5 inches	7*
6 inches	6
7 inches	5*
7 3/4 inches	4
8 1/2 inches	4

*When cutting an uneven number of triangles, cut the second strip beginning with the triangle you have the least of.

Tips For Accurate Cutting and Sewing

Accurate Cutting

It is important to keep the Starmaker 8 straight on the fabric. Here are some guidelines to help you do that:

Lines parallel to seamline.

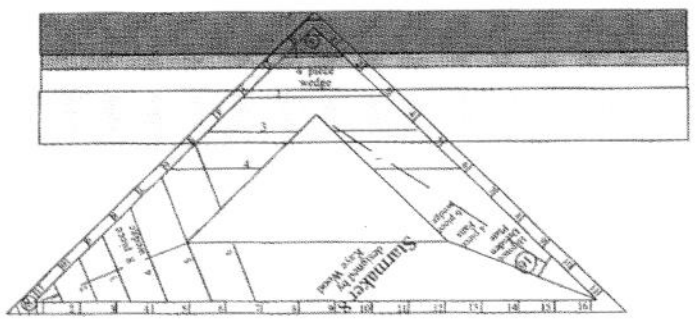

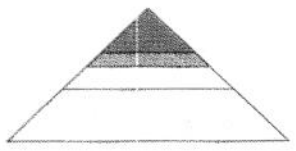

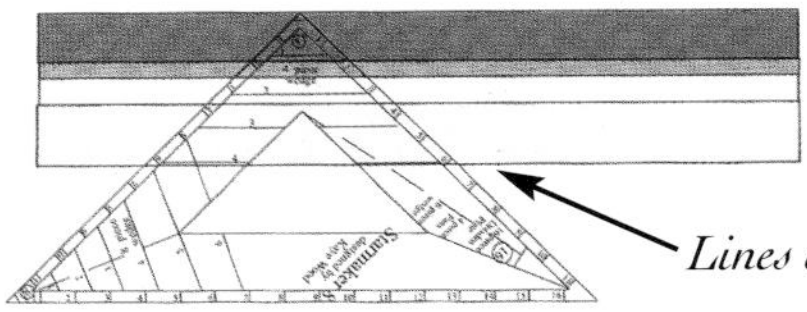

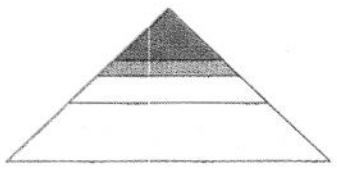

Lines on seamline.

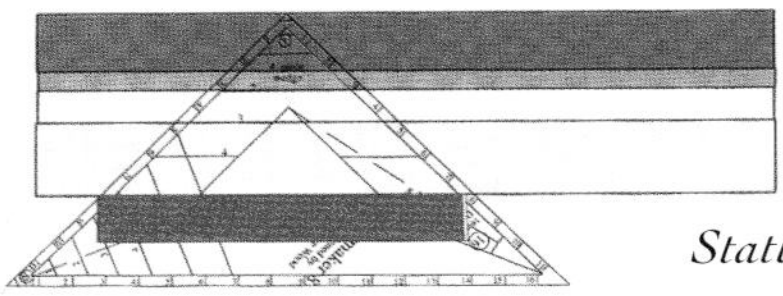

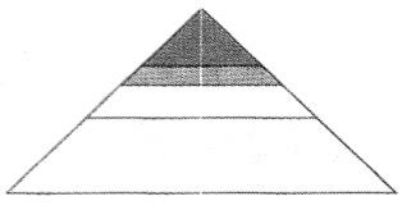

Static Sticker at bottom.

- ◆ Keep the horizontal lines on the Starmaker 8 parallel to the seamlines and to the edge of the strips.
- ◆ If one of the lines on the Starmaker 8 are exactly on the seamlines, use the line as a guide.
- ◆ If a line is not on the seamline, place a piece of Static Sticker or tape on the Starmaker 8 even with the bottom of the strip or on a seamline as a guide as you continue to cut triangles.
- ◆ Both sides of the bottom of the combination strip should end at the same marks on the ruled lines on the sides of the Starmaker 8. See page 303.

Point is 1/4 inch from edge.

Point is 1/4 inch from edge.

Matching Points

- ◆ Use 1/4-inch seam allowances.
- ◆ Match seamlines when necessary.
- ◆ Press accurately. See page 302.
- ◆ When sewing two blocks together, with diagonal seams coming together, the seams come to a "V" at 1/4 inch from the edge. This 1/4 inch is needed for the seam allowance when blocks or rows are sewn together.

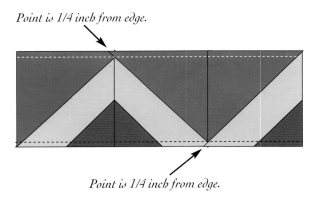

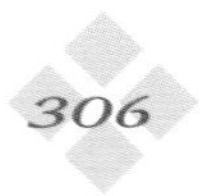

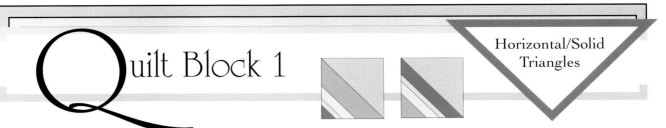

Quilt Block 1

1. **Make combination strips.**

   Sew two or more strips, right sides together, into a combination strip. Press seam allowances all in the same direction. See page 302.

2. **Cut solid strips.**

   Measure the width of the combination strip. Cut the solid fabric the same width.

Cut the solid strip the same width as the combination strip.

3. **Sew tubes.**

   Sew the combination strip and the solid strip, right sides together, along both long edges so it forms a tube.

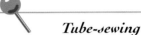

> ### Tube-sewing
> *It saves fabric, and you get two different quilt blocks. Strips can be solid, a stripe, or several strips sewn into a combination strip.*

4. **Cut triangles.**

   Cut with the combination strip on top; keep the seamlines parallel to the lines on the Starmaker 8. See page 305.

   "A" triangles—cut with the point of the 4-angle of the Starmaker 8 at the top of the strip.

   "B" triangles—cut with the Starmaker 8 upside-down and the point of the 4-angle at the bottom of the strip.

   Remove two or three stitches at each point. Press seam allowances toward the solid strip. See page 302.

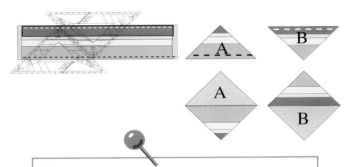

> *The solid fabric triangle is a great place to show off your quilting, your machine embroidery, or as an area to write names for a memory quilt.*

5. **Square up your blocks, if necessary.**

   If the blocks are not all the same size, square them up.
   Follow the directions on page 382.

> *The size of the block is determined by the width of the combination strip.*

6. **Lay out the design.**

   There are several possibilities, including those shown on the following pages. This quilt block is also great for border strips.

   Tubes make the triangles easier,
   but for accuracy sake, only use tubes
   when a solid strip is joined to a combination strip.

Yardages and sizes for Quilt Block 1 are on page 382.

Rainbow Sherbet

Finished size: 35-by-35 inches
A photo of this table cover or wallhanging,
by Kathleen Quinlan, is on the title page.

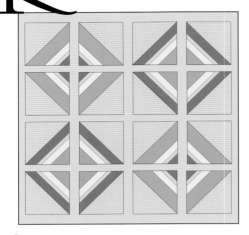

Fabric Requirements for Sixteen Blocks

Combination strips		
Purple	1/4 yard	Cut three 2-by-44-inch strips.
Blue	1/8 yard	Cut three 1-by-44-inch strips.
Yellow	1/4 yard	Cut three 1 1/2-by-44-inch strips.
Green	1/3 yard	Cut three 3-by-44-inch strips.
Solid strips	1/2 yard	Cut three 6-by-44-inch strips.
Sashing	1 yard	
Backing and sleeve	1 yard	
Binding	1/3 yard	
Batting	37-by-37 inches	

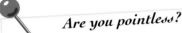

Are you pointless?
If you would rather not match seamlines and points, this design is for you!

Tip

If your combination strip is not 6 inches wide, cut the solid strips the width of your strip.

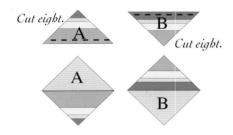

Cut eight.   Cut eight.

1. **Make combination strips.**
   Sew the four strips, right sides together, into three combination strips. Follow the directions for Quilt Block 1 on page 307.
   Cut three solid strips 6 inches wide (the width of the combination strip).

2. **Tube-sew strips.**
   Sew the solid strips to the combination strips, following the directions for Quilt Block 1 on page 307.

3. **Cut triangles.**
   Cut eight "A" and eight "B" quilt blocks. See page 307.
   Square up the blocks if necessary. See page 382.

4. **Lay out the design.**
   There are several possibilities, including the one above and those shown on the next page.

5. **Make short sashing strips.**
   See page 383 for instructions. Cut twelve sashing strips 2-by-8 inches (or the size of the block).

6. **Sew into rows.**
   Alternate four blocks and three short sashing strips.

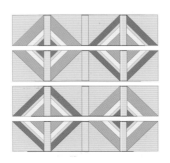

Kaye Wood's Strip-Cut Quilts

7. Make long sashing/border strips.

Cut seven sashing strips 2 inches wide. Pin-mark the strips (see page 383) to match seamlines.

8. Layer, quilt, and bind.

See page 386. For a wallhanging, add a sleeve before adding the binding.

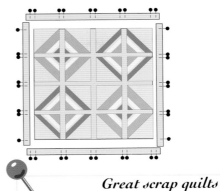

Great scrap quilts

The strips can be cut any size. Each set of triangles can be made from completely different fabric.

Try these designs.

Each one is made from eight "A" blocks and eight "B" blocks.
Experiment with different colors for the sashing and borders.

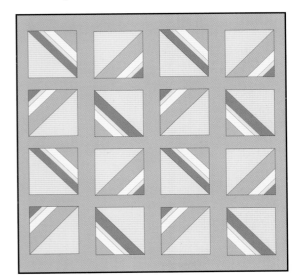
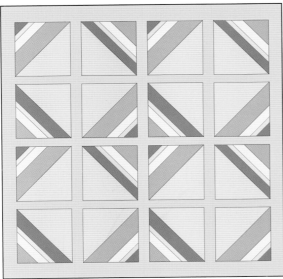
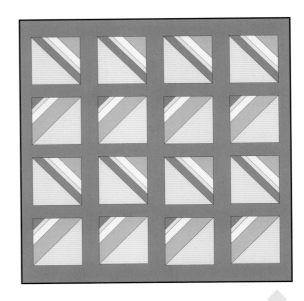

Quilt Block 2

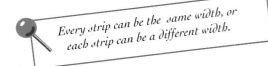

Every strip can be the same width, or each strip can be a different width.

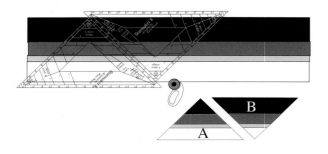

Sew "A" and "B" triangles together.

1. Make combination strips.

Sew two or more strips, right sides together, into a combination strip.
Press seam allowances all in the same direction. See page 302.

2. Cut triangles.

Cut "A" triangles with the point of the 4-angle of the Starmaker 8 at the top of the strip.
Cut "B" triangles with the Starmaker upside-down; the point of the 4-angle at the bottom of the strip.

3. Sew quilt blocks.

Sew one "A" and one "B" triangle, right sides together.
Press the seam allowance toward the darker fabric.

4. Square up the blocks, if necessary.

See page 382.

5. Lay out your design.

There are several possibilities, including those shown on the following pages. These blocks can also be used for border strips.

Yardages and sizes for Quilt Block 2 are on page 382.

Tablerunner Trio

Finished size: 22-by-42 inches
Photos of these quilts, made by Lori Jonsson,
are on the Table of Contents page (left edge).

Fabric Requirements for Each Quilt

Combination strips:

Black	1/3 yard	Cut three 3-by-44-inch strips.
Med. teal	1/8 yard	Cut three 1-by-44-inch strips.
Light teal	1/4 yard	Cut three 1 1/2-by-44-inch strips.
White	1/4 yard	Cut three 2-by-44-inch strips.
Sashing/borders	1/3 yard	
Backing and sleeve	1 yard	
Binding	1/3 yard	
Batting (optional)	24-by-44 inches	

1. Make combination strips.

Sew the strips, right sides together, into three
combination strips, as shown. Press seam
allowances toward the black strip. See page 302.

2. Cut and sew triangles.

Instructions for Quilt Block 2 are on page 310.
Cut eight "A" and eight "B" triangles.
Sew eight "A" and "B" triangles together.

3. Make short sashing strips.

Cut six sashing strips 2-by-8 inches (or size of
block). See page 383.

4. Sew into rows.

Sew two rows alternating blocks and sashing, following one of the above designs.

5. Make long sashing strips and borders.

Cut four strips 2-by-44 inches. Cut one of these
strips in half to use for the top and bottom border.
Pin-mark and sew the long sashing/border strips
to match seamlines. See page 383.
Pin-mark and sew the top and bottom border
strips.

6. Layer, quilt, and bind.

See page 386.
For a wallhanging, add a sleeve before adding the
binding.

Another pointless design!
Have fun with these designs.
They are great beginner projects.

Cut eight.
3 inches
1 inch
1 1/2 inches
2 inches
B
A
Cut eight.

Sew eight.

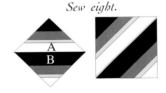

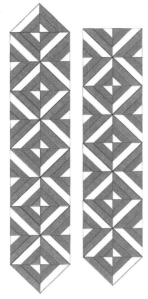

Christmas Tablerunners and Wallhangings

Finished size: 12 1/2-by-62 inches
A photo of the tablerunner, by Kaye Wood,
is on the Table of Contents page (lower right).

Fabric Requirements

Combination strips:
White	1/2 yard	Cut six 2-by-44-inch strips.
Red	1/2 yard	Cut six 2-by-44-inch strips.
Green	1/2 yard	Cut six 2-by-44-inch strips.
Backing	3/4 yard	Cut two 13-by-44-inch pieces.
Batting (optional)	14-by-64 inches	

1. Make combination strips.

Sew 2-inch strips, right sides together, into six combination strips. Press seam allowances all in the same direction. See page 302.

2. Cut triangles.

Follow the cutting directions on page 310. Tablerunner: Cut eighteen "A" triangles and eighteen "B" triangles.
Wallhanging: Cut seventeen "A" triangles and seventeen "B" triangles.

3. Sew quilt blocks.

Follow instructions on page 310 for Quilt Block 2.
Sew sixteen "A" and "B" triangles together to make sixteen blocks.
Tablerunner: Two "A" and two "B" blocks are used on the ends.
Wallhanging: One "A" and one "B" block is used on one end.

4. Sew into rows.

Sew blocks into two rows, each with eight blocks and one or two single triangles. Match seamlines. Press seam allowances.

5. Finish.

Tablerunner: Use an envelope finish and no batting.
Wallhanging: Layer, quilt, add a sleeve at the top, and bind. See page 386.

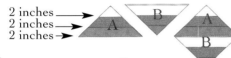

2 inches →
2 inches →
2 inches →

Merry Christmas!
Your Christmas table will look so festive. Be sure to make several of these for gifts. Try other seasonal colors!

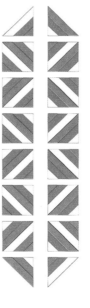

Reflections

Finished size: 42-by-67 inches

Fabric Requirements

Combination strips:

White	2/3 yard	Cut ten 2-by-44-inch strips.
Blue	2/3 yard	Cut ten 2-by-44-inch strips.
Black	2/3 yard	Cut ten 2-by-44-inch strips.
Borders	2/3 yard	Cut 3-by-44-inch strips.
Backing	46-by-70 inches	
Batting	46-by-70 inches	
Binding	1/3 yard	

1. ## Make combination strips.
   Sew 2-inch strips, right sides together, into ten combination strips.

2. ## Cut triangles.
   Cut sixty "A" and sixty "B" triangles, following the triangle cutting directions for Quilt Block 2 on page 310.

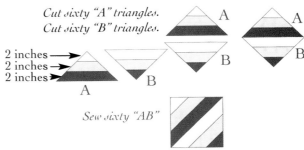

Cut sixty "A" triangles.
Cut sixty "B" triangles.

2 inches
2 inches
2 inches

A   B   A   B   A

Sew sixty "AB"

3. ## Sew blocks.
   Sew sixty "AB" blocks, following directions for Quilt Block 2, on page 310.

4. ## Sew into rows.
   Sew ten identical rows, matching seamlines.
   Turn every other row upside-down.
   Press seam allowances in opposite directions.

5. ## Finish.
   Add mitered or square borders, see pages 384 and 385.
   Cut six 3-inch strips. Pin-mark (see page 383) to match seamlines.
   Press seam allowances toward the border strip.
   Layer, quilt, and bind. See page 386.

Celebration Banner

(It's reversible!)

Front of quilt.

Back of quilt.

Fabric Requirements

White	2 yards
Light blue	2 yards
Dark blue	1-1/2 yards
Black	1/2 yard
Batting	60-by-50 inches

1. Cut strips.

Cut the 50-inch long strips lengthwise; cut the 44-inch long strips crosswise or lengthwise. (If necessary, two crosswise strips can be sewn together to get the 50-inch length.)

White	Cut four 5 1/2-by-50-inch strips, two 2-by-50-inch strips, and nine 2-by-44-inch strips.
Light blue	Cut four 4 1/2-by-50-inch strips, two 5 1/2-by-50-inch strips, and ten 2-by-44-inch strips.
Dark blue	Cut one 2-by-50-inch strip, two 4 1/2-by-50-inch strips, and fourteen 2-by-44-inch strips.
Black	Cut four 2-by-50-inch strips.
Batting	Cut three 2-by-50-inch strips, four 4 1/2-by-50-inch strips, and four 5-by-50-inch strips.

2. Make combination strips.

Sew four combination strips—2-by-44-inch strips of white/light blue/dark blue—for the "AB" triangles. Sew four combination strips—2-by-44-inch strips of white/dark blue/light blue/dark blue—for "CD" triangles. Press seam allowances all in the same direction. See page 302 for pressing instructions.

3. Cut triangles.

Cutting instructions are on page 310.
Cut twenty-four "A" and twenty-four "B" triangles. Cut twenty-six "C" and twenty-six "D" triangles.

4. Sew quilt blocks.

Sew twenty-four "AB" blocks. See page 310 for Quilt Block 2.
Sew only twenty "CD" blocks.

> **Reversible quilts are easy!**
> Both the front and back are joined and quilted at the same time. Get your serger out to save time. If not, just follow the instructions for sewing on a sewing machine.

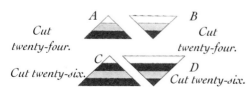

A — *Cut twenty-four.*
B — *Cut twenty-four.*
C — *Cut twenty-six.*
D — *Cut twenty-six.*

"C" and "D" triangles are larger than "A" and "B" triangles.

Sew twenty-four "AB."

Sew twenty "CD."

> **Tip**
> The rest of the "C" and "D" triangles will be used for the pointed edge at the bottom of the quilt.

5. **Sew the triangles into vertical rows.**
Sew two rows of twelve "AB" blocks.
Sew two rows of ten "CD" blocks.

6. **Sew the rows together.**
This quilt is reversible, and both front, back and the quilting are all done at the same time.

a. Start with the 2-inch center strip (right in the middle of the quilt). Make a sandwich with the 2-inch batting strip in the middle, the 2-inch fabric strips right side out. Serge or zigzag (down both long sides).

b. Add the next row in this manner:
Put the back strip right sides to the center back; Put the front strip right sides to the center front. Put a strip of batting underneath. Serge or straight-stitch all the layers together along one edge.

c. Open out the strips and batting.
The batting will be in the middle.
Serge or zigzag the long outside edge.

d. Repeat Steps b and c to continue adding rows.

7. **Square up the quilt.**
After all the rows are added, trim the top and bottom of the rows.

8. **Sew bottom border strip.**
Sew a 2-inch border strip to the bottom of the quilt, adding the back, front, and batting in the same way as the strips were added.
But do <u>not</u> serge or zigzag the outside edges closed.

9. **Sew the bottom triangle edging.**
Sew six triangles by sewing a "C" and a "D" triangle, right sides together with a triangle of batting underneath.
Sew along the two side edges, leaving the bottom open.
Turn the triangles right sides out (the batting will be in the middle).
Space, pin and sew the triangles right sides together to the bottom of just the front border strip.
Turn under the edge of the back border strip and hand-blindstitch or machine-topstitch the back border to the triangles.

10. **Finish.**
Cut the light blue into 3-inch binding strips.
Hanging tabs are on page 386.
Sew a binding on the two sides and top of the quilt, following instructions on page 386.

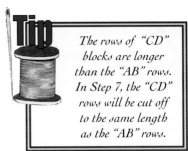

The rows of "CD" blocks are longer than the "AB" rows. In Step 7, the "CD" rows will be cut off to the same length as the "AB" rows.

Sew two rows of twelve "AB" blocks.

Sew two rows of ten "CD" blocks.

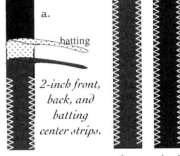

a.

batting

2-inch front, back, and batting center strips.

front   back

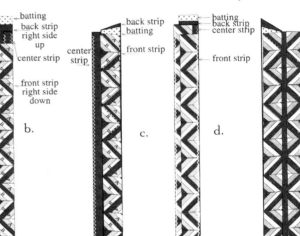

b.

batting
back strip right side up
center strip
front strip right side down

c.

back strip
batting
center strip
front strip

d.

batting
back strip
center strip
front strip

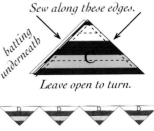

Check to see that serging stitches don't show on the right side. If stitching does show, just serge or straight-stitch a deeper seam.

Sew along these edges.

batting underneath

Leave open to turn.

Front of quilt.

Back of quilt.

Quilt Block 3

Random triangles

This is great for that scrap quilt look! Each triangle could be made from different fabrics. Just sew a bunch of strips together and cut triangles. Sew them together and see what you get. It's lots of fun!

Tip

It is easier to cut if you place the bottom of the Starmaker 8 at least a half-inch or more above or below a seamline.

Yardages and sizes for Quilt Block 3 are on page 382.

Randomly cut strips add excitement and movement to our quilts. Each triangle can be cut from a different section of the combination strip for a true scrap-looking quilt.

1. **Make combination strips.**
   Individual strips can be cut from 3/4 inch up to 3 inches wide. Cut and sew different width strips together into a combination strip that is at least 9 or 10 inches high.
   Press seam allowances toward the darker fabric. See pressing instructions, page 302.

2. **Cut triangles.**
   Cut triangles by placing the Starmaker 8 anywhere on the combination strip.
   The Starmaker 8 can be placed with the 4-angle even with the top or even with the bottom of the strip or anywhere on the combination strip. Triangles will be 8 1/2 inches high (the height of the Starmaker 8).

3. **Sew quilt blocks.**
   Sew any two triangles together to make a quilt block.
   Press seam allowances toward the darker fabric. See page 302.

4. **Square up the quilt blocks, if necessary.**
   See page 382.

5. **Lay out the design.**
   There are several possibilities, since every triangle can be different depending on where the Starmaker 8 was placed on the combination strip.

   These randomly cut quilt blocks can be used in many of the designs in this book. The triangles can also be combined with solid triangles, with vertical triangles, or with fussy-cut triangles.

Scrap Happy

Finished size: 70-by-74 inches
A photo of this quilt, made by Joyce Horn,
is on the Table of Contents page (upper right).

Make this any size from a lap robe, a couch throw, or a king-size bed.

Fabric Requirements

Combination strips (lots of scraps):

Solid strips	6-by-80 inches	
Brown	1 yard	Cut six 6-by-44-inch strips.
Beige	1 yard	Cut four 6-by-80-inch strips.
Backing	75-by-80 inches	
Batting	75-by-80 inches	
Binding	3/4 yard	Cut eight 3-by-44-inch strips.

1. **Make combination strips.**
   Cut strips from scraps. Strips can be any width.
   See page 316.

2. **Cut triangles.**
   Cut a total of sixty-four triangles following directions for Quilt Block 3 on page 316. Triangles cut from the combination strip will be 8 1/2 inches high (the height of the Starmaker 8).

   Cut sixty-four triangles.

3. **Sew the triangles into blocks.**
   Sew two triangles together to make thirty-two quilt blocks, following directions on page 316.

   Sew thirty-two blocks.

4. **Sew the blocks into rows.**
   Each of the four rows has seven blocks. Press the seam allowances

   Sew four rows.

5. **Add long solid strips between block rows.**
   Sew two 6-by-44-inch strips together to make each strip long enough. Pin-mark these strips. See page 383.

6. **Layer, quilt, and bind.**
   Cut eight 3-inch-wide binding strips. See instructions on page 386.

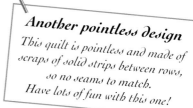

Another pointless design
This quilt is pointless and made of scraps of solid strips between rows, so no seams to match. Have lots of fun with this one!

Quilt Block 4

Horizontal
Scraps/Solid
Triangles

Scrap lovers:

*This quilt block is for you!
Use up some of your scraps and turn
them into a treasured quilt.*

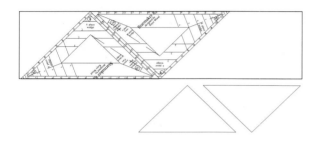

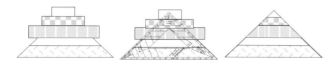

*Yardages and sizes for Quilt Block 4
are on page 382.*

1. **Cut solid triangles.**
   Cut strips 8 1/2 inches high.
   Place the point of the 4-angle of the Starmaker
   8 at the top of the strip. Cut on both sides of
   the Starmaker 8.
   Cut the second triangle by turning the
   Starmaker 8 upside-down and placing the
   point of the 4-angle of the Starmaker 8 at the
   bottom of the strip.

2. **Make scrap triangles.**
   Cut strips 1 1/2 to 2 1/2 inches wide from your
   scraps.
   Cut one of these strips 19-inch-long strip for
   the bottom of a triangle; this is the longest
   strip needed.
   Sew a strip to one side of the 19-inch strip by
   sewing the strips right sides together. Press the
   seams toward the bottom strip.
   Trim the length of these strips by placing the
   Starmaker 8 on the bottom of the 19-inch strip
   and cutting along the shape of the Starmaker
   8.
   Add more strips and trim the ends by placing
   the Starmaker 8 at the bottom of the long
   strip. Continue adding strips and trimming the
   sides until the triangle is complete.

3. **Sew triangles together.**
   Sew a solid triangle and a scrap triangle
   together to make a quilt block.
   Press seam allowances toward the solid triangle.

4. **Square up quilt blocks, if necessary.**
   See page 382.

5. **Lay out the design.**
   These quilt blocks can fit into any of the
   designs used in this book that are made from a
   solid/pieced triangle.

Rosebud Baby Quilt

Finished size: 32-by-45 inches
A photo of this quilt, made by
Kaye Wood, is on page 300.

Fabric Requirements

Strips (lots of scraps)		Need six 8 1/2-inch triangles.
Solid strips	1/2 yard	Cut two 8 1/2-by-44-inch strips.
Sashing/borders	2/3 yard	Cut five 3 1/2-by-44-inch strips.
Backing	35-by-48 inches	
Batting	35-by-48 inches	
Gathered eyelet	175 inches	

1. Create triangles.
   Sew strips together to make six 8 1/2-inch-high scrap triangles.
   Cut six triangles from the 8 1/2-inch-wide solid strips.
   See page 318.

2. Put together quilt blocks.
   Make six quilt blocks, following directions for Quilt Block 4 on page 318.

3. Make short sashing strips.
   Cut four 3 1/2-by-11 1/2-inch strips .
   Follow directions on page 383.
   Sew into two rows each with three blocks.

4. Make long sashing strip.
   Cut one 3 1/2-inch strip.
   Pin-mark the strip. See page 383.

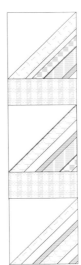

5. Finish.
   For the borders, pin-mark the top and bottom border strips. See page 383. Pin-mark the side border strips.
   To do the eyelet edging, see page 385.
   Do an envelope finish. See page 385.
   Machine tie as shown on page 386.

Chapter 2

Spool Quilts

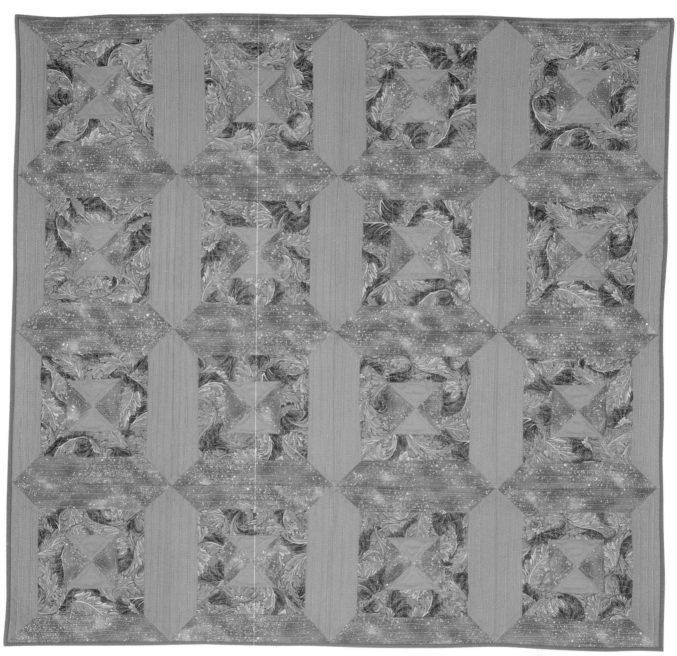

Emeralds and Amethysts, made by Kathleen Quinlan. Directions on page 525.

Kaye Wood's Strip-Cut Quilts

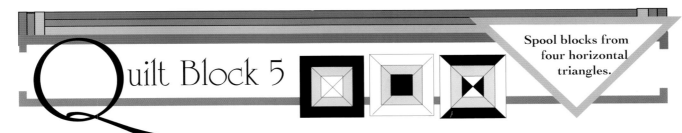

Quilt Block 5

Try the three blocks above for practice projects.

1. **Make combination strips.**
   Cut and sew three strips of fabric, right sides together into a combination strip.
   Press seam allowances toward the darker fabric. See pressing instructions, page 302.

2. **Cut triangles.**
   Cut "A" and "B" triangles (see page 305), or cut "A" and "B" triangles (see page 322).

Experiment with triangles—
Try both triangles and topless triangles.
Choose which you prefer and continue with one or more of the quilts on the following pages.
Practice blocks make great potholders!

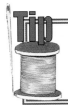

Notice the size of the small triangles coming together in the center of the spool block. Topless triangles have larger triangles so each piece in the triangle will finish up the same width.

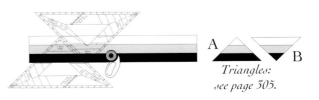

A / B *Triangles: see page 305.*

A / B *Topless triangles: see page 322.*

3. **Sew the quilt block.**
   Sew four triangles or four topless triangles together to make one or more of these spool designs.

   Sew two triangles, matching seamlines, together to make half of each quilt block. Press seam allowances on each half in opposite directions.

   Sew two halves together, matching seamlines, to make the quilt block. Press seam allowances.

4. **Square up the blocks, if necessary.**
   See page 382.

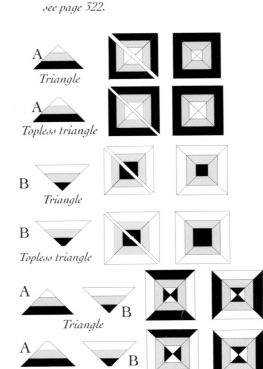

A *Triangle*

A *Topless triangle*

B *Triangle*

B *Topless triangle*

A *Triangle* B

A *Topless Triangle* B

Yardages and sizes for Quilt Block 5 are on page 382.

Topless triangles will be slightly larger so the quilted project will be a little larger than the sizes listed. Fabric amounts listed will be enough for either cutting method.

Topless Triangles

Use only when it is important for each piece in the triangle to finish the same width.

Triangle A

Cut with the top of the strip halfway between the point of the 4-angle and the first line on the Starmaker 8.

Triangle B

Cut with the bottom of the strip halfway between the point of the 4-angle and the first line on the Starmaker 8.

Do not confuse the #1 line on the Starmaker 8 with the first line from the point. See page 303.

Topless triangles are sometimes used for spool quilt blocks and for designs like this.

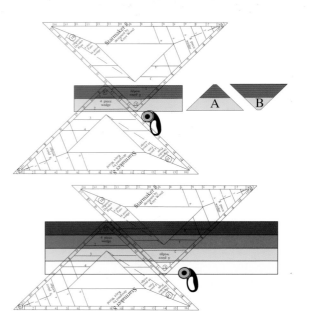

Topless triangles. The points at the top of the triangle are cut off.

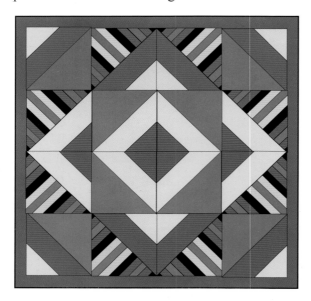

The size of the small pieces (solid brown and light green) in each triangle look best if they finish the same width as the other pieces in the triangle.

The advantage of using topless triangles is that each piece in the triangle finishes the same width.

If you cut triangles, with the point of the Starmaker 8 at the top or bottom of the strip, the small piece will be narrower than the rest of the pieces, which is okay for some designs.

Which cutting method?

Each project will specify whether to cut triangles or topless triangles. Some projects can use either, depending on the finished look you want.

Topless Triangles

combination strip width	number of triangles per 44-inch strip
2 1/2 inches	14
3 inches	13*
4 inches	8
5 inches	6
6 inches	5*
7 inches	4
7 3/4 inches	4
8 1/2 inches	3*

*When cutting an uneven number of triangles, cut the second strip beginning with the triangle you have the least of.

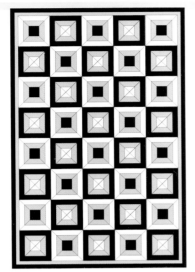

Two Fun Spool Quilts

(Instructions on this page and the next)

Finished size of both quilts: 47-by-74 inches

Fabric Requirements

Combination strips:
    White 1 3/4 yard Cut twenty-seven 2-by-44-inch strips.
    Blue   1 3/4 yard Cut twenty-seven 2-by-44-inch strips.
    Black 1 3/4 yard Cut twenty-seven 2-by-44-inch strips.
First border 1/2 yard Cut eight 2-by-44-inch strips.
Second border 1 yard Cut eight 3-by-44-inch strips.
Backing   50-by-78 inches
Batting   50-by-78 inches
Binding 1/2 yard

1. ## Make combination strips.
   Sew 2-inch strips, right sides together, into twenty-seven combination strips.

2. ## Cut triangles.
   Cut eighty "A" and eighty "B" topless triangles, following the directions on page 322.

3. ## Sew the triangles into blocks.
   Sew twenty "A" blocks and twenty "B" blocks, following the direction for Quilt Block 5, page 321.

4. ## Sew the blocks into rows.
   Alternate blocks, matching seamlines. Press the seam allowances for each row in opposite directions.

5. ## Sew the rows together.
   Match seamlines. Press seam allowances.

6. ## Finish.
   Add borders. See page 384.
       Cut eight 2-inch and eight 3-inch border strips, see above.
       Pin-mark the center and both ends of the border strips. See page 383.
   Press seam allowances toward the border strip.
   Layer, quilt, and bind. See page 386.

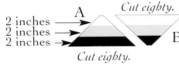
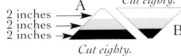

2 inches →   A   *Cut eighty.*
2 inches →
2 inches →   *Cut eighty.*   B

Sew twenty "A" blocks.

Sew twenty "B" blocks.

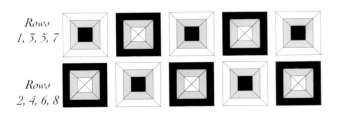

Rows 1, 3, 5, 7

Rows 2, 4, 6, 8

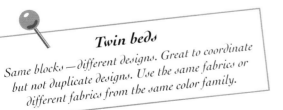

Twin beds
Same blocks — different designs. Great to coordinate but not duplicate designs. Use the same fabrics or different fabrics from the same color family.

Combination strips:

White	1 3/4 yard	Cut twenty-seven 2-by-44-inch strips.
Blue	1 3/4 yard	Cut twenty-seven 2-by-44-inch strips.
Black	1 3/4 yard	Cut twenty-seven 2-by-44-inch strips.

First border

	1/2 yard	Cut eight 2-by-44-inch strips.

Second border

	1 yard	Cut eight 3-by-44-inch strips.
Backing	50-by-78 inches	
Batting	50-by-78 inches	
Binding	1/2 yard	

1. **Make combination strips.**

   Sew 2-inch strips, right sides together, into twenty-seven combination strips.

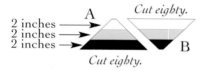

2 inches →
2 inches →
2 inches →

A

Cut eighty.

B

Cut eighty.

2. **Cut triangles.**

   Cut eighty "A" and eighty "B" topless triangles, following the directions on page 322.

Sew twenty "A" blocks.

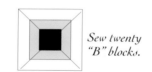

Sew twenty "B" blocks.

3. **Sew the triangles into blocks.**

   Sew twenty "A" blocks and twenty "B" blocks, following the direction for Quilt Block 5, page 321.

Rows 1, 3, 5, 7

Rows 2, 4, 6, 8

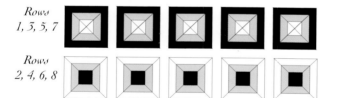

4. **Sew the blocks into rows.**

   Sew into rows of the same blocks.
   Press the seam allowances for each row in opposite directions.

5. **Sew the rows together.**

   Matching seamlines.
   Press seam allowances.

6. **Finish.**

   Add borders. See page 384.
   Cut eight 2-inch and eight 3-inch border strips, see above.
   Pin-mark the center and both ends of the border strips. See page 383.

   Press seam allowances toward the border strip.
   Layer, quilt, and bind. See page 386.

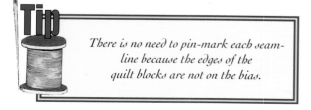

Tip

There is no need to pin-mark each seamline because the edges of the quilt blocks are not on the bias.

Emeralds and Amethysts

Finished size: 35 1/2-by-35 1/2 inches
A photo of this quilt, made by Kathleen Quinlan, is on page 320.

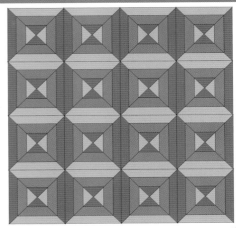

Fabric Requirements

Combination strips:

Purple	1 yard	Cut eleven 2-by-44-inch strips.
Green	1 yard	Cut eleven 2-by-44-inch strips.
Lavender	1 yard	Cut eleven 2-by-44-inch strips.
Backing	1 1/2 yards	40-by-40 inches
Batting	40-by-40 inches	
Binding	1/4 yard	Cut four 1 3/4-inch strips.

1. **Make combination strips.**
   Sew the 2-inch strips, right sides together, into eleven combination strips.

2. **Cut triangles.**
   Cut thirty-two "A" and thirty-two "B" topless triangles.
   Follow directions on page 322.

3. **Sew the triangles into blocks.**
   Sew sixteen "AB" blocks, following directions for Quilt Block 5 on page 321.

4. **Sew into rows.**
   Sew the blocks into four identical rows, matching seamlines.
   Press the seamlines, alternating direction with every row.

5. **Sew the rows together, matching seamlines.**

6. **Finish.**
   Layer, quilt, and bind. See page 386.

Shades of color
Try two different shades of one color together with a coordinating print.

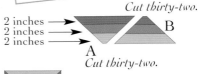

2 inches →
2 inches →
2 inches →

Cut thirty-two. B

A
Cut thirty-two.

Sew sixteen "AB" blocks.

Spools of Lace

Finished size: 33-by-48 inches
A photo of this quilt, made by Kaye Wood,
is on page Kaye Wood welcome page (at front).

(Trimmed with lace!)

Fabric Requirements

Combination strips:

Blue	3/4 yard	Cut eight 3-inch strips.
Beige	1/2 yard	Cut eight 1 1/2-inch strips.
Green	1/2 yard	Cut eight 1 1/2-inch strips.
Print	3/4 yard	Cut eight 3-inch strips.
Lace	20 yards	(1-inch wide)
Sashing/Borders	1 yard	Cut eleven 3-inch strips.
Backing	40-by-55 inches	
Batting	40-by-55 inches	

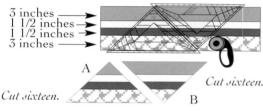

3 inches →
1 1/2 inches →
1 1/2 inches →
3 inches →

A

Cut sixteen.

Cut sixteen.

B

A   B

1. Make combination strips.

Sew four strips, right sides together, into eight combinations strips.

Press seam allowances. See page 302.

2. Cut triangles.

Cut sixteen "A" and sixteen "B" triangles. See page 302.

3. Add lace.

Sew flat or gathered lace, right sides together, to the bottom of each "A" and "B" triangle.

Press the seam allowances away from the lace and toward the triangles.

Trim the both ends of the lace with the Starmaker 8.

4. Sew quilt blocks.

Sew the triangles into eight "AB" blocks. See page 321 for quilt block 5.

Sew all the way to the end of the lace.

Be sure to sew with the seam allowances away from the lace.

Measure the quilt block, including seam allowances.

Sew eight "AB" blocks

5. Short sashing strips.

Cut four short sashing strips 3 inches by the quilt block measurement.

Press under 1/4 inch on both ends of the sashing strips.

Sew short sashing strips to four quilt blocks.

Stitch-in-the-ditch

Ends of sashing strips are pressed under 1/4 inch.

Sashing strip lays under the quilt block and lace.

Lay a quilt block on top of a sashing strip, both right sides up; line up one long raw edge of the sashing with the raw edge of the quilt block.

Pin the block to the sashing strip and stitch-in-the-ditch. (Sew on the seamline between the lace and the triangle.)

6. **Sew into rows.** Sew the blocks into four rows, each with two blocks and one sashing strip, following the directions in Step 6.

   Measure the row, including the outside seam allowances.

7. **Create sashing/borders.**

   Cut three sashing strips 3 inches by the row measurement. Press under 1/4 inch on both ends of the sashing strips. Pin-mark these strips. See page 383.

   Place the sashing strip under the row with the lace on top, both right sides up, with the raw edge of the sashing strip lined up with the raw edge of the quilt blocks.

   Pin through the quilt blocks and the sashing strip. Stitch-in-the-ditch only on the seamline between the lace and quilt block.

   Pin the folded end of the short sashing strips on top of the long sashing strips.

   Sew one of these ways:

   a. *The easy way* — Topstitch along the folded edge.

   b. *A little more difficult* — Bring the raw edges of the short and long sashing strips, right sides together. Sew along the creased fold of the short sashing strip, from seamline to seamline.

   Cut the top and bottom sashing strips 3-by-35 inches (to allow for mitered corners). Pin-mark. See page 383. Sew to the top and bottom rows, using the same techniques above.

   Cut four side border strips 3-by-44 inches. Sew two together to get the needed length — 3-by-55 inches. Sew to quilt, using the same techniques above.

Turn some of the spool blocks.
See how you can change the design.

8. **Finish.**

   Miter the corners of the border strips. See page 385.

   Sew lace, right sides together, to the outside edge of the quilt top.

   Pin lace in towards the quilt top to keep it from being caught in the seams.

   Use an envelope style finish. See page 385.

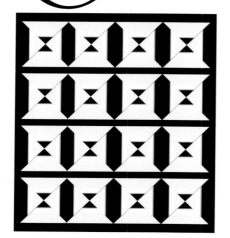

Glacier Ice

Finished size: 64-by-68 inches
A photo of this quilt, made by Lori Jonsson, is on
Table of Contents page (middle right).

Fabric Requirements

Combination strips:

Black	1 2/3 yard	Cut sixteen 3-inch strips.
Light teal	1/2 yard	Cut sixteen 1-inch strips.
White	1 yard	Cut sixteen 2-inch strips.
Teal	2 yards	Cut sixteen 4-inch strips.
Sashing/borders	1 yard	Cut fourteen 2-inch strips.
Backing	70-by-75 inches	
Batting	70-by-75 inches	
Binding	1/2 yard	

Another pointless design

Triangles from different width strips —3, 1, 2, and 4 inches —so when they go together, no seams will match. Sashing strips between rows, so no seams to match. Have lots of fun with this one!

3 inches
1 inch
2 inches
4 inches

A   B

Cut thirty-two of each "A" and "B".

Sew sixteen "AB" blocks.

1. Make combination strips.
Sew four strips, right sides together, into sixteen combination strips.

2. Cut triangles.
Cut thirty-two "A" and thirty-two "B" triangles, following directions on page 306.

3. Sew the triangles into blocks.
Sew the "A" and "B" triangles into sixteen blocks, following directions for Quilt Block 5 on page 321.

4. Sew the blocks into rows.
Sew four identical rows.
Press the seam allowances for each row in opposite directions.

5. Sashing strips.
Add long sashing strips between rows.
Cut fourteen sashing strips 2 inches wide.
Pin-mark the sashing strips. See page 383.

6. Finish quilt.
Pin-mark the center and both ends of the border strips. See page 383.
Add mitered or square borders. See pages 384 and 385.

Press seam allowances toward the border strip.
Layer, quilt, and bind. See page 386.

To make the border shown at the top of the page, cut "A" and "B" triangles. Sew together as shown in Quilt Block 2, page 310.

Chapter 3
Random Vertical Triangles

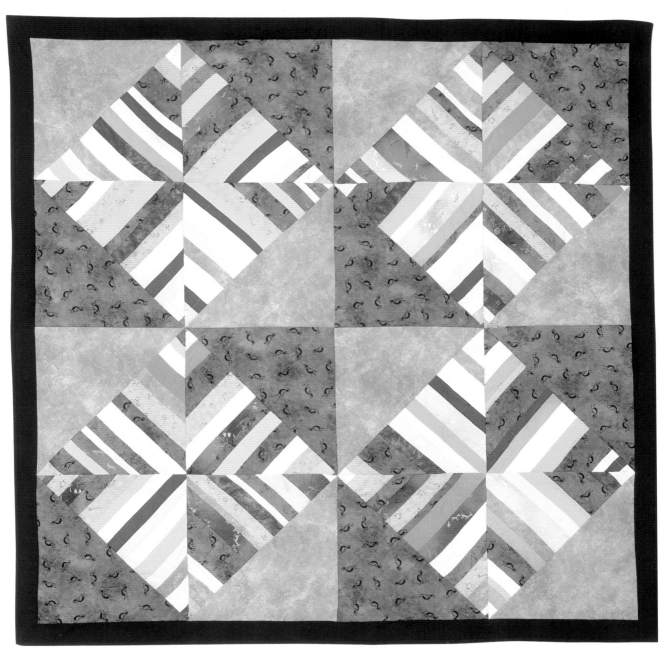

Ferris Wheel, made by Kaye Wood. Directions on page 332.

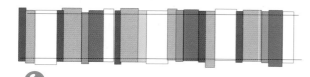

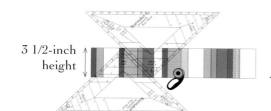

Another pointless design

No seams to match, so it's great for those pointless people. Use scraps of fabric or fat quarters, cut 9 inches long and random widths, from 1 to 4 inches.

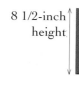

Tip

To keep the Starmaker 8 straight, line up the outside and inside points on the same strip. See page 303. The horizontal lines and the bottom of the Starmaker 8 should be parallel to the top and bottom of the strip.

Random-Width Vertical Triangles

1. **Make combination strips.**

   Sew strips of fabrics, all the same height, together into a combination strip approximately 42 to 44 inches long. The height of the strips (from 3 to 9 inches) is determined by the project. See below.

   Press seam allowances all in one direction. Trim the bottom and top edges to straighten the strip.

2. **Cut triangles with the Starmaker 8.**

   Cut the first triangle with the point of the 4-angle of the Starmaker 8 at the top of the strip. Cut the next triangle with the point of the 4-angle of the Starmaker 8 at the bottom of the strip.

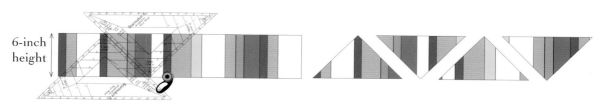

3 1/2-inch height

6-inch height

8 1/2-inch height

Quilt Block 6

Quilt Block 7

Quilt Block 8

These triangles can be used in several different ways—
joined with the same triangle into a quilt block,
combined with solid triangles,
or combined with horizontal strips.
See the following pages.

Quilt Block 6

Tube-sewing makes the triangles easier to cut, but for accuracy sake, only use tubes when one of the strips is a solid piece of fabric, such as this design.

> **Get rid of some fat.**
> The random strips are perfect for all those fat quarters you've been collecting.

1. **Make vertical strips.**
   Cut a strip vertically or follow instructions for sewing vertical strips on page 330.

2. **Cut solid strips.**
   Measure the width of the vertical combination strip.
   Cut the solid fabric the same width.

3. **Tube-sew.**
   Sew the vertical combination strip and the solid strip, right sides together, along both long edges so it forms a tube.

4. **Cut triangles.**
   Cut the tube into triangles with the point of the 4-angle of the Starmaker 8 first at the top of the strip. Cut the next triangle by turning the Starmaker upside-down with the point of the 4-angle at the bottom of the strip.

   Remove two or three stitches at each point. Press seam allowances toward the solid strip.

5. **Square up blocks, if necessary.**
   See page 382.

6. **Lay out the design.**
   There are several possibilities, including those shown on the following pages.
   The designs are also great for border strips.

   *Yardages and sizes for Quilt Block 6
   are on page 382.*

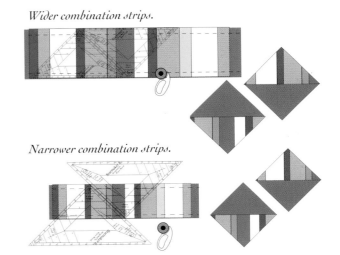

Wider combination strips.

Narrower combination strips.

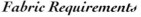

Ferris Wheel

Finished size: 47-by-47 inches
A photo of this quilt, made
by Kaye Wood, is on page 329.

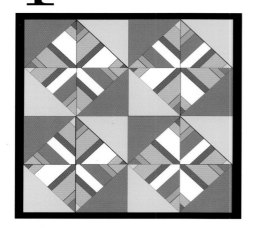

Fabric Requirements

Strips		Enough for four 9-by-44-inch strips.
Solid triangles		
light	1/2 yard	Cut two 8 1/2-by-44-inch strips.
dark	1/2 yard	Cut two 8 1/2-by-44-inch strips.
Borders	1/2 yard	Cut eight 2-by-44-inch strips.
Backing/sleeve	2 1/2 yards	
Batting	50-by-50 inches	
Binding	1/3 yard	

1. ## Make vertical combination strips.
   Directions are on page 330.
   Cut strips 9 inches high by various widths from 1 to 3 inches.
   Sew these strips into four vertical combination strips 44 inches long.
   Trim the vertical strips to make the height 8 1/2 inches.

2. ## Sew tubes.
   Cut solid-colored strips the same width (8 1/2 inches).
   Follow directions for Quilt Block 6 on page 331.
   Sew two tubes with light-colored solid strip.
   Sew two tubes with the dark-colored solid strip.

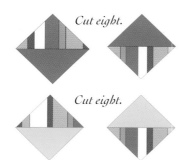

Cut eight.

Cut eight.

3. ## Cut triangles.
   Cut eight dark and eight light triangles using the Starmaker 8. Follow directions for Quilt Block 6 on page 331.

4. ## Sew the blocks into four rows.
   Match the diagonal seamlines.
   Press the seam allowances for each row in opposite directions.

5. ## Sew the rows together.
   Match the diagonal seamlines.
   Press seam allowances.

6. ## Finish.
   Add mitered or square borders. See pages 384 and 385.
      Cut eight 2-inch strips; sew two strips together for each border.
      Pin-mark to match seamlines. See page 383.
   Press seam allowances toward the border strip.
   Layer, quilt, and bind. See page 386.
   Add a sleeve if this is to be a wallhanging.
   See instructions on page 386.

Rows 1 and 3

Rows 2 and 4

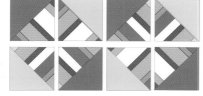

Quilt Block 7

Either the horizontal or the vertical strips, or both, may be cut randomly.

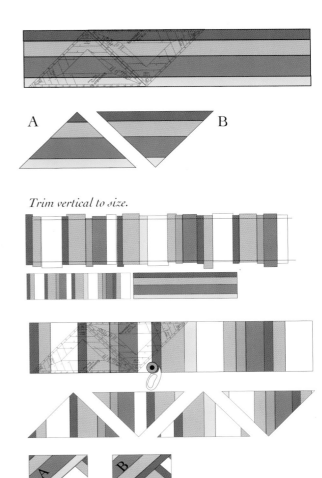

1. Make horizontal combination strips.

   Sew two or more strips together to make a horizontal combination strip.

2. Cut horizontal triangles.

   "A" triangles: Place the point of the 4-angle of the Starmaker 8 at the top of the strip.
   "B" triangles: Place the point of the 4-angle of the Starmaker 8 at the bottom of the strip.

3. Make vertical combination strips.

   Cut a stripe vertically or follow instructions for sewing vertical strips on page 330.
   Trim the vertical strip the same height as the horizontal strip.

4. Cut vertical triangles.

   Follow directions on page 330.

5. Sew quilt block.

   Sew each "A" and "B"horizontal triangle to a vertical triangle.
   Press seam allowances toward the horizontal triangle.
   Follow pressing instructions on page 302.

6. Square up quilt blocks, if necessary.

   See page 382.

Yardages and sizes for Quilt Block 7 are on page 382.

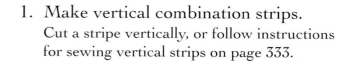

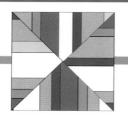

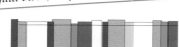

Quilt Block 8

Four Random Vertical/ Triangles

Scrap Happy Pillow

Make it from this quilt block; see photo on page 381.

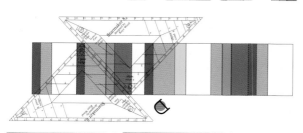

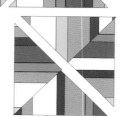

1. **Make vertical combination strips.**
   Cut a stripe vertically, or follow instructions for sewing vertical strips on page 333.

2. **Cut triangles.**
   Cut triangles with the point of the 4-angle of the Starmaker 8 first at the top of the strip. Cut the next triangle by turning the Starmaker upside-down with the point of the 4-angle at the bottom of the strip.

3. **Sew quilt block.**
   Sew two triangles, right sides together, to make each half of the quilt block.
   Press seam allowances in opposite directions.
   Sew two halves together, matching center seamlines.
   Press seam allowances.

4. **Square up quilt blocks.**
   If necessary, see page 382.

5. **Lay out the design.**
   Play with the blocks until you have a pleasing design.

Yardages and sizes for Quilt Block 8
are on page 382.

Scraps, Scraps, and More Scraps

Finished size:
51-by-51 inches

Fabric Requirements

Strips	Use assorted fabric scraps.
Border	1/2 yard Cut eight 2-by-44-inch strips.
Backing/sleeve	2 yards
Batting	55-by-55 inches
Binding	1/3 yard

1. Make combination strips.

Follow directions for cutting vertical strips on page 330.

Cut strips 9-inch-high by various widths from 1 to 3 inches.

Sew into nine combination strips 9-by-42 inches.

Trim these combination strips to 8 1/2 inches wide.

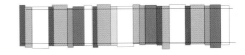

2. Cut triangles.

Cut thirty-six triangles using the Starmaker 8 and following instructions on page 334 for Quilt Block 8.

Cut thirty-six.

3. Sew quilt blocks.

Sew nine blocks, each made from four triangles.

Follow directions on page 334 for Quilt Block 8.

Sew nine.

4. Sew into rows.

Sew three quilt blocks each of three rows, matching seamlines.

Press seam allowances for each row in opposite directions.

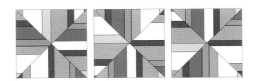

5. Finish.

Add mitered or square borders; see pages 384 and 385.

Cut eight 2-by-44-inch border strips.

Pin-mark to match seamlines. See page 383.

Press seam allowances toward the border strip.

Layer and quilt. See page 386.

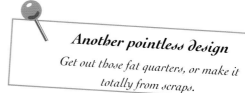

Another pointless design

Get out those fat quarters, or make it totally from scraps.

Chapter 4

Horizontal Fussy-Cut Triangles

Southwest Crossing, made by Lori Jonsson. Directions on page 339.

Large florals, stars, geometric shapes, or fabric scenes are all great for fussy-cuts.
The strips used for fussy-cuts can be any width.

With a strip or combination strip, the fabric motif is centered side-to-side in the middle of the Starmaker 8 with the point of the 4-angle of the Starmaker 8 at the top of the strip.

Some designs can also be used if they are cut upside-down, but this depends on your fabric motif pattern.

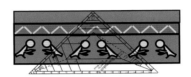 

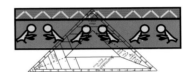 

Motifs can also be centered by cutting with one of the lines (instead of the point) of the 4-angle on the Starmaker 8 at the top of the strip. Strips are then sewn to the top and or bottom of this motif shape and the triangle is cut using the Starmaker 8.

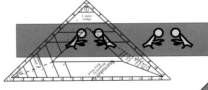 

When a motif is randomly spaced on the fabric, place the point of the 4-angle of the Starmaker 8 above the motif, with the design centered side-to-side.

Fussy-cut triangles can be used completely in a quilt, or they may be combined with solid triangles, randomly cut horizontal, or vertical triangles for interesting quilt designs.
Try several designs on the following pages.

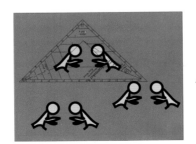 

Quilt Block 9

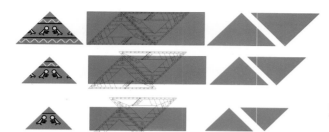

Tube-sewing

It saves fabric, and you get two different quilt blocks. Strips can be solid, a stripe, or several strips sewn into a combination strip.

1. Make horizontal fussy-cut triangles.
   The projects on the following pages will give strip or triangle sizes to cut.
   Follow directions on page 337.

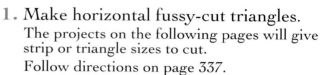

2. Cut solid-colored strips.
   Measure the height of the horizontal fussy triangle.
   Cut the solid fabric the same width.
   Cut this strip into triangles, by placing the point of the 4-angle of the Starmaker 8 at the top of the strip; cut the next triangle by turning the Starmaker upside-down with the point of the 4-angle at the bottom of the strip.

3. Sew the quilt blocks.
   Sew a horizontal fussy-cut triangle, right sides together, to a solid triangle. Press seam allowances toward the darker fabric.

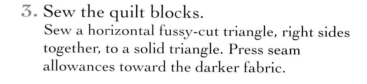

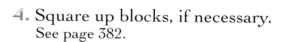

4. Square up blocks, if necessary.
   See page 382.

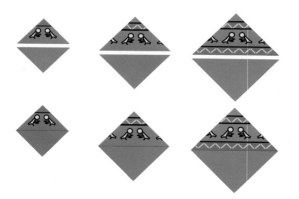

5. Lay out the design.
   There are several possibilities, including those shown on the following pages.
   These quilt blocks are also great for border strips.

Yardages and sizes for Quilt Block 9 are on page 382.

Southwest Crossing

Finished size: 26 1/2-by-26 1/2 inches
A photo of this quilt, made by
Lori Jonsson, is on page 336.

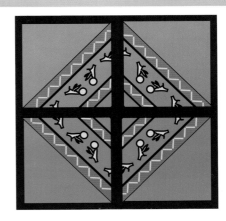

Fabric Requirements

Motif fabric   Enough for four 8 1/2-inch motifs.
Solid triangles   1/4 yard
Sashing/borders   1/2 yard
Backing/sleeve   1 yard
Batting   30-by-30 inches
Binding   1/4 yard

1. **Make fussy-cut triangles.**
   Cut four triangles, with the motif centered, the same size as the Starmaker 8 (height of 8 1/2 inches).
   For instructions, see page 337.

2. **Cut solid triangles.**
   Cut one solid-colored strip 8 1/2-by-44 inches.
   Cut four triangles, following the cutting directions for Quilt Block 9 on page 338.

3. **Sew quilt blocks.**
   Sew four quilt blocks, each made from a motif and a solid triangle.
   Press the seam allowances toward the solid fabric.

Cut four.

Cut four.

Sew four.

4. **Short sashing strips.**
   Cut two sashing strips 2-by-11 1/2 inches (or the size of your quilt block).
   Sew two rows of two blocks with a short sashing strip in between, as shown. See page 383.

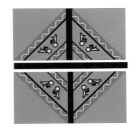

5. **Long sashing strip.**
   Cut one sashing strip 2-by-30 inches.
   Pin-mark to match seams. See page 383.

6. **Finish.**
   Add mitered or square borders. See pages 384 and 385.
   Cut four 2-inch strips. Pin-mark to match seamlines. See page 383.
   Press seam allowances toward the border strip.
   Layer, quilt, add sleeve, and bind. See page 386.

Chapter 5

Vertical Fussy-Cut Triangles

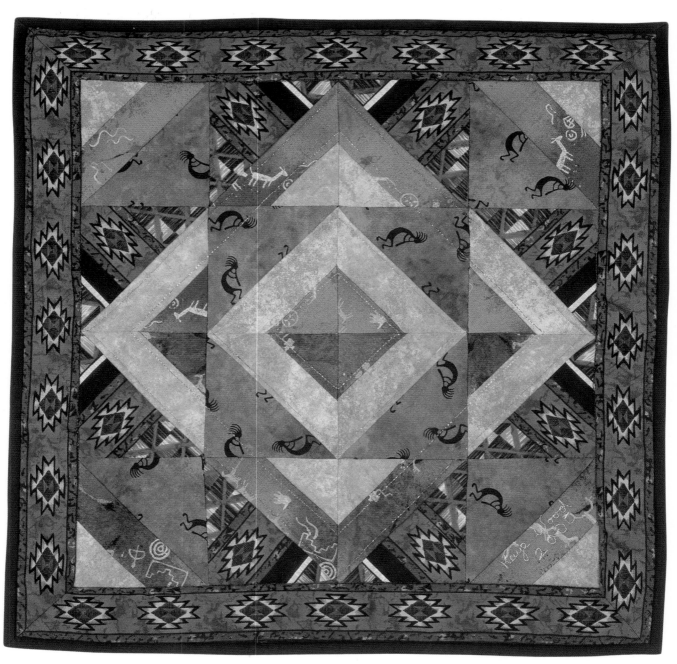

Painted Desert, made by Kaye Wood. Directions on page 344.

1. Make combination strips.

Choose an evenly striped fabric or sew together strips of fabric to make a striped combination.

Choose the "A" color strip you want in the very center of the triangle.
The "B" strips on either side of the center should be the same color and width. "C" strips should also be the same color and width, etc.

2. Cut triangles.

Cut triangles by centering the outside and inside points of the 4-angle of the Starmaker 8 on an "A" strip. See page 303.

Cut the next triangle by again centering the points of the Starmaker 8 on an "A" strip.

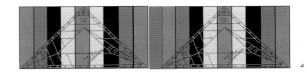

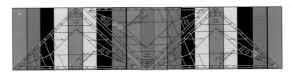

Second triangles: In-between the fussy-cut triangles, turn the Starmaker 8 upside-down to cut triangles with different color combinations. However, with careful strip placement, these second triangles can also have the same "A" strip centered in the triangle.

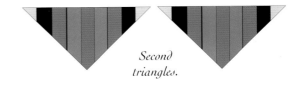

Second triangles.

Fussy-cut triangles can be used completely in a quilt, or they may be combined with solid triangles, randomly cut horizontal, or vertical triangles for interesting quilt designs.
Try several designs on the following pages.

Quilt Block 10

Vertical
Fussy/Horizontal
Triangles

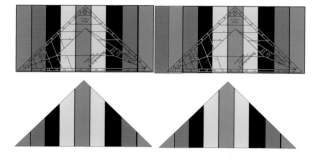

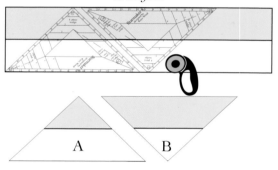

Triangles.

A   B

Topless triangles.

A   B

1. **Make vertical combination strip.**
   Choose a striped fabric or sew together strips
   of fabric to make a vertical combination strip.

2. **Cut vertical triangles.**
   See page 341.

3. **Make horizontal triangles.**
   Cut the horizontal triangles. See page 305.
   Or cut topless triangles. See page 322.
   Each project will suggest one or the other of
   these triangle methods.

4. **Sew the quilt blocks.**
   Sew one vertical and one horizontal triangle,
   right sides together, to make one block.
   Press seam allowances toward the horizontal
   stripped triangle.

5. **Square up the blocks, if necessary.**
   See page 382.

6. **Lay out the design.**
   There are several possibilities, including those
   shown on the following pages.
   The quilt blocks are also great for border
   strips.

*Yardages and sizes for Quilt Block 10
are on page 382.*

Quilt Block 11

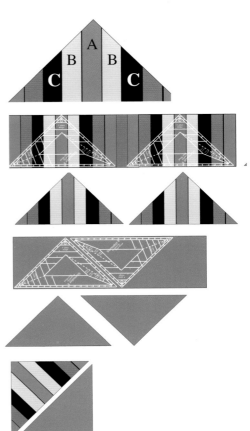

1. **Make vertical combination strip.**
   Choose a striped fabric or sew together strips of fabric to make a striped combination strip. See page 341.

2. **Cut vertical triangles.**
   Cut triangles from vertical stripes following directions on page 341.

3. **Make solid triangles.**
   Measure the height of the horizontal fussy triangle.
   Cut the solid fabric strip the same height.
   Cut triangles as shown on page 306.

4. **Sew the quilt blocks.**
   Sew a horizontal fussy-cut triangle, right sides together, to a solid triangle.
   Press seam allowances toward the solid fabric.

5. **Square up the blocks, if necessary.**
   See page 382.

6. **Lay out the design.**
   There are several possibilities, including those shown on the following pages.
   The quilt blocks are also great for border strips.

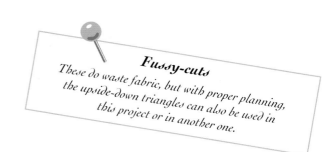

Fussy-cuts
These do waste fabric, but with proper planning, the upside-down triangles can also be used in this project or in another one.

Yardages and sizes for Quilt Block 11 are on page 382.

Painted Desert

Finished size: 15-by-15 inches
A photo of the top left quilt, made
by Kaye Wood, is on page 340.

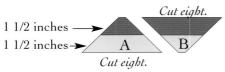

1 1/2 inches →
1 1/2 inches →

Cut eight.

A   B

Cut eight.

Cut eight.

Cut eight.

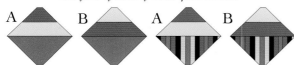

Sew four of each of these quilt blocks.

A   B   A   B

Quilt on left

Rows 1 and 4

Rows 2 and 3

Quilt on right

Rows 1 and 2

Rows 3 and 4

Fabric Requirements for Each Quilt

Horizontal combination strip:

Brown	Cut one 1 1/2-by-44-inch strip.
Light teal	Cut one 1 1/2-by-44-inch strip.
Stripe	Cut one 2 1/2-by-44-inch strip.
Solid	Cut one 2 1/2-by-44-inch strip.
Border	Cut two 2-by-44-inch strips.
Backing	17-by-17 inches
Batting	17-by-17 inches
Binding	Use two 1 3/4-by-44-inch strips.

1. Make horizontal triangles.

   Sew the two strips 1 1/2 inches wide.
   Sew right sides together, into a combination strip.
   Press seam allowances toward the darker fabric.
   Cut eight "A" and eight "B" topless triangles with the Starmaker 8, following the instructions on page 322.

2. Cut vertical triangles.

   Cut a stripe 2 1/2 inches high. See page 341.
   Fussy-cut or random-cut into eight topless triangles. See page 322.

3. Cut solid triangles.

   Cut a strip 2 1/2 inches wide.
   Cut eight topless triangles. See page 322.

4. Sew into quilt blocks.

   Sew the triangles into quilt blocks (shown at left).

5. Sew into rows.

   Match seamline where necessary. See page 306.
   Press the seam allowances for each row in opposite directions.

6. Sew the rows together.

   Match seamlines where necessary.
   Press seam allowances open to reduce the bulk from so many seams coming together.

7. Finish.

   Add mitered or square borders; see pages 384 and 385.
   Cut two 2-by-44-inch strips.
   Pin-mark to match seamlines. See page 383.
   Press seam allowances toward the border strip.
   Layer, quilt, add sleeve, and bind. See page 386.

Kokopelli Plays Again

Finished size: 76-by-102 inches
A photo of this quilt, made by Kaye Wood, is on page 347 and is also featured on the front cover.

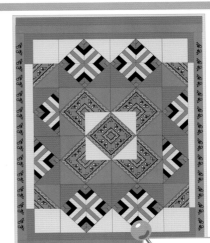

Fabric Requirements for Each Quilt

Motif fabric	Enough for twenty 8 1/2-inch fussy-cut triangles. Minimum of 1 1/4 yards	
Triangles:		
Brown	1 yard	Cut four 8 1/2-by-44-inch strips.
Tan	1 yard	Cut three 8 1/2-by-44-inch strips.
Teal	1 yard	Cut four 8 1/2-by-44-inch strips.
Vertical strips	Enough for twenty-four fussy-cut triangles. Minimum of 2 1/2 yards	
First borders:		
Brown	1/2 yard	Cut six 2-by-44-inch strips.
Tan	1/4 yard	Cut four 2-by-44-inch strips.
Second border:		
	1 1/2 yards	Cut ten 4 1/2-by-44-inch strips.
Backing	80-by-110 inches	
Batting	80-by-110 inches	
Binding	2/3 yard	Cut ten 1 3/4-inch strips.

1. **Cut motif triangles**
   Cut twenty triangles, with the motif centered, the same height as the Starmaker 8 (8 1/2 inches). See page 337.

2. **Cut vertical triangles.**
   Cut the striped fabric into 8 1/2-inch-high strips. Fussy-cut twenty-four triangles by centering the point of the 4-angle of the Starmaker 8 on a particular stripe or strip. See page 342.

3. **Cut solid-colored triangles.**
   Cut three 8 1/2-by-44-inch tan strips.
   Cut four 8 1/2-by-44-inch brown strips.
   Cut four 8 1/2-by-44-inch teal strips.
   Cut into triangles as shown on page 305.

4. **Sew the following quilt blocks:**
   Sixteen motif triangles "A" to solid triangles "E" (Quilt Block 9).
   Four motif triangles "A" to solid triangles "C" (Quilt Block 9).
   Eight striped triangles "B" to solid triangles "C" (Quilt Block 11).
   Sixteen striped triangles "B" to solid triangles "D" (Quilt Block 11).

   Press the seam allowances toward the solid fabric.

This Kokopelli fabric was perfect for my southwest quilt. Kokopelli is a legendary traveling salesman usually depicted playing a flute, possibly to alert a village that he was coming.

A — Cut twenty.

B — Cut twenty-four.

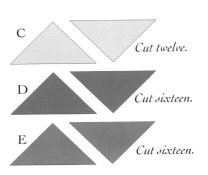

C — Cut twelve.

D — Cut sixteen.

E — Cut sixteen.

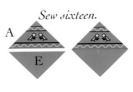

Sew sixteen. A, E

Sew eight. C, B

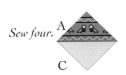

Sew four. A, C

Sew sixteen. D

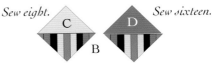

Kaye Wood's Strip-Cut Quilts

345

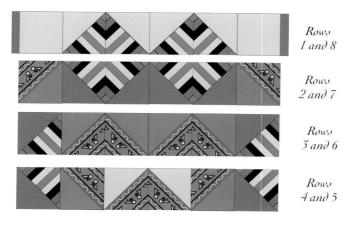

Cut four.

Rows 1 and 8

Rows 2 and 7

Rows 3 and 6

Rows 4 and 5

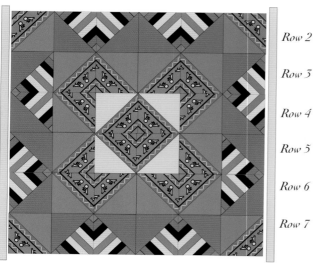

Row 2

Row 3

Row 4

Row 5

Row 6

Row 7

Completed Kokopelli quilt.

5. Cut squares.

Measure the finished quilt blocks. They should be approximately 11 1/2-by-11 1/2 inches.

Cut four squares this size.

6. Sew into rows.

Sew the rows together following the diagram at right.

The first border has an interesting division. Rows 1 and 8 have brown borders; sew a short brown sashing strip 2-by-11 1/2 inches to both ends. See page 383. Press the seam allowances of each row in opposite directions.

7. Sew rows 2 through 7.

Sew rows 2 through 7 together. Press seam allowances.

Rows 2 through 7 have tan side borders. Measure the length of rows 2 through 7. Cut four 2-inch tan border strips. Sew two strips together for each border to get the needed length. Pin-mark to match seamlines, following directions for long sashing strips on page 383.

Sew these strips to rows 2 through 7.

8. Sew all of the rows together.

9. Add the rest of the border strips.

The top and bottom brown border strips are cut 2 inches wide; sew two or more together to make the strip long enough. Pin-mark to match seamlines, in the same way the side borders are pinned. See page 383.

Cut the second border strips 4 1/2 inches wide; sew two or more together to make the strip long enough. Pin-mark. See page 383.

10. Finish.

Layer, quilt, and add binding. See page 386.

Chapter **6**

Vertical Divided Triangles

Illusions, made by Kaye Wood. Directions on page 351.

Jewel, made by Kaye Wood. Directions on page 350.

Shadows, made by Brenda Jonsson. Directions on page 354.

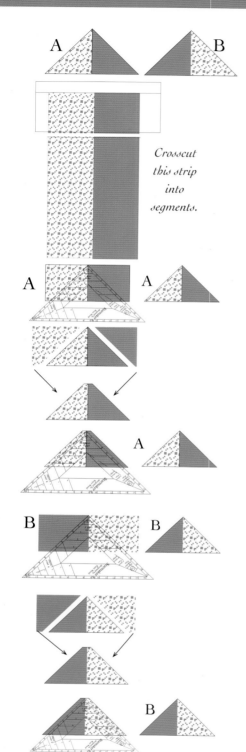

1. Make combination strips.

Sew two equal width strips, right sides together, into a combination strip.

Press seam allowances toward the darker fabric.

2. Crosscut combination strip.

Crosscut this combination strip into equal segments, using the chart below for the measurements.

For example, if the combination strip is 9 1/2 inches wide, crosscut the combination strip into 4-inch segments.

3. Cut "A" triangles.

Cut these segments into "A" triangles by placing the point of the 4-angle of the Starmaker 8 at the top of the piece, centered on the seamline between the two fabrics. Line up the outside point and the inside point (see page 303) on the Starmaker 8 with the seamline.

A second "A" triangle can be cut from each crosscut.

Bring the two ends of each piece together, as shown.

Turn the end pieces and sew them together.

Cut an "A" triangle.

4. Cut "B" triangles.

Follow step 1 and 2 above.

Turn the segments upside-down before cutting the "B" triangles.

Continue with Step 3 above.

Vertical Divided Triangles

each strip	combination strip*	triangles crosscut	per strip
3 inches wide	5 1/2 inches	2 inches	42
4 inches wide	7 1/2 inches	3 inches	28
5 inches wide	9 1/2 inches	4 inches	20
6 inches wide	11 1/2 inches	5 inches	16
7 inches wide	13 1/2 inches	6 inches	14

*If your combination strip is *slightly* wider or narrower than the measurement listed above (because of a difference in seam allowances), it's okay. This technique will still work; yardages will be the same.

Quilt Block 12

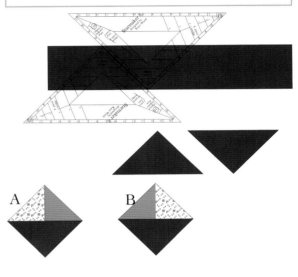

1. Vertical divided triangles.
Follow directions on page 348.

2. Solid-colored triangles.
Cut solid strips the same width as the crosscut segments from page 348.
Cut the solid strips into triangles, by placing the point of the 4-angle of the Starmaker 8 at the top of the strip; Cut the next triangle by turning the Starmaker upside-down with the point of the 4-angle at the bottom of the strip.

3. Sew quilt blocks.
Sew a divided triangle "A" and or "B" to each solid triangle, depending on the design. Press seam allowances toward the solid-colored triangle.

4. Square up the quilt blocks, if necessary.
See page 382.

5. Lay out the design.
There are several possibilities, including those shown on the following pages.
The designs are also great for border strips.

Embellishments
Show off your quilting or embroidery designs. The solid triangles are great for embellishing.

Vertical designs
These triangles can be combined with each other, or combined with solid or horizontal triangles.

Sizes for Quilt Blocks 12 and 13
Sizes for any vertical divided/triangle blocks

each strip	vertical combination strip	crosscut	block size	finished block size
3 inches wide	5 1/2 inches	2 inches	3 1/2 inches	3 inches
4 inches wide	7 1/2 inches	3 inches	4 inches	3 1/2 inches
5 inches wide	9 1/2 inches	4 inches	5 1/4 inches	4 3/4 inches
6 inches wide	11 1/2 inches	5 inches	6 3/4 inches	6 1/4 inches
7 inches wide	13 1/2 inches	6 inches	8 inches	7 1/2 inches

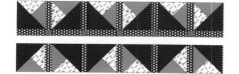

Jewel

Finished size: 61-by-80 inches
A photo of this quilt, made
by Kaye Wood, is on page 347.

Cut forty-eight.

Cut forty-eight.

Sew forty-eight.

Fabric Requirements

Combination strips:

Light mauve	1 yard	Cut four 7-by-44-inch strips.
Mauve	1 yard	Cut four 7-by-44-inch strips.
Blue	1 1/2 yards	Cut eight 6-by-44-inch strips.
Sashing/first border	1 yard	Cut seventeen 2-by-44-inch strips.
Sashing squares		Cut two 2-by-44-inch strips.
Second border	1 yard	Cut eight 3 1/4-inch strips.
Backing	65-by-85 inches	
Batting	65-by-85 inches	
Binding	1/2 yard	Cut 1 3/4-inch strips.

1. Make divided triangles.

Sew the two 7-inch strips, right sides together, into four combination strips. Crosscut these strips into twenty-four 6-inch segments and cut forty-eight "A" triangles. Directions are on page 348.

2. Cut solid triangles.

Cut blue strips into forty-eight triangles. Directions for Quilt Block 12 are on page 349.

3. Sew quilt blocks.

Sew a dark triangle to each "A" vertical divided triangle.

4. Make short sashing strips.

Cut the 2-inch sashing strips into forty 2-by-8-inch pieces.
Sew six blocks and sashing strips into rows.
Follow directions for short sashing strips on page 383.

5. Make long sashing strips.

Cut the 2-inch sashing strips into forty-two 2-by-8-inch pieces.
Sashing squares: Cut the 2-inch strips into thirty-five 2-inch squares.
Sew seven long sashing strips, each with six 8-inch strips and five 2-inch squares.

6. Sew rows together.

Sew together by alternating a row of quilt blocks with a long sashing strip. Match seamlines.

7. Finish.

Borders: Sew two sashing or border strips together to make the strip long enough. Match seamlines. Press seam allowances toward the border strip. Layer, quilt, and bind. See page 386.

Illusions

Finished size: 30-by-30 inches
A photo of this quilt, made
by Kaye Wood, is on page 347.

Fabric Requirements

Combination strip:

Light mauve	1/2 yard	Cut two 7-by-44-inch strips.
Mauve	1/2 yard	Cut two 7-by-44-inch strips.
Blue	1/2 yard	Cut three 6-by-44-inch strips.
Backing	1 yard	
Batting	36-by-36 inches	

Embellishments!

Try adding a decorative trim or lace doily in the solid triangles.

1. Make divided triangles.

Sew 7-inch strips, right sides together, into two combination strips.
Crosscut this strip into 6-inch segments. Cut ten "A" triangles and six "B" triangles.
Directions are on page 348.

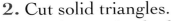

Cut ten. A   *Cut six.* B

2. Cut solid triangles.

Cut sixteen triangles from the blue strips, following directions on page 349.

3. Sew quilt blocks.

Sew a dark triangle to each "A" and "B" vertical divided triangle.
Directions for Quilt Block 12 are on page 349.

Rows 1 and 4

Rows 2 and 3

4. Sew into rows.

Sew four rows, as shown at right.

5. Sew rows together.

Match seamlines. See page 306.

6. Finish.

Layer, quilt, and bind. See page 386.

Same design, different fabrics!

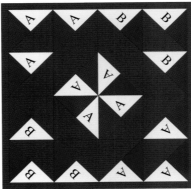

Different design, same blocks!

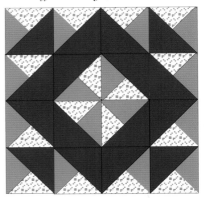

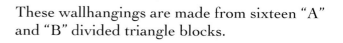

Try these designs, all made from "A" and "B" divided triangle blocks.

 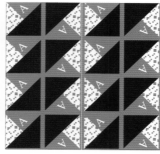

Both of these wallhangings are made from sixteen "A" divided triangle blocks.

The blocks in the quilt on the near left are divided by sashing strips.

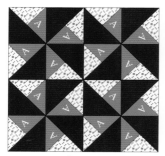 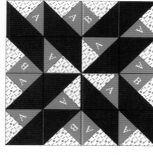

These wallhangings are made from sixteen "A" and "B" divided triangle blocks.

More embellishments!
Show off your quilting in the large triangles.

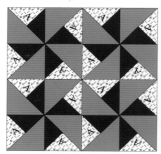 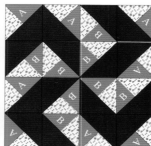 

On-point quilt blocks look entirely different.

Kaye Wood's Strip-Cut Quilts

Quilt Block 13

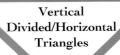

1. Cut vertical divided triangles.

Cut "A" and "B" triangles. See directions on page 348.

2. Make horizontal stripped triangles.

Sew strips together into a combination strip that equals the height of the segments from which the "A" and "B" triangles were cut. See page 348.

Cut into triangles, by placing the point of the 4-angle of the Starmaker 8 at the top of the strip. Cut the next triangle by turning the Starmaker upside-down with the point of the 4-angle at the bottom of the strip.

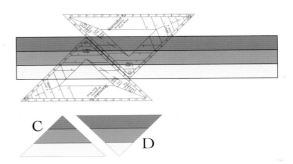

Mix and match.
Five different fabrics can be used in each of these quilts.

3. Sew quilt blocks.

Sew a divided triangle "A" or "B" to a horizontal triangle "C" or "D," depending on the design.
Press seam allowances toward the horizontal triangle.

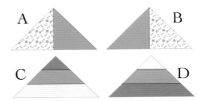

4. Square up the quilt blocks, if necessary.
See page 382.

5. Lay out the design.

There are several possibilities, including those shown on the following pages.
The quilt blocks are also great for border strips.

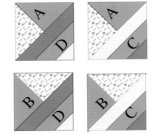

Yardages and sizes for Quilt Block 13 are on page 349.

Shadows

Finished size: 36-by-36 inches
A photo of this quilt, made
by Brenda Jonsson, is on page 347.

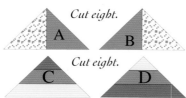

Cut eight.

Cut eight.

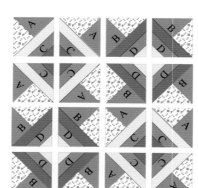

Fabric Requirements

Divided triangles:
 Light mauve Cut one 6-by-44-inch strip.
 Mauve   Cut one 6-by-44-inch strip.
Horizontal stripped triangles:
 Pink   Cut two 2-by-44-inch strips.
 Mauve   Cut two 2-by-44-inch strips.
Purple   Cut two 2-by-44-inch strips.
Backing   1 1/4 yard
Batting   40-by-40 inches
 (optional for table covers)

Tablecovers
These make perfect gifts!

1. Make divided triangles.
 Sew the 6-inch strips from the light and medium
 fabrics, right sides together, to make one 11 1/2-
 inch-wide combination strip.
 Crosscut this strip into 5-inch segments. Cut eight
 "A" triangles and eight "B" triangles.
 Directions are on page 348.

2. Make horizontal triangles.
 Sew a light, medium, and dark fabric together to
 make two 5-inch combination strips.
 Press seam allowances toward the darkest fabric.
 Cut eight "C" and eight "D" triangles. See page
 353.

3. Sew quilt blocks.
 Sew eight "AC" blocks and eight "BD" blocks.
 Directions for Quilt Block 13 are on page 353.

4. Sew into rows.
 Lay out the blocks in this design, or try one of
 your own designs.
 Sew four quilt blocks in each row.
 Match seamlines. See page 306.

5. Sew rows together
 Sew into four rows, as shown at right.
 Match seamlines.

6. Finish.
 Layer, quilt, and bind.
 See page 386.

Chapter 7

Vertical and Horizontal Triangles

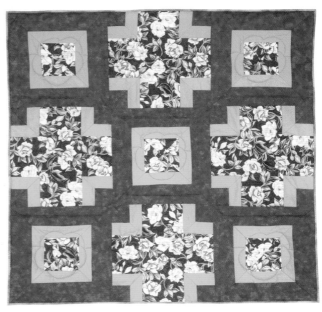

Hawaiian Fantasy (top left) and Spring Rain (lower left), made by Brenda Jonsson. Directions on pages 358 and 361, respectively.
Floral Windows (top right) and Crossroads (lower right), made by Kaye Wood. Directions on pages 359 and 365, respectively.

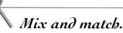

Vertical and horizontal triangles can be cut from the same combination strip. An overall design, such as a large floral, is best for the wide center stripe.

1. Make combination strips.

Sew an odd number of strips (three, five, seven, etc.) into a combination strip.

The two outside strips are the same width; these strips and the center motif strip should be at least 3 inches wide. The strips on both sides of the center should be the same fabric and the same width. Inside strips can be narrower (from 1 to 2 inches). Press seam allowances away from the center motif strip.

2. Cut squares.

Cut the combination strip into squares.

For example, if the combination strip is 10 inches wide, cut it into 10-by-10-inch squares. If it is 13 1/2 inches wide, cut it into 13 1/2-by-13 1/2-inch squares.

3. Fold the strip.

Fold the strip along the center of the motif strip. Press the center fold.

Pin seamlines together at the ends of the combination strip to keep the two layers from shifting.

4. Cut triangles.

Place the Starmaker 8 with the point of the 4-angle at the fold.

Cut along both edges of the Starmaker.

From one square, four triangles will be cut: two vertical and two horizontal.

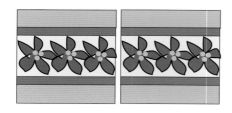

fold

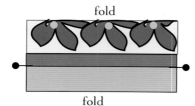

fold

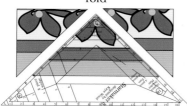

Two horizontal triangles.   *From each square:*   *Two vertical triangles.*

Sizes for Vertical/Horizontal Triangles

combination strip	square	height of triangles
8 inches	8 inches	4 inches
9 inches	9 inches	4 1/2 inches
10 inches	10 inches	5 inches
11 inches	11 inches	5 1/2 inches
12 inches	12 inches	6 inches
13 inches	13 inches	6 1/2 inches
14 inches	14 inches	7 inches
15 inches	15 inches	7 1/2 inches
16 inches	16 inches	8 inches
17 inches	17 inches	8 1/2 inches

Quilt Blocks 14 and 15

Quilt Block 14 *Quilt Block 15*
Vertical triangles. *Horizontal triangles.*

1. **Cut triangles.**
   Cut both vertical and horizontal triangles at the same time—and make both Quilt Blocks 14 and 15.
   See page 356.

2. **Sew quilt blocks.**
   Sew four vertical triangles together to make Quilt Block 14.
   Sew four horizontal triangles together to make Quilt Block 15.

    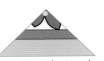

   Vertical triangles. *Horizontal triangles.*

   First sew two triangles together, matching seamlines, to make half of each quilt block. Press seam allowances on each half in opposite directions.
   Sew two halves together, matching seamlines, to make the quilt block.

3. **Square up these blocks.**
   Especially if the two different blocks are to be used in the same project, they must be the same size.
   See page 356.

4. **Lay out the design.**
   There are several possibilities, including those shown on the following pages.

   Yardages and sizes for Quilt Blocks 14 and 15 are on page 356.

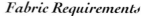

Hawaiian Fantasy

Finished size: 34-by-34 inches
A photo of this quilt, made by
Brenda Jonsson, is on page 355.

Fabric Requirements

Floral motif stripe	1 yard	
Borders	1/4 yard	Cut four 2-by-44-inch strips.
Backing	36-by-36 inches	
Batting	36-by-36 inches	
Binding	1/4 yard	Cut four 3-by-44-inch strips.

Did you know?
It is against the law to leave a state without buying fabric.
The stripes on this Hawaiian fabric were perfect for this design.
Only the one stripe was used for the quilt blocks.

1. **Cut stripes.**
   Cut two stripes 17 inches wide.
   Cut the stripes into four 17-inch squares. See
   page 356.

2. **Cut triangles.**
   Fold the strip and cut eight vertical triangles
   and eight horizontal side triangles. See page 356.

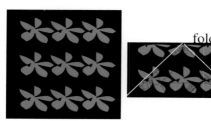

fold

Eight vertical triangles.   *Eight horizontal triangles.*

3. **Sew quilt blocks.**
   Sew four vertical triangles together to make
   each Quilt Block 14.
   Sew four horizontal triangles together to make
   each Quilt Block 15. See page 357.

4. **Sew into rows.**
   Sew one Quilt Block 14 and one Quilt Block
   15 together for each row.
   Press seam allowances in opposite directions.

5. **Sew rows together.**
   Match seamlines, and press seam allowances.

6. **Finish.**
   Add mitered or square borders; see pages 384
   and 385. Pin-mark the border strips to match
   seamlines and control the bias edges. See page
   383. Press seam allowances toward the border
   strip. Layer, quilt, and add sleeve; see page
   386. Cut binding strips 3-by-44 inches for a
   1/2-inch finished binding. See page 386.

Sew two.   *Sew two.*
vertical blocks.   *horizontal blocks.*

Floral Windows

**Finished size: 40-by-40 inches
A photo of this quilt, made by
Kaye Wood, is on page 355.**

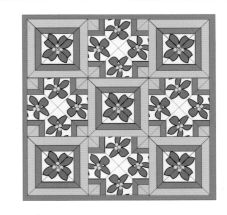

Fabric Requirements

Combination strip:

Floral motif	2/3 yard	Cut four 5 1/2-by-44-inch strips.
Dark	1/2 yard	Cut eight 2-by-44-inch strips.
Medium	2/3 yard	Cut eight 3-by-44-inch strips.
Borders	1/4 yard	Cut four 2-by-44-inch strips.
Backing/sleeve	1 1/2 yards	
Batting	43-by-43 inches	
Binding	1/4 yard	Cut into 1 3/4-inch strips.

1. Make combination strips.

   Cut a strip 13 1/2 inches wide, or sew combination strips together as follows: 3 inches to 2 inches to 5 1/2 inches to 2 inches to 3 inches.
   Press seam allowances away from the center (5 1/2-inch) strip.
   Measure the width of the combination strip. It should be approximately 13 1/2 inches; however, use your measurement to cut the combination strips into ten squares. See page 356.

2. Cut triangles.

   Cut twenty vertical triangles and twenty horizontal side triangles.
   Only sixteen of the vertical triangles will be used in the quilt. Use the four remaining vertical triangles to make a coordinating pillow.

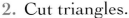

Cut twenty. *Cut twenty.*

3. Sew quilt blocks.

   Sew four vertical triangles together to make each Quilt Block 14.
   Sew four horizontal triangles together to make each Quilt Block 15. See page 356.

Sew four. *Sew five.*

4. Sew into rows.

   Sew three quilt blocks together into three rows.
   Press seam allowances in opposite directions.

 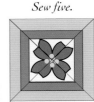

5. Sew rows together.

   Match seamlines, and press seam allowances.

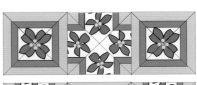

6. Finish.

   Add mitered or square borders; pages 384 and 385.
   Pin-mark the border strips to match seamlines. See page 383.
   Press seam allowances toward the border strip.
   Layer, quilt, and add sleeve and binding. See page 386.

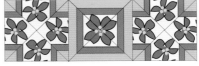

Quilt Block 16

1. **Make combination strips.**
   Sew an odd number of strips (three, five, seven, etc.) into a combination strip.
   Press seam allowances away from the center motif fabric.
   See page 356 for more information.
   Or use a geometric stripe instead of sewing a combination strip.

2. **Cut triangles.**
   Cut vertical and horizontal triangles, as shown on page 356.
   Both triangles are cut at the same time.

3. **Sew the quilt blocks.**
   Sew a vertical triangle to a horizontal triangle to make each quilt block.
   Press seam allowances toward the horizontal triangle.

4. **Square up blocks, if necessary.**
   See page 382.

Vertical triangles.

Horizontal triangles.

Yardages and sizes for Quilt Block 16 are on page 356.

Want to use stripes?
Look for fabrics that have both wide and narrow vertical stripes. The motif fabric should be wide enough to make a real statement in your quilt.

Spring Rain

Finished size: 22 1/2-by-22 1/2 inches
A photo of this quilt, made by
Brenda Jonsson, is on page 355.

Fabric Requirements for Each Quilt

Combination strips:

Floral	1/2 yard	Cut three 5-by-44-inch strips.
Dark	1/4 yard	Cut six 1 1/2-by-44-inch strips.
Medium	1/2 yard	Cut six 3-by-44-inch strips.
First border	1/3 yard	Cut four 2 1/2-by-44-inch strips.
Second border		
	1/4 yard	Cut four 1 1/2-by-44-inch strips.
Backing	40-by-40 inches	
Batting	40-by-40 inches	
Binding	1/4 yard	Cut 1 3/8-inch strips.

1. **Make combination strips.**
   Cut a stripe or sew combination strips together as follows: 3 inches to 1 1/2 inches to 5 inches to 1 1/2 inches to 3 inches.
   Cut the combination strip into squares. See page 356.

2. **Cut triangles.**
   Cut sixteen vertical and sixteen horizontal triangles.
   See page 356.

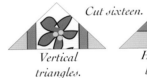

Cut sixteen.

Vertical triangles.   *Horizontal triangles.*

3. **Sew quilt blocks.**
   Sew sixteen vertical/horizontal triangle quilt blocks.
   Follow directions on page 360 for Quilt Block 16.

Sew sixteen.

4. **Sew into rows.**
   Sew four quilt blocks together into four identical rows.
   Turn every other row upside-down.
   Press seam allowances in opposite directions.

Quilt on bottom.

5. **Sew rows together.**
   Match seamlines, and press seam allowances.

6. **Finish.**
   Add mitered or square borders. See pages 384 and 385.
   Press seam allowances toward the border strip.
   Layer, quilt, and add sleeve and binding. See page 386.

Quilt on top.

Quilt Blocks 17 and 18

*Quilt Block 17
Vertical/Solid
Triangles.*

*Quilt Block 18
Horizontal/Solid
Triangles.*

*Vertical
triangles.*

*Horizontal
triangles.*

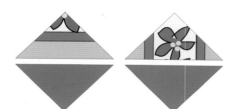

1. **Cut triangles.**
   Cut vertical and horizontal triangles, as shown on page 356. Both triangles are cut at the same time.

2. **Cut solid triangles.**
   Measure the height of the triangles.
   Cut the solid fabric the same width.
   Cut this strip into triangles, by placing the point of the 4-angle of the Starmaker 8 at the top of the strip. Cut the next triangle by turning the Starmaker upside-down with the point of the 4-angle at the bottom of the strip

3. **Sew the quilt blocks.**
   Sew a vertical or horizontal triangle to each solid triangle.
   Press seam allowances toward the solid triangle.

4. **Square up blocks, if necessary.**
   See page 382.

Embellishments
Add a decorative lace motif in the solid triangles.

*Yardages and sizes for Quilt Blocks 17 and 18
are on page 356.*

Dream Catchers

Finished size: 24-by-24 inches

Fabric Requirements for Both Quilts Combined

Combination strip:

Floral motif	Cut one 5-by-26-inch strip.
Dark	Cut two 1 1/2-by-26-inch strips.
Medium	Cut two 3-by-26-inch strips
Solid triangles	1/4 yard
Border	Cut four 1 1/2-by-26-inch strips.
Backing	8-by-28 inches
Batting	28-by-28 inches
Binding	Four 1 3/4-inch strips

1. Make combination strips.

Cut a stripe, or sew combination strips together as follows: 3 inches to 1 1/2 inches to 5 inches to 1 1/2 inches to 3 inches. Press seam allowances away from the center (5-inch) strip.

Measure the width of the combination strip. It should be approximately 12 inches. Use your measurement to cut the combination strips into two squares. See page 356.

2. Cut triangles.

Cut four vertical and four horizontal triangles. See page 356.

Cut eight solid triangles. See page 68, Quilt Blocks 17 and 18.

Cut 4. Cut 4.

Horizontal triangles. *Vertical triangles.*

3. Sew quilt blocks.

Sew four vertical triangles to four solid triangles.
Sew four horizontal triangles to four solid triangles
Follow directions on page 362, Quilt Blocks 17 and 18.

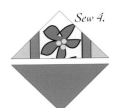

Sew 4. Sew 4.

4. Sew into rows.

Sew two quilt blocks together into two identical rows. Turn the second row upside-down. Press seam allowances in opposite directions.

5. Sew rows together.

Match seamlines, and press seam allowances.

Quilt on top. *Quilt on bottom.*

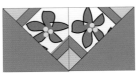 

6. Finish.

Add mitered or square borders; pages 384 and 385.
Pin-mark the border strips to match seamlines. See page 383.
Press seam allowances toward the border strip.
Layer, quilt, and add sleeve and binding. See page 386.

Quilt Block 19

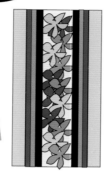

Diamonds

Cut diamonds whenever your motif fabric would look better in one piece instead of sewing two horizontal triangles together with a seam down the middle.

1. **Sew combination strips.**

   Sew an odd number of strips (three, five, seven, etc.) into a combination strip.

   The two outside strips and the center motif strip should be at least 3 inches wide.

   Inside strips should be narrower (from 1 to 2 inches).

   Press seam allowances away from the center motif strip.

2. **Fold combination strips.**

   Fold the strip along the center of the motif strip. Press the center fold.

   Pin seamlines together at the ends and in the middle of the combination strip to keep the two layers from shifting.

Step 2   *Step 3* Fold

Fold

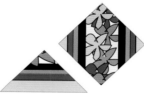

3. **Cut triangles.**

   Place the Starmaker 8 with the point of the 4-angle at the raw edges (the side opposite the fold).

   Cut along both edges of the Starmaker.

   From one square, a diamond and two horizontal triangles will be cut.

   The horizontal triangles can be used in any of the designs in this book that call for horizontal triangles, such as:

Quilt Block 1, see page 307.

Quilt Block 2, see page 310.

Quilt Block 5, see page 321.

Sizes for Diamonds

combination strip	width of diamonds	height of triangles
8 inches	8 inches	4 inches
9 inches	9 inches	4 1/2 inches
10 inches	10 inches	5 inches
11 inches	11 inches	5 1/2 inches
12 inches	12 inches	6 inches
13 inches	13 inches	6 1/2 inches
14 inches	14 inches	7 inches
15 inches	15 inches	7 1/2 inches
16 inches	16 inches	8 inches
17 inches	17 inches	8 1/2 inches

Crossroads

Finished size: 34-by-34 inches
A photo of this quilt, made by
Kaye Wood, is on page 355.

Fabric Requirements

Combination strip:

Floral	1/2 yard	Cut two 6 1/2-by-44 inch strips.
Dark	1/8 yard	Cut four 1 1/2-by-44-inch strips.
Medium	1/8 yard	Cut four 1 1/2-by-44-inch strips.
Medium	1/8 yard	Cut four 1 1/2-by-44-inch strips.
Light	1/8 yard	Cut four 2-by-44-inch strips.
Corner triangles	1/2 yard	
Border	1/2 yard	Cut four 3-by-44-inch strips.
Backing	1 yard	
Batting	36-by-36 inches	
Binding	1/4 yard	Cut 1 3/4-inch strips.

1. ## Make combination strips.

   Sew two combination strips, right sides together, each
   with the following strips: 2 inches to 1 1/2 inches to
   1 1/2 inches to 1 1/2 inches to 6 1/2 inches to 1 1/2
   inches to 1 1/2 inches to 1 1/2 inches to 2 inches.

2. ## Cut diamonds.

   Cut four diamonds. See page 364 for cutting Quilt
   Block 19.
   Use the horizontal triangles for coordinating pillows.

3. ## Sew into rows.

   Sew two quilt blocks together into two rows, matching
   seamlines.
   Press seam allowances in opposite directions.

4. ## Sew rows together.

   Match seamlines.

5. ## Finish.

   Corner triangles. Cut two 16-inch squares from the
   triangle fabric. Cut diagonally through both squares
   to get the four triangles needed for the corners.
   Pin-mark the center and edges along the diagonal side
   of these triangles, following the directions for pin-
   marking sashing strips. See page 383.
   Sew the diagonal side of each triangle to each side of
   the quilt, matching seamlines to pins.
   Square up the quilt 1/4 inches beyond the points of
   the diamond.
   Press seam allowances toward the triangles.
   Add a mitered border. See page 385.
   Layer, quilt, and add sleeve and binding. See page 386.

Looks like a cross ...
This would be perfect for a
liturgical banner for the
Easter holiday season.

Cut four.

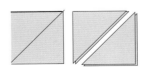

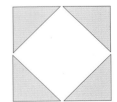

Chapter 8

Up-and-Down Triangles

Both quilts—Chill Out (above) and Mike's Quilt (right)—were made by Brenda Jonsson. Directions are on pages 369 and 370, respectively.

Fabric used for the up-and-down triangles can be an overall print, such as a one-directional floral vine or the wolf fabric in Mike's Quilt, or a fussy-cut motif. The design will be vertical (up and down) in the triangle.

1. Cut strip the desired width (up to 12 inches high).

2. Cut triangles.

   "C" triangle: Place the bottom of the Starmaker 8 along the bottom of the strip. The diagonal side of the Starmaker 8 should go to the corner, regardless of the width of the strip, see diagram below on left.

   "D" triangle: Turn the Starmaker 8 so the bottom of the Starmaker is now at the top of the strip. The vertical side of the Starmaker should go to the lower corner, regardless of the width of the strip.

   "E" triangle: The bottom of the Starmaker 8 is now at the top of the strip.
   The diagonal side of the Starmaker 8 should go to the lower corner.

   "F" triangle: Turn the Starmaker 8 so the bottom is now at the bottom of the strip.
   The vertical side of the Starmaker should go to the upper corner.

The design goes up and down.
The design will be up and down inside the triangle. Strips can be any height.

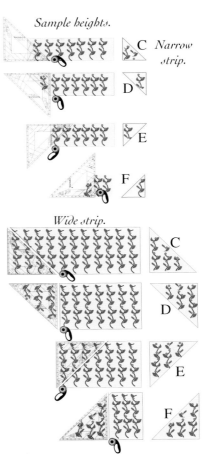

Sample heights.

C Narrow strip.

D

E

F

Wide strip.

C

D

E

F

If you cut two "C" and "D" triangles but only one "E" and one "F" triangle from a strip, start the second strip by cutting "E" and "F" triangle.

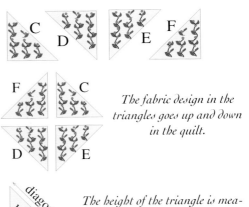

The fabric design in the triangles goes up and down in the quilt.

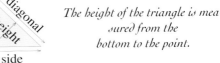

The height of the triangle is measured from the bottom to the point.

Sizes for Up-and-Down Triangles

strip width	*height	diagonal	side
5 inches	5 inches	3 1/2 inches	7 inches
6 inches	6 inches	4 1/4 inches	8 1/2 inches
7 inches	7 inches	5 inches	10 inches
8 inches	8 inches	5 5/8 inches	11 3/8 inches
9 inches	9 inches	6 1/2 inches	13 inches
10 inches	10 inches	7 inches	14 inches
11 inches	11 inches	7 3/4 inches	15 1/2 inches
12 inches	12 inches	8 1/2 inches	17 inches

*The height of the triangle is the measurement needed to combine

Quilt Block 20

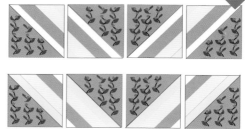

Lots of choices.

Four triangles are cut from one vertical strip — combine these with two different horizontal triangles, and you get eight different quilt blocks.

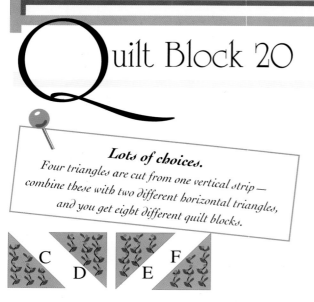

C

D

E

F

side
height
diagonal

A

B

1. **Cut up-and-down triangles.**
   Cutting directions are on page 367.

2. **Make horizontal triangles.**
   Sew strips together into a combination strip that equals the height of the vertical triangle. See page 367.

   Cut the combination strip into triangles by placing the point of the 4-angle of the Starmaker 8 at the top of the strip. Cut the next triangle by turning the Starmaker upside-down with the point of the 4-angle at the bottom of the strip.

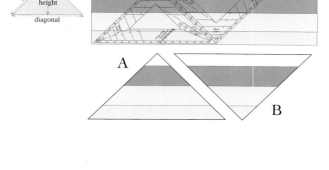

A-C   A-D   A-E   A-F

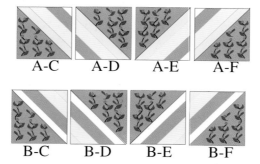

B-C   B-D   B-E   B-F

3. **Sew eight different quilt blocks.**
   Sew an "A" triangle to each of the up-and-down triangles "C," "D," "E," and "F."

   Sew a "B" triangle to each of the up-and-down triangles "C," "D," "E," and "F."

side
height
diagonal

Up-and-Down/Horizontal Triangles Size Chart

See page 367.

To use the chart on page 367, use the height of the triangle for the strip width.

Chill Out

It's an air conditioner cover!

Finished size: 31-by-31 inches
A photo of the finished quilt, made by Brenda Jonsson, is on page 366.

Fabric Requirements for Both Quilts

Up-and-down motif fabric 2/3 yard
Horizontal combination strips:

White		Cut two 3-by-44-inch strips.
Green		Cut two 2-by-44-inch strips.
Pink		Cut two 2-by-44-inch strips.
Light green		Cut two 3-by-44-inch strips.
Sashing		Cut two 1 1/2-by-44-inch strips.
First border	1/2 yard	Cut eight 2-by-44-inch strips.
Second border	1/2 yard	Cut eight 3-by-44-inch strips.
Backing		Cut two 34-by-34-inch pieces.
Batting		Cut two 34-by-34-inch pieces.
Binding	1/2 yard	Cut 1 3/4-inch strips.

1. **Cut up-and-down triangles.**
   Cut two strips 12 inches wide from the motif fabric. Cut two of each triangle— "C," "D," "E," and "F." See page 367.

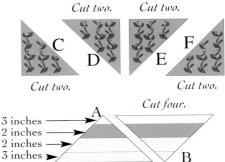

Cut two.   Cut two.

C   D   E   F

Cut two.   Cut two.

2. **Make horizontal triangles.**
   Sew two combination strips, as shown: 3 inches to 2 inches to 2 inches to 3 inches.
   Cut four "A" and four "B" triangles from the combination strips using the Starmaker 8. See Quilt Block 20, page 368.

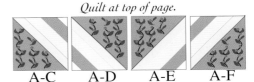

Cut four.

3 inches →   A
2 inches →
2 inches →
3 inches →   B

Cut four.

3. **Sew quilt blocks.**
   For the quilt on the left, sew "A" triangles to each of the four vertical triangles. For a variation, sew "B" triangles to each of the four vertical triangles.

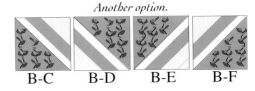

Quilt at top of page.

A-C   A-D   A-E   A-F

4. **Make short sashing strips.**
   For each quilt, cut two sashing strips 1 1/2-by-11 1/2 inches (or size of quilt block). Sew a sashing strip between two blocks. See page 383.
   Press seam allowances toward the sashing strips.

Another option.

B-C   B-D   B-E   B-F

5. **Make long sashing strips.**
   For each quilt, cut two sashing strips 1 1/2-by-24 inches. To match seamlines, pin-mark the sashing strip. See page 383.
   Sew the sashing strip, matching seamlines to pins. Press seam allowances toward the sashing strips.

6. **Finish.**
   Add borders. See page 383. Cut border strips 2 inches wide. To miter borders, sew both borders together before sewing them to the quilt top. Pin-mark to match seamlines. See page 383. Press seam allowances toward the border strip. Layer and quilt. See page 386.

Mike's Quilt

Finished size: 52-by-102 inches
A photo of this quilt, made by
Brenda Jonsson (Mike's mom), is on page 366.

Fabric Requirements

Up-and-down motif 2 yards (more for fussy-cuts)
Horizontal combination strips:

Beige	2/3 yard	Cut eight 2 1/2-by-44-inch strips.
Brown	2/3 yard	Cut eight 2 1/2-by-44-inch strips.
Rust	2/3 yard	Cut eight 2 1/2-by-44-inch strips.
Green	2/3 yard	Cut eight 2 1/2-by-44-inch strips.
Sashing	1 1/2 yard	Cut twenty-four 2-by-44-inch strips.
Borders	2/3 yard	Cut ten 2-by-44-inch strips.
Backing	55-by-105 inches	
Batting	55-by-105 inches	

1. Cut up-and-down triangles.
Cut six strips 12 inches wide from the motif fabric.
Cut eight of each triangle — "C," "D," "E," and "F." See page 367.

Cut eight of each.

2. Horizontal stripped triangles.
Sew eight combination strips, each made from four 2 1/2-inch strips.
Press seam allowances all in one direction. It will be slightly wider than the Starmaker 8.

Cut sixteen of each.

Cut sixteen "A" triangles with the bottom of the Starmaker along the bottom of the combination strip.
Cut sixteen "B" triangles with the bottom of the Starmaker 8 along the top of the combination strip.

Sew four of each block.

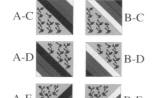

3. Sew quilt blocks.
Sew four each of the eight blocks shown. See Quilt Block 20, page 368.

4. Make sashing strips.
Cut long sashing strips first; cut fourteen 2-by-44-inch strips.
Sew two strips together to make seven longer strips; cut these longer strips into seven 2-by-52-inch strips, with the seam in the middle.
Cut twenty-eight short sashing strips 2-by-11 1/2 inches (or the size of the block). Some of the short sashing strips can be cut from leftover long sashing strip pieces.

5. Sew into rows
Sew blocks and short sashing strips together in rows. See page 383.

Rows 1, 4, 5, and 8

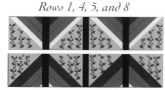

Rows 2, 3, 6, and 7

6. Sew rows together.
Pin-mark the three long sashing strips. See page 383.
Sew the rows and sashing strips together.

7. Finish.
Add mitered or square borders. See pages 384 and 385.
Sew two or three border strips together to make them long enough.
Pin-mark the border strips the same way as Step 6 above. See page 383.
Press seam allowances toward the border strip.
Layer and quilt.

Chapter 9

Flying Geese Triangles

The Geese Are Flying Along the Borders (top), made by Kaye Wood.
The Geese Are Flying North, South, East, and West, made by Brenda Jonsson.
Directions on pages 374 and 375, respectively.

Kaye Wood's Strip-Cut Quilts

Quilt Block 21

Flying Geese

Flying Geese

Use them as borders, or create a whole quilt from them.

No fabric waste and no math!

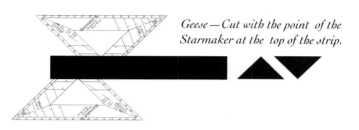

Geese—Cut with the point of the Starmaker at the top of the strip.

Background—Cut with the first line of the Starmaker at the top of the strip.

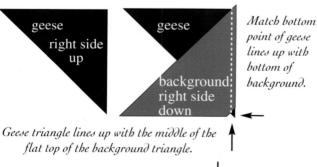

| geese
right side
up | geese | |
| | background;
right side
down | |

Match bottom point of geese lines up with bottom of background.

Geese triangle lines up with the middle of the flat top of the background triangle.

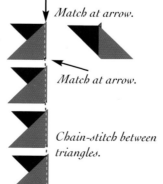

Match at arrow.

Match at arrow.

Chain-stitch between triangles.

To easily strip-cut the geese:

1. **Cut strips.**
   Cut a dark and a light strip the same width. One strip will become the background (teal); the other the geese (brown).

2. **Cut the geese.**
   Cut the geese strip by placing the point of the 4-angle of the Starmaker 8 at the top of the strip and cutting. Cut the second triangle by turning the Starmaker 8 upside-down with the point of the 4-angle at the bottom of the strip.

3. **Cut the background.**
   Cut the background strip into triangles by placing the first line from the 4-angle at the top of the strip and cutting. Cut the second triangle by turning the Starmaker 8 upside-down with the 1st line from the 4-angle at the bottom of the strip.

4. **Sew triangles into strips.**
   Sew a geese triangle to a background triangle, the background triangle on top, and the geese underneath. Match the triangles where they overlap; see the arrows on the diagram. Chain-sew these two triangles together.
   Press seam allowances away from geese and toward background triangle.

Chain-sew together these triangle sets, with the same background fabric, to form groups of four triangles; then groups of eight triangles.

Geese segments can be cut from this strip (see step 5), and then more triangles can be added to both ends of the strip.

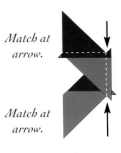

Match at arrow.

Match at arrow.

points

points

The strip will look like the one above:
The seamlines on the points of the geese (brown) will match 1/4 inch from the top of the strip. The seamlines on the points of the background will meet at the edge of the strip. This will give the seam allowance needed to cut the background triangles to make Flying Geese.

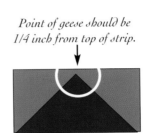

Point of geese should be 1/4 inch from top of strip.

Chain-stitch.

5. Cut Flying Geese.
Line up the Starmaker 8, as shown, with the side of the Starmaker 8 at the top of the strip, 4-angle at the center of the background triangle, and the #1, #2, and #3 lines on the Starmaker parallel to the seamline.

Cut one of the center Flying Geese by cutting the background triangle in half along the side of the Starmaker 8 (see dotted lines). Move the cut-off triangles from one end of the strip to the other end. Cut more Flying Geese blocks.

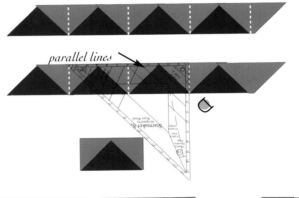

parallel lines

6. Continue to add and cut more geese and background triangles to the strip as needed.

Move the cut-off end to the other end of strip, and continue cutting geese.

Number of Triangles from Each Strip		
Strip width	Geese	Background
2 inches	19	16
3 inches	12	11
4 inches	9	9
5 inches	7	6
6 inches	6	5
7 inches	5	4
8 inches	4	4

Flying Geese Blocks		
Strip width	Width	Length
2 inches	1 7/8 inches	3 1/4 inches
3 inches	2 7/8 inches	5 1/4 inches
4 inches	3 7/8 inches	7 1/4 inches
5 inches	4 7/8 inches	9 1/4 inches
6 inches	5 7/8 inches	11 1/4 inches
7 inches	6 7/8 inches	13 1/4 inches

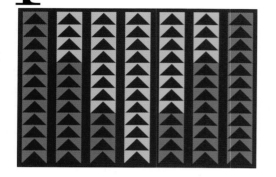

The Geese are Flying Along the Borders

Finished size: 39 1/2-by-28 1/2 inches
A photo of this quilt, by Kaye Wood, is on page 371.

Fabric Requirements

Geese	2/3 yard	Cut seven 3-by-44-inch strips.
Dark background	1//2 yard	Cut four 3-by-44-inch strips.
Light background	1/3 yard	Cut three 3-by-44-inch strips.
Sashing	1/3 yard	Cut six 1 1/2-by-44-inch strips.
Backing/sleeve	1 yard	
Batting	41-by-32 inches	
Binding	1/4 yard	

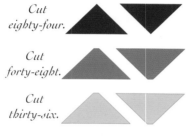

Cut eighty-four.

Cut forty-eight.

Cut thirty-six.

Forty-eight dark blocks.

Thirty-six light blocks.

1. **Cut triangles.**
   Cut eighty-four triangles from the 3-inch geese fabric strips.
   Cut forty-eight background triangles from the 3-inch dark strips. Cut thirty-six background triangles from the 3-inch light strips. Directions are on page 372.

2. **Sew Flying Geese strips.**
   Directions are on page 372.
   Sew a strip of geese (brown) and dark background.
   Sew a strip of geese (brown) and light background.

3. **Cut Flying Geese blocks.**
   Cut forty-eight blocks with dark background, and cut thirty-six blocks with light background.

Rows 1 and 7 *Rows 2 and 6* *Rows 3 and 5* *Row 4*

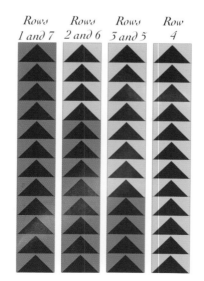

4. **Sew into vertical rows.**
   Sew twelve Flying Geese blocks into each row, as shown.
   The top points of the geese (brown) should come right to the seamline.

5. **Make sashing strips.**
   Cut sashing strips.
   Pin-mark to match the sashing strips at the center and both ends of the strips. See page 383.
   Press seam allowances toward the sashing strip.

6. **Finish.**
   Layer, quilt, add sleeve, and bind. See page 386.

The Geese are Flying North, South, East and West

Finished size: 19-by-19 inches

Fabric Requirements for Each Quilt

Geese	Cut one 3-by-44-inch strip.
Background:	
Dark	Cut one 3-by-22-inch strip.
Medium	Cut one 3-by-22-inch strip.
Light	Cut one 3-by-22-inch strip.
Large corner triangles:	
Dark	Cut one 5 3/4-by-44-inch strip.
Light	Cut one 5 3/4-by-44-inch strip.
Center square	6-by-6 inches
Backing	22-by-22 inches
Stretcher frame (for mounting)	
Batting	22-by-22 inches
Binding	2 1/4 yards

This quilt, made by Brenda Jonsson, has been stretched on a frame for an interesting wall-hanging. See photo on page 571.

1. **Cut Flying Geese triangles.**
   For each quilt:
   Cut twelve triangles from the 3-inch geese strip.
   Cut four triangles from each of the three background fabrics. See page 372.

Cut twelve.   *Cut four.*

Cut four.   *Cut four.*

2. **Sew Flying Geese strips.**
   See page 372 for sewing directions.

3. **Cut Flying Geese blocks.**
   Cut four blocks with each background color.
   Sew three flying geese together into rows as shown below.

Four blocks.   *Four blocks.*   *Four blocks.*

4. **Make large triangles.**
   Cut a 5 3/4-inch strip from both dark and light fabric.
   Cut each strip into four triangles. See page 305.
   Sew a light and dark triangle together into quilt blocks.

Cut four.

Cut four.

Four blocks.

5. **Cut center square.**
   Measure the width of the row of three flying geese blocks. Trim the square to this size.

6. **Sew into rows.**
   Choose the design on the right or on the left.
   Sew into three rows, as shown at right.

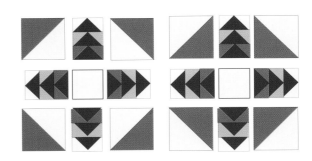

7. **Sew rows together.**

8. **Finish.**
   Layer, quilt, and bind, or make into a pillow.
   Finishing instructions are on page 386.

Chapter 10

Quilt Strip Blocks

Wildlife, made by Brenda Jonsson. Directions on page 380.

A quilt block can be made from quilt strips.
Shapes, like those shown on page 303, are cut using the 4-angle of the Starmaker 8.
The shapes are then sewn into strips; these are considered quilt blocks.

Strip blocks can be used within the quilt, much like other quilt blocks.
Strip blocks can also be used in sashing and border strips.

Quilt Block 22

Triangles are cut using the 4-angle of the Starmaker. The triangles are then sewn into strips, which are considered quilt blocks.

Strip Blocks
Try them as sashing strips in your next quilt.

1. Cut strips.
   Cut a strip for each different fabric.
   All strips are the same width.

2. Cut triangles.
   Cut the strip by placing the point of the 4-angle of the Starmaker 8 at the top of the strip and cutting. Cut the second triangle by turning the Starmaker 8 upside-down with the point of the 4-angle at the bottom of the strip.

3. Sew triangles into strips.
   Sew triangles, right sides together, lining up the edges where they overlap. See the arrows on the diagram.

   Chain-sew into sets of two triangles; chain-sew these into sets of four triangles, etc. Press seam allowances all in the same direction.

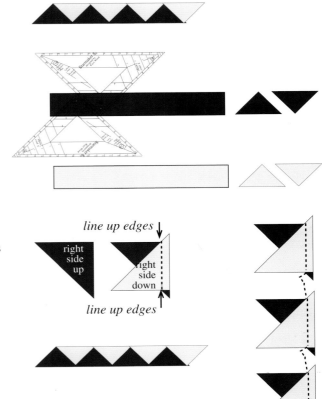

Number of Triangles from Each Strip

Strip width	Triangles
2 inches	19
3 inches	12
4 inches	9
5 inches	7
6 inches	6
7 inches	5
8 inches	4

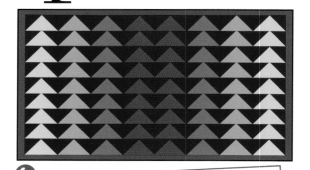

Flying Ganders

Finished size: 47-by-25 inches

Fabric Requirements

Triangles:		
Brown	2/3 yard	Cut seven 3-by-44-inch strips.
Light teal	4 1/4 yard	Cut two 3-by-44-inch strips.
Med. light teal	4 1/4 yard	Cut two 3-by-44-inch strips.
Medium teal	4 1/4 yard	Cut two 3-by-44-inch strips.
Dark teal	4 1/4 yard	Cut two 3-by-44-inch strips.
Border	1/3 yard	Cut five 2-by-44-inch strips.
Backing	48-by-30 inches	
Batting	48-by-30 inches	
Binding	1/4 yard	Cut five 1 3/4-by-44-inch strips.

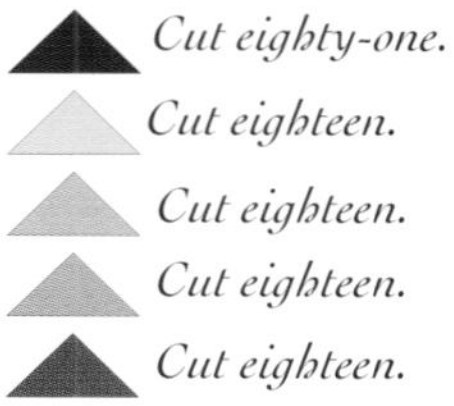

Make-Believe Flying Geese

Strips of triangles give an interesting variation to the traditional Flying Geese. Try these strips in your quilted clothing or as borders for your next quilt.

Cut eighty-one.

Cut eighteen.

Cut eighteen.

Cut eighteen.

Cut eighteen.

1. ## Cut triangles.
   Cut eighty-one brown triangles. Cut eighteen triangles from each of the other four fabrics. Follow directions on page 377.

2. ## Sew triangle strips.
   Sew the triangles together into nine identical strips, following the diagram at left. Sewing instructions are on page 377.

Sew nine strips.

3. ## Sew strips together.
   The points of the triangles at the bottom of the row line up with the center of the triangle in the next row.

4. ## Square up the edges.
   Using a ruler, trim both sides to cut off the points.

Square up both sides.

5. ## Finish.
   Add square or mitered borders, see pages 384 and 385.
   Cut border strips 2 inches wide. Pin-mark at the center and both ends of the border strips. See page 383. Press seam allowances toward the border strip.
   Layer and quilt. See page 386.

Quilt Block 23

These pieces are even more topless than the top-less triangles, (page 322), so we'll just call them "shapes."

1. **Cut strips.**
   Using two fabrics, cut three strips all the same width from each fabric.
   The wider the strips, the bigger the trees.

2. **Cut shapes.**
   "A"—Cut "A" shapes with the first line down from the 4-angle on the Starmaker 8 at the top of the strip. Cut the next shape by turning the Starmaker 8 upside-down with the first line down from the 4-angle at the bottom of the strip.

   "B"—Cut "B" shapes by placing the #1 line of the 4-angle of the Starmaker 8 at the top of the strip. Cut the next shape by turning the Starmaker 8 upside-down with the #1 line at the bottom of the strip.

   "C"—Cut "C" shapes by placing the #2 line of the 4-angle of the Starmaker 8 at the top of the strip. Cut the next shape by turning the Starmaker 8 upside-down with the #2 line at the bottom of the strip.

3. **Sew into strips.**
   Sew the shapes, right sides together, with a 3/8-inch seam allowance, lining up the edges as shown on the diagram at right.
   Chain-sew into sets of two shapes; chain-sew these into sets of four shapes, etc. Press seam allowances of the top and bottom strips away from the smallest shape.

4. **Sew strips together.**
   Sew strips, right sides together, using 1/4-inch seam allowances, matching the centers of each shape.

Trees are great for borders!
The secret is sewing the pieces into strips using 3/8-inch seam allowances.

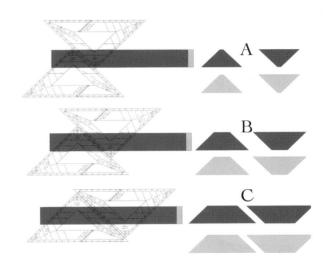

A

B

C

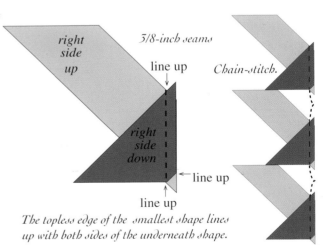

right side up

3/8-inch seams

line up

Chain-stitch.

right side down

← line up

line up

The topless edge of the smallest shape lines up with both sides of the underneath shape.

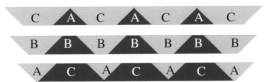

C A C A C A C

B B B B B B B

A C A C A C A

Wildlife

Finished size: 52 1/2-by-34 inches
A photo of this quilt, made by
Brenda Jonsson, is on page 376.

Fabric Requirements

Large print	Approximately 25-by-42 inches.	
Flying Geese		
Brown	1/4 yard	Cut two 3-by-44-inch strips.
Background	Eight gradated shades of teal.	
	From each, cut one 3-by-12 inches.	
Tree strip block		
Green	1/2 yard	Cut eight 2-by-44-inch strips.
Background	1/2 yard	Cut eight 2-by-44-inch strips.
Backing	55-by-38 inches	
Batting	55-by-38 inches	
Binding	1/3 yard	Cut five 1 3/4-inch strips.

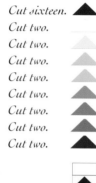

Cut sixteen.
Cut two.
Cut two.
Cut two.
Cut two.
Cut two.
Cut two.
Cut two.
Cut two.

1. ## Make Flying Geese border.
   Directions are on page 372. Cut sixteen triangles from the brown (geese) fabric strips. Cut
   two background triangles from each of the eight
   shades of teal strips.

   Sew Flying Geese strips. Directions are on page
   372.
   Sew a strip of two geese and two topless triangles of the same color together.
   Cut Flying Geese blocks; two with each background color.
   Sew two geese vertical rows, each with eight
   geese, shaded from light to dark.
   Measure the side of the large print. More geese
   can be added to make a longer border, or add
   an equal amount of fabric to the top and bottom
   of the row of geese to make the border fit the
   print, as shown.
   Sew geese rows to each side of the large print.

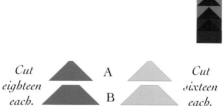

Cut eighteen each.   A   Cut sixteen each.
B
C

2. ## Put together tree border.
   Directions are on page 379. Cut eighteen "A,"
   eighteen "B," and eighteen "C" shapes from
   green.
   Cut sixteen "A," sixteen "B," and sixteen "C"
   shapes from the background.

   Sew into six rows, each with nine green shapes
   and eight blue shapes:
   - two rows with "A" and "C" shapes
   - two rows with "B" and "B" shapes
   - two rows with "C" and "A" shapes
   Add more shapes for a longer border.
   Sew rows together, matching center of shapes.
   Sew a tree border to the top and bottom of the
   large print.
   Trim the ends even with the rows of geese.

3. ## Layer, quilt, and bind. See page 386.

Chapter 11

Finishing Techniques

Scrap Happy Pillow, made by Kaye Wood. Directions on page 334.

Yardages for Quilt Blocks

All yardages given with projects are for strips cut 42 or 44 inches (across the width of the fabric).

To make any of these quilts larger or smaller, or to plan your very own quilt, use these charts.

To figure the amount of fabric needed for your special quilt, count the number of triangles in your design. The charts below tell you how many triangles you can cut from one 42/44-inch strip of fabric.

Square Up the Quilt Blocks

Each square in your project needs to be the same size. You can measure each quilt block by stacking a few at a time. They will probably be all the same. If they are the same, congratulations!

If they are not the same size, don't worry; just square up the blocks. To square up the blocks, use a square ruler that is larger than your block and has a diagonal line from corner to corner.

Place the square ruler on the block with the diagonal line of the ruler on the seamline between the two triangles.

If your block should be 8 inches, line up the 8-inch square lines on the ruler with two sides of the block.

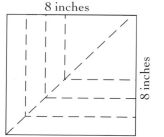
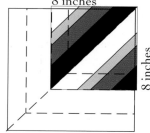

If the block measures less than the 8 inches, move the ruler so the 7 3/4-inch lines line up with two edges of the block. If this size will work, trim all your blocks to this size. If it is necessary to trim some or all of the blocks, it is best to trim a little equally on all four sides.

Yardages and Sizes for Quilt Blocks 1, 2, 3, 4, 6, 7, 9, 10 and 11

combination strip width	triangles per 44-inch strip	block size	finished size
3 inches	13*	4 1/4 inches	3 3/4 inches
4 inches	10	5 5/8 inches	5 1/8 inches
5 inches	7*	7 3/4 inches	7 1/4 inches
6 inches	6	8 inches	7 1/2 inches
7 inches	5*	9 1/2 inches	9 inches
8 inches	4	10 1/2 inches	10 inches
8 1/2 inches	4	11 1/2 inches	11 inches

Yardages and Sizes for Spool Quilt Blocks 5 and 8

combination strip width	triangles per 44-inch strip	block size	finished size
3 inches	13*	5 1/4 inches	4 3/4 inches
4 inches	10	7 1/4 inches	6 3/4 inches
5 inches	7*	9 1/4 inches	8 3/4 inches
6 inches	6	11 inches	10 1/2 inches
7 inches	5*	13 inches	12 1/2 inches
8 inches	4	15 1/2 inches	15 inches
8 1/2 inches	4	16-1/2 inches	16 inches

*When cutting an uneven number of triangles, cut the second strip beginning with the triangle you have the least of.

Sashing Strips

Pin-marking

Most of the these quilt blocks will have bias out-side edges. Pin-marking is used to control the bias when adding sashing strips, or when we add the first border.

Short Sashing Strips *(between quilt blocks)*

1. Measure the quilt blocks. Square up the blocks, if necessary; see page 382.

2. Cut sashing strips the exact length (size of the block). Sizes are given with each project, but measure your block because your sashing strip has to match your block.

3. Sew the sashing strips. Line up the top of the sashing strip and the top of the block. Start sewing with the sashing strip on top to control the stretch. After about an inch of sewing, stop and match up the bottom of the sashing strip with the bottom of the block.

Continue sewing.

Chain-stitch from one block to the next.

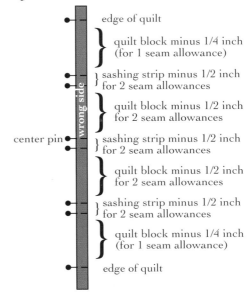

Chain-stitch: Sew from one block to the next without cutting threads.

Press the seam allowances toward the sashing strip.

Long Sashing Strips and Borders *(between rows or for the first border)*

1. Cut horizontal sashing and border strips across the width (40 or 44 inches wide). If nec-essary, sew sashing strips together to make a longer strip.

On small quilts, vertical sashing and border strips can be cut across the width of the fabric.

Vertical sashing strips and borders on large quilts should be cut lengthwise on the fabric. Cut the length of the sashing strip at least 4 inches longer than needed. For mitered corners, allow more.

2. Pin-Mark sashing/border strips to quilt blocks with bias edges. Pin-Marking the sashing and border strips will control the stretch in the bias edges. The pins will match up with the seamlines in the row of quilt blocks.

Place a pin in the center of the long sashing strip. If the sashing strip has been pieced together, the center pin should be on the seam-line.

From the center pin, measure and pin-mark along the left-hand side of the strip by placing pins that will line up with seamlines and both ends, as shown at below. The center pin should line up with a seamline.

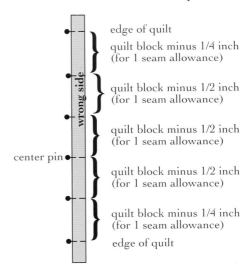

If there are no sashing strips, the pin-marks will be for the seamlines between the quilt blocks.

For borders and sashing strips on straight of grain edges, like the Spool Blocks or any second border, pins only need to mark the center, the ends, and halfway between the center and the ends of the strip.

3. Sew the right side of the sashing strip to one side of each row. Sew with the sashing strip on top to avoid stretching the bias edges.

Match pins to seamlines, but <u>do not</u> pin the sashing strip to the quilt blocks, and <u>do not</u> remove pins.

Press seam allowances toward the sashing strip.

4. Sew rows together by matching the pins on the left side of each sashing strip to the seamlines. Remove the pins as you come to the matching seamline. Trim the ends of the sashing strips even with the blocks.

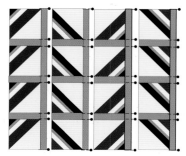

Border strips are pin-marked in the same way.

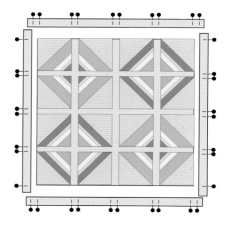

Borders

One or more borders can be added to adjust the finished size of the quilt and to frame the edges. Borders should be in scale with the rest of the quilt and should enhance the design. It is better to use two or more borders, than to make a wide border, unless the wide border is an interesting stripe.

Pieced Borders

Make the quilt fit the border. There are lots of ideas in this book for making pieced borders, but how do you make a pieced border that will fit your quilt? It is easier to enlarge the quilt to fit the border. After the quilt is pieced, make the pieced border strips. If the pieced border is too long, add a border strip to the quilt to make the size right. For example, if the quilt top is 36 inches high and the border strip is 40 inches high, add a top and bottom border to make the quilt fit the border.

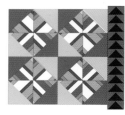

If the top and bottom pieced border strips are too long, add borders to each side to make the quilt fit the border. If the border strips are too short, add solid squares to make them longer.

Square Borders

Cut the top and bottom border strips the width of the quilt. Pin-mark both ends and the center and sew to the quilt, with the border strip on top. Press the seam allowances toward the border strips.

Measure, pin-mark, and sew the side border strips. Press the seam allowances toward the borders.

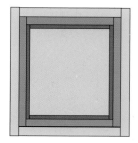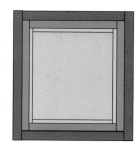

Mitered Borders

Add the top and bottom borders.
Cut the border strips the width of the quilt plus a 1-inch extension on each side, i.e. if the border is 2 inches wide, cut the border strip the width of the quilt plus 6 inches (*2-inch border + 1 inch = 3 inches x two ends = 6 inches*).

If several borders will be mitered, sew the border strips together first; then sew to quilt as if it is just one border.

1. Pin the strip to the quilt at the center and end points, leaving an extension at each end. Sew from edge to edge of the quilt. Press the seam allowances toward the border strip.

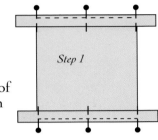

Step 1

Tip

Sewing two of the border strips all the way from edge to edge will lock in the corners and make the miters easier.

2. Add the side borders. Cut the side strips the length of the quilt plus an extension (the width of the border plus 1 inch) at both ends. Pin the strip to the quilt at the center and end points, leaving an extension at both ends. Lockstitch (3 or 4 stitches in one place) and start sewing at the seamline of the top border (do not backstitch to lock). Sew to the seamline of the bottom and lockstitch. Press seam allowances toward the border strip.

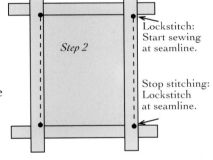

Step 2

Lockstitch: Start sewing at seamline.

Stop stitching: Lockstitch at seamline.

3. Trim the ends of the border strips even with each other. This will help you to miter the corners.

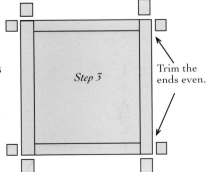

Step 3

Trim the ends even.

4. Fold the quilt diagonally, right sides together. The seam allowances should be toward the quilt and away from the border strips.
Pin both border strips together carefully along the seamlines on both sides of the diagonal stitching line. Lockstitch and start sewing at the seamline, and sew to the outside corner. Press the miter. Trim off the extra fabric in the seam allowance.

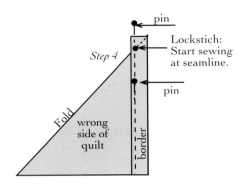

pin

Step 4

Lockstich: Start sewing at seamline.

pin

Fold

wrong side of quilt

border

Eyelet Edging

Eyelet is sewn, right sides together, to the quilt top. The band, or gathered part of the eyelet, should be even with the outside of the quilt. If your eyelet has a fabric band, you can get a nice full corner by removing about 9 inches of the eyelet band at the corner. Run a basting stitch by hand or machine where the band was removed. Gather the eyelet; then sew around the corner.

Envelopes or Pillowcase Finish

Cut a backing piece and batting the same size as the pieced top. Pin the top and backing, right sides together, with the batting underneath. Sew around the quilt, leaving an opening along one edge to turn the quilt right sides out. Turn right side out. Close the opening with hand stitches.

Get Ready to Quilt

There are several ways to finish your quilt: quilting by hand, quilting by home sewing machine, quilting on a professional quilting machine, hand tying or machine tying.

Professional quilting machine — Before sending your quilt top out to be quilted, take a look at a sample of the quilters work. Ask questions, such as can they do free motion quilting, pattern quilting, and straight or diagonal stitching? Who will furnish the batting and backing? Who will plan the quilting design? I send all of my quilts out to be machine-quilted on the American Professional Quilting System machine.

Batting

Batting comes in several different thicknesses—very thin to comforter thickness. Be sure to get the weight of batting that will give you the finish you want for your quilt. If you're not sure, go with the thinnest available. Remove the batting from the package the day before you use it, or put the batting in the dryer (no heat) for several minutes to allow it to breathe.

Backing Fabric

Backing fabric can be a plain muslin or a printed fabric. Quilt blocks can even be sewn together for a backing. If you are hand quilting, choose an all-cotton fabric for the backing; it will be easier to quilt. Backing fabrics can be pieced from one or more fabrics.

Layer the Quilt

To layer a quilt means to stack three layers (top, batting, backing) together. Cut the backing and batting approximately 4 inches larger than the finished top. The backing of the quilt should be held taut by using a quilt frame or by taping the fabric, right side down, to a flat surface, such as the floor or a pingpong table. The batting is laid on top of the backing; smooth the batting out but don't stretch it. The quilt top is placed right side up over the batting.

Hold the layers together

There are several ways to keep the layers (top, batting, backing) together: hand baste, safety pin baste or use a spray adhesive to hold the layers together.

A. Safety pin baste

Use small rust-proof safety pins. While the backing is still taped to a flat surface, insert but do not close the safety pins. After all the pins are in place, remove the tape from the backing and close the safety pins.

B. Spray adhesive

Spray adhesive eliminates the need for hand basting or safety pin basting. After the quilt back is held securely in place, spray the wrong side with a spray adhesive. Place the batting, and pat it in place. Spray the top side of the batting and place the quilt top, wrong side down, on top of the batting. Machine or hand quilt.

Machine Tie

To machine tie a quilt, drop or cover the feed dogs and set the machine for a zigzag stitch. Choose a washable yarn or use pearl cotton. Lay the yarn on top of the quilt. Take several zigzag stitches over the yarn. Tie in a knot or bow. If you want bows, tie the yarn into a bow before zigzagging over it.

Machine Quilting

To machine quilt, use an even-feed foot, lock your stitches, and use matching thread, decorative thread or invisible thread in the needle. Bring the bobbin thread through to the top of the quilt. Hold both bobbin and top thread. The bobbin thread should match the quilt back or the needle thread. Try a sample first; the stitch length is determined by the loft of the batting—lengthen if necessary.

Hanging Sleeve

Cut fabric 8 inches wide and 2 inches shorter than the width of the quilt. Turn the short ends under a 1/2 inch and topstitch. Press the strip in half (4 inches wide). Sew the raw edges of the sleeve to the top edge of the quilt. Hand stitch the folded edge 4 inches down from the top of the quilt.

For hanging tabs, cut 4-by-8-inch pieces, and attach several to the top of the quilt.

Binding

A binding finishes off the edges and frames the quilt. Binding strips can be cut on the straight of grain or on the bias. I prefer a straight-of-grain double binding. The finished binding (the width showing on the quilt top) can be very narrow to extra wide. However, the seam allowance must be the same width as the finished binding. If the finished binding is a 1/2 inch, then the seam allowance must be a 1/2 inch because the binding must be padded with the edge of the quilt. If you use a finished binding wider than 1/4 inch, the width of your last border may need to be adjusted; if your finished binding is 1 1/2 inches, the seam allowance will be 1 1/2 inches, and the last border will be 1 1/2 inches narrower than it is cut.

To use a double binding, cut the binding strips six times the finished width of the binding, i.e. if the finished width is 1/2 inch, the strip would be cut 3 inches wide, except when the finished binding is 1/4 inch, the strip needs to be cut 1 3/4 inches, as shown.

Double Binding	
Finished binding	Cut Strip
1/4 inch	1-3/4 inch
1/2 inch	3 inch
3/4 inch	4-1/2 inch
1 inch	6 inch
1-1/2 inch	9 inch

Cut enough binding strips to go around the quilt plus 12 inches. Sew two or more binding strips together on the diagonal (bias).

At the beginning of the strip, fold the end diagonally, and press a crease.

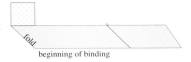

beginning of binding

Fold the binding strip in half, wrong sides together, and press.

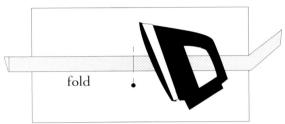

fold

To quickly get a folded strip:
Fold one end of the strip.
Put a pin in the ironing pad and up over the strip and into the pad.
Pull the folded strip under the pin and under an iron.

Sew the raw edges of the binding strip even with the edge of the quilt top. Leave a 6-inch tail at the beginning of the binding and start sewing on one side of the quilt — never at the corner. Sew with both raw edges of the binding even with the edge of the quilt.

Mitered Corners

To "perfect miter" the corners:

Step 1: Sew to a seam allowance width from the next side of the quilt. With the needle in the quilt, pivot and sew diagonally to the corner of the quilt. This forms a sewn-in miter.

Step 2: Fold the binding strip up so it lines up with the next side of the quilt.

Mitered Corners

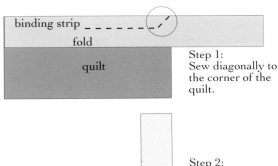

binding strip
fold
quilt

Step 1:
Sew diagonally to the corner of the quilt.

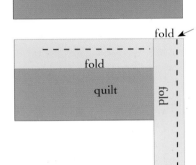

fold
fold
quilt

Step 2:
Fold the binding strip up at right angles along the diagonally sewn line, so it will line up with the next side of the quilt.

fold
fold
quilt
fold

Step 3:
Fold the binding strip down and start sewing at the folded edge, a seam allowance in from the side.

Step 3: Bring the binding strip down even with the next side. Start stitching from the edge of the quilt. Sew to the next corner. After mitering the last corner, lay the beginning and ending of the strip together. Fold a crease in the ending. Bring the folded crease lines right sides together, pin, and sew.

fold   end of binding   fold   beginning of binding   fold

Appendix

Available at quilt shops, or by calling 1-800-248-KAYE or sending e-mail www.kayewood.com

Strip Like A Pro
Strip-Quilting Books, Videos and Master Templates by Kaye Wood

Books

Quilt Like A Pro • *Turn Me Over—I'm Reversible* • *Serger Patchwork Projects*
Starmakers Ablaze 1—Log Cabin Triangles • *Starmakers Ablaze 2—Log Cabin Diamonds*
Savage Star • *6 Hour Quilt* book and video • *TwinStar Jacket* • *Stardust Quilt*
Strip Quilting Projects • *Strip Quilting Projects 2* • *Strip Quilting Projects 3* • *Strip Quilting Projects 4*
Strip Quilting Projects 5 • *Strip Quilting Projects 6* • *Strip Quilting Projects 7*
Strip Quilting Projects 8 • *Strip Quilting Projects 9* • *Strip Quilting Projects 10*
Easy Hexagon Designs book and video • *Fantastic Fans and Wedge Designs* book and video

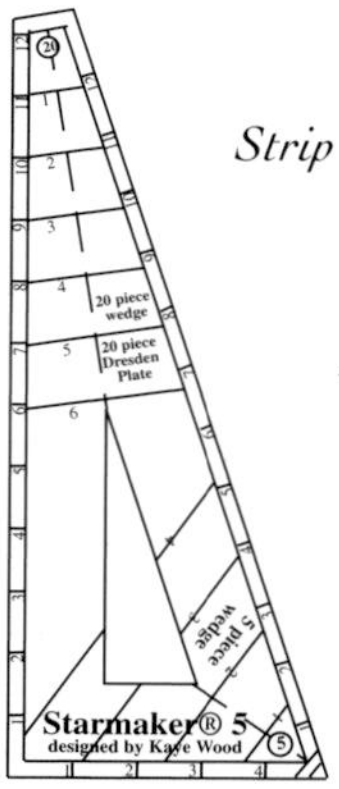

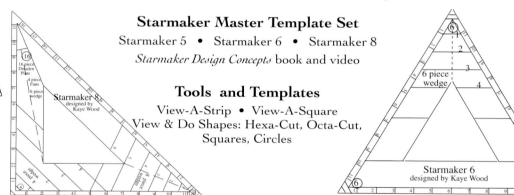

Starmaker Master Template Set

Starmaker 5 • Starmaker 6 • Starmaker 8
Starmaker Design Concepts book and video

Tools and Templates

View-A-Strip • View-A-Square
View & Do Shapes: Hexa-Cut, Octa-Cut, Squares, Circles

Other products that Kaye uses in her strip-quilting:

Rulers
Static Stickers
Spray Adhesive
Rotary cutter/mat
Frames for mounting quilt blocks
1/4-inch foot for the sewing machine

The quilts in this book were machine-quilted by:

Marilyn Badger
Carol Moss
Oregon Coast Quilting
(541) 412-1002

Jane Ehinger
West Branch, Michigan

Nancy Webster
Northwoods Quilting
Waters, Michigan
(517) 731-5166

The Cotton Patch
Tawas, Michigan
(517) 362-6779

FAST-FOLDED FLOWERS

Timesaving Techniques for a Quilted Bouquet

LAURA FARSON

Table of Contents

So many choices, so little time! And that is exactly why you need the timesaving techniques outlined in this book. Quilt units above made by Laura Farson.

Introduction

mong us quilters, there are those who have struggled with curved piecing. My interest was piqued in the early 1970s by the "Cathedral Window" pattern I had saved from a magazine.

It was brought to mind again about five years ago when I saw the pattern in a quilting book.

Fascinated, I bought the book and some fabric from the quilt shop. I made twenty-five blocks and joined them to make a 20-inch square.

It took me weeks!

Since I'm an "immediate gratification" type of person, my thoughts wandered to simpler methods. I began experimenting by sewing two squares of different fabrics together and turning them right sides out. After pressing and folding the corners to the center, I had trouble bending the petal edge.

Cutting the squares on the bias solved that problem.

Intrigued by the possibilities, I began further experiments with other shapes. I made lots of experimental blocks and small projects. Each one led to another with thoughts popping into my head at all hours of the day and night. I took to keeping a notebook with me at all times.

After a while, it occurred to me that I might do some research to see whether this kind of thing had been done before. I combed quilt shops, libraries, and bookstores and bought lots of books and fabric – all in the name of research!

And what fun I've had meeting and discussing this concept with other quilters and sewers.

Since it seemed unique, and I was looking for a career, I decided to write a book on how to make the very same quilts that have brought me so much joy.

There's a rich history of quilt patterns with circles and loops and curves. While looking into the background of curved-pieced quilts, patterns like "Orange Peel" and "Joseph's Coat" came to light. I was daunted by instructions that required cutting 600-plus pieces of part "A" and more than 400 pieces of "B." My future flashed before me – endless curved pieces with no finished projects in sight!

Not one to struggle, however, I've devised a simpler approach.

Fast-Folded Flowers will give you the skills to create beautiful curved-piece quilts without the agony. All techniques are performed with a sewing machine!

The emphasis is on simplicity, but the results look complicated. Curved edges are created when bias folds are turned back in gentle arcs and topstitched.

For the purist, all can be completed easily by hand, although not nearly as quickly.

Twelve different variations are explained in chapters featuring different geometric shapes. Each technique transforms the fabric into a unique petal-accented unit that is joined with others to complete a floral bouquet.

Basic information on terms, techniques, and tools is contained in Chapter One. Many of the terms and techniques are unique to this book, including instructions for: turning back the bias folds to make the petals; cutting fabric pieces with a rotary ruler on a paper template; snipping slashes; binding and borders; the many uses of temporary adhesive; and the insertion of batting within the unit. Review them before proceeding and refer back while making the projects. They are arranged in alphabetical order for easy reference.

Create the effect of a "Joseph's Coat" style in half the time and without sacrificing the quality of the resulting quilt. The block above was made by Laura Farson, 2001.

The use of photocopied templates that are used as guides for the rotary ruler is recommended. These paper templates are cut out and placed on the fabric with grain line indicators. The rotary ruler is placed over the template and acts as the guide for the rotary cutter.

Temporary adhesive spray is used to secure the templates on fabric while pieces are being cut. It's also used to tack batting in place during the construction.

Batting pieces are cut to fit inside each unit rather than layering after piecing.

Borders are filled with strips of batting to match the thickness with the project.

Patterns and projects are designed to utilize the greatest amount of fabric based on 40- to 45-inch widths. Although some of the cutting produces "waste," it is easily recycled into other projects.

Pieces are sized to match standard rotary rulers.

Chapters Two through Six contain instructions on different shapes, beginning with squares and triangles and progressing to hexagons and octagons. The largest is the dodecagon with twelve sides, more descriptively known as a "sunflower."

Within each chapter is the basic technique in which two shapes are cut from fabric, i.e. two squares or two stars. These are placed right sides together and sewn. A piece of batting is fused onto the inside surface, and the unit is flipped right-side out. Corners are folded to the center making flaps – and voila! – the block is ready to be joined to others like it. Once a group is joined, the folded flaps are turned back and topstitched to form lovely lined petal areas.

Once you have mastered the basic technique, the instructions move on to enhanced versions of each shape.

The second version is the accented-petal variation. Those petal areas that are turned back are lined with an accent fabric that makes a curved outline. Instructions for this technique are given for squares, hexagons, and octagons. Triangles are sewn onto the center fabric cut into a square, hexagon, or octagon, forming a star. These "stars" are placed right sides together with a back piece and are then sewn. After a cutout piece of batting is fused onto the inside surface, the unit is flipped to the right side and pressed flat. Points or corners are folded to the center forming flaps. The unit is ready to be joined with others like it.

Once a group is made, simply opening the flaps of touching units and sewing in the folds completes the joining. For hexagons and octagons, filler pieces are made using simple templates and joined in the open areas between units.

Two special variations are possible with squares. The simplest is the "Cutaway Square" variation. Using a template, the curved areas of the petal flaps are cut before construction. Once the units are sewn and folded, the petal flaps are already formed in an arc without the folded edge.

The "Petals and Ribbon" variation, featured in the background of the cover, is made by sewing accent strips onto four triangles. These pieces are inserted between the inside and outside fabric layers, and when folded, form the crossed accent stripes. The folded triangle edges are turned back to form petals. The whole looks like wrapped packages.

Each chapter features one or more projects for each technique. There is a full range of easy, intermediate, and advanced selections. Many variations in size and color are possible.

For any of the projects, be sure to select a group of fabrics that coordinate. Read through the instructions and construct a "sample" block or two. Such samples work wonderfully as hot pads when joined back to back. Or leave one end open on a pair and slip a tile into the pocket for a table trivet!

After completing some sample blocks by following the chapter instructions, begin with "Country Petals" or "Raggedy Edges," both easy projects to make.

Browse through the chapters and make a four-unit project such as "Peachy Petals" or "In the Pink."

Try a color study by making the three "Dreaming In Flowers" variations. A larger project, such as "Petals in the Ferns" has just twelve units.

For gift-giving, make the "Turkish Bazaar" or "Navy Blues" for pillows. Consider "Holly Berries" as a perfect gift for the holidays.

There are so many possibilities.

Have fun…play…enjoy!

basic
information

any of the techniques in Fast-Folded Flowers *are unique. They are described and illustrated in this chapter. It's worthwhile to review them before embarking on a project.*

I encourage you to make practice blocks. Not only will you build and refine your skills, you'll also produce a collection of handy mats to use!

In this chapter, you will also find definitions of terms and descriptions of tools. Some of the information will be review, but many items are special. They are organized in alphabetical order to make it easier for later reference.

Accessories

Needed tools and accessories include:

- an iron
- silk and flat-headed pins
- a medium (45 millimeter) and a large (60 millimeter) rotary cutter
- eye glasses
- pencils and permanent pens
- rotary rulers with ¼-inch, 60-degree, and 45-degree markings
- spare sewing machine needles
- bobbins
- thread
- ¼-inch foot for the sewing machine
- small 4-inch scissors and large sewing shears
- rotary cutting mat
- Fray Check™
- sewing machine
- a walking foot for the sewing machine.

Unique uses of these tools are discussed in the listing of the specific tool.

Adhesive/Basting

Temporary spray adhesive is used to "baste" batting to the inside fabric prior to turning a unit to the right side. It is also useful when applied to the backside of paper templates prior to cutting the fabric pieces of quilts.

Remember: Use spray adhesive in a well-ventilated area and avoid breathing the spray. Be sure to read the manufacturer's instructions.

1. Place the piece to be sprayed, usually the template or batting, in a shallow cardboard box.
2. Spray lightly and evenly over its surface.
3. Position the batting or template in place.
4. The piece can be repositioned for a few minutes. Most temporary adhesives dissipate quickly.

1.1 There are various types of batting on the market. Use the lightest and thinnest for these projects.

1.2 Batting is easily cut, using a ruler, template, and rotary cutter.

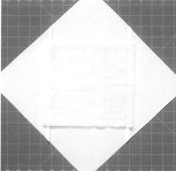

1.3 For best results, place your batting in the center of the block.

1.4 For star-based units, the batting should be centered.

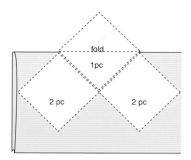

1.5 Follow this cutting diagram when working with a 1-yard piece of fabric.

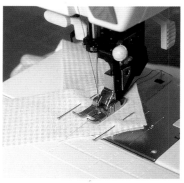

1.6 Use the line to guide you as you sew.

Batting

Batting is the layer of insulation and sometimes stiffening material placed between the front and back layers of a quilt. It can be cotton, wool, or polyester. The lightest and thinnest batting works best in flower units. (See 1.1)

Inserting batting is easy in flower units. A same-shaped piece is cut to fit within the inner boundary of the folded unit.

Fusible batting is especially desirable in the units that are turned right-side out through a slash.

Non-fusible batting can be temporarily attached using a spray adhesive.

Batting can be cut using a template, ruler, and rotary cutter. (See 1.2)

1. For square units, fold the batting onto itself to create four layers.
2. Cut a strip of batting the width of the square.
3. Crosscut the strip into squares.
4. Place the piece of batting in the center of the block according to the project instructions. (See 1.3) For star-based units, the batting is centered with equal space around all sides. (See 1.4)

Bias

Bias is the diagonal of the fabric grain. It has "give" and is very useful in your projects when turning back petals.

To facilitate the turning on square units, components of the unit are cut on the bias. Most commonly, 12½-inch squares are cut. At left is a cutting diagram to illustrate how to place the ruler on a 1-yard piece of fabric. (See 1.5)

Binding

A single layer of fabric is used for binding the projects. The step-by-step process is described in the following sequence of pictures and illustrations:

1. To find the number of strips needed, measure the total distance around the project, add them together plus 24 inches for joining the strips together and for turning the corners.
2. Once the total length of binding fabric is determined, divide that total by 40 inches (the net width of most fabrics).
3. Round up to the next whole number. This is the number of 40-inch strips needed.
4. Multiply this number by the width of the binding strip.

Usually, the projects in this book have a 1¾- or 2-inch strip. For example, if a project requires six strips, multiply six by 1½ inches for a total of 9 inches. You will need 9 inches of binding fabric.

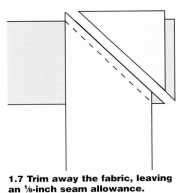

1.7 Trim away the fabric, leaving an ⅛-inch seam allowance.

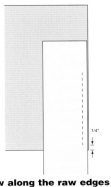

1.8 Press the seam allowance open.

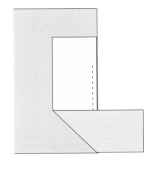

1.9 Sew along the raw edges to exactly ¼-inch from the corner.

Binding continued

5. Join the binding strips by placing the ends right sides together at a right angle ¼-inch in from the crossed pieces. Mark a line diagonally from the upper left intersection to the lower right intersection.
6. Sew along the line as indicated in the photo. (See 1.6)
7. Trim away the fabric, leaving an ⅛-inch seam allowance. (See 1.7)
8. Press the seam allowance open. (See 1.8)
9. Place a binding strip right-side down along the raw edge of the joined units of the project. Place it at least 6 inches from any corner. Leave a 6-inch tail of unsewn strip to be used for joining.
10. Sew along the raw edges to exactly ¼-inch from the corner. (See 1.9)
11. Fold the binding strip open at a 45-degree angle. The right side of the binding strip will be facing up. (See 1.10)
12. Refold the strip upon itself so that it turns the corner. The binding strip will be face down on the corner folds. (See 1.11)
13. Sew the next side of the project.
14. Repeat the sewing steps for each corner.
15. On the last side, leave 3 inches unsewn and a tail of binding strip. Lay the two loose pieces of binding strip along the raw edge until they meet in the center of the unsewn area.
16. Bend them back on each other and finger-press.
17. Join the two ends of the binding strip by placing them right sides together, and sewing the finger-pressed fold.
18. Trim the extra binding fabric.
19. Press the seam open.
20. Sew the joined binding strip onto the project.
21. Turn the binding right-side out and press open.
22. Turn the project to the backside, and fold the binding fabric onto itself so that the raw edge just touches the raw edge of the project.
23. At the corners, tuck the raw edge of the binding into the corner. (This may take a little fussing.)
24. Fold the binding again so that it's folded edge covers the stitching line on the back of the project.
25. At the corners, fold one side first and then the second side over the first, making a 45-degree fold.
26. Pin the binding. (See 1.12)
27. Topstitch either on the front or the backside of the project. When topstitching on the front, be sure that the folded binding is caught in the stitching.

1.10 Fold the binding strip open at a 45-degree angle.

1.11 Refold the strip upon itself so that it turns the corner.

1.12 Pin the binding and topstitch.

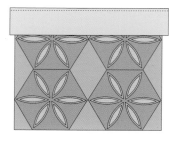

1.13 Place the first border strip right-side down on the long side of the project. Sew.

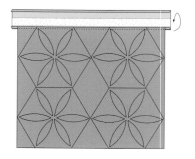

1.14 Turn a ¼-inch seam allowance along the raw edge of the border strip.

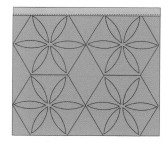

1.15 Trim the border pieces even with the project.

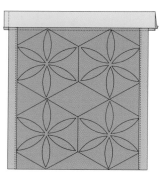

1.16 Fold the border strip back onto itself, right sides together, lining up the folded seam allowance with the sewn seam allowance.

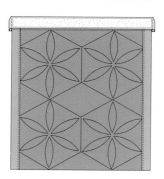

1.17 Stitch across both folded corners, trim the seam allowance, clip across the corners, and fuse batting strip between the seamed ends of the border strip.

Border

Borders are the frames around the outside of a project. Because they are finished on the outside edges, the addition of binding is not needed. The borders in this book are folded over a strip of batting to create a thickness that matches the depth of the units. Project instructions specify the width of a border strip.

1. To change the width of a border, cut the border strip at double the width of the desired finished border plus ½-inch. For example, you would cut strips 6½ inches wide for a 3-inch finished border.
2. Cut the batting filler strips ¼- to ½-inch narrower than the finished width (or 2½ to 2¾ inches for the 3-inch finished border described previously).
3. The length of two border strips is the same as two sides of the project. For a rectangular project, sew the longer sides first. The border looks more balanced with the other sides overlapping the first border strips. The length of the other sides is the distance along the remaining side of the project plus two times the finished width of the added border strips. (In the case of the 3-inch finished border, this would be 7½ inches – 6 inches plus 1½ inches – for a seam allowance long enough for trimming.)
4. Place the first border strip right-side down on the long side of the project, and sew. (See 1.13)
5. Press the border strip open and turn the project to the backside. (See 1.14)
6. Turn a ¼-inch seam allowance along the raw edge of the border strip.
7. Lay a strip of batting against the raw edge of the project. Spray or press-fuse the batting.
8. Fold the fold over the batting, covering the stitching line. Sew along the folded edge. Repeat for the opposite side.
9. Trim the border pieces even with the project. (See 1.15)
10. Turn the project over.
11. On the front side of the project, center the right side of the border strip along the raw edge of the project, across the first two border strips. Sew along the raw edge.
12. Press the border strip open.
13. Turn a ¼-inch seam allowance along the raw edge of the border strip.
14. Fold the border strip back onto itself, right sides together, lining up the folded seam allowance with the sewn seam allowance. (See 1.16)
15. Stitch across the folded corners so that the stitching is just outside the finished edge of the first border piece. (See 1.17)
16. Trim the seam allowance to approximately ⅛-inch and clip across the corners. (See 1.17)
17. Spray-fuse or press-fuse a 2¾-inch-wide strip of batting cut to fit flat between the seamed ends of the border strip. (See 1.17)
18. Turn the border piece right-side out. Smooth the batting inside the border.

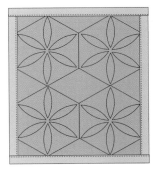

1.18 Turn the border piece right-side out and smooth the batting inside. Press and stitch along the folded seam. Repeat for other side.

1.19 To the second two border strips, sew a 3- by 4½-inch strip of outer fabric across each end. This end strip forms the corner.

Border continued

19. Press and stitch along the folded seam allowance. (See 1.18)

20. Repeat for the remaining side to complete the process. (See 1.20)

Borders With Corner Blocks

1. For borders with contrasting or coordinating corners, as in "Country Petals" on pages 410 and 411, cut a border strip from each color with the inner color 2 inches wide.

2. Cut the outer color 3 inches wide.

3. Cut two more inner and outer strips ½-inch plus the length of the other two sides.

4. With right sides together, sew an inner color strip to an outer color strip of the same length. You will have a 4½-inch-wide striped border strip.

5. Repeat for the other three two-color strips.

6. To the second two border strips, sew a 3- by 4½-inch strip of outer fabric across each end. This end strip forms the corner. (See 1.19)

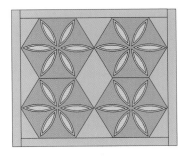

1.20 When completed, your project with borders will look like this.

When attaching the border strips to the project, place the inner fabric of the first two strips along the raw edge to be sewn. Continue with the border instructions.

When attaching the second (and following) pieced border strips, match the joints of the inner and outer border with the joints of the border corner pieces. (Refer to the picture of "Country Petals" in Chapter Two, page 411.)

Chain-Piecing

Chain-piecing is an efficient way to sew similar pieces. It consists of feeding similar pieces, one right after the other, through the sewing machine without cutting the thread between each piece.

1. Sew a first piece.

2. Follow with a second similar piece at the presser foot. Sew the second piece.

3. Continue placing pieces through the sewing machine without cutting the thread.

4. When you have finished a group, cut the thread at the end and in between each piece.

Cutting

Fabric is cut using a rotary cutter and ruler on a self-healing mat, with paper templates for guides. Project instructions will indicate how the fabric is to be folded.

For triangle-, hexagon-, and octagon-shaped pieces, most frequently the fabric will be folded matching the selvedge and then folded again matching the fold

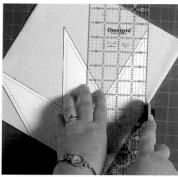

1.21 Place a clear-lined rotary ruler on the template, hold the ruler in place with your non-cutting hand, and cut with a rotary cutter.

1.22 For simple joining, open the adjacent flaps, match the fold lines, and sew in the fold.

Cutting continued

to the selvedge. This creates four layers and four pieces at a time when cut.

It's advisable to use the largest-diameter rotary cutter (60 millimeters) in this instance. A sharp blade is a must!

1. Place the paper template on the fabric, matching the grain line.
2. Place a clear-lined rotary ruler on the template so that the ¼-inch line of the ruler is directly on top of the ¼-inch line of the template. (See 1.21)
3. With your non-cutting hand, hold the ruler in place and then cut along the ruler with the rotary cutter. (See 1.21)

Dual-Feed

A built-in sewing machine feature that advances both the top and bottom layers of fabric. (Also see "Walking Foot," page 405.)

Fabric Preparation

Cotton fabric should be washed, dried, and pressed before cutting. Laundering should mimic the method you will use when the project is complete. (See Helpful Hint at left)

Fabric measurements for projects are rounded to the next-highest ¼- or ⅓-yard. The given yardage assumes that uneven edges have been removed.

Grain Line

The grain line of fabric runs parallel to the selvedge. The straight of grain is both parallel and at right angles to the selvedge. Many templates are marked with a designated grain line. Place the line of the template in the same direction as the fabric's straight of grain.

Joining

Completed units are joined by several methods. The simplest is to open the adjacent flaps, match the fold lines, and sew in the fold. This works for square, triangular, and hexagonal units. (See 1.22)

Join longer rows of units together first. Instructions for projects give specific joining plans.

Some topstitching of petals can be done through the middle of long rows before the rows are joined. These narrower strips are easier to manage in the sewing machine.

In projects where many flaps converge creating a space, a filler piece, which resembles a small pillow, is made to fit the space. Specific instructions for making filler pieces are included in the chapters and with the project instructions.

On the backside of the project, a filler piece is placed over the space between units. The edges of filler pieces are thinner so that the bulk falls into the space rather than in the seamed area. The corners are lined up, and the piece is pinned or taped into place.

On the front side, the flaps over the filler pieces are opened and pinned into place. Sewing through the folds of the flaps and the filler pieces joins the pieces. (See photo 6.16 on page 491 of Chapter Six.)

Petals

Petals are created when a folded flap of fabric is turned back on itself. The edge of the fabric layer is on the bias providing ease to the turning process. The turning takes place as you topstitch the petal in place. (See "Turning Back Petals," page 404.)

Quilting

Quilting may be desirable on the simpler projects such as two- or three-color squares. Shadow, or outline, quilting is quite lovely as it accentuates the petal effects and is easy to execute. Random meandering also works well as it puffs up the petal areas.

Rotary Cutter

A rotary cutter is a fabric-cutting tool that resembles a pizza cutter. It is placed against a plastic ruler, which acts as the guide, and rolled through a layer of fabric that is lying on a rotary mat. The blade slices the fabric in a straight line.

Rotary Mat

The rotary mat is made of a material that resists cutting and serves to protect the surface it covers from being cut by the rotary blade.

Rotary Ruler

Transparent rulers are the guides used to cut parts of the projects in this book. I find the most useful rulers to have increments of ⅛-inch and 30-, 45-, and 60-degree lines.

Seam Allowance

Seam allowances are always ¼-inch unless otherwise stated. Quite often the seam allowance will be trimmed to ⅛-inch. However, don't be tempted to change the seam allowance. They are specifically designed for successful construction. When sewing on the bias, the ¼-inch gives some leeway.

1.23 Create the slash by first pinching one layer of fabric and making a small clip across the pinch with the scissors.

1.24 Insert the scissors and cut across the bias for about 2 inches.

Sewing Machine

All stitching is done on a sewing machine. It is very helpful to have the ability to change stitch length.

Slash

The slash is used to turn a unit right-side out without having to sew up a seam allowance. Slashes should always be bias cut and should never be cut along the grain line; the latter will cause fraying.

It is also important to put the slash in a place that won't be seen and will be sealed inside a petal. Slash locations are indicated in the chapter illustrations. Place a slash under the area of a flap that will be folded completely over the slash after the petals are turned.

On star-shaped units, the slash can be cut in the central area of the inner petal fabric. Plan the location of the slash so that it can easily be cut on the bias. (See Helpful Hint at left)

1. Create the slash by first pinching one layer of fabric and making a small clip across the pinch with the scissors. (See 1.23)
2. Insert the scissors and cut across the bias for about 2 inches. (See 1.24)

When cutting a slash in a star-shaped piece, avoid cutting in the pointed area. Cut in the central part away from the fold. It is helpful to fold in one of the points to check which area will be covered when the unit is complete.

Spray-Basting

Batting is sprayed with temporary adhesive and placed on the inside fabric of a unit prior to turning the unit right-side out. The temporary adhesive keeps the batting in place while turning the units. It is also used to tack units in place prior to topstitching to the front of pillows. (Also see "Adhesive," page 395.)

Stitch Length

Set your stitch length at ten to twelve stitches per inch. The 2.5-millimeter setting on the newer computerized machines is fine. It is short enough to be secure but long enough to remove when necessary!

In areas that are later trimmed – such as the inside and outside corners of units – a shorter stitch length is preferred. As you sew the two layers together, reduce the stitch-length setting about ½-inch from the corner. (For manual machines fifteen to twenty stitches per inch would be recommended. Computer models read 1.5 millimeters.)

Strip

A strip is a piece of fabric cut from selvedge to selvedge. It is assumed to be 40 inches of usable fabric after shrinkage and removal of the selvedge edge.

Templates

The preferred method of making templates is to make photocopies and cut them out, rather than tracing onto plastic. Since all templates in this book (but one) consist of straight lines, I find it easier to cut fabric by using a rotary ruler placed over the paper template.

Line up the ruler's ¼-inch line on the dotted line of the template. The ruler acts as the guide for the rotary cutter, and the template remains under the ruler.

Full-size templates are located in the back section of the book. They are labeled and referenced in appropriate chapters or projects. Make the number of photocopies of templates required for the desired project. Cut on the solid lines.

When diamond-shaped pieces are joined to make a larger template, use your ruled rotary mat to line the pieces up before taping them together.

For a hexagon, three pieces make a straight line across the middle.

Four pieces of an octagon will be half the template.

Instructions for the dodecagon are given in Chapter Six, pages 486 to 491.

When instructed, cut an additional copy (or copies) of the template inside the dotted seam line for a batting template. (See Helpful Hint, top right)

Triangles

Corner and side triangles are used to fill in the sides of projects to make them "square." Instructions for their construction are included within the relevant chapters.

Trimming/Clipping

1. Trim straight sides of units by placing the rotary ruler along the seam line with the ⅛-inch line along the stitching.
2. Roll the rotary cutter along the edge of the ruler, cutting away the approximate ⅛-inch edge. (See 1.25)
3. At the corner of a square or the point of a star-shaped piece, cut the fabric at an angle in toward the point using a scissors.
4. Trim off the tip of the small point. Be careful to leave three or four threads outside the stitch line. (See Helpful Hint, bottom right)
5. At inside corners, while leaving a few threads uncut, clip straight into the corner with scissors.
6. Trim the seam allowance at an angle toward the clip.

1.25 Roll the rotary cutter along the edge of the ruler, cutting away the ⅛-inch edge.

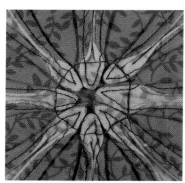

1.26 Pin the center corners or points. If desired, baste the points with machine stitching.

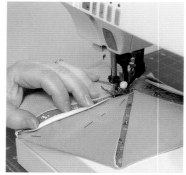

1.27 Sew over the folded fabric for about an inch.

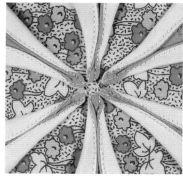

1.28 As you approach the center, return the fabric to the flat position and anchor the last area with three or four topstitches.

1.29 The petal area can be turned back to accentuate a "fussy-cut" design.

Turning Back Petals

1. Prepare to turn back the petals by pinning the center corners or points. If desired, baste the points with machine stitching. (See 1.26)
2. Pin the flaps in the middle area as well as near the corners and points to keep them from shifting during the topstitching process.
3. Begin at the corner or middle of a unit. Set the sewing machine needle through all the fabric layers at the center point or at the corner of the folded flap.
4. With the flap flat, take three or four stitches.
5. Leave the needle in the fabric and raise the presser foot. (A "needle-down" function is useful here.)
6. Fold the bias edge of the fabric back onto itself in a gentle arc.
7. Lower the presser foot, and sew over the folded fabric for about an inch. (See 1.27)
8. With the needle in the fabric, raise the presser foot and adjust the direction of the sewing and the arc of the folded fabric. The arc of the folded fabric will naturally be thinner at the corner, wider in the middle, and taper at the end.
9. Lower the presser foot, and continue sewing along the edge of the folded fabric.
10. When nearing the end of the folded flap, return the fabric to the flat position and anchor the last area with three or four topstitches. (See 1.28)
11. With the needle in the fabric, raise the presser foot and turn back along the other side of the petal flap.

You may wish to topstitch more and turn back less, depending on the pattern formed by the fabric. As you can see in the "fussy-cut" border fabric at right, the petal edges are neatly outlined by the stripes. (See 1.29)

Turning Right-Side Out

Once the slash is made (see "Slash" on page 402 for instructions), gently pull the fabric through the hole from the inside.

For star-shaped pieces, after the center area is flipped, pull the star points out of their "pockets" by gently grabbing the fabric inside the little tunnel and pulling it out.

The next section explains how to finish the points.

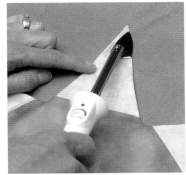

1.30 Use a miniature iron to assist with pressing the points flat.

Turning Out Corners and Points

Fully turn points by pulling the fabric to the surface with a pin. This takes a bit of practice. Avoid pulling the threads individually as they can pull out of the stitching. (If the trimming was too close to the stitching, this can easily happen.)

If your seam allowance shrunk to less than ⅛-inch, spread a little Fray Check with a toothpick along the cut edges of the thread before you turn the unit.

Press the points flat, making sure the seam allowances are fully open. A mini-iron is ideal for this step. (See 1.30)

Unit

The term "unit" refers to an individual part of a project.

Contrary to the term "block" used in the traditional quilting sense, a unit has a front and a back and often batting within.

Parts of units are described at the beginning of each chapter.

Walking Foot

A walking foot is a sewing machine attachment that advances both the lower and upper fabrics through the sewing machine. Its use is especially helpful when sewing across the bias of fabric. The seams lie flatter because the fabrics are even.

Sewing machines with a built in dual-feed feature function in the same manner as a walking foot but with greater visibility and ease of use.

Work Area Organization

Convenience is the key to organizing your workspace.

Place your sewing machine close to the ironing board. The more your sewing work is pressed between steps, the better the results.

Place a rotary mat next to your sewing machine. Many sizes are available; or if you have an old one, cut it to fit the workspace available.

squares

quares are simple, quick, and easy. Choose from many different fabric types. Many successful squares can be made from traditional quilt cottons, homespuns, loose weaves, and flannels.

"Glowing Embers" is an example of accented petal squares. This quilt was made by the author, who says this color combination isn't for everyone, but it does exemplify her wild side.

Basic Squares

The basic square is made from an inside and an outside fabric. The outside fabric is folded so that it forms the backside of the project and the front area that surrounds the petals. The inside fabric only shows inside the petal area. Some measure of contrast is desirable, and lots of contrast can be fun!

If you want an all-over pattern, choose two fabrics – one for the inside and one for the outside. The "Country Petals" project (page 411) is made this way.

More variety is possible by changing just the inside fabrics. "Batik Watercolor" (page 413) has many flower colors with just one outside fabric. It's a good example of a low-contrast combination.

Notice how much more the petal effects stand out in "Country Petals."

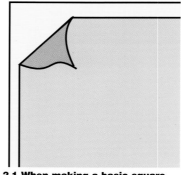

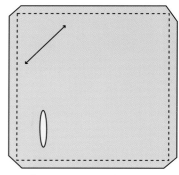

Helpful Hint

♦♦♦

For a first project, cutting these squares on point (with bias edges) is recommended. This method requires more fabric with leftover triangle-shaped pieces; they may be recycled as parts for other projects in later chapters. (Refer to "Bias," page 396.)

Helpful Hint

♦♦♦

To make step 5 easier, lift a single layer of fabric at about the center of where you would like the slash. Pinch it into a tiny fold and snip across the fold. (Be sure you have only one layer of fabric!) Insert your scissors and snip, cutting 1 inch first in one direction and then an inch in the opposite. Remember that cutting across the bias keeps the slash from fraying.

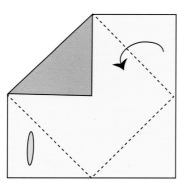

2.3 Press the folds by setting the iron on the folds. Be careful: Smearing the iron over the folded piece will cause distortion.

2.1 When making a basic square, place one inside and one outside fabric piece right sides together.

2.2 With the inner fabric facing up, cut a slash 2 inches wide through just one layer of fabric.

Traditional instructions

1. For the neat and tidy version of the basic square, start by cutting equal numbers of 12½-inch squares from the inside and outside fabrics. (See Helpful Hint, top left)
2. Place one of the inside and one of the outside fabric pieces right sides together. (See 2.1)
3. Pin at the corners and sew all four sides with a ¼-inch seam allowance.
4. Trim the seam allowance to ⅛-inch using a ruler and rotary cutter. Snip across the corners to smooth them.
5. With the inner fabric facing up, cut a slash 2 inches long through **just one layer**, across the bias in one of the corners about 1½ inches from the corner. (See 2.2 and the Helpful Hint)

Batting

The very lightest and thinnest works best. (Mountain Mist's® "Goldfuse"or "Quilt Light," or Thermore® by Hobbs.)

Use a medium-hot iron; too much heat can melt the batting.

1. If batting is required or desired, cut 8-inch squares of batting.
2. To position the batting, fold the fabric square in half in both directions, and finger-press the center points along the sides.
3. Line up the corners of the batting pieces with the center finger-pressed folds. Note that the batting square sits diagonally on the square just inside the dotted line shown in the illustration. (See 2.3)
4. Spray-fuse or press-fuse to the wrong side of the outside fabric. (See the "Basting" and "Batting" sections, pages 11 and 12.)
5. Turn the piece right-side out by gently pulling the fabric from the inside through the slash. Pay special attention to the corners so that all the fabric is turned to the seam allowance.
6. Press the square flat, making sure the seam allowances are fully open.
7. Fold the square in half, and finger-press a crease in the center. Fold in the opposite direction, and crease again to form a cross in the center of the square.
8. Open the square, and fold the four corners to the center crease forming a smaller square.
9. Press the folds by setting the iron on the folds. Be careful: Smearing the iron over the folded piece will cause distortion. (See 2.3)
10. Prepare the remaining square units in the same manner.
11. Once the squares are complete, arrange them as shown in the project or in your own pattern.

Joining

The units are sewn together in rows.

1. Open the flaps of two touching squares, match the folds.

2. Pin together, and sew in the fold. (See 2.4)
3. Fold the flaps back to their respective units.
4. Press again to set the seams and pin the flaps in the center.
5. Once all the rows are joined, line up two rows side by side.
6. Open the row of flaps on both sections.
7. Match the joints and the adjacent fold lines.
8. Pin across the folds.
9. Sew the two rows together by stitching in the fold.
10. Press the flaps back to their original unit, press, and pin the centers.
11. Repeat with the remaining rows.

Binding

1. Bind the outside edges of the project with a single layer of fabric. (See "Binding" on page 396 of Chapter One for photos and illustrations.)
2. After completing the binding, finish topstitching the petals.
3. Turn back the petals and topstitch by machine or a hand-sewn method.
4. Begin at the center or a corner of a square. Place three to four stitches in the flap before turning it back to reveal the inner fabric.
5. With the sewing machine needle in the fabric, raise the presser foot and turn back the bias edge.
6. Lower the presser foot, and sew along the edge of the turned-back flap.
7. As you approach the center or outside corner, return the flap to its original unturned position and topstitch for three to four stitches. This forms a flat center and flat outside corner.
8. Repeat this process without stopping by crossing over the corners and centers to turn back all the flaps. (See 2.5)

Raggedy Edges Version

It's simple with frayed edges! Use this for a group craft project. It has minimal sewing steps and will build confidence in new sewers.

Choose loose woven homespun or flannel fabric and don't wash or dry it. Plaids and prints look great when matched with a plain cream or other neutral for the inside.

1. Cut the 12½-inch squares as before, but they **must** be on the bias.
2. Place one inside square on an outside square, right sides out.
3. Find the center by alternately folding to the center and finger-pressing.
4. Fold all four of the two-layered corners to the center. Press the folds.
5. Or, cut an 8¼-inch square of heat resistant Templar® plastic and place it on the diagonal of the two layered squares.
6. Press the corners to the center of the plastic guide square.
7. Remove the Templar-square, and insert the batting.
8. Cut 8-inch squares of batting. This seems too small, but the bulk of the two fabric squares "eats up" some of the fabric in the folding.
9. Insert a square of batting between the layers of the folded squares. The batting will be set on the diagonal.
10. Arrange the squares according to the project or your plan.
11. Join the squares by opening the touching flaps and sewing on the fold line. Be careful not to rearrange the two layers of fabric and batting.
12. Once all the squares are joined, fold back the raw bias edges into petal shapes.
13. Like the traditional method, sew three to four stitches before turning back the petal. Finish by flattening the petal fabric for three to four stitches from the end.
14. Bind the same way as in the traditional method.
15. Throw the project in the washer and dryer for soft and fluffy edges!

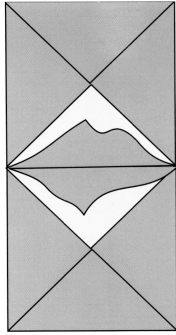

2.4 Open the flaps of two touching squares, match the folds, pin together, and sew in the fold.

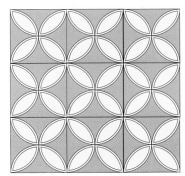

2.5 A completed basic square design, with units repeated and bound together, will look like the above illustration.

Country Petals
Basic Square

Finished size: 28 inches square
Difficulty level: Easy
Block size: 8-inch squares

Rich, deep burgundy and green give this quilt a homey country feel. Perk it up with a spring palette of yellow and white flowers. Or go old-fashioned with scrappy grandmotherly prints.

Do it up in plaids, but cut your squares on the bias if you do!

For bias-cut squares, you will need approximately one-and-a-half times as much fabric. A 12 ½-inch square cut on the bias is 17¾ inches across. (See the chart in "Raggedy Edges" on page 414 for fabric requirements.)

Choose contrasting colors for the inner and outer areas. Choose fabrics with small, consistent patterns for the inner areas. Large, busy prints will be lost.

Fabric requirements
(Yardages are given for squares cut on the straight of grain; variations in yardages for bias-cut squares are shown where necessary.)

Inside	1½ yards green; for bias cutting, add ½-yard
Outside	2 yards burgundy; for bias cutting, add ½-yard
Border	½-yard (included in burgundy)
Batting	⅔-yard of 45 inches wide

Cutting plan

Green	Nine 12½-inch squares
	Four 2-inch strips for border
Burgundy	Nine 12½-inch squares
	Four 3-inch strips for border
	Two 2½- by 4½-inch end blocks
Batting	Nine 8-inch squares
	Four 2½- by 27-inch strips for border

Layout
Three across and three down.

Specific instructions
1. Refer to the "Basic Square" instructions, beginning on page 407
2. Prepare nine square units and join in three rows of three units each.
3. The project is shown with a pieced border. Pieced strips are used in place of the solid strips shown in the "Border" instructions in Chapter One, page 398. To make a solid border for this project, substitute four 4½-inch strips for the pieced strips.

"Country Petals" uses the principles of the basic square. Shown here is a 28-inch square made by Laura Farson and quilted by Cindy Marshall.

4. Sew one 2-inch strip of green to one 3-inch strip of burgundy. Repeat with the remaining border strips.

5. Two sides of the project have border strips with the inner part green and the outer part burgundy. The other two sides have the green and burgundy strips with end blocks that form the corner squares when folded.

6. To prepare the strips with end blocks, cut two of the green/burgundy strips to ½-inch plus the length of the unfinished side.

7. Sew a 2½- by 4½-inch burgundy block across each end of these two cut strips. (Refer to illustration 1.19 in the "Borders with Corner Blocks" section of Chapter One, page 399.)

8. With the inner fabric along the raw edge of the project, sew the first two striped strips to the project's two opposite sides. Continue following the instructions in the "Border" section, page 398.

9. Insert a 1½-inch strip of batting between the folded border layers. Trim it to fit between the seam allowances.

10. With the inner fabric along the raw edge of the project, sew the pieced strips with burgundy corners to the remaining opposite sides of the quilt, matching the corners.

11. Fold back and topstitch as instructed in "Turning Back Petals," page 404.

Batik Watercolor
Basic Square

Finished size: 28 inches square
Difficulty level: Easy
Block size: 8-inch square

The beauty of Batik fabric is in its unpredictability. This is very evident in the petal area of this quilt.

Choose fabrics that are fairly consistent for the inner areas. Busier prints will be lost. Higher contrast between the inner and outer fabrics will highlight the petal shapes more.

This is also a perfect quilt to make any size. Just sew the desired number of blocks, sew into strips, and join.

Fabric requirements

Inside	Nine fat quarters mixed watermark Batiks (large enough for bias cutting)
Outside	1½-yard Batik coordinate; add ½-yard for bias cutting
Border	½-yard Batik, inner strip
Border	¼-yard of one of the inner fabrics, outer strip
Batting	⅔-yard of 45 inches wide

Cutting plan

Mixed fat quarter	One 12½-inch square of each fat quarter, preferably cut on the bias
	Four 3¾-inch-wide strips for border of one inner fabric
Batik	Nine 12½-inch squares, preferably cut on the bias
	Four 1½-inch-wide strips for border
Batting	Nine 8-inch squares

Layout

Three across and three down

Specific instructions

Prepare nine square units and join in three rows of three units each.

A basic square design does not have to be basic at all when you throw Batik fabric into the mix. Shown here is a finished "Batik Watercolor" 28-inch square made by Laura Farson and quilted by Cindy Marshall.

Border instructions

1. Sew one 1½-inch strip of Batik fabric to one 3¾-inch border strip.
2. Repeat with the remaining border strips. These pieced strips are used instead of a solid piece of border fabric.

In this project, corner blocks are not inserted, so the outside "binding" area is broken at the corners. If this does not appeal to you, substitute four 4¾-inch solid strips for the pieced border strips.

3. Sew the uncut strips to the first two opposite sides of the border by following the "Border" instructions in Chapter One, page 398.
4. Sew the remaining strips to the unfinished sides of the quilt.
5. Fold back and topstitch petals as instructed on page 404, "Turning Back Petals."

Raggedy Edges
Basic Square

Finished size: Four blocks makes a 16½-inch square. Six blocks by eight blocks (48) measures 50 by 66 inches.
Difficulty level: Easiest
Block size: 8¼-inch square

Make this one in every color! A 6- by 8-block group makes a great lap robe. Cozy flannels are as snuggly as one gets. Homespun means country! Make it manly with plaids. Or, try it in pastels for grandma and primaries for babies and school kids.

Fabric requirements for every five blocks

Note: In the "Bias" section of on page 396 there is a cutting diagram for 12½-inch blocks (See 1.5). For each yard of fabric, five 12½-inch blocks can be cut.

Inside	1 yard cream flannel or neutral homespun
Outside	1 yard plaid flannel or homespun
Binding	1¾-inch-wide strips multiplied by the number needed (See "Binding," page 396.)
Batting	(optional) ¼-yard for five blocks of 45-inch-wide batting

Cutting plan

Cream	Four 12½-inch squares, cut on the bias
Plaid	Four 12½-inch squares, cut on the bias
Batting	Four 8-inch squares

Specific instructions

See the "Raggedy Edge" section on page 409 of Chapter Two. The most important point is to cut the blocks on the bias. If you don't, you'll have spaghetti when you wash it!

1. Join the longest rows first.
2. Fold back the joined petal areas in the middle.
3. Sew the rows together in pairs.
4. Bind, wash, and dry.

Other sizes using common sizes of rulers

Block cut size	Batting cut size	Finished square	Fabric/No. of blocks
12½ inches	8 inches	8¼ inches	1 yard/5 squares
9½ inches	6 inches	6¼ inches	1 yard/10 squares
15 inches	9¾ inches	10 inches	2 yards/8 squares
6 inches	3½ inches	3¾ inches	1 yard/72 squares

Warm and fuzzy flannels are great made into "Raggedy Edges," shown here as a 16½-inch square made by Laura Farson, 2000.

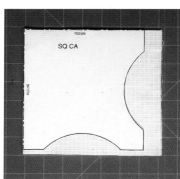

2.6 Place the template along the fold edges of the square, making sure there is no fabric showing on the straight edge of the template.

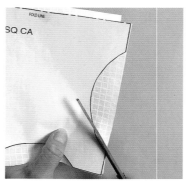

2.7 With scissors, cut through four layers along the raw edges of the template.

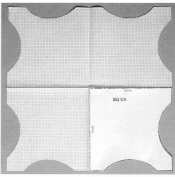

2.8 After cutting is complete, open the folded piece, and press it flat.

Helpful Hint

◆◆◆

A walking foot or dual-feed is useful for step 3 under "Construction."

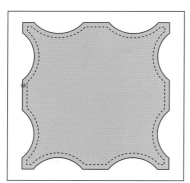

2.9 Follow the cutaway edges and curves of the outside fabric piece to sew a 1/4-inch seam. Reduce stitch length at points.

Cutaway Squares

For an elegant, clean look, choose the cutaway square. The fold-back area of the petal is eliminated, leaving an open, gentle arc of layered fabric.

This design lends itself to table linens as it has clean, sleek lines. Choose fabrics with larger prints for the outside and smaller prints or tone on tone for the inside. Because the design is so distinct, large busy prints detract from it.

Since larger petal areas are revealed, batting is desirable.

A finished block will measure 8½ inches square.

Template

Copy template CASQ12 (page 497) once and cut it out along the solid line.

Cutting plan

1. Cut 12½-inch squares of front fabric on the straight of grain.
2. Fold the square in half and then in half again to form a square with two folded sides. Press carefully so that the raw edges are very even.
3. Spray the backside of the template with temporary adhesive spray.
4. Place the solid sides of the template along the fold edges of the fabric square, checking to be sure that there is no fabric showing along the straight edge of the template. (See 2.6)
5. Cut through four layers along the cutaway sides (raw edges) of the template with scissors. Keep the layers of fabric even while cutting. Pinching the area near the scissors helps. If you have a circle-shaped plastic template matching the curve, cut on a mat with a rotary cutter along the curve. (See 2.7)
6. Once cut, open the folded piece. (See 2.8)
7. Press flat.
8. Cut the inside fabric into 12½-inch or larger squares.

Construction

1. Place a cutaway outside piece right-side down on an inside square, matching the straight edges.
2. Pin the corners and center areas along the sides.
3. Sew ¼-inch seam, following along the cutaway edges and curves of the outside fabric piece. Reduce the stitch length at the points. (See 2.9 and Helpful Hint)
4. Trim the seam allowance evenly with scissors to approximately ⅛-inch. Be careful not to get too close to the stitching. Snip across the outside corners.
5. Press flat.
6. With the inner fabric facing up, cut a slash 2 inches long through **just one layer**, across the bias at a point that will be hidden by a folded corner flap. Avoid cutting across the area that will fall into the fold. (See page 408 for a Helpful Hint to assist with this step.)

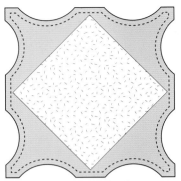

2.10 Be sure the batting is centered, and the edges are even.

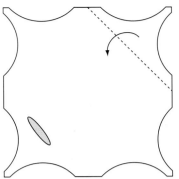

2.11 Gently pull the interior fabric through the slash to turn right-side out. Watch the corners and points.

2.12 Get fancy with your topstitching! Showcase those special stitches, or try an unique thread.

Batting

Batting is necessary in this style because of the larger exposed petal areas.

1. Fuse an 8-inch square of batting on the diagonal to the wrong side of the outside fabric.
2. Place the piece of batting so that it is centered, and edges are even. (See 2.10)
3. Turn the piece right-side out by gently pulling the interior fabric through the slash. Pay special attention to the corners and points so that all the fabric is turned to the seam allowance. (See 2.11)
4. Press the cutaway square flat, making sure the seam allowances are fully open.
5. Fold the corners to the center forming a square. Align the points in the center so that the corners lie flat and even. Press.
6. Prepare the remaining cutaway squares in the same manner.
7. Arrange the units as shown in the project or in your own pattern.

Joining

1. Once the arrangement is finished, join the units together. Joining the rows in the longest direction makes managing sections easier.
2. Open the touching flaps of two units. Match the fold lines and pin. (See 1.22 in "Joining," page 400)
3. Sew in the fold.
4. Replace the flaps and repeat for units along the row.
5. Once rows are joined, pin two rows together and sew in the folds for the length of the row.
6. Join rows into pairs, and then join the pairs into sections.
7. Once all the sections are joined, add binding, if desired.

Binding

1. Measure the four sides of the project. To this number add 24 inches for the corner turning. Divide this total by 40 inches, the length of a typical selvedge-to-selvedge strip.
2. Join the strips and bind as instructed in the "Binding" section of Chapter One, page 396.
3. Topstitch the outlines of the cutaway petals. This is the perfect place to show off special stitches and fancy threads! (See 2.12)
4. Press.

Floral Shadows
Cutaway Square

Finished size: 25 inches square
Difficulty level: Easy
Block size: 10 inches square and
5 inches square

Show off your fancy stitches by outlining the petal areas of this project. The smooth, arced edges give this a very tailored look. Use combinations of small and large squares to make table linens.

Fabric requirements

Inside	1½ yards cream
Outside	1½ yards blue
Binding	(optional) ⅓-yard blue
Batting	½-yard of 45 inches wide

Templates

CASQ15	Large cutaway square (page 500)
CASQ7	Small cutaway square (page 498)

Cutting plan

Cream	Four 15-inch squares
	Nine 7¾-inch squares
Blue	Four 15-inch squares folded twice and cut with template CASQ15
	Nine 7¾-inch squares folded twice and cut with template CASQ7
Binding	(optional) Four 1¾-inch-wide strips
Batting	Four 10-inch squares
	Nine 4¾-inch squares

Specific instructions

Follow the instructions in the "Cutaway Squares" section of Chapter Two, page 416. Prepare four large and nine small units.

Layout

See the project photograph on the next page.

Joining plan

1. Join four pairs of two small blocks.
2. Divide the joining into three rows. The first row includes one large block, two small blocks set vertically, and one large block. The second row includes five small blocks joined in a horizontal row. And the third row is the same as the first.
3. Join row one to row two and the bottom of row two to row three, matching the corners.
4. Bind, if desired.

This design may be called "Floral Shadows," but you'll certainly not want to hide it in the shadows! The cutaway square technique is optimal for showing off fancy stitching skills. This 25-inch square was made by Laura Farson, 2001.

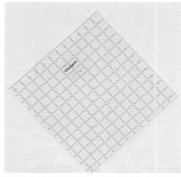

2.13 Cut a square of outside/background fabric

2.14 Press open with the seam allowance toward the center square.

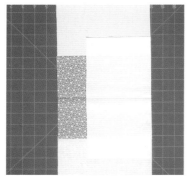

2.15 Center the rectangles on the remaining two sides of the square.

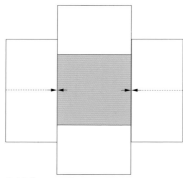

2.16 Sew and press the seam allowances toward the accent square. Trim bulky corners.

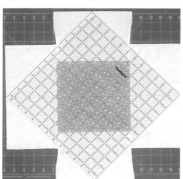

2.17 Place a square ruler on the diagonal. Place the outermost ¼-inch lines of the rotary ruler on the intersections between the accent fabric and the center square.

Accented-Petal Squares

This is a wonderful enhancement to the square. A petal outline fabric accents these pretty squares.

The color, when sufficiently contrasting to the background and inside, will show off the petal effect by forming an outlined area. Use colors that either contrast sharply or are otherwise well defined.

The petal-accent area, formed by turning back the inside of the triangle pieces, looks most attractive in a solid or tone-on-tone fabric.

The inside of the petals lends itself to small prints, as larger ones may not show consistent color throughout. One of the colors taken from the inside and outside print would produce a unifying look.

The outside fabric is the background for the petal area and the backside of the quilt; as such, it dominates the look of the project. Since this fabric is not manipulated like the petals, it lends itself to busier and/or larger prints. It can be either a coordinate or total contrast to the interior fabric.

Cutting plan

1. Cut one 8-inch square of inside petal fabric
2. From one 5½-inch strip of accent fabric, crosscut two 5½- by 8-inch rectangles and two 5½- by 11-inch rectangles.
3. Cut one 12½-inch bias square of outside/background fabric. (See 2.13)
   Also, refer to the "Bias" section of Chapter One, page 396, for a cutting diagram (illustration 1.5).

Construction

1. Place two 5½- by 8-inch accent rectangles right-side down on two opposite sides of an inside fabric square, matching the seam lines.
2. Sew ¼-inch seams along both sides.
3. Press open with the seam allowance toward the center square. (See 2.14)
4. Fold the square in half with one accent piece on top of the other.
5. Press crease lines in the center and edges of the square by lightly touching the iron to the center and both edges.
6. Using the crease lines to center them, place the 5½- by 11-inch rectangles centered on the remaining two sides of the square. (See 2.15)
7. Sew and press the seam allowances toward the accent square. Trim bulky corners. (See 2.16)
8. Place a 12½-inch square ruler on the diagonal. Place the outermost ¼-inch lines on the rotary ruler on the four intersections between the accent fabric and the center square. Visually verify the accurate placement of the ruler by checking to see that all the extra fabric around the edges is the same size. (See 2.17)
9. Trim excess fabric, using the ruler and rotary cutter. (See 2.18)

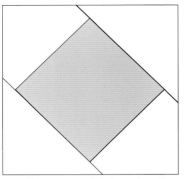

2.18 Trim excess fabric, using the ruler and rotary cutter.

2.19 Match the raw edges and pin.

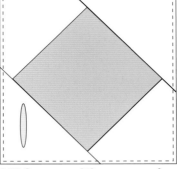

2.20 Sew around the square, using a dual-feed or walking foot and crossing the stitching at the corners.

10. With right sides together, place this 12½-inch outside square of fabric onto the right side of the trimmed square piece.
11. Match the raw edges and pin. (See 2.19)
12. Sew around the square, using a dual-feed or walking foot and crossing the stitching at the corners. (See 2.20)
13. Trim the seam to approximately ⅛-inch using a ruler and rotary cutter.
14. With the accent fabric facing up, cut a 3-inch-long slash through just one layer across the bias in one of the corners about 1 inch from the corner.

Note: Since the corner fabric is a bias-cut edge, your slash will be parallel to the side of the square.

Batting

The very lightest and thinnest works best. (Try Goldfuse, Quilt Light, or Thermore.)

1. If batting is desired, cut 8-inch squares of batting.
2. Spray-fuse or press-fuse to the inside of the backside fabric.
3. Turn the piece right-side out by gently pulling the fabric through the slash. Pay special attention to the corners so that all the fabric is turned to the seam allowance.
4. Press the square flat, making sure the seam allowances are fully open.
5. Fold the corners to the middle of the inside square so that the sides of the flaps lie flat and even. (See 2.21)
6. Press.
7. Prepare the remaining squares in the same fashion.
8. Once the squares are complete, arrange them as shown in the project or in your own pattern.

Joining

1. Once you have the arrangement complete, sew the units together.
2. First join across rows, and then join these groups in pairs of rows. This method keeps the sections manageable in the sewing machine.
3. Open the flaps of two touching squares.
4. Match the seam/fold lines, and pin across them.
5. Sew in the fold. (See 2.22)
6. Replace the flaps to their unit. It may be helpful to pin the flaps to keep them out of the way.
7. Repeat for all the squares in a row.
8. Join two rows at a time.
9. Join the pairs of rows together, using the joints as guides to match accurately.

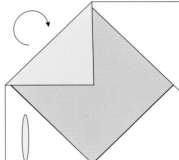

2.21 Fold the corners to the middle of the inside square so the sides of the flaps lie flat and even.

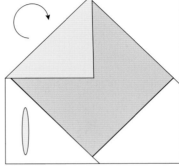

2.22 Once you have the arrangement complete, open the folds and sew the units together.

Binding

Bind the outside edges of the project with a single layer of fabric.

1. Cut a number of fabric strips 1¾ inches wide to equal the total distance around the project's borders plus 24 inches for the corners.
2. Refer to the "Binding" section in Chapter One, page 396.

Forming petals

1. Begin at the center or a corner of a square. Place three to four stitches in the flap before turning the edge back to reveal the inner fabric, and sew along this edge.
2. As you approach the center or outside corner, return the flap to its original unturned position and topstitch for three to four stitches. This forms a flat center and flat outside corner.
3. Repeat this process without stopping by crossing over the corners and centers to turn back all the flaps. (See 2.23)
4. Press.

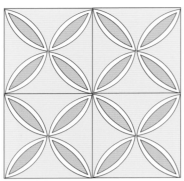

2.23 Completed accented-petal squares should look like this.

Granny's Yellow
Accented-Petal Square

Finished size: 50 by 67 inches
Difficulty level: Intermediate
Block size: 8⅜-inch square

If you love the reproduction fabrics, this is a great quilt to show off your stash! It's where mine is.

There are so many ways you can make this quilt. Change the outside color to match your décor. Mix and match using plaid shirting and make the petal areas plain. Petal-accents will glow when made of gold. Or for a dramatic effect, use black petal outlines and jewel color petals for a "stained-glass" look.

Fabric requirements

Inside	Twenty-four fat eighths
Outside	9 yards yellow in one length
Petal-accent	7⅓ yards white muslin
Binding	½-yard (included in yellow)
Batting	2 yards of 45 inches wide

Cutting plan

Fat eighths	Two 8-inch squares of each of twenty-four fabrics
Yellow	Forty-eight 12½-inch squares cut on the bias
	Seven 1¾-inch strips for binding
White	Forty-eight 5½-inch strips, and then crosscut each of them into two 5½- by 8-inch rectangles and two 5½- by 11-inch rectangles
Batting	Forty-eight 7¼-inch squares

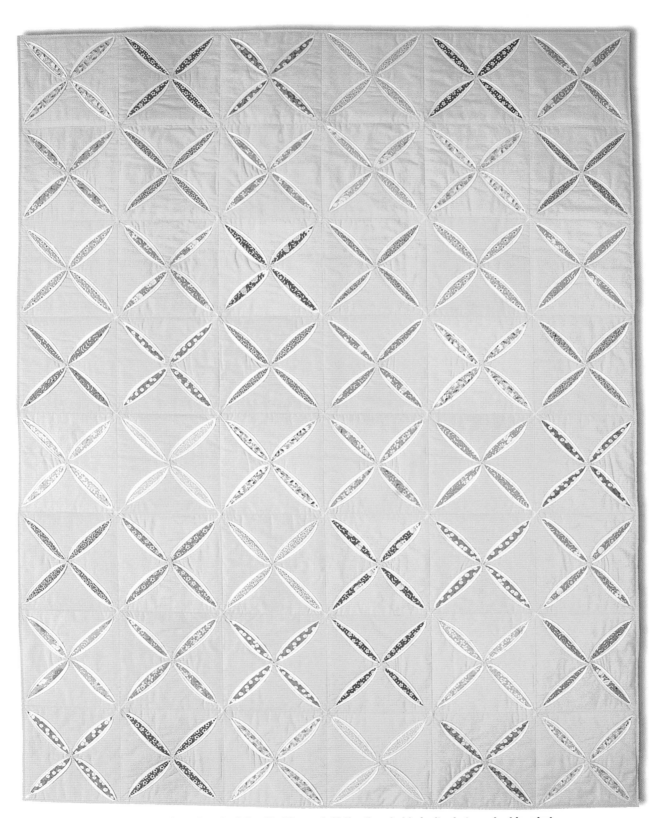

When you think of a typical "grandmotherly" quilt, "Granny's Yellow" probably isn't what you had in mind. Versitility is the key to this exciting design, shown here at 50 by 67 inches; made by Laura Farson, 2001.

Squares

Helpful Hint

♦♦♦

Chain-piecing saves time when doing a large number of units.

2.24 Variety will really enhance the "Petals and Ribbons" design. It is the most unique of the square-based units.

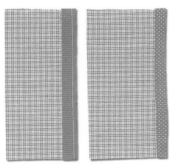

2.25 Place an accent strip right-side down on an outside rectangle, and sew along the long edge.

Specific instructions

1. Follow the instructions in the "Accented-Petal Squares" section of Chapter Two, page 420.
2. When cutting the forty-eight bias squares from one 9-yard piece, you will need to cut five squares from every yard. (Refer to the "Bias" section of Chapter One, page 396, for the cutting diagram plus the squares that fall "between" the five, illustration 1.5.)
3. Fold the fabric selvedge to selvedge.
4. Place a 12½-inch square ruler on point at the folded edge.
5. Cut through both layers (i.e. two squares at once).
6. Move the ruler so that its point meets the previous cut-point. There will be a triangle on the fold between the cut areas. This is a folded 12½-inch square.
7. Unfold and trim to size.
8. Repeat until you have forty-eight squares.

Layout

Six rows of eight blocks.

1. Arrange the blocks to scramble the colors as much as possible. Balance light and dark shades, but don't overplan. Be spontaneous! (Refer to the "Joining" and "Binding" sections of Chapter One, pages 400 and 396.)

Joining

1. Join eight blocks to make rows.
2. Join two rows.
3. Fold back the center-joined petal areas and topstitch. These long strips are easier to manage in the sewing machine at this point. Be careful not to sew down areas that need to be joined.
4. Join the paired rows, fold back the petals, and topstitch.
5. Bind with the seven joined 1¾-inch yellow strips.

Petals and Ribbons Squares

"Petals and Ribbons" is the most unique of the square-based designs. It has a little more going on during construction, but it's worth the extra effort.

Because there are four elements to the front side, there is a myriad of possibilities.

The "Petals and Ribbons" design works well with variety in the outside fabric, as well as in the accents. Fat quarters are perfect for mixing and matching these components. For a more geometric look, limiting to two sharply contrasting bold colors – such as navy and yellow – can work well. (See 2.24)

Cutting plan for each square

Four 11- by 5½-inch rectangles of outside fabric
Four 11- by 1-inch strips of accent fabric
One 12½-inch square of backing fabric, which will outline the front of each piece
One 12½-inch square of inside fabric

Construction

1. Place an accent strip right-side down on an outside rectangle, matching the long edges.
2. Sew along the long edge. (See 2.25)
3. Repeat for the other three rectangles and accent pieces. (See Helpful Hint)
4. Fold the pieces, right sides together, so that the accent strips are folded in half.

"Petals and Ribbons" designs will take extra effort to put together, but your diligence will be rewarded with the myriad of possibilities this design allows.

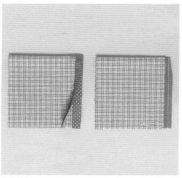

2.26 From the raw edge of the fold, sew along the accent strip.

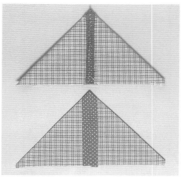

2.27 Flip to the right side and open to form a triangle.

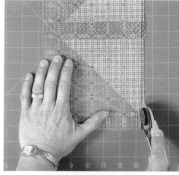

2.28 Use the 45-degree line on the ruler to trim the bottom edge of the triangle accurately.

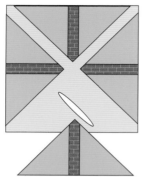

2.29 Match the center of the triangles to the center points onto outside edges of the square.

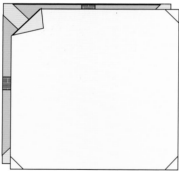

2.30 Place an outside fabric square right-side down on top of the pinned triangles.

2.31 Trim to 1/8-inch along the seam allowance and across the corners to reduce bulk.

Petals and Ribbons Squares construction continued

5. Sew along the raw edge of the accent strip from the raw edge to the fold. (See 2.26)
6. Chain-piece the three others.
7. Trim the point at the fold and finger-press the seam open.
8. Fold the rectangle in half and finger-press the center. Use this fold to center the front seam of the triangle.
9. Flip to the right side and open to form a triangle. (See 2.27)
10. Trim the bottom edge of the triangle with a rotary cutter and ruler so that both edges are even and the triangle measures $5\frac{1}{4}$ inches from base to point. Use the 45-degree line on the ruler, as illustrated in the picture. (See 2.28)
11. Assemble the pieces on a rotary mat so that you can cut the slash after step 15.
12. Fold the inside fabric square in half, and finger-press the center points along the sides.
13. Repeat in the other direction.
14. Place the four triangles right-side up along the outer edges on the right side of the inside square.
15. Match the center of the triangles to the center points pressed onto outside edges of the square. There will be gaps at the corners of the inside square. (See 2.29)

Cutting the slash

1. Lift one triangle and make a 2-inch slash with a rotary cutter across the bias in the center of the area covered by the triangle piece.
2. Pin the corners of the triangles to the square so that the pinheads are hanging over the outside edge of the square.
3. The corners of this block are not square. This "cut-off" corner is sewn using a guideline. To create this guideline, make a template by folding a $1\frac{1}{4}$-inch paper square in half diagonally.
4. Place the triangle template over the corner on the wrong side of the fabric.
5. Draw a line with a fabric marker along the angled edge of each corner.
6. Place an outside fabric square right-side down on top of the pinned triangles. (See 2.30)
7. Pin at the corners away from the seam line.
8. Sew along the raw edges and $\frac{1}{4}$-inch inside the drawn lines, crossing the stitching twice at each of the diagonal corners.
9. Trim to approximately $\frac{1}{8}$-inch along the seam allowance and across the corners to reduce bulk. (See 2.31)

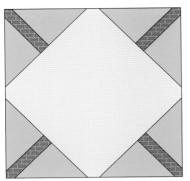

2.32 Turn the piece right-side out by gently pulling the fabric and triangles through the slash.

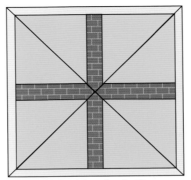

2.33 Fold the triangles to the center. Be sure to match the accent stripes and edge areas.

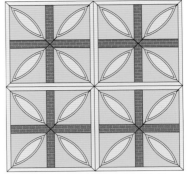

2.34 Repeat the process with the needle at the corner, folding over the petal and topstitching.

Batting

If batting is desired, the lightest/thinnest works best, as this design has lots of layers and seams.

1. Cut 10-inch squares of batting.
2. Spray-fuse or press to the wrong side of the outer fabric.
3. Turn the piece right-side out by gently pulling the fabric and triangles through the slash. (If you forgot to make the slash, make one now.) Pay special attention to the corner areas so that all the fabric is turned to the seam allowance, and the triangle flaps are flat. (See 2.32)
4. Press flat.
5. Fold the triangles to the center; match the accent stripes and edge areas. (See 2.33)
6. Repeat for the number of units in the project.
7. Arrange the units according to the project instructions or your plan.

Joining

1. Join units along the longer row first.
2. Open flaps that touch, match the accent stripes (which are between the layers being sewn together), and pin across the fold line.
3. Sew in the fold. (It is very helpful to use a walking foot at this point.)
4. Repeat for all the blocks in a row and then for all the rows. (See Helpful Hint)
5. Return the flaps to the center of their blocks and press.
6. Pin at the center of the accent stripes.
7. Topstitch along both edges of the accent stripes and across the points at the center of the units.

Binding

Bind the outside edges of the project with a single layer of fabric. (Refer to the "Binding" section of Chapter One, page 396.)

Turning back the petals

1. On the front side of the project, set the sewing machine needle into the corner where the triangle meets the edge of the project.
2. With the presser foot lifted, fold back the edge of the triangle.
3. Lower the presser foot and sew along the edge of the petal formed by this turned-back fabric. The flap will be narrower at the corners and wide in the center. The best look will be achieved when the fold is not forced, but gently eased for a consistent distance.
4. When one petal is complete, sew to the next corner.
5. Repeat the process with the needle at the corner, folding over the petal and topstitching. (See 2.34)
6. Press the project.

Helpful Hint

❖❖❖

When joining, it is easier to manage the sections in the sewing machine if you join two rows at a time and then join the two pairs. Join the rows together by opening the adjacent flaps, matching the joints and stripes (again, check between the layers being sewn together), and sewing in the fold close to the seam line.

Peachy Petals
Petals & Ribbons Square

Finished size: 22 inches square
Difficulty level: Intermediate
Block size: 11 inches square

Peachy describes just how yummy this project is. Because of the linear nature of this block, plaids and wavy stripe fabrics work wonderfully. Create warm masculine tones with flannels and homespun fabrics. Limit your colors for a very tailored look.

Fabric requirements

Inside	⅔-yard cream print
Front	1 yard peach plaid
Back	⅔-yard peach print
Accents	¼-yard peach dot
Batting	⅓-yard of 45 inches wide

Cutting plan

Cream	Four 12½-inch squares
Print	Four 12½-inch squares
Plaid	Cut three 11-inch strips and crosscut into sixteen 5½- by 11-inch rectangles
Peach dot	Cut six 1-inch strips and crosscut into sixteen 1- by 11-inch strips
Batting	Four 10-inch squares

Specific instructions

1. Follow the instructions in the "Petals and Ribbons" section of Chapter Two, beginning on page 424.
2. This block doesn't require binding. Secure the corners when joining by backstitching or using the "tie-off" feature of your sewing machine.

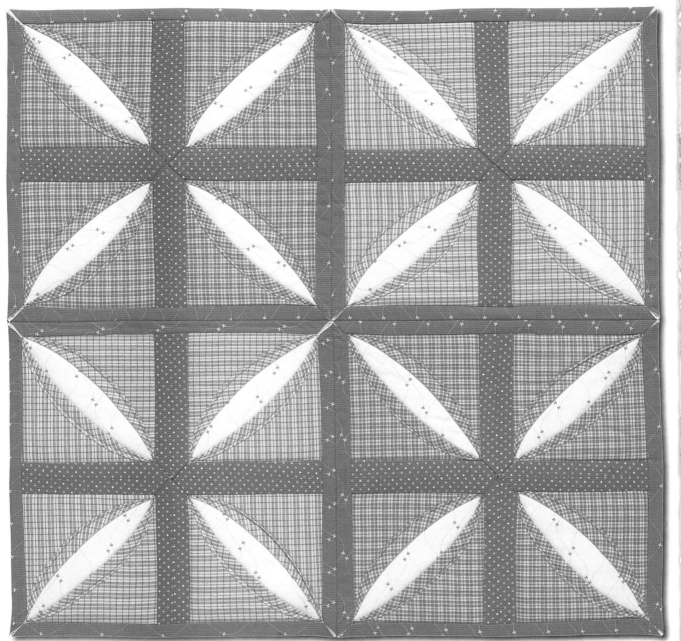

You will feel just peachy wrapped up in this "Peachy Petals" design. The example above was made by Laura Farson, 2000.

Hugs and Kisses
Petals & Ribbons Square

Finished size: 42 by 63½ inches
Difficulty level: Intermediate
Block size: Twenty-four
    10½-inch squares

This project has a very tidy and elegant look. These colors have a fresh, light, springtime feeling, but you could make it in reds and greens for the winter holidays. Feel free to add ribbons and bows, and give it as a "prewrapped" gift!

Fabric requirements

Green	2 yards
Blue	2 yards
Yellow	2 yards
Pink	2 yards
Purple	1½ yards
Inside	3 yards antique white
Batting	2 yards of 45 inches wide

Cutting plan

Cut from each of the first four colors:

	Twenty 5½- by 11-inch rectangles for fronts
	Twenty 1- by 11-inch strips for accents
	Five 12½-inch squares for backs
Purple	Sixteen 5½- by 11-inch rectangles for fronts
	Sixteen 1- by 11-inch strips for accents
	Four 12½-inch squares for backs
Antique white	Twenty four 12½-inch squares
Batting	Twenty-four 10-inch squares

Specific instructions

The instructions for this pattern have been updated to improve joining. As a result, there will be an outline of fabric surrounding the blocks as shown in the "Peachy Petals" photograph on page 429 and in the other examples on pages 424 (See 2.24) and 425.

The design of this pattern matches the back fabric square to the front fabric, which decreases the visibility of this outline. If you want to accentuate the outline, as in the other examples, scramble the backside pieces or choose a contrasting color fabric such as white or black.

Follow the instructions in the "Petals and Ribbons" section of this Chapter, beginning on page 424. There are five units of the first four colors and four units of purple. From each of the fabrics, cut front squares, accent strips, and a back square in the quantities shown in the cutting plan. Scramble the accent strips among the blocks.

"Hugs and Kisses" is likely what you'll receive from anyone getting this design as a gift. This example was made by Laura Farson, 2000.

Layout

Four rows of six blocks.

1. Join six blocks into a row and join rows in pairs.
2. Secure the edges by backstitching or using the "tie-off" feature of your sewing machine.

3 triangles

riangles provide more colors in smaller spaces, are easy to handle, and are easy to join in rows. With color variation and shading, they can look like tumbling blocks with flower petals.

Triangles are handy to use as filler pieces between hexagon units. When made with three petal flaps, they can be used to join groups of units. Triangle units create exciting variety.

This chapter will describe how to make basic triangles with two parts. It is possible to make triangles with cutaway or shadow petals, but the process is a bit tricky.

Choose two colors: one for the inside and one for the outside; one color for the outside and a variety for the inside; or mix and match colors for the inside and the outside. The "Golden Petals" centerpiece project uses only two fabrics.

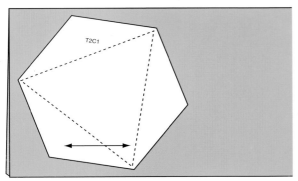

3.1 Place the hexagon-shaped template T2C1 on the folded fabric, being careful to orient the grain line marking.

Basic Two-Piece Triangles

By their nature, six equilateral triangles make a hexagon. The advantage of using triangles instead of hexagons is that you can include a greater number of colors in the background and/or in the petals. The outside piece forms the back of the unit and the area around the petal. The inside fabric forms the petal-reveal and the petal-outline areas.

In this chapter, you will learn how to make the equilateral triangle with three flaps. Two fabrics are cut into hexagon shapes. An outside fabric hexagon is sewn to an inside fabric hexagon. The unit is trimmed, batting applied, and a small slash cut before turning it right-side out and pressing. Sewing in the fold inside the flaps joins the units.

Equilateral Triangle Instructions

Once you have decided which fabric(s) will be outside and inside (those for the petals), fold the individual pieces selvedge to selvedge, and then fold again, matching the fold to the selvedge and creating four layers.

Template preparation

1. Make two photocopies of template T2C1 (page 501) and cut along the outer solid lines.
2. Tape the two halves together to make a hexagon-shaped template.

Cutting plan

1. Place the hexagon-shaped template T2C1 on the folded fabric, being careful to orient the template using the "grain line" marking. Edges are bias-cut to facilitate turning back the petals. (See 3.1)
2. Place a rotary ruler, with the ¼-inch line on top of the dotted line of the template.
3. Cut along the edge through all four layers, using the ruler and rotary cutter. You will have four pieces. Repeat this until you have the total number needed for your project.
4. Repeat this procedure with the petal fabric.

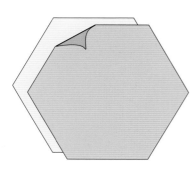

3.2 Place one hexagon-shaped piece of outside fabric on one of inside fabric, matching the straight edges and points.

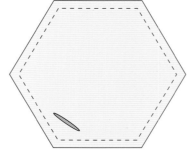

3.3 Sew along all sides, crossing the stitching at the corners. With the inner fabric facing up, cut a slash through one layer.

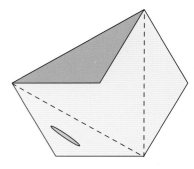

3.4 Press the hexagon flat, making sure the seam allowances are fully open.

Helpful Hint

◆◆◆

It's easy to trim using the ruler and rotary cutter.

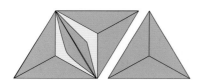

3.5 Open the flaps of two touching triangles.

Construction

1. Then, with the right sides together, place one hexagon-shaped piece of outside fabric on one of inside fabric, matching the straight edges and points. (See 3.2)
2. Pin at the corners to secure the bias edges.
3. Sew along all sides, crossing the stitching at the corners. (See 3.3)
4. Trim the seam allowance back to approximately ⅛-inch, being very careful not to get too close to the stitching. (Refer to the photo in the "Trimming" section of Chapter One, page 403.)
5. Snip across the corners to smooth them.
6. With the inner fabric facing up, cut a slash 2 inches long through just one layer, across the bias in one of the corners about 1½ inches in from the point. (See 3.3)

Batting

1. If batting is desired, prepare a batting template.
2. Make two photocopies of the hexagon-shaped template H3C1 and tape them together.
3. Cut it out along lines drawn between alternate corners that form a triangle. Use this triangle-shaped template to cut the batting.
4. Spray-fuse or press-fuse a triangle of batting to the wrong side of the outside fabric.
5. Turn the piece right-side out by gently pulling the fabric through the slash. Pay special attention to the corners so that all the fabric is turned to the seam allowance.
6. Press the hexagon flat, making sure the seam allowances are fully open.
7. Fold three alternate corners to meet in the center to form the triangle. Align the edges so that the corners lie flat. (See 3.4)
8. Press.
9. Prepare the remaining hexagons in the same manner. If you have many fabrics, separate them into two groups designated as background or petals.
10. Once the triangles are complete, arrange them as shown in the project or in your own pattern. Note that similar colors will blend together, and the pattern will be lost. More contrast will show the separate triangle shapes. (See 3.6)

Note that some of the petals are folded back into angular shapes rather than curves. This is another option.

Joining

1. Once you have the arrangement complete, sew the units together. Sewing the triangle units in rows makes joining simple.

3.6 Petals can be folded at angles as well as curves.

2. Once a row is joined, a second row can be sewn to it. Even with just six triangles, as in the centerpiece project, joining two groups of three units simplifies the process.
3. Open the flaps of two touching triangles. (See 3.5)
4. Match the fold lines of the flaps with right sides together. Pin across the fold.
5. Sew along the fold line. Fold back the flaps to their respective units.
6. Press again to set the seams, and pin the flaps at the center.
7. If desired, attach a binding as explained in the "Binding" section of Chapter One, page 396.
8. Turn back the petals and topstitch by machine or a hand-sewn method. (See 3.7)
9. Refer to the "Turning Back Petals" section of Chapter One, page 404, to complete the project.

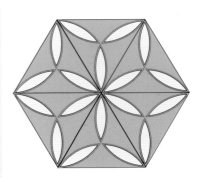

3.7 Turn back the petals and topstitch by machine or a hand-sewn method.

Golden Petals Centerpiece
Two-Color Triangle

Finished size: 17 by 19½ inches
Difficulty level: Easy
Block size: 8½ inches high by
  9¾ inches wide

This basic project is simple to make but lovely to look at. Six triangles join to make a hexagon centerpiece. Place a flower arrangement on it to complete the scene.

Fabric requirements
Inside   ⅔-yard gold
Outside   ⅔-yard green
Batting (optional) ⅓-yard of 45 inches wide

Templates
T2C1 (page 501)   Two copies
H3C1 (page 504)   Two copies (for batting)

Cutting plan
Gold   Six hexagons
Green   Six hexagons
Batting   Six 7½- by 9-inch triangles

Specific instructions
1. Follow the directions for the "Basic Two-Piece Triangle" in this chapter, beginning on page 433.
2. Batting, although optional, would be better protection for a table. If desired, spray-fuse or press a triangle of batting to the inside of the back fabric before flipping the unit right-side out.
3. A triangle template can be cut for the batting. On your H3C1 hexagon template, draw a line between every other corner of the stitching line.
4. Cut out this triangle template and use it for the batting template.
5. Join two rows of three triangles and then join the two rows in the center. This project is unbound; therefore, the joined areas should be secured by back-stitching.
6. Press.

It can't get any better than the "Golden Petals" project: simple to make, yet lovely to look at. The above example was made by Laura Farson, 2000.

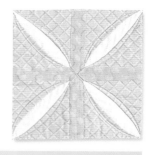

hexagons

he nifty thing about hexagons is that they look flowery, and they can nest together so there are fewer filler pieces to make.

The basic hexagon is made up of two six-pointed, star-shaped pieces of fabric. One color is for the inside and one for the outside.

There are two ways to make this unit. One is to cut both the inside and the outside fabric into star shapes. These cutout stars are placed right sides together and sewn along the edges. These edges are all on the bias.

As an alternative, you can cut out just the inside pieces into star shapes and then match them to outside fabric squares. The inside fabric star is placed on the bias of the outside fabric, but since only one piece has cut-bias edges, the sewing is easier. This way requires more fabric, but I recommend it for your first project.

Fast-Folded Flowers

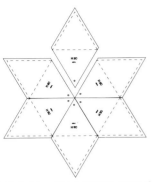

4.1 Matching the centers, tape the six diamonds together to form a star-shaped template.

4.2 Place the template on the fabric with no edges parallel to the grain line.

Basic Hexagon

Preparing the template

1. Photocopy template H2C on page 503 six times.
2. Cut along the solid lines on all six copies.
3. Matching the centers, tape the six diamonds together to form a star-shaped template. Three sections make a straight line. Use the lines on the rotary mat to line up each half of the template. (See 4.1)

Cutting plan

1. Organize your fabric choices into one pile for the inside and one for the outside.
2. Cut the outside fabric into enough 20-inch squares for the number of outside pieces needed.
3. After deciding which fabrics to use, fold the inside fabric selvedge to selvedge. This assumes that you will be cutting out two star shapes at a time. If only making one star piece of a color, use only a single layer of fabric.
4. Spray the backside of the paper template with temporary adhesive spray (See the "Adhesive" section in Chapter One, page 395.)
5. Place the template on the fabric with no edges parallel to the grain line. All edges are cut in a bias direction. (See 4.2)
6. Place a rotary ruler, with the ¼-inch line on top of the dotted line of the template and the end of the ruler stopped at the end of the template.
7. Cut through both layers of fabric along the edge of the ruler with a rotary cutter. Avoid cutting through the seam allowance at the inside corners. (Olfa's rotary-point cutter is handy to cut the inside corners.)
8. Move the ruler around the template and repeat the cutting until the entire star is cut. There are two layers and thus two stars.
9. Repeat this procedure for all the inside fabric(s) until you have the number of pieces required for your project.

Construction

1. Place one inside fabric star and one outside fabric square right sides together.
2. Rotate the star-shaped piece so that it does not have any edges going with the grain line of the outside fabric.
3. Pin in the points to secure the bias edges.
4. Sew along all sides, crossing the stitching at the points. (See 4.3)
5. Trim the seam allowance to approximately ⅛-inch from the stitching, being very careful not to get too close. (See Helpful Hint at right.)
6. Snip across the outside corners to smooth them and clip inside corners to ease the turning. This work is easily done while waiting for an appointment. Keep a roll of tape or lint roller handy to collect the debris!

Helpful Hint

♦♦♦

Use a walking foot to keep the edges flat. If you have a tie-down feature on your sewing machine, it is helpful to use it at both the inside and outside corners. Otherwise, decrease stitch length at these corners.

4.3 Sew along all sides, crossing the stitching at the points.

Helpful Hint

♦♦♦

I've done the trimming (step 5 of "Construction) with a rotary cutter and ruler, but invariably, I slip across the stitching at some point. Therefore, I recommend using a scissors.

4.4 Cut a slash 2 inches wide through just one layer, across the bias in the central area of the hexagon.

Basic Hexagons continued

At this point, check again to be sure which fabric is for the outside and which is for the inside.

Making the slash

1. With the inside fabric facing up, cut a slash 2 inches wide through just one layer, across the bias in the central area of the hexagon. (See 4.4)
2. Before cutting, check to be sure that it falls under a folded flap.
3. To make the slash, lift a single layer of fabric at about the center of its intended location.
4. Pinch it into a tiny fold and snip across the fold. (Again, be sure you only have one layer of fabric!)
5. Then, insert your scissors into the snip and cut first 1 inch in one direction and then 1 inch in the opposite. Cutting along the bias keeps the slash from fraying.

Batting

Use of batting is optional, but in many cases, it is desirable. It's very easy to include because it's added as a small piece within each unit. (Refer to the "Batting" section in Chapter One, page 396.)

1. The simplest way to cut batting is to make a template. Photocopy the H3C1 hexagon-shaped template on page 504 twice. Cut out the two halves on the dotted lines, and tape the halves together.
2. With the batting out of the package, carefully unfold it.
3. Refold into four layers.
4. Cut a strip of batting the same width as the batting template.
5. Place the batting template on the strip.
6. Place a rotary ruler on the template and line up the edge of the ruler with the edge of the template. Cut through four layers of batting.
7. Repeat until you have the number of batting pieces needed.

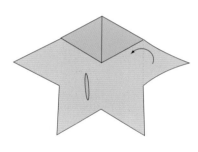

4.5 Align the points so that the corners lay flat.

Attaching the batting

1. Align the piece of batting on the wrong side of the outside fabric, so that it is centered.
2. Leave a ¼-inch space around the edge. This is the area that will be joined.
3. Fuse the batting to the fabric by pressing or by spraying it with temporary adhesive.
4. Turn the piece right-side out by gently pulling the fabric through the slash. Pay special attention to the points so that all the fabric is turned to the seam allowance. And be sure the batting is flat. If not, go inside the slash with your finger and smooth it out.
5. Press the star shape flat, making sure the seam allowances are fully open. (A mini-iron works well for this step.)
6. Fold the points to the center, forming a hexagon.
7. Align the points so that the corners lay flat. (See 4.5)
8. Press.
9. Prepare the remaining hexagon stars in the same manner.
10. Once the hexagons are complete, prepare the edge-filler triangles and corners.

Edge-Filler Triangles

Construction

1. Photocopy template HST on page 502 and cut along the solid lines.
2. For each edge-filler piece, cut two HST pieces: one from inside fabric and one from the outside fabric.
3. Place an inside and an outside piece with the right sides together. (See 4.6)

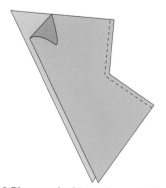

4.6 Place an inside and an outside piece with the right sides together. Sew along the seam line.

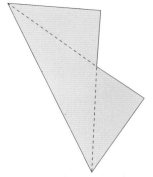

4.7 Turn right-sides out and press, making sure that the seam allowance is fully open.

4.8 Fold the upper points along the lines shown in the illustration to form a triangle.

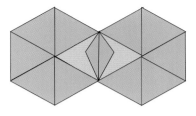

4.9 Open the folded points of two adjacent units. Match the fold, and sew in the fold.

4. Sew along the seam line, which is the angled area indicated along the top of the unit in the illustration. (See 4.6)
5. Trim along the seam allowance and clip the inside corner.

Batting

1. If you are using batting, prepare a batting template.
2. Make a photocopy of HST and cut it out on the inside of the triangle-shaped dotted line.
3. From the cutoffs of the hexagon-shaped batting pieces, cut enough triangle-shaped batting for the edge-filler triangles.
4. Keep the batting piece(s) about ¼-inch from the stitching line, as this is the area that will be sewn through when joined.
5. Spray-fuse or iron the batting onto the wrong side of the outside fabric of the filler triangle.
6. Turn right-sides out and press, making sure that the seam allowance is fully open. (See 4.7)
7. Fold the upper points along the lines shown in the illustration to form a triangle. (See 4.8)

Joining

1. Arrange the units as shown in the project or in your own pattern.
2. Once the arrangement is complete, sew the units together. (It is easier to join the horizontal seams first, creating vertical sets.)
3. Open the folded points of two adjacent units. Match the fold, and sew in the fold. (See 4.9)
4. Press.
5. Once all the horizontal seams are sewn together (See "A" in illustration 4.10), add the edge-filler triangles. (See "B" in 4.10)
6. Fold back and topstitch the flaps flat on the edge triangles.
7. Turn back and topstitch the center petal flaps on the vertical strips. (See "C" in illustration 4.10)
8. Join the vertical strips. You will zigzag back and forth between the hexagons.
9. Finish by folding back and topstitching the remaining petal areas. (See "D" in illustration 4.10)
10. Bind the outside edges with a single layer of fabric. Refer to the "Binding section of Chapter One, page 396.

As an alternative arrangement, make extra hexagon units and cut them horizontally or vertically as needed. (See 4.11)

4.10 Joining is made simple when you concentrate on one vertical grouping at a time.

4.11 There are numerous variations to the hexagon design, including this flowery project made from a circle of seven hexagons surrounded by four horizontal and six vertical halves. Five additional hexagons were cut to fit the edges, and a two-color binding was made without corner blocks.

Fall Festival
Basic Hexagon

Finished size: 47 by 50½ inches
Difficulty level: Intermediate
Block size: 11 inches wide by 9⅞ inches high

Put the accent on "Fest." Olé! It's a whirlwind of color – big and bright!

Make it in primary colors for the kids. This is the best example of mix-and-match colors.

Or, for a more subdued look, use just one color outside and mix up the petal colors.

Fabric requirements

Color	Yardage	Inside stars	Outside 20-inch squares	Total	Edge-fillers inside/outside
Gold	3½	7	5	12	3/3
Rust	3	4	6	10	0/2
Green	3	4	6	10	3/1
Multiprint	3	6	4	10	3/3
Brown	2½	4	4	8	1/1
Binding	½	Multiprint Eight 2-inch strips			
Batting (45 inches)	2½				

Templates

H2C	Hexagon	Six copies
HST	Side triangle	One copy
H3C1	Batting	Two copies taped together

Cutting plan

1. Following the chart above, cut twenty-five inside stars from the fabrics listed using the hexagon star template H2C, page 503.
2. Cut twenty-five 20-inch squares in the colors and quantities indicated.
3. Cut eight 2-inch-wide strips of the multicolor print for the binding.
4. Cut twenty-five batting pieces using a hexagon-shaped batting template prepared from H3C1, page 504.

Specific instructions

1. Follow the directions in the "Basic Hexagon" section of Chapter Four, beginning on page 439. You will also need ten edge-filler triangles.
2. Prepare twenty-five two-color hexagons, mixing the inside and outside colors. Use the project photo on the opposite page as a guide.
3. Make ten edge-filler triangles with mixed colors.

Looking to make a statement with big and bright colors? This "Fall Festival" design, shown above 47 by 50 inches, is your answer.

Layout

1. Arrange the hexagon units, half-hexagons, and edge-filler pieces according to the project photo.
2. Join vertical rows of hexagons first.
3. Turn back and topstitch the center petal flaps before joining the rows in pairs. As you join each pair of rows, turn back and topstitch the petal areas.
4. After all rows are joined, bind the quilt.

If you like color-placement options, try the "Accented-Petal Hexagon" like the 32- by 45-inch example above made by Laura Farson and quilted by Cindy Marshall.

Helpful Hint

♦♦♦

Try white muslin. I often make petal outlines using white muslin for the triangle pieces because it has such a high contrast, and white goes with almost everything!

Accented-Petal Hexagons

The "Accented-Petal Hexagon" pattern has more options for color placement than a basic hexagon design. The third color of fabric can be positioned to outline the edge of the petal area or focus attention on the petal background area surrounding the petals. Switching the inside and outside of the unit's construction shifts the position of the third fabric. By mixing and matching color options, diverse effects are possible.

The project "Petals in the Ferns" is an accented-petal hexagon, Version One. The petal-reveal areas are outlined with contrasting fabrics. The outside piece that forms the backside and the petal-surround is a folded hexagon star. The backside pieces and fillers are all green to serve as a background for the flower shapes.

Selective petal turning and subtle differences in the petal-accent fabric make this window and "broken glass" effect, as in the "French Petals" design pictured on the opposite page.

For a leaded glass look, use black for the petal-accent triangles and bright colors for the petal-reveal of the inner hexagon piece.

The accented-petal unit is a hexagonal, star-shaped piece.

In Version One, the inside of the star is a hexagon with six triangles sewn to it. These triangles form the outline of the flower petal when turned back. The hexagon fabric shows as the center of the petals. The outside of the star is a single piece of fabric that, when folded, forms the back of the unit and the front side of the triangles.

In Version Two, the pieced hexagon and triangle are on the outside of the unit. The front-facing triangles can be fussy-cut to create a fancy pattern. The hexagon

"French Petals" uses an accented-petal hexagon design to create a window effect. The above quilt is 40 inches square; made by Laura Farson, 1999.

part forms the back of the unit and folds over the outer edge of the front to form an outline. The inner fabric is a single, whole, hexagon-shaped star. It shows as the petal-reveal and the petal turn-back areas.

The construction of the two versions differs only in the placement of the turning slash. To keep the slash hidden within the folds of the unit, the slash is cut in the hexagon piece for Version One. For Version Two, the slash is cut in the star piece that forms the inner portion of that unit. The instructions for both versions are included in this section of the chapter.

Preparing the templates

1. Photocopy template H3C1 on page 504 twice and H3CT on page 505 once.
2. Cut the two half-hexagons and the triangle shapes along the outside solid lines.
3. Tape the two halves of the hexagon together along the centerline.
4. With a pointed object, such as the tip of a stiletto or the point of a compass, poke a hole at each of the six corners of the dotted line of the hexagon template. These points form the intersection of the fold line and the seam allowance. They will be used to mark the corners of the seam line on the fabric hexagons.

Fabric preparation

1. Choose three fabrics (one for the hexagon, one for the triangles, and one for the outside). When choosing your fabrics, keep in mind that there will be many triangle-shaped pieces left from cutting out the hexagons. (See 4.12 on the next page) These can be used with other hexagons in the same project, or

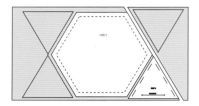

4.12 Place the hexagon-shaped template H3C1 on the folded fabric designated for the hexagon. Because triangles form when the hexagon is cut, you will want to save these end scraps for later use.

Helpful Hint

◆◆◆

In step 15, you may notice that the 60-degree line of the ruler will line up with the edge of the fabric. If you are familiar with the use of this line, the triangles may be cut by alternating the 60-degree line of the ruler along the long edge of the fabric strip.

Helpful Hint

◆◆◆

Spray a little temporary adhesive on the back of the template to keep it from slipping while cutting.

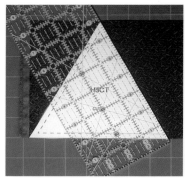

4.13 Place a rotary ruler on top of the template, with the ¼-inch line on top of the dotted template line.

plan to use them in another project teamed up with other fabric hexagons.

2. Fold the outside fabric selvedge to selvedge.

3. Cut two 18½-inch squares through both layers, along the selvedge edge. Cutting the squares along the selvedge leaves a nice long piece along the folded side.

4. Fold the hexagon and triangle fabrics, selvedge to selvedge and fold to selvedge, creating four layers.

5. Place the hexagon-shaped template H3C1 on the folded fabric designated for the hexagon, being careful to orient the template with the grain line. Note that there is a natural triangle formed when the hexagon is cut. These triangles can be used with other color hexagons to make the petal turn-back area. (See 4.12)

6. Place a rotary ruler on top of the template with the ½-inch line on top of the dotted line of the template.

7. Using the ruler as the rotary cutter guide, cut along its edge.

8. Cut around all six sides, through all four layers. You will have four pieces.

9. Repeat this until you have the total number needed for your project.

10. Place the H3C1 hexagon-shaped template on the backside of a fabric hexagon.

11. With a fabric-marking pencil, mark the points where the seam allowance meets the fold line, using the holes you poked into the template. Repeat this marking for all the hexagons.

12. Cut the triangle fabric into 5-inch selvedge-to-selvedge strips.

13. With the grain line along the cut edge of the fabric, place template H3CT on the fabric strip.

14. Place a rotary ruler on top of the template with the ¼-inch line on top of the dotted line of the template. (See 4.13)

15. Using the ruler as the rotary cutter guide, cut along its edge.

16. Repeat until you have six triangles for every hexagon piece.

17. After cutting the four layers, unfold the 5-inch strip and cut the remaining fabric into two triangles.

Fussy-cut triangles

One of the reasons to use a Version One unit is that you can fussy-cut your triangles. By cutting the six triangles from the same part of the fabric design, you can create a whirled or kaleidoscope appearance.

1. Make a plastic triangle template by tracing template H3CT onto template plastic with a permanent marker.

2. Pick a place on the fabric that looks interesting. Cut it out using the plastic triangle template.

3. Trace a part of the fabric design onto the plastic with the marker.

4. Use this marked triangle to cut five more triangles that are exact replicas of

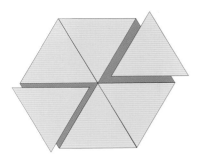

4.14 For ordinary triangles, place six triangles on top of a hexagon piece with right sides together.

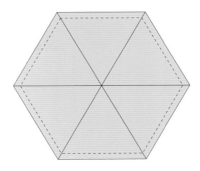

4.15 Join the triangles to the hexagon by sewing 1/4-inch from the edge around all six sides.

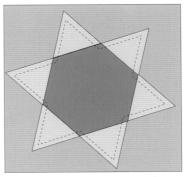

4.16 Rotate the star-shaped piece so that all edges are cut on the bias. Pin at the points.

the first one.

5. In the next step, place the fabric triangles right-side up on the hexagon, so that the "top" of each is in the center of the hexagon. Preview other patterns formed by the duplicated triangles, by rotating the part of the pattern that is placed in the center of the hexagon. Choose the arrangement that pleases you, and flip the triangles over to match right sides together. Skip to step 2 in the next section.

Construction

1. For ordinary triangles (not fussy-cut), place six triangles on top of a hexagon piece with the right sides together and the grain line of the triangles along the cut edge of the hexagon. (See 4.14)
2. Join the triangles to the hexagon by sewing ¼-inch from the edge around all six sides, crossing the stitching lines at the corners. It's helpful to use a dual-feed or walking foot. (See 4.15)
3. Trim the seam to approximately ⅛-inch along the sides of the hexagon.
4. Press the triangles open with the seam allowance toward the triangles. This forms a six-pointed star.
5. Place this star-shaped piece onto the square of star fabric, right sides together.
6. Rotate the star-shaped piece so that all edges are cut on the bias. (See 4.16)
7. Pin at the points to secure the bias edges.
8. Sew along all the edges of the pieced star, making the inner corner turns at the dots marked on the hexagon.
9. Decrease the stitch length as you approach the corner dot and for a ½-inch after making the turn. This is an inside corner that will be stressed during the turning process. (See Helpful Hint)
10. Cross the stitching lines at the points. These areas will be trimmed quite close, and the shorter stitches will keep them from pulling out when turned.
11. Using scissors, cut out the star-shaped piece ⅛-inch from the seam line, being careful not to get too close to the stitching.
12. Trim the outside points and clip the inside corners to ease the turning.

Batting

Use of batting is optional, but in many cases, it is desirable. It's very easy to include because it's added as a small piece within each unit.

1. For ease, use a template. Photocopy the H3C1 template (hexagon-shaped) made previously, and cut it out inside the dotted line.
2. Unfold the batting as it comes out of the package.
3. Refold it into four smoothed layers.
4. Cut a strip of batting the same width as the batting template.
5. Place the batting template on the strip.
6. Place a rotary ruler on the template and line up the edge of the ruler with the

Helpful Hint

❖❖❖

In step 9, it's a good idea to shorten your machine's stitch length around the outside of the points and at the inside of the corners. These areas will be trimmed quite close, and the shorter stitches will keep them from pulling out

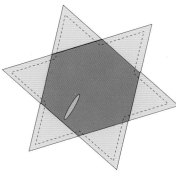

4.17 For Version One, cut a slash 2 inches wide through just one layer, across the bias in the hexagon-shaped piece.

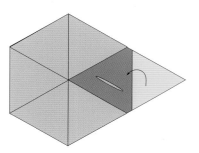

4.18 Fold the six points to the center so that the flaps lie flat and the points meet without gaps. Version One will look like this.

4.19 For Version Two, face the star-shaped piece up and cut the slash through just one layer.

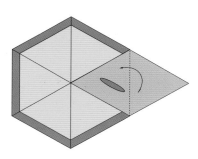

4.20 A Version Two unit will look like this when the flaps are folded flat.

edge of the template.

7. Cut through four layers of batting.
8. Repeat until you have the number of batting pieces needed. (Save the cutoffs for use later in filler pieces.)

Attaching the batting

1. Align the piece of batting on the wrong side of the fabric so that it is centered between the inner corners of the backside star.
2. Leave a little space all around the edge.
3. Spray-fuse or press-fuse the batting to the fabric.

Cutting the slash (Version One)

For Version One, the slash is cut on the bias in the hexagon-shaped center piece of fabric.

1. Before cutting, fold a point over the area to be sure a folded petal will cover the slash.
2. With the inner fabric facing up, cut a slash 2 inches wide through just one layer, across the bias in the hexagon-shaped piece about 1½ inches in from where the fold will be. (See 4.17)
3. Turn the piece right-side out by gently pulling the fabric through the slash. Pay special attention to the corners so that all the fabric is turned to the seam allowance. (See "Turning Right-Side Out," page 404.)
4. Carefully finger-press the seam open before pressing with an iron to make the process easier. Press the star shape flat.
5. Fold the six points to the center so that the flaps lie flat and the points meet without gaps. (See 4.18)
6. Press.

Cutting the slash (Version Two)

For Version Two, the slash is cut in the center area of the star-shaped inner piece.

1. Before cutting the slash, fold a point over the area to be sure that the folded flap will cover the slash.
2. With the star-shaped piece facing up, cut the slash through just one layer. Refer to the "Slash" section of Chapter Once, page 402. (See 4.19)

Turn right-side out, and press as instructed in steps 3 through 6 in the Version One slash-cutting instructions. A Version Two unit will look like illustration 4.20.

4.21 Place two rectangle halves right sides together and stitch across the short side, leaving a 1½-inch opening.

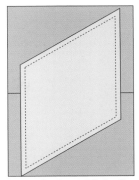

4.22 Place the front-fabric diamond on the rectangle, right sides together.

Filler Pieces

Hexagons can be arranged two ways. Units can be nestled together as in the "Fall Festival" project shown in the "Basic Hexagon" section, page 442. Or, they can be set point-to-point as in the "Petals in the Ferns" project at the end of this section, page 452.

Instructions for the side filler pieces and half-hexagons used in the nestled version are included in the Basic Hexagon section.

In this section, instructions are given for diamond-shaped filler pieces.

Diamond Filler Pieces

Pillow-style filler pieces are advantageous over the awkward joining of multi-sided, flapped pieces. Diamond filler pieces have no flaps. Rather, they are like little pillows with double layers of batting inside to match the thickness of the adjacent hexagonal units.

Diamond filler pieces are used whole between four hexagons set point to point.

Cut in half horizontally, they fill in at the top and bottom edges.

Along the side, diamonds are cut vertically. These filler pieces are set on the backside of the project overlapping the space between units.

On the front side, the hexagon-flaps are opened and the pieces are joined through the overlapped area under the flaps.

Construction

1. Photocopy template H3CD on page 506 and cut it out on the outer solid line.
2. Cut front fabric into diamonds, using the template, ruler, and rotary cutter.
3. Cut the back fabric into 6- by 11-inch rectangles and cut these in half, leaving 5½- by 6-inch rectangles.
4. Place two rectangle halves right sides together and stitch across the short side, leaving a 1½-inch opening. This opening will be used later to flip the diamonds right-side out. (See 4.21)
5. Press the rectangle open and flat.
6. Place the front-fabric diamond on the rectangle, right sides together. (See 4.22)
7. Sew along the outside edges, crossing the stitching at the corners.
8. Trim the seam allowance to approximately ⅛-inch.
9. Spray-fuse or press a smaller diamond-shaped piece of batting to the inside of the front fabric. There are usually enough cutoffs from the hexagon batting to fill in the center area of the diamond. Use two triangle-shaped pieces or four right triangles for this area.
10. Leave ¼-inch along the edge of the seam lines free of batting, as this area will

4.23 Flip the diamond to the right side by gently pulling the outer fabric through the opening left in the back fabric.

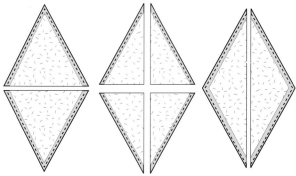

4.24 Cut the sewn diamond horizontally or vertically, depending on the number needed for your project.

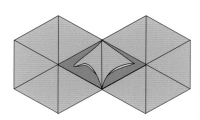

4.25 Open the petal flaps of two touching hexagons. Match the fold lines, pin together, and sew in the fold.

be sewn through during the joining process. Having batting too near the fold causes lumps.

11. Flip the diamond to the right side by gently pulling the outer fabric through the opening left in the back fabric. Pay special attention to the points and corners so that all the fabric is turned to the seam allowance. (See 4.23)

12. Press.

Diamonds that are to be cut horizontally or vertically can be made by sewing two whole diamond-shaped pieces together.

1. Cut front and back diamond-shaped pieces.
2. With right sides together, place a front diamond on a back diamond.
3. Sew around all sides.
4. Fuse a double layer of batting to the center area. Use the cutoffs from the hexagons.
5. Cut the sewn diamond horizontally or vertically, depending on the number needed for your project. (See 4.24)
6. Cutting a diamond into four pieces makes corner triangles. The finished edge will be at the corner.
7. The cut edges will be bound.

Joining

1. Arrange the pieces according to the project or your own design.
2. Once the arrangement is complete, sew the units together. (It is easier to join the horizontal seams first, creating vertical strips.)
3. Open the petal flaps of two touching hexagons. (See 4.25)
4. Match the fold lines, pin together, and sew in the fold.
5. Join all the touching hexagons into vertical strips. You may want to fold back and topstitch the center petal areas before joining. (See part "A" in illustration 4.26)

Joining the filler diamonds

1. Place two joined strips of hexagons right-side down on your work area with the points of the hexagons touching.
2. With the opening facing the back of the project, place whole diamond-filler pieces so they evenly overlap the space between the hexagons. The top and bottom points of adjacent diamonds will overlap.
3. Pin the diamonds onto the back of the hexagons, catching just one layer of hexagon fabric.
4. Alternatively, place masking or other easily removable tape at 2-inch intervals along the diamonds. For photos of this technique, refer to the "Filler Units" section in Chapter Six, pages 489 through 491.
5. Turn the grouped pieces to the front. Open the petal flaps of the hexagon

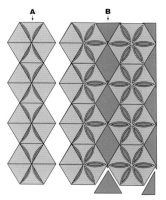

4.26 Join touching hexagons into vertical strips. Then use filler diamonds to join strips together.

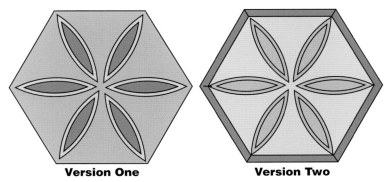

Version One   **Version Two**

4.27 Version One hexagons have contrasting outlines around the petal areas. Version Two units, with triangles on the outside, have an outline around the edge of the hexagon.

units that lie over the filler piece and pin across the fold of the flaps.

6. Sew along the fold lines and through the overlapping areas of the filler unit, being careful not to catch the petal flaps in the seam.

7. Return the flaps to their original folded position and pin to the center of the hexagon.

8. Repeat for each of the filler diamonds. Some adjustment to the upper and lower overlapping points may be necessary.

9. Once you have joined two vertical strips of hexagons, you may want to fold back and topstitch the petal flaps in those hexagons that are already joined. (See "B" in illustration 4.26)

10. Press.

Border/Binding

1. Refer to the "Border" and "Binding" sections of Chapter One for instructions, pages 398 and 396.

2. Prepare and apply border or binding fabric strips per the project instructions.

3. Complete the petal flap turning and topstitching.

The Version One hexagons have contrasting outlines around the petal areas.

Version Two units, with triangles on the outside, have an outline around the edge of the hexagon. (See 4.27)

Helpful Hint

◆◆◆

In larger projects, the joined fabric pieces become quite large and unwieldy. By doing some of the topstitching as you go, you can avoid some of the wrestling with the larger pieces later.

Petals in the Ferns
Accented-Petal Hexagon
(Version One)

Finished size: 34 by 38 inches
Difficulty level: Intermediate
Block size: 8⅜ by 9¾ inches

This quilt evokes memories of a spring hike through dense woods. It's shear delight to find a cluster of bright blossoms poking through the damp leaves.

Choosing a mix of shades creates light and dark areas. For overall consistency in appearance, limit the petal areas to just two colors.

Fabric requirements

Inside	⅔-yard each of four shades of pink, or 2⅔- yard of one fabric
Outside	3⅓ yards green for squares
	¾-yard green for backside of diamonds
Border	½-yard fern/leaf green for border
Diamonds	¾-yard fern/leaf green
Batting	2 yards of 45 inches wide

Templates

H3C1	Hexagon	Two copies taped together
H3CT	Triangle	One copy
H3CD	Diamond	One copy

Cutting plan

Green (tone on tone)		Twelve 18½-inch squares
		Twelve 6- by 11-inch rectangles for diamonds
Pink	H3C1	Three hexagons each of four shades of pink
Pink	H3CT	Twenty-four triangles from each of four shades of pink
Fern	H3CD	Twelve 6- by 11-inch diamonds
		Four 4½-inch-wide border strips
Batting		Twelve hexagons cut on the inside line of template H3C1
		Four 1¾- by 38-inch strips for border
		Save cutoffs for filling diamond pieces

Specific instructions

1. Follow the instructions in the "Accented-Petal Hexagon" section of this chapter, beginning on page 444.
2. Make twelve pink and green hexagon units and twelve diamond-shaped filler pieces.
3. Make six whole diamonds with openings.
4. Cut the other six diamonds as follows: two horizontally, one into fourths for the corners, and three vertically for the sides.
5. Arrange the pieces as shown in the project photo.

"Petals in the Ferns," shown above 34 by 38 inches, expresses the delight experienced by finding a cluster of bright blossoms poking through fern leaves on the floor of the forest.

6. Join the units in three columns of four units each. You may wish to fold back the petals and topstitch the center areas of each strip before joining them. This makes it easier to manage in the sewing machine at this stage.

7. Sew the four border strips as instructed in the "Border" section of Chapter One, page 398.

Helpful Hint

◆◆◆

Be sure to read through the special instructions for four-color hexagons before starting your project.

Four-Part Hexagons

The "Four-Part Hexagon" pattern gives you the greatest flexibility for color choice and placement. Because each part of the flower is a different color, really exciting effects are possible.

You can choose to make subtle shades for the outlines, or stark contrast for bright and dramatic looks.

You can use just two triangle colors and two hexagon colors for allover consistency.

It's the ultimate for a leaded glass effect, as every area is outlined.

You also may mix up the inside hexagon colors to vary the flower effects; and, as with all the other techniques, you may choose to mix and match all parts. This may turn out to be scrappy or raucous!

In the "Turkish Bazaar" project, at the end of this chapter, note how the dark petal edges stand out against the red background, and the outer edge is defined by the second red print.

The technique for making these units is very similar to the "Accented-Petal Hexagon." In this case, two-pieced stars are sewn together. There is an inside-pieced star and an outside-pieced star. Both are made by sewing six triangles to a center hexagon.

The inside triangles are the turn-back part of the flower petal. The inside hexagon will show as the center of the petals.

The hexagon part of the outside-pieced star shows as the backside of the project and the outline at the edge of the hexagon. The triangles sewn to it are folded toward the front and form the background for the flower.

Special instructions for four colors

Follow the instructions for "Accented-Petal Hexagons" in the previous setion of this chapter, page 444, with the following modifications. (Read through them thoroughly before beginning your project.)

1. Choose four fabrics. The inner hexagon is the petal-reveal. The inner triangle fabric forms the petal-accent. The front triangle fabric surrounds the petals, and the backside fabric outlines the outer edge of the front.

2. Using hexagon-shaped template H3C1 on page 503 and triangle template H3CT on page 504, cut each fabric into the shape designated for its position in the unit. For each unit, you will need one inner and one outer hexagon, and six each of the inner and outer triangles.

3. Mark dots through the holes in the template at the corners on the wrong side of the inner hexagon.

4. Sort your inner and outer hexagons and triangles into groups. If you are using several fabrics in more than one position, label which fabric goes where.

5. Skip the step that prepares outer squares.

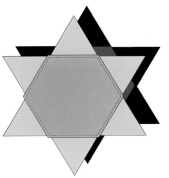

4.28 With right sides together, place an inside star on an outside star.

4.29 These two illustrations show the same unit, but with different hexagon colors in the slash. One has the red for the inner petal color and the other has orange. Note how the areas switch places when reversed.

Construction

1. Prepare an inner star-shaped unit. Following the instructions in the "Accented-Petal" section (page 444), construct an inner star from the inner hexagon and six inner triangles.
2. Press the seam allowance in toward the hexagon.
3. Prepare an outer star-shaped unit. Place six outer triangles around an outer hexagon piece with the right sides together and the grain line of the triangles along the cut edges of the hexagon. (See 4.14)
4. After trimming the triangles, press the seam allowance out toward the triangles. This is opposite from the inner piece star. In the next step, these seams will lie flat against one another.
5. With right sides together, place an inside star on an outside star. (See 4.28)
6. Match the triangles at the points and at the seam allowances that were pressed in opposite directions. Pin at the points to secure the bias edges.
7. Sew along all the outside edges of the pieced-star, making the inner corner turns at the dots marked on the hexagon and crossing the stitching at the points.
8. Trim around the sides of the joined star-shaped pieces to approximately ⅛-inch, being careful not to get too close to the stitching.
9. Trim the outside points and clip the inside corners to ease the turning.

Batting

1. With a batting template cut from a copy of H3C1, cut a piece of batting.
2. Attach the batting to the wrong side of the outer hexagon fabric with temporary adhesive or by pressing.
3. Cut the slash in the inner hexagon at a point that will be covered by a folded petal flap.
4. Continue with the turning, pressing, and folding of the hexagon unit.
5. Prepare filler units as needed by following the instructions in either or both of the "Filler Piece" sections of the "Basic Hexagon" and/or "Accented-Petal Hexagon" sections of this chapter, pages 440 and 449.

Assembly

1. Arrange the pieces according to the project or your own design.
2. Join the units and add a border or binding per the instructions in Chapter One, page 398 or 396.
3. Turn back and topstitch petals.

This unit has two looks, depending on which hexagon color is slashed and designated as the inner color. (See 4.29)

Helpful Hint

❖❖❖

It's a good idea to shorten your machine's stitch length around the outside of the points and at the inside of the corners. These areas will be trimmed quite close and the shorter stitches will keep them from pulling out when turned.

Turkish Bazaar Pillow
Four-Part Hexagon

Finished size: 18 inches square
Difficulty level: Intermediate
Block size: 10-inch hexagon

Brighten up a room with this high-contrast pillow! Red, yellow, and black look rich and exotic.

Change to primary colors for kids, or to pastels for a sunny porch. It's easy to make with just one hexagon block. Use tone-on-tone black for a rich-textured background.

Fabric requirements

Inside petals	½-yard large red print
Front triangles	¼-yard yellow print
Hexagon border	½-yard red and black small figure
Petal-accent	black (included in background)
Background	½-yard black
Backing	½-yard muslin (inside pillow lining)
Border	½-yard red small figure
Backside	½-yard black
Batting	18 inches square
Pillow form	16 inches square

Templates

H3C1	Hexagon	Two copies taped together
H3CT	Triangle	One copy

Cutting plan

Red print	One hexagon
Red outline	One hexagon
Yellow print	Six triangles
Red border	Two 3-inch-wide strips
Black backside	Two 12½- by 18-inch rectangles
Black background	One 13½-inch square
	Six triangles
Muslin	One 18-inch square

The high contrast in fabric colors of the "Turkish Bazaar" design add drama to your home decor. Pillow shown above is 18 inches square; made by Laura Farson, 2001.

Specific instructions

1. Follow the instructions in the "Four-Part Hexagons" section of Chapter Five, page 454, to make the center hexagon block.
2. Sew the six yellow triangles onto the small, red-figured outline fabric hexagon. The black triangles are sewn onto the inner large red print hexagon.
3. Complete the petal turn-back and topstitching steps.

Continued on next page.

Make this design with country ginghams and lace for a feminine pillow.

Turkish Bazaar Pillow project continued
Pillow front

1. Sew the 3-inch red outer border fabric to the 13½-inch black square.
2. With right sides together, place a red strip along one edge and sew.
3. Trim the extra fabric from the strip even with the edge of the square.
4. Repeat on the opposite side of the square.
5. Open the strips and press the seam allowance toward the red.
6. Sew the second strip along one of the remaining sides across both red strips.
7. Trim.
8. Repeat for the last side.
9. Open the seams.
10. Press the seam allowance toward the red.
11. Place the hexagon on the center of the black square.
12. Find the center by folding in half both directions and finger-pressing the folds along the edge of the black square.
13. Line up the petals with the finger-pressed folds.
14. Spray-baste the block onto the fabric or pin at the corners.
15. Turn the pieces over and layer the 18-inch piece of batting on top of the backside.
16. Cut out and remove the batting behind the hexagon.
17. Layer the muslin over the batting.
18. Spray-fuse or press-fuse the batting and muslin backing. If using temporary adhesive spray, just lift the batting and spritz with a little spray to keep it in place. Do the same for the muslin layer.
19. Turn the layered group to the front. Topstitch along the outer edge of the hexagon block with monofilament thread. (I use the hemstitch with a narrow width.)
20. Sew a straight stitch with the monofilament thread through all layers around the inside edge of the outer border.

Change the fabrics to match your home's color scheme. Above is a variation in yellow.

Pillow back

The backside of the pillow has a slotted opening for ease of turning now and for changing or laundering later.

1. Prepare the back piece by folding over 2 inches on the long side of one of the black rectangles.
2. Topstitch along the raw edge of the turned piece. It will measure 10½ by 18 inches.
3. Place this hemmed rectangle right-side down on the front of the layered piece with three raw edges even with the front square.
4. Place the unhemmed piece on top so that its sides are even with the opposite side of the square. It will overlap about 4½ inches.
5. Pin the raw edges.
6. Sew around the square.
7. Trim the corners and flip to the outside through the slot in the black square.
8. Insert the 16-inch pillow form into the slot and arrange the front so that it is unwrinkled.

5 octagons

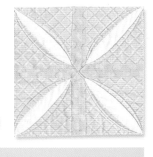

ctagons are so much fun because they have more petals and interesting filler pieces. In this chapter, you will learn how to make octagons with two, three, and four parts.

Like the other shapes, octagons can be made with as many color combinations as desired.

The procedure is identical to that of the hexagon; but as previously mentioned; filler pieces are of different shapes.

Eight is great! That could be you're mantra as you tackle the exciting possibilities an octagon can provide. Shown above is a quilt by Laura Farson that utilizes the "Basic Octagon" technique of two fabric colors.

Basic Octagons

The octagon or "stop sign" shape has eight sides. The middle space between connected units is a square. The edge units are right triangles or half-squares.

By having more petals than a hexagon, the shape is rounder and more flowery.

As with the basic hexagon, you may choose just two colors: one for the inside and one for the outside. Or, you can vary just the inside, while keeping the outside the same.

Finally, both the inside and outside can be different for a scrappier look.

Preparing the template

1. Photocopy template O2C on page 507 eight times.
2. Cut along the solid lines on all eight copies.

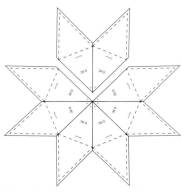

5.1 Join the halves into a star-shaped template.

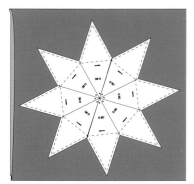

5.2 Place the template on one of the fabrics, rotated so no edge is parallel to the grain line.

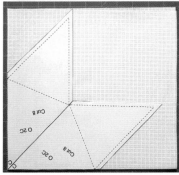

5.3 Place the template on the folded square with the center on the fabric. Line up the right-angled sides along the folded fabric edges.

3. Place two cutout copies on your rotary mat at right angles using the crossed lines of the mat as guides.

4. Matching the centers, tape the diamonds together two at a time. Four pieces form a straight line.

5. Join the halves into a star-shaped template. (See 5.1)

Fabric preparation

Organize your fabric choices into one pile for the inside pieces and one for the outside.

Outside fabric

1. After deciding which fabrics to use, fold the fabric selvedge to selvedge, and then fold again, matching the fold to the selvedge.

2. Using 45-inch-wide fabric, two 21-inch squares can be cut from each 21-inch length. Cut the outside fabric into the number of 21-inch squares needed. (I use the inch marks built into the rotary mat to make these cuts easier.)

3. Line up the fabric parallel to a horizontal line on the mat. Place the cut edge of the fabric just over the zero line.

4. Line up a ruler on the 21-inch line and cut along the edge of the ruler. This will give you a folded piece 21 inches by the width of the fabric. The easiest thing to do is just cut along the fold line. This piece will work just fine as an outside "square."

Inside fabric

From the inside fabric(s), you will cut out two stars of the same fabric at one time. If you don't want two star fabrics alike, unfold the fabric and cut through just one layer.

1. Spray the backside of the paper template with temporary adhesive spray.

2. Place the template on one of the fabrics, rotated so no edge is parallel to the grain line. All edges will be cut on the bias. (See 5.2)

3. Place a rotary ruler on top of the template, lining up the ¼-inch line with the dotted line of the template. Refer to the "Cutting" section in Chapter One, beginning on page 399.

4. Cut through both layers of fabric along the edge of the ruler with a rotary cutter. Avoid cutting through the seam allowance at the inside corners. (Olfa's rotary-point cutter is handy to cut these inside corners.)

5. Move the ruler around the template and repeat the cutting until the entire star is cut out. If you used folded fabric, there are two pieces.

6. Repeat this procedure for the number of star units needed.

5.4 Place one inside fabric star onto an outside fabric square.

5.5 Trim the seam allowance back to about 1/8-inch from the stitching, being very careful not to get too close.

Helpful Hint

♦♦♦

When sewing around the star, use your tie-down feature on your sewing machine at both the inside and outside corners; or, if not, decrease stitch length before and after crossing the corners.

Helpful Hint

♦♦♦

Trimming, as detailed in step 4 of "Construction," can be done with a rotary cutter and ruler, but there's a tendency to slip across the stitching, so I recommend using a scissors.

Alternative star-cutting procedure

This alternative is easier to cut out as four layers are cut at once, so there are fewer inside and outside corners. However, some of the edges are on the straight of grain and will be harder to turn. I suggest that you make a practice unit of each method and decide which you prefer.

1. Cut the inside fabric into 21-inch squares.
2. Fold one square in half and fold again to form a square.
3. Press the folds so that the cut edges are even.
4. Photocopy template O2C, page 507, twice.
5. Using the lines on your rotary mat, place each piece at right angles and tape together.
6. Spray some temporary adhesive on the back of the template.
7. Place this two-piece template on the folded square with the center on the folded corner. Be sure to line up the right-angled sides along the edges of the folded fabric square. (See 5.3)
8. Cut along the solid lines through all the layers.
9. Unfold, press open, and proceed.

Construction of octagon units

1. With right sides together, place one inside fabric star onto an outside fabric square, rotating the star so that all edges are on the bias. (See 5.4)
2. Pin the points of the star to secure the bias edges.
3. Sew along all the edges of the star, crossing the stitching at the points. Use a walking foot to keep the edges flat.
4. Trim the seam allowance back to approximately ⅛-inch from the stitching, being very careful not to get too close. (See 5.5 and Helpful Hint)
5. Snip across the outside corners to smooth them and clip inside corners to ease the turning.

Making the slash

1. At this point, remind yourself which fabric is for the outside and which is for the inside.
2. With the inner fabric facing up, cut a slash 2 inches wide through just one layer across the bias in the center in an area that will be covered by a folded flap.

Batting

Use of batting is optional, but in many cases is desirable. It's very easy to include because it's added as a small piece within each unit. (Refer to the "Batting" section in Chapter One, page 396.)

1. Begin by photocopying template O3C on page 508 twice.
2. Cut the two halves on the dotted line and tape them together.
3. With the batting out of the package, open and refold it so there are four layers.

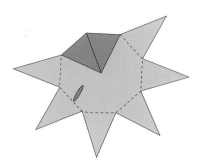

5.6 Fold the points to the center, forming an octagon as you go. Be sure to align the points so the corners lay flat.

5.7 Place these squares right sides together and sew around all but 1½ inches in the center of one side.

4. Cut a strip of batting the same width as the batting template.
5. Place the batting template on the cut strip.
6. Place a rotary ruler on the template and line up the edge of the ruler with the edge of the template.
7. Cut through four layers of batting.
8. Repeat until you have the number of batting pieces needed.

Attaching the batting

1. Fuse a piece of batting to the center of the inside surface of the outside fabric.
2. Align the piece of batting so that it is centered in the octagon.
3. Leave a little space all around the edge. This is the area that will be sewn through in the joining step.
4. Turn the piece right-side out by gently pulling the fabric through the slash. Pay special attention to the points so that all the fabric is turned to the seam allowance.
5. Press the star shape flat, making sure the seam allowances are fully open. A mini-iron is useful for this step.
6. Fold the points to the center, forming an octagon. (See 5.6)
7. Align the points so that the corners lay flat.
8. Press.

Prepare the remaining octagon stars in the same manner.

Once the octagons are complete, prepare the filler squares and side- and corner-triangle units.

Filler Pieces

The spaces and edges around the octagons are filled with fabric pieces. Such pieces include:

○ Pillow fillers
    a. Pillow squares – squares without flaps
    b. Edge triangle pillows – triangles without flaps
    c. Corner triangle pillows – small triangles without flaps

○ Flapped fillers
    a. Squares with flaps
    b. Triangles with flaps
    c. Corner triangles

The square and triangle pillow-filler pieces are plain without flaps. The insides are filled with two layers of batting to make up for the lack of layers. These filler, or connector, pieces are overlapped on the backside of the project and sewn through the inside of the octagon flaps. (Directions follow.)

The other style of filler piece is constructed with flaps just like the octagons. The flaps of the middle squares are folded to the center and can be turned back to

The spaces and edges around the octagons are filled with flapped squares, edge triangle pillows, and corner triangle pillows. Adding a binding will finish this piece.

make smaller petal units.

Side triangles also have flaps.

When all these filler flaps are turned back, they create a very busy floral look!

Pillow Squares

On pillow squares, all edges are finished.

1. Cut two 4¾-inch squares of fabric, one each of the front and the back fabrics.

2. Place these squares right sides together and sew around all but 1½ inches in the center of one side. (See 5.7)

3. Cut and fuse together two 3¾-inch squares of batting. The batting is cut smaller so that the edge of the filler piece is not too thick. This is the area that

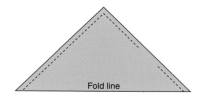

Fold line

5.8 Sew along the diagonal sides, leaving a 1-inch opening along one side.

is sewn through when joining the units.

4. Spray-baste or press-fuse the batting onto the center of the square.
5. Flip to the right side through the opening in the seam allowance. Pay special attention to the corners so that they are fully open.
6. Turn the seam allowance at the opening to the inside of the square.
7. Hand- or machine-stitch to close the opening.
8. Press the square flat.

Pillow Triangles

The fabric chosen for this piece will be the same on the back as on the front. Choose a fabric that looks good on both sides of the quilt. Even if it contrasts with the backside, the pieced effect can be quite nice.

1. Cut a 4¾-inch fabric square.
2. Fold it in half diagonally with the right sides together.
3. Sew along the diagonal sides, leaving a 1-inch opening along one side. (See 5.8)
4. Cut a 3¾-inch square piece of batting, and then cut it in half diagonally.
5. Fuse these two triangles of batting to make a double-thick triangle.
6. Fuse this triangle of batting to the center of the inside of the filler triangle.
7. Flip the piece right-side out through the opening in the seam allowance. Pay special attention to the corners so that all the fabric is turned to the seam allowance.
8. Press the edges of the seam allowance so they open to the inside of the triangle.
9. Hand- or machine-stitch to close the opening.

Pillow Triangle Corners

Corner triangles are the same color on the front and backside.

1. Cut a 4¾-inch square of fabric.
2. Cut the square in half diagonally.
3. Fold each triangle in half with the right sides together.
4. Sew along the two open sides leaving a 1-inch opening. This is a half-size version of the previous example.
5. Cut a 3¾-inch square piece of batting.
6. Cut the square of batting in half diagonally, and then cut each triangle of batting in half.
7. Fuse two quarters to make a double-thick triangle. Fuse this layered batting piece to the center of the triangle.
8. Flip the triangle to the right side. Pay special attention to the corners.
9. Tuck the seam allowance at the opening to the inside and press flat.
10. Sew the opening closed with a few hand or machine stitches.

Fast-Folded Flowers

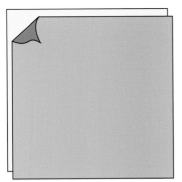

5.9 Cut two 6½-inch squares: one each of the inside and outside fabrics.

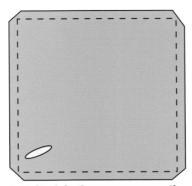

5.10 Slash in the corner across the bias and turn right-side out. Pay attention to the corners so all fabric is turned to seam allowance.

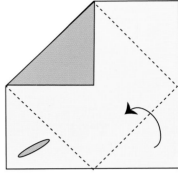

5.11 Press flat and then press the corners to the middle.

Squares with Flaps

1. Cut two 6½-inch squares: one each of the inside and outside fabrics. (See 5.9)
2. Place the two squares right sides together and stitch all the way around.
3. Spray-baste a 3¾-inch square of batting to the wrong side of the outer fabric on the diagonal.
4. Slash in the corner across the bias and turn right-side out. Pay special attention to the corners so that all the fabric is turned to the seam allowance. (See 5.10)
5. Press flat and then press the corners to the middle. (See 5.11)

Corner Triangles

The corner triangle is the easiest to make. It is simply two squares of fabric folded diagonally with a triangle of batting tucked in between the layers. Because it is only used for corners, the edges can remain raw as they are incorporated into the binding.

1. Cut two 4-inch squares of fabric. One of the two must be the front fabric. The other can be the front or any inner color, as it doesn't show. Use a fabric from the project, though, so that any shadowing through will be consistent in color.
2. Place the two squares wrong sides together, matching the sides.
3. With the proper fabric on the outside, fold the squares in half on the diagonal, matching the corners.
4. Cut a 3½-inch square of batting in half on the diagonal.
5. Insert one of the batting triangles into the space between the inner and outer fabric pieces.
6. Press the fold. The cut edges will be enclosed in the border or binding.

Filler Triangles with Flaps

1. Follow steps 1 through 3 in the "Squares with Flaps" section above.
2. Cut the squares in half. (See 5.12)
3. Turn the rectangles right-side out.
4. Press, having fully turned the corner fabric to the outside.
5. Fold the rectangle in half again with the background fabric on the outside, and gently crease the center. (See 5.13)
6. Open.
7. Fold the seamed corners to the crease on the diagonal, forming the triangle by keeping the short-seamed sides perpendicular to the base of the triangle. (See 5.14)

5.12 Cut the squares in half.

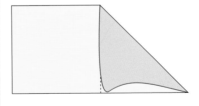

5.13 Fold the rectangle in half again with the background fabric on the outside, and gently crease the center.

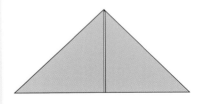

5.14 Fold the seamed corners to the crease on the diagonal, forming the triangle.

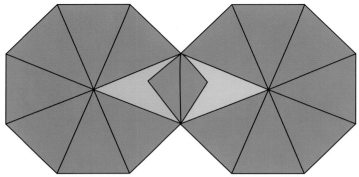

5.15 Match the fold, pin, and sew in the fold.

Organizing the pieces

1. Arrange all the pieces according to the project layout or your plan.
2. Once the arrangement is complete, sew the octagon units together. It is easier to join the horizontal seams first, creating vertical strips.
3. Open the petal flaps of two touching octagons.
4. Match the fold, pin, and sew in the fold. (See 5.15)
5. Return the petal flaps to their folded position.

Joining the filler pieces

These instructions apply to either pillow-filler pieces or flapped-filler pieces. Once all the horizontal lines of the octagon pieces are sewn together, the center squares and edge triangles are added. The filler pieces are designed to overlap the space between the octagon pieces. It is placed over the hole between the four joined octagon pieces on the backside of the project. This makes the joints fully covered.

1. Place a filler square over the space between the octagon-shaped units with the flaps of the square left folded throughout the process. Slip it through the hole to the back and line up the corners of the square with those on the octagon pieces.
2. Pin the square in position.(Refer to the photographs 6.14 through 6.16 in the "Joining" section of Chapter Six, page 491.)
3. Turn the group of pieces over and fasten the square on the back with masking tape.
4. Flip the group of pieces back to face the front.
5. Open the four petal flaps of just the octagons and pin across the fold of the flaps. I remove the tape at this point, because some tapes gum up the sewing machine needle.
6. Sew along the fold lines inside the octagon flaps and through the center square, being careful not to catch the octagon petal flaps in the seam.
7. Return the petal flaps to their original folded position and pin at their centers.
8. Repeat for each of the center square units.

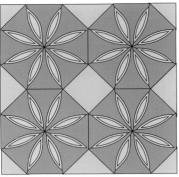

5.16 Insert filler pieces.

Attaching filler triangles

Pillow and flapped triangles can be joined just like squares.

1. Leave the flaps folded and overlap the triangle on the backside of the project.
2. Open the two octagon flaps that touch the triangle.
3. Sew through the inside of the octagon flaps. The octagon flaps are folded back to their original positions.

As an alternative, flapped triangles can be joined by sewing between the folds of the touching flaps of the triangle and the two octagons.

1. Open the flaps and match the fold lines.
2. Pin.
3. Sew through the folds. The flaps are folded back to their original positions.

This method is a little harder to do, as you have to make a turn at the peak of the triangle. Its advantage is a neater appearance when finished. (See 5.16)

4. Bind according to the "Binding" section in Chapter One, page 396.
5. Once all the pieces are joined and the binding is complete, fold back the petals on the main pieces and on the filler triangles, if desired. The flaps can be left "straight" and topstitched in place creating contrasting lines of petal fabric. Where the filler pieces are small, this is a very pleasing effect.

In the Pink
Basic Octagon

Finished size: 21½ inches square
Difficulty level: Intermediate
Block size: 8¾ inches square

Three different pinks of the same fabric group exhibit just enough shading to highlight the subtle flowery shapes. This monochromatic project has a very rich and elegant look.

Fabric requirements:

Inside	1½ yards light pink
Outside	1⅓ yards medium pink
	1 yard dark pink
Border	(included with outside fabric)
Batting	⅓-yard of 45 inches wide

Template

O2C	Octagon	Eight copies

Cutting plan

Light pink	Four octagon stars
	Three 6½-inch squares
Medium pink	Four 21-inch squares
Dark pink	Three 6½-inch squares
	Four 3½-inch squares
	Four 3½-inch strips
Batting	Four 9-inch octagons

Layout
Two rows of two.

Specific instructions
Follow the instructions in the "Basic Octagon" section of Chapter Five, page 461.

This project is made with folded filler squares. Make three whole squares. You will need one whole square and two that will be cut in half.

Making whole squares
1. Place one 6½-inch light pink square and one 6½-inch dark pink square right sides together and sew a ¼-inch seam allowance. (Refer to the instructions for flapped filler squares in Chapter Five, page 467.)
2. Make a slash; flip to the right side, press, and fold.
3. Repeat for the other two squares.

Use "In the Pink" as a throw on your little girl's bed, or add a sleeve and hang it on the wall. Either way, it brings a feminine elegance to her bedroom. The above quilt was made by Laura Farson, 2000.

Making half-squares

1. Make the four half-squares, by the same method as used for the whole squares, except cut them in half rather than making a slash.

2. Flip to the right side through the cut side, press, and fold.

3. Each corner triangle is made from two 3½-inch squares, placed right-side out and folded diagonally. These are joined with no seamed edge, as they will be encased in the border.

4. After assembling, add the 3½-inch border strips per the instructions in Chapter One, page 398.

5. Turn back and topstitch the petals.

Switching Blue
Basic Octagon

Finished size: 26½ inches square
Difficulty level: Intermediate
Block size: 8¾ inches square

This nine-block quilted wall hanging is a lesson in contrast and how it affects the appearance of a block.

Note that the center block in the example is actually made with the three-color octagon instructions. It's the same shape and size of the other eight blocks, but it looks completely different due to the reversal of dark and light.

Fabric requirements

Inside	⅝-yard light blue
	⅝-yard medium blue
	⅝-yard medium dark blue
	1¼ yards dark blue
Outside	3⅓ yards cream print
Binding	Scrap strips
Batting	¾-yard of 45 inches wide

Template

O2C	Large octagon	Eight copies

Cutting plan

Light blue	Two octagon stars
Medium blue	Two octagon stars
	Eight 3½-inch squares
Medium/dark blue	Two octagon stars
Dark blue	Three octagon stars
Cream	Nine 21-inch squares
	Sixteen 6½-inch squares
Batting	Nine 9-inch octagons

Layout

Three rows of three.

Experimenting with different contrast fabrics can dramatically affect the appearance of a block, as is evidenced in "Switching Blue," made by Laura Farson, 2000.

Specific instructions

Follow the instructions in the "Basic Octagon" section of Chapter Five, page 461.

This project is made with flapped filler squares. There is no batting in the filler squares. Make eight squares. You will need four whole squares and four that will be cut in half.

Making whole squares

1. Place two 6½-inch cream-colored squares with right sides together and sew. Refer to the instructions for "Squares with Flaps" in Chapter Five, page 467.
2. Make a slash, flip to the right side, press, and fold.
3. Repeat for the remaining three whole squares.

Continued on next page.

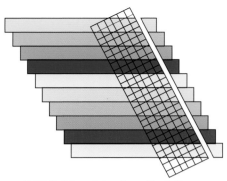

5.17 Cut ten strips from the left-over fabric scraps. Sew these strips together along the long sides with a 1-inch offset at one edge. Staggering saves fabric.

Switching Blue project continued

Making half-squares

1. To make the eight half-squares, repeat step 1 of "whole squares" (previous page). Then, cut them in half before the slash-making step.
2. Flip to the right side through the cut side, press, and fold.

Corner triangles

Each corner triangle is made from two 3½-inch squares, placed right-side out and folded diagonally. These are joined with no seamed edge, as they will be encased in the binding.

Multicolor center block

The cutting plan has an extra dark blue octagon star in lieu of the multicolor version.

1. To make a multicolor block in the center, use the "Accented-Petal Octagon" instructions on the next page.
2. Cut two triangle pieces from each of the blue fabrics. The center octagon and the inside fabric square are cream.

Special binding instructions

1. Cut ten 1¾- by at least 15-inch strips from the leftover fabric scraps. If you don't have sufficient length, join some scraps.
2. Sew these strips together along the long sides with a 1-inch offset at one edge. Staggering saves fabric. (See 5.17)
3. Press seams to one side.
4. Place a rotary ruler on the strips with the 30-degree line along the horizontal edge of the striped piece.
5. Trim off the uneven edges, and then cut eight 1½-inch strips at a 30-degree angle.
6. Sew two strips together, keeping the color sequence in order.
7. Use the four strips to bind the four sides of the project. Use the "Borders" instructions in Chapter One, page 398, to apply this binding. The striped strips are cut like border pieces rather than folded around the corners like binding.
8. Finish by turning back the petals and topstitching.
9. Press.

Accented-Petal Octagons

The "Accented-Petal Octagon" pattern can be folded two ways.

Version One

Version One forms an outline of the flower petals with a third color. This is comparable to the "Petals in the Ferns" hexagon project, page 453.

The basic unit is a star-shaped piece.

The inside of the star is an octagon with eight triangles sewn to it. These triangles form the outline of the flower petal.

The inside central octagon is the inner part of the petal that is revealed when turned back.

The triangle fabric outlines the petals.

The outside of the star is a single piece of fabric that, when folded, forms the back of the unit and the front area surrounding the petals.

Version Two

Version Two's star-shaped unit is folded the opposite way of Version One. The octagon and triangles are on the outside, and the single star-shaped fabric piece is on the inside.

The octagon-shaped piece that forms the back of the unit folds over to the front and outlines the unit.

The triangles form the front outlines of the petal area. By fussy-cutting these triangles, you can create some whirling patterns. The petal-outline and petal-reveal are the same inner fabric.

In the three Version Two projects called "Dreaming in Flowers," pages 479 through 481, notice how the front areas formed by the triangles are whirling designs. These triangles are fussy-cut. Each quilt in the series has front triangles of the same floral print. The inner fabric and the filler pieces were changed to create different effects.

Preparing the templates

1. Photocopy template O3C on page 508 twice and O3CT on page 499 once.
2. Cut the half-octagons and the triangle shapes along the outside solid lines.
3. Tape the octagon halves together to make a whole.
4. With a pointed object, such as the tip of a stiletto or the point of a compass, poke a hole at each of the eight corners of the dotted line of the octagon template. These points mark the intersection of the fold line and the seam allowance. They will be used to mark the corners of the seam line on the cut fabric octagon.

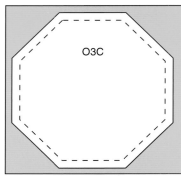

O3C

5.18 Place the octagon-shaped template O3C on the folded fabric designated for the octagon. Orient it with the grain line marking.

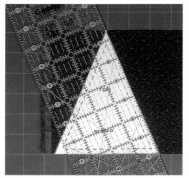

5.19 With the grain line along the cut edge of the fabric, place template O3CT on the fabric strip.

Helpful Hint

◆◆◆

Spray a little temporary adhesive on the back of the template to keep it from slipping while cutting. Place a rotary ruler on top of the template with the ¼-inch line on top of the dotted line of the template.

Construction

1. Choose three fabrics: one for the octagon, one for the triangles, and one for the star.
2. Fold the fabric chosen for the star selvedge to selvedge and then turn the fold to selvedge.
3. Cut 21-inch lengths of the folded fabric. Use the horizontal line of your rotary mat to line up the selvedge edge of the fabric. Place the cut edge just over the zero line and line up fabric along the horizontal.
4. Place a rotary ruler on the fabric at the 21-inch mark. Be sure it lines up with both the upper and lower indicator.
5. Cut along the edge of the ruler.
6. Open this 21-inch length and cut it on the first fold. The square will measure approximately 21 inches both ways, as most fabric is about 44 to 45 inches wide. Unless there is a significant shortage, this should be adequate to match with the octagon star piece.
7. Fold the octagon and triangle fabrics, selvedge to selvedge, and then turn the fold to selvedge, creating four layers.
8. Place the octagon-shaped template O3C on the folded fabric designated for the octagon, being careful to orient the template with the grain line. (See 5.18)
9. Place a rotary ruler on top of the template with the ½-inch line on top of the dotted line of the template.
10. Using the ruler as the rotary cutter guide, cut along its edge.
11. Cut around all eight sides through all four layers. You will have four pieces.
12. Repeat this until you have the total number needed for your project.
13. Place the O3C octagonal template on the backside of the fabric octagon. With a fabric marking pencil, mark the points where the seam allowance meets the fold line, using the holes you poked into the template.
14. Cut the triangle fabric into 5⅛-inch selvedge-to-selvedge strips.
15. With the grain line along the cut edge of the fabric, place template O3CT on the fabric strip. (See 5.19 and Helpful Hint)
16. Repeat until you have eight triangles for every octagon piece.

Fussy-cut triangles

1. To make fussy-cut triangles, trace template O3CT onto template plastic.
2. Use the seam lines as a guide when finding a motif on your fabric. When you find a pleasing area outlined by the triangle, mark the template with an outline of a prominent part of the pattern.
3. Cut out eight identical triangles from the same part of the pattern.
4. Arrange the triangles in a pleasing pattern so that all the center points are the same motif.

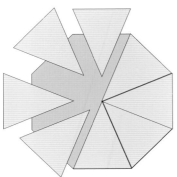

5.20 Place eight triangles on top of an octagonal piece with the right sides together and the grain line of the triangles along the cut edge of the octagon.

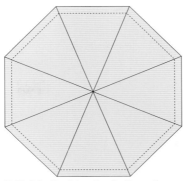

5.21 Join the triangles to the octagon by sewing around the eight sides.

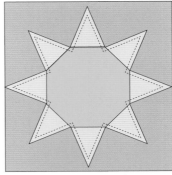

5.22 Place star-shaped piece onto the fabric, right sides together, rotating the star so all edges are on the bias. Sew along all edges.

Construction

1. Place eight triangles on top of an octagonal piece with the right sides together and the grain line of the triangles along the cut edge of the octagon. Note: You may ignore the grain line for fussy-cut triangles. (See 5.20)
2. Join the triangles to the octagon by sewing ¼-inch from the edge around all eight sides. (See 5.21)
3. Trim the seam to approximately ⅛-inch along the sides of the octagon.
4. Press the triangles open with the seam allowance toward the triangles. This forms an eight-pointed star.
5. Place this star-shaped piece onto the 21-inch fabric square, right sides together, rotating the star so all edges are on the bias. Pin at the points to secure the bias edges.
6. Sew along all the edges of the pieced-star, making the inner corner turns at the dots marked on the octagon piece. Cross the stitching at the points. (See 5.22)
7. Using scissors, cut out the star-shaped piece ⅛-inch from the seam line, being careful not to get too close to the stitching.
8. Trim the outside points and clip the inside corners to ease the turning.

Batting

1. Photocopy the O3C template made earlier and cut it inside the dotted line.
2. With the batting out of the package, unfold it carefully.
3. Refold it into four smooth layers.
4. Cut a strip of batting the same width as the batting template – approximately 9¼ inches.
5. Place the batting template on the strip.
6. Place a rotary ruler on the template and line up the edge of the ruler with the edge of the template. Cut through four layers of batting.
7. Repeat until you have the number of batting pieces needed.

Attaching the batting

In Version One, the backside of the unit will be the whole star-shaped piece. In Version Two, the octagon piece is the back of the unit.

1. Fuse a piece of batting to the fabric that will form the backside of the unit by pressing or by spraying it with temporary adhesive.
2. Align the piece of batting so that it is centered.

Helpful Hint

◆◆◆

In step 6 of "Construction," it's a good idea to shorten your machine's stitch length around the outside of the points and at the inside of the corners. These areas will be trimmed quite close, and the shorter stitches will keep them from pulling out when turned.

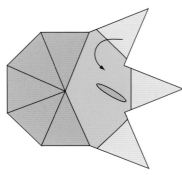

5.23 Fold the eight points to the center so that the triangles lie flat and the points meet without gaps in this Version One octagon.

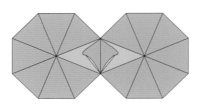

5.24 Join the pieces.

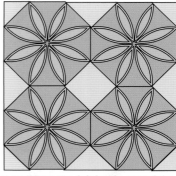

5.25 When the joining is complete, bind if desired, and turn back the petal areas.

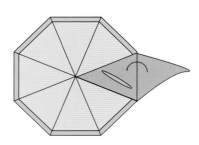

5.26 Press the folded points to complete a Version Two octagon.

Cutting the slash (Version One)

For Version One, the slash is cut in the octagon piece. For Version Two, cut the slash in the center area of the whole star-shaped piece in the center area. In both cases, this is the fabric without the batting attached.

1. Before cutting, fold a point over the area to be sure that a folded petal will cover the slash. Refer to the "Slash" section of Chapter One, page 402.
2. Cut the slash on the bias in the octagon-shaped piece. (See 5.23 for a suggested location.)
3. Turn the piece right-side out by gently pulling the fabric through the slash. Pay special attention to the corners so that all the fabric is turned to the seam allowance.
4. Press the star shape flat, making sure the seam allowances are fully open. A mini-iron is helpful with this step.
5. Fold the eight points to the center so that the triangles lie flat and the points meet without gaps. (See 5.23)
6. Press.
7. Prepare the remaining octagons in the same manner.
8. Once all are complete, prepare center squares and side-filler triangles per the instructions in the "Basic Octagon" section of this chapter, page 461.
9. Arrange the pieces according to the instructions in the project or to your own plan.
10. Join the pieces. Refer to "Joining" section in Chapter One, beginning on page 16. (See 5.24)
11. When the joining is complete, bind if desired. For Version Two projects, the outlined octagons can be left unbound, but secure the joined pieces carefully with backstitches at the outside joints.
12. Turn back the petal areas. (See 5.25)

Cutting the slash (Version Two)

1. Before cutting, check the slash location so that the folded petal will completely cover it.
2. Cut the slash on the bias in the center area of the star-shaped inner fabric piece. (Refer to 5.26 for a suggested location.)
3. Repeat steps 3, 4, and 5 of Version One.
4. Press the folded points to complete a Version Two octagon. (See 5.26)
5. Prepare the remaining octagons in the same manner.
6. Follow Version One steps 8 through 12 to complete this version.

You can dream up a number of variations to the "Accented-Petal Octagon" design, as evidenced by the three "Dreaming In Flowers" designs. Two are shown here, "Dreaming in Flowers I" (above) and "Dreaming in Flowers II" (below). Directions for these projects and a third variation follow on the next two pages.

Dreaming in Flowers
I, II & III
Accented-Petal Octagon

(Version Two)

Finished size: 17½ inches square
Difficulty level: Advanced
Block size: 8¾ inches square

Each color selection reminds me of a different time of the year: rich reds for Valentine's Day, white for summer, and dusty rose for fall. These three projects are a study in background color.

The triangles in all three projects are cut from the same floral fabric. Just the backgrounds have been changed!

These also would look pretty using a tiny, multicolored, flowered print.

Fabric requirements

Floral	1½ yards for three four-block projects
Inside/filler piece	1⅓ yards for each project
Burgundy back	⅓-yard for each project
Batting	⅓-yard of 45 inches wide

Templates

O3C	Large octagon	Two copies
O3CT	Octagon triangle	One copy

Cutting plan for each project

Floral	Four sets of eight fussy-cut triangles
Inside	Four 21-inch squares
Filler pieces	Two 4½-inch squares
	Four 4½-inch squares for triangles
Burgundy	Four octagons
Batting	Four octagons

Note how the cream-colored background makes the flower shapes fade away in this variation, "Dreaming In Flowers III."

Specific instructions

1. Follow the instructions in the "Accented-Petal Octagon" section of Chapter Five, page 475. Pay particular attention to the "Fussy-cut triangles" section.
2. Prepare four Version Two octagons, one filler square, and four filler triangles. The filler pieces in this project are made like little pillows.
3. Save your batting cutoffs from the large octagons and use them to fill the triangles.
4. Arrange the pieces and join.
5. Fold back and topstitch the petal areas. (This project is not bound.)

Helpful Hint

◆◆◆

When constructing four-part octagons, be sure to read through all the modifications before beginning.

Four-Part Octagons

The "Four-Part Octagon" pattern gives you the greatest flexibility for color choice and placement.

Because each part of the flower is a different color, very exciting effects are possible. You can choose to make subtle shades for the outlines or stark contrast for bright and dramatic looks. You can use just two triangle colors and two octagon colors for allover consistency. It's the ultimate for a leaded-glass effect, as every area is outlined. You may choose to mix up the inside octagon colors to vary the flower effects, or as with all the other techniques, mix and match all parts. The results will be very interesting!

Note how the dark green petal edges stand out against the red background and the outer edge is defined by the second red print in the "Holly Berry Petals" project, pages 484 and 485.

The technique for making these units is very similar to the "Accented-Petal Octagon." In this case, two pieced-stars are sewn together. There is an inside pieced-star and an outside pieced-star. Both are made by sewing eight triangles to a center octagon.

The inside triangles are the turn-back part of the flower petal. The inside octagon will show as the center of the petals.

The octagonal part of the outside pieced-star shows as the backside of the project and the outline at the edge of the octagon.

The triangles sewn to it are folded toward the front and form the background for the flower.

Special instructions

Follow the instructions for "Accented-Petal Octagons" in the previous section of this chapter, page 475, with the following modifications:

1. Choose four fabrics. The inner octagon is the petal-reveal. The inner triangle fabric forms the petal-accent. The front triangle fabric surrounds the petals, and the backside fabric outlines the outer edge of the front.

2. Using photocopied templates O3C (two halves taped together) and O3CT, cut each fabric into the shape designated for its position in the octagon. For each unit, you will need one inner and one outer octagon and eight each of the inner and outer triangles.

3. Mark dots through the holes in the template at the corners on the inside surface of the inner octagon.

4. Sort your inner and outer octagons and triangles into groups. If you are using several fabrics in more than one position, label which fabric goes where.

5. Skip the step that prepares the 21-inch outer squares.

5.27 With right sides together, place an inside star on an outside star.

5.28 Join the units together and add a border or binding. Turn back the petals and topstitch.

Construction

1. Prepare an inner star-shaped unit. Following the instructions in the "Accented-Petal" section, page 475, construct an inner star from the inner octagon and eight inner triangles.
2. Press the seam allowance toward the octagon.
3. Prepare an outer star-shaped unit. Place eight outer triangles around an outer octagon piece with the right sides together and the grain line of the triangles along the cut edges of the octagon. (See 5.20, page 477.)
4. After sewing and trimming the triangles, press the seam allowance toward the triangles. This is opposite from the inner-pieced star. In the next step, these seams will lie flat against one another.
5. With right sides together, place an inside star on an outside star. (See 5.27)
6. Match the triangles at the points and at the seam allowances that were pressed in opposite directions. Pin at the points to secure the bias edges.
7. Sew along all the outside edges of the pieced-star, making the inner corner turns at the dots marked on the octagon and crossing the stitching at the points.
8. Trim around the sides of the joined star-shaped pieces to approximately ⅛-inch, being careful not to get too close to the stitching.
9. Trim the outside points and clip the inside corners to ease the turning.

Batting

1. Follow the batting instructions for star-shaped pieces in the "Batting" section of Chapter One, page 396.
2. Attach the batting octagon to the inside surface of the outer octagon fabric piece.
3. Cut the slash in the inner octagon at a point that will be covered by a folded petal flap.
4. Continue with the turning, pressing, and folding of the octagon unit.
5. Prepare filler units as needed by following the instructions in either or both of the "Filler Piece" sections of the "Basic Octagon" section of this chapter, page 464.

Assembly

1. Arrange the pieces according to the project or your own design.
2. Join the units and add a border or binding per the instructions in Chapter One, pages 398 and 396.
3. Turn back and topstitch petals. (See 5.28)

This unit has two looks depending on which fabrics are folded to the inside.

Holly Berry Petals
Four-Part Octagon

Finished size: 18 inches square
Difficulty level: Intermediate
Block size: 9-inch octagon

Rosy red accents give this floral fabric holiday cheer. Make it as a wall or door hanging or convert it into a pillow.

The four-color octagon pattern allows you to have each part of the block in the color you choose. The background outline and the inner petals in this project are the same rosy fabric. The visual illusion ties these areas together.

Fabric requirements

Front triangles	⅓-yard floral
Background	½-yard white on white
Backing	½-yard muslin
Inside petals/back	½-yard rosy red
Border and accent	½-yard green
Binding	4 inches (included in inside petals)
Batting	18 inches square

Templates

O3C	Octagon	Two copies
O3CT	Triangle	One copy

Cutting plan

Floral	Eight outer triangles
Muslin	One 18-inch square
Rosy red	Two octagons: one inner, one outer; Two 1¾-inch strips
Green	Eight inner triangles; Two 3-inch strips
White	One 13½-inch square
Batting	One 18-inch square

Specific instructions

1. Follow the instructions in the "Four-Part Octagon" section of Chapter Five, page 482, to make the center block.
2. Complete the petal turn-back and topstitching steps.
3. Sew the 3-inch green strips to the 13½-inch white print square.
4. With right sides together, place a green strip along one edge and sew.
5. Trim the extra fabric from the strip even with the edge of the square.
6. Repeat on the opposite side of the square.
7. Open the strips and press the seam allowance toward the green strips.
8. Sew the second strip along one of the remaining sides across both green strips.
9. Trim.
10. Repeat for the last side.

Deck your halls with "Holly Berry Petals," made above by Laura Farson, for a splash of holiday good cheer.

11. Open the green strips and press the seam allowance toward the green strip.

12. Place the octagon on the center of the white print square. Find the center by folding in half both directions and finger-pressing the folds along the edge of the white square.

13. Line up the petals with the finger-pressed folds.

14. Spray-baste the block onto the fabric or pin at the corners.

15. Turn the pieces over and layer the 18-inch piece of batting on top of the backside.

16. Cut out and remove the batting behind the octagon.

17. Layer the muslin over the batting.

18. Spray-fuse or press-fuse the batting and muslin backing. If using temporary adhesive spray, just lift the batting and spritz with a little spray to keep it in place. Do the same for the muslin layer.

19. Turn the layered group to the front.

20. Topstitch along the outer edge of the block with monofilament thread. (I use the hemstitch with a narrow width.)

21. Sew a straight stitch with the monofilament thread through all layers around the inside edge of the border.

22. Bind with the two 1¾-inch rosy red strips.

Hanging option

1. From cutoffs, fold three strips of 6-inch-long fabric so that all the raw edges are inside.

2. Topstitch.

3. Fold each of the three strips in the center.

4. Pin one of the strips to each of the upper corners of the square and one in the center.

5. Tack with a few stitches.

6. Place a rod through the loops to hang the project.

6 dodecagons

It's difficult to pick a favorite, but the sunflower design vies for mine! Inspired by the lush yellow fields of Kansas, it's hard to resist.

The sunflower, with its twelve sides, is called a "dodecagon."

Once you get past the odd name, you realize that they can look great in quilting projects as yellow sunflowers, creamy daisies, and red poinsettias.

Thus, color choice determines the desired flower outcome. The dramatic contrast of green and yellow, enhanced by shading, in "Sunny Days in Kansas" (page 493) gives a very summery appearance. Deep rich reds opposite leafy green create the impression of Christmas. For spring, choose light yellow, pale grassy green, and white on white for a crisp, clean look.

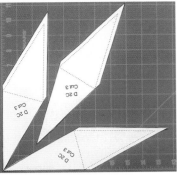

6.1 Matching the centers, arrange the template pieces as shown here.

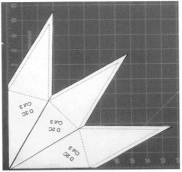

6.2 Tape the three diamonds together to form a quarter of a star-shaped template.

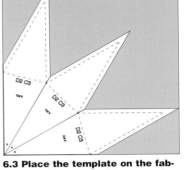

6.3 Place the template on the fabric, matching the inside corner to the folds.

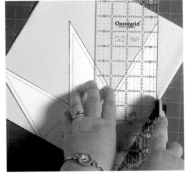

6.4 Place a rotary-cutting ruler on top of the template.

Basic Dodecagons

Although a twelve-sided shape can appear a bit daunting, the extra effort in constructing this variation yields a beautiful flower blossom with twelve petals.

Preparing the template

1. Photocopy template D2C3 on page 509 three times.
2. Cut along the solid lines on all copies.
3. Matching the centers, arrange the template pieces, first with two outside star points and then inserting the third piece between the two. (See 6.1)
4. Tape the three diamonds together to form a quarter of a star-shaped template. It is helpful to align the two outside pieces, using removable tape, on your cutting mat lines so that they are at right angles. (See 6.2)

Construction

1. Organize your fabric choices into a group for the inside pieces and one for the outside.
2. After folding the fabric selvedge to selvedge, cut 22-inch lengths from both the front and back fabrics. Cut the length in half to make a roughly 22- by 22-inch square.
3. Fold one piece of the inside fabric two times to form a "square." Be sure that the raw edges are exactly even. Press each fold as you make it.
4. Spray the backside of the paper template with temporary adhesive spray.
5. Place the template on the fabric, matching the inside corner to the folds. (See 6.3)
6. Place a rotary-cutting ruler on top of the template, lining up the ¼-inch line with the dotted line of the template. (See 6.4)
7. Cut through four layers of fabric along the edge of the ruler with a rotary cutter.
8. Repeat along the outside lines, outlining the points. Do not cut on the fold lines.
9. Remove the template and unfold the fabric. You should have a star with twelve points.
10. Press.
11. Place this star-shaped fabric piece, with right sides together, on a 22-inch square of the background fabric. Avoid aligning the straight edges of the star along the grain line of the back fabric so that all the angles fall on the bias. (See 6.5)
12. Pin the points to the inside piece to secure the bias edges.
13. Sew along all star points ¼-inch from the edges, crossing the stitching. Use a walking foot to keep the edges flat. (See Helpful Hint)

Helpful Hint

◆◆◆

If you have a tie-down feature on your sewing machine, it's helpful to use it at both the inside and outside corners. Otherwise, decrease stitch length in the corners and at the points.

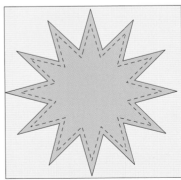

6.5 Place this star-shaped fabric piece, right-side down on a 22-inch square of the background fabric.

Helpful Hint

❖❖❖

After step 14 of "Construction," remind yourself which fabric is for the outside and which is for the inside. This is very important when using multiple fabrics.

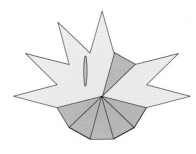

6.6 Trim the seam allowance back to 1/8-inch, being very careful not to get too close to the stitching.

6.7 Turn the piece right-side out by gently pulling the fabric through the slash.

14. Trim the seam allowance back to approximately ⅛-inch, being very careful not to get too close to the stitching. Snip across the outside corners and at an angle to smooth them. Make a clip and trim at an angle into the inside corners to ease the turning. (See 6.6 and Helpful Hint)

15. With the inner fabric facing up, cut a slash 2 inches long through just one layer across the bias in the center area of the star-shaped piece.

16. Locate the slash so that it will be hidden under a folded petal flap.

17. Lift a single layer of fabric at about the center of where you would like the slash.

18. Pinch it into a tiny fold and snip across the fold. Be sure you only have one layer of fabric!

19. Then insert your scissors into the snip and cut first 1 inch in one direction and then an inch in the opposite. Cutting across the bias keeps the slash from fraying.

Batting

If batting is desired, the lightest/thinnest ("Gold Fuse" or Thermore) works best, as there are many layers of fabric close together in this design.

1. Cut batting pieces using a paper template cut ¼-inch smaller than the center dodecagon.

2. Create the template by tracing around an unturned, folded unit and cutting it ¼-inch smaller. To do this, fold the points to the center of an unturned unit.

3. Place on a piece of paper and trace around it.

4. Place the ¼-inch line of a rotary ruler on the line so that the ¼-inch line is on the inside of the traced dodecagon.

5. Draw a line.

6. Repeat for the twelve sides.

7. Cut on the inside lines.

8. Carefully unfold the batting.

9. Refold it two times creating four smoothed layers.

10. With a large rotary ruler and cutter, cut a strip the width of the batting template.

11. Place the template on the batting strip with a rotary ruler along the edge.

12. Cut along the ruler with a rotary cutter. Save the cutoffs to use later for the middle filler pieces.

13. Spray-fuse or press-fuse the batting to the center of the wrong side of the outside fabric.

14. Turn the piece right-side out by gently pulling the fabric through the slash. Pay special attention to the points so that all the fabric is turned to the seam allowance. (See 6.7)

15. Press the star shape flat, making sure the seam allowances are fully open.

16. Fold the points to the center to form a dodecagon (twelve-sided figure).

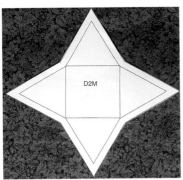

6.8 Photocopy template D2M, cut along the solid lines, and use it to cut the front fabric.

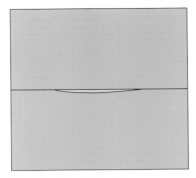

6.9 Matching right sides, sew one-third of the seam, back-tack, skip one-third, back-tack, and finish.

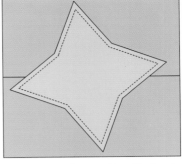

6.10 Place a front unit on the back square with right sides together, alingned so the opening doesn't intersect with the points of the star.

17. Align the points so that the corners lie flat. Press.

18. Prepare the remaining stars in the same manner.

19. Once the dodecagons are complete, prepare the filler units.

Filler units

Filler units are made two ways.

When a whole center unit is needed, as in the situation where four flowers meet, the filler unit is made with an opening used to turn it right-side out.

Because side- and corner-filler units can be cut in half or fourths before turning, they don't need an opening. The two methods are explained here.

Whole center filler unit

The front fabric of a center unit is cut with a template into a star shape. This star is placed right-side down on a square that has been seamed to provide an opening for turning. Batting is fused to the wrong side of the front fabric, and the unit is turned to the right side through the opening in the back piece.

1. Photocopy the star-shaped template labeled D2M, page 510, and cut it along the solid lines.

2. Cut front fabric using the D2M template. (See 6.8)

3. Cut back fabric into 10-inch squares. Cut the squares in half one time.

4. Matching the right sides, sew the square halves together along the long side as follows: sew one-third of the seam, back-tack, skip one-third of the seam, back-tack, and finish the seam. (See 6.9)

5. Open flat and press the seam allowance to one side. The skipped area becomes a finished-edged opening that will be used later to flip the unit to the right side.

6. Place a front unit on the back square with right sides together and aligned so that the opening doesn't intersect with the points of the star. In other words, offset the star so that the seam is below or above the points. (See 6.10)

7. Sew ⅛-inch around the edge of the star-shaped front unit.

8. Cut out the star-shaped piece ⅛-inch from the stitching, trim the points, and clip the inner corners.

9. Cut a piece of batting ½-inch smaller than the sewn unit or use the cutoffs from the large center batting pieces.

10. Place the pieces on the wrong side of the front fabric to arrange them before fusing. (See 6.11)

11. Spray-fuse or press-fuse the batting pieces to the wrong side of the front fabric.

12. Turn the piece right-side out by gently pulling the fabric through the opening in the seam of the back piece. Pay special attention to the points so that the fabric is fully turned to the seam allowance.

13. Sew some quilting lines in the center to close the opening, and press.

6.11 Place batting pieces on wrong side of the front fabric and arrange them before fusing. Then, spray-fuse or press-fuse.

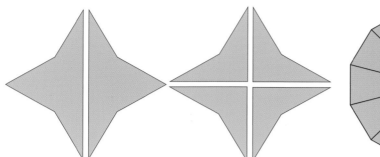

6.12 For edge units, cut the star in half. For corner units, cut again perpendicular to first cut.

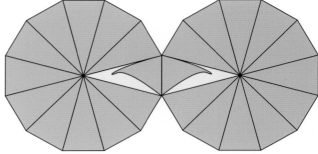

6.13 Match the folds and sew in the fold.

Edge and corner units

Edge and corner units are made using the D2M template on page 510. The finished opening is not necessary because the whole pieces are cut in half. The star-shaped front fabric is sewn to a back square. Once the batting is fused onto it, it is cut into smaller pieces. Then, it is turned right-side out.

1. Cut front fabric using the D2M template.
2. Cut back fabric into 7-inch squares.
3. Place a front piece on a back square with right sides together, pin, and sew ⅛-inch seam around the outside.
4. Trim away any extra fabric ⅛-inch from the stitching line.
5. Spray-baste a piece, or pieces, of batting to the wrong side of the outside fabric. These batting pieces are also the same size as the cutoffs of the larger piece.
6. For edge units, cut the star in half with the ruler placed from point to point through the middle of the star. For the corner units, cut again perpendicular to the first cut. (See 6.12)
7. Flip the pieces to their right sides.
8. Be sure to fully open the seam allowances and press flat.

Joining

1. Arrange the units as shown in the project or in your own pattern.
2. Once the arrangement is complete, sew the units together. (It is easier to join the horizontal seams first, creating vertical strips.)
3. Open the folded points of two touching flower units.
4. Match the folds and sew in the fold. (See 6.13)
5. Return the petal flaps to their folded position and pin in place.
6. Once all the horizontal seams are sewn together, repeat with the vertical

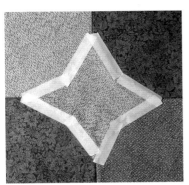

6.14 Place a center connector unit over each space, with the seam opening facing up on the backside.

6.15 Once turned over to the front side, you can see how nicely the units are aligned.

6.16 Open the petal flaps and pin across the flap folds. Remove tape and sew along the fold lines and through the filler unit.

seams.

7. There will be large spaces between the dodecagon units.

8. Turn the joined units over to the back.

9. Place a center filler unit over each of these spaces with the seam opening facing up on the backside. Make sure that the middle unit is centered by lining up the corners of the star with the joining seams of the flower units. (See 6.14 and Helpful Hint)

10. Turn the units over to the front side. (See 6.15)

11. Open the petal flaps of the flower units that lie over the filler piece and pin across the fold of the flaps. Remove the tape, as it will gum up the sewing machine needle. (See 6.16)

12. Sew along the fold lines and through the filler unit, being careful not to catch the petal flaps in the seam.

13. Return the flaps to their original folded positions and pin at their centers.

14. Repeat for each of the center units and then for any edge-filler units.

Finishing

1. Add a border and/or bind, as instructed on pages 398 and 396 of Chapter One.

2. Finish by topstitching the petal flaps. Refer to the "Turning Back Petals" section of Chapter One, page 404. (See 6.17)

Helpful Hint

◆◆◆

I usually secure the center units in place with masking tape along the outside edges.

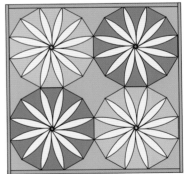

6.17 The finished quilt will look like this.

Sunny Days in Kansas
Two-Color Dodecagon

Finished size: 40 inches square
Difficulty level: Advanced
Block size: 10 inches square

This quilt was inspired by a drive across Kansas in late-summer, when the sunflower fields were laden with blooms. Mix and match shades of gold, yellow, and green.

Fabric requirements

Yellow/gold	1¼ yards of four shades
Green	1¼ yards of four shades
Dark green	2 yards (⅓-yard binding; 1⅔ yards filler pieces)
Batting	1½ yards of 45 inches wide

Templates

D2C3	Dodecagon	Three copies
D2M	Filler-star piece	One copy

Cutting plan

Green	Sixteen 21-inch squares (four of each shade)
Yellow	Sixteen 21-inch squares folded and cut into dodecagon stars
Dark green	Five 1¾-inch strips binding
	Nine 9- by 10-inch rectangles for filler stars with turning slots
	Seven 7-inch squares for cut filler stars
Sixteen filler stars	
Batting	Sixteen small dodecagons
	Sixteen filler stars (can use cutoffs from dodecagon)

Specific instructions

1. Follow the instructions in Chapter Six for dodecagons, page 487.
2. Prepare sixteen dodecagons, nine whole filler stars with turning slots, and seven filler stars to be divided as follows.
3. Cut six stars in half. Cut the seventh one twice to make four corner pieces.
4. Arrange the parts as shown in the photo.
5. Join the pieces in rows.
6. Join rows into pairs and then join the two pairs.
7. Although it is more awkward, turn back the petals and topstitch after you bind the quilt.

A drive through the bloom-laden coutryside can inspire the clever quilter. Such was the case for this 40-inch square quilt, "Sunny Days in Kansas," made by Laura Farson, 2001.

Navy Blues Pillow
Two-Color Dodecagon

Finished size: 18 inches square
Difficulty level: Intermediate
Block size: 10-inch dodecagon

If joining unit after unit for an entire quilt seems too daunting or is going to take more time than you have planned for, just use a single unit for a smaller project—like a pillow!

Make this tailored-looking pillow for a formal living room. Its simplicity of color lends itself to blend in with a cream-colored sofa or chair.

Fabric requirements

Inside	⅔-yard cream print
Outside	⅔-yard navy print
Background	½-yard cream figure
Backing	½-yard muslin
Border	½-yard navy dot
Back side	½-yard plain navy
Batting	18 inches square
Pillow form	16 inches square

Templates

D2C3	Dodecagon	Three copies

Cutting plan

Cream print	One 22-inch square cut into one dodecagon star
Navy print	One 22-inch square
Cream figure	One 14-inch square
Navy dot	Two 3-inch strips
Navy solid	Two 12½- by 18-inch rectangles
Muslin	One 18-inch square

Specific instructions

1. Follow the instructions in Chapter Six to make the center dodecagon block, page 487.
2. Complete the petal turn-back and topstitching steps.
3. Sew the 3-inch navy-dotted strips to the 14-inch white-print square.
4. With right sides together, place a navy strip along one edge and sew.

A single flower unit can be used all on its own, as was the case here in "Navy Blues Pillow," made by Laura Farson, 2001.

5. Trim the extra fabric from the strip even with the edge of the square.

6. Repeat on the opposite side of the square.

7. Open the strips and press the seam allowance toward the navy.

8. Sew the second strip along one of the remaining sides across both navy strips.

9. Trim.

10. Repeat for the last side.

Continued on next page.

Continued on next page.

Navy Blues Pillow continued

11. Open the seams.
12. Press the seam allowance toward the navy.
13. Place the octagon on the center of the white print square. Find the center by folding in half in both directions and finger-pressing the folds along the edge of the white square.
14. Line up the petals with the finger-pressed folds.
15. Spray-baste the block onto the fabric or pin at the corners.
16. Turn the pieces over and layer the 18-inch piece of batting on top of the backside.
17. Cut out and remove the batting behind the dodecagon.
18. Layer the muslin over the batting.
19. Spray-fuse or press-fuse the batting and muslin backing. (See Helpful Hint)
20. Turn the layered group to the front. Topstitch along the outer edge of the block with monofilament thread. (I use the hemstitch with a narrow width.)
21. Sew a straight stitch with monofilament thread through all layers around the inside edge of the border.
22. The backside of the pillow has a slotted opening for ease of turning now and for changing or laundering later. Prepare the back piece by folding over 2 inches on the long side of one of the navy rectangles.
23. Topstitch along this raw edge of the turned piece. The piece now measures 10½ by 18 inches.
24. With right sides facing each other, place the hemmed piece on the front square so that the raw edges are matched.
25. Lay the unhemmed piece on top of the hemmed piece so that its center overlaps about 4½ inches and its edges line up with the other end of the front square. Sew around all the edges.
26. Trim the corners and flip to the outside through the slot in the navy square.
27. Insert the 16-inch pillow form into the slot and smooth the front so that it is unwrinkled.

Templates

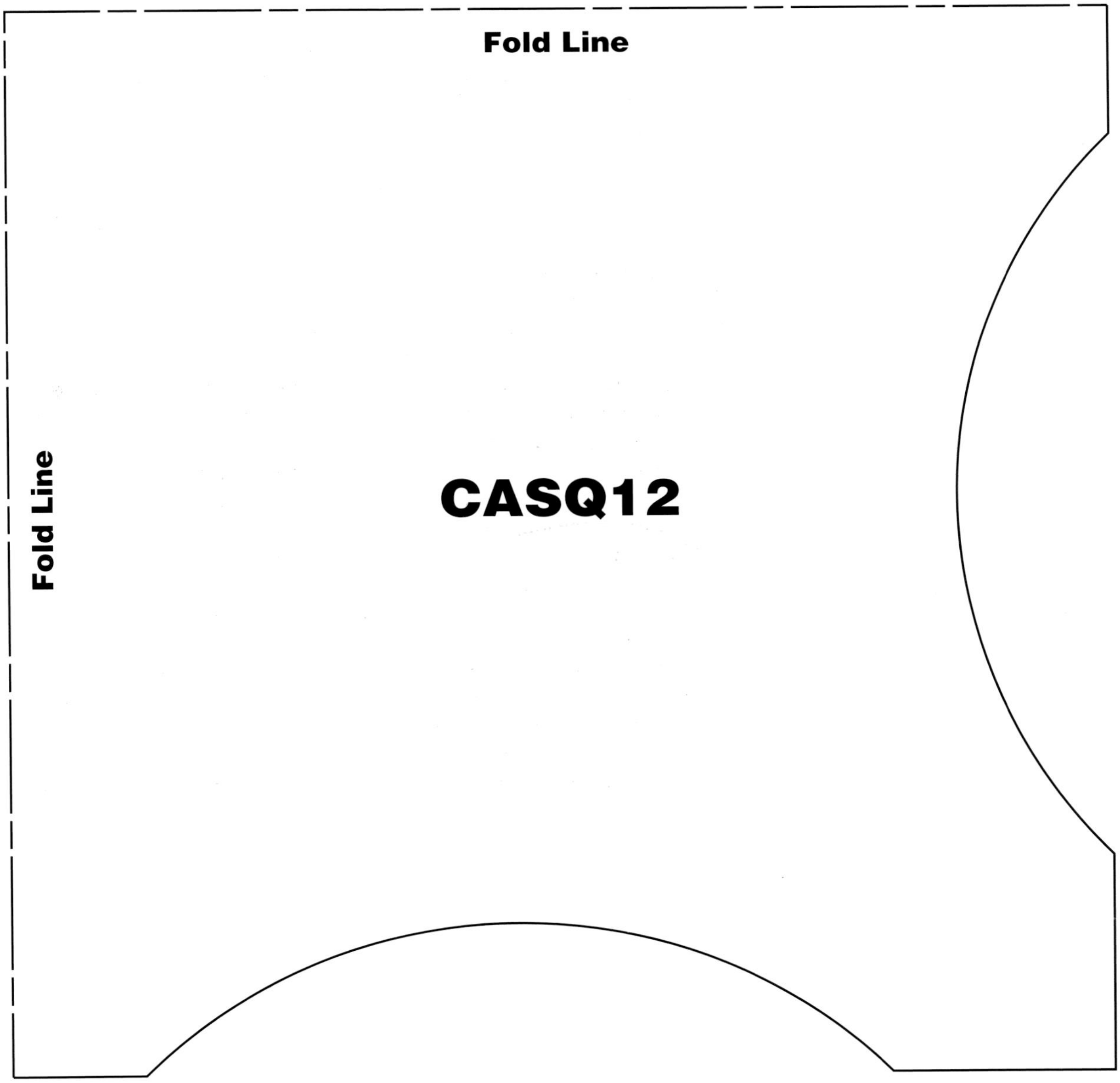

Fold Line

Fold Line

CASQ12

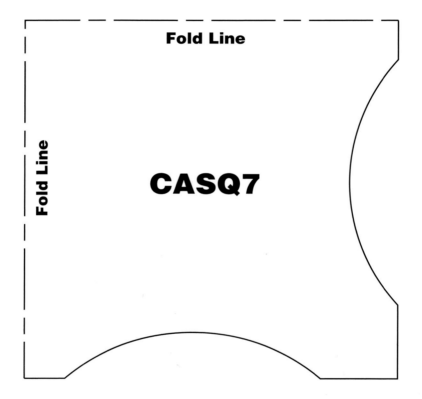

Fold Line

Fold Line

CASQ7

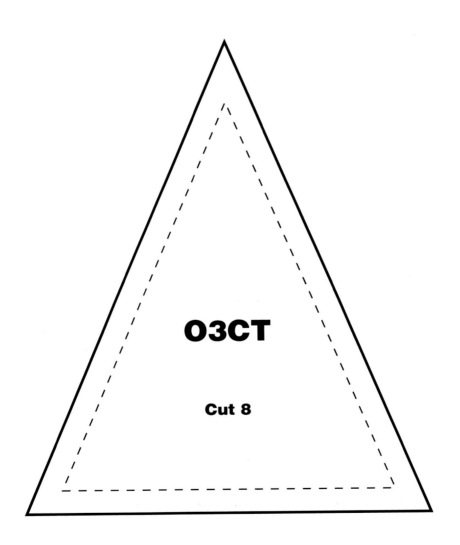

O3CT

Cut 8

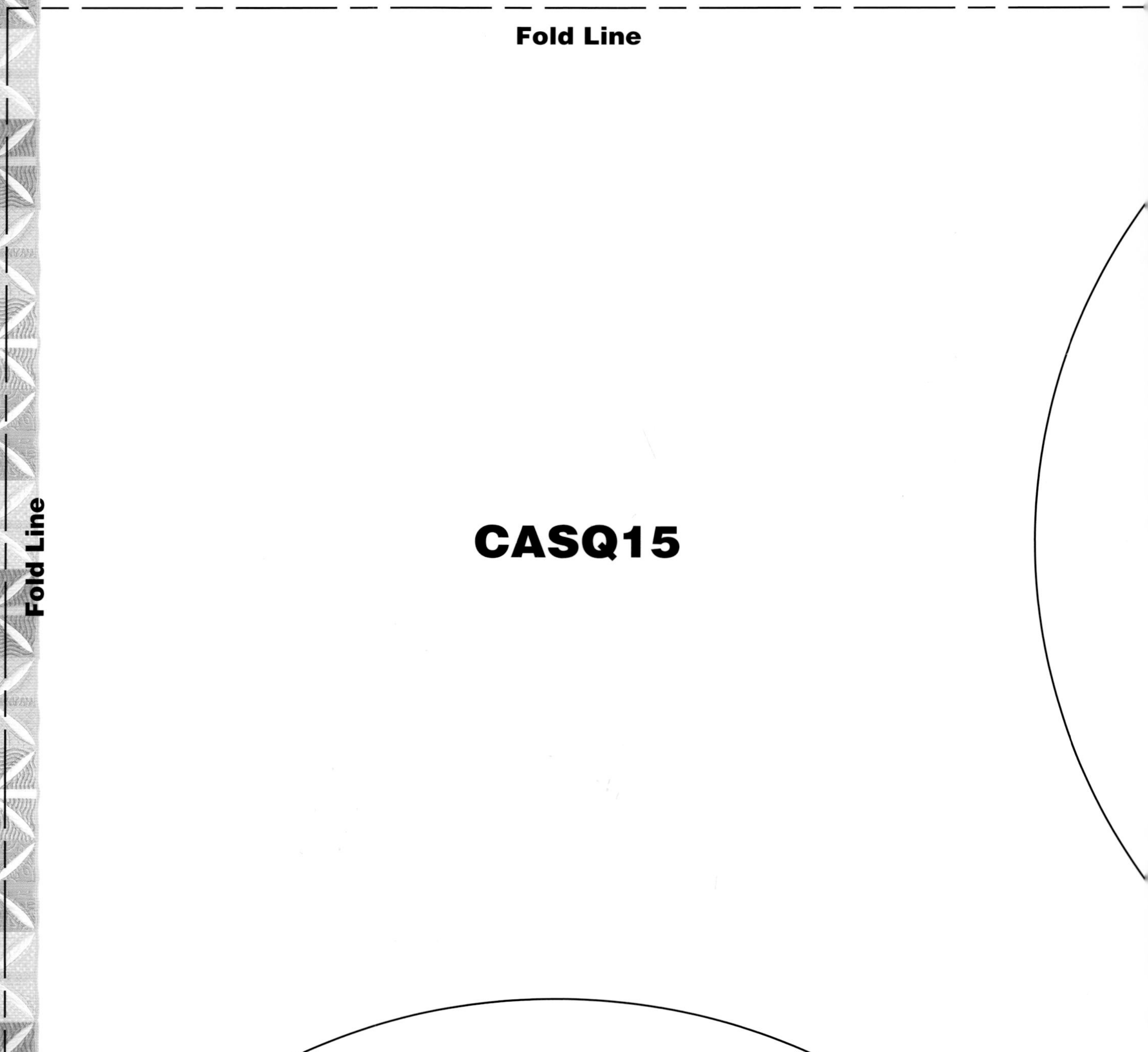

Fold Line

Fold Line

CASQ15

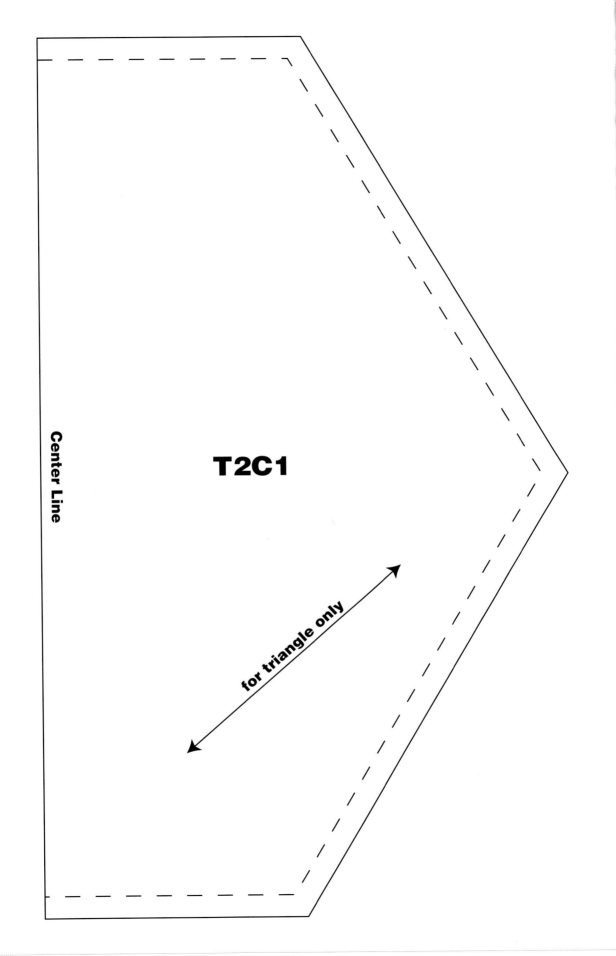

Center Line

T2C1

for triangle only

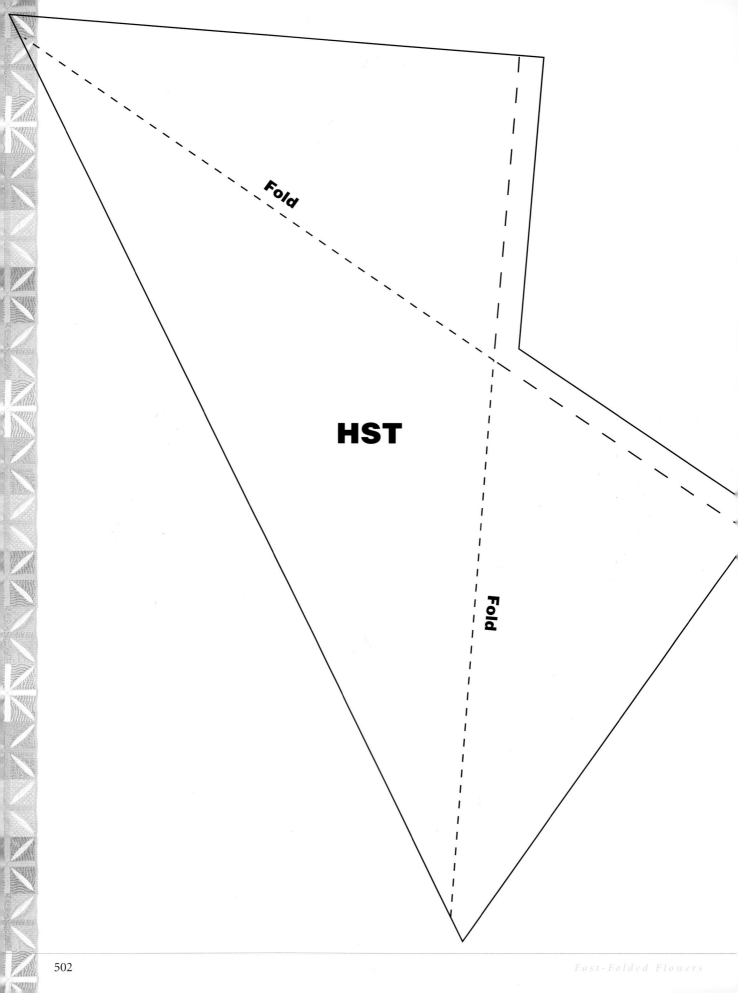

HST

Fold

Fold

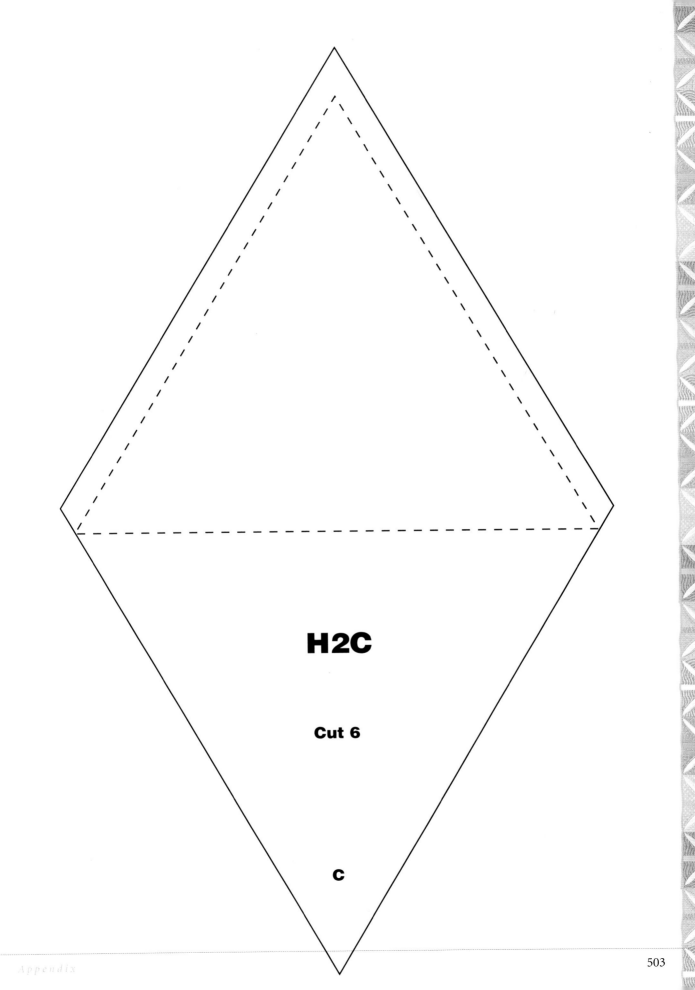

H2C

Cut 6

c

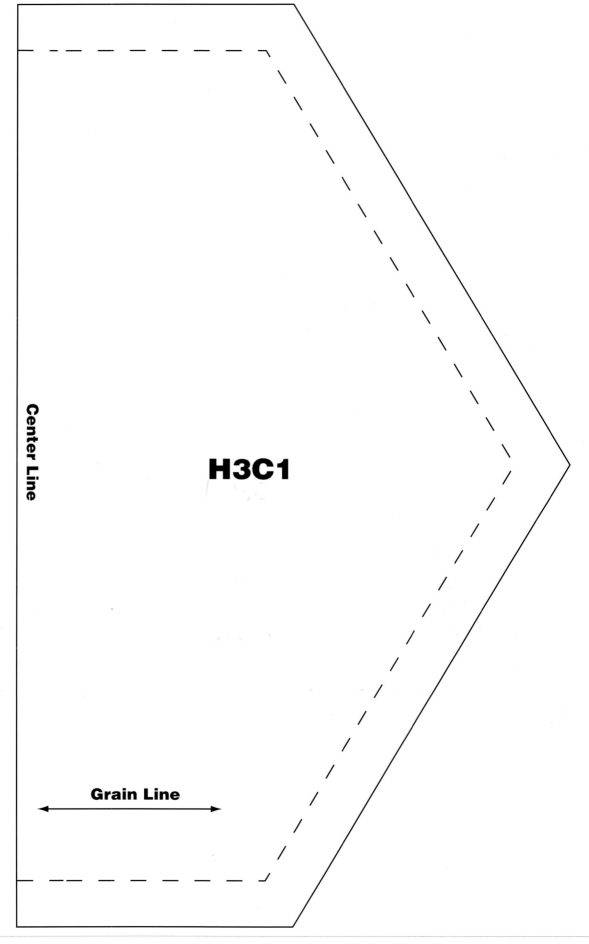

H3C1

Center Line

Grain Line

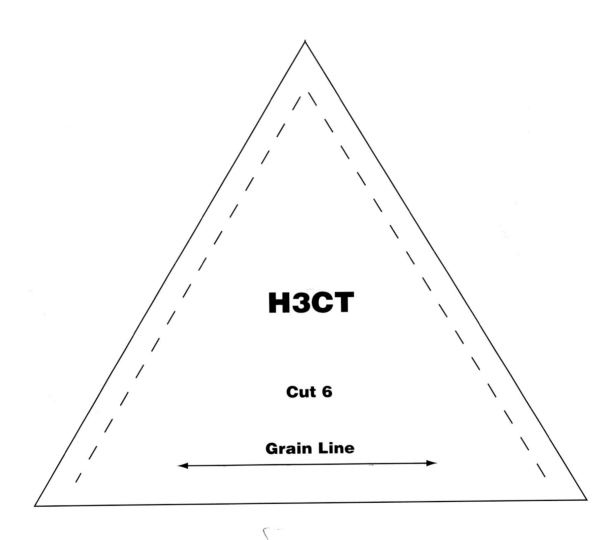

H3CT

Cut 6

Grain Line

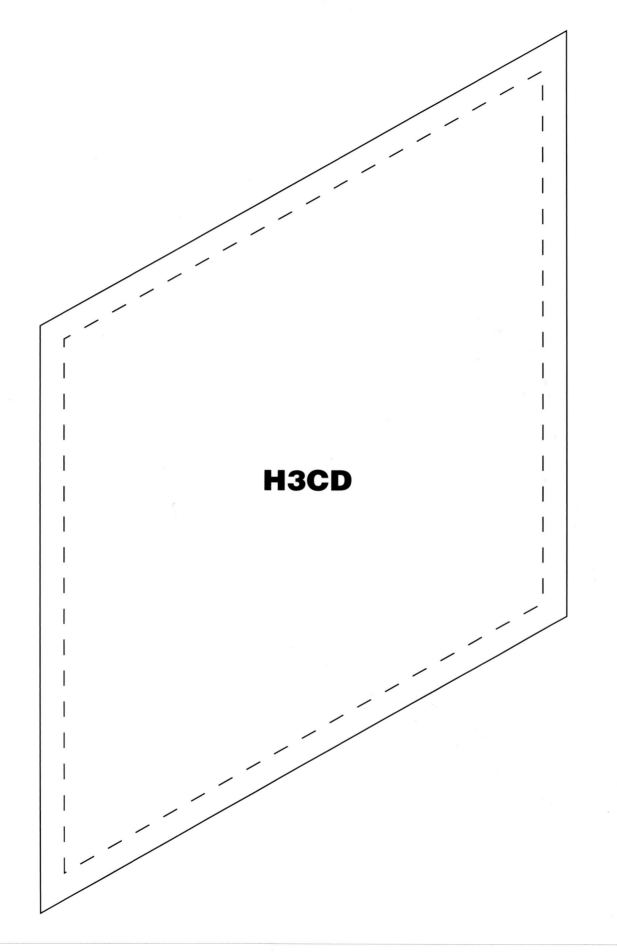

H3CD

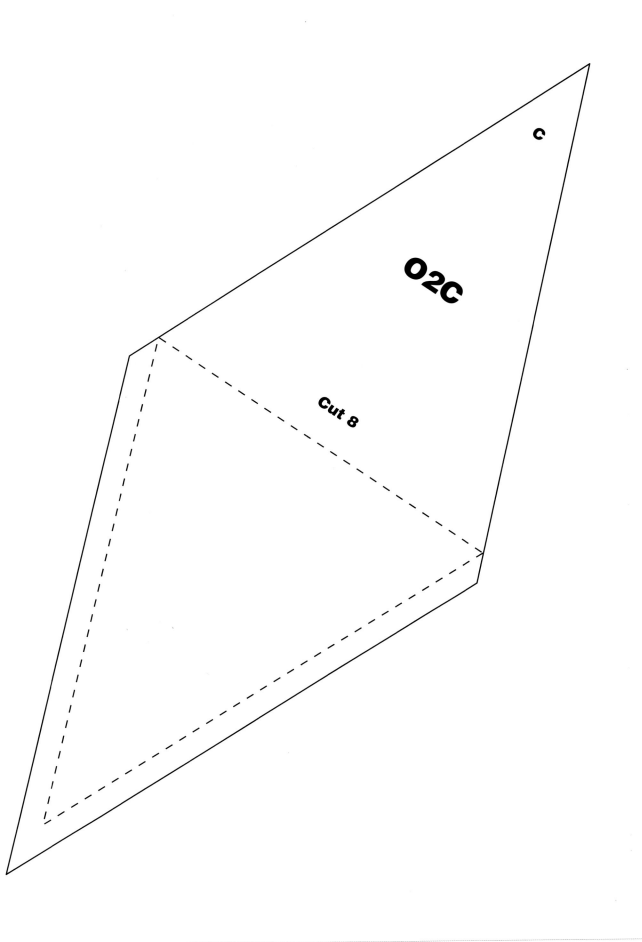

C

O2C

Cut 8

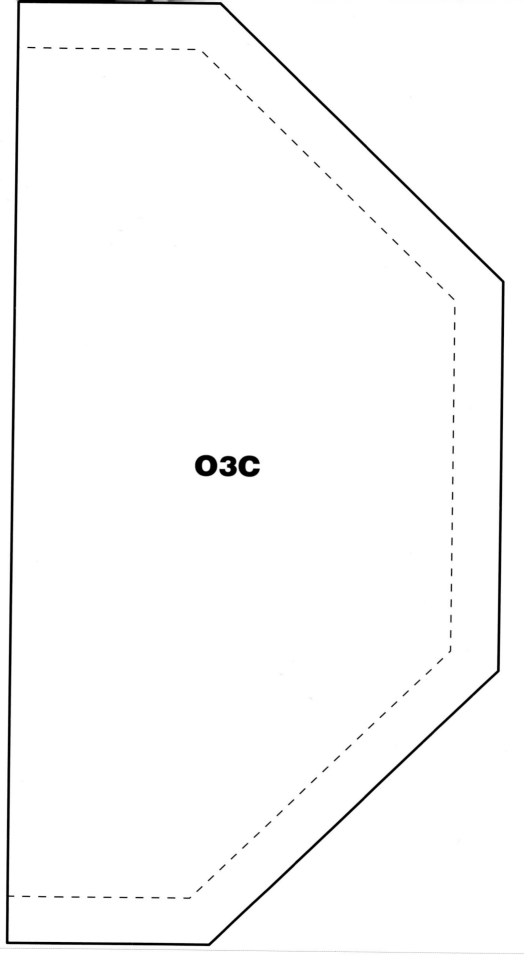

O3C

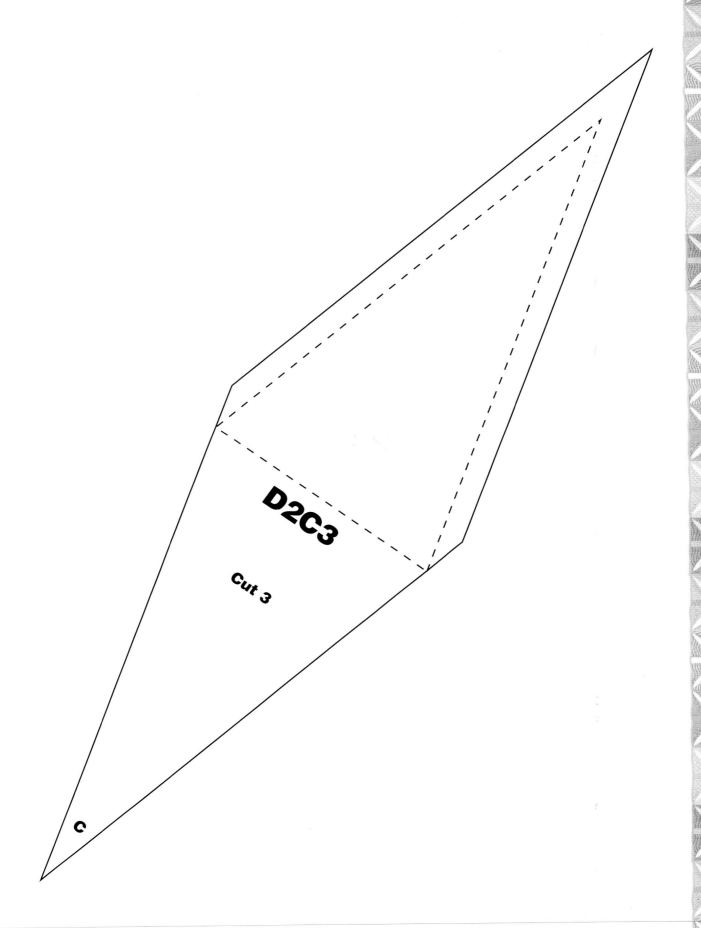

D2C3

Cut 3

C

D2M

The material in this compilation appeared in the following previously published Krause Publications and appears here by permission of the authors. (The initial page numbers given refer to pages in the original work; page numbers in parentheses refer to pages in this book.)

Harer, Michele Morrow	The Essential Guide to Practically Perfect Patchwork © 2002	Pages 1, 4-160 (5-162)
Michler, J. Marsha	The Magic of Crazy Quilting © 1998	Pages 1, 5-137 (163-295)
Wood, Kaye	Kaye Wood's Strip-Cut Quilts © 2001	Pages 1, 3-94 (296-388)
Farson, Laura	Fast-Folded Flowers © 2001	Pages 1, 4-127 (389-510)

 Published by Krause Publications, an imprint of F & W Publications, Inc., 700 East State Street, Iola, WI 54990. (800) 289-0963. First edition.

Other fine Krause Publications are available from your local bookstore, art supply store or direct from the publisher.

08 07 06 05 04 5 4 3 2

A catalog record for this book is available from the Library of Congress at <http://catalog.loc.gov>.